BASEBALLHQ.COM'S 2016

MINOR LEAGUE BASEBALL ANALYST

ROB GORDON AND JEREMY DELONEY | BRENT HERSHEY, EDITOR | 11TH EDITION

TRIUMPH
BOOKS

This book is available in quantity at special discounts for your group or organization. For further information, contact:

Triumph Books LLC
814 North Franklin Street
Chicago, Illinois 60610
(312) 337-0747
www.triumphbooks.com

Printed in U.S.A.
ISBN: 978-1-62937-139-9

Data provided by TheBaseballCube.com and Baseball Info Solutions

Cover design by Brent Hershey
Front cover photograph by Jayne Kamin-Oncea/USA TODAY Sports Images

Acknowledgments

Jeremy Deloney:

I've been doing this for seven years and the amount of time and effort spent seems to increase every year. Whether that is due to attention to detail or being afraid to fail, I don't know if I could draw a conclusion. The book is essentially a year-round venture, but the bulk of the work takes place in a four month window from September through December.

Nobody comes close to the amount of thanks and gratitude that I owe my wife, Amy. My world is better with her by my side. She is the most selfless person I know and she continuously supports me regardless of what I'm doing. Amy is a franchise player who the GM of the World would build around. She touches so many lives with her giving and nurturing nature and I'm absolutely a lucky benefactor. She deserves all kinds of awards and accolades that a paragraph in the Acknowledgments doesn't do her justice. Those that know her, love her. Those that don't know her, should. I love her with all of my being.

My three wonderful children—Owen, Ethan, and Madeline—have led me on a whirlwind journey and have made me realize my greatest job is as a father. I love that they are different from one another. I love that they laugh together. I love that they love together. At times I'm the student in this household and I'm always willing to learn. All three of you make me very proud. Yes, I do brag.

I owe a great deal of gratitude to my parents, Bill and Nancy, who modeled the work ethic, belief system, and love of life that I share with my kids today. Regardless of how old I am—and I'm not sharing that unimportant detail—I always strive to make my parents proud.

My brothers—BJ and Andy—are both older than me and paved the way in the struggles of adolescence. They always had my back and they still do today. As we all live our lives, they also exemplify the same characteristics our parents model every day. They are successes in life.

I'm forever grateful for the gang at BaseballHQ who took a chance on me several years ago. Yes, writing is time-consuming and can be difficult, but part of that can be attributed to keeping up with the quality work that is consistently churned out every day by the BHQ staff.

I always end with thanking the readers of this book as well as BaseballHQ.com. I always appreciate the support and feedback, whether positive or negative.

Rob Gordon:

In 2003 Ron Shandler and Deric McKamey gave me the opportunity to do something I'd wanted to do all of my life—write about baseball. Ron and Deric showed me the ropes, and spent countless hours explaining what scouts look for. Deric's total recall of the most obscure minor league players still amazes me. They have both moved on to bigger and better things, but their imprint on the structure and content of this book lives on.

Jeremy and I are now in our seventh edition of the Minor League Baseball Analyst and each year I'm more and more impressed with his comprehensive and astute knowledge of the minor leagues. Over the past couple of years Jeremy and I have gotten invaluable help from the rest of the HQ minor league team: Brent Hershey, Chris Blessing, and Alec Dopp. I would especially like to thank Brent Hershey. Brent serves as our editor at BaseballHQ.com and has been the glue that holds this project together.

Many other baseball people provided invaluable support and encouragement over the years. They include Jeff Barton, Jim Callis, John Sickels, Ray Murphy, Rick Wilton, Patrick Davitt, Todd Zola, Jason Grey, Joe Sheehan, Jeff Erickson, Kimball Crossley, Steve Moyer, Phil Hertz, Jock Thompson and Doug Dennis.

Some day someone will write a story about Baseball Unlimited. Until then I'll just have to thank the boys—Michael Hartman, Kegan Hartman, Steve Hartman, Michael Cooney, Bob Hathaway, Doug Hathaway, Raj Patel, Derald Cook, Dave Dannemiller, Ted Maizes, Randy Jones, and John Mundelius. Rest in peace Greg and may BU live forever!

My oldest son Bobby had a blast playing JV baseball for Dearborn High and the coaches—Kyle Jenks, Eric Jenks, and Matt McKay—did a great job with the boys, as did his travel baseball coaches Rob Stockman, John Schneider, and Rob Septor.

I would especially like to thank my family. My two boys—Bobby and Jimmy—make the sky bluer, the sun brighter, and the crack of the bat all the more sweet. My sister Susan Arntson helped raise me and tried to keep me out of trouble, which wasn't always easy. Thanks to the Arntson clan—Jeff, Rachel, Josh, Marissa, and Jake. My mother Sandra Gordon took me on an annual birthday trip to see the Cubs play and drove me to countless Little League games and my father Robert W. Gordon III has shared my passion for the game of baseball. Finally, a huge thank you to my amazing and beautiful wife Paula. This may sound like a cliché, but I really would not have been able to do this without her in my life.

TABLE OF CONTENTS

by Jeremy Deloney

We are beyond excited to share the eleventh edition of the Minor League Baseball Analyst (MLBA). For the new readers here, it all started in 2005 with Deric McKamey, now a scout with the St. Louis Cardinals. His unique and expert insights added a lot of color to the ambiguous world of minor league prospects and the tradition continues today. Deric passed the torch to Rob Gordon and me seven years ago and we've done our best to maintain the consistent, objective perspective that Deric brought to the table. While we've added several names to the mix, the goal remains the same: to bring readers fresh ideas in an inimitable format while adding our own personal assessments. Brent Hersey, the editor of the MLBA and General Manager of Content for BaseballHQ.com, continues to bring out the best in all of us.

For the 2016 edition, we are excited to add the expertise and knowledge of Alec Dopp and Chris Blessing to the MLBA. As you will see in the pages that follow, these new contributors have keen eyes and the ability to articulate scouting observations in a clear, succinct manner. Both were tremendous additions to the BaseballHQ.com staff in 2015 and have continued their incredible work with this 11th edition of the book. Chris and Alec spend a lot of time at minor league parks in different parts of the country, which makes our coverage that much more well-rounded.

The space for prospect coverage has gotten awfully crowded— and that is a good thing. Not only does it give all of us plenty of resources and insight, it also forces us at BaseballHQ.com to remain consistent and find new ways to keep our readers informed and entertained. I believe we've done that with the MLBA as well as the coverage at the site. You'll see some new features in both in 2016 and we're excited to bring you along for the ride.

There is little doubt the MLBA attracts fantasy baseball players with its statistical focus and valuable compilation of lists and rankings. However, the MLBA also is a poignant resource for any minor league baseball fan. With assessments on over 1,000 prospects, most any minor league game you might attend in 2016 will have at least a few players featured in this book. I've actually seen the MLBA at a few games myself.

We truly appreciate the thirst for prospect information and we enjoy bringing our assessments to you. While we also understand there are several other qualified prospect sites and outlets available to you, we encourage you to make the MLBA a staple of your annual routine, whether it be taking it with you to a minor league game or enjoying the daily and weekly analysis via BaseballHQ. com. Rob and I have done this for a long time and have several connections within the game.

That's why we believed it to be important to gather new voices and add them to the MLBA. Chris and Alec both have different perspectives that add to the overall experience of the book as well as to BHQ.

While the general format of the book remains the same with valuable statistical information, impactful essays, and a multitude of lists, you'll see some slight tweaks to our coverage. The player commentaries are more structured and will tell you more of the hows and whys behind the statistical outputs of the various prospects. The essays are written from different perspectives and will shine a different kind of light on the topics.

Because of more contributors to the MLBA, we believe this allows us to have greater coverage all across the U.S. Most of us have contacts within the game that can provide us with scouting tips and valuable information on various prospects and organizations. All of us attend games each year and like to chat with the scouts in attendance. While we all have our own personal biases and likes/dislikes, the collaboration of this project is more evident than usual.

The organizational coverage continues to be diverse and well-rounded, as each writer was responsible for the write-ups on players from on a per-team basis. I took the entire American League and SD, while the rest of the National League was split up between Rob (MIA, CHC, PIT, STL, COL, LA), Chris (NYM, ATL, CIN, ARI), Alec (MIL and SF), and Brent (PHI and WAS). Because of our year-round sharing of information, there is definitely more of a collaborative feel for the coverage. After all, the competition in this industry forces us to be at the top of our game.

The BaseballHQ.com rating system (detailed at the beginning of the Batters and Pitchers sections) continues to be a source of debate, but also an effective way to evaluate minor league prospects. The Potential Ratings is a two-part system in which a player is assigned a number rating based on his upside potential (1-10) and a letter rating based on the probability of reaching that potential (A-E). A 10 implies Hall of Fame potential whereas a 1 is minor league roster filler. Given our coverage of 1,000+ prospects, you won't find any player with less than a 6 in this book. The letter/probability ratings, on the other hand, are all across the board and for good reason.

Rating minor league baseball players can be a difficult exercise, just like any assessment system dealing with 17-24 year-old individuals. Some prospects improve. Some prospects regress. That's just the nature of the business. That's why this system wasn't designed to be your only way to assess prospects. We rate players first by the upside potential. We absolutely have internal debates on whether any certain five-tool player should be a 9 or an 8, for example. The letter/probability rating comes next, and we have just as much debate over that. We consider all kinds of factors and variables including, but not limited to: athleticism, tools, ability to improve, and historical performance. Ratings can and will change, though not typically in a drastic fashion from year to year. Our goal is to give you a snapshot of a player's ultimate upside and likelihood of success. A player's final rating—made by the team author—can be a difficult decision. But in the end, it is just a rating, given at one moment in a player's development. The more valuable information is in the player boxes and commentary.

As mentioned previously, the outline of the book will look and feel similar to previous editions of the MLBA. The Insights section is filled with premium essays designed to shine a spotlight on more free-form assessments. Some of the essays are topics from previous years—this is, in large part, by design as we've gotten positive feedback from our readers—such as Sleepers Outside the HQ100, Top 20 International Prospects, 2016 College Baseball

Names to Know, and a team-by-team 2015 Draft Recap. We also have added an article on the December Rule 5 draft; as a way for fantasy leaguers to become familiar with those players who have switched organizations, and their likelihood for success both in 2016 and over the long haul.

One of the more difficult exercises this year was the Organizational Ratings/Rankings section. As most of you know, the player movement during—and after—the Winter Meetings was unprecedented and we had to continually revise the rankings. From the Rule 5 draft to trades to free agent acquisitions, all created havoc with the ratings and rankings. But we stayed current through mid-December, and those grades reflect the player movement.

The bulk of the book continues to be made up of the hitter and pitcher profiles. We bring you expanded stats, tool assessments, expected arrival dates, draft into, potential roles, and the BaseballHQ rating. While a player's skills may improve or regress from year to year, our goal is to qualify/quantify and measure a player at one certain point in time. Equally important as the statistical tables is the tool analysis. Over-analysis of statistics in the minor leagues can be a dangerous proposition. Not only are there severe hitters/pitchers environments, but these are mostly still young players who are developing their bodies and their games. Don't get too caught up in a hitter's BA or a pitcher's ERA—look deeper at their skills and how their tools project. That's where the BHQ team comes into play. It's one thing to look at an OBP and draw conclusions. It's another thing to provide reasons why the OBP is at a certain level and why it may get better or get worse.

As mentioned previously, the player commentaries have become more consistent and provide more information on how a prospect's tools and skills project rather than just a regurgitation of their statistical outputs from previous seasons. While stats are certainly important, they don't tell the full story. There has to be some consideration for hitting/pitching environments as well as age-to-level analysis. A powerful position player prospect in the spacious ballparks of the Florida State League may not hit many HR while a so-so prospect in the hitter-friendly California League may hit 25 HR. The player commentaries are meant to provide insights into this type of situation.

Major League Equivalents remains a staple of the MLBA and provides MLEs on several prospects. Used correctly, MLEs are excellent indicators of potential. But just like we cannot take traditional major league statistics at face value, the same goes for MLEs. Compare what you see in this space versus what you see in the batter/pitcher profiles and commentaries. You'll often notice eerie similarities. Fun stuff.

The section that always generates constructive debate is the Mega-Lists. Here you will find lists such as the HQ100, Top Prospects by Organization, Top Positional Prospects, Top Prospects by Category, Best Fantasy Prospects, and the Top 100 Archives. Everybody loves lists—we do as well—and this section brings all of the assessments and analytics together. Let the debates begin.

The HQ100 is a combination of five individual contributor Top 100 lists. All five of our writers submitted his own Top 100 list—without consulting or reviewing any other list—and the HQ100 is the end result. This continues to be an interesting exercise. Sixty-three prospects that are listed in the HQ100 appeared on all five ballots—that's remarkably consistent given the large universe of minor league players.

One caveat with the HQ100 – you will notice that a prospect's placement on this list may run contrary to their placement on the organizational rankings. This is because the top prospect by organization list was constructed by one individual contributor. For example, I ranked the Top 15 prospects in each organization in the American League. My opinion will obviously differ from the four other writers when submitting a Top 100 list.

This is also evident in the lists of Top Prospects by Position. These lists were generated and formulated directly from the HQ100 as opposed to from an individual writer's opinion. Some prospects play multiple positions currently or may change positions in the future. This was captured in these lists. A difficult position to rank is relief pitchers. Many of the best relievers in the majors were starters in the minors and never would've been ranked as a top relief pitching prospect. Of similar difficulty was ranking second baseman. Many major league second basemen have slid over from shortstop.

We hope you enjoy the 11th edition of the Minor League Baseball Analyst. This is a result of year-round hard work and constant communication with each other. We are always open to your feedback on what we can do to make your reading experience more enjoyable. It is OK to disagree with some of our assessments and ratings—we welcome it. Let us know what you think. We look forward to the 2016 baseball season and hope you do as well. Enjoy!

The 2015 Rule 5 Draft Recap

by Jeremy Deloney

The 2015 MLB Winter Meetings concluded, as they do every year, with the annual Rule 5 Draft. Though the MLB on-the-field impact over the recent years has been inconsistent, the 2014 Rule 5 draft included two players who emerged as fantasy contributors in 2015: Odubel Herrera (OF, PHI), Delino Deshields (OF, TEX). Perhaps it's worth taking a closer look at the 2015 Rule 5 class.

A quick refresher: In almost all cases, players have four years from the time they were signed to their first professional contract before they become eligible for the Rule 5 Draft. Once a team places a player on its 40-man roster, that player is protected.

Clubs select in reverse order of standings from the preceding season; each club may select as many players as it so chooses until it reaches the 40-man roster limit; many teams pass on their chance to select. The catch is that players selected in the Rule 5 Draft must remain on a club's active 25-man roster for the entire season, unless the player becomes injured and is subsequently placed on the MLB disabled list; the player may not be optioned to the minor leagues. If the selecting team chooses not to keep the player on the 25-man roster, the player is offered back to his original organization.

On to the first-round picks of the MLB phase, which is where the most likely impact players come from:

Tyler Goeddel (OF, PHI); selected from Tampa Bay

Profile: He was coming off his best season to date, with a solid line of .279/.350/.433 with a career-high 12 HR in 473 AB in Double-A. He also contributed 28 stolen bases. Goeddel is a wiry strong prospect who converted from 3B to the outfield and he looked comfortable defensively, tracking balls with average range and arm strength. He only projects to average pop, but his hitting instincts are sound.

2016 Fantasy Impact: There is a very good chance that Goeddel will make the Phillies Opening Day roster in 2016; he could even win a starting job. He can play all OF positions.

Long-term Impact: His well-rounded game and athleticism should keep him in the big leagues for several years. He should be able to hit for a decent BA, average pop, and nice SB totals at his peak.

Jake Cave (OF, CIN); selected from New York (AL)

Profile: Doesn't bring much bat to the table, but he has value in his speed and defense. Cave has a slashing, choppy swing without power, but he can hit for an acceptable BA. He's not a burner, but he runs well underway and has good instincts. While he has played some CF, his best position may be LF because of his average range and arm strength.

2016 Fantasy Impact: He fits more of a reserve outfielder profile because of his defense and lack of offensive punch, so it may behoove the Reds to keep him around.

Long-term Impact: Without offensive juice (his career-high in HR is 7), he won't have much of an impact in fantasy terms.

Evan Rutckyj (LHP, ATL); selected from New York (AL)

Profile: Rutckyj was converted to a reliever in 2014 and has used a more effective fastball with added ticks and a slider for more strikeouts. He has a big frame, but maintains his mechanics well and exhibited much better control in 2015.

2016 Fantasy Impact: Rutckyj could stick—though likely as a lefty specialist, which severely limits his fantasy value.

Long-term Impact: Unlikely to return to the rotation, he could develop into a quality situational reliever or set-up guy.

Luis Perdomo (RHP, SD, via COL); selected from St. Louis

Profile: The 22-year-old has almost exclusively been used as a starter, though he may move to the bullpen to take advantage of his 92-96 mph fastball. He appeared in the 2015 Futures Game in 2015 and has some potential, backing up his heater with a hard, though inconsistent, slider. His change-up and command are both well below average.

2016 Fantasy Impact: In the bullpen, he would likely be used in low-leverage situations, thus greatly reducing his fantasy value. As a starter, he'd have to put together an outstanding spring to make the team.

Long-term Impact: If he ever learns to command his pitches and develop just an average change-up, he could be a #3-4 starter in the big leagues. However, his best chance for success is as a late-innings reliever.

Colin Walsh (2B, MIL); selected from Oakland

Profile: The 26-year-old turned himself into an on-base machine in 2015, leading the Texas League with a .447 OBP (124 walks). The switch-hitter also set a career high with 39 doubles and hit 13 HR. The Brewers plan to add to his versatility by getting him action at 3B and the outfield. He's not a particularly strong defender with limited range and hands.

2016 Fantasy Impact: Walsh is a favorite of the MIL analytics department, but he has fringy skills. He will have to prove he can hit upper level pitching in order to make the squad.

Long-term Impact: Outside of his extreme plate discipline, he doesn't offer much. He lacks offensive punch and his stolen bases (17 in 2015) are more a byproduct of shrewd baserunning than frontline speed.

Jabari Blash (OF, SD, via OAK); selected from Seattle

Profile: He hit .271/.370/.576 with 32 HR between Double-A and Triple-A, and his power could be useful if he can make better contact. At 6'5", the right-handed hitter has long arms which leaves him vulnerable to pitches inside. He has enough arm for RF, but doesn't run well and has limited range.

2016 Fantasy Impact: He has enough tools and talent to make the team and could hit some HR. His BA may be problematic, however, as MLB pitchers will likely have their way with him.

Long-term Impact: Blash has never been a top prospect because he has too many holes in his swing. But if he can make improvements to his approach, he could become an everyday player.

Josh Martin (RHP, SD); selected from Cleveland
Profile: The bulldog reliever has been consistent throughout his career and though without filthy stuff, he does have an appetite for throwing strikes, locating his three pitches, and keeping hitters off-guard.
2016 Fantasy Impact: Relievers who can pitch multiple innings and throw strikes have MLB value, but little fantasy value.
Long-term Impact: He won't have much relevance in most fantasy formats.

Joey Rickard (OF, BAL); selected from Tampa Bay
Profile: Rickard was selected not based on his offensive production, but his defensive ability and OBP. The right-handed hitter sees a lot of pitches and draws walks, but has little HR power.
2016 Fantasy Impact: Rickard could stick as a reserve who can get on base and steal a few bags, but seems more likely that he'll be returned to the Rays.
Long-term Impact: Rickard will not play every day, but may steal an occasional base. He's a better real-life than fantasy player.

Deolis Guerra (RHP, LAA); selected from Pittsburgh
Profile: The former Mets and Twins prospect signed with the Pirates for 2015 and dominated Triple-A, but got hit in his MLB debut. His change-up remains his best pitch; also has a 90-94 mph fastball. His curveball remains a distant third pitch.
2016 Fantasy Impact: Guerra is unlikely to play a prominent role in the Angels bullpen, but he may stick as a low-leverage, middle innings guy. He doesn't have closer stuff.
Long-term Impact: Because he doesn't project as a closer, his impact will be minimal.

Joe Biagini (RHP, TOR); selected from San Francisco
Profile: Biagini has a tall frame that allows him to pitch downhill and induce groundballs. He has a deep repertoire of pitches to keep hitters off-guard, though he lacks an out pitch. He has done a better job of repeating his delivery and throwing strikes.
2016 Fantasy Impact: Because of his arm strength, he has a good chance to make the Blue Jays, but as a reliever. He could potentially spot start, but won't contribute much in fantasy terms.
Long-term Impact: Biagini has average stuff, but could eventually make it as a #4 starter. He won't register many strikeouts, but his walk rate and oppBA could be moderately good.

Matt Bowman (RHP, STL); selected from New York (NL)
Profile: The 24-year-old got lit up (5.53 ERA) in his first full season in Triple-A. He's a command-control pitcher with average velocity and no knockout offering, though he induces a lot of ground balls. Bowman is at his best when he mixes efficiently and works quickly.
2016 Fantasy Impact: Despite the poor production, he has a chance to make the Cardinals roster as a long reliever. If he earns a spot, he'll have low to non-existent fantasy value.
Long-term Impact: Bowman could eventually grow into a back-end starter, but since he relies on deception and sequencing rather than stuff, he won't have a huge impact.

Sleepers Outside the HQ100

by Rob Gordon

Every year when we put together the HQ100 top prospect list there are a handful of players who are on the brink of a breakout and have the potential to develop into elite prospects. Some of these "sleeper" prospects were high draft picks in 2014 or 2015 and haven't had time to establish themselves, while others haven't gotten the attention they should, and others are just working out flaws in their game.

The ten players highlighted below aren't likely to appear on many top prospect lists and many should be available to fantasy owners, even those in long-term keeper formats. All have the potential to establish themselves as top 100 prospects in 2017 and beyond.

Because he doesn't have the elite level power most teams and fantasy owners are looking for, **Harold Ramirez** (OF, PIT) tends to get lost in the shuffle when it comes to ranking the top OF prospects in the NL. That's in part because at 5-10, 210, he doesn't have the frame or the swing plane to develop more than average power, but he can do everything else and profiles as an excellent table-setter. In 2015, Ramirez had a slash line of .337/.399/.458 with 22 SB for High-A Bradenton. He has been injury-prone early in his career and has a below-average arm, but he should be able to stick in CF and offers a nice package of speed, contact ability, and track record of hitting for average.

The Houston Astros picked up **Joe Musgrove** (RHP) as part of a 10-player deal with the Blue Jays in 2012. The supplemental 1st rounder from 2011 had one of the more impressive breakout seasons of 2015, going 12-1 with a 1.88 ERA across three different levels. The 6-5 righty comes after hitters with a good 92-94 mph fastball that has late life and backs it up with a plus, swing-and-miss slider, and a change-up that shows potential. More important than the raw stuff is the fact that Musgrove has pinpoint control and command of both the fastball and the slider. He walked just eight batters in 100.2 innings and has walked just 31 batters since turning pro in 2011. Musgrove isn't flashy, but he is one of the best strike-throwers in the minors and should develop into a solid mid-rotation starter.

The Chicago Cubs have done an excellent job scouting the collegiate ranks and they look to have found another gem in **Ian Happ** (OF/2B). Happ was the 9th overall pick in the 2015 draft after a standout career at the University of Cincinnati. The switch-hitting Happ has an aggressive approach at the plate, but also has a good understanding of the strike zone and rips line drives to all fields. Happ played primarily 2B in college, but was used exclusively in the OF after being drafted. The Cubs still have hopes that he will be able to stick at 2B and he has been compared to Ben Zobrist, and more optimistically, Chase Utley.

The Cubs have also been aggressive on the international free agent market and in 2013 landed SS Gleyber Torres and OF **Eloy Jimenez.** Torres quickly established himself as the organization's top prospect and Jimenez could soon follow. The 18-year-old Jimenez was signed out of the Dominican Republic for $2.8 million and at 6-4, 205 he has a similar profile to the Cubs Jorge Soler. He has plus bat speed and the raw power to hit 20+ HR in the majors, but like Soler he can be overly aggressive at the plate, and scouts are mixed on his ability to hit for average as he moves up. Club President Theo Epstein has instilled an emphasis on plate discipline and strike zone judgment throughout the system and if Jimenez can put that to use, he has the tools to be an impact major leaguer.

The Baltimore Orioles haven't had a ton of success on the international free agent market, but 3B **Jomar Reyes** has some nice offensive tools. Signed out of the Dominican Republic in 2014 for just $350,000, Reyes was impressive as one of the youngest players in the SAL, hitting .278/.334/.440 in 89 games before a broken hamate bone shut him down. At 6-3, 220 Reyes has good bat speed and plus raw power to all fields. Like most young players, he can be overly aggressive at the plate and needs to make more consistent contact, but his power tool is legit and he should continue to move up quickly.

Over the past decade the Cardinals have received a lot of praise for their scouting and player development—and rightfully so. Despite not having a top 10 draft pick since 1988, the Cardinals have been able to consistently restock their system with major league talent. They seem to have found another reliable arm in **Jack Flaherty** (RHP). Flaherty was a 1st round pick in 2014, played on the same Harvard-Westlake high school team as Lucas Giolioto and Max Fried, has a good 90-93 mph fastball and could add more velocity as he fills out his 6-4, 205 pound frame. Flaherty held his own in the MWL, going 9-3 with a 2.84 ERA in 18 starts and will move up to the FSL in 2016. He has a nice four-pitch mix and could develop into a low-end #2 starter.

The Kansas City Royals **Ashe Russell** (RHP) didn't get a lot of pre-draft hype but he quietly emerged as one of the best prep arms in the country. The Royals were eager to snatch him up with the 21st pick in the draft. Russell already features a plus 92-95 mph fastball that has been clocked as high as 97 mph with nice arm-side run. He could add more velocity as he matures and fills out his lean 6-4, 200 pound frame. His slider and change-up are works in progress, but the slider has swing-and-miss potential and he gets plus movement from his low ¾ delivery. Russell is less polished than Flaherty or Musgrove, but has more projectability and could develop into a #2 starter.

The L.A. Dodgers were excoriated in the press for failing to sign Zack Grienke, the botched Aroldis Chapman and Hisashi Iwakuma deals, and then not being able to land starters Johnny Cueto or Jeff Samardzija. But they did manage to trade for **Frankie Montas** (RHP) as part of the three-team Todd Frazier deal. Montas has an electric arm and can blow away hitters with a plus 93-97 mph sinking fastball that has been clocked as high as 102 mph. He backs it up with an above-average, but inconsistent, hard slider and a change-up that shows some potential. Like a lot of young fireballers, Montas struggles with control and was used mostly in relief in his brief stint with the White Sox in 2015. It remains to be seen how the Dodgers will use Montas, but he certainly has the velocity to make an impact either as a starter or in relief.

The Washington Nationals have done an excellent job of stockpiling high upside prospects to bolster their already deep MLB roster. Most of the attention goes to Lucas Giolito and Trea Turner. **Erick Fedde** (RHP) is likely to lead the next wave of Nationals prospects and is a name you need to know. Fedde, the 18th overall pick in the 2014 draft, had Tommy John surgery in 2014. He finally made his pro debut in 2015 and looked relatively sharp, despite the long layoff, going 5-3 with a 3.38 ERA in 14 starts. He has seen most of his velocity come back and features a plus 91-94 mph heater that reached 97 mph pre-surgery. He backs up the heat with a good, but inconsistent slider and an improved change-up, and walked just 16 batters in 64 innings, a good sign when recovering from TJS. Fedde has the size and stuff to develop into a #2 starter and could be in-line for a breakout in 2016.

The Cleveland Indians have quietly developed a solid farm system. Nineteen-year-old **Justus Sheffield** (RHP) is the nephew of former big leaguer Gary Sheffield and was the Indians 1st round pick in 2014. He had a solid full-season debut, going 9-4 with a 3.31 ERA in 26 starts for Low-A Lake County in the MWL. Sheffield has a good 90-93 mph fastball that has been clocked as high as 96 mph, and backs it up with an above-average curveball and a change-up that shows potential. He commands the strike zone well and walked just 38 while striking out 138 in 127.2 innings. If Sheffield can refine his change-up, he has the stuff to be a good mid-rotation starter despite his 5-10, 200 pound frame.

Top 20 International Prospects for 2016

by Jeremy Deloney

Major League Baseball has implemented changes to the signing of international players over the past few years, some in part for the purposes of leveling the playing field. Given the potential for change with respect to the U.S. relationship with Cuba, there may be more Cuban players entering the U.S. in the next few years. Listed below are various international prospects who inked contracts during the international signing period in 2015 or players who could make the jump to the U.S. in the next two seasons. Because of the uncertainty of defections and eligibility, some top Cuban prospects may not be profiled below.

Note that some signed players eligible for this list have player boxes in this book. For additional info on Vladimir Guerrero, Jr. (OF, TOR), Lucius Fox (SS, SF), Jhailyn Ortiz (OF, PHI), Eddy Martinez (OF, CHC), Leodys Taveras (OF, TEX), Yadier Alvarez (RHP, LA), and Starling Heredia (OF, LA), see their player boxes in the sections to follow. In alphabetical order:

Aramis Ademan (SS, CHC)
A smooth, quick defender, the 17-year-old should be able to climb the ladder as a shortstop and not have to switch positions. He possesses admirable defensive attributes led by his soft hands and nimble feet. He also has a strong, accurate arm. He uses a compact stroke from the left side to put bat to ball easily. Ademan has a fast bat, but his thin, lean frame lacks the strength and leverage to hit the ball over the fence. Rather, he focuses on line drives to the gaps.
Signing bonus/status: Signed for $2 million
MLB Debut: 2021

Lazaro Armenteros (OF, Cuba)

The 16-year-old has yet to sign a contract with a major league club, but he has scouts abuzz based upon his five tools and sky-high ceiling. He already possesses a mature frame at 6'2" 205, but plays the game with passion and polish. Arementeros has present power that could grow to plus-plus and he runs well. He has the type of tools that could lead to .300+ seasons with 30+ HR and 20+ SB. The jury is out on his future defensive home —some see him in an outfield corner, others at 3B or 1B.
Signing bonus/status: Defected from Cuba; seeking free agency
MLB Debut: 2021

Randy Arozarena (SS/OF, Cuba)

The 20-year-old has a chance to be a high-caliber leadoff hitter, as he works counts and draws a large number of walks while making simple contact with a short swing. He uses the entire field and has the instincts and bat control to be a sound situational hitter. Arozarena could develop average power, though he's at his best when hitting hard line drives to the gaps. He's played all over the diamond, but he's not proficient at any one position. Second base may be his ultimate destination.
Signing bonus/status: Defected from Cuba, seeking free agency
MLB Debut: 2018

Gilberto Celestino (OF, HOU)

Long and lean, the 16-year-old's glove is ahead of his bat, but he has offensive upside with above average bat speed and advanced pitch recognition. The right-handed hitter should be able to maintain a moderate to high BA. His power potential is in question, however, as his swing mechanics aren't conducive to plus pop. Celestino is a very good CF with intelligence and savvy to get good jumps and take efficient routes. He has an average, accurate arm.
Signing bonus/status: Signed for $2.5 million
MLB Debut: 2021

Derian Cruz (SS, ATL)

The 17-year-old has double-plus speed that allows him to be a stolen base threat every time he's on. A switch-hitter with a choppy swing, he makes consistent contact. Though he has the bat speed, he will need to add significant strength for power. As a defender, Cruz has fundamental footwork and clean, quick hands, though his lack of arm strength may push him to 2B long-term.
Signing bonus/status: Signed for $2 million
MLB Debut: 2022

Yusniel Diaz (OF, LA)

The 18-year-old right-handed hitter has a bevy of tools, and could evolve into a leadoff or a #3-type batter. The main question is power projection. Diaz has exceptional hand-eye coordination, makes contact and covers the plate well. His swing can get long at times and he often struggles with breaking balls. He hits a lot of doubles now, though there is some natural strength that could result in HR down the line. Diaz can patrol CF with plus speed, strong arm, and sound reads.
Signing bonus/status: Signed for $15.5 million
MLB Debut: 2019

Omar Estevez (2B, LA)

Though not blessed with plus tools or athleticism, the 17-year-old does everything well and maximizes his ability. Estevez works counts to his advantage and uses his simple swing to put bat to ball which should result in BA and doubles power. He won't hit many HR, but he recognizes pitches and draws walks. Estevez is a fundamentally-sound defender who could play shortstop in a pinch, but is best at 2B. He has a fringe-average arm and adequate range and quickness.
Signing bonus/status: Signed for $6 million
MLB Debut: 2020

Yonathan Sierra Estiwal (OF, CHC)

The long and lanky 17-year-old looks the part of a prototypical RF because of his power potential and raw arm strength. At 6'3" 205 pounds, he has the room to grow and fill out his frame. He possesses a quick, clean stroke from the left side with the hitting instincts to use the entire field. There are concerns about whether he'll make enough contact. His swing mechanics and pitch recognition need attention, though he's athletic enough to improve. His speed is only average, but he tracks balls well in the outfield.
Signing bonus/status: Signed for $2.5 million
MLB Debut: 2022

Jose Fernandez (2B, Cuba)

When he signs with a major league club, the 27-year-old won't need much time in the minors. He is a bat-first player who sees a lot of pitches and rarely swings and misses. Bat control and plate coverage are his specialties and he uses his level stroke to hit hard line drives to the gaps. He won't hit for much long ball pop and his speed is fringe-average at best. 2B is his best position as he lacks pure arm strength.
Signing bonus/status: Defected from Cuba; seeking free agency
MLB Debut: 2017

Andres Gimenez (SS, NYM)

The 17-year-old is a pure shortstop with plenty of athleticism and agility in his lean frame. His natural actions, above average range, and strong arm will keep him at the position for the long-term. The left-handed hitter has very good offensive potential with his quick bat and mature approach at the plate Gimenez projects to gap power with a quick, level swing path and has a feel for contact with advanced pitch recognition skills. His speed and eye at the plate could allow him to hit in the leadoff position.
Signing bonus/status: Signed for $1.2 million
MLB Debut: 2021

Gregory Guerrero (SS, NYM)

The polished 16-year-old has good skills that should translate well to the U.S. He stands out on defense with his quick, smooth actions and plus agility. He may eventually move to 2B or 3B because his range may not be enough. His arm is playable at any position and could also work in the outfield. Guerrero, a right-handed hitter, makes hard contact and exhibits raw power to the pull side, though mostly in the gaps. He sees pitches and is willing to draw walks.
Signing bonus/status: Signed for $1.5 million
MLB Debut: 2021

Vladimir Gutierrez (RHP, Cuba)
The 20-year-old has mostly been a reliever in Cuba, though most scouts project him to be a starter because of three average-to-plus offerings and durability. Gutierrez stands 6'3" and has a lean frame that oozes projection, though his mechanics can get rough which may hinder his potential to hit the mid-to-high 90s with his fastball (currently 89-93 mph). His curveball is a plus pitch that misses bats and his change-up is average.
Signing bonus/status: Declared free agent by MLB, but has not yet signed
MLB Debut: 2018

Andy Ibanez (2B, TEX)
The short, thick infielder may turn out to be a value sign for the Rangers as he could be major league ready soon. He exhibits above average athleticism and body control. His arm is a little short for any position other than 2B, but he has a quick release and makes routine plays. Offensively, he's a sound hitter who understands the strike zone. Ibanez can hit breaking balls and possesses ideal patience at the plate. Because he makes consistent contact, he should be able to hit for a high BA. He has more doubles power than long ball pop.
Signing bonus/status: Signed for $1.6 million
MLB Debut: 2018

Wander Javier (SS, MIN)
The 16-year-old has one of the highest ceilings of any prospect on this list. Javier has all five tools in his repertoire and could grow into a middle-of-the-order run producer. He may stick at short-stop because of his athleticism and quickness, though some see a move to 3B because of his cannon arm. He swings a very fast bat and has raw power that could allow him to hit 25+ HR at his peak. However, he has a long swing and he struggles with breaking balls. His approach could be better as he is an aggressive hitter.
Signing bonus/status: Signed for $4 million
MLB Debut: 2021

Kenta Maeda (RHP, LA)
With command of four pitches, the 27-year-old has the goods to become an immediate #4 starter. He doesn't wow with premium velocity, but he relies on sequencing and pitch location. His fastball sits between 88-94 mph and he mixes in a slider, slow curveball, and change-up. He adds and subtracts well from each offering and keeps hitters off-guard. Because of Maeda's command, his pitch effectiveness plays up. He won't be a pitcher who contends for strikeout titles, but his oppBA could be low and he'll pitch a lot of innings.
Signing info: Eight years, $24M with performance bonuses
MLB Debut: 2016

Seuly Matias (OF, KC)
With a look at the 17-year-old's frame and plus arm, one can see the star potential. Matias has a long, slender frame with the room to add muscle. As a result, he owns a significant amount of power projection. He has a chance to stick in CF because of his speed and range, but most see an eventual move to RF. He exhibits above

average bat speed and raw power, but can get pull-happy and has some contact issues due to his long stroke.
Signing bonus/status: Signed for $2.25 million
MLB Debut: 2022

Daniel Montano (OF, COL)
The lean 16-year-old will take time to develop, but the Rockies will be patient. Though he may not have a loud tool, he has good fundamentals and feel for the game. Montano, a left-handed hitter, has a balanced approach with a quick, level swing. He has a discerning eye at the plate and can make contact. He doesn't have much power at present and may only grow into average pop at his peak. His fringy arm may move him from CF to LF, but he has above average instincts and range.
Signing bonus/status: Signed for $2 million
MLB Debut: 2022

Jorge Ona (OF, Cuba)
Despite not playing much against advanced competition, the 19-year-old shows advanced skills and plenty of power projection in his 6'2" 195 pound frame. Ona has exceptional bat speed and loft in his stroke to hit for power to all fields. As he continues to add strength and learn to read pitches better, he could become a middle-of-the-order hitter. He knows the strike zone, though he can lunge at breaking balls. Ona is a good defender in RF with a very strong arm. He only has average speed at best and will likely slow down as he ages.
Signing bonus/status: Has not yet signed – defected from Cuba – seeking free agency
MLB Debut: 2019

Byung Ho Park (1B, MIN)
The 29-year-old Park is a two-time MVP of the Korean Baseball Organization and last season, he led the league in both HR (53) and strikeouts (161). The right-handed hitter is all about power as he owns an uppercut swing and plenty of strength. His bat speed is well above average, but his tendency to swing and miss is a concern. He can struggle with upper-tier velocity and good breaking balls. Park does have a disciplined eye at the plate and will draw walks. Defensively, he's an adequate 1B, though the Twins will also use him as a DH.
Signing bonus/status: Signed 4-year contract worth $12 million
MLB Debut: 2016

Norge Ruiz (RHP, Cuba)
The short, compact pitcher has mid-rotation potential due to a four-pitch mix and above average control. Ruiz, 21, doesn't have great size and has some durability concerns, but his arm action gives his pitches some extra movement and he sequences them well. He lacks a true out pitch, though his above average change-up gives hitters fits. His slider shows nice break at times, but it is too inconsistent. Ruiz is athletic and has advanced pitchability and will only need a few years in the minors.
Signing bonus/status: Has not yet signed – defected from Cuba – seeking free agency
MLB Debut: 2017

2015 First-Year Player Draft Recap

by Jeremy Deloney (AL) and Rob Gordon (NL)

AMERICAN LEAGUE

BALTIMORE ORIOLES

The Orioles made it a priority to draft power bats, and three of their first five picks satisfied that desire. OF D.J. Stewart (1st), 3B Ryan Mountcastle (supp 1st) and OF Jason Heinrich (5th) all bring offensive punch to the table. Stewart was the only collegian, while the other two will take time to develop. The Orioles selected several high schoolers, including RHP Gray Fenter (7th) who received a $1 million bonus. The most polished arm drafted was LHP Garrett Cleavinger (3rd) who could reach the majors quickly if he stays in the bullpen. This draft may not have been filled with high ceiling, five-tool talents or flamethrowers, but the overall haul was solid. If the prep picks pan out, it could be even better.
Sleeper: RHP Ryan Meisinger (11th) had a stellar pro debut, with two pitches (fastball, slider) that give him a chance to ascend the ladder quickly.
Grade: B

BOSTON RED SOX

The Red Sox used their early pick wisely on OF Andrew Benintendi (1st), 7th overall. He immediately becomes one of the better prospects in the system after a .313 BA/11 HR debut (198 AB). The Red Sox continued the college bat trend with C Austin Rei (3rd) and OF Tate Matheny (4th). Due to new MLB rules, teams can now trade drafted players within a year and the Red Sox did that during the offseason, when they sent LHP Logan Allen (8th) to the Padres in the Craig Kimbrel deal. This was a college-heavy draft that lacks upside and included several high-floor picks.
Sleeper: RHP Travis Lakins (6th) is a very good athlete who has a chance to regain the velocity he showed in the past. If he improves his change-up, he could have three average to above average pitches.
Grade: C+

CHICAGO WHITE SOX

Due to free agent signings, the White Sox were left without 2nd and 3rd round picks. Their 4th rounder, LHP Zack Erwin, was shipped to Oakland in the Brett Lawrie deal during the offseason. On the bright side, they did sign their first 32 picks and have a potential frontline starter in RHP Carson Fulmer (1st). He was their only draftee to sign for a bonus over $510,000. It was a college heavy draft, though they did select prep 1B Corey Zangari (6th) who could develop into a 30+ HR hitter down the line. Outside of Fulmer, the White Sox chose a good college arm in RHP Jordan Stephens (5th) who has a solid fastball and plus curveball. To add backstop depth to their organization, they selected two fundamentally-sound catchers in Casey Schroeder (8th) and Seby Zavala (12th).
Sleeper: RHP Chris Comito (15th) is a very projectable high school arm that will take years of development. However, he has feel for a curveball and throwing strikes.
Grade: C-

CLEVELAND INDIANS

The Indians had three of the top 59 picks and selected high-ceiling high school arms with all three. This was one of the best draft hauls, attributable to solid late-round picks. 15 picks signed for at least $100,000. The class is headlined by the three arms – LHP Brady Aiken (1st), RHP Triston McKenzie (supp 1st), and LHP Juan Hillman (2nd). Due to Tommy John surgery, Aiken won't return to action until late 2016, but he will be worth the wait. McKenzie and Hillman both have lean frames that figure to add strength and more ticks to their fastballs. In rounds 3 and 4, they opted for college middle infielders in 2B Mark Mathias (3rd) and SS Tyler Krieger (4th). Mathias was impressive in his pro debut while Krieger did not play due to a shoulder injury.
Sleeper: SS Luke Wakamatsu (20th) was a steal and though he needs to add a lot of strength, already is a force defensively.
Grade: A-

DETROIT TIGERS

After drafting a high school pitcher, RHP Beau Burrows (1st) with their first pick, the Tigers went with college players until the 17th round. In fact, of the 27 players they signed, only Burrows was from the prep ranks. Burrows gives the club a high-upside power arm they can develop. The best pro debut belonged to LHP Tyler Alexander (2nd) who was the third draftee to sign for $1 million+ and used his savvy to dominate low-level hitters. The Tigers signed OF Christin Stewart (1st) as their second first round pick and he showcased his immense power by hitting 10 HR in 256 AB. As usual, Detroit also selected hard-throwing relievers, led by RHP Drew Smith (3rd) who can touch the high-90s. The ultimate grade on this draft will depend on Burrows and Stewart.
Sleeper: SS A.J. Simcox (14th) was best known for his outstanding glovework in college, but opened eyes with his level stroke and easy contact skills. He signed for $600,000.
Grade: B-

HOUSTON ASTROS

Due to the inability (or unwillingness) to sign LHP Brady Aiken in 2014, the Astros were rewarded with another first round pick. Thus, they had two picks in the top five and five in the first 79. All five of those picks received signing bonuses of at least $1 million and another—LHP Patrick Sandoval (11th)—received $900,000. The Astros selected position players with their top three picks—SS Alex Bregman (1st), OF Kyle Tucker (1st), and OF Daz Cameron (supp 1st). All three received bonuses of at least $4 million. Tucker and Cameron were from the prep ranks and Bregman was a highly-touted college infielder. The Astros used RHP Thomas Eshleman (2nd) in a deal to acquire RHP Ken Giles from Philadelphia. Given the number of high picks, it would be tough not to be one of the top classes, at least on paper.
Sleeper: OF Johnny Sewald (14th) is a leadoff hitter who gets on base a lot and uses his speed well. He is also an outstanding defensive CF.
Grade: A

KANSAS CITY ROYALS

Few teams can match the pitching the Royals have added to their ranks over the past two years. They selected prep pitchers with their two first round picks and added possibly the best arm in the entire draft in the 2nd round. Because of the early round focus on hurlers, the Royals didn't draft any high ceiling position players outside of OF Anderson Miller (3rd) who is starting to emerge. RHP Ashe Russell (1st) and RHP Nolan Watson (1st) highlight the class and give the Royals two more prep arms that could deliver huge pay-offs. Russell has more electricity whereas Watson shows more polish. RHP Josh Staumont (2nd) can easily reach triple digits with his fastball and can dominate. LHP Garrett Davila (4th) is another projectable prep star and he signed for a $746,000 bonus.

Sleeper: LHP Joey Markus (9th) is long and angular (6'7") and will need to refine his mechanics and find a consistent release point. However, the raw stuff is there for him to succeed.

Grade: B+

LOS ANGELES ANGELS

With one of the weakest farm systems in baseball, the Angels stockpiled position players. They picked only two pitchers in the top 10 rounds while selecting seven college hitters and one prep position player. The Angels signed all but one of their 40 selections. Their top pick, C Taylor Ward (1st), had as good of a debut as any and immediately becomes one of their top prospects. They are excited about OF Jahmai Jones (2nd), a prepster with excellent athleticism and an ability to play CF. Candidates that could ascend through the minors quickly include OF Brendon Sanger (4th) and SS David Fletcher (6th). There may not be many—if any—stars in this class, but some should be contributors. RHP Grayson Long (3rd) was the highest pitcher selected and he has a chance to be a back-end starter with three average offerings.

Sleeper: C Dalton Blumenfeld (12th) has a large frame and the raw power and pure arm strength to match, though he'll take several years to develop.

Grade: C

MINNESOTA TWINS

The Twins had a number of options on their draft board with the #6 overall pick, but decided on LHP Tyler Jay (1st). They'll need to decide whether to move the college reliever to the rotation to take advantage of his arm strength and plus arsenal or keep him in the bullpen where he could help them quickly. They failed to sign their 2nd round pick, RHP Kyle Cody, but then focused their attention on high school infielders. 3B Travis Blankenhorn (3rd) and 3B Trey Cabbage (4th) both have good tools with the bat and glove. The Twins are excited about two college teammates at Maryland, LHP Alex Robinson (5th) and OF LaMonte Wade (9th). The latter had a spectacular pro debut with power and plate discipline. Power arms and power hitters highlight this draft class.

Sleeper: 1B Kolton Kendrick (8th) can hit the ball farther than most any prep pick in the draft, but he'll need to work on his approach and defense.

Grade: B-

NEW YORK YANKEES

With two first round picks, the Yankees had a chance to set a positive tone and they certainly did with RHP James Kaprielian (1st) and SS Kyle Holder (1st) that cost the club $2.65 million and $1.8 million respectively. Kaprielian has excellent arm strength and has #2-3 starter stuff. While questionable with the bat, Holder is a potential Gold Glove-caliber defender. Overall, the Yankees took college players with nine of their first 11 picks. To add to the haul, they drafted a few intriguing players in later rounds. OF Jhalan Jackson (7th) and 3B Donny Sands (8th) had solid pro debuts and could climb prospect charts in years to come. Three other pitchers, LHP Jeff Degano (2nd), RHP Drew Finley (3rd), and RHP Chance Adams (5th) could pay dividends in short order.

Sleeper: 1B Isiah Gilliam (20th) has potential to evolve into a corner infielder with plus power to all fields due to his strong build and incredible bat speed.

Grade: B+

OAKLAND ATHLETICS

It was quite evident the Athletics wanted college players, as only one of their top ten picks was from high school. With their top two picks, they chose college shortstops, Richie Martin (1st) and Mikey White (2nd). Martin is ultra-athletic with a chance to produce with the bat while White is likely to switch positions to 2B or 3B. RHP Dakota Chalmers (3rd) was their only prep player in the top ten rounds. He can hit the mid-90s with his fastball, but needs a lot of work with his mechanics. The Athletics had to give him $1.2 million to buy him out of his Georgia commitment. After the top three, there were a number of safer college picks. OF Skye Bolt (4th) was a solid pick and has exciting tools. Whether he can develop into an everyday player is another story.

Sleeper: RHP Bubba Derby (6th) isn't very big, but gets the job done with a quality fastball, two breaking balls that miss bats, and a very good change-up.

Grade: C+

SEATTLE MARINERS

The Mariners weren't able to make a selection until the 2nd round at pick #60. They spread out their bonus pool to acquire solid talent with some exceeding expectations in their pro debuts. The top pick was prep RHP Nick Neidert (2nd) who signed for $1.2 million and has good feel for pitching. They went with college players with five of their next six picks with RHP Dylan Thompson (4th) the only high schooler. OF Braden Bishop (3rd) could turn out to be the jewel of the class as he shows nice tools with both the bat and glove. One of the best debuts of any draftee was SS Drew Jackson (5th) who led the NWL in BA while flashing a good glove. The Mariners hope that some of their later round picks develop to ease the pain of not having a first rounder.

Sleeper: RHP Kyle Wilcox (6th) pitched out of the bullpen upon signing and sat in the mid-90s with his fastball. He has a fresh arm that could be special.

Grade: C-

TAMPA BAY RAYS

After selecting prep bats with their top two selections, the Rays almost exclusively focused on college picks with their remaining selections. Between OF Garrett Whitley (1st) and C Chris Betts (2nd), the Rays spent over $4.4 million, but they still were able to obtain quality picks, especially in the top 10 rounds. Whitley has significant upside while Betts supplies well above average raw power. 2B Brandon Lowe (3rd) might have been a higher pick if not for a broken ankle and OF Joe McCarthy (5th) exhibits nice tools, including speed, patience, and bat speed. There weren't many high-profile arms selected, though RHP Brandon Koch (4th) and RHP Ian Gibaut (11th) can reach the mid-90s with their heaters. Koch pitches out of the bullpen and could reach the majors within a few years.

Sleeper: 2B Jake Cronenworth (7th) was a two-way player in college, but played both middle infield spots upon signing. He has a smooth bat, but not much power projection.

Grade: B

TEXAS RANGERS

If some of the high-risk pitchers pan out, this draft class could be among the best in baseball. With the fourth overall pick, the Rangers selected RHP Dillon Tate (1st), a hard-throwing and athletic pitcher who could front a rotation someday. In rounds 3 and 4, they opted to take big chances with two injured college pitchers, RHPs Michael Matuella (3rd) and Jake Lemoine (4th). Matuella was a first round talent before he succumbed to Tommy John surgery in April. Lemoine encountered a shoulder injury, but did not have surgery. Both can fire their fastballs into the mid-to-high 90s when healthy. The Rangers gave prep OF Eric Jenkins (2nd) a $2 million bonus and he has impact speed that makes him a very good CF and basestealer. They did well with mixing college and high school and position players and pitchers.

Sleeper: OF Chad Smith (5th) was young for the class and has the tools that could be cultivated into a top-notch player, whether at 1B or an outfield corner.

Grade: B

TORONTO BLUE JAYS

The Blue Jays certainly did not expect RHP Jon Harris (1st) to fall into their lap, but they were happy to nab him. He could fit at the top of the rotation due to his plus fastball and ability to miss bats. Toronto failed to sign their 2nd round selection, RHP Brady Singer, a long and lanky prep arm with a feel for pitching. There was a focus on arms and there are a handful that could become legitimate prospects. RHP Justin Maese (3rd) and RHP Jose Espada (5th) were two high school picks who will likely spend a few years in rookie ball, but have upside. The Blue Jays didn't have any eye-popping position players picked early, but paid big money to late round picks 3B Christian Williams (16th) and OF Reggie Pruitt (24th).

Sleeper: 3B Carl Wise (4th) has some kinks to work out with the bat, but he exhibits power potential with above average bat speed and an innate feel for the strike zone.

Grade: C

NATIONAL LEAGUE

ARIZONA DIAMONDBACKS

With the team's 1st overall pick, the only time they've had it since 2005, the Diamondbacks took Vanderbilt SS Dansby Swanson, the top collegiate player. Swanson was the draft's most polished player, and was traded in December to Atlanta. The Diamondbacks also added TCU lefty Alex Young (2nd), College of Charleston righty Taylor Clarke (3rd) and ASU reliever Ryan Burr (5th). Burr has a fastball that tops out at 100 mph, was lights out in his pro debut, and could reach the majors by late 2016.

Sleeper: OF Jason Morozowski (13th) was a Division II All-American and belted 21 HR in his junior year. He had an impressive pro debut, hitting .292/.369/.479 in 240 AB.

Grade: A-

ATLANTA BRAVES

The Braves are in rebuilding mode, and in addition to making numerous trades to restock their farm system, the Braves had five of the first 75 picks in the draft. With the first two picks they landed prep hurlers Kolby Allard and Mike Soroka for a combined $5.01 million and then added 3B Austin Riley (supp 1st) and C Lucas Herbert (2nd). Allard and Herbert were teammates at San Clemente High School and Allard has the highest upside of any of the Braves 2015 picks. Texas A&M closer A.J. Minter (supp 2nd) is recovering from Tommy John surgery, but prior to the injury showed a plus mid-90s fastball that topped out at 98 mph. The Braves invested heavily in projectable high school players and pitching. They took 12 pitchers in their first 14 picks and will have to be patient with their development, but overall this was a good haul.

Sleeper: OF Justin Ellison (12th) might be the best athlete in the Braves draft class. The Western Oklahoma State JC standout has a nice mix of power and speed, but will need to prove he can hit as a professional.

Grade: B+

CHICAGO CUBS

The Cubs invested heavily in the draft, spending a combined $7.6 million in bonuses, including dishing out over-slot bonuses to prep lefty Bryan Hudson (3rd) and OF D.J. Wilson (4th). The Cubs stayed the course with their first two picks and took advanced collegiate hitters Ian Happ (1st) and Donnie Dewees (2nd). Both impressed in their pro debuts and are among the Cubs top 15 prospects. The Cubs saved money in later rounds by drafting inexpensive college seniors with picks 6-10. The development of Hudson and Wilson will be key to this draft class. Wilson has above-average raw tools, but at 5-8, 175, he'll have to work hard to make an impact in the majors. At 6-8, 220, Hudson has the size and projection that scouts dream on, but will take time to develop. The only weakness in this draft class is the lack of impact arms.

Sleeper: RHP Preston Morrison (8th) doesn't have overpowering stuff, but the 4-year starter at TCU knows how to pitch and could develop into a viable back-end starter. He held his own in his pro debut, going 1-1 with a 0.81 ERA with 3 BB/30 K in 22.1 IP.

Grade: B+

CINCINNATI REDS

Taking a high school catcher in the first round of the draft is always a risky proposition. The Reds nabbed Tyler Stephenson with the 11th overall pick and paid him $3.1 million, knowing that it could take a while for him to reach the majors. At 6-4, 225 he's bigger than most big league catchers and will have to work hard to stick behind the plate. The Reds added high school RHP Antonio Santillan (2nd) and college RHP Tanner Rainey (supp 2nd) before picking their next position player, SS Blake Trahan (3rd). Rainey and Santillan both have power stuff and bolster a system otherwise thin on starting pitching, but the development of Stephenson will be the key to this draft.

Sleeper: 1B James Vasquez (25th) was a college senior from UCF who has good raw power. He showed good plate discipline but underwhelmed in his senior season and fell to the 25th round. His pro debut (.359/.415/.669) shows there is some potential.

Grade: C+

COLORADO ROCKIES

The Rockies had the 3rd pick in the draft and wisely opted for the top prep position player, SS Brendan Rodgers. He has the most upside of any player in the draft. He has plus bat speed, a good approach at the plate and the potential to stick at short while hitting 25+ home runs. The Rockies followed up with talented righty Mike Nikorak (1st) and prep 3B Tyler Nevin (supp 1st)—son of former big leaguer Phil Nevin. Both were compensation picks. Righties Peter Lambert (2nd) and David Hill (4th) have good velocity and were impressive in their pro debuts. The Rockies took advantage of their extra picks, taking high-upside high schoolers and shelling out a club record $13.6 million in draft bonuses.

Sleeper: 1B Collin Ferguson (17th) was drafted twice previously and has nice offensive potential. The college senior from St. Mary's impressed in his pro debut, hitting .346/.463/.605 with 9 HR in 185 AB.

Grade: A

LOS ANGELES DODGERS

The Dodgers had a solid game plan going into the 2015 draft—take the best players available. Unfortunately, the plan backfired. They took RHP Walker Buehler with the 24th overall pick. He was considered a potential top 5 pick and was a key member of Team USA and Vanderbilt's national championship team in 2014, but his stuff was off all spring. After signing Buehler to a below-slot deal, it was announced that he would need Tommy John surgery. The club followed that pick with Louisville ace Kyle Funkhouser (supp 1st). Funkhouser fell in the draft due to concerns about his ability to throw strikes consistently. The two sides were ultimately unable to work out a deal and he will head back to campus. Buehler still has the potential to develop into a reliable mid-rotation starter and the Dodgers landed some nice complementary players in OF Mitch Hansen (2nd), RHP Josh Sborz (supp 2nd), and 2B Willie Calhoun (4th).

Sleeper: RHP Imani Abdullah (11th) was inked to an over-slot bonus of $647,500. He comes after hitters with a good 88-92 mph fastball that tops out at 94 mph.

Grade: C

MIAMI MARLINS

The Marlins turned more than a few heads when they took high school slugger Josh Naylor with the 12th overall pick. At 6-0, 225 Naylor is physically mature and had some of the best power in the draft class, but he is a big-bodied player and lacks the athleticism typical of a 1st round pick. Most pre-draft evaluations had him going towards the end of round two. The dearth of young power hitters convinced the Marlins that Naylor was worth the gamble. He hit .327 in his pro debut and has impressive raw power and an advanced ability to make consistent, hard contact. The Marlins followed by taking ASU lefty Brett Lilek (2nd), high school OF Isaiah White (3rd), and UCLA righty Cody Peteet (4th). The cost-conscious Marlins spent just $6.6 million in bonuses and almost half of that total went to Naylor and Lilek.

Sleeper: RHP Jordan Hillyer (14th) was the ace of the Kennesaw State staff and has a good low-90s sinking fastball with a slider and change-up. The Marlins used him exclusively in relief and his sinker/slider package should be effective as he moves up.

Grade: C

MILWAUKEE BREWERS

New Scouting Director Ray Montgomery went into the 2015 draft with the goal of adding high-upside prospects after the organization had been criticized for not adding enough high-end talent. For now, it looks like Brewers did exactly that. They took high school OF Trent Clark with the 14th overall pick and then Virginia lefty Nathan Kirby (supp 1st) and Cal Poly righty Cody Ponce (2nd). Kirby was projected to be a top 15 pick, but an elbow injury slowed him and he ended up having Tommy John surgery after being a brief stint in the MWL. The club is also excited about Nigerian-born Demi Orimoloye (4th) who went to high school in Canada and has plus raw power. He impressed in his pro debut, hitting .292 with 6 HR and 19 SB in 137 AB. If Kirby can come back at 100%, this could be an excellent draft.

Sleeper: RHP Jon Perrin (27th) has a funky short-arm delivery with a decent slider. His velocity jumped into the mid-90s in his pro debut and he struck out 42 while walking just 7 in 49.2 IP.

Grade: B+

NEW YORK METS

The Mets did not have a pick until #53 due to the free agent signing of Michael Cuddyer. With it, the Mets took high school OF Desmond Lindsay, a toolsy, athletic prospect. They followed that up with high school lefty Max Wotell (3rd) and Miami 3B David Thompson (4th), who belted 19 HR in his junior season. The club went over-slot for Jake Simon (11th), a projectable high school lefty who has a nice three pitch mix. The lack of impact talent will be felt down the road, but the Mets have moved into win-now mode and have an impressive nucleus, so one sub-par draft isn't a huge concern.

Sleeper: C Patrick Mazeika (8th) was a freshman All-American at Stetson, but struggled to duplicate those results over the next two seasons. His pro debut was impressive and he hit .354/.451/.540 in the Appalachian League, finishing second in the league in BA.

Grade: D

PHILADELPHIA PHILLIES

For years the Phillies have tended to draft toolsy high school players. Those gambles have not always paid off, but second year Scouting Director Johnny Almaraz looks to have hit a homerun with prep OF Cornelius Randolph (10th overall). Randolph played SS in high school, but was drafted as an OF and has an advanced bat. He impressed in his debut, hitting .302 with 32 BB/32 K and should add more power as he matures. The club then added Arizona 2B Scott Kingery (2nd), high school SS Lucas Williams (3rd), and South Carolina 1B Kyle Martin (4th). Kingery won the Pac-12 batting title for the second time, is a plus defender, and could develop into a solid big league regular in time. The team didn't draft a pitcher until the 5th round and added only three hurlers in their first 11 picks, so Kingery and Randolph will need to hit for this draft to be a success.

Sleeper: OF Mark Laird (9th) has 70 grade speed and profiles as a Ben Revere type. He swiped 11 bags while hitting .285.

Grade: B

PITTSBURGH PIRATES

In 2014 the team drafted unheralded high school SS Cole Tucker and in 2015 they went with Arizona SS Kevin Newman. Unlike Tucker, who was not considered highly regarded pre-draft, Newman was a consensus first-rounder after winning two batting titles in the Cape Cod League. Scouts like his bat, but his other tools only grade out as average. The club added Ke'Bryan Hayes (1st) with their compensation pick. He is the son of former big leaguer Charlie Hayes and projects to have moderate power and should hit for average. They also added UCLA SS Kevin Kramer (2nd), Alabama OF Casey Hughston (3rd), and Virginia lefty Brandon Waddell (5th). Seven of their first nine picks came from the collegiate ranks.

Sleeper: RHP Seth McGarry (8th) pitched mostly in relief for Florida Atlantic, but the Pirates hope to convert him to a starting role. He held his own in 12 starts, going 3-3 with a 3.88 ERA and has a good mid-90s fastball.

Grade: B

SAN DIEGO PADRES

The Padres attempted to put together a playoff contender in 2015, but failed at almost every level. Unfortunately the experiment cost the Padres 12 of their top 20 prospects as well as their first round draft pick in 2015. When the Padres finally picked, they went with high upside high school arms Austin Smith (2nd) and Jacob Nix (3rd). Smith features a good 94-96 mph fastball, but needs to develop his secondary offerings and throw more strikes. Nix—a 5th round pick in 2014—has a 92-94 mph fastball, but his secondary offerings need work. The club took Florida Tech C Austin Allen and prep OF Josh Magee in rounds four and five, but Smith and Nix will be key to the draft and both struggled in their pro debuts.

Sleeper: RHP Trevor Megill (7th) was a 3rd round pick in 2014, but was unable to reach a deal with the Cardinals and fell to the 7th round in 2015. At 6-8, 235 he has excellent size and competes well with a good low-90s fastball and above-average change-up.

Grade: D

ST. LOUIS CARDINALS

The Cardinals rolled the dice in 2015 and took high school players with five of their first six picks. They started in round one with Michigan prep OF Nick Plummer and followed up with RHP Jake Woodford (supp 1st), and 3B Bryce Denton (2nd). Plummer has good athleticism, but didn't face the stiffest competition in high school and could take time to develop. Woodford has a good 90-93 mph fastball and profiles as a solid mid-rotation starter. The Cardinals first collegiate pick, Florida OF Harrison Bader (3rd), is a polished player with nice tools across the board. They also added Illinois State 3B Paul DeJong (4th). Bader and DeJong might be the two best players added in 2015.

Sleeper: C Chris Chinea (17th) has the potential to stick behind the plate with an advanced bat. He hit .313/.356/.506 in his pro debut and should move up to full-season ball in 2016.

Grade: B

SAN FRANCISCO GIANTS

The Giants are often unconventional in their draft strategy, but it's hard to argue with the results. The club had two first round picks and went with Southern Nevada righty Phil Bickford at #18. Bickford was the 10th pick in 2013, but failed to reach an agreement with the Blue Jays. He has big-time stuff that includes a plus 93-96 mph fastball, but struggles with consistency. The Giants then grabbed Boston College 1B Chris Shaw (1st) who led the Cape Cod league in HR. At 6-4, 235 he has advanced power and can play 1B or the OF. They also picked up Miami lefty Andrew Suarez (2nd), prep SS Jalen Miller (3rd) and juco lefty John Marshall (4th). Bickford, Suarez, and Marshall give the Giants three high-upside hurlers and they have a solid track record of developing their young arms.

Sleeper: SS C.J. Hinojosa (11th) struggled in his junior year at Texas, but had previously shown solid offensive potential. He fared well in his pro debut and could still develop into a serviceable player.

Grade: A

WASHINGTON NATIONALS

The Nationals had to wait longer than any other team to make their first pick and took LSU CF Andrew Stevenson (2nd) with the 58th pick. The Nationals went college heavy early in the draft, adding Vanderbilt OF Rhett Wiseman (3rd), Iona RHP Mariano Rivera (4th), and Oklahoma Baptist lefty Taylor Hearn (5th). In fact the Nationals took just one high school player, Blake Perkins (2nd), before round 14. Stevenson has some of the best speed in the draft and swiped 23 bases in his debut and showed a solid approach at the plate. Hearn was drafted for the 4th time and has a nice 92-95 mph fastball. The Nationals added three athletic OF in Stevenson, Perkins, and Wiseman and three interesting LHP, nicely addressing organizational needs.

Sleeper: RHP Koda Glover (8th) has a plus fastball that tops out at 98 mph and mixes in a slider that shows potential. He worked in relief in his debut and struck out 38 in 30 innings of work.

Grade: B+

2016 College Names to Know

by Chris Lee

This year seems to bring us a deeper crop of college players as compared to last year's class, though like last season, there's no superstar talent on the level of Kris Bryant (3B, CHC) or David Price (LHP, BOS). Also, there's not even a lot of the Michael Conforto (OF, NYM) types—players with star upside, but whose base skills suggest a high floor.

That said, there is also a wisdom that comes from watching college baseball for years, and realizing that base skills from 20-year-old collegians are very volatile—and different from those already in the professional ranks. Matt LaPorta's base skills as a collegian at Florida never translated the way most thought, while Dallas Keuchel broke out as a pro in a way that his junior stats at Arkansas never even suggested.

So, this list is an attempt to explore to a wide range of possibilities as we look into these players' MLB futures. Don't get too hung up on the rankings; though a pitcher with only two great months tops this list, my eyes told me that A.J. Puk figured some things out in 2015. To get the most out of this list, use it as a starting point and mix with your own observations as the college season progresses.

1. A.J. Puk, LHP

Florida, L/L, Jr., 6-7, 225

Puk was one of the highest-rated pitchers in the country two years ago, and sported a 5.87 ERA around midseason of 2015 until a silly arrest for climbing a campus crane served as an awakening. After regaining focus, Puk's fastball started climbing into the upper-90s. Given the downward plane and the huge stride created by someone his size, it's tough to square up. Puk's secondary offerings—a rapidly-improving slider and a change-up—are quality pitches with a chance to get better.

The bottom line: Once the switch flipped, Puk was flat-out dominant in leading the Gators deep into the postseason. A 2016 follow-up could make him the No. 1 overall pick in 2016, and he has the ingredients to be a legitimate MLB ace.

2. Corey Ray, OF

Louisville, L/L, Jr., 5-11, 185

Ray shot up draft boards after a terrific sophomore campaign followed by a summer during which he slugged .548 and led Team USA with 11 SBs and nine extra-base hits. A mature, disciplined, hard-working player, Ray's calling card has been his speed, but he's now a well-rounded player who many considered the best position player on Team USA. He's played right field, but may have the tools to make it in center.

The bottom line: Ray could be a coveted speed-power guy, but the cautions are his 77% ct% and short track record. That said, after his summer, Ray might be the first position player off the board if the draft were held before the season.

3. Kyle Lewis, OF

Mercer, R/R, Jr., 6-4, 195

Lewis may be this draft's Andrew Benintendi (OF, BOS), a guy whose stock soared overnight. Undrafted out of high school, Lewis played sparingly as a freshman, and then exploded to nearly win the Southern Conference triple crown as a sophomore. His swing is a bit noisy, but Lewis makes solid contact and has enough loft to generate home runs as a professional. Right now, his first step isn't quick, but he's got enough athleticism and overall speed that this could change. Playing in the outfield won't be an issue.

The bottom line: The short track record in a smaller conference make evaluating Lewis a bit tougher, but he had a great summer (.300, 7 HRs) in the Cape Cod League, and many dubbed him the league's top prospect. Perhaps the most intriguing collegiate player entering the 2016 season, Lewis seems to have worked himself into the first round.

4. Nick Banks, OF

Texas A&M, L/L, Jr., 6-0, 215

Banks followed up on a Freshman All-American campaign by leading the Southeastern Conference in batting average in league games (.417) in 2015, and then paced Team USA in batting (.386) and on-base percentage (.491). A line-drive hitter with above-average raw power, Banks has started to become more aggressive, trading some contact for home runs. He is a good collegiate center fielder who could play there in the professional ranks, though right field may be where he lands.

The bottom line: With good-but-not-great speed and his evolving approach at the plate, there's some power/speed potential here. The ceiling is not be huge—think 20/20 if things work out, and that could be pushing it on the steals—but Banks does everything well and is likely to be one the higher-floor collegians in the class.

5. Alec Hansen, RHP

Oklahoma, R/R, Jr., 6-7, 235

Another fast-rising prospect, the former Colorado prep star threw just 11.1 innings as a freshman before becoming one of its top starters last year. In 2015, Hansen's fastball, which gets elite grades, sat between 94-98, and he'll touch triple digits at times. In between seasons, he developed a slider and also improved his control. He also throws a change-up; though one health note: Hansen didn't pitch last summer and then was held out of Oklahoma's fall baseball scrimmage series due to a forearm issue that was termed "precautionary."

The bottom line: Consistency, which seems to be tied to fastball command, is the biggest issue with Hansen. It's far more about potential than past production, but his rate of improvement combined with his size, athleticism and velocity are exciting. A great junior season would put him in the discussion for the draft's top overall pick.

6. Buddy Reed, OF

Florida, S/R, Jr., 6-3, 200

Reed spent his freshman year at Florida as a reserve shortstop. But he moved to center field as a sophomore, changed from contact lenses to prescription glasses, and took off against top competition as the season progressed. He's still raw, but he's one of the faster, more athletic players in the class, a terrific center fielder with some flashes of developing power.

The bottom line: It's hard to say what Reed can be because optimism centers more around his tools than his production, but the pace at which he's developed has been remarkable. Reed's value will likely be greater in the real game than the fantasy version, but there's probably a 20-plus stolen base guy in here with the potential to add a little pop.

7. Bryan Reynolds, OF
Vanderbilt, S/R, Jr., 6-2, 210

Reynolds started for Vanderbilt from Day 1 in its national title season of 2014, hitting .338/.395/.480 as a freshman. He had a massive slump in mid-season 2015 due to a lot of swing and miss, but made adjustments and hit well against good pitching as VU advanced through the postseason. He followed that up with a good Cape Cod League season. Defensively, he has great instincts and covers a lot of ground, though his arm may limit him to playing left field.

The bottom line: A smart player with great vision, Reynolds has advanced in terms of pitch recognition and selectivity throughout his first two years. The latest improvement came this summer and fall, when he focused on learning to hit pitches to the opposite field with authority from both sides of the plate. Reynolds has solid skills in most areas and should be an MLB contributor who'll hit line drives and steal some bases with a chance for average power.

8. Nick Senzel, 2B/3B
Tennessee, R/R, Jr., 6-1, 205

Senzel put himself squarely on the prospect radar after his Freshman All-American season of 2014, followed by a summer during which he hit .364 in the Cape Cod League, after which he was named Perfect Game's Summer Collegiate Player of the Year. He's a good athlete with a strong, quick bat with some power and the ability to hit to all fields. Some think he can stay in the infield, though it's not a sure thing.

The bottom line: Senzel's hit tool is his biggest gift, but he seems to project more as a do-a-bit-of-everything hitter rather than a standout in any area. Some believe him to be the safest college bat in the class given that there's not a clear weakness outside the defensive questions.

9. Cal Quantrill, RHP
Stanford, L/R, Jr., 6-3, 185

The son of former MLB hurler Paul Quantrill, Cal spent most of his 2015 season watching from the dugout after Tommy John surgery in March. The year before, Quantrill posted a 2.68 ERA in 110.2 IP, with 98 Ks and 34 BBs, earning Freshman All-American honors while showing tremendous pitchability for his age due to a low-to-mid-90s fastball, a curve, a slider and a quality change-up.

The bottom line: Quantrill doesn't have the "Wow!" factor of a Puk or a Hansen, but knows how to pitch. Assuming Quantrill has no health complications and can pick up where he left off, he's easily one of the most polished guys in the draft class. He may get a late start to the season, though.

10. Connor Jones, RHP, Virginia
Virginia, R/R, Jr., 6-3, 200

Jones was a big reason why an injury-plagued Virginia team won its first College World Series in 2015. He throws a heavy four-seam fastball that sits in the low-90s but can touch the mid-90s, has an excellent change-up and both a slider and a show-me

curve. His Ctl (4.0 in '15, 3.8 in '14) could be better, but that's the only real negative.

The bottom line: After UVA's run into late June, Jones sat out the summer, so there's a bit of "wait-and-see," as he pitched out of the bullpen as a freshman. And the Cavaliers haven't had a great track record of producing MLB starters. That said, most believe Jones to be one of the more polished arms out in the class, and while others have more upside, he should be one of the quickest guys to the majors.

11. Will Craig, 1B
Wake Forest, R/R, Jr., 6-3, 230

After a good-but-not-great freshman year, Craig exploded with a monster sophomore season that earned him Atlantic Coast Conference Player of the Year honors in 2015. A patient hitter who can hit to all fields with power with a reputation for being able to handle any type of pitch and not chase, Craig also pitched 44.1 innings with 39 Ks for the Demon Deacons (albeit with a 6.09 ERA), automatically sparking the A.J. Reed comparisons. He's good enough defensively to hold down first given the way he hits.

The bottom line: The Reed comparison is an easy one because there aren't many like either; Craig's sophomore hitting stats were actually better, though Reed took his two-way game to an entirely different level the next year. He came out of nowhere last season and scouts want to see a repeat, and others are skeptical because outstanding college first basemen have a well-earned recent track record of underperformance. As of winter 2015, he's not considered a first-rounder, so this slot hedges bets between his outstanding production now and the things that may work against him later.

12. Matt Krook, LHP
Oregon, L/L, Jr., 6-3, 205

In the 2013 MLB Draft, Krook passed on Miami after the Marlins found an issue in his shoulder which resulted in a $650k offer rather than the slot value of $1.6 million. Krook then whiffed 60 hitters in 45.1 IP with 19 walks and just 22 hits allowed as an Oregon freshman in 2014, before requiring Tommy John surgery that April. When he was healthy, Krook sat 90-92 (and touched 95) with his fastball, complementing it with a hard curve that may grade as a plus pitch, and a change-up.

The bottom line: Krook had his fastball up into the low-90s in 2015 showings at the Cape, and that was encouraging. The injury issues are an obvious concern, giving Krook one of the biggest ranges of potential outcomes heading to the 2016 draft and beyond.

13. Kyle Funkhouser, RHP
Louisville, R/R, Sr., 6-3, 225

Previously having Ctl troubles, Funkhouser's problem in 2015 was that as he threw more strikes but showed less velocity, he became quite mortal against the better teams on the Cardinals' schedule. Consequently, Funkhouser fell from what looked like being a top-5 pick to more of a middle-of-the-first-round consideration, and then slid all the way to 35th overall (Dodgers), and chose not to sign. His fastball sits low-to-mid-90s and can go to 98, with respectable secondary offerings of a slider, curve and change.

The bottom line: Funkhouser bet on himself, spurning an offer reported to be between $1.7 and $2 million to return for his senior year and lose all negotiating leverage in the process. Perhaps that's telling of the Funkhouser's self-confidence. We shall see in 2016.

14. Bobby Dalbec, 3B
Arizona, R/R, Jr., 6-4, 219
There may not be a collegian with more power than Dalbec, who hit .315/.432/.728 with a league-leading 12 HRs in the Cape in 2015, and also showed pop for Team USA. The problem with Dalbec is simple: he doesn't make consistent contact, whiffing 72 times in 183 summer plate appearances. Dalbec also pitched and fanned 48 in 61.2 sophomore innings at Arizona with a low-90s fastball.

The bottom line: There's no question that Dalbec has big-league power; he's not Kris Bryant, but he's got about as much raw power as any collegiate since. His arm gives him a chance to play a corner infield spot, though that may be at first. The issue obviously is whether he can make enough contact to make the bigs. If so, he could have fantasy value in a Mark Reynolds-kind-of-way but if not… well, power's useless if one can't make contact.

15. Chris Okey, C
Clemson, R/R, Jr., 5-11, 195
An athletic catcher with good defensive skills who was a first team All-American pick in 2015, Okey's not exceptional at anything, but some believe he could smack 15 HRs at the big-league level. Has good bat speed and base running instincts.

The bottom line: As a fantasy commodity, he could have value by virtue of being a catcher who may not hurt your average, with a little pop and perhaps a small handful of steals thrown in.

Others to watch:

Zack Collins, C, Jr., Miami: The National Freshman of the Year in 2014 followed up with a .302/.445/.507, 15-HR, 0.89-Eye sophomore season after a slow start. His defense is improving but it may not be enough, prompting many to peg him as a first base prospect.

Jordan Sheffield, RHP, Rs-So., Vanderbilt: His raw stuff, which includes a fastball that sits mid-90s and can approach triple-digits, may be as good as anyone's in the draft. Next step: cutting down on the walks (8.3 bb/9), which returned with a vengeance after missing 2014 to Tommy John surgery.

Mike Shawaryn, RHP, Jr., Maryland: Based on stats (138/29 K/BB in 116 IP in 2015, with a 1.71 ERA) and size (6-3, 211), Shawaryn belongs somewhere on the top 15. The problem is a fastball that sits 87-93, which has many doubting his ability to be a successful MLB starter. That said, he's got an excellent change-up and the fastball was reportedly hitting 94 in the summer.

Logan Shore, RHP, Jr., Florida: Outstanding collegiate hurler will likely be a first-rounder, if not a top-half first-rounder, but lack of strikeouts (6.6 Dom) limits his fantasy upside.

Matt Thaiss, C, Jr., Virginia: The lefty's 2015 season (.323/.413/.512, 10 HR, 1.27 Eye) put him in the discussion; doubts about his arm strength cloud his future behind the plate, and lack of foot speed could hamper him elsewhere.

Robert Tyler, RHP, Jr., Georgia: Based on raw talent (11.0 Dom in 23.2 IP in '15), an upper-90s fastball and size (6-4, 225), Tyler could be a top-5 pick. But his secondary stuff isn't nearly refined enough, and he's been shut down each of the last three seasons with health concerns.

ORGANIZATION RATINGS/RANKINGS

Each organization is graded on a standard A-F scale in four separate categories, and then after weighing the categories and adding some subjectivity, a final grade and ranking are determined. The four categories are the following:

Hitting: The quality and quantity of hitting prospects, the balance between athleticism, power, speed, and defense, and the quality of player development.

Pitching: The quality and quantity of pitching prospects and the quality of player development.

Top-End Talent: The quality of the top players within the organization. Successful teams are ones that have the most star-quality players. These are the players who are a teams' above average regulars, front-end starters, and closers.

Depth: The depth of both hitting and pitching prospects within the organization.

Overall Grade: The four categories are weighted, with top-end talent being the most important and depth being the least.

TEAM	Hitting	Pitching	Top-End Talent	Depth	Overall
Atlanta	B+	A+	A+	A	A
Colorado	A	A-	A	A	A
Los Angeles (N)	B+	A	A	A	A
Pittsburgh	A-	B	A	A-	A-
Chicago (N)	A-	B-	B	A	B+
Washington	B	B+	A	B-	B+
Philadelphia	B+	B	B	A	B+
Texas	B+	B+	A-	B+	B+
San Francisco	B	A-	B+	B+	B+
Minnesota	B	B+	A-	B	B+
Tampa Bay	A-	B-	B+	B	B+
Boston	B+	C	A-	B	B+
Cincinnati	B	A-	B	B-	B
Oakland	A-	C	B	B	B
Houston	B+	B-	B	B+	B
Kansas City	B-	B	B+	B	B
St. Louis	C	B+	B	C+	B-
Cleveland	B-	C+	B	B-	B-
New York (N)	B-	C+	B	B-	B-
Milwaukee	B-	C+	B-	C+	B-
New York (A)	B-	C	C+	B-	C+
Toronto	C+	C+	C+	B-	C+
San Diego	B	D	C-	C	C
Arizona	C	B-	C	C	C
Chicago (A)	C-	C+	C-	D	C-
Seattle	C	C-	D	C	C-
Detroit	D	C+	D	D+	D
Miami	D	C-	C-	D	D
Baltimore	C-	D	D	D	D
Los Angeles (A)	D	D-	D-	D	D

POSITIONS: Up to four positions are listed for each batter and represent those for which he appeared (in order) the most games at in 2011. Positions are shown with their numeric designation (2=CA, 3=1B, 7=LF, 0=DH, etc.)

BATS: Shows which side of the plate he bats from—right (R), left (L) or switch-hitter (S).

AGE: Player's age, as of April 1, 2016.

DRAFTED: The year, round, and school that the player performed at as an amateur if drafted, or where the player was signed from, if a free agent.

EXP MLB DEBUT: The year a player is expected to debut in the major leagues.

H/W: The player's height and weight.

FUT: The role that the batter is expected to have for the majority of his major league career, not necessarily his greatest upside.

SKILLS: Each skill a player possesses is graded and designated with a "+", indicating the quality of the skills, taking into context the batter's age and level played. An average skill will receive three "+" marks.

- **PWR:** Measures the player's ability to drive the ball and hit for power.
- **BAVG:** Measures the player's ability to hit for batting average and judge the strike zone.
- **SPD:** Measures the player's raw speed and base-running ability.
- **DEF:** Measures the player's overall defense, which includes arm strength, arm accuracy, range, agility, hands, and defensive instincts.

PLAYER STAT LINES: Player statistics for the last five teams that he played for (if applicable), including college and the major leagues.

TEAM DESIGNATIONS: Each team that the player performed for during a given year is included.

LEVEL DESIGNATIONS: The level for each team a player performed is included. "AAA" means Triple-A, "AA" means Double-A, "A+" means high Class-A, "A-" means low Class-A, and "Rk" means rookie level.

SABERMETRIC CATEGORIES: Descriptions of all the sabermetric categories appear in the glossary.

CAPSULE COMMENTARIES: For each player, a brief analysis of their skills/statistics, and their future potential is provided.

ELIGIBILITY: Eligibility for inclusion is the standard for which Major League Baseball adheres to; 130 at-bats or 45 days on the 25-man roster, not including the month of September.

POTENTIAL RATINGS: The Potential Ratings are a two-part system in which a player is assigned a number rating based on his upside potential (1-10) and a letter rating based on the probability of reaching that potential (A-E).

Potential

10:	Hall of Famer	5:	MLB reserve
9:	Elite player	4:	Top minor leaguer
8:	Solid regular	3:	Average minor leaguer
7:	Average regular	2:	Minor league reserve
6:	Platoon player	1:	Minor league roster filler

Probability Rating

- A: 90% probability of reaching potential
- B: 70% probability of reaching potential
- C: 50% probability of reaching potential
- D: 30% probability of reaching potential
- E: 10% probability of reaching potential

SKILLS: Scouts usually grade a player's skills on the 20-80 scale, and while most of the grades are subjective, there are grades that can be given to represent a certain hitting statistic or running speed. These are indicated on this chart:

Scout Grade	HR	BA	Speed (L)	Speed (R)
80	39+	.320+	3.9	4.0
70	32-38	.300-.319	4.0	4.1
60	25-31	.286-.299	4.1	4.2
50 (avg)	17-24	.270-.285	4.2	4.3
40	11-16	.250-.269	4.3	4.4
30	6-10	.220-.249	4.4	4.5
20	0-5	.219-	4.5	4.6

CATCHER POP TIMES: Catchers are timed (in seconds) from the moment the pitch reaches the catcher's mitt until the time that the middle infielder receives the baseball at second base. This number assists both teams in assessing whether a base-runner should steal second base or not.

1.85	+
1.95	MLB average
2.05	–

Abreu,Osvaldo — 46 — Washington

EXP MLB DEBUT: 2018 | H/W: 6-0 170 | FUT: Starting SS | 7C

Bats R | Age 21 | 2012 FA (DR)

Pwr ++ | BAvg +++ | Spd +++ | Def +++

Year	Lev	Team	AB	R	H	HR	RBI	Avg	OB	Slg	OPS	bb%	ct%	Eye	SB	CS	x/h%	Iso	RC/G
2013	Rk	GCL Nationals	147	24	42	0	24	286	367	381	748	11	84	0.79	16	6	31	95	5.12
2014	A-	Auburn	210	31	48	1	15	229	260	305	565	4	80	0.22	10	6	23	76	2.35
2015	A	Hagerstown	442	74	121	6	47	274	348	412	759	10	80	0.56	30	11	37	138	5.10

Breakout year in full-season ball puts him on the prospect map. While he has a good eye at the plate, he swings aggressively, which can throw him out of sync. Present doubles power, and speed found its way to SB. Solid SS actions; could also end up at 2B. Under the radar until 2015, needs to prove at higher levels.

Adames,Cristhian — 6 — Colorado

EXP MLB DEBUT: 2014 | H/W: 6-0 185 | FUT: Starting SS | 7B

Bats B | Age 24 | 2007 FA (DR)

Pwr ++ | BAvg +++ | Spd +++ | Def ++++

Year	Lev	Team	AB	R	H	HR	RBI	Avg	OB	Slg	OPS	bb%	ct%	Eye	SB	CS	x/h%	Iso	RC/G
2014	AA	Tulsa	330	42	88	2	38	267	326	336	662	8	82	0.50	7	9	17	70	3.76
2014	AAA	Colorado Springs	145	19	49	1	14	338	392	441	834	8	83	0.52	5	1	27	103	5.88
2014	MLB	Colorado	15	1	1	0	0	67	67	67	133	0	67	0.00	0	0	0	0	-4.22
2015	AAA	Albuquerque	463	62	144	11	51	311	361	438	799	7	88	0.64	11	7	24	127	5.31
2015	MLB	Colorado	53	4	13	0	3	245	286	302	588	5	79	0.27	0	1	15	57	2.67

Slender Dominican had a solid season at AAA. Quick, agile fielder with soft hands and a strong arm. Defense is major league ready now. Nice spike in power with a career high 11 HR gives him a chance. Good strike zone judgment and puts the ball in to play consistently. Held his own in 53 AB with the Rockies.

Adames,Willy — 6 — Tampa Bay

EXP MLB DEBUT: 2017 | H/W: 6-1 180 | FUT: Starting SS/3B | 9D

Bats R | Age 20 | 2012 FA (DR)

Pwr ++ | BAvg +++ | Spd +++ | Def +++

Year	Lev	Team	AB	R	H	HR	RBI	Avg	OB	Slg	OPS	bb%	ct%	Eye	SB	CS	x/h%	Iso	RC/G
2013	Rk	DSL Tigers	200	48	49	1	21	245	410	370	780	22	78	1.27	9	12	37	125	6.03
2014	A	West Michigan	353	40	95	6	50	269	342	428	770	10	73	0.41	3	6	34	159	5.31
2014	A	Bowling Green	97	15	27	2	11	278	375	433	808	13	69	0.50	3	0	33	155	6.08
2015	A+	Charlotte	396	51	102	4	46	258	347	379	725	12	69	0.44	10	1	33	121	4.88

Advanced, yet young INF who has tools to be superstar. Has power potential despite limited HR output and has bat to hit for high BA. Knows strike zone and works counts to get on base consistently. Swings very fast bat and can go to opposite field. Flashes good glove with above average range and strong arm. Could move to 2B or 3B.

Adams,Lane — 789 — Kansas City

EXP MLB DEBUT: 2014 | H/W: 6-4 190 | FUT: Starting OF | 7D

Bats R | Age 26 | 2009 (13) HS (OK)

Pwr +++ | BAvg ++ | Spd ++++ | Def +++

Year	Lev	Team	AB	R	H	HR	RBI	Avg	OB	Slg	OPS	bb%	ct%	Eye	SB	CS	x/h%	Iso	RC/G
2014	Rk	Burlington	10	3	5	0	4	500	643	1100	1743	29	90	4.00	0	0	80	600	18.67
2014	AA	NW Arkansas	405	65	109	11	36	269	342	427	769	10	79	0.52	38	9	36	158	5.13
2014	MLB	KC Royals	3	1	0	0	0	0	0	0	0	0	33	0.00	0	0		0	-9.58
2015	AA	NW Arkansas	373	58	111	12	49	298	359	466	826	9	74	0.37	29	6	32	169	5.86
2015	AAA	Omaha	115	14	26	4	13	226	305	374	679	10	82	0.62	2	1	35	148	3.93

Premium athlete who who struggled in AAA, but was terrific in AA. Set career high in HR with average pull power and can hit for BA with level swing. Very solid against LHP and likes to shoot gaps with hard line drives. Plays all OF spots with plus speed and tracks down balls well. Has talent, but needs polish.

Adolfo,Micker — 89 — Chicago (A)

EXP MLB DEBUT: 2019 | H/W: 6-3 200 | FUT: Starting OF | 8D

Bats R | Age 19 | 2013 FA (DR)

Pwr +++ | BAvg ++ | Spd ++ | Def ++

Year	Lev	Team	AB	R	H	HR	RBI	Avg	OB	Slg	OPS	bb%	ct%	Eye	SB	CS	x/h%	Iso	RC/G
2014	Rk	Azl White Sox	179	27	39	5	21	218	275	380	654	7	53	0.16	0	0	44	162	4.47
2015	Rk	Azl White Sox	83	14	21	0	10	253	303	313	617	7	70	0.24	3	2	19	60	3.07

Athletic and strong prospect with tantalizing upside predicated on plus raw power, he struggled to make contact in 2nd year in rookie ball. Has holes in swing and can't read spin well, though fits RF profile with very strong arm. Power gives him upside, but should improve in other areas with more time.

Aguilar,Jesus — 3 — Cleveland

EXP MLB DEBUT: 2014 | H/W: 6-3 250 | FUT: Starting 1B | 7D

Bats R | Age 25 | 2010 FA (VZ)

Pwr ++++ | BAvg ++ | Spd + | Def ++

Year	Lev	Team	AB	R	H	HR	RBI	Avg	OB	Slg	OPS	bb%	ct%	Eye	SB	CS	x/h%	Iso	RC/G
2013	AA	Akron	499	66	137	16	105	275	348	427	775	10	79	0.52	0	1	32	152	5.14
2014	AAA	Columbus	427	69	130	19	77	304	395	511	906	13	78	0.67	0	0	38	206	6.98
2014	MLB	Cleveland	33	2	4	0	3	121	216	121	337	11	61	0.31	0	0	0	0	-1.35
2015	AAA	Columbus	510	57	136	19	93	267	329	439	768	8	77	0.41	0	0	36	173	4.96
2015	MLB	Cleveland	19	0	6	0	2	316	316	368	684	0	63	0.00	0	0	17	53	3.95

Large, strong 1B who is sound hitter with bat speed and power, but struggles with pitch recognition. Uses entire field with clean swing mechanics, though bat head doesn't stay in zone long. Hasn't stolen base in last 4 years and is very poor runner. Provides sufficient defense, though arm strength is limited.

Alberto,Hanser — 456 — Texas

EXP MLB DEBUT: 2015 | H/W: 5-11 215 | FUT: Utility player | 6A

Bats R | Age 23 | 2009 FA (DR)

Pwr ++ | BAvg +++ | Spd +++ | Def +++

Year	Lev	Team	AB	R	H	HR	RBI	Avg	OB	Slg	OPS	bb%	ct%	Eye	SB	CS	x/h%	Iso	RC/G
2013	AA	Frisco	356	37	76	4	40	213	247	287	534	4	88	0.39	13	5	18	73	2.20
2014	A+	Myrtle Beach	262	37	71	5	43	271	298	408	706	4	90	0.40	10	4	32	137	4.15
2014	AA	Frisco	178	23	49	2	15	275	299	354	653	3	90	0.35	6	4	18	79	3.50
2015	AAA	Round Rock	310	42	96	4	32	310	329	435	765	3	89	0.27	5	5	28	126	4.72
2015	MLB	Texas	99	12	22	0	4	222	238	263	500	2	83	0.12	1	0	14	40	1.50

Short, strong INF who played first year above AA and reached TEX. Solid defender who played SS in AAA and 2B in majors. Shows improving range and above average, accurate arm. Has hand-eye coordination and barrel control for consistent, hard contact, but rarely draws walks. SB have declined and won't hit many HR.

Albies,Ozhaino — 6 — Atlanta

EXP MLB DEBUT: 2018 | H/W: 5-9 150 | FUT: Starting SS | 9C

Bats B | Age 19 | 2013 FA (CUR)

Pwr + | BAvg ++++ | Spd +++++ | Def ++++

Year	Lev	Team	AB	R	H	HR	RBI	Avg	OB	Slg	OPS	bb%	ct%	Eye	SB	CS	x/h%	Iso	RC/G
2014	Rk	Danville	135	25	48	1	14	356	428	452	879	11	87	1.00	15	3	17	96	6.60
2014	Rk	GCL Braves	63	16	24	0	5	381	473	429	902	15	90	1.83	7	2	13	48	7.14
2015	A	Rome	394	64	122	0	37	310	367	404	771	8	86	0.64	29	8	24	94	5.20

Switch-hitting SS burst on the prospect scene with a tremendous full-season debut. Makes solid contact utilizing a short stroke, quick hands and tremendous balance. Best hand-eye coordination in SAL. Generously listed at 5'9", there isn't much room to develop power. Has plus-plus speed and the potential to be a strong defender.

Alcantara,Sergio — 46 — Arizona

EXP MLB DEBUT: 2019 | H/W: 5-10 170 | FUT: Starting SS | 8E

Bats B | Age 19 | 2012 FA (DR)

Pwr + | BAvg +++ | Spd +++ | Def ++++

Year	Lev	Team	AB	R	H	HR	RBI	Avg	OB	Slg	OPS	bb%	ct%	Eye	SB	CS	x/h%	Iso	RC/G
2013	Rk	Azl DBacks	169	31	41	0	16	243	399	320	719	21	79	1.22	3	2	22	77	5.15
2014	Rk	Missoula	266	48	65	1	18	244	360	297	657	15	77	0.77	8	4	18	53	3.98
2015	A-	Hillsboro	257	34	65	1	23	253	317	327	644	9	82	0.52	6	0	23	74	3.58
2015	A	Kane County	71	5	8	0	5	113	160	127	287	5	76	0.24	1	0	13	14	-1.33

Glove-first defender with developing hit tool. Aggressively promoted to full-season ball to start '15 and was overmatched by MWL pitching. Solid bat control and good plate discipline are best attributes as hitter. Struggles making solid-contact. Sticks at SS with advanced range and strong throwing arm.

Alfaro,Jorge — 2 — Philadelphia

EXP MLB DEBUT: 2017 | H/W: 6-2 225 | FUT: Starting C/OF | 8D

Bats R | Age 22 | 2010 FA (CB)

Pwr ++++ | BAvg ++ | Spd ++ | Def ++

Year	Lev	Team	AB	R	H	HR	RBI	Avg	OB	Slg	OPS	bb%	ct%	Eye	SB	CS	x/h%	Iso	RC/G
2014	A+	Myrtle Beach	398	63	104	13	73	261	302	440	741	5	75	0.23	6	5	38	178	4.55
2014	AA	Frisco	88	12	23	4	14	261	309	443	752	6	74	0.26	0	0	35	182	4.62
2015	Rk	GCL Phillies	4	0	2	0	1	500	500	750	1250	0	100		0	0	50	250	9.68
2015	AA	Frisco	190	22	48	5	21	253	286	432	718	5	68	0.15	2	1	46	179	4.45

Lost significant development time in 2015 with ankle injury in June. Has elite arm behind the plate, but receiving skills lag behind. Has plus raw power and bat speed, but pitch recognition and contact issues have yet to improve. Potential impact C, but not as close as his experience might suggest.

Alford,Anthony — 8 — Toronto

EXP MLB DEBUT: 2017 | H/W: 6-1 205 | FUT: Starting CF | 8C

Bats R | Age 21 | 2012 (3) HS (MS)

Pwr ++ | BAvg +++ | Spd ++++ | Def +++

Year	Lev	Team	AB	R	H	HR	RBI	Avg	OB	Slg	OPS	bb%	ct%	Eye	SB	CS	x/h%	Iso	RC/G
2013	Rk	GCL Blue Jays	22	4	5	0	2	227	393	409	802	21	73	1.00	2	0	60	182	6.46
2014	Rk	Bluefield	29	5	6	1	2	207	324	310	634	15	55	0.38	1	0	17	103	3.64
2014	A	Lansing	25	3	8	1	3	320	320	480	800	0	68	0.00	4	0	25	160	5.18
2015	A	Lansing	188	49	55	1	16	293	414	394	808	17	68	0.65	12	1	29	101	6.36
2015	A+	Dunedin	225	42	68	3	19	302	379	444	824	11	78	0.57	15	6	29	142	5.99

Exciting, breakout star whose tools are translating into plus skills. Has disciplined feel for game and will draw walks with discerning eye. Power should continue to blossom as he learns pitches and uses plus bat speed to advantage. Has easy plus speed for SB and true CF range. Needs polish, but has very high ceiling.

Allen,Austin — 2 — San Diego

EXP MLB DEBUT: 2018 | H/W: 6-4 225 | FUT: Starting C | 7D

Bats L Age 22 — 2015 (4) Florida Tech — Pwr +++ | BAvg ++ | Spd + | Def ++

Year	Lev	Team	AB	R	H	HR	RBI	Avg	OB	Slg	OPS	bb%	ct%	Eye	SB	CS	x/h%	Iso	RC/G
2015	A-	Tri-City	196	23	47	2	34	240	313	332	645	10	81	0.55	1	2	28	92	3.61

Tall, strong backstop whose bat is ahead of glove. Has shown good receiving skills, but crude footwork hinders blocking and throwing. Throws with accuracy, but slow release mutes average arm strength. Exhibits plus raw power, mostly to pull side, and has patient eye at plate. Has some upside, but needs significant polish.

Allen,Greg — 8 — Cleveland

EXP MLB DEBUT: 2018 | H/W: 6-0 175 | FUT: Fourth OF | 6B

Bats B Age 23 — 2014 (6) San Diego St — Pwr ++ | BAvg ++ | Spd ++++ | Def +++

Year	Lev	Team	AB	R	H	HR	RBI	Avg	OB	Slg	OPS	bb%	ct%	Eye	SB	CS	x/h%	Iso	RC/G
2013	NCAA	San Diego St	254	51	76	0	28	299	386	350	737	12	84	0.90	25	9	16	51	4.98
2014	NCAA	San Diego St	255	52	77	0	26	302	375	380	756	11	88	0.97	25	5	18	78	5.18
2014	A-	Mahoning Val	225	46	55	0	19	244	325	298	623	11	88	1.04	30	5	18	53	3.66
2015	A	Lake County	479	83	131	7	45	273	346	382	728	10	88	0.93	43	16	27	109	4.75
2015	A+	Lynchburg	13	2	2	0	0	154	267	231	497	13	77	0.67	3	0	50	77	1.85

Slashing OF who is all about speed and defense. Finished 2nd in MWL in SB and played solid CF with plus speed. Baserunning needs polish. Gets on base with mature eye, though swing not tailored for much pop. Has enough strength to shoot gaps and uses wheels to leg out doubles. Has tendency to flail at breaking balls.

Almora,Albert — 8 — Chicago (N)

EXP MLB DEBUT: 2016 | H/W: 6-2 180 | FUT: Starting CF | 8B

Bats R Age 21 — 2012 (1) HS (FL) — Pwr +++ | BAvg +++ | Spd +++ | Def ++++

Year	Lev	Team	AB	R	H	HR	RBI	Avg	OB	Slg	OPS	bb%	ct%	Eye	SB	CS	x/h%	Iso	RC/G
2012	A-	Boise	65	9	19	1	6	292	292	446	738	0	92	0.00	0	1	42	154	4.32
2013	A	Kane County	249	39	82	3	23	329	372	466	838	6	88	0.57	4	4	29	137	5.81
2014	A+	Daytona	367	55	104	7	50	283	306	406	712	3	87	0.26	6	3	28	123	4.09
2014	AA	Tennessee	141	20	33	2	10	234	245	355	599	1	84	0.09	0	1	33	121	2.67
2015	AA	Tennessee	405	69	110	6	46	272	325	400	725	7	88	0.68	8	4	33	128	4.58

Undervalued all-around player with quick hands and smooth line-drive stroke. Sprays balls to all fields and makes consistent contact. Needs to be more selective at the plate, but did double his BB rate. Has yet to hit for power, but should develop more as he matures. Has good range and has a strong arm that will allow him to stay in CF.

Alvarez,Dariel — 89 — Baltimore

EXP MLB DEBUT: 2015 | H/W: 6-2 180 | FUT: Starting OF | 7B

Bats R Age 27 — 2013 FA (CU) — Pwr +++ | BAvg +++ | Spd ++ | Def +++

Year	Lev	Team	AB	R	H	HR	RBI	Avg	OB	Slg	OPS	bb%	ct%	Eye	SB	CS	x/h%	Iso	RC/G
2014	AA	Bowie	359	52	111	14	68	309	333	487	821	3	90	0.37	7	4	32	178	5.27
2014	AAA	Norfolk	173	23	52	1	19	301	331	439	771	4	84	0.30	1	1	38	139	4.95
2015	A+	Frederick	16	2	5	0	1	313	421	500	921	16	81	1.00	1	0	40	188	7.66
2015	AAA	Norfolk	512	61	141	16	72	275	297	424	721	3	88	0.25	7	3	30	148	4.13
2015	MLB	Baltimore	29	3	7	1	1	241	290	379	670	6	72	0.25	0	0	29	138	3.57

Aggressive hitter who covers plate well and makes hard contact to all fields. Exhibits power from pole to pole, but can be fooled by spin. Should be able to contribute with bat at major league level, but could use a more discerning eye. Has shown ability in OF with strong arm and average range. Can steal occasional bag with OK speed.

Alvarez,Eliezer — 4 — St. Louis

EXP MLB DEBUT: 2019 | H/W: 5-11 165 | FUT: Starting 2B | 8E

Bats B Age 21 — 2011 FA (DR) — Pwr ++ | BAvg +++ | Spd ++++ | Def +++

Year	Lev	Team	AB	R	H	HR	RBI	Avg	OB	Slg	OPS	bb%	ct%	Eye	SB	CS	x/h%	Iso	RC/G
2013	Rk	GCL Cardinals	67	12	14	1	7	209	254	373	627	6	79	0.29	6	2	43	164	3.24
2014	Rk	GCL Cardinals	68	11	24	1	15	353	405	632	1038	8	90	0.86	3	1	50	279	8.36
2015	Rk	Johnson City	204	32	64	2	31	314	349	451	800	5	84	0.34	9	4	36	137	5.30

Breakout season at the plate and does everything well on the diamond. At the plate has a short, compact LH stroke that allows him to barrel the ball with surprising gap power. Plus speed on the bases and in the field. Solid defender with good range, nice hands, and a strong arm. Nice sleeper prospect.

Amaya,Gioskar — 2 — Chicago (N)

EXP MLB DEBUT: 2017 | H/W: 5-11 175 | FUT: Utility player | 6B

Bats R Age 23 — 2009 FA (VZ) — Pwr + | BAvg +++ | Spd ++ | Def ++

Year	Lev	Team	AB	R	H	HR	RBI	Avg	OB	Slg	OPS	bb%	ct%	Eye	SB	CS	x/h%	Iso	RC/G
2012	A-	Boise	272	61	81	8	33	298	374	496	870	11	76	0.51	15	5	32	199	6.57
2012	AAA	Iowa	1	1	1	0	0	1000		2000	3000	0	100		0	0	100	1000	27.71
2013	A	Kane County	453	65	114	5	28	252	315	369	684	8	76	0.39	13	6	32	117	4.03
2014	A+	Daytona	369	56	102	4	35	276	367	369	736	13	76	0.59	14	7	23	92	4.89
2015	A	South Bend	400	45	104	4	43	260	333	345	678	10	82	0.60	17	5	23	85	4.04

Short, athletic player was moved behind the plate and split time at 1B. Has a quick bat and makes consistent contact, but lacks power. Transition to catcher is very much a work in progress, though he continues to show above-average speed. At 23, the clock is ticking and a UT role seems most likely.

Anderson,Blake — 2 — Miami

EXP MLB DEBUT: 2019 | H/W: 6-3 180 | FUT: Starting C | 7D

Bats R Age 20 — 2014 (1) HS (MS) — Pwr ++ | BAvg ++ | Spd ++ | Def +++

Year	Lev	Team	AB	R	H	HR	RBI	Avg	OB	Slg	OPS	bb%	ct%	Eye	SB	CS	x/h%	Iso	RC/G
2014	Rk	GCL Marlins	74	6	8	0	5	108	233	135	368	14	55	0.36	0	1	25	27	-0.96
2015	A-	Batavia	118	9	26	2	16	220	240	322	562	2	64	0.07	0	0	31	102	2.10

Backstop has yet to hit as a pro. Has a balanced approach at the plate with a nice line-drive swing, but lacks the bat speed needed to drive the ball and struggles to make consistent contact. Has good blocking and receiving skills with a plus arm and should be able to stick behind the dish, if only he could hit.

Anderson,Brian — 457 — Miami

EXP MLB DEBUT: 2018 | H/W: 6-3 185 | FUT: Starting 3B | 7D

Bats R Age 22 — 2014 (3) Arkansas — Pwr +++ | BAvg +++ | Spd ++ | Def +++

Year	Lev	Team	AB	R	H	HR	RBI	Avg	OB	Slg	OPS	bb%	ct%	Eye	SB	CS	x/h%	Iso	RC/G
2013	NCAA	Arkansas	209	47	68	4	36	325	436	488	924	16	84	1.24	6	1	31	163	7.49
2014	NCAA	Arkansas	241	39	79	7	51	328	379	498	877	8	83	0.50	9	2	30	170	6.27
2014	A-	Batavia	77	11	21	3	12	273	325	455	780	7	86	0.55	1	1	33	182	5.04
2014	A	Greensboro	153	27	48	8	37	314	367	516	884	8	82	0.46	0	0	31	203	6.23
2015	A+	Jupiter	477	50	112	8	62	235	294	340	634	8	77	0.37	2	2	29	105	3.27

Scrappy infielder has a good approach at the plate and makes consistent contact. Has surprising power for his size. Was moved to 3B and was one of the better defenders in the league with good range and a strong arm. Was skipped over Low-A and the jumped proved too much so will need to regroup in 2016.

Anderson,Tim — 6 — Chicago (A)

EXP MLB DEBUT: 2016 | H/W: 6-1 185 | FUT: Starting SS | 9D

Bats R Age 22 — 2013 (1) EastCentComm — Pwr +++ | BAvg ++++ | Spd +++++ | Def ++

Year	Lev	Team	AB	R	H	HR	RBI	Avg	OB	Slg	OPS	bb%	ct%	Eye	SB	CS	x/h%	Iso	RC/G
2013	A	Kannapolis	267	45	74	1	21	277	334	363	698	8	71	0.29	24	4	22	86	4.26
2014	Rk	Azl White Sox	15	2	3	2	2	200	294	600	894	12	67	0.40	0	1	67	400	6.63
2014	A+	Winston-Salem	286	48	85	6	31	297	314	472	786	2	76	0.10	10	3	36	175	5.03
2014	AA	Birmingham	44	7	16	1	7	364	364	500	864	0	80	0.00	0	1	25	136	5.63
2015	AA	Birmingham	513	79	160	5	46	312	343	429	771	4	78	0.21	49	13	24	117	4.92

Plus athlete who could hit .300+ annually due to short, quick stroke. Best present attribute is double plus speed, but exhibits some raw power and contact skills. Draws few walks in aggressive approach, but shoots gaps. Led SL in SB and finished 3rd in BA. Has arm and range for SS, but also led league in errors.

Andujar,Miguel — 5 — New York (A)

EXP MLB DEBUT: 2018 | H/W: 6-0 175 | FUT: Starting 3B | 8E

Bats R Age 21 — 2011 FA (DR) — Pwr +++ | BAvg ++ | Spd ++ | Def ++

Year	Lev	Team	AB	R	H	HR	RBI	Avg	OB	Slg	OPS	bb%	ct%	Eye	SB	CS	x/h%	Iso	RC/G
2012	Rk	GCL Yankees	177	21	41	1	19	232	284	299	584	7	79	0.35	1	3	24	68	2.66
2013	Rk	GCL Yankees 2	133	18	43	4	25	323	357	496	853	5	84	0.33	4	1	35	173	5.80
2014	A	Charleston (Sc)	484	75	129	10	70	267	316	397	713	7	83	0.42	5	1	30	130	4.26
2015	A+	Tampa	485	54	118	8	57	243	286	363	649	6	81	0.32	12	1	31	120	3.44

Athletic INF who was young for level and proved to be too aggressive with stick. Uses above average bat speed to project to at least average pop, but won't hit for high BA without more patience. Has shown improving defensive skills, though can get careless with glove. More tools than performance at this point.

Aplin,Andrew — 8 — Houston

EXP MLB DEBUT: 2016 | H/W: 6-0 205 | FUT: Fourth OF | 6B

Bats L Age 25 — 2012 (5) Arizona St — Pwr + | BAvg +++ | Spd +++ | Def +++

Year	Lev	Team	AB	R	H	HR	RBI	Avg	OB	Slg	OPS	bb%	ct%	Eye	SB	CS	x/h%	Iso	RC/G
2013	A+	Lancaster	500	102	139	9	107	278	381	424	805	14	87	1.32	24	6	35	146	5.92
2014	AA	Corpus Christi	356	49	95	6	50	267	380	354	734	15	84	1.16	21	8	19	87	5.03
2014	AAA	Oklahoma City	96	14	25	0	15	260	360	313	673	14	84	1.00	5	3	16	52	4.28
2015	AA	Corpus Christi	105	27	36	0	12	343	465	448	913	19	88	1.85	12	3	19	105	7.60
2015	AAA	Fresno	233	37	64	2	28	275	392	348	740	16	82	1.10	20	7	17	73	5.17

Savvy OF who lacks profile to be starting OF, but has usable skills. Plays game hard with above average speed and shrewd plate discipline. Sees pitches and can hang in against LHP. Recognizes and hits spin, but swing lacks punch and speed. Tools enhanced by keen instincts. Mostly singles hitter at present. Good defender in CF who can track balls.

Aquino,Aristides — 9 — Cincinnati

EXP MLB DEBUT: 2019 | H/W: 6-4 190 | FUT: Starting RF | 8E

Bats R Age 21 — 2011 FA (DR)

Pwr ++++ | BAvg ++ | Spd ++++ | Def +++

Year	Lev	Team	AB	R	H	HR	RBI	Avg	OB	Slg	OPS	bb%	ct%	Eye	SB	CS	x/h%	Iso	RC/G
2013	Rk	AZL Reds	194	37	54	4	38	278	314	479	793	5	79	0.25	4	3	46	201	5.27
2013	Rk	Billings	69	13	14	3	10	203	225	377	602	3	67	0.09	1	1	36	174	2.55
2014	Rk	Billings	284	48	83	16	64	292	328	577	905	5	77	0.23	21	5	53	285	6.57
2015	Rk	Billings	52	7	16	2	13	308	333	558	891	4	83	0.22	0	1	38	250	6.24
2015	A	Dayton	231	25	54	5	27	234	269	364	632	5	77	0.21	6	1	31	130	3.10

Struggled after suffering a broken wrist in April. Emerged in '14; then impressed in 2015's full-season debut. Pitch recognition skills and in-game power regressed due to injury. Bat didn't barrel ball as much after injury. Profiles in RF despite plus speed. Throws laser beams from the OF.

Aracena,Ricky — 6 — Kansas City

EXP MLB DEBUT: 2019 | H/W: 5-8 160 | FUT: Starting SS | 7E

Bats S Age 18 — 2014 FA (DR)

Pwr + | BAvg +++ | Spd ++++ | Def +++

Year	Lev	Team	AB	R	H	HR	RBI	Avg	OB	Slg	OPS	bb%	ct%	Eye	SB	CS	x/h%	Iso	RC/G
2015	Rk	Azl Royals	109	14	32	0	9	294	306	349	655	2	81	0.10	8	3	13	55	3.29

Diminutive INF who plays small ball extremely well and effectively uses plus speed. Makes consistent contact with quick, level stroke and sprays balls to all fields Swings aggressively and doesn't take many walks, but differentiates between balls and strikes. Owns good glove at SS with strong arm and sufficient range.

Arauz,Jonathan — 6 — Houston

EXP MLB DEBUT: 2021 | H/W: 6-0 147 | FUT: Starting SS | 8D

Bats L Age 17 — 2014 FA (Panama)

Pwr ++ | BAvg +++ | Spd ++ | Def +++

Year	Lev	Team	AB	R	H	HR	RBI	Avg	OB	Slg	OPS	bb%	ct%	Eye	SB	CS	x/h%	Iso	RC/G
2015	Rk	GCL Phillies	173	21	44	2	18	254	306	370	676	7	83	0.45	2	0	32	116	3.91

Despite diminutive size and young age, showed a surprisingly refined hit tool in his first stateside action, with a line-drive stroke and more power than one would expect. Doesn't run particularly well, but has enough defensive tools (good hands and arm) to play in the middle of the diamond. More instinct than flash.

Arcia,Orlando — 6 — Milwaukee

EXP MLB DEBUT: 2016 | H/W: 6-0 165 | FUT: Starting SS | 9C

Bats R Age 21 — 2010 FA (VZ)

Pwr ++ | BAvg ++++ | Spd +++ | Def ++++

Year	Lev	Team	AB	R	H	HR	RBI	Avg	OB	Slg	OPS	bb%	ct%	Eye	SB	CS	x/h%	Iso	RC/G
2013	A	Wisconsin	442	67	111	4	39	251	306	333	639	7	91	0.88	20	9	21	81	3.67
2014	A+	Brevard County	498	65	144	4	50	289	344	392	736	8	87	0.65	31	11	26	102	4.72
2015	AA	Biloxi	512	74	157	8	69	307	345	453	798	6	86	0.41	25	8	33	146	5.27

Young SS who made seamless jump to the SL. High contact, line-drive swing and mature approach translated to career high BA/ISO. Raw power projects as below average, but has strength to expose gaps regularly. Speed and athleticism bode well for SB value. Flaunts plus range and arm in the field. With more maturation, value will increase.

Arroyo,Christian — 6 — San Francisco

EXP MLB DEBUT: 2017 | H/W: 5-11 185 | FUT: Starting SS | 8C

Bats R Age 20 — 2013 (1) HS (FL)

Pwr ++ | BAvg ++++ | Spd +++ | Def +++

Year	Lev	Team	AB	R	H	HR	RBI	Avg	OB	Slg	OPS	bb%	ct%	Eye	SB	CS	x/h%	Iso	RC/G
2013	Rk	Azl Giants	184	47	60	2	39	326	389	511	900	9	83	0.59	3	2	42	185	6.86
2014	A-	Salem-Kaizer	243	39	81	5	48	333	379	469	848	7	87	0.58	6	1	26	136	5.88
2014	A	Augusta	118	10	24	1	14	203	230	271	501	3	81	0.18	1	2	21	68	1.51
2015	A+	San Jose	381	48	116	9	42	304	338	459	797	5	81	0.26	5	3	34	155	5.16

Former 1st rounder whose bat impressed in AFL action. Has advanced barrel control vs. array of offerings, giving him BA upside. Mostly gap power with line-drive approach, but raw pop projects as an average tool. Great instincts and strong arm help fringe-average defensive range play at SS, where he profiles best long-term. Fallback option is 2B.

Ascanio,Rayder — 6 — Seattle

EXP MLB DEBUT: 2018 | H/W: 5-11 155 | FUT: Starting SS | 7D

Bats B Age 20 — 2012 FA (VZ)

Pwr + | BAvg ++ | Spd +++ | Def ++++

Year	Lev	Team	AB	R	H	HR	RBI	Avg	OB	Slg	OPS	bb%	ct%	Eye	SB	CS	x/h%	Iso	RC/G
2014	Rk	Azl Mariners	145	28	36	0	15	248	359	310	669	15	68	0.54	5	3	25	62	4.16
2015	A	Clinton	24	6	7	0	2	292	433	333	767	20	88	2.00	0	1	14	42	5.87
2015	A+	Bakersfield	297	28	68	1	30	229	275	286	562	6	76	0.27	6	2	21	57	2.29

Light-framed INF who showed glimpses of talent in first full season as pro. Likely best defender in system with quick, clean actions, plus arm, and above average range to both sides. Footwork is textbook which allows for accurate throws. Not a threat with bat and needs to add strength. No present pop, but has good speed.

Asuaje,Carlos — 45 — San Diego

EXP MLB DEBUT: 2016 | H/W: 5-9 160 | FUT: Utility player | 6B

Bats L Age 24 — 2013 (11) Nova SouthEstrn

Pwr ++ | BAvg +++ | Spd +++ | Def ++

Year	Lev	Team	AB	R	H	HR	RBI	Avg	OB	Slg	OPS	bb%	ct%	Eye	SB	CS	x/h%	Iso	RC/G
2013	NCAA	Nova SouthEstrn	178	40	57	2	33	320	440	449	889	18	93	2.92	32	3	30	129	7.24
2013	A-	Lowell	171	19	46	1	21	269	369	368	737	14	81	0.82	4	3	30	99	5.03
2014	A	Greenville	325	59	99	11	73	305	383	542	924	11	83	0.73	7	4	45	237	7.15
2014	A+	Salem	155	27	50	4	28	323	393	516	909	10	78	0.53	1	3	40	194	7.02
2015	AA	Portland	495	60	124	8	61	251	327	374	700	10	82	0.64	9	6	31	123	4.34

Short, smart INF who has value with bat and glove. Gap power, though can pull ball out on occasion. Works counts and knows strike zone. Has controlled swing for contact, though bat speed is limited. Plays 2B and 3B, though not ace at either spot. Arm and range best suited for 2B. Uses average speed, but not many SB.

Avelino,Abiatal — 46 — New York (A)

EXP MLB DEBUT: 2018 | H/W: 5-11 186 | FUT: Starting 2B/SS | 7C

Bats R Age 21 — 2011 FA (DR)

Pwr + | BAvg +++ | Spd ++++ | Def +++

Year	Lev	Team	AB	R	H	HR	RBI	Avg	OB	Slg	OPS	bb%	ct%	Eye	SB	CS	x/h%	Iso	RC/G
2013	A-	Stn Island	70	10	17	0	6	243	284	271	555	5	91	0.67	2	0	12	29	2.65
2014	Rk	GCL Yankees	31	7	11	0	3	355	394	548	942	6	87	0.50	0	0	55	194	7.16
2014	A	Charleston (Sc)	220	31	51	2	12	232	287	323	610	7	80	0.39	11	5	29	91	3.03
2015	A	Charleston (Sc)	83	16	25	0	4	301	341	398	738	6	81	0.31	16	3	32	96	4.62
2015	A+	Tampa	405	64	102	4	23	252	307	321	628	7	84	0.51	38	15	18	69	3.31

Short, stocky INF whose defense is ahead of bat at present. Versatility will be key as he may not have enough punch to warrant starting role. Has long swing and doesn't read spin well. Has ability to hit to all fields and can bunt to get on base. Exhibits plus speed, but has high CS%. Owns impressive range and plus arm.

Aybar,Yoan — 89 — Boston

EXP MLB DEBUT: 2019 | H/W: 6-2 165 | FUT: Starting OF | 8E

Bats L Age 18 — 2013 FA (DR)

Pwr ++ | BAvg ++ | Spd +++ | Def +++

Year	Lev	Team	AB	R	H	HR	RBI	Avg	OB	Slg	OPS	bb%	ct%	Eye	SB	CS	x/h%	Iso	RC/G
2015	Rk	GCL Red Sox	157	19	42	0	16	268	299	338	636	4	71	0.15	6	6	19	70	3.24

Toolsy OF who showed raw talent in first season in US. Has potential to evolve into middle of order hitter with loose, powerful stroke. Has room to add muscle to lean frame. Bat speed and barrel control are very good, but has raw approach with little feel for spin. Runs well now and tracks down balls efficiently in OF.

Bader,Harrison — 8 — St. Louis

EXP MLB DEBUT: 2018 | H/W: 6-0 195 | FUT: Starting CF | 8D

Bats R Age 21 — 2015 (3) Florida

Pwr +++ | BAvg +++ | Spd +++ | Def +++

Year	Lev	Team	AB	R	H	HR	RBI	Avg	OB	Slg	OPS	bb%	ct%	Eye	SB	CS	x/h%	Iso	RC/G
2015	NCAA	Florida	256	53	76	17	66	297	377	566	944	11	79	0.61	8	5	45	270	7.23
2015	A-	State College	29	6	11	2	4	379	379	655	1034	0	83	0.00	2	0	36	276	7.41
2015	A	Peoria	206	34	62	9	28	301	348	505	853	7	79	0.34	15	6	35	204	5.92

Has a good approach at the plate with surprising pop for his size. Blasted 17 HR in college and then launched another 11 as a pro. Can be aggressive and sells out for power, resulting in some swing and misses, but the end results were good. Runs well and played all three OF spots in his debut.

Baez,Leudys — 789 — Atlanta

EXP MLB DEBUT: 2020 | H/W: 6-0 160 | FUT: Starting CF | 7D

Bats S Age 19 — 2014 FA (DR)

Pwr ++ | BAvg ++ | Spd +++ | Def +++

Year	Lev	Team	AB	R	H	HR	RBI	Avg	OB	Slg	OPS	bb%	ct%	Eye	SB	CS	x/h%	Iso	RC/G
2015	Rk	Danville	148	19	46	4	13	311	325	473	797	2	79	0.10	5	1	30	162	5.00
2015	A	Rome	107	12	22	1	6	206	227	318	545	3	72	0.10	1	4	36	112	1.93

Made his professional debut this season, posting solid numbers in the APPY before an Aug promotion to the SAL, where he was overmatched. Has plus raw power despite smallish frame. Should grow into body. Needs to cut length down on swing and improve feel for the strike zone. A solid defender with a strong arm, he is capable of playing CF.

Baldoquin,Roberto

6 | **Los Angeles (A)** | EXP MLB DEBUT: 2017 | H/W: 5-11 185 | FUT: Starting 2B/SS | **7C**

Bats R Age 21
2014 FA (CU)
Pwr ++
BAvg ++
Spd +++
Def +++

Year	Lev	Team	AB	R	H	HR	RBI	Avg	OB	Slg	OPS	bb%	ct%	Eye	SB	CS	x/h%	Iso	RC/G
2015	A+	Inland Empire	289	23	68	1	27	235	258	294	553	3	76	0.13	4	5	21	59	2.02

Strong INF who missed time with rib cage injury and struggled when healthy. Expands strike zone with overzealous swing and needs to hone approach. Has natural gap power that could develop into average long ball pop. Stayed at SS all season, though may be better at 2B due to average arm and range. Could steal bases if he got on base more.

Bandy,Jett

2 | **Los Angeles (A)** | EXP MLB DEBUT: 2015 | H/W: 6-4 235 | FUT: Backup C | **6B**

Bats R Age 26
2011 (31) Arizona
Pwr +++
BAvg ++
Spd +
Def +++

Year	Lev	Team	AB	R	H	HR	RBI	Avg	OB	Slg	OPS	bb%	ct%	Eye	SB	CS	x/h%	Iso	RC/G
2012	A+	Inland Empire	324	42	80	7	46	247	291	386	677	6	84	0.39	1	1	38	139	3.81
2013	AA	Arkansas	245	26	59	4	28	241	282	376	657	5	84	0.36	0	1	39	135	3.60
2014	AA	Arkansas	312	38	78	13	40	250	322	413	735	10	80	0.52	2	4	32	163	4.54
2015	AAA	Salt Lake	309	47	90	11	60	291	326	466	792	5	80	0.25	0	0	36	175	5.06
2015	MLB	LA Angels	2	1	1	1	1	500	500	2000	2500	0	100		0	0	100	1500	20.12

Big, strong catcher with improving bat that resulted in September callup. Not a liability in any part of game, but not a standout either. Good catch-and-throw skills enhance defense, where he has agility and mobility. Offense all about power as he has leveraged swing to mask fringy bat speed. Doesn't read spin well, but makes acceptable contact.

Barnes,Austin

2 | **Los Angeles (N)** | EXP MLB DEBUT: 2015 | H/W: 5-11 185 | FUT: Starting C | **7D**

Bats R Age 26
2011 (9) Arizona St
Pwr ++
BAvg +++
Spd ++
Def +++

Year	Lev	Team	AB	R	H	HR	RBI	Avg	OB	Slg	OPS	bb%	ct%	Eye	SB	CS	x/h%	Iso	RC/G
2013	AA	Jacksonville	62	10	21	1	7	339	446	484	930	16	84	1.20	0	0	24	145	7.56
2014	A+	Jupiter	180	24	57	1	14	317	382	417	799	10	86	0.76	3	3	25	100	5.57
2014	AA	Jacksonville	284	56	84	12	43	296	401	507	908	15	87	1.39	8	0	40	211	7.06
2015	AAA	Oklahoma City	292	40	92	9	42	315	388	479	868	11	88	0.97	12	2	30	164	6.33
2015	MLB	LA Dodgers	29	4	6	0	1	207	343	276	619	17	79	1.00	1	0	33	69	3.67

Athletic C was traded as part of the Dee Gordon deal. Nice season hitting .315 at AAA and earned a late-season call-up. Shows patience at the plate and makes hard contact going gap-to-gap. Power and speed will never be a big part of his game. Has good hands and receiving skills that will keep him behind the plate.

Barnes,Barrett

8 | **Pittsburgh** | EXP MLB DEBUT: 2017 | H/W: 5-11 210 | FUT: Starting CF | **8E**

Bats R Age 24
2012 (1) Texas Tech
Pwr +++
BAvg +++
Spd +++
Def +++

Year	Lev	Team	AB	R	H	HR	RBI	Avg	OB	Slg	OPS	bb%	ct%	Eye	SB	CS	x/h%	Iso	RC/G
2014	Rk	GCL Pirates	16	5	5	2	5	313	500	813	1313	27	81	2.00	1	0	80	500	12.57
2014	A	West Virginia	13	1	2	0	2	154	267	154	421	13	85	1.00	2	0	0	0	1.17
2014	A+	Bradenton	21	3	5	0	1	238	333	333	667	13	76	0.60	1	0	40	95	4.07
2015	A+	Bradenton	234	45	61	6	24	261	340	423	763	11	82	0.68	13	5	39	162	5.11
2015	AA	Altoona	126	17	31	3	17	246	331	365	696	11	80	0.64	4	4	29	119	4.24

The oft-injured Barnes was mostly healthy in '15 and put up respectable numbers between A+/AA. Has good bat speed, solid plate discipline, and plus raw power. Has above-avg speed, covers ground well, and should be able to stick in CF. Loads of potential, but checkered injury history makes him unreliable.

Barnum,Keon

3 | **Chicago (A)** | EXP MLB DEBUT: 2017 | H/W: 6-5 225 | FUT: Starting 1B | **7D**

Bats L Age 23
2012 (1) HS (FL)
Pwr +++
BAvg ++
Spd +
Def ++

Year	Lev	Team	AB	R	H	HR	RBI	Avg	OB	Slg	OPS	bb%	ct%	Eye	SB	CS	x/h%	Iso	RC/G
2012	Rk	Bristol	43	6	12	3	8	279	354	512	866	10	70	0.38	0	0	33	233	6.37
2013	A	Kannapolis	201	22	51	5	26	254	318	403	721	9	68	0.29	0	0	37	149	4.61
2014	A+	Winston-Salem	491	49	124	8	60	253	305	365	669	7	67	0.23	3	0	31	112	3.83
2015	A+	Winston-Salem	382	40	98	9	67	257	319	390	709	8	71	0.31	0	1	34	134	4.33

Large-framed INF who set career high in HR, but has plenty in tank for more. Made more consistent contact with better approach, though projected power hasn't materialized. Long arms result in exploitable stroke, but can hang in against LHP. Offers well below average speed and commits lot of errors at 1B despite soft hands.

Barreto,Franklin

6 | **Oakland** | EXP MLB DEBUT: 2017 | H/W: 5-9 175 | FUT: Starting INF | **9D**

Bats R Age 20
2012 FA (VZ)
Pwr +++
BAvg ++++
Spd +++
Def ++

Year	Lev	Team	AB	R	H	HR	RBI	Avg	OB	Slg	OPS	bb%	ct%	Eye	SB	CS	x/h%	Iso	RC/G
2013	Rk	GCL Blue Jays	174	30	52	4	19	299	348	529	876	7	76	0.31	10	4	50	230	6.56
2013	Rk	Bluefield	54	4	11	0	7	204	232	333	565	4	74	0.14	0	2	55	130	2.39
2014	A-	Vancouver	289	65	90	6	61	311	368	481	849	8	78	0.41	29	5	37	170	6.13
2015	A+	Stockton	338	50	102	13	47	302	331	500	831	4	80	0.22	8	3	37	198	5.51

Short, strong INF who bypassed Low-A and set career high in HR. Above average bat speed and use of all fields should lead to high BA. Power projects to average due to line drive stroke. SB output dropped, but could increase with more walks. Commits careless errors despite solid range and arm. Has things to tidy up, but has makings of All-Star.

Basabe,Luis

789 | **Boston** | EXP MLB DEBUT: 2019 | H/W: 6-0 160 | FUT: Starting OF | **8D**

Bats B Age 19
2012 FA (VZ)
Pwr +++
BAvg ++
Spd +++
Def ++

Year	Lev	Team	AB	R	H	HR	RBI	Avg	OB	Slg	OPS	bb%	ct%	Eye	SB	CS	x/h%	Iso	RC/G
2013	Rk	DSL Red Sox	209	49	47	1	19	225	372	321	693	19	72	0.84	18	5	34	96	4.64
2014	Rk	GCL Red Sox	105	15	26	1	13	248	331	324	654	11	78	0.57	2	4	23	76	3.73
2014	Rk	DSL Red Sox	148	38	42	0	26	284	404	480	884	17	76	0.83	13	2	43	196	7.38
2015	A-	Lowell	222	36	54	7	23	243	339	401	739	13	70	0.48	15	4	33	158	4.91

Developing prospect who has exciting athleticism and power potential. Frame is very lean and has room to pack on muscle. Has controlled swing, but struggles with breaking balls. Draws walks with nice approach and has pretty swing from both sides. Plays mostly CF with above average arm, though reads and jumps are unpolished.

Bauers,Jake

3 | **Tampa Bay** | EXP MLB DEBUT: 2017 | H/W: 6-1 195 | FUT: Starting 1B | **7B**

Bats L Age 20
2013 (7) HS (CA)
Pwr ++
BAvg +++
Spd ++
Def +++

Year	Lev	Team	AB	R	H	HR	RBI	Avg	OB	Slg	OPS	bb%	ct%	Eye	SB	CS	x/h%	Iso	RC/G
2013	Rk	Azl Padres	163	22	46	1	25	282	339	374	713	8	81	0.45	2	0	24	92	4.39
2014	A	Fort Wayne	406	59	120	8	64	296	374	414	788	11	80	0.64	5	6	24	118	5.42
2015	A+	Charlotte	217	33	58	6	38	267	354	433	787	12	85	0.88	2	3	38	166	5.47
2015	AA	Montgomery	257	36	71	5	36	276	331	405	736	8	84	0.51	6	3	32	128	4.61

Patient, advanced hitter who grinds out at bats and is very tough out. May not have ideal power for 1B, but can lace doubles to all fields with direct swing. Can pull balls out, but at best when using entire field. Has been solid defender with mobility and good hands. May be candidate to see time in LF.

Bautista,Claudio

4 | **Cleveland** | EXP MLB DEBUT: 2018 | H/W: 5-11 170 | FUT: Starting 2B | **7D**

Bats R Age 22
2011 FA (DR)
Pwr ++
BAvg ++
Spd +++
Def +++

Year	Lev	Team	AB	R	H	HR	RBI	Avg	OB	Slg	OPS	bb%	ct%	Eye	SB	CS	x/h%	Iso	RC/G
2013	A-	Mahoning Val	250	36	68	4	24	272	326	416	742	7	78	0.36	3	1	35	144	4.72
2013	A	Lake County	51	6	8	1	5	157	204	255	459	6	73	0.21	0	2	38	98	0.75
2014	A	Lake County	461	65	115	13	54	249	268	410	678	3	78	0.12	11	3	36	161	3.57
2015	A	Lake County	253	39	76	7	39	300	352	466	818	7	81	0.41	5	4	36	166	5.57
2015	A+	Lynchburg	178	24	35	2	12	197	263	287	549	8	71	0.31	3	2	34	90	2.13

Fundamentally-sound INF who hit well in Low-A before struggling in High-A. Possesses BA potential thanks to quick wrists and stroke. Has feel for contact, though can get himself out by swinging at bad pitches. Can pull ball over wall, but only profiles to gap power. Instincts allow average tools to play up.

Bautista,Rafael

8 | **Washington** | EXP MLB DEBUT: 2017 | H/W: 6-2 165 | FUT: Starting CF | **7C**

Bats R Age 23
2012 FA (DR)
Pwr +
BAvg +++
Spd ++++
Def +++

Year	Lev	Team	AB	R	H	HR	RBI	Avg	OB	Slg	OPS	bb%	ct%	Eye	SB	CS	x/h%	Iso	RC/G
2013	Rk	GCL Nationals	202	44	65	1	27	322	377	391	768	8	83	0.53	26	7	15	69	5.05
2014	A	Hagerstown	487	97	141	5	54	290	335	382	717	6	85	0.46	69	15	21	92	4.34
2015	Rk	GCL Nationals	16	3	5	1	2	313	313	500	813	0	94	0.00	0	0	20	188	4.79
2015	A-	Auburn	33	6	9	0	4	273	294	364	658	3	79	0.14	3	0	33	91	3.46
2015	A+	Potomac	206	23	56	0	8	272	309	325	634	5	89	0.50	23	4	16	53	3.44

Broken finger in the season's first week cost him almost three months. Primarily a singles hitter with very little power projection, he does have fantastic speed that benefits him in CF and on the bases. A decent plate approach and contact skills, but question will be whether he can handle the bat at higher levels.

Becerra,Wuilmer

9 | **New York (N)** | EXP MLB DEBUT: 2018 | H/W: 6-4 190 | FUT: Starting RF | **8D**

Bats R Age 21
2011 FA (VZ)
Pwr +++
BAvg +++
Spd +++
Def +++

Year	Lev	Team	AB	R	H	HR	RBI	Avg	OB	Slg	OPS	bb%	ct%	Eye	SB	CS	x/h%	Iso	RC/G
2012	Rk	GCL Blue Jays	32	5	8	0	4	250	333	375	708	11	78	0.57	0	1	50	125	4.61
2013	Rk	GCL Mets	173	21	42	1	25	243	321	295	616	10	65	0.33	5	6	17	52	3.17
2014	Rk	Kingsport	207	37	62	7	29	300	344	469	812	6	73	0.25	7	3	31	169	5.53
2015	A	Savannah	449	67	130	9	63	290	338	423	761	7	79	0.34	16	8	30	134	4.87

Talented OF had a breakout season in first taste of full-season ball. Made adjustments to swing to maximize power potential. More upper-cut than before. Struggles identifying breaking pitch. Won't swing even at hangers unless 2-strikes. Raw power shows signs of developing. Has the arm to stay in RF.

Bell,Josh | 3 | Pittsburgh | EXP MLB DEBUT: 2016 | H/W: 6-4 235 | FUT: Starting 1B | 9D

Bats B Age 23	Year	Lev	Team	AB	R	H	HR	RBI	Avg	OB	Slg	OPS	bb%	ct%	Eye	SB	CS	x/h%	Iso	RC/G
2011 (2) HS (TX)	2013	A	West Virginia	459	75	128	13	76	279	352	453	805	10	80	0.58	1	2	41	174	5.60
Pwr ++++	2014	A+	Bradenton	331	45	111	9	53	335	382	502	884	7	87	0.58	5	4	30	166	6.28
BAvg ++++	2014	AA	Altoona	94	13	27	0	7	287	343	309	652	8	87	0.67	4	1	7	21	3.70
Spd ++	2015	AA	Altoona	368	47	113	5	60	307	381	427	808	11	86	0.88	7	4	25	120	5.71
Def +++	2015	AAA	Indianapolis	121	20	42	2	18	347	444	504	948	15	88	1.40	2	0	29	157	7.66

Imposing switch hitter has plus bat speed and raw power. Level swing plane and plus bat control has generated line drives so far, but has worked on getting more lift in hopes of more home runs. Hit .317 between AA/AAA; Was moved from OF to 1B in '15. If the power comes, he could be a stud.

Bellinger,Cody | 38 | Los Angeles (N) | EXP MLB DEBUT: 2018 | H/W: 6-4 180 | FUT: Starting 1B/OF | 8C

Bats L Age 20	Year	Lev	Team	AB	R	H	HR	RBI	Avg	OB	Slg	OPS	bb%	ct%	Eye	SB	CS	x/h%	Iso	RC/G
2013 (4) HS (AZ)																				
Pwr ++++	2013	Rk	Azl Dodgers	162	25	34	1	30	210	337	358	695	16	72	0.67	3	3	47	148	4.63
BAvg +++	2014	Rk	Azl Dodgers	20	2	3	0	0	150	190	200	390	5	75	0.20	0	0	33	50	0.01
Spd ++	2014	Rk	Ogden	195	49	64	3	34	328	373	503	876	7	82	0.40	8	0	34	174	6.34
Def ++++	2015	A+	RanchoCuca	478	97	126	30	103	264	336	538	874	10	69	0.35	10	2	53	274	6.68

Put up ridiculous power numbers in the CAL, launching 33 doubles and 30 HR after just 3 HR in '14. Huge raw power and a quick LH stroke. Got more loft from his swing, but sacrificed contact for power and struck out 150 times. Plus defender who moves well and has Gold Glove potential and can also play the OF.

Benintendi,Andrew | 8 | Boston | EXP MLB DEBUT: 2017 | H/W: 5-11 175 | FUT: Starting CF | 8B

Bats L Age 21	Year	Lev	Team	AB	R	H	HR	RBI	Avg	OB	Slg	OPS	bb%	ct%	Eye	SB	CS	x/h%	Iso	RC/G
2015 (1) Arkansas																				
Pwr ++++																				
BAvg +++	2015	NCAA	Arkansas	226	62	85	20	57	376	489	717	1206	18	86	1.56	24	4	41	341	10.61
Spd +++	2015	A-	Lowell	124	19	36	7	15	290	409	540	950	17	88	1.67	7	1	36	250	7.59
Def +++	2015	A	Greenville	74	17	26	4	16	351	429	581	1010	12	88	1.11	3	2	35	230	7.94

Short, athletic OF who made pro ball look easy with balanced approach and plus ability to hit. Brings power and speed to table and is solid all-around player. Knows strike zone and puts bat to ball consistently. Owns plus, raw power, but will need to prove he can hit LHP. Played CF and has good instincts, but not a standout.

Beras,Jairo | 9 | Texas | EXP MLB DEBUT: 2018 | H/W: 6-5 178 | FUT: Starting OF | 8D

Bats R Age 21	Year	Lev	Team	AB	R	H	HR	RBI	Avg	OB	Slg	OPS	bb%	ct%	Eye	SB	CS	x/h%	Iso	RC/G
2012 FA (DR)																				
Pwr +++																				
BAvg ++	2013	Rk	Azl Rangers	64	11	16	2	15	250	304	438	742	7	70	0.26	1	0	38	188	4.78
Spd +++	2014	A	Hickory	389	38	94	7	33	242	301	342	643	8	66	0.25	5	4	27	100	3.45
Def ++	2015	A	Hickory	327	45	95	9	43	291	329	440	770	5	73	0.22	9	4	31	150	4.95

Rangy, tall OF who repeated Low-A and was much better, increasing BA, HR, and SB. Missed time early with quad injury, but was good when healthy. Made better contact and flashed plus raw power. Covers plate well with long arms, but has holes in swing. Not a strong defender at present, though has average speed and strong arm.

Bernard,Wynton | 78 | Detroit | EXP MLB DEBUT: 2016 | H/W: 6-2 195 | FUT: Starting OF | 7D

Bats R Age 25	Year	Lev	Team	AB	R	H	HR	RBI	Avg	OB	Slg	OPS	bb%	ct%	Eye	SB	CS	x/h%	Iso	RC/G
2012 (35) Niagara	2013	A-	Eugene	136	19	34	1	10	250	338	324	661	12	76	0.55	7	4	21	74	3.85
Pwr +	2013	A	Fort Wayne	15	1	3	0	3	200	250	333	583	6	67	0.20	1	1	33	133	2.78
BAvg +++	2013	A+	Lake Elsinore	14	4	3	0	0	214	267	357	624	7	86	0.50	0	1	33	143	3.49
Spd ++++	2014	A	West Michigan	507	91	164	6	47	323	391	442	833	10	83	0.65	45	19	26	118	5.96
Def +++	2015	AA	Erie	534	78	161	4	36	301	348	408	756	7	86	0.52	43	16	25	107	4.88

Speedy OF who is all about making contact and keeping ball on ground. Led EL in SB due to plus speed and shows polished instincts as baserunner. Can be too aggressive on base and needs to pick spots better. Career .300 hitter, though power is below average. Drives gaps with level swing path. Plus range in OF and arm strength is limited.

Betancourt,Javier | 4 | Milwaukee | EXP MLB DEBUT: 2017 | H/W: 5-10 180 | FUT: Starting 2B | 7C

Bats R Age 20	Year	Lev	Team	AB	R	H	HR	RBI	Avg	OB	Slg	OPS	bb%	ct%	Eye	SB	CS	x/h%	Iso	RC/G
2011 FA (VZ)																				
Pwr ++																				
BAvg +++	2013	Rk	GCL Tigers	177	28	59	2	22	333	376	441	816	6	92	0.86	5	3	22	107	5.56
Spd ++	2014	A	West Michigan	558	67	150	6	54	269	301	344	645	4	85	0.32	9	6	18	75	3.37
Def +++	2015	A+	Lakeland	491	45	129	3	48	263	304	336	640	6	91	0.66	4	1	19	73	3.58

Intelligent INF whose limited tools play up due to instincts. Uses whole field with contact approach and is a tough out. Swings early in count and often makes weak contact, but has some pull power potential. Fringy speed limits SB output, but doesn't impact defense. Very competent defender with textbook hands and footwork.

Betts,Chris | 2 | Tampa Bay | EXP MLB DEBUT: 2019 | H/W: 6-2 215 | FUT: Starting C | 8D

Bats L Age 19	Year	Lev	Team	AB	R	H	HR	RBI	Avg	OB	Slg	OPS	bb%	ct%	Eye	SB	CS	x/h%	Iso	RC/G
2015 (2) HS (CA)																				
Pwr +++																				
BAvg ++																				
Spd +																				
Def ++	2015		*Did not play; injured*																	

Powerful backstop who did not play upon signing after TJ surgery in July. Has vicious, quick stroke that produces easy power to all fields. Has ability to grow into double-plus pop with better and cleaner approach. Can expand strike zone with poor pitch recognition and can get pull happy. Showing improving glovework behind plate with easy plus arm.

Bishop,Braden | 8 | Seattle | EXP MLB DEBUT: 2018 | H/W: 6-1 190 | FUT: Starting OF | 8E

Bats R Age 22	Year	Lev	Team	AB	R	H	HR	RBI	Avg	OB	Slg	OPS	bb%	ct%	Eye	SB	CS	x/h%	Iso	RC/G
2015 (3) Washington																				
Pwr ++																				
BAvg ++																				
Spd ++++	2015	NCAA	Washington	193	38	57	4	25	295	370	440	811	11	81	0.64	15	5	33	145	5.71
Def +++	2015	A-	Everett	219	34	70	2	22	320	335	393	728	2	85	0.15	13	3	16	73	4.15

Lean, strong athlete who had promising pro debut and starting to turn tools into production. Current swing doesn't project to much pop, but could revise to take advantage of strength and bat speed. Makes good contact, but doesn't see many pitches. Will need to shorten swing with 2 strikes. True CF with plus arm and solid range.

Blandino,Alex | 456 | Cincinnati | EXP MLB DEBUT: 2017 | H/W: 6-0 190 | FUT: Starting 2B | 8C

Bats R Age 23	Year	Lev	Team	AB	R	H	HR	RBI	Avg	OB	Slg	OPS	bb%	ct%	Eye	SB	CS	x/h%	Iso	RC/G
2014 (1) Stanford	2014	NCAA	Stanford	226	49	70	12	44	310	391	531	922	12	85	0.91	2	1	37	221	6.92
Pwr ++	2014	Rk	Billings	110	20	34	4	16	309	397	527	924	13	84	0.89	6	3	44	218	7.18
BAvg +++	2014	A	Dayton	134	20	35	4	16	261	327	440	767	9	69	0.31	1	2	43	179	5.26
Spd ++	2015	A+	Daytona	299	46	88	7	35	294	361	438	799	9	81	0.55	7	10	31	144	5.46
Def ++	2015	AA	Pensacola	115	15	27	3	18	235	338	374	712	14	82	0.86	2	2	37	139	4.60

Average tools across the board. Bat plays up despite fringe-average bat speed due to advanced pitch recognition skills and plate discipline. Power is fringe-average at current projection. Arm plays at SS/3B but fringy range limits him to 2B long term. Likely a long-term answer for CIN at 2B.

Blankenhorn,Travis | 5 | Minnesota | EXP MLB DEBUT: 2019 | H/W: 6-1 208 | FUT: Starting 3B | 8E

Bats L Age 19	Year	Lev	Team	AB	R	H	HR	RBI	Avg	OB	Slg	OPS	bb%	ct%	Eye	SB	CS	x/h%	Iso	RC/G
2015 (3) HS (PA)																				
Pwr +++																				
BAvg +++																				
Spd ++	2015	Rk	Elizabethton	144	14	35	3	20	243	297	326	623	7	78	0.34	1	0	17	83	3.03
Def ++	2015	Rk	GCL Twins	49	6	12	0	3	245	339	408	747	13	78	0.64	2	0	50	163	5.25

Tall, athletic INF with sound instincts for game. Moved from SS to 3B as pro and could eventually move to OF. Balanced swing and strong eye allow him to hit for BA while he has above average pop potential thanks to quick stroke and natural strength. Holes in swing result in Ks and needs to read LHP better. Doesn't run well at present.

Bohn,Justin | 6 | Miami | EXP MLB DEBUT: 2017 | H/W: 6-0 180 | FUT: Utility Infielder | 6C

Bats R Age 23	Year	Lev	Team	AB	R	H	HR	RBI	Avg	OB	Slg	OPS	bb%	ct%	Eye	SB	CS	x/h%	Iso	RC/G
2013 (7) FeatherRvr	2013	A	Greensboro	48	5	12	0	2	250	308	271	579	8	75	0.33	4	0	8	21	2.53
Pwr ++	2014	A	Greensboro	239	39	70	6	47	293	392	452	844	14	79	0.80	4	2	34	159	6.32
BAvg +++	2014	A+	Jupiter	199	29	59	0	12	296	349	372	721	7	77	0.36	7	3	20	75	4.48
Spd ++	2015	A+	Jupiter	340	40	89	4	34	262	312	338	651	7	82	0.40	10	1	19	76	3.49
Def ++	2015	AA	Jacksonville	87	5	14	1	6	161	215	218	433	6	66	0.20	0	0	14	57	0.24

7th round pick continues to make steady progress. Pro hitter with a short, compact stroke. Stays behind the ball and shoots line drives to all fields. Approach doesn't project for much power. Average defender spent most of the season at SS, but doesn't have the range or arm to stick. Profiles as a UT infielder with a nice bat.

Bolt,Skye — 789 — Oakland

EXP MLB DEBUT: 2018 | H/W: 6-1 180 | FUT: Starting OF | 8E

Bats B Age 22
2015 (4) North Carolina

- Pwr + + +
- BAvg + +
- Spd + + +
- Def + + +

Year	Lev	Team	AB	R	H	HR	RBI	Avg	OB	Slg	OPS	bb%	ct%	Eye	SB	CS	x/h%	Iso	RC/G
2015	NCAA	North Carolina	205	44	53	10	45	259	380	449	828	16	80	1.00	7	3	36	190	6.06
2015	A-	Vermont	181	26	43	4	19	238	327	381	708	12	76	0.55	2	1	37	144	4.45

Rangy, athletic OF who has tools to be exciting player, but will need significant polish. Can be solid defender with ideal routes and reads off bat. Arm strength good enough for corner OF. Offers some power to pull side, though pitch recognition is a tad short. Has chance to steal bases with above average speed.

Bonifacio,Jorge — 79 — Kansas City

EXP MLB DEBUT: 2016 | H/W: 6-1 195 | FUT: Starting OF | 8D

Bats R Age 22
2009 FA (DR)

- Pwr + + +
- BAvg + +
- Spd + +
- Def + + +

Year	Lev	Team	AB	R	H	HR	RBI	Avg	OB	Slg	OPS	bb%	ct%	Eye	SB	CS	x/h%	Iso	RC/G
2013	Rk	Azl Royals	30	4	9	0	6	300	382	533	916	12	80	0.67	1	0	56	233	7.45
2013	A+	Wilmington	206	32	61	2	29	296	367	408	775	10	81	0.58	0	2	26	112	5.27
2013	AA	NW Arkansas	93	15	28	2	19	301	375	441	816	11	75	0.48	2	1	32	140	5.83
2014	AA	NW Arkansas	505	49	116	4	51	230	299	309	608	9	75	0.39	8	3	24	79	3.01
2015	AA	NW Arkansas	483	60	116	17	64	240	301	416	717	8	74	0.33	3	2	42	176	4.33

Strong OF who repeated AA and posted similar stats with exception of significant increase in HR. Exhibits plus bat speed and repeatable stroke to offer above average pop, pulling ball more and focusing on hard contact. BA potential in question. Plus arm and average range are assets in outfield corner.

Bostick,Chris — 47 — Washington

EXP MLB DEBUT: 2017 | H/W: 5-11 185 | FUT: Backup 2B/OF | 7C

Bats R Age 23
2011 (44) HS (NY)

- Pwr + + +
- BAvg + +
- 4.26 Spd + + +
- Def + +

Year	Lev	Team	AB	R	H	HR	RBI	Avg	OB	Slg	OPS	bb%	ct%	Eye	SB	CS	x/h%	Iso	RC/G
2012	A-	Vermont	279	41	70	3	29	251	317	369	686	9	76	0.41	12	5	33	118	4.09
2013	A	Beloit	489	75	138	14	89	282	350	452	802	9	75	0.42	25	8	34	170	5.57
2014	A+	Myrtle Beach	495	81	124	11	62	251	315	412	728	9	77	0.41	24	11	40	162	4.59
2015	A+	Potomac	234	23	64	4	18	274	328	393	721	8	81	0.43	15	3	27	120	4.41
2015	AA	Harrisburg	296	34	73	8	40	247	276	402	678	4	81	0.21	16	5	34	155	3.66

Sparkplug type that swings hard, and good things happen when he connects. Pull power despite smallish build, but overaggressiveness and impatient approach lead to many Ks. Steals bases more on instinct than straight-line speed. Some rough patches at 2B, and logged some time in OF to increase versatility.

Bousfield,Auston — 78 — San Diego

EXP MLB DEBUT: 2017 | H/W: 5-10 185 | FUT: Fourth OF | 6B

Bats R Age 22
2014 (5) Mississippi

- Pwr + +
- BAvg + + +
- Spd + + + +
- Def + + +

Year	Lev	Team	AB	R	H	HR	RBI	Avg	OB	Slg	OPS	bb%	ct%	Eye	SB	CS	x/h%	Iso	RC/G
2013	NCAA	Mississippi	242	45	61	2	25	252	335	343	678	11	84	0.77	9	4	25	91	4.16
2014	NCAA	Mississippi	286	61	96	6	50	336	379	476	855	7	91	0.74	19	1	27	140	5.95
2014	A-	Eugene	166	36	50	3	13	301	389	512	902	13	78	0.65	12	4	48	211	7.17
2015	A+	Lake Elsinore	400	53	109	3	32	273	353	335	688	11	80	0.63	22	6	16	63	4.20
2015	AA	San Antonio	73	6	18	0	1	247	321	288	609	10	77	0.47	1	0	17	41	3.10

Athletic OF with plus speed and polished defensive skills. Can play all OF spots with excellent range and average, accurate arm. Reads balls off bat and can track down flyballs to gaps. Uses level swing to hit hard line drives, but bat speed a little short for power. Has too much swing and miss for below average pop, but will draw walks.

Boyd,B.J. — 7 — Oakland

EXP MLB DEBUT: 2018 | H/W: 5-10 220 | FUT: Starting OF | 7E

Bats L Age 22
2012 (4) HS (CA)

- Pwr + +
- BAvg + + +
- Spd + + +
- Def + +

Year	Lev	Team	AB	R	H	HR	RBI	Avg	OB	Slg	OPS	bb%	ct%	Eye	SB	CS	x/h%	Iso	RC/G
2012	Rk	Azl Athletics	143	37	43	1	20	301	398	434	831	14	75	0.64	16	4	30	133	6.36
2013	A-	Vermont	260	39	74	8	32	285	369	442	812	12	75	0.53	8	6	31	158	5.80
2014	A	Beloit	464	57	105	6	38	226	299	319	618	9	80	0.51	15	9	25	93	3.21
2015	A+	Stockton	458	67	127	5	52	277	337	389	725	8	81	0.46	18	5	26	111	4.54

Stocky OF who has advanced one level per year and has shown incremental improvement. Turning raw tools into production by using natural strength and speed to advantage. Set high in SB and has tweaked swing to use whole field and make consistent contact. Stuck in LF with crude routes and fringy arm.

Boyd,Jayce — 37 — New York (N)

EXP MLB DEBUT: 2016 | H/W: 6-3 185 | FUT: Reserve OF/1B | 6C

Bats R Age 25
2012 (6) Florida St

- Pwr +
- BAvg + + +
- Spd + +
- Def + + +

Year	Lev	Team	AB	R	H	HR	RBI	Avg	OB	Slg	OPS	bb%	ct%	Eye	SB	CS	x/h%	Iso	RC/G
2013	A	Savannah	249	40	90	5	46	361	440	494	934	12	87	1.09	0	4	24	133	7.26
2013	A+	St. Lucie	209	28	61	4	37	292	370	421	791	11	86	0.90	2	0	30	129	5.51
2014	AA	Binghamton	413	60	121	8	59	293	372	414	786	11	84	0.78	2	1	26	121	5.42
2015	AA	Binghamton	161	18	49	1	16	304	356	422	779	7	90	0.81	2	1	35	118	5.27
2015	AAA	Las Vegas	138	12	35	0	12	254	313	333	647	8	83	0.52	0	2	31	80	3.66

Has hit at every level until promotion to Triple-A in 2015. Has always displayed a high BB and LD rate. Lacks corner OF power. Despite barreling balls, ball comes off bat with top spin, depressing loft. Excellent defensive 1B. Has transitioned to OF to maximize overall profile.

Bradley,Bobby — 3 — Cleveland

EXP MLB DEBUT: 2018 | H/W: 6-1 225 | FUT: Starting 1B | 8D

Bats L Age 19
2014 (3) HS (MS)

- Pwr + + + +
- BAvg + +
- Spd + +
- Def + +

Year	Lev	Team	AB	R	H	HR	RBI	Avg	OB	Slg	OPS	bb%	ct%	Eye	SB	CS	x/h%	Iso	RC/G
2014	Rk	AZL Indians	155	39	56	8	50	361	421	652	1073	9	77	0.44	3	0	45	290	9.04
2015	A	Lake County	401	62	108	27	92	269	359	529	888	12	63	0.38	3	0	43	259	7.30
2015	A+	Lynchburg	8	0	0	0	0	0	111	0	111	11	75	0.50	0	0		0	-3.61

Big and burly 1B who led MWL in HR by 11 despite missing 20 games. Also was 2nd in K. Uppercut stroke could be exploited at higher levels. Knows strike zone and willing to work counts. Needs to improve against LHP and should get better with using all fields. Not a defensive liability, but lacks footwork to be asset. Currently a bat-only prospect.

Bray,Colin — 8 — Arizona

EXP MLB DEBUT: 2018 | H/W: 6-4 197 | FUT: Reserve OF | 6C

Bats B Age 22
2013 (6) FaulknerSt CC

- Pwr +
- BAvg + +
- Spd + + + +
- Def + + +

Year	Lev	Team	AB	R	H	HR	RBI	Avg	OB	Slg	OPS	bb%	ct%	Eye	SB	CS	x/h%	Iso	RC/G
2012	NCAA	South Alabama	50	5	12	0	3	240	309	280	589	9	64	0.28	0	0	17	40	2.78
2013	NCAA	FaulknerStComm	143	44	58	2	24	406	472	531	1004	11	85	0.82	15	1	19	126	8.07
2013	Rk	Missoula	268	43	74	4	29	276	340	373	713	9	77	0.42	15	9	22	97	4.36
2014	A	South Bend	30	3	8	1	5	267	290	467	757	3	60	0.08	2	1	38	200	5.48
2015	A	Kane County	490	78	151	3	52	308	369	410	779	9	78	0.43	27	9	24	102	5.28

Speedy CF put broken foot suffered in 2014 behind him to post an excellent season at the plate. Took up switch-hitting late in collegiate career & has doubles power to the gaps, especially from LH side. Struggles against breaking pitches and elevating balls into the air. 70-grade runner still learning base stealing craft. Can stick in CF.

Bregman,Alex — 6 — Houston

EXP MLB DEBUT: 2017 | H/W: 5-11 180 | FUT: Starting SS | 8B

Bats R Age 22
2015 (1) Louisiana St

- Pwr + +
- BAvg + + + +
- Spd + + +
- Def + + +

Year	Lev	Team	AB	R	H	HR	RBI	Avg	OB	Slg	OPS	bb%	ct%	Eye	SB	CS	x/h%	Iso	RC/G
2015	NCAA	LSU	260	59	84	9	49	323	405	535	940	12	92	1.64	38	10	40	212	7.31
2015	A	Quad Cities	112	18	29	1	13	259	357	330	687	13	88	1.31	5	2	21	71	4.49
2015	A+	Lancaster	160	19	51	3	21	319	366	475	841	7	89	0.71	8	4	29	156	5.87

Consistent INF with impressive bat and glove. Will stick at SS due to quick actions, solid range, and strong, accurate arm. Makes easy contact with compact stroke and has enough bat speed and strength. Knows strike zone and has plus hand-eye coordination. Flat bat path mutes pop, but could grow to average power. Safe bet to be very good MLB player.

Brett,Ryan — 4 — Tampa Bay

EXP MLB DEBUT: 2015 | H/W: 5-9 180 | FUT: Starting 2B | 7B

Bats R Age 24
2010 (3) HS (WA)

- Pwr + +
- BAvg + + +
- Spd + + +
- Def + + +

Year	Lev	Team	AB	R	H	HR	RBI	Avg	OB	Slg	OPS	bb%	ct%	Eye	SB	CS	x/h%	Iso	RC/G
2013	AA	Montgomery	105	19	25	3	16	238	292	400	692	7	87	0.57	4	0	40	162	4.10
2014	AA	Montgomery	422	64	128	8	38	303	341	448	789	5	82	0.32	27	7	30	145	5.12
2015	A+	Charlotte	3	2	2	0	0	667	667	1000	1667	0	100		0	1	50	333	13.79
2015	AAA	Durham	328	48	81	5	30	247	280	354	634	4	80	0.23	4	3	30	107	3.15
2015	MLB	Tampa Bay	3	0	2	0	0	667	750	1000	1750	25	100		0	0	50	333	17.49

Consistent INF with average tools. Missed time with shoulder injury, yet still reached TAM. Uses compact stroke to make consistent contact and has discerning eye at plate. Not reflected in BB/K ratio, but likes to swing early in count. Offers some pop and shoots gaps with line drives. Runs well despite drop in SB and is steady defender at 2B.

Briceno,Jose — 2 — Los Angeles (A)

EXP MLB DEBUT: 2018 | H/W: 6-0 210 | FUT: Starting C | 7E

Bats R Age 23
2009 FA (VZ)

- Pwr + +
- BAvg + +
- Spd + +
- Def + +

Year	Lev	Team	AB	R	H	HR	RBI	Avg	OB	Slg	OPS	bb%	ct%	Eye	SB	CS	x/h%	Iso	RC/G
2012	Rk	Grand Junction	23	5	9	2	5	391	440	652	1092	8	91	1.00	0	0	22	261	8.29
2013	Rk	Grand Junction	153	32	51	9	30	333	354	614	969	3	80	0.17	8	2	49	281	7.07
2013	A	Asheville	91	12	24	1	8	264	302	363	665	5	78	0.25	1	0	29	99	3.58
2014	A	Asheville	315	38	89	12	50	283	317	476	793	5	82	0.28	8	4	40	194	5.06
2015	A+	Carolina	311	32	57	4	20	183	214	267	481	4	83	0.23	2	0	32	84	1.36

Big, strong backstop who fared poorly in first taste of A+. HR output regressed, though still maintains power projection due to bat speed and strong forearms. Lacks semblance of selectivity and rarely draws walks. Owns strong arm, but receiving and blocking need attention.

Brinson,Lewis — 789 — Texas
EXP MLB DEBUT: 2016 | H/W: 6-3 170 | FUT: Starting OF | 9D

Bats R Age 21 — 2012 (1) HS (FL)
Pwr ++++ | BAvg +++ | Spd +++ | Def +++

Year	Lev	Team	AB	R	H	HR	RBI	Avg	OB	Sig	OPS	bb%	ct%	Eye	SB	CS	x/h%	Iso	RC/G
2014	A	Hickory	164	36	55	10	28	335	401	579	980	10	72	0.39	7	4	35	244	7.96
2014	A+	Myrtle Beach	183	17	45	3	22	246	303	350	653	8	73	0.30	5	5	27	104	3.50
2015	A+	High Desert	258	51	87	13	42	337	408	628	1036	11	75	0.48	13	6	48	291	8.76
2015	AA	Frisco	110	14	32	6	23	291	328	545	873	5	75	0.21	2	1	47	255	6.20
2015	AAA	Round Rock	30	9	13	1	4	433	541	567	1107	19	80	1.17	3	0	15	133	9.93

Vastly improving OF who put bat to ball consistently and showed greater feel for bat control. Raw tools are well above average and can be impact player. Can still lunge at breaking balls, but tapping into power while using opposite field. Played mostly CF with plus speed, range, and arm. Still crude with reads and angles, but will get better.

Brito,Socrates — 789 — Arizona
EXP MLB DEBUT: 2015 | H/W: 6-2 200 | FUT: Starting CF | 8C

Bats L Age 23 — 2010 FA (DR)
Pwr +++ | BAvg +++ | Spd ++++ | Def ++++

Year	Lev	Team	AB	R	H	HR	RBI	Avg	OB	Sig	OPS	bb%	ct%	Eye	SB	CS	x/h%	Iso	RC/G
2012	Rk	Missoula	279	47	87	4	39	312	360	444	804	7	74	0.29	15	9	28	133	5.57
2013	A	South Bend	523	61	138	2	49	264	313	356	668	7	76	0.30	27	9	25	92	3.75
2014	A+	Visalia	518	82	152	10	62	293	339	429	768	6	79	0.33	38	10	30	135	4.94
2015	AA	Mobile	490	70	147	9	57	300	339	451	790	6	83	0.35	20	6	28	151	5.17
2015	MLB	Arizona	33	5	10	0	1	303	324	455	778	3	79	0.14	1	0	40	152	5.06

Athletic OF languished in system until '14 breakout in CAL. Proved breakout was real with solid '15, leading to MLB callup in Sept. Slight uppercut in swing produces solid line drives off bat. Added strength has improved power projection. Could hit 15-20 HRs at full development. Range works in CF and arm can stick in RF. Plus run tool.

Brown,Aaron — 8 — Philadelphia
EXP MLB DEBUT: 2017 | H/W: 6-2 220 | FUT: Starting RF | 7D

Bats L Age 23 — 2014 (3) Pepperdine
Pwr +++ | BAvg ++ | Spd ++ (4.37) | Def +++

Year	Lev	Team	AB	R	H	HR	RBI	Avg	OB	Sig	OPS	bb%	ct%	Eye	SB	CS	x/h%	Iso	RC/G
2013	NCAA	Pepperdine	46	10	15	2	3	326	340	500	840	2	74	0.08	2	0	27	174	5.55
2014	NCAA	Pepperdine	242	44	76	13	49	314	339	554	892	4	79	0.17	5	3	38	240	6.19
2014	A-	Williamsport	180	23	46	3	16	256	280	356	635	3	77	0.15	8	4	24	100	3.05
2014	A	Lakewood	55	3	17	1	5	309	321	473	794	2	65	0.05	0	1	41	164	5.62
2015	A+	Clearwater	389	52	100	11	47	257	305	406	711	6	77	0.31	10	8	32	149	4.18

Intense, hard-nosed player with fluid LH swing with average hit and power tools that have yet to materialize. Hit for more power in 2015, but still has a lot of swing-and-miss. Did make big strides in plate patience. Former college pitcher has plus arm strength; has handled CF but likely ends up on a corner. Needs to make a bigger impression at AA.

Brugman,Jaycob — 789 — Oakland
EXP MLB DEBUT: 2017 | H/W: 5-11 195 | FUT: Starting OF | 7D

Bats L Age 24 — 2013 (17) Brigham Young
Pwr ++ | BAvg +++ | Spd +++ | Def +++

Year	Lev	Team	AB	R	H	HR	RBI	Avg	OB	Sig	OPS	bb%	ct%	Eye	SB	CS	x/h%	Iso	RC/G
2013	NCAA	Brigham Young	202	39	64	11	52	317	405	609	1014	13	76	0.63	8	2	50	292	8.50
2013	A-	Vermont	165	13	43	1	23	261	291	382	673	4	71	0.15	7	0	33	121	3.78
2014	A	Beloit	248	33	69	8	37	278	367	484	851	12	74	0.54	5	2	45	206	6.45
2014	A+	Stockton	195	34	55	13	35	282	336	533	870	8	74	0.32	3	3	38	251	6.17
2015	AA	Midland	500	61	130	6	63	260	342	382	724	11	82	0.70	11	7	32	122	4.71

Fundamental OF who saw power decline despite better contact and more patient eye at plate. Hits doubles and uses balanced, compact stroke to smoke line drives to gaps. Set high in SB, though average speed doesn't project well. Knows strike zone and willing to draw walks. LHP eat him up (.213 BA) and will need more bat to profile to ML starter.

Burns,Andy — 456 — Toronto
EXP MLB DEBUT: 2016 | H/W: 6-1 205 | FUT: Starting 2B | 7C

Bats R Age 25 — 2011 (11) Arizona
Pwr +++ | BAvg +++ | Spd +++ | Def ++

Year	Lev	Team	AB	R	H	HR	RBI	Avg	OB	Sig	OPS	bb%	ct%	Eye	SB	CS	x/h%	Iso	RC/G
2013	A+	Dunedin	248	45	81	8	53	327	388	524	912	9	85	0.66	21	9	35	198	6.79
2013	AA	New Hampshire	265	40	67	7	32	253	313	419	731	8	79	0.42	12	5	42	166	4.56
2014	AA	New Hampshire	495	71	126	15	63	255	312	430	742	8	80	0.41	18	8	41	176	4.65
2015	AA	New Hampshire	21	5	5	1	1	238	333	381	714	13	86	1.00	0	0	20	143	4.46
2015	AAA	Buffalo	478	60	140	4	45	293	345	372	717	7	86	0.55	6	9	21	79	4.41

Versatile, athletic prospect who can play all over diamond. Natural hitter with line drive swing and plenty of contact. HR declined in '15, but has strength to hit for average pop. Hits loads of doubles and can use average speed well on base. Has mostly played 3B and 2B in career and may fit best at 2B with decent quickness and hands.

Buxton,Byron — 8 — Minnesota
EXP MLB DEBUT: 2015 | H/W: 6-2 190 | FUT: Starting OF | 9A

Bats R Age 22 — 2012 (1) HS (GA)
Pwr +++ | BAvg ++++ | Spd +++++ | Def ++++

Year	Lev	Team	AB	R	H	HR	RBI	Avg	OB	Sig	OPS	bb%	ct%	Eye	SB	CS	x/h%	Iso	RC/G
2014	A+	Fort Myers	121	19	29	4	16	240	298	405	703	8	73	0.30	6	2	34	165	4.14
2014	AA	New Britain	3	0	0	0	0	0	0	0	0	0	0	0.00	0	0		0	
2015	AA	Chattanooga	237	44	67	6	37	283	354	489	843	10	78	0.51	20	2	37	207	6.16
2015	AAA	Rochester	55	11	22	1	8	400	441	545	986	7	78	0.33	2	1	23	145	7.73
2015	MLB	Minnesota	129	16	27	2	6	209	244	326	570	4	66	0.14	2	2	37	116	2.32

Elite athlete who just needs to stay healthy to realize vast potential. Has game-changing speed on base and in CF where he has plus range and arm. Swings very fast bat to make easy contact and has at least average power potential. Swing path more conducive to line drives, but has strength in wrists and arms to impact game.

Cabbage,Trey — 5 — Minnesota
EXP MLB DEBUT: 2019 | H/W: 6-3 204 | FUT: Starting 3B | 7D

Bats L Age 18 — 2015 (4) HS (TN)
Pwr ++ | BAvg +++ | Spd ++ | Def +++

Year	Lev	Team	AB	R	H	HR	RBI	Avg	OB	Sig	OPS	bb%	ct%	Eye	SB	CS	x/h%	Iso	RC/G
2015	Rk	GCL Twins	119	8	30	0	13	252	294	269	563	6	69	0.19	1	5	7	17	2.16

Strong, athletic INF who has skill set to project well at next level. Brings crude approach to plate and long swing could impact BA potential. Lots of power in lefty stroke and has projection and upside. Can be solid defender with nice arm and textbook footwork. Played mostly 3B, but saw action at SS and LF.

Cabrera,Gustavo — 8 — San Francisco
EXP MLB DEBUT: 2018 | H/W: 6-2 190 | FUT: Starting OF | 8E

Bats R Age 20 — 2012 FA (DR)
Pwr ++ | BAvg + | Spd ++++ | Def ++++

Year	Lev	Team	AB	R	H	HR	RBI	Avg	OB	Sig	OPS	bb%	ct%	Eye	SB	CS	x/h%	Iso	RC/G
2015	Rk	Azl Giants	7	0	2	0	0	286	375	571	946	13	71	0.50	0	0	50	286	8.37

Wrist injury sidelined him for all of '14 and most of '15, but intriguing skills remain. Has premium athleticism and top-end speed, projecting him as a future SB asset and plus CF glove. Bat is raw, but has strong wrists and good bat speed that should allow for solid-avg power as he hones his swing and approach. Chance to impact several categories.

Calhoun,Willie — 4 — Los Angeles (N)
EXP MLB DEBUT: 2018 | H/W: 5-9 187 | FUT: Starting 2B | 7D

Bats L Age 21 — 2015 (4) Yavapai JC
Pwr +++ | BAvg ++ | Spd ++ | Def ++

Year	Lev	Team	AB	R	H	HR	RBI	Avg	OB	Sig	OPS	bb%	ct%	Eye	SB	CS	x/h%	Iso	RC/G
2015	Rk	Ogden	151	28	42	7	26	278	374	517	890	13	88	1.28	2	1	50	238	6.74
2015	A	Great Lakes	61	9	24	1	8	393	439	492	931	8	89	0.71	0	0	17	98	6.83
2015	A+	RanchoCuca	73	11	24	3	14	329	388	548	935	9	82	0.54	0	0	42	219	7.04

4th round JuCo pick where he hit 31 HR in 61 games. Impressed at three levels and for the year hit .316/.390/.519. Played 3B in college, but is better suited at 2B where he has avg range, but will need to work hard to stick on the dirt. Speed is not part of his game, but he barrels the ball consistently with good strike zone judgment.

Calixte,Orlando — 456 — Kansas City
EXP MLB DEBUT: 2015 | H/W: 5-11 160 | FUT: Starting SS | 7D

Bats R Age 24 — 2010 FA (DR)
Pwr ++ | BAvg ++ | Spd +++ | Def +++

Year	Lev	Team	AB	R	H	HR	RBI	Avg	OB	Sig	OPS	bb%	ct%	Eye	SB	CS	x/h%	Iso	RC/G
2012	A+	Wilmington	256	38	72	4	28	281	321	426	747	6	75	0.23	8	3	35	145	4.73
2013	AA	NW Arkansas	484	59	121	8	36	250	310	368	678	8	73	0.32	14	11	31	118	3.89
2014	AA	NW Arkansas	374	43	90	11	37	241	292	374	666	7	75	0.29	9	5	30	134	3.56
2015	AAA	Omaha	354	38	81	8	27	229	283	339	622	7	76	0.32	22	3	26	110	3.04
2015	MLB	KC Royals	3	1	0	0	0	0	0	0	0	0	100		0	0		0	-2.66

Short, lean INF who is smooth defender with quick hands and average range. Arm strength works at any infield spot. Shows surprising pop in quick righty stroke, but lacks approach at plate and strikes out in bunches. Long swing gets exploited by good pitching and can be pull happy. Has versatility and played all over diamond in '15.

Camargo,Johan — 6 — Atlanta
EXP MLB DEBUT: 2017 | H/W: 6-0 160 | FUT: Reserve SS | 6D

Bats B Age 22 — 2010 FA (PN)
Pwr + | BAvg ++ | Spd +++ | Def +++

Year	Lev	Team	AB	R	H	HR	RBI	Avg	OB	Sig	OPS	bb%	ct%	Eye	SB	CS	x/h%	Iso	RC/G
2013	Rk	Danville	228	28	67	0	14	294	346	360	705	7	86	0.58	3	3	16	66	4.33
2014	A	Rome	420	53	112	0	40	267	322	324	645	7	88	0.68	7	6	18	57	3.70
2014	A+	Lynchburg	58	7	15	1	6	259	271	345	616	2	78	0.08	0	0	20	86	2.69
2015	A+	Carolina	391	50	101	1	32	258	311	335	646	7	86	0.56	4	2	22	77	3.64

Switch-hitter struggled to separate himself from the pack in a relatively weak High-A lineup. Has good contact skills and feel for the strike zone but lacks consistent hard contact. Does not get out of the box well. Questions about headiness have been questioned in past. Fields position well with a strong arm. Should stick at the position.

Cameron,Daz | 78 | Houston | EXP MLB DEBUT: 2019 | H/W: 6-2 185 | FUT: Starting OF | 8C

Bats R Age 19	Year	Lev	Team	AB	R	H	HR	RBI	Avg	OB	Slg	OPS	bb%	ct%	Eye	SB	CS	x/h%	Iso	RC/G
2015 (1) HS (GA)																				
Pwr ++																				
BAvg ++																				
Spd +++	2015	Rk	Greeneville	103	20	28	0	11	272	370	350	719	13	70	0.52	11	6	18	78	4.85
Def ++++	2015	Rk	GCL Astros	70	13	15	0	6	214	304	243	547	11	76	0.53	12	4	13	29	2.31

Smooth, athletic OF with tools that can impact game with bat and glove. Ranges well in CF with plus instincts and has speed to track down balls to gaps. Uses exceptional bat speed to drive balls to all fields and should develop average pop at maturity. Needs to be more selective to hit for BA. Thrown out stealing a lot in pro debut.

Candelario,Jeimer | 5 | Chicago (N) | EXP MLB DEBUT: 2017 | H/W: 6-1 210 | FUT: Starting 3B | 7D

Bats B Age 22	Year	Lev	Team	AB	R	H	HR	RBI	Avg	OB	Slg	OPS	bb%	ct%	Eye	SB	CS	x/h%	Iso	RC/G
2010 FA (DR)	2013	A	Kane County	500	71	128	11	57	256	345	396	741	12	82	0.77	1	0	37	140	4.92
Pwr ++	2014	A	Kane County	244	32	61	6	37	250	302	426	728	7	82	0.40	0	1	46	176	4.49
BAvg ++	2014	A+	Daytona	218	24	42	5	26	193	270	326	595	10	80	0.52	0	3	40	133	2.92
Spd ++	2015	A+	Myrtle Beach	318	42	86	5	39	270	314	415	729	6	81	0.32	0	1	38	145	4.47
Def ++++	2015	AA	Tennessee	158	21	46	5	25	291	378	462	840	12	87	1.05	0	0	35	171	6.11

Switch-hitter has plus power, an easy contact-oriented swing, and a good understanding of the strike zone. Plus defender at 3B with good hands and a strong arm, but limited speed. Gap power limits his short-term upside.

Canelo,Malquin | 6 | Philadelphia | EXP MLB DEBUT: 2018 | H/W: 5-10 156 | FUT: Starting SS | 8D

Bats R Age 21	Year	Lev	Team	AB	R	H	HR	RBI	Avg	OB	Slg	OPS	bb%	ct%	Eye	SB	CS	x/h%	Iso	RC/G
2012 FA (DR)	2014	A-	Williamsport	13	1	2	0	1	154	214	154	368	7	69	0.25	0	0	0	0	-0.58
Pwr ++	2014	A	Lakewood	152	19	41	1	18	270	319	355	674	7	80	0.35	4	1	24	86	3.81
BAvg +++	2014	A+	Clearwater	48	2	10	0	3	208	255	271	526	6	75	0.25	1	1	30	63	1.84
Spd +++	2015	A	Lakewood	264	48	82	5	23	311	361	466	827	7	85	0.54	10	2	35	155	5.72
Def ++++	2015	A+	Clearwater	248	24	62	3	24	250	295	323	618	6	79	0.30	7	6	18	73	2.99

Previously a glove-only MIF, he added strength in the offseason that resulted in increased bat speed. With loose hands and level swing, he projects to an average hitter with doubles power. Could still improve pitch recognition. Smooth on defense, with great range and a plus arm. Some speed, but not an efficient base stealer. Pleasant surprise.

Caratini,Victor | 2 | Chicago (N) | EXP MLB DEBUT: 2017 | H/W: 6-1 215 | FUT: Starting C | 8D

Bats B Age 22	Year	Lev	Team	AB	R	H	HR	RBI	Avg	OB	Slg	OPS	bb%	ct%	Eye	SB	CS	x/h%	Iso	RC/G
2013 (2) Miami-Dade	2013	NCAA	Miami-Dade	175	44	66	6	66	377	463	549	1012	14	85	1.08	10	1	27	171	8.24
Pwr ++	2013	Rk	Danville	200	29	58	1	25	290	406	430	836	16	76	0.80	0	2	43	140	6.57
BAvg +++	2014	A	Kane County	53	7	14	0	13	264	316	377	693	7	81	0.40	0	0	36	113	4.19
Spd +	2014	A	Rome	323	42	90	5	42	279	347	406	753	10	82	0.58	1	1	30	127	4.95
Def +++	2015	A+	Myrtle Beach	393	39	101	4	53	257	339	372	711	11	81	0.65	0	0	36	115	4.55

Uses a line-drive swing to shoot balls into the gaps and has good patience. Could develop more power as he matures, but his swing can get long. Compensates with above-avg bat speed and makes solid contact. Still developing behind the plate, but shows good instincts and a strong, accurate arm.

Carpio,Luis | 6 | New York (N) | EXP MLB DEBUT: 2019 | H/W: 6-0 165 | FUT: Starting SS | 9E

Bats R Age 18	Year	Lev	Team	AB	R	H	HR	RBI	Avg	OB	Slg	OPS	bb%	ct%	Eye	SB	CS	x/h%	Iso	RC/G
2013 FA (VZ)																				
Pwr ++																				
BAvg +++																				
Spd ++++																				
Def ++++	2015	Rk	Kingsport	181	31	55	0	22	304	364	359	723	9	81	0.50	9	7	18	55	4.54

Advanced hitter with line drive approach. Finds gaps. Power tool lags behind other tools. Frame has room for 15-20 llbs of muscle, adding to his power projection. A plus runner and defender. Softest hands in APPY. Will easily stick at SS with strong throwing arm.

Cave,Jake | 78 | Cincinnati | EXP MLB DEBUT: 2016 | H/W: 6-0 200 | FUT: Fourth OF | 6B

Bats L Age 23	Year	Lev	Team	AB	R	H	HR	RBI	Avg	OB	Slg	OPS	bb%	ct%	Eye	SB	CS	x/h%	Iso	RC/G
2011 (6) HS (VA)	2013	A	Charleston (Sc)	464	69	131	2	31	282	339	401	740	8	76	0.36	18	9	34	119	4.80
Pwr ++	2014	A+	Tampa	385	50	117	3	24	304	351	395	746	7	79	0.35	10	3	21	91	4.70
BAvg +++	2014	AA	Trenton	176	24	48	4	18	273	340	455	795	9	75	0.41	2	3	40	182	5.55
Spd +++	2015	AA	Trenton	505	68	136	2	37	269	327	345	671	8	81	0.44	17	3	21	75	3.86
Def +++	2015	AAA	Scranton/WB	24	4	11	0	2	458	519	667	1185	11	67	0.38	0	0	36	208	12.13

Aggressive OF who doesn't bring much bat to table, but has value in speed and defense. Doesn't project power due to choppy swing and lack of loft, but can hit for BA. Needs to fine-tune approach against breaking balls and keep ball on ground. Not a burner, but runs well underway. Possesses average range and arm. Selected from NYY in Rule 5.

Cecchini,Garin | 357 | Milwaukee | EXP MLB DEBUT: 2014 | H/W: 6-3 220 | FUT: Starting 3B | 7C

Bats L Age 24	Year	Lev	Team	AB	R	H	HR	RBI	Avg	OB	Slg	OPS	bb%	ct%	Eye	SB	CS	x/h%	Iso	RC/G
2010 (4) HS (LA)	2013	AA	Portland	240	36	71	2	28	296	419	404	823	18	78	0.98	8	2	27	108	6.35
Pwr ++	2014	AAA	Pawtucket	407	52	107	7	57	263	335	371	706	10	76	0.44	11	1	27	108	4.31
BAvg +++	2014	MLB	Boston	31	6	8	1	4	258	324	452	775	9	65	0.27	0	0	50	194	5.59
Spd +++	2015	AAA	Pawtucket	422	34	90	7	28	213	281	296	578	9	76	0.40	9	0	23	83	2.54
Def ++	2015	MLB	Boston	4	0	0	0	0	0	0	0	0	0	25	0.00	0	0		0	-10.45

Regressing prospect with two poor seasons in a row. Learning to play new positions for versatility, but bat will be ticket. Has patient approach, but lacks consistent pop and struggles with LHP. Uses entire field when at top of his game, but has been pull conscious. Lacks range and quickness with erratic arm. Best at 3B, but not a standout.

Cecchini,Gavin | 6 | New York (N) | EXP MLB DEBUT: 2016 | H/W: 6-2 200 | FUT: Starting SS | 8C

Bats R Age 22	Year	Lev	Team	AB	R	H	HR	RBI	Avg	OB	Slg	OPS	bb%	ct%	Eye	SB	CS	x/h%	Iso	RC/G
2012 (1) HS (LA)	2013	A-	Brooklyn	194	18	53	0	14	273	322	314	637	7	85	0.47	2	3	15	41	3.42
Pwr ++	2014	A	Savannah	228	42	59	3	25	259	332	408	740	10	82	0.61	7	1	41	149	4.87
BAvg +++	2014	A+	St. Lucie	233	36	55	5	31	236	328	352	680	12	83	0.80	3	3	29	116	4.15
Spd +++	2014	AA	Binghamton	4	1	1	0	0	250	250	250	500	0	75	0.00	0	0	0	0	1.07
Def +++	2015	AA	Binghamton	439	64	139	7	51	317	376	442	818	9	87	0.76	3	4	27	125	5.70

Fmr 1st rd pick had a breakout 2015. Average tools across the board. Short, compact swing and advanced approach could help exceed hit tool projections. Sprays the ball to all fields. Power maxes out with single digit HR potential despite getting most out of slight frame.

Chang,Yu-Cheng | 6 | Cleveland | EXP MLB DEBUT: 2018 | H/W: 6-1 175 | FUT: Starting 3B | 7D

Bats R Age 20	Year	Lev	Team	AB	R	H	HR	RBI	Avg	OB	Slg	OPS	bb%	ct%	Eye	SB	CS	x/h%	Iso	RC/G
2013 FA (TW)																				
Pwr ++																				
BAvg ++																				
Spd +++	2014	Rk	AZL Indians	159	39	55	6	25	346	412	566	978	10	82	0.64	6	1	35	220	7.68
Def +++	2015	A	Lake County	393	52	91	9	52	232	281	361	642	6	74	0.26	5	6	32	130	3.29

Lean, rangy INF who was inconsistent in first full season. Needs to add strength, but has bat speed to hit for potential average power. Has feel for barrel and puts ball in play with line drive swing. Can be free swinger and get himself into pitchers counts. Solid defender with strong arm and enough range and instincts to stick at SS long-term.

Chapman,Matt | 5 | Oakland | EXP MLB DEBUT: 2016 | H/W: 6-1 205 | FUT: Starting 3B | 8C

Bats R Age 22	Year	Lev	Team	AB	R	H	HR	RBI	Avg	OB	Slg	OPS	bb%	ct%	Eye	SB	CS	x/h%	Iso	RC/G
2014 (1) Cal St Fullerton	2014	NCAA	Cal St Fullerton	205	37	64	6	48	312	392	498	890	12	87	1.04	6	2	38	185	6.70
Pwr ++++	2014	Rk	Azl Athletics	14	1	6	0	0	429	467	643	1110	7	93	1.00	0	0	33	214	8.97
BAvg ++	2014	A	Beloit	190	22	45	5	20	237	264	389	653	4	76	0.15	2	1	36	153	3.31
Spd ++	2014	AA	Midland	3	0	0	0	0	0	0	0	0	0	100		0	0		0	-2.66
Def ++++	2015	A+	Stockton	304	60	76	23	57	250	335	566	901	11	74	0.49	4	1	62	316	6.82

Tall, strong INF who missed time with nagging injuries, but saw power emerge for impressive all-around game. Added loft to quick stroke to realize natural pop and continues to make consistent contact. Pitch recognition needs work. Isn't much of a SB threat as his foot speed is below average, but has quick actions at 3B with double plus arm.

Chavis,Michael | 5 | Boston | EXP MLB DEBUT: 2018 | H/W: 5-10 190 | FUT: Starting 3B | 7C

Bats R Age 20	Year	Lev	Team	AB	R	H	HR	RBI	Avg	OB	Slg	OPS	bb%	ct%	Eye	SB	CS	x/h%	Iso	RC/G
2014 (1) HS (GA)																				
Pwr ++++																				
BAvg ++																				
Spd ++	2014	Rk	GCL Red Sox	134	21	36	1	16	269	342	425	768	10	72	0.39	5	3	44	157	5.42
Def ++	2015	A	Greenville	435	56	97	16	58	223	272	405	676	6	67	0.20	8	5	47	182	3.83

Powerful hitter with explosive bat speed and natural strength. Can hit balls out to any part of park, though will need to make more contact to realize potential. Doesn't work counts and lacks feel for spin. Lacks BA potential, but power in play. Fits bill at 3B, though has limited range and inaccurate arm.

Ciuffo,Nick | 2 | Tampa Bay | EXP MLB DEBUT: 2018 | H/W: 6-1 205 | FUT: Starting C | 8E

Bats L Age 21
2013 (1) HS (SC)
Pwr ++
BAvg ++
Spd ++
Def +++

Year	Lev	Team	AB	R	H	HR	RBI	Avg	OB	Slg	OPS	bb%	ct%	Eye	SB	CS	x/h%	Iso	RC/G
2013	Rk	GCL Devil Rays	159	11	41	0	25	258	298	308	606	5	75	0.23	0	0	17	50	2.83
2014	Rk	Princeton	192	25	43	4	20	224	287	333	620	8	77	0.38	2	1	28	109	3.08
2015	A	Bowling Green	356	30	92	1	32	258	273	326	599	2	85	0.13	2	3	24	67	2.71

Athletic backstop who got hot at end of season in first full year in minors. Hits lots of doubles with line drive stroke, yet has enough leverage to project to at least average pop. Needs better approach against LHP and struggles to read spin. Can be too aggressive, though makes good contact. Has plus arm strength with quick release.

Clark,Trent | 8 | Milwaukee | EXP MLB DEBUT: 2019 | H/W: 6-0 205 | FUT: Starting OF | 8E

Bats L Age 19
2015 (1) HS (TX)
Pwr ++
BAvg ++++
Spd +++
Def +++

Year	Lev	Team	AB	R	H	HR	RBI	Avg	OB	Slg	OPS	bb%	ct%	Eye	SB	CS	x/h%	Iso	RC/G
2015	Rk	Helena	42	5	13	1	5	310	431	381	812	18	81	1.13	5	3	8	71	6.01
2015	Rk	Azl Brewers	165	34	51	1	16	309	415	442	858	15	78	0.83	20	5	27	133	6.74

Former dual-sport star excelled in debut. Swing is unorthodox, but bat speed, level barrel path to all fields project BA as easy plus tool. Sturdy build should allow for so-so power. Instincts, above-average speed add to his SB upside and help his range in CF, where he profiles best. If advanced approach stays intact, he'll move quickly.

Coats,Jason | 7 | Chicago (A) | EXP MLB DEBUT: 2016 | H/W: 6-2 200 | FUT: Fourth OF | 6B

Bats R Age 26
2012 (29) Texas Christian
Pwr ++
BAvg +++
Spd ++
Def ++

Year	Lev	Team	AB	R	H	HR	RBI	Avg	OB	Slg	OPS	bb%	ct%	Eye	SB	CS	x/h%	Iso	RC/G
2013	A	Kannapolis	516	63	140	12	84	271	313	426	739	6	84	0.36	12	3	38	155	4.54
2014	A+	Winston-Salem	429	64	125	15	72	291	345	487	832	8	85	0.54	5	2	42	196	5.72
2014	AA	Birmingham	68	5	18	0	9	265	296	338	634	4	87	0.33	1	1	22	74	3.35
2015	AA	Birmingham	47	6	16	0	2	340	354	532	886	2	87	0.17	0	2	56	191	6.23
2015	AAA	Charlotte	489	56	132	17	81	270	311	438	748	6	81	0.31	11	2	36	168	4.55

Emerging prospect who set career high in HR and has hit exactly 38 doubles in each of last three seasons. Hits LHP well with consistent approach, though doesn't recognize pitches and has limited bat speed. Can be free swinger at times. Played all OF spots in '15, but lacks speed and arm strength. Profiles as extra OF.

Cole,Hunter | 479 | San Francisco | EXP MLB DEBUT: 2017 | H/W: 6-1 190 | FUT: Starting LF | 7C

Bats R Age 23
2014 (26) Georgia
Pwr ++
BAvg +++
Spd ++
Def +++

Year	Lev	Team	AB	R	H	HR	RBI	Avg	OB	Slg	OPS	bb%	ct%	Eye	SB	CS	x/h%	Iso	RC/G
2014	Rk	Azl Giants	9	2	4	0	1	444	444	556	1000	0	89	0.00	1	0	25	111	7.10
2014	A-	Salem-Kaizer	92	17	22	4	10	239	300	424	724	8	78	0.40	1	0	41	185	4.33
2015	A	Augusta	40	4	11	0	5	275	356	425	781	11	70	0.42	2	1	55	150	5.77
2015	A+	San Jose	217	28	68	6	37	313	369	493	862	8	81	0.45	4	3	32	180	6.18
2015	AA	Richmond	192	23	56	3	21	292	340	464	803	7	76	0.30	1	1	41	172	5.56

Former 26th-rounder lacks standout tool, but is well-rounded and could have future avg value. Has decent bat speed and line-drive pop to all fields; added muscle projects 15 HR upside. Swing is long, though, which will limit ct% at next level against quality secondaries. Solid glove/arm, but fringy range likely puts him in LF, limiting his impact.

Contreras,Willson | 2 | Chicago (N) | EXP MLB DEBUT: 2017 | H/W: 6-1 175 | FUT: Starting C | 7B

Bats R Age 23
2009 FA (VZ)
Pwr +++
BAvg +++
Spd ++
Def ++

Year	Lev	Team	AB	R	H	HR	RBI	Avg	OB	Slg	OPS	bb%	ct%	Eye	SB	CS	x/h%	Iso	RC/G
2011	A-	Boise	222	31	58	2	27	261	296	347	643	5	82	0.27	3	2	19	86	3.32
2012	A-	Boise	249	32	68	3	39	273	304	357	661	4	78	0.20	3	2	21	84	3.44
2013	A	Kane County	310	46	77	11	46	248	307	423	729	8	79	0.39	8	3	35	174	4.44
2014	A+	Daytona	281	40	68	5	37	242	311	359	670	9	77	0.42	5	5	31	117	3.82
2015	AA	Tennessee	454	71	151	8	75	333	407	478	885	11	86	0.92	4	4	30	145	6.65

Looks to be a late bloomer; hit below .250 the past two seasons and then won the SL batting title. Improved contact, but was also more selective, posting a career best Eye. Solid bat speed and the ability to barrel the ball. Moves well with a strong arm and has a chance to stick behind the dish.

Cooper,Garrett | 3 | Milwaukee | EXP MLB DEBUT: 2017 | H/W: 6-6 230 | FUT: Backup 1B | 7D

Bats R Age 25
2013 (6) Auburn
Pwr +++
BAvg ++
Spd +
Def +++

Year	Lev	Team	AB	R	H	HR	RBI	Avg	OB	Slg	OPS	bb%	ct%	Eye	SB	CS	x/h%	Iso	RC/G
2014	Rk	Azl Brewers	16	3	6	1	3	375	474	625	1099	16	81	1.00	0	0	33	250	9.41
2014	A	Wisconsin	30	2	10	1	8	333	333	533	867	0	87	0.00	0	0	40	200	5.59
2014	A+	Brevard County	164	23	39	2	16	238	313	341	655	10	69	0.35	1	0	33	104	3.71
2015	A+	Brevard County	422	55	124	8	54	294	348	436	784	8	79	0.40	1	1	34	142	5.22
2015	AA	Biloxi	29	3	16	0	5	552	639	690	1329	19	93	3.50	0	0	19	138	12.44

Tall, physically mature 1B enjoyed bounce-back year in FSL after injury-marred '14. Raw power is plus with tons of loft to all fields. Long swing still a concern for his contact skills, which could limit his ability to hit for enough average against advanced pitching. Solid defensive chops and a strong arm will allow him to stick at 1B long term.

Cordell,Ryan | 58 | Texas | EXP MLB DEBUT: 2016 | H/W: 6-3 205 | FUT: Starting OF | 7B

Bats R Age 24
2013 (11) Liberty
Pwr +++
BAvg +++
Spd +++
Def ++

Year	Lev	Team	AB	R	H	HR	RBI	Avg	OB	Slg	OPS	bb%	ct%	Eye	SB	CS	x/h%	Iso	RC/G
2013	A-	Spokane	232	34	56	5	23	241	310	358	668	9	77	0.43	19	4	30	116	3.75
2014	A	Hickory	274	53	88	8	40	321	382	504	886	9	81	0.51	18	3	34	182	6.52
2014	A+	Myrtle Beach	62	12	19	5	19	306	377	645	1022	10	79	0.54	3	1	47	339	8.13
2015	A+	High Desert	286	58	89	13	57	311	373	528	901	9	81	0.53	10	5	35	217	6.59
2015	AA	Frisco	221	26	48	5	18	217	258	335	592	5	67	0.16	10	1	27	118	2.57

Thin, tall prospect who can play all over diamond. Profiles in CF due to plus speed, range, and average arm. Shows plenty of athleticism with quick actions and could play 2B or 3B. Uses smooth swing to hit for BA, and he understands strike zone. Can lengthen swing at times and will fan. Set career-high in HR and could become 20/20 player at peak.

Cordero,Franchy | 67 | San Diego | EXP MLB DEBUT: 2018 | H/W: 6-3 175 | FUT: Starting OF | 8E

Bats L Age 21
2011 FA (DR)
Pwr ++
BAvg ++
Spd +++
Def ++

Year	Lev	Team	AB	R	H	HR	RBI	Avg	OB	Slg	OPS	bb%	ct%	Eye	SB	CS	x/h%	Iso	RC/G
2013	Rk	Azl Padres	141	23	47	3	17	333	377	511	888	7	77	0.30	11	0	28	177	6.58
2014	A-	Eugene	240	40	67	9	35	279	319	458	777	6	69	0.19	13	5	31	179	5.17
2014	A	Fort Wayne	85	5	16	0	9	188	225	235	460	4	58	0.11	3	3	19	47	0.74
2015	A	Fort Wayne	481	59	117	5	34	243	289	306	595	6	75	0.26	22	11	16	62	2.64

Tall, rangy prospect who hasn't lived up to lofty billing. Spent most of season in LF after signing as SS. Still shows impressive, raw power, but rarely taps into it due to long swing and aggressive approach. Strikes out far too often and struggles with LHP. Runs well for SB, but careless errors led him to OF.

Coulter,Clint | 9 | Milwaukee | EXP MLB DEBUT: 2017 | H/W: 6-3 222 | FUT: Starting OF | 8D

Bats R Age 22
2012 (1) HS (WA)
Pwr +++
BAvg +++
Spd ++
Def +++

Year	Lev	Team	AB	R	H	HR	RBI	Avg	OB	Slg	OPS	bb%	ct%	Eye	SB	CS	x/h%	Iso	RC/G
2013	Rk	Azl Brewers	60	12	21	3	15	350	400	617	1017	8	75	0.33	1	1	43	267	8.28
2013	Rk	Helena	74	8	16	1	8	216	256	311	567	5	81	0.29	1	0	31	95	2.40
2013	A	Wisconsin	116	18	24	3	13	207	276	345	620	9	73	0.35	1	0	38	138	3.08
2014	A	Wisconsin	429	84	123	22	89	287	390	520	910	15	76	0.71	6	6	43	233	7.14
2015	A+	Brevard County	499	63	123	13	59	246	310	397	707	8	82	0.50	6	6	37	150	4.27

Switched from C to OF and held his own in pitcher-friendly FSL. Discipline, barrel control continue to improve and raw power remains an intriguing tool. Profiles best in RF with plus arm but questionable range. Could need more time in FSL to adjust to OF, but the bat appears just about ready for the next step.

Cousino,Austin | 8 | Seattle | EXP MLB DEBUT: 2018 | H/W: 5-10 178 | FUT: Starting OF | 7D

Bats L Age 22
2014 (3) Kentucky
Pwr +
BAvg ++
Spd +++
Def ++++

Year	Lev	Team	AB	R	H	HR	RBI	Avg	OB	Slg	OPS	bb%	ct%	Eye	SB	CS	x/h%	Iso	RC/G
2013	NCAA	Kentucky	209	42	52	6	27	249	329	402	731	11	78	0.54	14	1	37	153	4.65
2014	NCAA	Kentucky	263	58	81	4	38	308	341	441	782	5	85	0.33	19	1	28	133	5.01
2014	A-	Everett	271	40	72	6	28	266	334	402	737	9	80	0.52	23	4	33	137	4.69
2015	Rk	Azl Mariners	21	6	9	0	4	429	500	524	1024	13	71	0.50	2	1	11	95	9.13
2015	A	Clinton	232	23	44	0	12	190	251	254	505	8	80	0.41	9	4	30	65	1.81

Aggressive OF who has tangible skills, but needs polish. Missed time with shoulder injury and wasn't effective when healthy. Failed to hit HR, though has loose swing with some pop to pull side. Goes mostly gap to gap and uses speed to leg out infield hits and xbh. Solid runner and CF with keen routes and reads. Tools play up due to all-out style.

Cowart,Kaleb | 5 | Los Angeles (A) | EXP MLB DEBUT: 2015 | H/W: 6-3 225 | FUT: Starting 3B | 7B

Bats B Age 23
2010 (1) HS (GA)
Pwr +++
BAvg ++
Spd ++
Def +++

Year	Lev	Team	AB	R	H	HR	RBI	Avg	OB	Slg	OPS	bb%	ct%	Eye	SB	CS	x/h%	Iso	RC/G
2013	AA	Arkansas	498	48	110	6	42	221	276	301	577	7	75	0.31	14	5	25	80	2.48
2014	AA	Arkansas	435	48	97	6	54	223	293	324	617	9	77	0.43	26	7	29	101	3.14
2015	A+	Inland Empire	194	32	47	2	23	242	319	387	706	10	78	0.51	10	2	43	144	4.47
2015	AAA	Salt Lake	220	35	71	6	45	323	402	491	893	12	71	0.45	2	1	31	168	7.09
2015	MLB	LA Angels	46	8	8	1	4	174	255	283	538	10	59	0.26	1	1	38	109	1.96

Athletic, strong INF who began in A+ and finished in LAA. Revised swing mechanics and improved approach to make more contact and tap into raw power. Will still swing and miss and make weak contact at times, but flashing power that made him top prospect previously. Runs well for size and will steal bases. Possesses good glove with cannon arm.

Coyle,Sean — 45 — Boston

EXP MLB DEBUT: 2016 | H/W: 5-8 175 | FUT: Starting 2B | **7C**

Bats R Age 24 — 2010 (3) HS (PA)

Skills	Year	Lev	Team	AB	R	H	HR	RBI	Avg	OB	Slg	OPS	bb%	ct%	Eye	SB	CS	x/h%	Iso	RC/G
Pwr +++	2013	A+	Salem	195	41	47	14	28	241	324	513	837	11	67	0.37	11	0	51	272	6.19
BAvg ++	2014	AA	Portland	336	60	99	16	61	295	366	512	878	10	72	0.40	13	1	40	217	6.65
Spd +++	2015	Rk	GCL Red Sox	38	10	11	1	8	289	341	474	815	7	50	0.16	0	0	45	184	8.02
Def +++	2015	A-	Lowell	12	2	3	0	1	250	308	333	641	8	75	0.33	1	0	33	83	3.48
	2015	AAA	Pawtucket	126	21	20	5	16	159	274	302	576	14	65	0.45	4	1	40	143	2.41

Short, compact INF who has been injury prone, including elbow injury in '15. Drives ball to all fields with plus bat speed. Can reach seats, mostly to pull side. Not a standout, though does everything relatively well. Swings and misses frequently and could limit BA potential. Handles 2B adequately with average speed quickness and arm.

Cozens,Dylan — 9 — Philadelphia

EXP MLB DEBUT: 2018 | H/W: 6-6 235 | FUT: Starting RF | **8D**

Bats L Age 21 — 2012 (2) HS (AZ)

Skills	Year	Lev	Team	AB	R	H	HR	RBI	Avg	OB	Slg	OPS	bb%	ct%	Eye	SB	CS	x/h%	Iso	RC/G
	2013	A-	Williamsport	245	50	65	9	35	265	341	469	810	10	74	0.44	11	6	46	204	5.73
Pwr ++++	2014	A	Lakewood	509	69	126	16	62	248	302	415	717	7	71	0.27	23	7	37	167	4.37
BAvg ++	2015	Rk	GCL Phillies	15	1	3	0	4	200	200	267	467	0	73	0.00	0	0	33	67	0.78
Spd +++	2015	A+	Clearwater	365	52	103	5	46	282	330	411	741	7	78	0.33	18	5	31	129	4.65
Def ++	2015	AA	Reading	40	6	14	3	9	350	395	625	1020	7	83	0.43	2	1	36	275	7.71

With the strength one would expect from this frame, he hits the ball hard when he connects. His movements are stiff rather than fluid, but made better contact at expense of pop. Pitch selection an issue; breaking balls give him fits. Has some speed, but unlikely to hold it as body matures. Upside due to power projection.

Crawford,J.P. — 6 — Philadelphia

EXP MLB DEBUT: 2016 | H/W: 6-2 180 | FUT: Starting SS | **9B**

Bats L Age 21 — 2013 (1) HS (CA)

Skills	Year	Lev	Team	AB	R	H	HR	RBI	Avg	OB	Slg	OPS	bb%	ct%	Eye	SB	CS	x/h%	Iso	RC/G
	2013	A	Lakewood	53	10	11	0	2	208	300	226	526	12	81	0.70	2	1	9	19	2.23
Pwr ++	2014	A	Lakewood	227	37	67	3	19	295	394	405	799	14	84	1.00	14	7	28	110	5.80
BAvg ++++	2014	A+	Clearwater	236	32	65	8	29	275	352	407	759	11	84	0.76	10	7	23	131	4.95
4.25 Spd +++	2015	A+	Clearwater	79	15	31	1	8	392	484	443	927	15	89	1.56	5	2	6	51	7.33
Def ++++	2015	AA	Reading	351	53	93	5	34	265	355	407	762	12	87	1.09	7	2	35	142	5.33

One of baseball's top prospects; features the instincts and field awareness, along with range, arm and hands necessary for a top SS. Advanced hit tool starts with pitch recognition and knowledge of the strike zone; works deep counts and rarely chases. Plus bat speed, smooth left-handed swing hits gaps now, but should mature into moderate power.

Cruz,Johan — 56 — Chicago (A)

EXP MLB DEBUT: 2019 | H/W: 6-2 170 | FUT: Starting 3B | **8E**

Bats R Age 20 — 2012 FA (DR)

Skills	Year	Lev	Team	AB	R	H	HR	RBI	Avg	OB	Slg	OPS	bb%	ct%	Eye	SB	CS	x/h%	Iso	RC/G
Pwr ++	2013	Rk	DSL White Sox	244	29	30	0	7	123	204	160	364	9	77	0.44	18	7	27	37	-0.12
BAvg +++	2014	Rk	DSL White Sox	85	10	28	1	7	329	412	471	883	12	79	0.67	5	4	32	141	6.83
Spd ++	2014	Rk	Azl White Sox	78	12	14	1	7	179	264	256	521	10	77	0.50	0	1	29	77	1.92
Def +++	2015	Rk	Great Falls	269	40	84	6	38	312	342	442	784	4	77	0.20	0	0	27	130	4.98

Long INF who has yet to see time in full-season, but continues to improve as he adds strength. Offers some present pop, but projects to more as he learns swing and adds loft. Limited foot speed hurts SB and may end up at 3B long-term where cannon arm best used. Could be dynamite 3B with quick hands. Lot of potential, but long way from CHW.

Cruzado,Victor — 789 — New York (N)

EXP MLB DEBUT: 2017 | H/W: 5-11 180 | FUT: Reserve OF | **7D**

Bats B Age 23 — 2010 FA (DR)

Skills	Year	Lev	Team	AB	R	H	HR	RBI	Avg	OB	Slg	OPS	bb%	ct%	Eye	SB	CS	x/h%	Iso	RC/G
Pwr ++	2013	Rk	Kingsport	137	21	45	3	22	328	418	467	885	13	81	0.81	1	2	27	139	6.78
BAvg +++	2014	A	Savannah	359	64	98	7	50	273	374	404	778	14	78	0.74	10	7	28	131	5.48
Spd +++	2015	A+	St. Lucie	324	51	88	3	34	272	360	401	762	12	79	0.67	2	3	33	130	5.27
Def +++	2015	AA	Binghamton	15	1	3	0	2	200	333	267	600	17	87	1.50	0	0	33	67	3.68

Former SS at Dominican Academy has done nothing but hit since stateside debut. Has a skill to get on base. Works deep counts and will take pitches to where they are pitched. Utilizes short, compact swing to hit for solid average. Doesn't generate loft off bat, severely depressing power potential. Can play all 3 OF positions.

Cuthbert,Cheslor — 35 — Kansas City

EXP MLB DEBUT: 2015 | H/W: 6-1 190 | FUT: Starting 3B | **7C**

Bats R Age 23 — 2009 FA (NI)

Skills	Year	Lev	Team	AB	R	H	HR	RBI	Avg	OB	Slg	OPS	bb%	ct%	Eye	SB	CS	x/h%	Iso	RC/G
	2013	AA	NW Arkansas	237	25	51	6	28	215	276	359	635	8	78	0.39	5	2	43	143	3.30
Pwr +++	2014	AA	NW Arkansas	355	35	98	10	48	276	343	420	762	9	81	0.54	9	3	31	144	4.96
BAvg +++	2014	AAA	Omaha	91	12	24	2	16	264	330	385	715	9	87	0.75	1	1	29	121	4.46
Spd ++	2015	AAA	Omaha	397	55	110	11	51	277	339	421	759	9	85	0.62	5	2	31	144	4.91
Def ++	2015	MLB	KC Royals	46	6	10	1	8	217	280	370	650	8	80	0.44	0	0	40	152	3.57

Despite age, has been good prospect for years, but upside isn't nearly as high. Brings simple approach to box and swings line drive bat. Makes easy contact and won't strike out much thanks to plus bat control. Power is fringy and could hit more HR by pulling more. Lack of speed, range, and quickness limit defensive upside, though arm is strong.

Daal,Carlton — 46 — Cincinnati

EXP MLB DEBUT: 2017 | H/W: 6-2 160 | FUT: Reserve INF | **7E**

Bats R Age 22 — 2012 FA (CUR)

Skills	Year	Lev	Team	AB	R	H	HR	RBI	Avg	OB	Slg	OPS	bb%	ct%	Eye	SB	CS	x/h%	Iso	RC/G
Pwr +	2013	Rk	AZL Reds	21	3	3	0	3	143	182	143	325	5	71	0.17	0	0	0	0	-1.16
BAvg ++	2013	Rk	Billings	51	5	13	0	4	255	296	275	571	6	75	0.23	2	0	8	20	2.31
Spd +++	2014	A	Dayton	345	46	102	1	29	296	332	351	683	5	83	0.32	13	3	14	55	3.83
Def +++	2015	A+	Daytona	381	38	103	0	30	270	308	286	595	5	84	0.34	21	5	6	16	2.77

Solid defensive SS may not have enough bat to stick as a regular. Struggles working deep counts and making solid contact and virtually no power in package. Makes most of above-average speed. Defensively, glove will stick at SS. Defense could get better with improved footwork.

Dahl,David — 8 — Colorado

EXP MLB DEBUT: 2016 | H/W: 6-2 195 | FUT: Starting CF | **9C**

Bats L Age 22 — 2012 (1) HS (AL)

Skills	Year	Lev	Team	AB	R	H	HR	RBI	Avg	OB	Slg	OPS	bb%	ct%	Eye	SB	CS	x/h%	Iso	RC/G
	2013	A	Asheville	40	9	11	0	7	275	310	425	735	5	80	0.25	2	0	45	150	4.63
Pwr ++++	2014	A	Asheville	392	69	121	10	41	309	347	500	847	6	83	0.35	18	5	40	191	5.84
BAvg ++++	2014	A+	Modesto	120	14	32	4	14	267	296	467	763	4	78	0.19	3	0	44	200	4.74
Spd +++	2015	A-	Boise	24	1	3	0	1	125	125	167	292	0	63	0.00	0	0	33	42	-2.00
Def +++	2015	AA	New Britain	288	46	80	6	24	278	304	417	721	4	75	0.15	22	7	31	139	4.22

Ugly collision cost him a month of action and was slow to return to form. Has the tools to hit for BA due to plus bat speed and a short compact stroke, but can be overly aggressive. Swing produces plenty of line drives, but has over-the-fence power as well. He is a solid-average CF with plus speed and a good arm.

Davidson,Braxton — 79 — Atlanta

EXP MLB DEBUT: 2018 | H/W: 6-2 210 | FUT: Starting LF | **8D**

Bats L Age 19 — 2014 (1) HS (NC)

Skills	Year	Lev	Team	AB	R	H	HR	RBI	Avg	OB	Slg	OPS	bb%	ct%	Eye	SB	CS	x/h%	Iso	RC/G
Pwr ++++																				
BAvg ++	2014	Rk	Danville	36	1	6	0	3	167	333	222	556	20	72	0.90	0	0	33	56	2.67
Spd ++	2014	Rk	GCL Braves	111	23	27	0	8	243	368	324	693	17	71	0.69	0	0	30	81	4.58
Def ++	2015	A	Rome	401	51	97	10	45	242	373	374	747	17	66	0.62	1	6	34	132	5.32

Struggled mightily with the swing and miss in his first taste of full season ball. Raw power will play in any ballpark and should start to translate to live pitching soon. Combining plus power with an elongated-looping swing and fantastic batter's eyes, gives him a three true outcome projection. A former 1B, his OF defense is shaky.

Davidson,Matt — 5 — Chicago (A)

EXP MLB DEBUT: 2013 | H/W: 6-3 230 | FUT: Starting 3B | **7E**

Bats R Age 25 — 2009 (1) HS (CA)

Skills	Year	Lev	Team	AB	R	H	HR	RBI	Avg	OB	Slg	OPS	bb%	ct%	Eye	SB	CS	x/h%	Iso	RC/G
	2012	AA	Mobile	486	81	127	23	76	261	353	469	822	12	74	0.55	3	4	42	208	5.90
Pwr ++++	2013	AAA	Reno	443	55	124	17	74	280	348	481	828	9	70	0.34	1	0	42	201	6.07
BAvg +	2013	MLB	Arizona	76	8	18	3	12	237	326	434	760	12	68	0.42	0	1	50	197	5.20
Spd +	2014	AAA	Charlotte	478	59	95	20	55	199	273	362	635	9	66	0.30	0	0	40	163	3.24
Def ++	2015	AAA	Charlotte	528	63	107	23	74	203	286	375	661	11	64	0.32	1	0	42	172	3.72

Big, strong INF who led IL in HR and Ks in another disappointing year. Matched high in HR despite hitting under .200 in July and August. Can go opposite way, but expands strike zone. Uppercut stroke and aggressive swinging not conducive to BA. Has decent glove at 3B with average range and arm. Time is running out if power not playable.

Davis,Brendon — 6 — Los Angeles (N)

EXP MLB DEBUT: 2019 | H/W: 6-4 155 | FUT: Starting 3B | **7D**

Bats R Age 18 — 2015 (5) HS (CA)

Skills	Year	Lev	Team	AB	R	H	HR	RBI	Avg	OB	Slg	OPS	bb%	ct%	Eye	SB	CS	x/h%	Iso	RC/G
Pwr +++																				
BAvg ++																				
Spd ++	2015	Rk	Azl Dodgers	90	14	25	0	14	278	309	322	631	4	71	0.15	2	0	12	44	3.10
Def ++	2015	Rk	Ogden	24	5	4	1	3	167	231	333	564	8	67	0.25	0	0	50	167	2.14

5th round pick fell in the draft due a broken wrist that caused him to miss his senior season. Tall, lanky SS projects to have at least avg power once he matures. Moves well with avg speed and a strong arm, but isn't likely to stick at SS due to his size. Swing mechanics need refinement, but he has good athleticism and had a solid pro debut.

Davis,D.J. | 78 | **Toronto** | EXP MLB DEBUT: 2018 | H/W: 6-1 180 | FUT: Starting OF | **8E**

Bats L Age 21	Year	Lev	Team	AB	R	H	HR	RBI	Avg	OB	Slg	OPS	bb%	ct%	Eye	SB	CS	x/h%	Iso	RC/G
2012 (1) HS (MS)	2012	Rk	Bluefield	47	9	16	1	6	340	392	511	903	8	79	0.40	6	2	31	170	6.76
Pwr ++	2012	A-	Vancouver	18	3	3	0	0	167	348	167	514	22	67	0.83	1	1	0	0	1.84
BAvg ++	2013	Rk	Bluefield	225	35	54	6	25	240	319	418	737	10	66	0.34	13	8	39	178	5.00
Spd ++++	2014	A	Lansing	494	56	105	8	52	213	266	316	582	7	66	0.22	19	20	27	103	2.52
Def +++	2015	A	Lansing	496	77	140	7	59	282	335	391	726	7	76	0.33	21	10	24	109	4.47

Ultra-athletic OF who repeated Low-A and provided much better contact. Was consistent all year and showed improvement in baserunning. Bat speed very evident and has wiry strength to hit for semblance of power. Instincts and pitch recognition a little short. Plays solid CF, though reads and routes need polish.

Davis,Dylan | 79 | **San Francisco** | EXP MLB DEBUT: 2017 | H/W: 6-0 205 | FUT: Starting RF | **7C**

Bats R Age 22	Year	Lev	Team	AB	R	H	HR	RBI	Avg	OB	Slg	OPS	bb%	ct%	Eye	SB	CS	x/h%	Iso	RC/G
2014 (3) Oregon St	2014	NCAA	Oregon St	237	33	67	7	64	283	341	430	771	8	87	0.68	4	4	31	148	5.04
Pwr +++	2014	Rk	Azl Giants	37	6	11	0	8	297	350	486	836	8	68	0.25	0	0	64	189	6.62
BAvg ++	2014	A-	Salem-Kaizer	85	11	17	4	7	200	261	341	602	8	73	0.30	1	0	24	141	2.58
Spd ++	2015	A	Augusta	256	37	64	9	30	250	324	406	730	10	70	0.37	2	1	34	156	4.62
Def +++	2015	A+	San Jose	107	18	22	3	11	206	298	318	615	12	74	0.50	0	1	27	112	3.06

Former Cape Cod League standout has muscular build, strong wrists, good bat speed and above-avg raw power. Aggressive approach often leads to ct% issues and a high K-rate, limiting his BA upside. Has plus arm to profile well in RF and enough athletic ability to stick. Future value tied to HR/ISO.

Davis,J.D. | 5 | **Houston** | EXP MLB DEBUT: 2017 | H/W: 6-3 215 | FUT: Starting 3B | **8D**

Bats R Age 22	Year	Lev	Team	AB	R	H	HR	RBI	Avg	OB	Slg	OPS	bb%	ct%	Eye	SB	CS	x/h%	Iso	RC/G
2014 (3) Cal St Fullerton	2013	NCAA	Cal St Fullerton	211	40	67	4	50	318	405	436	841	13	82	0.84	1	1	24	118	6.19
Pwr ++++	2014	NCAA	Cal St Fullerton	237	34	80	6	43	338	416	523	940	12	78	0.60	7	0	34	186	7.51
BAvg ++	2014	A-	Tri City	111	18	31	5	20	279	365	495	861	12	77	0.60	1	0	42	216	6.34
Spd +	2014	A	Quad Cities	155	20	47	8	32	303	357	516	873	8	74	0.32	4	0	36	213	6.33
Def +++	2015	A+	Lancaster	485	93	140	26	101	289	360	520	880	10	68	0.34	5	2	41	231	6.85

Tall INF who had solid campaign, especially in August when he broke out in big way. Finished 2nd in CAL in K due to long swing and struggles with breaking balls. Owns above average pop to all fields and has patient approach to get on base. Exhibits plus arm at 3B and is average defender. Won't steal many bases, but bat should carry him.

De Leon,Michael | 46 | **Texas** | EXP MLB DEBUT: 2019 | H/W: 6-1 160 | FUT: Starting SS | **7D**

Bats B Age 19	Year	Lev	Team	AB	R	H	HR	RBI	Avg	OB	Slg	OPS	bb%	ct%	Eye	SB	CS	x/h%	Iso	RC/G
2013 FA (DR)																				
Pwr +	2014	A	Hickory	336	42	82	1	26	244	302	295	597	8	88	0.70	3	3	16	51	3.13
BAvg ++	2014	A+	Myrtle Beach	24	5	7	1	6	292	370	542	912	11	83	0.75	0	0	57	250	6.94
Spd ++	2014	AA	Frisco	3	1	1	0	0	333	333	667	1000	0	67	0.00	0	0	100	333	9.06
Def +++	2015	A	Hickory	306	29	68	1	29	222	277	281	558	7	85	0.49	1	1	21	59	2.53

Lean, reliable SS who repeated Low-A and was slightly worse. Played mostly SS and has good fundamentals, but no flashy tools. Range may be best at 2B, but has quick hands and arm. Focuses on contact in basic approach and can shorten swing when behind in count. Offers minimal power and will struggle to drive ball. Speed is below average.

Dean,Austin | 7 | **Miami** | EXP MLB DEBUT: 2017 | H/W: 6-1 190 | FUT: Fourth OF | **7C**

Bats R Age 22	Year	Lev	Team	AB	R	H	HR	RBI	Avg	OB	Slg	OPS	bb%	ct%	Eye	SB	CS	x/h%	Iso	RC/G
2012 (4) HS (TX)	2012	Rk	GCL Marlins	148	15	33	2	15	223	331	338	669	14	76	0.69	2	2	39	115	4.07
Pwr +++	2013	A-	Batavia	213	28	57	2	19	268	322	418	740	7	78	0.36	0	2	37	150	4.77
BAvg +++	2013	A	Greensboro	20	4	4	1	3	200	333	400	733	17	75	0.80	0	0	50	200	4.81
Spd ++	2014	A	Greensboro	403	67	124	9	58	308	367	444	812	9	82	0.53	4	4	27	136	5.56
Def +++	2015	A+	Jupiter	519	67	139	5	52	268	319	366	685	7	85	0.51	18	10	28	98	4.04

Solid hitter with good bat speed but limited power. Has just 19 HR in 4 seasons, but did blast 32 doubles. Drives the ball up the middle with a contact oriented approach. Has above-average speed but that isn't going to be part of his game as he moves up. Covers ground well in the OF, but a below-avg arm limits him to LF.

Dean,Matt | 35 | **Toronto** | EXP MLB DEBUT: 2017 | H/W: 6-3 215 | FUT: Starting 1B | **8D**

Bats R Age 23	Year	Lev	Team	AB	R	H	HR	RBI	Avg	OB	Slg	OPS	bb%	ct%	Eye	SB	CS	x/h%	Iso	RC/G
2011 (13) HS (TX)																				
Pwr ++++	2012	Rk	Bluefield	167	22	37	2	24	222	274	353	627	7	64	0.20	3	2	38	132	3.37
BAvg ++	2013	Rk	Bluefield	210	37	71	6	35	338	379	519	899	6	73	0.25	8	5	32	181	6.79
Spd ++	2014	A	Lansing	448	58	126	9	51	281	322	429	751	6	74	0.23	2	1	34	147	4.76
Def +++	2015	A+	Dunedin	478	53	121	14	63	253	305	410	715	7	71	0.26	3	1	36	157	4.34

Strong INF who set career high in HR and starting to realize natural power to all fields. Pitch recognition remains a little short and may struggle to hit for BA. Power will play at 1B or 3B. Has potential to become above average defender at 1B because of athleticism and ability to scoop balls out of dirt. Lacks foot speed for SB.

DeJong,Paul | 5 | **St. Louis** | EXP MLB DEBUT: 2019 | H/W: 6-0 195 | FUT: Starting 3B | **7C**

Bats R Age 22	Year	Lev	Team	AB	R	H	HR	RBI	Avg	OB	Slg	OPS	bb%	ct%	Eye	SB	CS	x/h%	Iso	RC/G
2015 (4) Illinois St																				
Pwr +++																				
BAvg +++	2015	NCAA	Illinois St	210	47	70	14	48	333	412	605	1017	12	76	0.56	2	1	41	271	8.31
Spd ++	2015	Rk	Johnson City	37	10	18	4	15	486	558	973	1531	14	76	0.67	0	0	56	486	15.32
Def ++	2015	A	Peoria	219	32	63	5	26	288	355	438	794	10	80	0.53	13	4	32	151	5.42

Solid in his debut, hitting .316 with 30 extra-base hits. Has a quick RH stroke that generates lift to go along with raw power. Can be overly aggressive, but also walked 29 times. Played C and 2B in college, but profiles better at 3B where he has good hands and a strong arm.

Delgado,Natanael | 79 | **Los Angeles (A)** | EXP MLB DEBUT: 2018 | H/W: 6-1 170 | FUT: Starting OF | **8E**

Bats L Age 20	Year	Lev	Team	AB	R	H	HR	RBI	Avg	OB	Slg	OPS	bb%	ct%	Eye	SB	CS	x/h%	Iso	RC/G
2012 FA (DR)																				
Pwr ++																				
BAvg ++	2013	Rk	Azl Angels	192	23	52	3	33	271	310	422	732	5	78	0.26	4	0	40	151	4.51
Spd ++	2014	Rk	Orem	153	23	46	3	21	301	323	464	787	3	78	0.15	4	0	33	163	5.04
Def ++	2015	A	Burlington	411	32	99	6	46	241	274	355	630	4	75	0.18	2	2	30	114	3.08

Raw OF who lost steam late in season. Possesses plus bat speed and has leverage and loft to profile to above average pop. Needs work on approach and swing consistency to produce. Free swinger who rarely draws walks and can't solve LHP. Speed is regressing and arm most suitable for LF. Potential impact and role solely based on bat development.

Demeritte,Travis | 4 | **Texas** | EXP MLB DEBUT: 2017 | H/W: 6-0 180 | FUT: Starting 2B | **7C**

Bats R Age 21	Year	Lev	Team	AB	R	H	HR	RBI	Avg	OB	Slg	OPS	bb%	ct%	Eye	SB	CS	x/h%	Iso	RC/G
2013 (1) HS (GA)																				
Pwr ++++	2013	Rk	Azl Rangers	144	31	41	4	20	285	405	444	849	17	66	0.59	5	1	29	160	6.92
BAvg ++	2014	A	Hickory	398	77	84	25	66	211	299	450	749	11	57	0.29	6	2	51	239	5.49
Spd +++	2015	A-	Spokane	20	0	3	0	0	150	227	150	377	9	45	0.18	0	2	0	0	-0.70
Def ++	2015	A	Hickory	170	27	41	5	19	241	338	412	750	13	59	0.36	10	1	44	171	5.62

Compact INF who repeated Low-A and was suspended 80 games for PED. Works counts and uses quick bat and natural strength to generate pop. Plate coverage is sub par and lot of swing-and-miss in game. Needs to use entire field more. Played mostly 2B with some 3B in '15 and profiles best at 2B due to quick feet. Runs well and will steal occasional bag.

Denton,Bryce | 5 | **St. Louis** | EXP MLB DEBUT: 2020 | H/W: 6-0 190 | FUT: Starting LF | **7D**

Bats R Age 18	Year	Lev	Team	AB	R	H	HR	RBI	Avg	OB	Slg	OPS	bb%	ct%	Eye	SB	CS	x/h%	Iso	RC/G
2015 (2) HS (TN)																				
Pwr ++																				
BAvg +++																				
Spd ++																				
Def ++	2015	Rk	GCL Cardinals	155	21	30	1	14	194	247	245	492	7	79	0.34	3	0	13	52	1.49

Looked over-matched in his pro debut. Showed good bat speed and raw power in HS, but swing is long and struggled to make consistent contact as a pro with just 4 x-base hits. Below average defender at 3B and profiles better as a corner OF. Was young even for the GCL, but will need to show more in '16.

Devers,Rafael | 5 | **Boston** | EXP MLB DEBUT: 2018 | H/W: 6-0 195 | FUT: Starting 3B | **9C**

Bats L Age 19	Year	Lev	Team	AB	R	H	HR	RBI	Avg	OB	Slg	OPS	bb%	ct%	Eye	SB	CS	x/h%	Iso	RC/G
2013 FA (DR)																				
Pwr ++++																				
BAvg +++	2014	Rk	DSL Red Sox	104	26	35	3	21	337	448	538	986	17	81	1.05	4	1	34	202	8.32
Spd ++	2014	Rk	GCL Red Sox	157	21	49	4	36	312	368	484	852	8	81	0.47	1	0	35	172	6.07
Def ++	2015	A	Greenville	469	71	135	11	70	288	323	443	766	5	82	0.29	3	2	37	156	4.80

Strong INF with high ceiling based on incredible offensive talent. Doubles should evolve into plus HR production due to all-fields pop and natural strength. Elite bat speed and hand-eye coordination should allow for high BA. Could stand to be more patient, but should get better. Not a strong defender, though has hands and arm to improve.

Dewees,Donnie | 8 | Chicago (N)

Bats L Age 22 — 2015 (2) North Florida
EXP MLB DEBUT: 2018 | H/W: 6-0 180 | FUT: Starting CF | 8D

Pwr + + + | BAvg + + + | Spd + + + + | Def + +

Year	Lev	Team	AB	R	H	HR	RBI	Avg	OB	Slg	OPS	bb%	ct%	Eye	SB	CS	x/h%	Iso	RC/G
2015	NCAA	North Florida	251	88	106	18	68	422	484	749	1233	11	94	1.88	23	3	36	327	10.21
2015	A-	Eugene	282	42	75	5	30	266	301	376	677	5	81	0.26	19	7	27	110	3.68

Three sport star in HS has good across-the-board tools. Scouts are mixed on his long-term power upside, but he does show an advanced feel for hitting and a good understanding of strike zone. Makes consistent hard contact, but currently has more of a line-drive approach. Plus speed should allow him to stick in CF, though he has a below average arm.

Diaz,Elias | 2 | Pittsburgh

Bats R Age 25 — 2008 FA (VZ)
EXP MLB DEBUT: 2015 | H/W: 6-1 210 | FUT: Starting C | 7A

Pwr + + | BAvg + + + | Spd + + | Def + + + +

Year	Lev	Team	AB	R	H	HR	RBI	Avg	OB	Slg	OPS	bb%	ct%	Eye	SB	CS	x/h%	Iso	RC/G
2013	A+	Bradenton	183	30	51	2	15	279	383	399	782	14	82	0.94	4	4	31	120	5.64
2014	AA	Altoona	326	41	107	6	54	328	385	445	830	8	84	0.59	3	2	24	117	5.76
2014	AAA	Indianapolis	33	4	5	0	0	152	222	182	404	8	82	0.50	0	1	20	30	0.62
2015	AAA	Indianapolis	325	33	88	4	47	271	331	382	712	8	86	0.62	1	4	27	111	4.43
2015	MLB	Pittsburgh	2	0	0	0	0	0	0	0	0	0	50	0.00	0	0		0	-7.85

Strong defensive CA had a breakout year at the plate and rocketed up prospect charts. Blocks and receives well and has a plus arm, nailing 30% of runners. Frames pitches well and calls a good game. Widely considered one of the best defenders in the minors. Showed an improved ability to hit over the past two years.

Diaz,Isan | 46 | Arizona

Bats L Age 19 — 2014 (3) HS (MA)
EXP MLB DEBUT: 2019 | H/W: 5-10 185 | FUT: Starting 2B | 9E

Pwr + + + | BAvg + + + + | Spd + + | Def + + +

Year	Lev	Team	AB	R	H	HR	RBI	Avg	OB	Slg	OPS	bb%	ct%	Eye	SB	CS	x/h%	Iso	RC/G
2014	Rk	Azl DBacks	182	22	34	3	21	187	285	330	615	12	69	0.45	6	5	44	143	3.23
2015	Rk	Missoula	272	58	98	13	51	360	431	640	1071	11	76	0.52	12	7	45	279	9.20

Organization's breakout performer in '15. Led PIO in most offensive categories. Advanced approach at plate; quick, easy swing lends itself to high BA. Consistently makes hard contract. Generates incredible loft despite short, stocky stature. Ball carries naturally off bat. Presently a SS, but lacks range and speed to stay at position long term.

Diaz,Lewin | 3 | Minnesota

Bats L Age 19 — 2013 FA (DR)
EXP MLB DEBUT: 2020 | H/W: 6-3 200 | FUT: Starting 1B | 9E

Pwr + + + + | BAvg + + | Spd + | Def + +

Year	Lev	Team	AB	R	H	HR	RBI	Avg	OB	Slg	OPS	bb%	ct%	Eye	SB	CS	x/h%	Iso	RC/G
2015	Rk	GCL Twins	111	12	29	1	15	261	344	369	713	11	78	0.58	2	0	31	108	4.56
2015	Rk	Elizabethton	48	7	8	3	5	167	216	375	591	6	65	0.18	0	0	50	208	2.37

Big-bodied slugger who struggled in first year in U.S. before breaking out in August. Has incredible raw power with natural loft and plus bat speed. Has BA potential as well with advanced feel for contact. Exhibits strong arm, but lack of mobility and instincts limit him to 1B. Will likely spend another year in rookie ball.

Diaz,Yandy | 5 | Cleveland

Bats R Age 24 — 2013 FA (CU)
EXP MLB DEBUT: 2016 | H/W: 6-2 185 | FUT: Utility player | 6B

Pwr + + | BAvg + + + | Spd + + | Def + + +

Year	Lev	Team	AB	R	H	HR	RBI	Avg	OB	Slg	OPS	bb%	ct%	Eye	SB	CS	x/h%	Iso	RC/G
2014	A+	Carolina	283	42	81	2	37	286	392	367	759	15	88	1.40	3	3	17	81	5.44
2015	AA	Akron	476	61	150	7	55	315	412	408	819	14	86	1.20	8	7	17	92	6.02
2015	AAA	Columbus	19	1	3	0	1	158	158	263	421	0	74	0.00	0	0	67	105	0.30

Tall, lean INF who may not have power for 3B, but is sound defender with BA ability. Very selective hitter who rarely chases bad pitches and can put bat on ball. Doesn't have much pop, but can hit LHP and has feel for contact. Provides below average speed and won't steal many bases. Arm strength is good and could play any INF spot.

Dickerson,Alex | 37 | San Diego

Bats L Age 25 — 2011 (3) Indiana
EXP MLB DEBUT: 2015 | H/W: 6-3 230 | FUT: Starting OF | 7C

Pwr + + + | BAvg + + + | Spd + | Def + +

Year	Lev	Team	AB	R	H	HR	RBI	Avg	OB	Slg	OPS	bb%	ct%	Eye	SB	CS	x/h%	Iso	RC/G
2014	Rk	Azl Padres	14	3	4	0	0	286	286	643	929	0	79	0.00	0	0	75	357	7.19
2014	A-	Eugene	10	3	3	0	2	300	462	400	862	23	80	1.50	0	0	33	100	7.22
2014	AA	San Antonio	137	20	44	3	24	321	363	496	859	6	80	0.32	0	1	36	175	6.09
2015	AAA	El Paso	459	82	141	12	71	307	369	503	872	9	79	0.47	4	0	40	196	6.44
2015	MLB	San Diego	8	0	2	0	0	250	250	250	500	0	63	0.00	0	0	0	0	1.04

Large, consistent hitter who produced all year and earned AB with SD. Only has average power despite strong build, but knows how to hit. Makes easy, hard contact with balanced swing and also draws walks by solid selectivity. Has few secondary skills as he moved to LF from 1B despite lack of foot speed. Defense may keep him from full-time job.

Difo,Wilmer | 6 | Washington

Bats B Age 24 — 2010 FA (DR)
EXP MLB DEBUT: 2015 | H/W: 6-0 195 | FUT: Starting SS | 8C

Pwr + + + | BAvg + + + | Spd + + + + | Def + + + +

Year	Lev	Team	AB	R	H	HR	RBI	Avg	OB	Slg	OPS	bb%	ct%	Eye	SB	CS	x/h%	Iso	RC/G
2013	A+	Potomac	18	2	4	0	1	222	300	278	578	10	83	0.67	0	1	25	56	2.91
2014	A	Hagerstown	559	91	176	14	90	315	357	470	828	6	88	0.57	49	9	30	156	5.60
2015	A+	Potomac	75	13	24	3	14	320	386	533	919	10	83	0.62	4	1	42	213	6.89
2015	AA	Harrisburg	359	48	100	2	39	279	302	387	689	3	78	0.15	26	1	29	109	3.85
2015	MLB	Washington	11	1	2	0	0	182	182	182	364	0	82	0.00	0	0	0	0	-0.33

High-energy player with life in his legs and surprising sting in his bat. Stroke is short, quick as LHH; a bit longer from RH side. Has strength to lace balls into the gaps (59 doubles, 2014-15) and shows willingness to run. Can handle SS with smooth, quick actions and plus arm.

Dixon,Brandon | 4 | Cincinnati

Bats R Age 24 — 2013 (3) Arizona
EXP MLB DEBUT: 2018 | H/W: 6-1 215 | FUT: Utility player | 6C

Pwr + + + | BAvg + + | Spd + + + | Def + +

Year	Lev	Team	AB	R	H	HR	RBI	Avg	OB	Slg	OPS	bb%	ct%	Eye	SB	CS	x/h%	Iso	RC/G
2013	A	Great Lakes	211	28	39	1	17	185	225	261	486	5	69	0.17	6	2	33	76	1.14
2014	Rk	Azl Dodgers	3	0	0	0	0	0	0	0	0	0	100		0	0		0	-2.66
2014	A+	RanchoCuca	390	59	102	9	46	262	284	410	694	3	74	0.12	8	7	35	149	3.85
2015	A+	RanchoCuca	174	37	52	11	30	299	358	575	933	8	74	0.35	10	0	44	276	7.17
2015	AA	Tulsa	336	33	82	8	38	244	270	375	645	3	71	0.12	16	6	32	131	3.21

Moved from 3B to 2B and had a solid season between A+/AA, hitting .263/.303/.443 with 19 HR and 26 SB. Has some pop in his bat, but swings and misses a ton - 28 BB/144 K. Has above-average speed and should be able to stick at 2B despite his size. Power uptick gives him some potential, but will need to prove it wasn't a fluke.

Dosch,Drew | 5 | Baltimore

Bats L Age 23 — 2013 (7) Youngstown St
EXP MLB DEBUT: 2017 | H/W: 6-2 200 | FUT: Starting 3B | 7E

Pwr + + | BAvg + + + | Spd + + | Def + +

Year	Lev	Team	AB	R	H	HR	RBI	Avg	OB	Slg	OPS	bb%	ct%	Eye	SB	CS	x/h%	Iso	RC/G
2012	NCAA	Youngstown St	224	36	79	8	42	353	413	527	940	9	91	1.10	5	2	28	174	7.02
2013	NCAA	Youngstown St	201	40	68	3	30	338	439	488	926	15	88	1.44	3	3	31	149	7.44
2014	A	Delmarva	500	76	157	5	50	314	373	404	777	9	81	0.48	5	3	20	90	5.17
2015	A+	Frederick	207	30	57	2	34	275	348	372	720	10	82	0.62	4	2	23	97	4.58
2015	AA	Bowie	231	17	55	1	21	238	285	307	592	6	81	0.33	2	1	20	69	2.77

Smooth-hitting INF with good size and strength, but focuses more on contact than power. Has been mostly a singles hitter with slappy, short swing. Uses entire field and is sound situational hitter. Lacks power projection and doesn't fit mold of typical 3B. Agility and glovework are below par, though arm and hands may work at 2B.

Downes,Brandon | 89 | Kansas City

Bats R Age 23 — 2014 (7) Virginia
EXP MLB DEBUT: 2017 | H/W: 6-2 195 | FUT: Starting OF | 8E

Pwr + + + | BAvg + + | Spd + + + | Def + + +

Year	Lev	Team	AB	R	H	HR	RBI	Avg	OB	Slg	OPS	bb%	ct%	Eye	SB	CS	x/h%	Iso	RC/G
2013	NCAA	Virginia	253	67	80	10	59	316	382	569	951	10	76	0.45	6	1	46	253	7.56
2014	NCAA	Virginia	237	31	57	7	40	241	313	388	701	10	80	0.52	9	2	33	148	4.20
2014	Rk	Idaho Falls	169	31	52	3	23	308	346	485	832	6	76	0.24	6	4	38	178	5.85
2015	A	Lexington	391	52	98	14	59	251	306	448	753	7	71	0.27	19	7	47	197	4.91
2015	A+	Wilmington	1	0	0	0	0	0	0	0	0	0	0	0.00	0	0		0	

Physical OF who started slow, but caught fire at end of season. Can be doubles machine with impressive bat speed and strength. Reaches seats mostly on pull side, though has chance to develop more pop. Struggles with breaking balls and doesn't see many pitches in approach. K totals need to be curbed. Runs well, which enhances OF play.

Dozier,Hunter | 5 | Kansas City

Bats R Age 24 — 2013 (1) Stephen F. Austin
EXP MLB DEBUT: 2016 | H/W: 6-4 220 | FUT: Starting 3B | 8D

Pwr + + + | BAvg + + | Spd + + + | Def + + +

Year	Lev	Team	AB	R	H	HR	RBI	Avg	OB	Slg	OPS	bb%	ct%	Eye	SB	CS	x/h%	Iso	RC/G
2013	Rk	Idaho Falls	218	43	66	7	43	303	399	509	908	14	85	1.09	3	1	47	206	7.07
2013	A	Lexington	55	6	18	0	9	327	362	436	798	5	91	0.60	0	0	33	109	5.36
2014	A+	Wilmington	224	36	66	4	39	295	390	429	819	14	75	0.63	7	3	33	134	6.06
2014	AA	NW Arkansas	234	33	49	4	21	209	302	312	614	12	70	0.44	3	2	33	103	3.12
2015	AA	NW Arkansas	475	65	101	12	53	213	281	349	630	9	68	0.30	6	2	40	137	3.24

Tall INF who has struggled in AA for 1 1/2 seasons. Set high in HR, but did not have one good month in '15. Will draw walks and smash line drives to gaps, but swing gets out of whack and will chase pitches out of zone. Led TL in Ks. Has good speed, but rarely steals bags. Has found home at 3B where he has enough arm and quick hands.

Drury,Brandon — 45 — Arizona

EXP MLB DEBUT: 2015 | H/W: 6-2 215 | FUT: Starting 2B/3B | 8C

Bats R Age 23
2010 (13) HS (OR)

- Pwr + +
- BAvg + + +
- Spd + +
- Def + + +

Year	Lev	Team	AB	R	H	HR	RBI	Avg	OB	Sig	OPS	bb%	ct%	Eye	SB	CS	x/h%	Iso	RC/G
2014	A+	Visalia	430	73	129	19	81	300	361	519	880	9	82	0.54	4	3	43	219	6.33
2014	AA	Mobile	105	12	31	4	14	295	339	476	815	6	82	0.37	0	0	35	181	5.39
2015	AA	Mobile	273	22	76	3	36	278	306	370	676	4	85	0.27	4	5	24	92	3.70
2015	AAA	Reno	251	43	83	2	25	331	382	458	841	8	86	0.60	0	2	34	127	5.95
2015	MLB	Arizona	56	3	12	2	8	214	241	375	616	3	86	0.25	0	0	42	161	2.93

Former 3B struggled during Sept call-up but has bat and glove to stick at 2B. Heady hitter with terrific bat control needs to work deeper counts. Hit 41 doubles total, peppering the ball to both gaps. Below average HR power, shouldn't hamper slugging in MLB. Projects as a above-average regular at 2B.

Dubon,Mauricio — 46 — Boston

EXP MLB DEBUT: 2018 | H/W: 6-0 160 | FUT: Starting 2B/SS | 7C

Bats R Age 21
2013 (26) HS (CA)

- Pwr + +
- BAvg + + +
- Spd + + + +
- Def + + +

Year	Lev	Team	AB	R	H	HR	RBI	Avg	OB	Sig	OPS	bb%	ct%	Eye	SB	CS	x/h%	Iso	RC/G
2013	Rk	GCL Red Sox	53	8	13	0	4	245	259	302	561	2	77	0.08	6	2	23	57	2.12
2014	A-	Lowell	256	40	82	3	34	320	343	395	738	3	90	0.35	7	8	15	74	4.40
2015	A	Greenville	236	43	71	4	29	301	350	428	778	7	86	0.53	18	4	27	127	5.11
2015	A+	Salem	237	27	65	1	18	274	338	325	663	9	84	0.61	12	3	15	51	3.83

Quick, lean INF who played mostly 2B in Low-A before moving to SS in High-A. Had promising first full season with both bat and glove. Hits hard line drives to gaps and shows enough strength for pull power. Covers plate well and can beat out infield grounders. Possesses average range and quick, nimble feet.

Duggar,Steven — 89 — San Francisco

EXP MLB DEBUT: 2018 | H/W: 6-2 195 | FUT: Starting OF | 7C

Bats L Age 22
2015 (6) Clemson

- Pwr + +
- BAvg + + +
- Spd + + + +
- Def + + +

Year	Lev	Team	AB	R	H	HR	RBI	Avg	OB	Sig	OPS	bb%	ct%	Eye	SB	CS	x/h%	Iso	RC/G
2015	NCAA	Clemson	227	56	69	5	43	304	438	432	869	19	78	1.10	10	5	26	128	6.94
2015	A-	Salem-Kaizer	229	40	67	1	27	293	386	367	753	13	77	0.67	6	3	21	74	5.18

Lean, athletic 6th-round pick exhibits a sound approach and decent contact skills. Uses bat speed to spray the ball to all fields, but load and swing will need shortening to handle velocity and tap into fringy power. Has plus speed for future SB value. Has range for CF, but his strong, accurate arm likely makes a solid defender in RF.

Eaves,Kody — 45 — Los Angeles (A)

EXP MLB DEBUT: 2017 | H/W: 6-0 175 | FUT: Starting 2B | 7D

Bats L Age 22
2012 (16) HS (TX)

- Pwr + +
- BAvg + +
- Spd + + +
- Def + +

Year	Lev	Team	AB	R	H	HR	RBI	Avg	OB	Sig	OPS	bb%	ct%	Eye	SB	CS	x/h%	Iso	RC/G
2012	Rk	Azl Angels	165	25	43	2	19	261	326	400	726	9	79	0.47	6	0	33	139	4.62
2013	Rk	Orem	264	45	73	1	24	277	327	386	714	7	85	0.50	22	6	29	110	4.44
2014	A	Burlington	549	74	147	10	45	268	304	415	720	5	74	0.20	25	10	37	148	4.33
2015	A+	Inland Empire	520	70	129	11	71	248	308	387	695	8	71	0.30	21	9	30	138	4.13

Strong, quick INF who is becoming more selective, but still has holes in swing. Lot of Ks as he struggles with LHP and pull-happy tendencies. Lacks loft in swing, though hits line drives to all fields and can pull ball out of park occasionally. Instincts enhance average speed and has potential to become average defender at 2B.

Engel,Adam — 8 — Chicago (A)

EXP MLB DEBUT: 2017 | H/W: 6-1 215 | FUT: Starting CF | 7C

Bats R Age 24
2013 (19) Louisville

- Pwr + +
- BAvg + +
- Spd + + + +
- Def + + +

Year	Lev	Team	AB	R	H	HR	RBI	Avg	OB	Sig	OPS	bb%	ct%	Eye	SB	CS	x/h%	Iso	RC/G
2013	Rk	Great Falls	239	44	72	3	30	301	358	414	772	8	86	0.62	31	8	25	113	5.11
2014	Rk	Azl White Sox	33	6	12	1	3	364	417	727	1144	8	82	0.50	2	0	58	364	9.90
2014	A	Kannapolis	307	54	80	6	30	261	324	410	735	9	72	0.34	28	11	34	150	4.75
2014	A+	Winston-Salem	88	11	21	0	5	239	287	239	526	6	76	0.29	9	1	0	0	1.76
2015	A+	Winston-Salem	529	90	133	7	43	251	330	369	699	10	75	0.47	65	11	29	117	4.31

Athletic OF who led CAR in both SB and K. Matched career high in HR, but at best when keeping ball on ground and using plus speed. Owns natural pop, but choppy swing limits output. Ranges well in CF, though arm strength is a little short.

Ervin,Phil — 78 — Cincinnati

EXP MLB DEBUT: 2017 | H/W: 5-10 205 | FUT: Starting OF | 8E

Bats R Age 23
2013 (1) Samford

- Pwr + + +
- BAvg + +
- Spd + + + +
- Def + + +

Year	Lev	Team	AB	R	H	HR	RBI	Avg	OB	Sig	OPS	bb%	ct%	Eye	SB	CS	x/h%	Iso	RC/G
2013	Rk	Billings	129	27	42	8	29	326	404	597	1001	12	81	0.71	12	0	43	271	7.94
2013	A	Dayton	43	7	15	1	6	349	451	465	916	16	77	0.80	2	1	20	116	7.37
2014	A	Dayton	498	68	118	7	68	237	301	376	677	8	78	0.42	30	5	41	139	3.96
2015	A+	Daytona	405	68	98	12	63	242	330	375	705	12	80	0.64	30	7	31	133	4.33
2015	AA	Pensacola	51	7	12	2	8	235	391	412	802	20	71	0.87	4	3	42	176	6.05

Former high pick struggling to recover lost bat speed from '14 wrist surgery. Plate discipline & walk rate returned to pre-surgery levels, but has struggled with getting the barrel through the zone, resulting in soft contact. Combination of power and speed unheard of from many prospects. Defensively, struggled in CF with routes. Tweener prospect.

Escalera,Alfredo — 789 — Kansas City

EXP MLB DEBUT: 2018 | H/W: 6-1 185 | FUT: Starting OF | 7D

Bats R Age 21
2012 (8) HS (FL)

- Pwr + +
- BAvg + +
- Spd + + +
- Def + + +

Year	Lev	Team	AB	R	H	HR	RBI	Avg	OB	Sig	OPS	bb%	ct%	Eye	SB	CS	x/h%	Iso	RC/G
2012	Rk	Azl Royals	119	26	36	0	11	303	331	361	692	4	76	0.17	2	1	14	59	3.89
2013	Rk	Burlington	184	23	51	1	13	277	328	380	709	7	77	0.33	3	2	31	103	4.30
2014	A	Lexington	438	62	97	9	38	221	252	340	592	4	75	0.16	11	3	31	119	2.53
2015	A	Lexington	262	40	82	8	33	313	338	477	815	4	78	0.17	12	2	29	164	5.32
2015	A+	Wilmington	199	18	41	2	14	206	269	291	560	8	69	0.28	7	3	27	85	2.26

Versatile OF who showed more consistent pop and put himself on prospect map. Dominated Low-A before struggling in High-A. Exhibits decent power to all fields that should grow to at least average. Plate discipline is a bit short and possesses raw offensive abilities, but has instincts to improve. Runs well and owns solid range at all OF spots.

Evans,Zane — 2 — Kansas City

EXP MLB DEBUT: 2016 | H/W: 6-3 210 | FUT: Platoon C | 6B

Bats R Age 24
2013 (4) Georgia Tech

- Pwr + + +
- BAvg + +
- Spd +
- Def + +

Year	Lev	Team	AB	R	H	HR	RBI	Avg	OB	Sig	OPS	bb%	ct%	Eye	SB	CS	x/h%	Iso	RC/G
2013	NCAA	Georgia Tech	244	47	88	14	66	361	437	590	1027	12	84	0.83	0	1	31	230	8.20
2013	Rk	Idaho Falls	162	26	57	4	31	352	393	537	930	6	85	0.44	1	0	39	185	6.85
2014	A+	Wilmington	371	34	84	5	36	226	279	332	610	7	75	0.29	2	1	35	105	2.94
2015	A+	Wilmington	107	12	29	4	15	271	310	458	768	5	79	0.27	0	0	41	187	4.79
2015	AA	NW Arkansas	238	21	60	6	41	252	276	387	663	3	73	0.13	1	0	33	134	3.41

Large-framed backstop who set high in HR and was much improved from poor '14. Recognizes pitches well, but swings hard early in count. Exhibits average power, mostly to pull side, and can shoot gaps with level swing. Strikeouts have been issue and needs to exhibit more patience. Footwork and receiving still below par, but slowly improving.

Farmer,Kyle — 2 — Los Angeles (N)

EXP MLB DEBUT: 2017 | H/W: 6-0 200 | FUT: Backup C | 6C

Bats R Age 25
2013 (8) Georgia

- Pwr + +
- BAvg + + +
- Spd + +
- Def + + +

Year	Lev	Team	AB	R	H	HR	RBI	Avg	OB	Sig	OPS	bb%	ct%	Eye	SB	CS	x/h%	Iso	RC/G
2013	Rk	Ogden	167	37	58	4	36	347	374	533	906	4	87	0.33	1	1	40	186	6.38
2013	A	Great Lakes	229	25	71	2	35	310	352	441	794	6	90	0.63	9	3	31	131	5.33
2014	A+	RanchoCuca	130	8	31	0	15	238	293	292	585	7	78	0.36	2	0	19	54	2.71
2015	A+	RanchoCuca	163	33	55	1	27	337	383	515	898	7	85	0.48	5	2	38	178	6.67
2015	AA	Tulsa	283	25	77	2	39	272	306	392	699	5	81	0.25	0	1	38	120	4.06

Converted backstop put up solid numbers between A+/AA, hitting .296/.343/.437. Continues to progress behind the plate with good hands and a strong arm, but his release and blocking skills need work. Barrels the ball well and makes decent contact. A work in progress.

Field,Johnny — 789 — Tampa Bay

EXP MLB DEBUT: 2016 | H/W: 5-10 190 | FUT: Fourth OF | 6B

Bats R Age 24
2013 (5) Arizona

- Pwr + +
- BAvg + +
- Spd + +
- Def + +

Year	Lev	Team	AB	R	H	HR	RBI	Avg	OB	Sig	OPS	bb%	ct%	Eye	SB	CS	x/h%	Iso	RC/G
2013	NCAA	Arizona	222	58	77	5	39	347	413	527	940	10	90	1.14	16	6	30	180	7.21
2013	A-	Hudson Valley	238	22	60	2	24	252	288	370	658	5	84	0.32	14	6	38	118	3.61
2014	A	Bowling Green	317	62	92	7	41	290	357	461	818	9	77	0.45	18	4	38	170	5.81
2014	A+	Charlotte	150	33	48	5	17	320	374	547	921	8	81	0.46	5	4	44	227	6.91
2015	AA	Montgomery	432	68	110	14	66	255	312	447	759	8	75	0.33	18	3	46	192	4.92

Undersized grinder who set career high in HR while continuing to use entire field. Plays all OF positions equally well and has good feel for game. No tool stands out and may struggle to hit for BA due to limited bat speed. Has instincts to get jumps and reads in OF, though arm and speed are iffy.

Fields,Roemon — 78 — Toronto

EXP MLB DEBUT: 2016 | H/W: 5-11 180 | FUT: Reserve OF | 6B

Bats L Age 25
2013 NDFA Bethany

- Pwr +
- BAvg + +
- Spd + + + +
- Def + + + +

Year	Lev	Team	AB	R	H	HR	RBI	Avg	OB	Sig	OPS	bb%	ct%	Eye	SB	CS	x/h%	Iso	RC/G
2014	A-	Vancouver	294	64	79	1	26	269	330	350	681	8	79	0.44	48	9	23	82	4.01
2015	A+	Dunedin	264	34	71	1	21	269	311	348	659	6	80	0.31	21	9	21	80	3.59
2015	AA	New Hampshire	202	28	52	1	11	257	318	292	610	8	83	0.53	23	5	8	35	3.11
2015	AAA	Buffalo	23	1	5	0	1	217	308	261	569	12	83	0.75	2	0	20	43	2.84

Elite speed merchant who impacts game with legs, both on base and in OF. Spent most of year in CF and exhibits incredible range. Arm may be a little short, but tracks balls well and gets great jumps. Can be too aggressive at plate and needs to get on base more consistently. Lacks punch in stroke and won't hit HR. Made it to AAA in first full year.

Fisher,Derek — 78 — Houston

EXP MLB DEBUT: 2017 | H/W: 6-3 210 | FUT: Starting OF | 8C

Bats L Age 22 — 2014 (1) Virginia
Pwr ++++ / BAvg +++ / Spd ++++ / Def ++

Year	Lev	Team	AB	R	H	HR	RBI	Avg	OB	Slg	OPS	bb%	ct%	Eye	SB	CS	x/h%	Iso	RC/G
2014	NCAA	Virginia	177	24	46	3	29	260	307	362	668	6	84	0.43	5	3	24	102	3.72
2014	Rk	GCL Astros	3	0	2	0	0	667	750	1000	1750	25	100		0	0	50	333	17.49
2014	A-	Tri City	152	31	46	2	18	303	369	408	777	10	77	0.46	17	4	20	105	5.25
2015	A	Quad Cities	151	32	46	6	24	305	382	510	892	11	75	0.51	8	2	39	205	6.81
2015	A+	Lancaster	344	74	90	16	63	262	350	471	821	12	72	0.49	23	5	37	209	5.92

Emerging OF who impressed with power output and speed. Can be impact hitter with 20/20 potential thanks to double plus bat speed and knowledge of strike zone. Smooth swing makes hard contact, though can flail at breaking balls. Split time between LF and CF and remains below average. Arm is fringy at best and will likely be OK in LF.

Fletcher,David — 6 — Los Angeles (A)

EXP MLB DEBUT: 2018 | H/W: 5-10 175 | FUT: Utility player | 6B

Bats R Age 21 — 2015 (6) Loyola Marymount
Pwr + / BAvg +++ / Spd +++ / Def ++++

Year	Lev	Team	AB	R	H	HR	RBI	Avg	OB	Slg	OPS	bb%	ct%	Eye	SB	CS	x/h%	Iso	RC/G
2015	NCAA	Loyola Marymount	221	32	68	2	27	308	373	416	789	9	92	1.28	14	3	26	109	5.52
2015	Rk	Orem	160	28	53	0	30	331	392	456	848	9	94	1.78	11	4	30	125	6.27
2015	A	Burlington	120	18	34	1	10	283	348	358	707	9	89	0.92	6	1	18	75	4.48

Fundamentally-sound INF who has no weakness in glove, but may not hit enough to be every day regular. Ranges well to both sides and has instincts to be premium defender. Makes very easy contact with plus bat control, but has no power in compact stroke. Bunts well and has enough speed to beat out some infield grounders.

Flores,Ramon — 79 — Milwaukee

EXP MLB DEBUT: 2015 | H/W: 5-10 190 | FUT: Starting OF | 7D

Bats L Age 24 — 2008 FA (VZ)
Pwr ++ / BAvg +++ / Spd ++ / Def ++

Year	Lev	Team	AB	R	H	HR	RBI	Avg	OB	Slg	OPS	bb%	ct%	Eye	SB	CS	x/h%	Iso	RC/G
2014	Rk	GCL Yankees	8	2	3	1	2	375	375	1000	1375	0	75	0.00	0	0	100	625	12.46
2014	AAA	Scranton/WB	235	30	58	7	23	247	340	443	782	12	81	0.73	3	2	48	196	5.45
2015	AAA	Scranton/WB	276	43	79	7	34	286	375	417	791	12	84	0.91	3	2	25	130	5.52
2015	AAA	Tacoma	52	11	22	2	7	423	524	654	1178	17	88	1.83	0	0	36	231	10.45
2015	MLB	NY Yankees	32	3	7	0	0	219	219	250	469	0	88	0.00	0	0	14	31	1.19

Short, strong OF who broke leg at end of '15 and will open season late. Lacks ideal power profile of corner OF and doesn't have speed or range for CF. Knows how to hit and uses entire field in contact approach. Works counts to get on base. Has value, but may not have enough tools to win starting spot.

Fontana,Nolan — 456 — Houston

EXP MLB DEBUT: 2016 | H/W: 5-11 205 | FUT: Utility player | 6B

Bats L Age 24 — 2012 (2) Florida
Pwr ++ / BAvg ++ / Spd ++ / Def +++

Year	Lev	Team	AB	R	H	HR	RBI	Avg	OB	Slg	OPS	bb%	ct%	Eye	SB	CS	x/h%	Iso	RC/G
2012	NCAA	Florida	243	59	69	9	30	284	402	444	847	16	89	1.78	13	1	29	160	6.43
2012	A	Lexington	151	37	34	2	25	225	458	338	796	30	71	1.48	12	2	35	113	6.47
2013	A+	Lancaster	386	88	100	8	60	259	414	399	813	21	74	1.02	16	5	32	140	6.32
2014	AA	Corpus Christi	229	33	60	1	26	262	417	376	793	21	67	0.80	5	8	38	114	6.34
2015	AAA	Fresno	361	56	87	3	40	241	370	357	727	17	73	0.75	6	11	34	116	5.05

Steady, consistent INF who can play any infield spot. Lacks ideal quickness and range, but maximizes talent with soft hands and accurate arm. Not much of threat with bat, though works counts and gets on base. Understands strike zone and his own limitations as power not part of equation. Erratic contact hinders BA potential.

Forbes,Ti'quan — 5 — Texas

EXP MLB DEBUT: 2019 | H/W: 6-3 180 | FUT: Starting 3B | 8E

Bats R Age 19 — 2014 (2) HS (MS)
Pwr ++ / BAvg ++ / Spd ++++ / Def ++

Year	Lev	Team	AB	R	H	HR	RBI	Avg	OB	Slg	OPS	bb%	ct%	Eye	SB	CS	x/h%	Iso	RC/G
2014	Rk	Azl Rangers	174	27	42	0	16	241	330	282	612	12	73	0.49	10	1	12	40	3.17
2015	A-	Spokane	217	25	57	0	19	263	307	323	630	6	75	0.26	2	2	21	60	3.20

Lean INF who moved to 3B in '15. Lacks power at present, but has wiry strength and plus bat speed to project to above average pop. Owns above average speed and will need to get on base more to utilize. Has little feel for contact and swing gets out of whack. Has range for 3B and will need more reps.

Fowler,Dustin — 8 — New York (A)

EXP MLB DEBUT: 2018 | H/W: 6-0 185 | FUT: Fourth OF | 6B

Bats L Age 21 — 2013 (18) HS (GA)
Pwr ++ / BAvg +++ / Spd ++++ / Def +++

Year	Lev	Team	AB	R	H	HR	RBI	Avg	OB	Slg	OPS	bb%	ct%	Eye	SB	CS	x/h%	Iso	RC/G
2013	Rk	GCL Yankees	112	8	27	0	9	241	267	384	651	3	79	0.17	3	1	44	143	3.52
2014	A	Charleston (Sc)	257	33	66	9	41	257	293	459	752	5	79	0.25	3	2	42	202	4.62
2015	A	Charleston (Sc)	241	35	74	4	31	307	337	419	756	4	80	0.23	18	7	22	112	4.63
2015	A+	Tampa	246	29	71	1	39	289	330	370	699	6	83	0.35	12	6	21	81	4.10

Versatile, athletic OF who has solid skills, though no plus tool other than speed. Plays true CF with excellent range and average arm. Hasn't hit many long balls, but can reach seats on occasion. Plate discipline needs attention and could benefit by drawing more walks. Ability to hit LHP gives him some upside.

Fox,Lucius — 6 — San Francisco

EXP MLB DEBUT: 2019 | H/W: 6-1 165 | FUT: Starting SS | 9D

Bats B Age 18 — 2015 FA (Bahamas)
Pwr ++ / BAvg +++ / Spd +++++ / Def +++

Year	Lev	Team	AB	R	H	HR	RBI	Avg	OB	Slg	OPS	bb%	ct%	Eye	SB	CS	x/h%	Iso	RC/G
2015		*Did not play in minors*																	

Raw SS with plus-plus athleticism who signed for $6,000,000 in July. Elite speed, agility foretell of legit SB upside. Has soft hands, good range and strong enough arm to stick at SS long-term, with CF as a possible fallback. Shows nice barrel control as switch-hitter for BA potential. Raw power is below avg, but has good bat speed to expose gaps.

Franco,Anderson — 5 — Washington

EXP MLB DEBUT: 2019 | H/W: 6-3 190 | FUT: Starting 3B | 8D

Bats R Age 18 — 2013 FA (DR)
Pwr +++ / BAvg ++ / Spd ++ / Def ++++

Year	Lev	Team	AB	R	H	HR	RBI	Avg	OB	Slg	OPS	bb%	ct%	Eye	SB	CS	x/h%	Iso	RC/G
2015	Rk	GCL Nationals	153	19	43	4	19	281	341	412	753	8	83	0.54	2	3	26	131	4.80
2015	A-	Auburn	40	0	9	0	4	225	340	300	640	15	95	3.50	0	0	22	75	4.42

Teenager held up well in first stateside action, with athleticism, hands, and a plus arm that should allow him to stay at 3B. Strength in swing leads to raw power, though will need to focus on making better contact and not chasing unhittable pitches. Praised for work ethic and demeanor, and has a history of playing against older competition.

Frazier,Clint — 89 — Cleveland

EXP MLB DEBUT: 2017 | H/W: 6-1 190 | FUT: Starting CF | 9D

Bats R Age 21 — 2013 (1) HS (GA)
Pwr ++++ / BAvg +++ / Spd +++ / Def +++

Year	Lev	Team	AB	R	H	HR	RBI	Avg	OB	Slg	OPS	bb%	ct%	Eye	SB	CS	x/h%	Iso	RC/G
2013	Rk	AZL Indians	172	32	51	5	28	297	360	506	866	9	65	0.28	3	2	41	209	7.06
2014	A	Lake County	474	70	126	13	50	266	343	411	755	11	66	0.35	12	6	29	146	5.21
2015	A+	Lynchburg	501	88	143	16	72	285	371	465	836	12	75	0.54	15	7	38	180	6.14

Pure-hitting OF who was better in all phases after ho-hum '14. Cut K rate while showing more consistent pop. Finished 2nd in CAR in HR despite age and has bat speed and strength to project to more pop. Owns good speed and can patrol CF, though also has arm for corner spot. Swing can get long at times, but has tweaked swing enough to make contact.

Fuenmayor,Balbino — 3 — Kansas City

EXP MLB DEBUT: 2016 | H/W: 6-3 230 | FUT: Starting 1B | 7D

Bats R Age 26 — 2006 FA (VZ)
Pwr ++++ / BAvg +++ / Spd + / Def +

Year	Lev	Team	AB	R	H	HR	RBI	Avg	OB	Slg	OPS	bb%	ct%	Eye	SB	CS	x/h%	Iso	RC/G
2015	AA	NW Arkansas	291	50	103	15	51	354	380	591	971	4	84	0.26	1	0	37	237	7.01
2015	AAA	Omaha	69	12	26	2	15	377	377	580	957	0	81	0.00	0	0	35	203	6.77

Mammoth slugger who set career high in HR after 2 years in indy ball. Makes easy contact for power hitter and destroys LHP with short, quick swing. Not likely to sustain extreme BA, but has value with stick. Secondary skills lag far behind. Is very slow on base and has poor footwork and agility at 1B. Will begin '16 late due to knee surgery.

Fuentes,Reymond — 78 — Kansas City

EXP MLB DEBUT: 2013 | H/W: 6-0 160 | FUT: Fourth OF | 6A

Bats L Age 25 — 2009 (1) HS (PR)
Pwr ++ / BAvg +++ / Spd ++++ / Def +++

Year	Lev	Team	AB	R	H	HR	RBI	Avg	OB	Slg	OPS	bb%	ct%	Eye	SB	CS	x/h%	Iso	RC/G
2013	AAA	Tucson	55	17	23	0	8	418	508	491	999	15	82	1.00	6	1	17	73	8.44
2013	MLB	San Diego	33	4	5	0	1	152	222	152	374	8	52	0.18	3	0	0	0	-0.88
2014	AA	San Antonio	170	25	55	4	17	324	382	453	835	9	78	0.43	12	1	22	129	5.86
2014	AAA	El Paso	157	29	41	1	16	261	333	376	709	10	83	0.63	13	2	32	115	4.51
2015	AAA	Omaha	396	70	122	9	46	308	357	422	779	7	82	0.42	29	6	19	114	5.01

Wiry strong OF who has solid approach at plate that allows him to hit for BA. Knows K zone and has discerning eye to get on base and use plus speed. Uses entire field and has shown ability to hit LHP. Set career high in HR, but power not his forte and doesn't hit many xbh. Arm strength is weak, though is solid defender with plus range and routes.

Fukofuka, Amalani — 89 — Kansas City

EXP MLB DEBUT: 2019 | H/W: 6-1 180 | FUT: Starting OF | 8E

Bats R Age 20 — 2013 (5) HS (CA)
Pwr ++ / BAvg +++ / Spd +++ / Def +++

Year	Lev	Team	AB	R	H	HR	RBI	Avg	OB	Slg	OPS	bb%	ct%	Eye	SB	CS	x/h%	Iso	RC/G
2013	Rk	Azl Royals	156	28	38	1	12	244	355	346	701	15	70	0.57	10	2	32	103	4.62
2014	Rk	Burlington	180	19	33	1	12	183	261	289	550	10	63	0.29	7	7	30	106	2.27
2015	Rk	Idaho Falls	280	33	95	3	38	339	395	500	895	8	75	0.37	10	3	32	161	6.92

Thin, athletic OF who has spent 3 years in short-season ball, but showed vast improvement in '14. Starting to turn tools into production as he's adding strength and allowing bat speed to impact ball. Projects to fringe-average pop, but makes contact and can use all fields. Can play all OF spots and is good defender with average speed and arm.

Gallo, Joey — 57 — Texas

EXP MLB DEBUT: 2015 | H/W: 6-5 230 | FUT: Starting 3B | 9C

Bats L Age 22 — 2012 (1) HS (NV)
Pwr +++++ / BAvg ++ / Spd ++ / Def ++

Year	Lev	Team	AB	R	H	HR	RBI	Avg	OB	Slg	OPS	bb%	ct%	Eye	SB	CS	x/h%	Iso	RC/G
2014	A+	Myrtle Beach	189	53	61	21	50	323	467	735	1202	21	66	0.80	5	3	54	413	12.07
2014	AA	Frisco	250	44	58	21	56	232	329	524	853	13	54	0.31	2	0	53	292	7.56
2015	AA	Frisco	121	21	38	9	31	314	428	636	1064	17	60	0.49	1	0	53	322	10.82
2015	AAA	Round Rock	200	20	39	14	32	195	291	450	741	12	55	0.30	1	0	59	255	5.47
2015	MLB	Texas	108	16	22	6	14	204	301	417	717	12	47	0.26	3	0	45	213	6.10

Tall, strong hitter who is all about power and can hit any pitch to any part of park. Showcased double-plus pop in trial with TEX and along with continued plate discipline. Long swing and struggles against LHP ding some value, but has incredible bat speed and loft to be threat. Doesn't run well, but shows athleticism and arm for either 3B or LF.

Garcia, Aramis — 2 — San Francisco

EXP MLB DEBUT: 2017 | H/W: 6-2 220 | FUT: Starting C | 8C

Bats R Age 23 — 2014 (2) Florida Intl
Pwr +++ / BAvg +++ / Spd ++ / Def ++

Year	Lev	Team	AB	R	H	HR	RBI	Avg	OB	Slg	OPS	bb%	ct%	Eye	SB	CS	x/h%	Iso	RC/G
2014	NCAA	Florida Intl	163	34	60	8	37	368	452	626	1078	13	86	1.09	4	1	40	258	8.96
2014	Rk	Azl Giants	32	6	7	0	3	219	324	313	637	14	81	0.83	0	0	43	94	3.82
2014	A-	Salem-Kaizer	70	5	16	2	12	229	280	357	637	7	73	0.26	0	0	31	129	3.18
2015	A	Augusta	319	42	87	15	61	273	345	467	812	10	76	0.45	0	1	36	194	5.57
2015	A+	San Jose	75	10	17	0	5	227	310	280	590	11	71	0.41	1	0	24	53	2.83

Strong, well-built C with intriguing bat skills. Has mature approach with good pitch recognition; subtle kick and load allow for quick bat speed and quality contact. Showed massive pull-side pop in '15; added muscle could peg raw power as solid-average tool. Defensive skills lacking, but has work ethic to stay behind plate.

Garcia, Dermis — 5 — New York (A)

EXP MLB DEBUT: 2019 | H/W: 6-3 200 | FUT: Starting 3B | 9E

Bats R Age 18 — 2014 FA (DR)
Pwr +++ / BAvg ++ / Spd ++ / Def +++

Year	Lev	Team	AB	R	H	HR	RBI	Avg	OB	Slg	OPS	bb%	ct%	Eye	SB	CS	x/h%	Iso	RC/G
2015	Rk	GCL Yankees	69	7	11	0	6	159	256	188	445	12	64	0.36	0	1	18	29	0.55

Tall INF who already moved off SS to 3B. Has quick, smooth actions with glove and could become plus defender. Strong arm enhanced by quick transfer. Owns soft hands and agility as well. Needs work with bat as he sells out for power and struggles with contact. Swing mechanics are raw. Has below average speed that limits SB.

Garcia, Eudor — 5 — New York (N)

EXP MLB DEBUT: 2018 | H/W: 6-0 225 | FUT: Starting 1B/3B | 8E

Bats L Age 21 — 2014 (4) El Paso CC
Pwr +++ / BAvg ++ / Spd ++ / Def ++

Year	Lev	Team	AB	R	H	HR	RBI	Avg	OB	Slg	OPS	bb%	ct%	Eye	SB	CS	x/h%	Iso	RC/G
2014	Rk	Kingsport	202	22	53	2	28	262	317	347	663	7	84	0.50	0	0	23	84	3.75
2015	A	Savannah	398	57	118	9	59	296	333	442	776	5	76	0.23	5	2	31	146	4.98

Has hit in his first two professional seasons. Unorthodox swing, but an improved load, leaves him less susceptible to high heat. Questions remain whether swing translates to upper minors. Physically, he's at projection; has 15-20 HR in bat. Lacks reactions needed for 3B. Might end up at 1B.

Garcia, Greg — 46 — St. Louis

EXP MLB DEBUT: 2014 | H/W: 5-11 190 | FUT: Utility player | 6C

Bats L Age 26 — 2010 (7) Hawaii
Pwr + / BAvg ++ / Spd ++ / Def +++

Year	Lev	Team	AB	R	H	HR	RBI	Avg	OB	Slg	OPS	bb%	ct%	Eye	SB	CS	x/h%	Iso	RC/G
2014	AA	Springfield	15	2	5	0	1	333	375	467	842	6	73	0.25	1	0	40	133	6.20
2014	AAA	Memphis	382	60	104	8	40	272	343	382	725	10	75	0.43	7	5	22	110	4.53
2014	MLB	St. Louis	14	2	2	0	1	143	200	214	414	7	57	0.17	0	0	50	71	0.05
2015	AAA	Memphis	330	47	97	6	36	294	384	364	747	13	83	0.87	16	3	22	70	4.59
2015	MLB	St. Louis	75	7	18	2	4	240	329	387	716	12	84	0.83	0	0	39	147	4.59

Has a knack for hitting and getting on base and made his MLB debut. Has a good understanding of the strike zone and made strides in making contact, walking almost as many times as he K'd. Has a short, compact stroke, but below-average power that will likely keep him in a UT role. Is an average defender, but his arm and range are light for SS.

Garcia, Julio — 6 — Los Angeles (A)

EXP MLB DEBUT: 2020 | H/W: 6-0 175 | FUT: Starting SS | 8E

Bats R Age 18 — 2014 FA (DR)
Pwr ++ / BAvg ++ / Spd ++ / Def +++

Year	Lev	Team	AB	R	H	HR	RBI	Avg	OB	Slg	OPS	bb%	ct%	Eye	SB	CS	x/h%	Iso	RC/G
2015	Rk	Azl Angels	58	5	13	0	6	224	250	259	509	3	72	0.13	4	0	15	34	1.39

Lean, quick INF who is all about projection as he grows into frame. Can be plus defender at times with smooth, quick actions and strong arm. Can get sloppy with glove and make careless errors. Can drive ball to all fields with quick swing and focuses on contact. May need to be more aggressive to tap into any pop potential.

Garcia, Wilkerman — 6 — New York (A)

EXP MLB DEBUT: 2019 | H/W: 6-0 176 | FUT: Starting SS | 8D

Bats B Age 18 — 2014 FA (VZ)
Pwr ++ / BAvg +++ / Spd +++ / Def +++

Year	Lev	Team	AB	R	H	HR	RBI	Avg	OB	Slg	OPS	bb%	ct%	Eye	SB	CS	x/h%	Iso	RC/G
2015	R	DSL Yankees	6	3	4	0	1	667	714	667	1381	14	100		5	1	0	0	12.11
2015	R	GCL Yankees	121	20	34	0	18	281	400	347	747	17	84	1.26	6	8	21	66	5.38

Athletic INF who has good tools, yet has keen baseball IQ for young age. Solid hitter from both sides and can hit for BA by using all fields with line drive stroke. Should eventually grow into average power as he adds loft and backspin. Runs well and has quickness to handle any infield spot. May move to 2B or 3B where he'll have enough bat.

Garcia, Willy — 9 — Pittsburgh

EXP MLB DEBUT: 2016 | H/W: 6-3 215 | FUT: Starting RF | 8D

Bats R Age 23 — 2010 FA (DR)
Pwr ++++ / BAvg ++ / Spd ++ / Def ++

Year	Lev	Team	AB	R	H	HR	RBI	Avg	OB	Slg	OPS	bb%	ct%	Eye	SB	CS	x/h%	Iso	RC/G
2012	A	West Virginia	459	57	110	18	77	240	289	403	692	7	71	0.24	10	8	34	163	3.90
2013	A+	Bradenton	449	51	115	16	60	256	292	437	729	5	66	0.15	13	6	37	180	4.62
2014	AA	Altoona	439	59	119	16	63	271	309	478	787	5	67	0.17	8	4	42	207	5.42
2015	AA	Altoona	204	26	64	5	29	314	349	441	790	5	77	0.23	3	2	22	127	5.09
2015	AAA	Indianapolis	276	36	68	10	38	246	278	424	702	4	72	0.16	1	4	37	178	3.96

Started slow when moved up to AAA, but finished strong (.281 with 8 HR in Aug). Has good speed and raw power, but is overly aggressive, raising concerns about his ability to hit for average (23 BB/123 K). Solid defender with good range and a plus arm. The power is legit, but will need to refine his approach at some point.

Garrett, Stone — 8 — Miami

EXP MLB DEBUT: 2020 | H/W: 6-2 195 | FUT: Starting LF | 8D

Bats R Age 20 — 2014 (8) HS (TX)
Pwr ++++ / BAvg ++ / Spd +++ / Def ++

Year	Lev	Team	AB	R	H	HR	RBI	Avg	OB	Slg	OPS	bb%	ct%	Eye	SB	CS	x/h%	Iso	RC/G
2014	Rk	GCL Marlins	148	17	35	0	11	236	271	270	541	5	79	0.23	4	1	11	34	2.00
2015	A-	Batavia	222	36	66	11	46	297	353	581	934	8	73	0.32	8	5	53	284	7.35

Physically mature OF showed ability to hit for BA, but needs to make more consistent contact. Does have short, quick stroke, good raw power, and plus bat speed and stroked 35 extra-base hits. Struggles with breaking balls and off-speed stuff. Runs well, is a hard worker, but a below-avg arm will likely limit him to LF.

Gasparini, Marten — 6 — Kansas City

EXP MLB DEBUT: 2019 | H/W: 6-0 165 | FUT: Starting SS | 8E

Bats B Age 18 — 2013 FA (IT)
Pwr ++ / BAvg ++ / Spd ++++ / Def ++++

Year	Lev	Team	AB	R	H	HR	RBI	Avg	OB	Slg	OPS	bb%	ct%	Eye	SB	CS	x/h%	Iso	RC/G
2014	Rk	Idaho Falls	11	4	5	1	3	455	500	727	1227	8	82	0.50	2	0	20	273	10.18
2014	Rk	Burlington	68	11	13	0	1	191	225	250	475	4	53	0.09	4	1	23	59	1.20
2015	Rk	Idaho Falls	197	36	51	2	25	259	342	411	754	11	59	0.31	26	9	31	152	5.86

Athletic, slender INF who is emerging. Can be elite defender in time due to exceptional instincts and ranges well to both sides. Has strong, accurate arm and can be a tad careless. Has significant contact issues and is very raw with stick. Can be too patient and needs to add strength to be consistent gap producer. Very nice upside.

Gatewood,Jake — 6 — Milwaukee

EXP MLB DEBUT: 2019 | H/W: 6-5 190 | FUT: Starting 3B | **8E**

Bats R Age 20
2014 (1) HS (CA)
Pwr ++++
BAvg ++
Spd ++
Def +++

Year	Lev	Team	AB	R	H	HR	RBI	Avg	OB	Slg	OPS	bb%	ct%	Eye	SB	CS	x/h%	Iso	RC/G
2014	Rk	Azl Brewers	204	19	42	3	32	206	253	279	533	6	65	0.18	7	8	21	74	1.72
2015	Rk	Helena	212	38	58	6	41	274	330	476	807	8	68	0.26	3	5	52	203	5.90
2015	A	Wisconsin	177	16	37	4	16	209	267	316	583	7	63	0.22	5	0	27	107	2.54

Easy to dream 20-25 HR future on his plus raw power and bat speed alone, but MWL debut exposed some of his recurring flaws. Long swing not conducive to much contact; questionable, aggressive approach still very much intact. Solid arm, glove, range at SS at present, but future is at 3B with that 6'5" build.

Gerber,Michael — 9 — Detroit

EXP MLB DEBUT: 2017 | H/W: 6-2 175 | FUT: Starting OF | **7C**

Bats L Age 23
2014 (15) Creighton
Pwr +++
BAvg +++
Spd +++
Def +++

Year	Lev	Team	AB	R	H	HR	RBI	Avg	OB	Slg	OPS	bb%	ct%	Eye	SB	CS	x/h%	Iso	RC/G
2013	NCAA	Creighton	134	20	44	5	31	328	379	567	946	8	83	0.48	2	1	36	239	7.15
2014	NCAA	Creighton	208	34	57	11	49	274	320	500	820	6	83	0.39	2	2	40	226	5.39
2014	A-	Connecticut	217	40	62	7	37	286	338	493	831	7	78	0.35	8	4	44	207	5.80
2014	A	West Michigan	31	4	12	0	5	387	457	484	941	11	90	1.33	1	0	25	97	7.38
2015	A	West Michigan	513	74	150	13	76	292	354	468	822	9	81	0.51	16	4	36	175	5.74

Athletic OF who improved across board and does everything well. Plate approach centers around using entire field, and has strength and bat speed to hit HR. Recognizes spin and puts bat to ball easily. Struggles against LHP (.212) with limited pop, but has instincts to get better. Strong arm and average range suitable for RF.

Gettys,Michael — 8 — San Diego

EXP MLB DEBUT: 2019 | H/W: 6-1 203 | FUT: Starting OF | **8C**

Bats R Age 20
2014 (2) HS (GA)
Pwr +++
BAvg ++
Spd ++++
Def +++

Year	Lev	Team	AB	R	H	HR	RBI	Avg	OB	Slg	OPS	bb%	ct%	Eye	SB	CS	x/h%	Iso	RC/G
2014	Rk	Azl Padres	213	29	66	3	38	310	355	437	792	7	69	0.23	14	2	24	127	5.56
2015	A	Fort Wayne	494	62	114	6	44	231	272	346	618	5	67	0.17	20	10	34	115	3.07

Plus athlete who struggled in first full season, but showed improvement by years-end. Was young for level and seem overmatched, but has plus bat speed and foot speed to project well. Pitch recognition and selectivity are sub-par and his K rate was high. Hits gaps with natural strength and plays excellent CF defense with strong arm.

Gillaspie,Casey — 3 — Tampa Bay

EXP MLB DEBUT: 2017 | H/W: 6-4 240 | FUT: Starting 1B | **8C**

Bats B Age 23
2014 (1) Wichita St
Pwr ++++
BAvg +++
Spd +
Def ++

Year	Lev	Team	AB	R	H	HR	RBI	Avg	OB	Slg	OPS	bb%	ct%	Eye	SB	CS	x/h%	Iso	RC/G
2014	NCAA	Wichita St	211	50	82	15	50	389	520	682	1203	22	87	2.07	8	0	38	294	10.90
2014	A-	Hudson Valley	263	27	69	7	42	262	364	411	775	14	75	0.65	2	3	35	148	5.40
2015	Rk	GCL Devil Rays	6	0	0	0	0	0	0	0	0	0	67	0.00	0	0		0	-6.12
2015	A	Bowling Green	234	37	65	16	44	278	355	530	885	11	82	0.65	4	0	42	252	6.36
2015	A+	Charlotte	41	3	6	1	4	146	222	268	491	9	78	0.44	0	0	33	122	1.48

Hulking 1B who finished 2nd in MWL in HR despite promotion to High-A in June. Missed time after promotion due to hand injury. Has plus power from both sides and has hitting instincts and barrel control to hit for BA. Draws walks and gets on base. Secondary skills are far behind. Has limited athleticism and well below average speed.

Giron,Ruddy — 6 — San Diego

EXP MLB DEBUT: 2019 | H/W: 5-11 175 | FUT: Starting SS | **8C**

Bats R Age 19
2013 FA (DR)
Pwr ++
BAvg ++++
Spd +++
Def ++

Year	Lev	Team	AB	R	H	HR	RBI	Avg	OB	Slg	OPS	bb%	ct%	Eye	SB	CS	x/h%	Iso	RC/G
2014	Rk	Azl Padres	185	23	31	0	13	168	202	222	424	4	77	0.19	1	2	32	54	0.51
2015	A	Fort Wayne	386	58	110	9	49	285	335	407	742	7	82	0.43	15	14	23	122	4.58

Young, talented SS who exceeded expectations in first full season in U.S. Started strong and faded late, but showed impressive tools. Exhibits natural strength and bat speed and makes easy contact with simple, line drive stroke. Can go opposite way, but most power is to pull side. Makes careless errors, but has tools to be exceptional with glove.

Goeddel,Tyler — 789 — Philadelphia

EXP MLB DEBUT: 2016 | H/W: 6-4 185 | FUT: Starting OF | **7C**

Bats R Age 23
2011 (1) HS (CA)
Pwr ++
BAvg +++
Spd +++
Def ++

Year	Lev	Team	AB	R	H	HR	RBI	Avg	OB	Slg	OPS	bb%	ct%	Eye	SB	CS	x/h%	Iso	RC/G
2012	A	Bowling Green	329	52	81	6	46	246	324	371	695	10	71	0.40	30	5	33	125	4.24
2013	A	Bowling Green	450	63	112	7	65	249	310	389	699	8	78	0.41	30	5	33	140	4.21
2014	A+	Charlotte	424	41	114	6	61	269	340	408	748	10	77	0.47	20	9	34	139	4.95
2015	AA	Montgomery	473	68	132	12	72	279	345	433	779	9	79	0.49	28	9	30	154	5.21

Wiry prospect who broke out after middling seasons in low minors. Converted from 3B and looked comfortable tracking balls with average range and arm. Kills LHP (.398) and set career high in HR. Only projects to average pop, but can hit for BA. Has long swing and approach isn't polished. Steals bases on instincts and average speed. Rule 5 pick from TAM.

Gonzalez,Erik — 6 — Cleveland

EXP MLB DEBUT: 2016 | H/W: 6-3 195 | FUT: Utility player | **6A**

Bats R Age 24
2008 FA (DR)
Pwr ++
BAvg ++
Spd +++
Def +++

Year	Lev	Team	AB	R	H	HR	RBI	Avg	OB	Slg	OPS	bb%	ct%	Eye	SB	CS	x/h%	Iso	RC/G
2013	A+	Carolina	153	16	37	0	27	242	266	366	632	3	75	0.13	1	2	38	124	3.22
2014	A+	Carolina	308	44	89	3	46	289	338	409	747	7	79	0.35	15	6	27	120	4.77
2014	AA	Akron	129	21	46	1	16	357	390	473	863	5	82	0.30	6	1	22	116	6.03
2015	AA	Akron	311	38	87	6	46	280	304	421	726	3	82	0.20	10	5	32	141	4.24
2015	AAA	Columbus	238	32	53	3	23	223	269	311	580	6	80	0.32	8	2	23	88	2.57

Tall, lean INF who is solid defender with strong arm and ample range. Has nice fundamentals and rarely makes careless errors. Likes to swing early in count and won't draw many walks, but has developing strength to hit ball over fence. Matched career high in HR and exhibits average speed for doubles and SB.

Gonzalez,Luis — 6 — Cincinnati

EXP MLB DEBUT: 2018 | H/W: 6-0 175 | FUT: Starting SS | **6D**

Bats R Age 21
2012 FA (DR)
Pwr +
BAvg ++
Spd +++
Def ++++

Year	Lev	Team	AB	R	H	HR	RBI	Avg	OB	Slg	OPS	bb%	ct%	Eye	SB	CS	x/h%	Iso	RC/G
2013	Rk	DSL Rojos	264	32	62	2	28	235	268	326	594	4	89	0.40	18	14	26	91	2.94
2014	Rk	AZL Reds	94	7	26	0	11	277	292	362	653	2	77	0.09	5	3	27	85	3.34
2015	A	Dayton	497	55	122	2	50	245	266	306	572	3	84	0.17	7	4	19	60	2.40

Made his full-season debut in '15. Glove-first SS with little power and a weak bat. Makes a lot of soft contact and struggles with pitches out of the zone. Will be a plus defender at projection. Will stick at SS. Bat may hold back from reaching potential. Broke his ankle during the last week of the season.

Goodwin,Brian — 8 — Washington

EXP MLB DEBUT: 2016 | H/W: 6-0 195 | FUT: Reserve OF | **6B**

Bats L Age 25
2011 (1) Miami-Dade JC
Pwr +++
BAvg ++
Spd +++
Def ++++

Year	Lev	Team	AB	R	H	HR	RBI	Avg	OB	Slg	OPS	bb%	ct%	Eye	SB	CS	x/h%	Iso	RC/G
2012	A	Hagerstown	216	47	70	9	38	324	436	542	978	17	82	1.10	15	4	40	218	8.07
2012	AA	Harrisburg	166	17	37	5	14	223	299	373	672	10	70	0.36	3	3	38	151	3.84
2013	AA	Harrisburg	457	82	115	10	40	252	346	407	753	13	74	0.55	19	11	35	155	5.14
2014	AAA	Syracuse	274	31	60	4	32	219	340	328	668	15	65	0.53	6	4	30	109	4.13
2015	AA	Harrisburg	429	58	97	8	46	226	289	340	629	8	78	0.41	15	7	30	114	3.25

Reminder of the downside risk of "tools" players. While the pieces are there—bat speed, foot speed, plate patience, and defense—he's not been able to make adjustments in the high minors. Struggles with off-speed especially. Reserve outfielder at this point.

Gordon,Nick — 6 — Minnesota

EXP MLB DEBUT: 2018 | H/W: 6-0 160 | FUT: Starting 3B/LF | **8C**

Bats L Age 20
2014 (1) HS (FL)
Pwr ++
BAvg ++++
Spd +++
Def ++++

Year	Lev	Team	AB	R	H	HR	RBI	Avg	OB	Slg	OPS	bb%	ct%	Eye	SB	CS	x/h%	Iso	RC/G
2014	Rk	Elizabethton	235	46	69	1	28	294	325	366	691	4	81	0.24	11	7	16	72	3.89
2015	A	Cedar Rapids	481	79	133	1	58	277	331	360	690	8	82	0.44	25	8	23	83	4.11

Smooth athlete who got better as season progressed. Has bat speed, wiry strength, and hand-eye coordination that profiles for BA and pop. Needs to pull more to hit HR, but at best when using entire field and using legs to get on base. Works counts and makes simple contact. Has the quickness, hands, arm, and instincts to stick at SS.

Gregor,Conrad — 3 — Houston

EXP MLB DEBUT: 2016 | H/W: 6-2 225 | FUT: Platoon 1B | **6B**

Bats L Age 24
2013 (4) Vanderbilt
Pwr +++
BAvg +++
Spd +
Def ++

Year	Lev	Team	AB	R	H	HR	RBI	Avg	OB	Slg	OPS	bb%	ct%	Eye	SB	CS	x/h%	Iso	RC/G
2013	A-	Tri City	270	36	78	4	35	289	375	385	760	12	84	0.86	2	2	22	96	5.16
2014	A	Quad Cities	161	26	48	1	28	298	402	410	812	15	79	0.82	0	0	31	112	6.07
2014	A+	Lancaster	180	43	66	12	45	367	449	678	1127	13	86	1.08	1	1	44	311	9.44
2014	AA	Corpus Christi	109	14	26	3	13	239	320	376	696	11	81	0.62	0	1	31	138	4.21
2015	AA	Corpus Christi	435	57	104	10	73	239	338	384	722	13	77	0.64	5	1	39	145	4.69

Lumbering slugger who had strong start, but faded down stretch. Draws lots of walks with ultra-patient approach and makes acceptable contact. Exhibits raw power, but focused more on line drives to gaps than HR. Can hit LHP, though mostly weak contact. Speed defense are well below average and he'll need to hit for more pop to stick at 1B.

Greiner,Grayson — 2 — Detroit
EXP MLB DEBUT: 2018 | H/W: 6-5 220 | FUT: Starting C | 8E

Bats R Age 23	Year	Lev	Team	AB	R	H	HR	RBI	Avg	OB	Slg	OPS	bb%	ct%	Eye	SB	CS	x/h%	Iso	RC/G
2014 (3) South Carolina	2012	NCAA	South Carolina	194	26	43	6	32	222	326	392	718	13	75	0.63	0	1	47	170	4.61
Pwr +++	2013	NCAA	South Carolina	205	32	61	4	38	298	371	424	796	10	86	0.86	5	4	26	127	5.52
BAvg ++	2014	NCAA	South Carolina	212	39	66	8	50	311	394	486	880	12	82	0.74	0	0	32	175	6.54
Spd +	2014	A	West Michigan	90	11	29	2	16	322	396	444	840	11	80	0.61	0	0	24	122	6.05
Def +++	2015	A+	Lakeland	312	24	57	3	21	183	248	250	498	8	71	0.30	0	0	26	67	1.37

Very tall backstop who struggled to hit for BA and may have been impacted by broken wrist at end of '14. Offers size and strength with raw power despite limited bat speed. Has chance to hit for above average pop, but needs to make better contact. Has good agility and is sound receiver, though slow release mutes plus arm.

Grullon,Deivi — 2 — Philadelphia
EXP MLB DEBUT: 2019 | H/W: 6-1 180 | FUT: Starting C | 7C

Bats R Age 20	Year	Lev	Team	AB	R	H	HR	RBI	Avg	OB	Slg	OPS	bb%	ct%	Eye	SB	CS	x/h%	Iso	RC/G
2012 FA (DR)	2013	Rk	GCL Phillies	121	13	33	1	14	273	328	364	692	8	85	0.56	0	0	27	91	4.15
Pwr ++	2014	A-	Williamsport	187	14	42	0	18	225	260	283	544	5	79	0.23	3	0	24	59	2.09
BAvg ++	2014	A	Lakewood	76	9	18	1	7	237	266	342	608	4	83	0.23	0	0	33	105	2.88
Spd +	2014	A+	Clearwater	10	0	2	0	1	200	200	200	400	0	90	0.00	0	0	0	0	0.52
Def ++++	2015	A	Lakewood	394	38	87	8	50	221	264	335	599	6	73	0.22	0	0	32	114	2.67

Defensive stalwart who shuts down the running game with premium arm and continues to improve blocking/receiving skills. Though hit tool and pitch recognition shaky, a strong upper body led to some HR power in 2015, which is encouraging. Still young for his level, has time for hitting to catch up to advanced defensive skills.

Guerra,Javier — 6 — San Diego
EXP MLB DEBUT: 2018 | H/W: 5-11 155 | FUT: Starting SS | 7B

Bats L Age 20	Year	Lev	Team	AB	R	H	HR	RBI	Avg	OB	Slg	OPS	bb%	ct%	Eye	SB	CS	x/h%	Iso	RC/G
2012 FA (PN)																				
Pwr ++																				
BAvg +++	2013	Rk	DSL Red Sox	210	27	52	0	23	248	350	290	640	14	81	0.83	7	4	17	43	3.78
Spd ++	2014	Rk	GCL Red Sox	201	21	54	2	26	269	286	408	694	2	79	0.12	1	5	37	139	3.89
Def ++++	2015	A	Greenville	434	64	121	15	68	279	325	449	775	6	74	0.27	7	9	34	171	5.01

Instinctual, quick SS who will likely compete for Gold Glove awards. Exhibits nimble, smooth actions at SS and has positioning and arm to be impact defender. Surprised with power output as he drives balls to all fields and can pull out of park. Can expand zone and lunge at breaking balls. Speed is fringy at best and has been caught stealing often.

Guerrero,Gabriel — 89 — Arizona
EXP MLB DEBUT: 2017 | H/W: 6-3 190 | FUT: Starting RF | 8E

Bats R Age 22	Year	Lev	Team	AB	R	H	HR	RBI	Avg	OB	Slg	OPS	bb%	ct%	Eye	SB	CS	x/h%	Iso	RC/G
2011 FA (DR)	2012	Rk	Azl Mariners	75	17	25	4	18	333	359	560	919	4	83	0.23	0	0	36	227	6.40
Pwr +++	2013	A	Clinton	469	60	127	4	50	271	302	358	660	4	76	0.19	12	3	24	87	3.47
BAvg ++	2014	A+	High Desert	538	97	165	18	96	307	348	467	814	6	76	0.26	18	6	29	160	5.46
Spd +++	2015	AA	Jackson	177	22	38	2	15	215	265	305	570	6	73	0.25	3	0	32	90	2.35
Def +++	2015	AA	Mobile	283	29	64	5	32	226	255	367	623	4	79	0.18	8	2	39	141	3.01

Acquired in trade with SEA mid-season, athletic OF has strong bloodlines (Vlad Guerrero is his uncle). From batting stance to lack of plate discipline, overall game is reminiscent of uncle. However, makes lots of weak contact on balls out of zone. Plus raw power has yet to translate to games.

Guerrero,Vladimir — 7 — Toronto
EXP MLB DEBUT: 2020 | H/W: 6-1 210 | FUT: Starting OF | 9E

Bats R Age 17	Year	Lev	Team	AB	R	H	HR	RBI	Avg	OB	Slg	OPS	bb%	ct%	Eye	SB	CS	x/h%	Iso	RC/G
2015 FA (DR)																				
Pwr ++++																				
BAvg ++																				
Spd ++																				
Def +	2015		*did not play in U.S.*																	

High-ceiling OF who could become offensive behemoth with strength and bat speed. Has hitting profile similar to his father. Can make contact any where ball is thrown. Expansion of strike zone could limit BA potential. Secondary skills are far behind bat. Has little athleticism and may eventually move to 1B due to poor arm. Won't steal many bases.

Guillorme,Luis — 6 — New York (N)
EXP MLB DEBUT: 2018 | H/W: 5-10 170 | FUT: Starting SS | 7C

Bats L Age 21	Year	Lev	Team	AB	R	H	HR	RBI	Avg	OB	Slg	OPS	bb%	ct%	Eye	SB	CS	x/h%	Iso	RC/G
2013 (10) HS (FL)																				
Pwr +	2013	Rk	GCL Mets	159	22	41	0	11	258	330	283	613	10	89	1.00	6	4	10	25	3.46
BAvg +++	2014	Rk	Kingsport	238	38	67	0	17	282	329	324	653	7	88	0.61	6	4	15	42	3.70
Spd +++	2014	A	Savannah	9	2	3	0	0	333	400	333	733	10	100		0	0	0	0	5.15
Def ++++	2015	A	Savannah	446	67	142	0	55	318	392	354	746	11	84	0.77	18	8	11	36	4.96

Glove-first SS with bat that made tremendous strides in '15. 2015 SAL MVP. Struggled with consistent hard contact before move to Single-A. All he did was hit, punching line drives to all fields. Lacks power and is maxed out physically. Average speed, but struggles out of box. Tremendous defender. Doesn't make mistakes. Plus makeup.

Gushue,Taylor — 2 — Pittsburgh
EXP MLB DEBUT: 2018 | H/W: 6-2 215 | FUT: Starting C | 6C

Bats B Age 22	Year	Lev	Team	AB	R	H	HR	RBI	Avg	OB	Slg	OPS	bb%	ct%	Eye	SB	CS	x/h%	Iso	RC/G
2014 (4) Florida	2012	NCAA	Florida	141	21	29	5	21	206	317	383	700	14	77	0.70	1	2	48	177	4.37
Pwr +++	2013	NCAA	Florida	216	27	58	5	33	269	336	417	753	9	81	0.54	3	3	34	148	4.89
BAvg ++	2014	NCAA	Florida	222	30	71	6	49	320	389	473	862	10	83	0.68	1	0	31	153	6.24
Spd ++	2014	A-	Jamestown	199	25	48	5	29	241	332	402	734	12	81	0.73	0	1	42	161	4.82
Def ++	2015	A	West Virginia	360	35	83	5	47	231	281	342	622	6	78	0.32	1	2	31	111	3.12

Strong, compact swing for this switch-hitter with above-average power. Struggled again on offense and now has a career slash line of .234/.305/.363 and his ability to hit for average is very much in doubt. Has made progress as he attempts to learn the position and has a strong arm, but if he can't stick he has limited fantasy appeal.

Guzman,Ronald — 3 — Texas
EXP MLB DEBUT: 2017 | H/W: 6-5 205 | FUT: Starting 1B | 7C

Bats L Age 21	Year	Lev	Team	AB	R	H	HR	RBI	Avg	OB	Slg	OPS	bb%	ct%	Eye	SB	CS	x/h%	Iso	RC/G
2011 FA (DR)	2012	Rk	Azl Rangers	212	29	68	1	33	321	377	434	811	8	80	0.45	7	1	28	113	5.66
Pwr +++	2013	A	Hickory	173	17	47	4	26	272	315	387	703	6	84	0.41	0	0	26	116	4.07
BAvg +++	2014	A	Hickory	445	46	97	6	63	218	278	330	608	8	76	0.35	6	3	39	112	2.98
Spd +	2015	A	Hickory	97	10	30	3	14	309	350	433	783	6	85	0.40	2	0	20	124	4.93
Def +++	2015	A+	High Desert	422	54	117	9	73	277	321	434	754	6	76	0.27	3	0	35	156	4.79

Tall INF who is turning tools into production. Spent two years in Low-A before emerging late in season in High-A. Free-swinging approach still evident, but can shorten stroke and make hard contact. More of a pure hitter than HR guy, though has bat speed and leverage to hit for pop. Foot speed well below average, but is dependable defender.

Hager,Jake — 46 — Tampa Bay
EXP MLB DEBUT: 2017 | H/W: 6-1 170 | FUT: Starting SS | 7D

Bats R Age 23	Year	Lev	Team	AB	R	H	HR	RBI	Avg	OB	Slg	OPS	bb%	ct%	Eye	SB	CS	x/h%	Iso	RC/G
2011 (1) HS (NV)	2012	A	Bowling Green	442	63	124	10	72	281	340	412	752	8	86	0.67	17	11	28	131	4.85
Pwr ++	2013	Rk	GCL Devil Rays	4	1	2	0	1	500	500	750	1250	0	100		0	0	50	250	9.68
BAvg +++	2013	A+	Charlotte	449	56	116	0	33	258	316	305	621	8	82	0.47	12	8	16	47	3.26
Spd +++	2014	AA	Montgomery	447	42	121	4	47	271	317	376	692	6	80	0.33	4	4	29	105	4.03
Def +++	2015		*Did not play—injured*																	

Tall, lean INF who missed season after knee surgery. Close to majors with impressive, all-around skill set. Keeps bat head in strike zone to make good contact. Controlled swing enhances BA and has hand-eye coordination. Not much power or strength in game, but can hit doubles to all fields. Has soft hands and range for either middle infield spot.

Haniger,Mitch — 789 — Arizona
EXP MLB DEBUT: 2017 | H/W: 6-2 215 | FUT: Platoon OF | 7C

Bats R Age 25	Year	Lev	Team	AB	R	H	HR	RBI	Avg	OB	Slg	OPS	bb%	ct%	Eye	SB	CS	x/h%	Iso	RC/G
2012 (1) Cal Poly	2014	Rk	Azl DBacks	15	4	3	1	4	200	250	467	717	6	60	0.17	0	0	67	267	4.66
Pwr +++	2014	AA	Huntsville	243	41	62	10	34	255	309	416	725	7	83	0.46	4	0	29	160	4.31
BAvg ++	2014	AA	Mobile	24	5	8	0	5	333	407	458	866	11	83	0.75	0	0	38	125	6.56
Spd ++	2015	A+	Visalia	202	40	67	12	36	332	384	619	1002	8	81	0.44	8	2	46	287	7.78
Def +++	2015	AA	Mobile	153	23	43	1	19	281	349	379	728	9	79	0.50	4	4	28	98	4.67

Split 2015 between two levels. Hit tool took off in High-A and came down to earth against age appropriate competition in Double-A. Hitch in swing slows bat considerably. Forced to be a guess hitter against FB. Has power to pull field to slug 10-15 HR at projection. Doesn't hurt self in OF with clean routes to balls.

Hanneman,Jacob — 8 — Chicago (N)
EXP MLB DEBUT: 2017 | H/W: 6-1 200 | FUT: Starting OF | 7D

Bats L Age 24	Year	Lev	Team	AB	R	H	HR	RBI	Avg	OB	Slg	OPS	bb%	ct%	Eye	SB	CS	x/h%	Iso	RC/G
2013 (3) Brigham Young	2013	A-	Boise	62	8	18	1	5	290	313	468	780	3	82	0.18	3	1	39	177	4.97
Pwr ++	2014	A	Kane County	342	57	87	6	39	254	316	377	694	8	77	0.40	32	4	29	123	4.10
BAvg ++	2014	A+	Daytona	145	17	35	2	12	241	295	345	640	7	77	0.32	5	3	31	103	3.34
Spd ++++	2015	A+	Myrtle Beach	61	12	20	0	4	328	388	393	782	9	75	0.40	7	1	20	66	5.36
Def ++	2015	AA	Tennessee	434	60	101	6	41	233	285	362	647	7	74	0.28	17	1	35	129	3.47

Quick, athletic CF started the season strong, hitting .328 at High-A, but scuffled when moved up to Double-A. Smooth LH stroke and good bat speed generates solid power, but can be overly aggressive and a 23% K rate has prevented him from reaching his potential. Runs well and swiped 24 bases in 26 attempts and should be able to stick in CF.

Hansen,Mitch | 7 | Los Angeles (N)

EXP MLB DEBUT: 2020 | H/W: 6-4 195 | FUT: Starting LF | 8E

Bats L Age 19
2015 (2) HS (TX)
Pwr ++++
BAvg ++
Spd +++
Def ++

Year	Lev	Team	AB	R	H	HR	RBI	Avg	OB	Slg	OPS	bb%	ct%	Eye	SB	CS	x/h%	Iso	RC/G
2015	Rk	Azl Dodgers	149	23	30	0	17	201	274	282	556	9	66	0.29	6	1	30	81	2.35

Two-sport star in HS remains raw on the diamond. Has good size and above-average raw power, but his swing can get long. Struggled in his pro debut, hitting just .201 with 51 K in 149 AB. Runs well and has the arm for CF, but needs to take better routes and a move to a corner spot seems likely. Lots of work to do yet.

Hanson,Alen | 4 | Pittsburgh

EXP MLB DEBUT: 2016 | H/W: 5-11 180 | FUT: Starting 2B | 8C

Bats B Age 23
2009 FA (DR)
Pwr ++
BAvg +++
Spd ++++
Def ++

Year	Lev	Team	AB	R	H	HR	RBI	Avg	OB	Slg	OPS	bb%	ct%	Eye	SB	CS	x/h%	Iso	RC/G
2012	A	West Virginia	489	99	151	16	62	309	379	528	906	10	79	0.52	35	19	41	219	6.93
2013	A+	Bradenton	367	51	103	7	48	281	340	444	784	8	81	0.47	24	14	37	163	5.29
2013	AA	Altoona	137	13	35	1	10	255	297	380	676	6	81	0.31	6	2	29	124	3.85
2014	AA	Altoona	482	64	135	11	58	280	324	442	765	6	82	0.35	25	11	33	162	4.89
2015	AAA	Indianapolis	475	66	125	6	43	263	316	387	704	7	81	0.41	35	12	28	124	4.23

Held his own in a full season at AAA. Has plus speed and a nice line-drive approach. Is aggressive at the plate and can put a charge into the ball, but makes enough contact that he should be able to hit for average and steal bases. Struggled in the field at SS, so the move to 2B was inevitable. Has good range and a strong arm.

Happ,Ian | 4 | Chicago (N)

EXP MLB DEBUT: 2017 | H/W: 6-0 205 | FUT: Starting 2B | 8B

Bats B Age 21
2015 (1) Cincinnati
Pwr +++
BAvg ++++
Spd ++
Def ++

Year	Lev	Team	AB	R	H	HR	RBI	Avg	OB	Slg	OPS	bb%	ct%	Eye	SB	CS	x/h%	Iso	RC/G
2015	NCAA	Cincinnati	198	47	73	14	44	369	494	672	1166	20	75	1.00	12	8	44	303	10.88
2015	A-	Eugene	106	26	30	4	11	283	411	491	901	18	74	0.82	9	0	43	208	7.36
2015	A	South Bend	145	24	35	5	22	241	321	448	769	10	73	0.44	1	1	49	207	5.23

Balanced approach at the plate, though could make better contact. Shows a good understanding of the strike zone and good bat speed, so power should develop as he moves up. Below average range prompted the Cubs to use him in the OF, but he was back at 2B in instructional ball. His future position will determine his long-term fantasy potential.

Harrison,Monte | 89 | Milwaukee

EXP MLB DEBUT: 2019 | H/W: 6-3 220 | FUT: Starting RF | 8E

Bats R Age 20
2014 (2) HS (MO)
Pwr +++
BAvg +++
Spd ++++
Def ++++

Year	Lev	Team	AB	R	H	HR	RBI	Avg	OB	Slg	OPS	bb%	ct%	Eye	SB	CS	x/h%	Iso	RC/G
2014	Rk	Azl Brewers	180	37	47	1	20	261	370	339	709	15	73	0.65	32	2	21	78	4.66
2015	Rk	Helena	97	20	29	3	13	299	387	474	862	13	76	0.61	14	2	31	175	6.49
2015	A	Wisconsin	162	18	24	2	11	148	216	247	463	8	52	0.18	6	4	42	99	0.91

Season-ending broken ankle isn't encouraging, but tools are still exciting. Premium athleticism, solid reads and strong arm make him a plus OF defender and future SB asset. Quick hands and decent contact, but struggled with approach in MWL stint. Power is below average at present, but should grow to an average tool. Patience needed, but could be worth the wait.

Harrison,Travis | 79 | Minnesota

EXP MLB DEBUT: 2016 | H/W: 6-1 215 | FUT: Starting 3B/LF | 7C

Bats R Age 23
2011 (1) HS (CA)
Pwr +++
BAvg ++
Spd +
Def ++

Year	Lev	Team	AB	R	H	HR	RBI	Avg	OB	Slg	OPS	bb%	ct%	Eye	SB	CS	x/h%	Iso	RC/G
2012	Rk	Elizabethton	219	39	66	5	27	301	370	461	832	10	77	0.47	3	0	32	160	5.99
2013	A	Cedar Rapids	450	66	114	15	59	253	351	416	767	13	72	0.54	2	4	38	162	5.27
2014	A+	Fort Myers	458	80	123	3	59	269	358	365	723	12	81	0.74	7	5	30	96	4.77
2015	AA	Chattanooga	396	64	95	5	54	240	347	356	703	14	74	0.64	3	9	34	116	4.54

Strong, muscular hitter whose power output has drastically fallen, but still possesses bat speed and plate patience. Power projection still evident, but shortens swing to make hard contact to gaps. Mostly bat only and can get on base with discerning eye. Moved from 3B to OF and reads and routes still quite crude.

Hart,Josh | 78 | Baltimore

EXP MLB DEBUT: 2017 | H/W: 6-1 180 | FUT: Starting CF | 8E

Bats L Age 21
2013 (1) HS (GA)
Pwr +
BAvg ++
Spd ++++
Def ++++

Year	Lev	Team	AB	R	H	HR	RBI	Avg	OB	Slg	OPS	bb%	ct%	Eye	SB	CS	x/h%	Iso	RC/G
2013	Rk	GCL Orioles	123	14	28	0	9	228	301	301	602	10	81	0.57	11	3	25	73	3.15
2013	A-	Aberdeen	10	0	1	0	0	100	182	100	282	9	60	0.25	0	0	0	0	-2.30
2014	Rk	GCL Orioles	24	2	4	0	0	167	200	250	450	4	92	0.50	2	0	25	83	1.55
2014	A	Delmarva	326	22	83	1	28	255	300	285	585	6	74	0.24	11	5	8	31	2.50
2015	A+	Frederick	424	43	108	1	28	255	274	311	585	3	81	0.14	30	15	18	57	2.48

Athletic, fast OF who hasn't lived up to lofty expectations, but shows flashes. Thrives with wheels and above average defense in OF. Has outstanding range and improved reads. Arm may not be good enough for CF. Only hit 2 HR in career and is mostly singles hitter at present. Owns gap power potential, but has zero patience at plate.

Hawkins,Courtney | 7 | Chicago (A)

EXP MLB DEBUT: 2016 | H/W: 6-3 220 | FUT: Starting OF | 8D

Bats R Age 22
2012 (1) HS (TX)
Pwr ++++
BAvg ++
Spd ++
Def ++

Year	Lev	Team	AB	R	H	HR	RBI	Avg	OB	Slg	OPS	bb%	ct%	Eye	SB	CS	x/h%	Iso	RC/G
2012	A	Kannapolis	65	11	20	4	15	308	348	631	979	6	74	0.24	3	2	55	323	7.74
2012	A+	Winston-Salem	17	3	5	1	2	294	294	588	882	0	88	0.00	0	1	60	294	5.74
2013	A+	Winston-Salem	383	48	68	19	62	178	235	384	619	7	58	0.18	10	5	56	206	3.22
2014	A+	Winston-Salem	449	65	112	19	84	249	329	450	779	11	68	0.37	11	3	43	200	5.42
2015	AA	Birmingham	300	39	73	9	41	243	291	410	701	6	67	0.20	1	4	41	167	4.24

Muscular OF whose season ended in July after foot injury. Saw HR output drop and he continued to struggle from poor pitch recognition, which limits his BA. Can crush mistakes to all fields and has as much raw pop as any in org, but athleticism has slowed. Was still young for level and has upside despite flaws.

Hayes,Ke'Bryan | 5 | Pittsburgh

EXP MLB DEBUT: 2019 | H/W: 6-1 210 | FUT: Starting 3B | 8D

Bats R Age 19
2015 (1) HS (TX)
Pwr +++
BAvg +++
Spd ++
Def +++

Year	Lev	Team	AB	R	H	HR	RBI	Avg	OB	Slg	OPS	bb%	ct%	Eye	SB	CS	x/h%	Iso	RC/G
2015	Rk	GCL Pirates	144	24	48	0	13	333	422	375	797	13	83	0.92	7	1	10	42	5.73
2015	A-	West Virginia	41	8	9	0	7	220	319	244	563	13	83	0.86	1	1	11	24	2.82

Son of former major leaguer Charlie Hayes, he has a strong frame and the bat speed for plus raw power, though he's yet to realize it as a pro. Patient approach at the plate and ability to barrel the ball give him a chance to hit and hit for power in the majors. Good feet and range at 3B with a strong arm.

Healy,Ryon | 35 | Oakland

EXP MLB DEBUT: 2016 | H/W: 6-5 225 | FUT: Starting 1B | 7C

Bats R Age 24
2013 (3) Oregon
Pwr +++
BAvg +++
Spd +
Def ++

Year	Lev	Team	AB	R	H	HR	RBI	Avg	OB	Slg	OPS	bb%	ct%	Eye	SB	CS	x/h%	Iso	RC/G
2013	NCAA	Oregon	228	44	76	11	56	333	406	566	972	11	89	1.17	5	3	41	232	7.49
2013	Rk	Azl Athletics	28	4	6	2	8	214	290	500	790	10	86	0.75	0	0	50	286	5.20
2013	A-	Vermont	146	12	34	4	21	233	243	384	627	1	84	0.08	2	1	41	151	2.93
2014	A+	Stockton	561	73	160	16	83	285	319	428	747	5	86	0.35	0	0	29	143	4.52
2015	AA	Midland	507	63	153	10	62	302	341	426	767	6	84	0.37	0	1	27	124	4.83

Contact-oriented hitter who uses short, compact stroke and natural strength to hit for average power. Uses whole field with slight loft in swing, but tends to be free swinger and pull happy at times. Lacks any semblance of foot speed which limits SB and range. Saw most of time at 3B, though fits better at 1B.

Heathcott,Slade | 789 | New York (A)

EXP MLB DEBUT: 2015 | H/W: 6-1 190 | FUT: Starting OF | 7D

Bats L Age 25
2009 (1) HS (TX)
Pwr ++
BAvg ++
Spd +++
Def ++++

Year	Lev	Team	AB	R	H	HR	RBI	Avg	OB	Slg	OPS	bb%	ct%	Eye	SB	CS	x/h%	Iso	RC/G
2013	AA	Trenton	399	59	104	8	49	261	322	411	733	8	73	0.34	15	8	36	150	4.67
2014	AA	Trenton	33	4	6	0	1	182	250	242	492	8	61	0.23	0	1	33	61	1.32
2015	A	Charleston (Sc)	9	0	2	0	0	222	222	222	444	0	100		0	0	0	0	1.56
2015	AAA	Scranton/WB	251	25	67	2	27	267	316	343	659	7	76	0.30	6	5	18	76	3.56
2015	MLB	NY Yankees	25	6	10	2	8	400	444	720	1164	7	80	0.40	0	1	40	320	9.65

Aggressive OF who can't stay healthy. Most AB in season is 399 ('13) and all-out style may be cause. Has good tools and performance when healthy. Is plus defender at all three OF spots with above average range and arm. Uses whole field in simple approach and has strength to hit for fringy pop. Breaking balls give him fits.

Heim,Jonah | 2 | Baltimore

EXP MLB DEBUT: 2018 | H/W: 6-3 189 | FUT: Starting C | 8E

Bats B Age 20
2013 (4) HS (NY)
Pwr ++
BAvg ++
Spd +
Def +++

Year	Lev	Team	AB	R	H	HR	RBI	Avg	OB	Slg	OPS	bb%	ct%	Eye	SB	CS	x/h%	Iso	RC/G
2013	Rk	GCL Orioles	81	8	15	0	4	185	275	247	522	11	84	0.77	1	1	33	62	2.33
2014	Rk	GCL Orioles	78	8	19	0	5	244	298	359	657	7	88	0.67	3	0	47	115	3.91
2014	A-	Aberdeen	70	2	10	1	2	143	167	214	381	3	79	0.13	0	0	30	71	-0.12
2015	Rk	GCL Orioles	6	2	2	0	2	333	429	500	929	14	100		0	0	50	167	7.68
2015	A	Delmarva	149	13	37	1	16	248	277	336	613	4	83	0.23	0	0	27	87	2.95

Tall, lean backstop who missed big chunk of season with foot injury. Long way away from reaching potential, but could be special. Has pretty swing from both sides and has bat speed to produce pop. Mostly gap power now, but should add more pop as he gains strength. Aggressive approach mutes OBP. Solid glove with strong arm and ideal footwork.

Heinrich, Jason — 7 — Baltimore
EXP MLB DEBUT: 2019 | H/W: 6-1 205 | FUT: Starting OF | 7D

Bats R | Age 19 | 2015 (5) HS (FL)

			Pwr	+++
BAvg	++
Spd	
Def	++

Year	Lev	Team	AB	R	H	HR	RBI	Avg	OB	Slg	OPS	bb%	ct%	Eye	SB	CS	x/h%	Iso	RC/G
2015	Rk	GCL Orioles	153	14	41	2	23	268	337	379	716	9	74	0.40	0	1	27	111	4.49

Powerful OF is all about bat and offensive production. Not gifted athletically and lack of range may move him to 1B eventually despite strong arm. Likes to swing bat and will fan, but acceptable trade off for average power. Mostly pop to the pull side, but can turn on any pitch. Needs to hit to have value, especially if he moves away from OF.

Hendrix, Jeff — 8 — New York (A)
EXP MLB DEBUT: 2018 | H/W: 5-11 195 | FUT: Starting OF | 7D

Bats L | Age 22 | 2015 (4) Oregon St

Pwr	++
BAvg	++
Spd	++++
Def	+++

Year	Lev	Team	AB	R	H	HR	RBI	Avg	OB	Slg	OPS	bb%	ct%	Eye	SB	CS	x/h%	Iso	RC/G
2015	NCAA	Oregon St	139	33	45	4	20	324	413	518	930	13	83	0.91	3	0	36	194	7.32
2015	A-	Stn Island	236	42	54	0	14	229	311	254	565	11	72	0.43	17	1	11	25	2.45

Speedy OF who plays game aggressively and can stick in CF long-term. Works counts and uses slashing stroke to make contact. Has trouble with breaking balls and can swing and miss. Lacks power despite strong frame and has experienced trouble with LHP (.177). Weak arm may move him to LF, but has instincts and range for CF.

Herbert, Lucas — 2 — Atlanta
EXP MLB DEBUT: 2019 | H/W: 6-1 200 | FUT: Starting C | 7C

Bats R | Age 19 | 2015 (2) HS (CA)

Pwr	++
BAvg	++
Spd	
Def	++++

Year	Lev	Team	AB	R	H	HR	RBI	Avg	OB	Slg	OPS	bb%	ct%	Eye	SB	CS	x/h%	Iso	RC/G
2015	Rk	GCL Braves	4	1	2	1	1	500	500	1250	1750	0	75	0.00	0	0	50	750	16.26

Tremendous defender. Blocks daylight with the best of them. Soft hands, advanced presentation skills and a plus throwing arm gives him chance to eventually be a Gold-Glove caliber performer. Simple approach with the bat. Quick wrists will aid in development as a hitter. Caught fellow prospect Kolby Allard in HS.

Heredia, Starling — 8 — Los Angeles (N)
EXP MLB DEBUT: 2021 | H/W: 6-0 215 | FUT: Starting CF | 9E

Bats R | Age 17 | 2015 FA (DR)

Pwr	++++
BAvg	+++
Spd	++
Def	+++

Year	Lev	Team	AB	R	H	HR	RBI	Avg	OB	Slg	OPS	bb%	ct%	Eye	SB	CS	x/h%	Iso	RC/G
2015		Did not play in U.S.																	

Physically mature Dominican OF signed with the Dodgers for $2.6 million. Plus athlete with good raw power and impressive bat speed. Crushes quality FB, but struggles with off-speed stuff. Above-average speed and a strong arm should allow him to stick in CF. Definitely a player to keep an eye on.

Hernandez, Brayan — 89 — Seattle
EXP MLB DEBUT: 2020 | H/W: 6-2 175 | FUT: Starting OF | 9E

Bats B | Age 18 | 2014 FA (VZ)

Pwr	++
BAvg	+++
Spd	+++
Def	+++

Year	Lev	Team	AB	R	H	HR	RBI	Avg	OB	Slg	OPS	bb%	ct%	Eye	SB	CS	x/h%	Iso	RC/G
2015	Rk	DSL Mariners	174	32	39	2	22	224	297	328	624	9	75	0.41	9	6	31	103	3.26

Gifted OF with very high upside who has yet to play in U.S. Shows polished bat for age and could grow into offensive behemoth. Has strong, quick bat to produce present gap power that could evolve into plus pop with strength. Has good eye at plate with average speed for SB and range. Arm is playable in CF or RF.

Hernandez, Elier — 9 — Kansas City
EXP MLB DEBUT: 2017 | H/W: 6-3 200 | FUT: Starting OF | 8D

Bats R | Age 21 | 2011 FA (DR)

Pwr	+++
BAvg	+++
Spd	+++
Def	++

Year	Lev	Team	AB	R	H	HR	RBI	Avg	OB	Slg	OPS	bb%	ct%	Eye	SB	CS	x/h%	Iso	RC/G
2012	Rk	Idaho Falls	250	30	52	0	34	208	250	280	530	5	74	0.21	2	0	27	72	1.86
2013	Rk	Idaho Falls	289	44	87	3	44	301	342	439	781	6	79	0.29	9	2	30	138	5.16
2014	A	Lexington	420	54	111	9	34	264	291	393	684	4	76	0.16	5	5	29	129	3.70
2015	A	Lexington	290	37	84	5	42	290	322	421	743	5	75	0.19	6	5	31	131	4.58
2015	A+	Wilmington	177	15	41	1	12	232	273	311	583	5	73	0.21	4	2	24	79	2.53

Improving prospect who was very good in Low-A but struggled after promotion in July. Still lacks selectivity, but swings hard and makes hard contact. Owns plus power potential, though aggressive approach hinders its use. Can be an average defender in RF with sufficient arm and range. Age works in his favor, but KC is expecting more pop.

Hernandez, Marco — 46 — Boston
EXP MLB DEBUT: 2016 | H/W: 6-0 170 | FUT: Utility player | 6B

Bats L | Age 23 | 2009 FA (DR)

Pwr	++
BAvg	+++
Spd	+++
Def	+++

Year	Lev	Team	AB	R	H	HR	RBI	Avg	OB	Slg	OPS	bb%	ct%	Eye	SB	CS	x/h%	Iso	RC/G
2012	A	Peoria	157	18	33	2	12	210	253	299	552	5	75	0.23	2	1	21	89	2.08
2013	A	Kane County	417	45	106	4	34	254	282	338	620	4	83	0.22	21	3	23	84	2.99
2014	A+	Daytona	441	61	119	3	45	270	316	351	668	6	80	0.33	22	8	19	82	3.70
2015	AA	Portland	282	30	92	5	31	326	347	482	829	3	83	0.18	4	2	33	156	5.48
2015	AAA	Pawtucket	181	27	49	4	22	271	302	409	710	4	78	0.21	1	0	31	138	4.07

Free-swinging INF who set highs in doubles and HR in solid season. Lacks plate patience to draw walks, but has quick, loose stroke to make sufficient contact. Mostly gap guy who uses speed to leg out xbh. More of a function of OBP than speed. Commits lazy errors and has the tools to play either 2B or SS. Has strong arm and range.

Hernandez, Teoscar — 89 — Houston
EXP MLB DEBUT: 2017 | H/W: 6-2 180 | FUT: Starting OF | 8E

Bats R | Age 23 | 2011 FA (DR)

Pwr	+++
BAvg	++
Spd	++++
Def	+++

Year	Lev	Team	AB	R	H	HR	RBI	Avg	OB	Slg	OPS	bb%	ct%	Eye	SB	CS	x/h%	Iso	RC/G
2012	A	Lexington	25	2	6	1	5	240	321	440	761	11	52	0.25	1	0	50	200	6.50
2013	A	Quad Cities	499	97	135	13	55	271	326	435	761	8	73	0.30	24	11	35	164	4.99
2014	A+	Lancaster	391	72	115	17	75	294	373	550	923	11	70	0.42	31	6	50	256	7.53
2014	AA	Corpus Christi	95	12	27	4	10	284	299	474	773	2	62	0.06	2	3	33	189	5.36
2015	AA	Corpus Christi	470	92	103	17	48	219	270	362	632	7	73	0.26	33	7	30	143	3.50

Athletic, toolsy OF who had production regression, though was better late in season. Has ideal power and speed for above average corner OF, but poor pitch recognition has led to ton of Ks (3rd in TL). Chases pitches out of zone and can be jammed inside. Raw power and plus speed could be cultivated and has the range and arm to play either CF or RF.

Herrera, Carlos — 6 — Colorado
EXP MLB DEBUT: 2019 | H/W: 6-0 155 | FUT: Starting SS | 7D

Bats L | Age 19 | 2013 FA (VZ)

Pwr	++
BAvg	+++
Spd	++++
Def	+++

Year	Lev	Team	AB	R	H	HR	RBI	Avg	OB	Slg	OPS	bb%	ct%	Eye	SB	CS	x/h%	Iso	RC/G
2014	Rk	DSL Rockies	139	18	32	0	11	230	287	281	567	7	82	0.44	6	4	22	50	2.59
2015	Rk	DSL Rockies	53	12	18	0	5	340	364	377	741	4	79	0.18	10	2	11	38	4.40
2015	A-	Boise	221	35	59	2	21	267	311	339	650	6	79	0.30	28	5	19	72	3.41

Has plus speed and good raw athleticism. Held his own in state-side debut in the NWL, hitting .267 with 28 SB. Should develop at least average power once he matures and has the range and arm to stick at short, but needs to work on his mechanics and footwork. Plus speed and ability to stick at SS give decent fantasy potential.

Herrera, Juan — 6 — St. Louis
EXP MLB DEBUT: 2018 | H/W: 5-11 165 | FUT: Utility player | 7D

Bats R | Age 22 | 2010 FA (DR)

Pwr	++
BAvg	+++
Spd	+++
Def	++++

Year	Lev	Team	AB	R	H	HR	RBI	Avg	OB	Slg	OPS	bb%	ct%	Eye	SB	CS	x/h%	Iso	RC/G
2013	A-	Mahoning Val	149	20	41	1	11	275	345	369	715	10	80	0.53	2	1	27	94	4.50
2013	A	Peoria	85	5	23	0	3	271	326	318	644	8	74	0.32	2	0	17	47	3.43
2014	A	Peoria	379	50	104	2	56	274	318	364	682	6	85	0.42	27	13	26	90	3.95
2014	A+	Palm Beach	31	3	6	0	0	194	219	194	412	3	84	0.20	1	0	0	0	0.51
2015	A+	Palm Beach	185	18	49	0	8	265	303	292	594	5	82	0.29	8	3	10	27	2.73

Quick, athletic SS. Has the tools to make all of the plays on D. Has good range, quick feet, soft hands, and a strong arm. Good approach at the plate and makes consistent contact, but is not likely to ever hit for much power. Has good speed and is a threat on the bases. Injury limited him to just 54 games and a likely repeat of the FSL in '16.

Herrera, Rosell — 7 — Colorado
EXP MLB DEBUT: 2017 | H/W: 6-3 195 | FUT: Starting LF | 8E

Bats B | Age 23 | 2009 FA (DR)

Pwr	+++
BAvg	+++
Spd	++
Def	+++

Year	Lev	Team	AB	R	H	HR	RBI	Avg	OB	Slg	OPS	bb%	ct%	Eye	SB	CS	x/h%	Iso	RC/G
2012	A-	Tri-City	194	30	55	1	30	284	332	351	682	7	82	0.41	7	3	16	67	3.92
2012	A	Asheville	213	22	43	1	26	202	274	272	546	9	77	0.43	6	3	26	70	2.25
2013	A	Asheville	472	83	162	16	76	343	418	515	933	11	80	0.64	21	8	30	172	7.23
2014	A+	Modesto	275	31	67	4	31	244	304	335	639	8	81	0.46	9	7	24	91	3.41
2015	A+	Modesto	466	55	121	4	36	260	314	354	668	7	79	0.38	9	8	25	94	3.77

Toolsy switch-hitter was pedestrian in 2nd stint in the CAL and moved from SS to OF. Has good size and above-avg power, but can be overly aggressive. Improved vs. LHP and was better in the 2nd half, but his development has stalled. Speed is not part of his game, but does have good instincts. Move to the OF hurts his long-term fantasy value.

Hicks,John — 2 — Minnesota

EXP MLB DEBUT: 2015 | H/W: 6-1 210 | FUT: Reserve C | **6B**

Bats R Age 26	Year	Lev	Team	AB	R	H	HR	RBI	Avg	OB	Slg	OPS	bb%	ct%	Eye	SB	CS	x/h%	Iso	RC/G
2011 (4) Virginia	2013	AA	Jackson	296	40	70	4	29	236	289	331	620	7	79	0.35	13	4	27	95	3.10
Pwr ++	2014	AA	Jackson	189	29	56	3	27	296	364	418	782	10	78	0.48	6	3	27	122	5.31
BAvg +++	2014	AAA	Tacoma	101	13	28	2	20	277	324	376	700	6	76	0.29	1	0	18	99	4.02
Spd ++	2015	AAA	Tacoma	298	39	73	6	35	245	286	362	648	5	76	0.24	9	2	30	117	3.33
Def +++	2015	MLB	Seattle	32	1	2	0	1	63	91	94	185	3	44	0.06	1	1	50	31	-4.53

Strong backstop who earned time in SEA, but lacks tools to project to starter. Has become solid backstop with good catch-and-throw skills. Blocks and receives while while footwork adequate for quick release. Hasn't realized power potential and lacks trigger to project. Chases pitches out of zone and is free swinger.

Hill,Derek — 8 — Detroit

EXP MLB DEBUT: 2018 | H/W: 6-2 195 | FUT: Starting CF | **8D**

Bats R Age 20	Year	Lev	Team	AB	R	H	HR	RBI	Avg	OB	Slg	OPS	bb%	ct%	Eye	SB	CS	x/h%	Iso	RC/G
2014 (1) HS (CA)																				
Pwr ++																				
BAvg +++	2014	Rk	GCL Tigers	99	12	21	2	11	212	322	333	655	14	81	0.84	9	1	29	121	3.91
Spd ++++	2014	A-	Connecticut	74	8	15	0	3	203	224	243	467	3	65	0.08	2	1	13	41	0.73
Def ++++	2015	A	West Michigan	210	33	50	0	16	238	304	314	619	9	79	0.45	25	7	22	76	3.27

Ultra athletic OF who saw limited action after May due to injuries. Presently, game revolves around plus speed and defense, where he has great CF range and an average arm. Plate approach is fringy, and power may never develop due to lack of loft in swing. But BA has potential due to quick stroke and ability to make contact.

Hinshaw,Chad — 8 — Los Angeles (A)

EXP MLB DEBUT: 2017 | H/W: 6-1 205 | FUT: Starting OF | **7D**

Bats R Age 25	Year	Lev	Team	AB	R	H	HR	RBI	Avg	OB	Slg	OPS	bb%	ct%	Eye	SB	CS	x/h%	Iso	RC/G
2013 (15) Illinois St	2013	Rk	Orem	89	24	23	0	8	258	353	281	634	13	76	0.62	9	1	9	22	3.53
Pwr ++	2014	A	Burlington	206	51	58	6	24	282	368	461	829	12	69	0.44	25	8	38	180	6.26
BAvg +++	2014	A+	Inland Empire	264	49	69	10	46	261	301	489	790	5	75	0.23	16	7	46	227	5.21
Spd ++++	2015	Rk	Azl Angels	26	7	8	0	4	308	438	462	899	19	77	1.00	3	0	38	154	7.59
Def ++	2015	AA	Arkansas	263	48	76	1	26	289	377	365	742	12	71	0.49	27	5	24	76	5.05

Under-the-radar OF who maximizes average tools with intellect and instincts. Best tool is plus speed which enhances OF play. Plays mostly CF with good arm and range. Steals bases consistently and makes enough contact to beat out grounders and leg out doubles. Power is below average and is at best when putting ball in play.

Hoelscher,Shane — 5 — Colorado

EXP MLB DEBUT: 2018 | H/W: 6-0 195 | FUT: Backup 3B/LF | **6B**

Bats R Age 24	Year	Lev	Team	AB	R	H	HR	RBI	Avg	OB	Slg	OPS	bb%	ct%	Eye	SB	CS	x/h%	Iso	RC/G
2014 (17) Rice	2013	NCAA	Rice	150	21	48	0	25	320	389	380	769	10	85	0.77	3	2	17	60	5.24
Pwr ++	2014	NCAA	Rice	227	43	75	0	27	330	380	423	802	7	85	0.55	0	2	28	93	5.49
BAvg +++	2014	A-	Tri-City	193	31	64	2	27	332	419	466	885	13	80	0.74	11	6	31	135	6.89
Spd ++	2015	A	Asheville	348	64	114	11	61	328	416	529	945	13	85	1.00	14	9	42	201	7.47
Def ++	2015	A+	Modesto	17	3	2	0	1	118	167	176	343	6	71	0.20	1	0	50	59	-0.78

Professional hitter with a good understanding of strike zone. Isn't likely to develop more than average power, though he did walk as many times as he K'd. Left quad injury cost him a month. Moves well at 3B with good hands and a strong arm. Has hit at every stop, but at 23 was old for this level.

Holder,Kyle — 6 — New York (A)

EXP MLB DEBUT: 2017 | H/W: 6-1 185 | FUT: Starting SS | **7C**

Bats L Age 21	Year	Lev	Team	AB	R	H	HR	RBI	Avg	OB	Slg	OPS	bb%	ct%	Eye	SB	CS	x/h%	Iso	RC/G
2015 (1) San Diego																				
Pwr +																				
BAvg ++																				
Spd +++	2015	NCAA	San Diego	224	45	78	4	31	348	399	482	881	8	92	1.00	5	6	26	134	6.36
Def +++++	2015	A-	Stn Island	225	23	48	0	12	213	269	253	522	7	85	0.50	6	2	17	40	2.12

Athletic, smooth INF who could stick in majors with glove alone. Quick actions, textbook footwork, and strong arm are best attributes and can make flashy and routine plays look easy. Bat production not nearly in same league. Focuses on line drives, but doesn't have strength or bat speed to be threat. Swing not conducive to power or BA.

Hoskins,Rhys — 3 — Philadelphia

EXP MLB DEBUT: 2018 | H/W: 6-4 225 | FUT: Starting 1B | **7C**

Bats R Age 23	Year	Lev	Team	AB	R	H	HR	RBI	Avg	OB	Slg	OPS	bb%	ct%	Eye	SB	CS	x/h%	Iso	RC/G
2014 (5) Sacramento St	2013	NCAA	Sacramento St	198	37	56	3	22	283	333	404	737	7	79	0.36	1	0	32	121	4.60
Pwr +++	2014	NCAA	Sacramento St	213	45	68	12	53	319	425	573	997	15	85	1.26	6	0	44	254	8.09
BAvg +++	2014	A-	Williamsport	245	30	58	9	40	237	297	408	705	8	78	0.39	3	3	41	171	4.13
Spd +	2015	A	Lakewood	255	39	82	9	51	322	384	525	910	9	80	0.52	2	4	37	204	6.82
Def ++	2015	A+	Clearwater	243	47	77	8	39	317	390	510	900	11	80	0.59	2	0	38	193	6.81

As RH college 1B, the bar is high, but rose to occasion in first full season. Long swing, great extension, but without normal huge holes. No noticeable platoon split, but speed not part of his game. Good agility around the bag on defense. Has surprised with hitting acumen so far, but upper-level arms will be the true test.

Hughston,Casey — 8 — Pittsburgh

EXP MLB DEBUT: 2020 | H/W: 6-2 200 | FUT: Starting CF | **7D**

Bats L Age 21	Year	Lev	Team	AB	R	H	HR	RBI	Avg	OB	Slg	OPS	bb%	ct%	Eye	SB	CS	x/h%	Iso	RC/G
2015 (3) Alabama																				
Pwr +++																				
BAvg ++																				
Spd +++	2015	NCAA	Alabama	235	39	78	6	44	332	389	502	891	9	77	0.40	12	2	31	170	6.68
Def +++	2015	A-	West Virginia	219	23	49	2	28	224	267	311	578	6	68	0.18	4	1	27	87	2.45

Collegiate OF from Alabama has solid tools across the board tools, but none that grade as plus. Speed and raw power give him interesting potential and he has the range and arm strength to stick in CF for now. Quick LH bat, but can be overly aggressive and pull-conscious and that was exploited in his debut and he whiffed 71 times in 219 AB.

Jackson,Alex — 79 — Seattle

EXP MLB DEBUT: 2018 | H/W: 6-2 215 | FUT: Starting OF | **9D**

Bats R Age 20	Year	Lev	Team	AB	R	H	HR	RBI	Avg	OB	Slg	OPS	bb%	ct%	Eye	SB	CS	x/h%	Iso	RC/G
2014 (1) HS (CA)																				
Pwr ++++																				
BAvg +++	2014	Rk	Azl Mariners	82	11	23	2	16	280	352	476	827	10	71	0.38	0	1	43	195	6.17
Spd ++	2015	A-	Everett	163	31	39	8	25	239	326	466	792	11	63	0.34	2	4	51	227	5.94
Def ++	2015	A	Clinton	108	10	17	0	13	157	202	213	415	5	68	0.17	1	1	35	56	0.11

Aggressive hitter who struggled in Low-A before demotion in June. Has significant power potential with clean swing and plus bat speed. Can hit for BA due to hand-eye coordination and ability to read spin. Controls bat well, but can expand strike zone. Moved to OF after draft and owns plus arm strength. Still working on reads and routes.

Jackson,Drew — 6 — Seattle

EXP MLB DEBUT: 2018 | H/W: 6-2 200 | FUT: Starting SS | **7C**

Bats R Age 22	Year	Lev	Team	AB	R	H	HR	RBI	Avg	OB	Slg	OPS	bb%	ct%	Eye	SB	CS	x/h%	Iso	RC/G
2015 (5) Stanford																				
Pwr +																				
BAvg +++																				
Spd +++	2015	NCAA	Stanford	147	27	47	0	9	320	383	388	770	9	85	0.68	6	2	17	68	5.21
Def +++	2015	A-	Everett	226	64	81	2	26	358	434	447	880	12	85	0.86	47	4	19	88	6.63

Tall, athletic SS who led NWL in BA. Focuses on working counts and finding pitches to drive to gaps. Has instincts and feel for contact and is tough out. Only has average speed, but reads pitchers well for SB. Power not part of game and needs to change swing and add loft for HR. Has cannon for arm, but makes errors due to fringy footwork.

Jackson,Jhalan — 9 — New York (A)

EXP MLB DEBUT: 2018 | H/W: 6-3 220 | FUT: Starting OF | **7D**

Bats R Age 23	Year	Lev	Team	AB	R	H	HR	RBI	Avg	OB	Slg	OPS	bb%	ct%	Eye	SB	CS	x/h%	Iso	RC/G
2015 (7) Florida Southern																				
Pwr +++																				
BAvg ++																				
Spd +++																				
Def +++	2015	A-	Stn Island	177	35	47	5	34	266	326	452	778	8	67	0.27	4	0	45	186	5.53

Athletic OF who has tools that could be cultivated to become sound player. Doesn't have any loud tools, but semblance of all. Has average power to all fields, though too much swing and miss to game. Can be exploited inside and will need to shorten stroke. Plus arm is highlight of RF defense and has average speed for range and SB.

Jagielo,Eric — 5 — Cincinnati

EXP MLB DEBUT: 2016 | H/W: 6-2 215 | FUT: Starting 3B | **8D**

Bats L Age 23	Year	Lev	Team	AB	R	H	HR	RBI	Avg	OB	Slg	OPS	bb%	ct%	Eye	SB	CS	x/h%	Iso	RC/G
2013 (1) Notre Dame	2013	Rk	GCL Yankees	2	1	0	0	0	0	0	0	0	0	100		0	0		0	-2.66
Pwr ++++	2013	A-	Stn Island	184	19	49	6	27	266	357	451	808	12	71	0.48	0	0	43	185	5.91
BAvg +++	2014	Rk	GCL Yankees	23	3	5	2	4	217	308	478	786	12	96	3.00	0	0	40	261	5.33
Spd +	2014	A+	Tampa	309	43	80	16	54	259	340	460	800	11	70	0.41	0	0	38	201	5.57
Def ++	2015	AA	Trenton	222	36	63	9	35	284	338	495	833	8	74	0.31	0	0	43	212	5.88

Smooth-swinging INF who ended season in June with knee injury. Has plus power at present thanks to natural strength and leveraged stroke. Swings and misses a lot, but can shorten swing and use entire field. Lacks foot speed and may not have quickness or agility for 3B. All about offense and will need to exhibit more plate patience.

Jankowski,Travis | 8 | **San Diego** | EXP MLB DEBUT: 2015 | H/W: 6-2 190 | FUT: Starting OF | **7B**

Bats L Age 24	Year	Lev	Team	AB	R	H	HR	RBI	Avg	OB	Slg	OPS	bb%	ct%	Eye	SB	CS	x/h%	Iso	RC/G
2012 (1) Stony Brook	2014	A+	Lake Elsinore	18	2	3	0	1	167	375	222	597	25	83	2.00	1	0	33	56	3.87
Pwr +	2014	AA	San Antonio	100	14	24	0	10	240	296	300	596	7	86	0.57	10	2	21	60	3.08
BAvg + + +	2015	AA	San Antonio	282	50	89	1	13	316	393	401	794	11	86	0.90	23	8	19	85	5.62
Spd + + + +	2015	AAA	El Paso	97	19	38	0	12	392	464	495	958	12	90	1.30	9	3	21	103	7.62
Def + + + +	2015	MLB	San Diego	90	9	19	2	12	211	245	344	589	4	73	0.17	2	1	32	133	2.51

Smart OF who gets on base and uses plus wheels to advantage. Offers little power, but hit 2 HR in 90 AB in SD (only 3 career HR in minors). Game revolves around speed and plus-plus contact. Rarely swings and misses due to simple, level stroke. Can be impact CF with advanced routes and jumps, though arm strength is fringe average at best.

Jansen,Dan | 2 | **Toronto** | EXP MLB DEBUT: 2018 | H/W: 6-2 230 | FUT: Starting C | **7D**

Bats R Age 20	Year	Lev	Team	AB	R	H	HR	RBI	Avg	OB	Slg	OPS	bb%	ct%	Eye	SB	CS	x/h%	Iso	RC/G
2013 (16) HS (WI)																				
Pwr + + +	2013	Rk	GCL Blue Jays	114	19	28	0	18	246	363	281	644	16	91	2.10	0	0	14	35	4.28
BAvg + +	2014	Rk	Bluefield	124	22	35	5	17	282	364	484	848	11	86	0.94	2	1	43	202	6.12
Spd + +	2015	Rk	GCL Blue Jays	21	4	5	1	3	238	304	429	733	9	76	0.40	0	0	40	190	4.46
Def + +	2015	A	Lansing	160	19	33	4	27	206	291	331	622	11	86	0.86	2	0	36	125	3.45

Physical backstop who missed time again with injuries. Has raw skills to be dependable receiver, but can't stay healthy. Frames pitches well and has catch-and-throw skills. Needs repetitions to improve. Knows strike zone as hitter and puts bat to ball with ease. Power mostly to pull side and has bat speed to generate more pop.

Jenkins,Eric | 8 | **Texas** | EXP MLB DEBUT: 2020 | H/W: 6-1 170 | FUT: Starting OF | **8E**

Bats L Age 19	Year	Lev	Team	AB	R	H	HR	RBI	Avg	OB	Slg	OPS	bb%	ct%	Eye	SB	CS	x/h%	Iso	RC/G
2015 (2) HS (NC)																				
Pwr +																				
BAvg + +																				
Spd + + + +	2015	Rk	Azl Rangers	177	35	44	0	13	249	335	339	674	12	68	0.40	27	3	23	90	4.18
Def + + +	2015	A	Hickory	18	3	7	0	1	389	421	444	865	5	78	0.25	1	0	14	56	6.12

Athletic, lean OF who profiles as leadoff hitter with on base skills and plus speed. Recognizes pitches and can drive ball to gaps with barrel control. Too much swing and miss to game at present and lacks strength for HR. Raw approach needs to be cleaned up, though plus speed allows him to beat out infield grounders. Patrols CF with plus range.

Jhang,Jin-De | 2 | **Pittsburgh** | EXP MLB DEBUT: 2018 | H/W: 5-11 220 | FUT: Starting C | **7C**

Bats L Age 22	Year	Lev	Team	AB	R	H	HR	RBI	Avg	OB	Slg	OPS	bb%	ct%	Eye	SB	CS	x/h%	Iso	RC/G
2011 FA (TW)																				
Pwr + +	2012	Rk	GCL Pirates	128	12	39	1	23	305	373	398	772	10	88	0.88	1	1	21	94	5.26
BAvg + +	2013	A-	Jamestown	184	22	51	5	34	277	338	413	751	8	87	0.71	0	1	27	136	4.83
Spd + +	2014	A+	Bradenton	269	29	59	2	35	219	261	301	562	5	87	0.42	3	0	27	82	2.55
Def + + +	2015	A+	Bradenton	370	45	108	5	41	292	332	381	713	6	88	0.51	2	4	20	89	4.27

Short, stocky Taiwanese backstop rebounded in a repeat of the FSL. Has a nice line-drive approach and double-digit HR potential. Despite his stocky frame, he moves well behind the plate with a plus arm and quick release. Frames the ball well and should stick at catcher.

Jimenez,Eloy | 9 | **Chicago (N)** | EXP MLB DEBUT: 2018 | H/W: 6-4 205 | FUT: Starting RF | **9D**

Bats R Age 19	Year	Lev	Team	AB	R	H	HR	RBI	Avg	OB	Slg	OPS	bb%	ct%	Eye	SB	CS	x/h%	Iso	RC/G
2013 FA (DR)																				
Pwr + + + +																				
BAvg + +																				
Spd + + +	2014	Rk	Azl Cubs	150	13	34	3	27	227	275	367	642	6	79	0.31	3	1	38	140	3.35
Def + + +	2015	A-	Eugene	232	36	66	7	33	284	328	418	746	6	81	0.35	3	2	26	134	4.53

Talented OF justified his $2.8 million bonus, and was one of the most dynamic players in the NWL. Lean and projectable with plus raw power, he makes consistent contact with plus bat speed and hunts for pitches he can drive. Proved willing to use the entire field. Can still be beaten on breaking balls down and away and hard stuff inside.

Jimenez,Emerson | 6 | **Colorado** | EXP MLB DEBUT: 2018 | H/W: 6-1 160 | FUT: Starting SS | **7E**

Bats L Age 21	Year	Lev	Team	AB	R	H	HR	RBI	Avg	OB	Slg	OPS	bb%	ct%	Eye	SB	CS	x/h%	Iso	RC/G
2011 FA (DR)	2013	Rk	DSL Rockies	36	3	8	0	4	222	243	250	493	3	89	0.25	1	2	13	28	1.69
Pwr + +	2013	Rk	Grand Junction	181	32	56	3	20	309	342	414	756	5	77	0.21	6	3	21	105	4.67
BAvg + + +	2014	A	Asheville	266	36	69	1	28	259	273	342	615	2	78	0.09	16	7	23	83	2.81
Spd + + + +	2015	A	Asheville	232	33	43	1	17	185	203	254	457	2	78	0.10	16	5	30	69	0.83
Def + + + +	2015	A+	Modesto	153	18	33	1	12	216	231	307	538	2	67	0.06	1	3	30	92	1.79

Slick fielding SS struggled offensively in repeat of Low-A. Has good bat speed and the potential to develop avg power, but needs a better understanding of the strike zone. Plus speed gives him SB potential and range at short. Makes all the plays on defense and glove is his standout tool. He gets a do-over due to age, but his slash line was ugly.

Joe,Connor | 3 | **Pittsburgh** | EXP MLB DEBUT: 2018 | H/W: 6-0 205 | FUT: Starting 1B | **7D**

Bats R Age 23	Year	Lev	Team	AB	R	H	HR	RBI	Avg	OB	Slg	OPS	bb%	ct%	Eye	SB	CS	x/h%	Iso	RC/G
2014 (1) San Diego																				
Pwr + +																				
BAvg + +																				
Spd + + +																				
Def + +	2015	A	West Virginia	290	38	71	1	20	245	356	303	659	15	88	1.47	0	4	20	59	4.29

Short, strong 1B finally made his pro debut after a back injury kept him out of action after '14 draft. Was a collegiate catcher, but played 1B as pro. Has avg speed, good glove and a strong arm. Quick bat with solid plate discipline and gap power, but looked rusty after a long layoff.

Johnson,Micah | 4 | **Los Angeles (N)** | EXP MLB DEBUT: 2015 | H/W: 6-0 210 | FUT: Starting 2B | **7C**

Bats L Age 25	Year	Lev	Team	AB	R	H	HR	RBI	Avg	OB	Slg	OPS	bb%	ct%	Eye	SB	CS	x/h%	Iso	RC/G
2012 (9) Indiana	2014	AA	Birmingham	146	18	48	3	16	329	413	466	879	13	82	0.78	10	7	27	137	6.66
Pwr + +	2014	AAA	Charlotte	273	30	75	2	28	275	315	370	685	6	85	0.38	12	6	23	95	3.94
BAvg + + +	2015	Rk	Azl White Sox	15	4	5	0	0	333	412	467	878	12	87	1.00	0	0	40	133	6.75
Spd + + + +	2015	AAA	Charlotte	311	54	98	8	36	315	379	466	845	9	80	0.51	28	7	29	151	6.03
Def + +	2015	MLB	Chi White Sox	100	10	23	0	4	230	294	270	564	8	70	0.30	3	2	17	40	2.34

Opening Day 2B, but was demoted in May due to inconsistent glovework. Exhibits plus athleticism and quickness, but poor hands and footwork lead to a below average defender. Set career high in HR, but game is about getting on base and using plus speed. Has strength and bat speed and makes acceptable contact.

Jones,JaCoby | 6 | **Detroit** | EXP MLB DEBUT: 2016 | H/W: 6-2 205 | FUT: Starting SS/OF | **7C**

Bats R Age 23	Year	Lev	Team	AB	R	H	HR	RBI	Avg	OB	Slg	OPS	bb%	ct%	Eye	SB	CS	x/h%	Iso	RC/G
2013 (3) Louisiana St	2013	A-	Jamestown	61	14	19	1	10	311	344	459	803	5	77	0.21	3	2	26	148	5.34
Pwr + + +	2014	A	West Virginia	445	72	128	23	70	288	337	503	840	7	70	0.25	17	9	37	216	5.98
BAvg + +	2015	A+	Bradenton	379	48	96	10	58	253	310	396	706	8	70	0.27	14	4	32	142	4.24
Spd + + + +	2015	AA	Altoona	10	2	5	0	2	500	545	500	1045	9	100		1	0	0	0	8.18
Def + +	2015	AA	Erie	136	26	34	6	20	250	333	463	797	11	62	0.33	10	3	44	213	6.09

Versatile prospect who will sit for 50 games due to drug suspension. Has all-or-nothing approach, but drives ball consistently and has all-fields pop. Exhibits plus speed on base and set high in SB. Has 20/20 potential, but BA could be issue. Strikes out often and has trouble reading spin. May end up in OF or 2B, but has range for any spot.

Jones,Jahmai | 8 | **Los Angeles (A)** | EXP MLB DEBUT: 2020 | H/W: 5-11 210 | FUT: Starting OF | **8E**

Bats R Age 18	Year	Lev	Team	AB	R	H	HR	RBI	Avg	OB	Slg	OPS	bb%	ct%	Eye	SB	CS	x/h%	Iso	RC/G
2015 (2) HS (GA)																				
Pwr + +																				
BAvg + +																				
Spd + + +																				
Def + + +	2015	Rk	Azl Angels	160	28	39	2	20	244	316	344	660	10	79	0.52	16	7	26	100	3.77

Athletic OF who has some upside, but will need lot of development time. Has quick bat to make hard contact to gaps and uses speed to leg out doubles and steal bases. Power potential predicated upon whether he can add loft to level stroke. Has bat speed to catch up to FB, though struggles with breaking balls. Patrols CF well, but may move to corner.

Jones,Ryder | 5 | **San Francisco** | EXP MLB DEBUT: 2018 | H/W: 6-3 215 | FUT: Backup IF | **7D**

Bats L Age 21	Year	Lev	Team	AB	R	H	HR	RBI	Avg	OB	Slg	OPS	bb%	ct%	Eye	SB	CS	x/h%	Iso	RC/G
2013 (2) HS (NC)																				
Pwr + + +	2013	Rk	Azl Giants	145	29	46	1	18	317	377	400	777	9	74	0.37	0	0	22	83	5.29
BAvg + +	2014	A-	Salem-Kaizer	107	17	26	3	18	243	289	393	682	6	80	0.33	1	0	35	150	3.80
Spd +	2014	A	Augusta	369	43	81	7	49	220	256	339	595	5	75	0.19	6	1	36	119	2.61
Def + + +	2015	A+	San Jose	406	49	109	6	47	268	296	394	690	4	80	0.20	2	2	34	126	3.84

Tall, strong IF has struggled since nice '13 system debut. Has leverage and natural loft in swing to hit for power, but poor contact skills and approach paint ugly picture for future BA/Eye. Has a good enough arm to make tough throws at 3B, but range limited by poor athleticism. If contact woes aren't rectified, future limited to a utility IF bat.

Judge,Aaron — 9 — New York (A)

EXP MLB DEBUT: 2016 | H/W: 6-7 265 | FUT: Starting RF | 8B

Bats R Age 23	Year	Lev	Team	AB	R	H	HR	RBI	Avg	OB	Slg	OPS	bb%	ct%	Eye	SB	CS	x/h%	Iso	RC/G
2013 (1) Fresno St	2013	NCAA	Fresno St	206	45	76	12	36	369	461	655	1116	15	74	0.66	12	2	41	286	10.04
Pwr ++++	2014	A	Charleston (Sc)	234	36	78	9	45	333	429	530	958	14	75	0.66	1	0	33	197	7.90
BAvg ++	2014	A+	Tampa	233	44	66	8	33	283	410	442	852	18	69	0.69	0	0	29	159	6.77
Spd +++	2015	AA	Trenton	250	36	71	12	44	284	347	516	863	9	72	0.34	1	0	44	232	6.38
Def +++	2015	AAA	Scranton/WB	228	27	51	8	28	224	311	373	684	11	68	0.39	6	2	35	149	4.05

Huge-framed OF who fits mold of ideal RF with plus-plus power and plus arm strength. Set career high in HR and more to come. Has advanced approach and shows sound hitting skills by going other way and shortening stroke with 2 strikes. Has long arms that lead to holes in swing. Struggled in AAA, but nearly big league ready.

Kelly,Carson — 2 — St. Louis

EXP MLB DEBUT: 2017 | H/W: 6-2 200 | FUT: Reserve C | 6C

Bats R Age 21	Year	Lev	Team	AB	R	H	HR	RBI	Avg	OB	Slg	OPS	bb%	ct%	Eye	SB	CS	x/h%	Iso	RC/G
2012 (2) HS (OR)	2012	Rk	Johnson City	213	24	48	9	25	225	260	399	659	4	85	0.30	0	0	40	174	3.42
Pwr +++	2013	A-	State College	271	35	75	4	32	277	326	387	714	7	89	0.65	1	0	28	111	4.40
BAvg ++	2013	A	Peoria	146	18	32	2	13	219	283	301	584	8	83	0.52	0	0	25	82	2.80
Spd ++	2014	A	Peoria	363	41	90	6	49	248	318	366	684	9	85	0.69	1	0	30	118	4.13
Def ++	2015	A+	Palm Beach	389	30	85	8	51	219	260	332	592	5	84	0.34	0	0	32	113	2.74

Converted backstop made impressive strides behind the plate. Moves well and calls a good game. Won the minor league Gold Glove at C. Offensive game has regressed and has failed to hit a pro. Does have good raw power, but it hasn't shown up in game action. Makes consistent contact, but lacks an advanced feel for hitting.

Kemp,Tony — 478 — Houston

EXP MLB DEBUT: 2016 | H/W: 5-6 160 | FUT: Utility player | 6A

Bats L Age 24	Year	Lev	Team	AB	R	H	HR	RBI	Avg	OB	Slg	OPS	bb%	ct%	Eye	SB	CS	x/h%	Iso	RC/G
2013 (5) Vanderbilt	2013	A	Quad Cities	98	21	25	1	9	255	376	316	692	16	82	1.06	4	2	12	61	4.53
Pwr +	2014	A+	Lancaster	295	79	99	4	37	336	424	468	891	13	88	1.29	28	7	27	132	6.89
BAvg +++	2014	AA	Corpus Christi	233	42	68	4	21	292	368	425	793	11	86	0.88	13	6	28	133	5.53
Spd ++++	2015	AA	Corpus Christi	193	36	69	0	19	358	456	420	876	15	85	1.25	15	8	16	62	6.87
Def ++	2015	AAA	Fresno	271	42	74	3	29	273	325	362	687	7	86	0.57	20	6	20	89	4.06

Short prospect who continues to produce despite slight frame and lack of pop. Played mostly 2B and also saw action in OF. Hits consistent line drives to gaps and has approach that leads to walks and extreme contact. Uses above average speed to steal bases. Not a strong defender, but versatility and quickness are assets.

Kepler,Max — 378 — Minnesota

EXP MLB DEBUT: 2015 | H/W: 6-4 215 | FUT: Starting OF | 8C

Bats L Age 23	Year	Lev	Team	AB	R	H	HR	RBI	Avg	OB	Slg	OPS	bb%	ct%	Eye	SB	CS	x/h%	Iso	RC/G
2010 FA (GE)	2013	A	Cedar Rapids	236	35	56	9	40	237	308	424	731	9	82	0.56	2	0	41	186	4.57
Pwr +++	2014	A+	Fort Myers	364	53	96	5	59	264	327	393	719	9	83	0.55	6	2	32	129	4.52
BAvg ++++	2015	A+	Fort Myers	24	4	6	0	0	250	308	333	641	8	79	0.40	1	0	33	83	3.51
Spd +++	2015	AA	Chattanooga	407	76	131	9	71	322	418	531	948	14	85	1.06	18	4	41	209	7.67
Def +++	2015	MLB	Minnesota	7	0	1	0	0	143	143	143	286	0	57	0.00	0	0	0	0	-2.36

Emerging, consistent prospect who combines mature approach with ideal contact skills to be offensive threat. Added more strength and started to hit for more power while keeping keen eye at plate. Uses all fields with smooth swing and can hit LHP. Plays all OF positions with average arm and ranges well.

Kingery,Scott — 4 — Philadelphia

EXP MLB DEBUT: 2018 | H/W: 5-10 180 | FUT: Starting 2B | 8C

Bats R Age 21	Year	Lev	Team	AB	R	H	HR	RBI	Avg	OB	Slg	OPS	bb%	ct%	Eye	SB	CS	x/h%	Iso	RC/G
2015 (2) Arizona																				
Pwr ++																				
BAvg +++																				
Spd ++++	2015	NCAA	Arizona	237	53	93	5	36	392	415	561	976	4	92	0.50	11	6	27	169	7.06
Def +++	2015	A	Lakewood	252	43	63	3	21	250	300	337	637	7	83	0.42	11	1	22	87	3.37

Pure hitter that ranked near top of NCAA BA leaderboards in 2015. Lightning wrists can square up velocity; can also recognize spin. Short stroke produces hard line drives, and has enough speed to play the top of the lineup. Slight build, but good instincts and range at 2B; enough athleticism to move to OF if necessary.

Kivlehan,Patrick — 357 — Texas

EXP MLB DEBUT: 2016 | H/W: 6-2 210 | FUT: Starting 3B | 7B

Bats R Age 26	Year	Lev	Team	AB	R	H	HR	RBI	Avg	OB	Slg	OPS	bb%	ct%	Eye	SB	CS	x/h%	Iso	RC/G
2012 (4) Rutgers	2013	A	Clinton	223	26	63	3	31	283	333	386	719	7	81	0.40	5	3	25	103	4.36
Pwr +++	2014	A+	High Desert	266	48	85	13	59	320	380	530	910	9	76	0.40	10	3	33	211	6.83
BAvg +++	2014	A+	High Desert	142	24	40	9	35	282	338	563	901	8	77	0.38	2	0	50	282	6.58
Spd +++	2014	AA	Jackson	377	60	113	11	68	300	373	485	858	10	79	0.56	9	4	36	186	6.30
Def ++	2015	AAA	Tacoma	472	58	121	22	73	256	309	453	762	7	76	0.32	14	3	40	197	4.79

Versatile, athletic prospect who set high in HR and continues to show BA potential with compact stroke. K rate increased and walk rate declined, but has bat speed and barrel control to be acceptable. Uses average speed well and will need to find defensive home. Played all OF positions and INF corners.

Knapp,Andrew — 2 — Philadelphia

EXP MLB DEBUT: 2016 | H/W: 6-1 190 | FUT: Starting C | 7B

Bats B Age 24	Year	Lev	Team	AB	R	H	HR	RBI	Avg	OB	Slg	OPS	bb%	ct%	Eye	SB	CS	x/h%	Iso	RC/G
2013 (2) California	2013	A-	Vermont	217	30	55	4	23	253	322	401	723	9	74	0.39	7	5	44	147	4.59
Pwr ++	2014	A	Lakewood	283	39	82	5	25	290	352	438	790	9	75	0.38	3	3	34	148	5.44
BAvg +++	2014	A+	Clearwater	83	7	13	1	7	157	205	205	409	6	69	0.19	1	0	15	48	-0.08
Spd +	2015	A+	Clearwater	244	38	64	2	28	262	341	369	710	11	74	0.46	0	1	30	107	4.50
Def ++	2015	AA	Reading	214	39	77	11	56	360	419	631	1050	9	80	0.51	1	0	44	271	8.56

An unconscious Aug (8 HR, 1.227 OPS) skewed final results, but grades as slightly above average in both hit and power. Uses whole field w/ short LH stroke, often sending balls to the gaps. As RHH, loses some punch; can become impatient and chase. Defense still a question mark; has improved with glove, but arm still suspect.

Krause,Kevin — 2 — Pittsburgh

EXP MLB DEBUT: 2019 | H/W: 6-2 190 | FUT: Starting C | 7D

Bats R Age 23	Year	Lev	Team	AB	R	H	HR	RBI	Avg	OB	Slg	OPS	bb%	ct%	Eye	SB	CS	x/h%	Iso	RC/G
2014 (9) Stony Brook	2012	NCAA	Stony Brook	209	38	69	3	40	330	404	431	835	11	85	0.84	6	2	22	100	6.01
Pwr +++	2013	NCAA	Stony Brook	71	4	15	0	6	211	317	268	585	13	75	0.61	0	0	27	56	2.93
BAvg ++	2014	NCAA	Stony Brook	198	46	70	8	51	354	429	551	979	12	86	0.93	8	3	33	197	7.66
Spd +++	2014	A-	Jamestown	134	22	37	7	32	276	353	560	913	11	79	0.57	6	2	54	284	6.96
Def ++	2015			*Did not play; injured*																

Injured his elbow in spring training and had TJS in June. In '14 showed a mature approach at the plate with above-average power, good plate discipline, and the ability to make consistent contact. Moves well behind the plate with good hands, but even before the surgery he struggled getting basestealers out. Will need to reboot in 2016.

Krieger,Tyler — 4 — Cleveland

EXP MLB DEBUT: 2018 | H/W: 6-0 155 | FUT: Starting 2B | 7C

Bats S Age 22	Year	Lev	Team	AB	R	H	HR	RBI	Avg	OB	Slg	OPS	bb%	ct%	Eye	SB	CS	x/h%	Iso	RC/G
2015 (4) Clemson																				
Pwr +																				
BAvg +++																				
Spd +++																				
Def ++	2015			*Did not play; injured*																

Quick and athletic INF who did not play upon signing due to shoulder injury. Focuses on hard line drives to gaps with bat speed and short stroke. Knows strike zone and has ability to hit for BA from both sides. Needs to add strength to produce HR. Owns average speed and exhibits sound instincts. Arm limits defensive upside, but is sufficient at 2B.

Kubitza,Kyle — 457 — Los Angeles (A)

EXP MLB DEBUT: 2015 | H/W: 6-3 210 | FUT: Starting 2B/3B | 7C

Bats L Age 25	Year	Lev	Team	AB	R	H	HR	RBI	Avg	OB	Slg	OPS	bb%	ct%	Eye	SB	CS	x/h%	Iso	RC/G
2011 (3) Texas St	2012	A	Rome	448	68	107	9	59	239	345	393	738	14	72	0.57	18	11	39	154	5.03
Pwr +++	2013	A+	Lynchburg	435	75	113	12	57	260	375	434	809	16	70	0.61	8	16	41	175	6.12
BAvg +++	2014	AA	Mississippi	440	76	130	8	55	295	400	470	871	15	70	0.58	21	6	38	175	7.10
Spd ++	2015	AAA	Salt Lake	457	63	124	7	50	271	356	433	789	12	73	0.48	7	1	44	162	5.69
Def +++	2015	MLB	LA Angels	36	6	7	0	1	194	256	194	451	8	58	0.20	0	0	0	0	0.48

Polished INF who was getting work at 2B in instructionals. Has balanced approach at plate and will hit ton of doubles thanks to level swing path and quick wrists. Draws walks with mature eye and can drive ball to gaps. Can be too patient at plate and get behind in counts, resulting in Ks. Soft hands and strong arm suitable for any INF spot.

Lambo,Andrew — 379 — Oakland

EXP MLB DEBUT: 2013 | H/W: 6-3 215 | FUT: Reserve 1B/OF | 6B

Bats L Age 27	Year	Lev	Team	AB	R	H	HR	RBI	Avg	OB	Slg	OPS	bb%	ct%	Eye	SB	CS	x/h%	Iso	RC/G
2007 (4) HS (CA)	2013	MLB	Pittsburgh	30	4	7	1	2	233	303	400	703	9	63	0.27	0	1	43	167	4.47
Pwr +++	2014	A-	Jamestown	12	2	2	0	1	167	375	167	542	25	83	2.00	0	0	0	0	3.11
BAvg +++	2014	AAA	Indianapolis	238	44	78	11	42	328	385	563	948	8	80	0.47	3	2	41	235	7.20
Spd +	2014	MLB	Pittsburgh	39	3	10	0	1	256	256	359	615	0	79	0.00	0	0	40	103	2.80
Def ++	2015	MLB	Pittsburgh	25	1	1	0	0	40	111	80	191	7	68	0.25	0	0	100	40	-3.10

Big, strong prospect who missed most of season with foot injury. Has chance to provide offensive muscle with good pop, but struggles with pitch recognition and inconsistent approach. Has appeared in majors in each of past three seasons and awaiting opportunity. Secondary skills are lagging as he is poor runner and lacks range at 1B and OF corners.

Lara,Gilbert

56 | **Milwaukee** | **EXP MLB DEBUT:** 2019 | **H/W:** 6-2 190 | **FUT:** Starting 3B | **8E**

Bats R Age 18
2014 FA (DR)

- Pwr ++++
- BAvg ++
- Spd +++
- Def +++

Year	Lev	Team	AB	R	H	HR	RBI	Avg	OB	Slg	OPS	bb%	ct%	Eye	SB	CS	x/h%	Iso	RC/G
2015	Rk	Azl Brewers	202	29	50	1	25	248	280	332	611	4	80	0.22	3	3	20	84	2.91
2015	Rk	Helena	44	2	9	0	5	205	286	273	558	10	73	0.42	0	0	33	68	2.43

Raw, but has plus bat speed and leverage for impact power at next level. Swing will need fine-tuning, as he swings and misses often and could be challenged by off-speed. Athletic with some range at SS, but projects as 3B/LF down the road with a strong arm. If barrel control progresses, he could have .250 BA/25 HR upside potential.

Lara,Jordy

359 | **Atlanta** | **EXP MLB DEBUT:** 2016 | **H/W:** 6-3 215 | **FUT:** Starting 3B | **7D**

Bats R Age 24
2008 FA (DR)

- Pwr +++
- BAvg +++
- Spd +
- Def ++

Year	Lev	Team	AB	R	H	HR	RBI	Avg	OB	Slg	OPS	bb%	ct%	Eye	SB	CS	x/h%	Iso	RC/G
2013	A	Clinton	339	39	88	10	63	260	318	440	757	8	80	0.43	3	0	43	180	4.87
2013	A+	High Desert	61	11	19	3	9	311	323	492	814	2	79	0.08	0	0	26	180	5.01
2014	A+	High Desert	399	77	141	22	80	353	410	609	1019	9	79	0.46	1	3	38	256	8.07
2014	AA	Jackson	126	14	36	4	24	286	328	492	820	6	85	0.42	0	0	50	206	5.53
2015	AA	Jackson	443	48	107	7	56	242	300	377	677	8	81	0.44	0	0	37	135	3.92

Versatile and tall INF who is developing slowly. Power magnified by home park in '14, but has average pop at best. Can hit breaking balls and works best when using gap approach. Can be tough out as he works counts. Defensive home in question. Range is limited, though has strong arm. Foot speed is well below average.

LaValley,Gavin

35 | **Cincinnati** | **EXP MLB DEBUT:** 2019 | **H/W:** 6-3 235 | **FUT:** Starting 1B | **8E**

Bats R Age 21
2014 (4) HS (OK)

- Pwr ++++
- BAvg ++
- Spd +
- Def ++

Year	Lev	Team	AB	R	H	HR	RBI	Avg	OB	Slg	OPS	bb%	ct%	Eye	SB	CS	x/h%	Iso	RC/G
2014	Rk	Billings	21	2	4	1	2	190	190	333	524	0	52	0.00	0	0	25	143	1.71
2014	Rk	AZL Reds	189	29	54	5	30	286	372	439	811	12	77	0.59	3	0	31	153	5.80
2015	A	Dayton	469	52	125	4	53	267	337	358	695	10	76	0.44	4	1	27	92	4.22

Potential to be power-hitting corner INF. Showed good plate discipline and an ability to barrel pitches in his debut. Long swing caused plenty of swings and misses, and raw power hasn't translated yet to in-game power. HR numbers could escalate as he generates loft. Size and lack of speed will likely regulate him to 1B long term.

Lee,Hak-Ju

6 | **San Francisco** | **EXP MLB DEBUT:** 2016 | **H/W:** 6-2 170 | **FUT:** Starting SS | **7D**

Bats L Age 25
2008 FA (KR)

- Pwr +
- BAvg ++
- Spd +++
- Def ++++

Year	Lev	Team	AB	R	H	HR	RBI	Avg	OB	Slg	OPS	bb%	ct%	Eye	SB	CS	x/h%	Iso	RC/G
2011	AA	Montgomery	100	16	19	1	7	190	270	310	580	10	78	0.50	5	2	32	120	2.80
2012	AA	Montgomery	475	68	124	4	37	261	333	360	693	10	79	0.50	37	9	23	99	4.21
2013	AAA	Durham	45	13	19	1	7	422	536	600	1136	20	80	1.22	6	2	26	178	10.51
2014	AAA	Durham	315	36	64	4	23	203	287	276	563	11	73	0.43	12	5	22	73	2.38
2015	AAA	Durham	313	33	69	3	27	220	299	304	602	10	66	0.33	20	3	28	83	2.96

Lean, quick SS who has spent last 3 years in AAA and cannot stay healthy. Regressed considerably last 2 seasons, though defense remains above average. Ranges well to both sides and has clean, quick hands. Plus arm accentuated by quick release. Offense predicated on slap approach and little pop. Plate discipline is disappointing.

Leon,Julian

2 | **Los Angeles (N)** | **EXP MLB DEBUT:** 2017 | **H/W:** 5-11 200 | **FUT:** Starting C | **7D**

Bats R Age 20
2012 FA (MX)

- Pwr +++
- BAvg +++
- Spd +
- Def ++

Year	Lev	Team	AB	R	H	HR	RBI	Avg	OB	Slg	OPS	bb%	ct%	Eye	SB	CS	x/h%	Iso	RC/G
2013	Rk	Azl Dodgers	81	12	20	3	19	247	307	420	727	8	74	0.33	0	1	35	173	4.43
2014	Rk	Ogden	223	39	74	12	57	332	413	565	978	12	76	0.58	1	1	36	233	7.89
2015	A	Great Lakes	309	30	62	5	26	201	254	298	552	7	65	0.21	0	1	32	97	2.06

Short, athletic C was completely over-matched in full-season ball. Has plus present power and drives the ball to all fields. Moves well behind the dish with a strong arm, but needs to improve his footwork and blocking skills. Showed enough to stick behind the plate and but needs to prove that '15 was a fluke.

Leonard,Patrick

35 | **Tampa Bay** | **EXP MLB DEBUT:** 2017 | **H/W:** 6-4 225 | **FUT:** Starting 3B/1B | **7D**

Bats R Age 23
2011 (5) HS (TX)

- Pwr ++
- BAvg +++
- Spd ++
- Def ++

Year	Lev	Team	AB	R	H	HR	RBI	Avg	OB	Slg	OPS	bb%	ct%	Eye	SB	CS	x/h%	Iso	RC/G
2012	Rk	Burlington	235	37	59	14	46	251	336	494	829	11	77	0.55	6	2	44	243	5.82
2013	A	Bowling Green	440	52	99	9	57	225	293	345	638	9	73	0.36	4	1	35	120	3.34
2014	A+	Charlotte	455	79	129	13	58	284	353	448	802	10	76	0.46	14	0	34	165	5.55
2015	AA	Montgomery	446	72	114	10	43	256	336	408	744	11	71	0.42	11	3	39	152	4.97

Strong corner INF who has advanced one level per year. Mostly played 3B, but saw action at 1B and RF. Has strong, leveraged stroke and offers average power potential. Focuses more on contact with hard line drives and has nice pitch recognition. Will strike out due to long swing. Has strong arm and decent hands, but not polished defender.

Leyba,Domingo

6 | **Arizona** | **EXP MLB DEBUT:** 2018 | **H/W:** 5-11 160 | **FUT:** Starting SS | **8D**

Bats B Age 20
2012 FA (DR)

- Pwr ++
- BAvg +++
- Spd +++
- Def +++

Year	Lev	Team	AB	R	H	HR	RBI	Avg	OB	Slg	OPS	bb%	ct%	Eye	SB	CS	x/h%	Iso	RC/G
2013	Rk	DSL Tigers	201	51	70	5	36	348	443	577	1020	14	87	1.31	16	8	40	229	8.51
2014	A-	Connecticut	144	20	38	1	17	264	303	375	678	5	88	0.47	1	2	34	111	3.95
2014	A	West Michigan	116	20	46	1	7	397	426	483	909	5	89	0.46	1	2	17	86	6.41
2015	A+	Visalia	514	60	122	2	43	237	274	309	583	5	82	0.29	10	6	23	72	2.65

Athletic SS struggled with aggressive promotion to High-A in '15. Advanced approach at plate. Short contact-oriented swing and plate discipline should aid in '16 rebound. Added strength should tap into XBH totals. Will stick at SS but could be effective at 2B as well.

Liberato,Luis

789 | **Seattle** | **EXP MLB DEBUT:** 2018 | **H/W:** 6-1 175 | **FUT:** Starting OF | **8D**

Bats L Age 20
2012 FA (DR)

- Pwr ++
- BAvg ++
- Spd +++
- Def +++

Year	Lev	Team	AB	R	H	HR	RBI	Avg	OB	Slg	OPS	bb%	ct%	Eye	SB	CS	x/h%	Iso	RC/G
2013	Rk	DSL Mariners	204	39	52	2	17	255	330	353	683	10	75	0.46	14	8	25	98	4.09
2014	Rk	Azl Mariners	175	28	37	2	14	211	324	314	638	14	73	0.62	14	2	30	103	3.63
2015	A-	Everett	181	34	47	5	31	260	346	453	799	12	74	0.51	10	3	43	193	5.73
2015	A	Clinton	30	3	4	0	0	133	188	233	421	6	67	0.20	1	0	50	100	0.31
2015	AA	Jackson	10	0	0	0	0	0	0	0	0	0	80	0.00	0	0		0	-4.74

Lean, wiry OF who exhibits promising tools and could be sleeper. Needs to add muscle to realize average power potential and could benefit by working deeper counts. Has feel for bat and produces fast swing thanks to quick wrists. Could be impact player with bat at peak. Can play all OF positions and has range and arm to be solid-average at any spot.

Lien,Connor

89 | **Atlanta** | **EXP MLB DEBUT:** 2017 | **H/W:** 6-3 205 | **FUT:** Starting CF | **7D**

Bats R Age 22
2012 (12) HS (FL)

- Pwr +++
- BAvg ++
- Spd ++++
- Def +++

Year	Lev	Team	AB	R	H	HR	RBI	Avg	OB	Slg	OPS	bb%	ct%	Eye	SB	CS	x/h%	Iso	RC/G
2012	Rk	GCL Braves	149	30	34	0	11	228	315	282	597	11	67	0.39	15	3	18	54	2.97
2013	Rk	Danville	212	32	48	6	27	226	274	401	675	6	67	0.20	10	3	44	175	3.89
2014	A	Rome	309	41	85	5	36	275	321	398	719	6	73	0.25	16	4	29	123	4.39
2015	A+	Carolina	453	72	129	9	47	285	333	415	748	7	72	0.26	34	12	28	130	4.81

Under-the-radar prospect who broke out in '15. Solid tools at the plate. Tapped into raw power, slugging 9 HRs. Length in swing leaves him vulnerable to better FBs, especially up in the zone. Has plus speed but has struggled to translate into a high SB percentage. Has the range to play CF but could easily become a 4th OF on a first division club.

Lindsay,Desmond

8 | **New York (N)** | **EXP MLB DEBUT:** 2020 | **H/W:** 6-0 200 | **FUT:** Starting CF | **9E**

Bats R Age 19
2015 (2) HS (FL)

- Pwr +++
- BAvg ++++
- Spd ++++
- Def +++

Year	Lev	Team	AB	R	H	HR	RBI	Avg	OB	Slg	OPS	bb%	ct%	Eye	SB	CS	x/h%	Iso	RC/G
2015	Rk	GCL Mets	69	10	21	1	6	304	400	464	864	14	70	0.52	3	2	33	159	6.97
2015	A-	Brooklyn	45	3	9	0	7	200	308	267	574	13	58	0.37	0	1	33	67	2.83

Raw, athletic CF with 5-tool potential. Struggled with health as an amateur. Had a solid debut in the GCL. Makes hard loud contact. Line drive approach to RCF. Has gap power presently; as he learns to use his legs, power should develop. A prep infielder. Plus run speed should make transition to OF easier. Work in progress in CF.

Lindsey,Taylor

4 | **San Diego** | **EXP MLB DEBUT:** 2016 | **H/W:** 6-0 195 | **FUT:** Starting 2B | **7D**

Bats L Age 24
2010 (1) HS (AZ)

- Pwr ++
- BAvg +++
- Spd ++
- Def ++

Year	Lev	Team	AB	R	H	HR	RBI	Avg	OB	Slg	OPS	bb%	ct%	Eye	SB	CS	x/h%	Iso	RC/G
2013	AA	Arkansas	508	68	139	17	56	274	336	441	777	9	82	0.53	4	4	32	167	5.10
2014	AAA	El Paso	146	18	32	2	17	219	265	315	580	6	90	0.60	0	2	28	96	2.87
2014	AAA	Salt Lake	295	50	73	8	30	247	319	400	719	10	85	0.70	7	2	34	153	4.52
2015	AA	San Antonio	199	21	34	5	15	171	257	302	558	10	81	0.61	1	0	47	131	2.50
2015	AAA	El Paso	92	8	21	0	7	228	343	283	625	15	80	0.89	3	1	19	54	3.66

Natural hitting INF who had worst season as pro and demoted to AA in June. Needs to hit in order to play in majors as he is below average defender with fringy speed. Swing mechanics can get out of whack and disrupt timing. Bat to ball skills are admirable and has some power to pull side. Lacks ideal quickness and arm for SS and still limited at 2B.

Liriano,Rymer — 9 — San Diego

EXP MLB DEBUT: 2014 | H/W: 6-0 230 | FUT: Starting OF | **8D**

Bats R Age 24	Year	Lev	Team	AB	R	H	HR	RBI	Avg	OB	Slg	OPS	bb%	ct%	Eye	SB	CS	x/h%	Iso	RC/G
2007 FA (DR)	2012	AA	San Antonio	183	24	46	3	20	251	325	377	702	10	73	0.40	10	1	33	126	4.33
Pwr ++++	2014	AA	San Antonio	371	55	98	14	53	264	328	442	770	9	73	0.34	17	7	37	178	5.08
BAvg +++	2014	AAA	El Paso	62	14	28	0	13	452	514	661	1176	11	77	0.57	3	1	43	210	10.84
Spd +++	2014	MLB	San Diego	109	13	24	1	6	220	280	266	546	8	64	0.23	4	1	13	46	1.97
Def +++	2015	AAA	El Paso	472	85	138	14	64	292	377	460	837	12	72	0.48	18	8	35	167	6.24

Toolsy OF who can do everything on diamond, but has holes in game. Projects as ideal RF with power and speed, but lack of contact negatively impacts upside. Works counts, but could stand to be more aggressive. Strong frame produces pop to all fields and still runs well despite severe drop in SB (66 SB in '11). Has average range and strong arm.

Locastro,Tim — 4 — Los Angeles (N)

EXP MLB DEBUT: 2018 | H/W: 6-1 200 | FUT: Utility player | **6B**

Bats R Age 23	Year	Lev	Team	AB	R	H	HR	RBI	Avg	OB	Slg	OPS	bb%	ct%	Eye	SB	CS	x/h%	Iso	RC/G
2013 (13) Ithaca																				
Pwr ++	2013	Rk	Bluefield	138	28	39	1	13	283	344	384	728	9	91	1.08	12	2	23	101	4.79
BAvg +++	2014	A-	Vancouver	256	49	80	1	27	313	343	367	710	4	91	0.52	32	4	15	55	4.24
Spd +++	2015	A	Lansing	242	48	75	5	25	310	365	421	787	8	90	0.84	30	11	21	112	5.25
Def +++	2015	A+	RanchoCuca	156	30	35	1	14	224	288	327	615	8	81	0.47	11	5	34	103	3.22

Strong, hard-nosed ball player was traded for international bonus slots. Was not young for the level, but impressed in the MWL, hitting .310/.409/.421. Crowds the plate and has a solid approach with moderate bat speed and the ability to make consistent contact. Solid defender with above-average speed with a good idea of how to run the bases.

Longhi,Nick — 39 — Boston

EXP MLB DEBUT: 2018 | H/W: 6-2 205 | FUT: Starting 1B/RF | **8E**

Bats R Age 20	Year	Lev	Team	AB	R	H	HR	RBI	Avg	OB	Slg	OPS	bb%	ct%	Eye	SB	CS	x/h%	Iso	RC/G
2013 (30) HS (FL)																				
Pwr +++																				
BAvg +++	2013	Rk	GCL Red Sox	45	4	8	1	4	178	229	356	585	6	73	0.25	1	0	75	178	2.63
Spd ++	2014	A-	Lowell	109	19	36	0	10	330	392	440	832	9	80	0.50	0	3	31	110	6.03
Def +	2015	A	Greenville	442	52	124	7	62	281	332	403	735	7	80	0.39	2	0	30	122	4.57

Consistent prospect who split time between 1B and RF in first full season. Has impressive upside predicated on bat alone. Offers power potential with strength in wrists and forearms. Uses all fields and could hit more HR by pulling more. Swing is crisp and clean and has enough control to make contact. Currently a poor defender with strong arm.

Lopez,Jesus — 46 — Oakland

EXP MLB DEBUT: 2019 | H/W: 5-11 170 | FUT: Starting 2B | **7D**

Bats B Age 19	Year	Lev	Team	AB	R	H	HR	RBI	Avg	OB	Slg	OPS	bb%	ct%	Eye	SB	CS	x/h%	Iso	RC/G
2013 FA (NI)																				
Pwr ++																				
BAvg ++																				
Spd ++	2014	Rk	Azl Athletics	136	18	30	0	13	221	316	272	588	12	79	0.66	4	1	20	51	3.01
Def +++	2015	A-	Vermont	202	14	41	0	10	203	226	228	454	3	80	0.15	2	1	12	25	0.87

Quick INF whose glove is ahead of bat at present. Displays smooth, athletic actions in middle infield. Hands work well and has footwork to turn double plays. Offers little to no punch in bat and struggles to get extra base hits. Has yet to HR as pro, though has natural feel for contact. Doesn't work counts and below average speed limits upside.

Lora,Edwin — 6 — Washington

EXP MLB DEBUT: 2019 | H/W: 6-1 150 | FUT: Starting SS | **7C**

Bats R Age 20	Year	Lev	Team	AB	R	H	HR	RBI	Avg	OB	Slg	OPS	bb%	ct%	Eye	SB	CS	x/h%	Iso	RC/G
2012 FA (DR)																				
Pwr +																				
BAvg ++	2013	Rk	DSL Nationals	185	29	38	2	13	205	276	281	557	9	76	0.41	6	4	26	76	2.32
Spd ++++	2014	Rk	GCL Nationals	181	27	53	0	15	293	333	337	670	6	80	0.30	13	6	15	44	3.68
Def ++++	2015	A-	Auburn	116	19	30	2	17	259	295	414	709	5	72	0.18	7	0	40	155	4.26

A very good defender who makes use of his excellent speed to cover ground in the infield. Can make the spectacular play yet let down on the routine. Hasn't yet actualized speed on the bases, and diminutive frame lacks present strength in hit tool. Power projects as below average.

Lowe,Brandon — 4 — Tampa Bay

EXP MLB DEBUT: 2018 | H/W: 5-10 178 | FUT: Starting 2B | **7C**

Bats L Age 21	Year	Lev	Team	AB	R	H	HR	RBI	Avg	OB	Slg	OPS	bb%	ct%	Eye	SB	CS	x/h%	Iso	RC/G
2015 (3) Maryland																				
Pwr ++																				
BAvg +++																				
Spd +++																				
Def ++	2015		*Did not play; injured*																	

Instinctual INF who did not play upon signing due to broken ankle. Brings mature approach to plate with discerning eye, balanced swing, and pitch recognition. Can hit for BA by hitting to all fields. Has some punch in bat, but mostly of gap variety. Exhibits average speed and quickness. Has been passable defender with fringy arm and ample range.

Lugo,Dawel — 6 — Arizona

EXP MLB DEBUT: 2018 | H/W: 6-0 190 | FUT: Reserve INF | **7D**

Bats R Age 21	Year	Lev	Team	AB	R	H	HR	RBI	Avg	OB	Slg	OPS	bb%	ct%	Eye	SB	CS	x/h%	Iso	RC/G
2011 FA (DR)	2013	A-	Vancouver	69	6	17	1	8	246	257	348	605	1	81	0.08	0	0	29	101	2.65
Pwr ++	2014	A	Lansing	474	40	123	4	53	259	287	329	616	4	85	0.25	3	3	19	70	2.97
BAvg +++	2015	A	Kane County	81	12	27	0	3	333	365	370	735	5	84	0.31	2	2	7	37	4.41
Spd ++	2015	A	Lansing	122	15	41	2	23	336	362	451	813	4	80	0.21	3	1	22	115	5.29
Def ++	2015	A+	Dunedin	260	16	57	2	21	219	245	292	538	3	81	0.18	1	3	23	73	1.96

Strong-armed INF was acquired mid-season in Cliff Pennington deal. Struggled w/ bat in High-A debut; was demoted. Has great hand-eye coordination but swings at anything remotely close to zone. Scouts believe power will come despite stocky frame. Doesn't have the range or speed to stick at SS and could find 2B difficult to man as well.

Luplow,Jordan — 5 — Pittsburgh

EXP MLB DEBUT: 2018 | H/W: 6-0 195 | FUT: Starting 3B | **7C**

Bats R Age 22	Year	Lev	Team	AB	R	H	HR	RBI	Avg	OB	Slg	OPS	bb%	ct%	Eye	SB	CS	x/h%	Iso	RC/G
2014 (3) Fresno St	2012	NCAA	Fresno St	233	33	65	2	34	279	311	386	698	5	79	0.23	10	1	29	107	3.99
Pwr +++	2013	NCAA	Fresno St	151	23	42	3	21	278	335	437	772	8	79	0.42	6	1	36	159	5.11
BAvg +++	2014	NCAA	Fresno St	215	40	81	9	48	377	466	609	1075	14	90	1.64	10	4	38	233	8.96
Spd +++	2014	A-	Jamestown	220	31	61	6	30	277	356	423	779	11	80	0.61	10	6	31	145	5.27
Def ++	2015	A	West Virginia	390	74	103	12	67	264	361	464	825	13	83	0.88	11	2	50	200	6.02

Moved to 3B in '15 and held his own. Has above-average bat speed, good plate discipline, and showed surprising power in his full-season debut. Shows average speed, good range, and a strong arm and should be able to stick at the hot corner. Lack of org depth at the position increases his chances of moving up quickly.

Machado,Dixon — 6 — Detroit

EXP MLB DEBUT: 2015 | H/W: 6-0 170 | FUT: Utility player | **6A**

Bats R Age 24	Year	Lev	Team	AB	R	H	HR	RBI	Avg	OB	Slg	OPS	bb%	ct%	Eye	SB	CS	x/h%	Iso	RC/G
2008 FA (VZ)	2013	A+	Lakeland	149	19	32	1	12	215	264	295	559	6	87	0.53	1	0	25	81	2.61
Pwr ++	2014	A+	Lakeland	159	30	40	1	8	252	346	333	679	13	79	0.68	2	1	25	82	4.19
BAvg ++	2014	AA	Erie	292	45	89	5	32	305	389	442	830	12	88	1.11	8	5	33	137	6.07
Spd +++	2015	AAA	Toledo	509	61	133	4	48	261	310	332	642	7	83	0.42	15	3	20	71	3.43
Def ++++	2015	MLB	Detroit	68	6	16	0	5	235	307	279	586	9	79	0.50	1	0	19	44	2.84

Defensive-oriented INF who offers some offensive talent. Swing geared more towards line drives to gaps and uses speed to leg out extra base hits. Makes consistent contact with level stroke and knows value of working counts and being selective. Terrific SS with sure hands and plus range to both sides. Stands out for quickness and smooth actions.

Mahtook,Mikie — 789 — Tampa Bay

EXP MLB DEBUT: 2015 | H/W: 6-1 200 | FUT: Starting OF | **7B**

Bats R Age 26	Year	Lev	Team	AB	R	H	HR	RBI	Avg	OB	Slg	OPS	bb%	ct%	Eye	SB	CS	x/h%	Iso	RC/G
2011 (1) Louisiana St	2012	AA	Montgomery	153	17	38	4	25	248	299	405	704	7	80	0.35	4	3	39	157	4.13
Pwr +++	2013	AA	Montgomery	511	71	130	7	68	254	312	386	698	8	80	0.42	25	8	35	131	4.19
BAvg +++	2014	AAA	Durham	489	56	143	12	68	292	353	458	811	9	72	0.34	18	5	36	166	5.78
Spd +++	2015	AAA	Durham	385	35	96	4	45	249	290	366	656	5	75	0.22	10	1	35	117	3.53
Def +++	2015	MLB	Tampa Bay	105	22	31	9	19	295	333	619	952	5	70	0.19	4	3	48	324	7.34

All-around prospect who maximizes abilities with solid feel for game. Can hit for BA with all-fields approach and is smart baserunner. Performed better in majors than AAA with surprising power output. Can impact game defensively with speed and quality routes to ball. Has plus range to play CF.

Mancini,Trey — 3 — Baltimore

EXP MLB DEBUT: 2016 | H/W: 6-4 215 | FUT: Starting 1B | **7B**

Bats R Age 24	Year	Lev	Team	AB	R	H	HR	RBI	Avg	OB	Slg	OPS	bb%	ct%	Eye	SB	CS	x/h%	Iso	RC/G
2013 (8) Notre Dame	2013	A-	Aberdeen	256	43	84	3	35	328	377	449	826	7	83	0.47	3	1	27	121	5.71
Pwr +++	2014	A	Delmarva	268	30	85	3	42	317	351	422	773	5	81	0.27	1	1	22	104	4.90
BAvg ++++	2014	A+	Frederick	275	37	69	7	41	251	287	396	684	5	84	0.33	0	1	38	145	3.81
Spd +	2015	A+	Frederick	207	28	65	8	32	314	343	527	869	4	83	0.26	4	2	38	213	5.93
Def ++	2015	AA	Bowie	326	60	117	13	57	359	399	586	985	6	82	0.38	2	1	38	227	7.49

Natural-hitting 1B who had breakout season with easy highs in doubles and HR. Hit at least .331 each month except April and made consistent contact. Has feel for bat and nice approach, though power may only be average. Can be too aggressive at times. Not a great athlete and doesn't run well, but holds own with glove.

Margot,Manuel — 8 — San Diego

EXP MLB DEBUT: 2017 | H/W: 5-11 170 | FUT: Starting CF | 8C

Bats R Age 21	Year	Lev	Team	AB	R	H	HR	RBI	Avg	OB	Slg	OPS	bb%	ct%	Eye	SB	CS	x/h%	Iso	RC/G
2011 FA (DR)	2013	A-	Lowell	185	29	50	1	21	270	348	351	699	11	78	0.55	18	8	22	81	4.34
Pwr ++	2014	A	Greenville	370	61	106	10	45	286	351	449	800	9	87	0.76	39	13	33	162	5.47
BAvg +++	2014	A+	Salem	50	4	17	2	14	340	365	560	925	4	90	0.40	3	2	41	220	6.49
Spd ++++	2015	A+	Salem	181	35	51	3	17	282	323	420	743	6	92	0.73	20	5	27	138	4.74
Def ++++	2015	AA	Portland	258	38	70	3	33	271	326	419	745	8	86	0.58	19	8	40	147	4.84

Lean, quick OF who makes extreme contact and uses plus speed to wreak havoc on base. Profiles as leadoff hitter, but puts bat to ball so easily he swings early in count. Power hasn't yet developed, but could get to at least average. Plays well above average defense in CF with plus range and average arm. Has chance to be impact player.

Marin,Adrian — 6 — Baltimore

EXP MLB DEBUT: 2017 | H/W: 6-0 180 | FUT: Starting SS | 7D

Bats R Age 22	Year	Lev	Team	AB	R	H	HR	RBI	Avg	OB	Slg	OPS	bb%	ct%	Eye	SB	CS	x/h%	Iso	RC/G
2012 (3) HS (FL)	2012	Rk	GCL Orioles	178	24	51	0	13	287	328	360	688	6	81	0.32	6	1	20	73	3.97
Pwr ++	2012	A	Delmarva	21	5	6	0	2	286	318	286	604	5	90	0.50	2	0	0	0	3.02
BAvg ++	2013	A	Delmarva	388	30	103	4	48	265	307	356	662	6	77	0.26	11	4	24	90	3.56
Spd +++	2014	A+	Frederick	431	40	100	5	42	232	268	341	609	5	76	0.20	12	4	36	109	2.85
Def +++	2015	A+	Frederick	416	57	99	4	41	238	278	344	622	5	82	0.31	25	8	31	106	3.14

Instinctual and fundamental INF who relies on quickness and speed. Set career high in SB, though could be higher with better plate discipline and OBP. Makes easy contact with compact stroke and can read spin. Strong arm is best defensive attribute and has hands and enough range to stick at SS.

Marlette,Tyler — 2 — Seattle

EXP MLB DEBUT: 2016 | H/W: 5-11 195 | FUT: Starting C | 7C

Bats R Age 23	Year	Lev	Team	AB	R	H	HR	RBI	Avg	OB	Slg	OPS	bb%	ct%	Eye	SB	CS	x/h%	Iso	RC/G
2011 (5) HS (FL)	2013	A	Clinton	270	36	82	6	37	304	361	448	809	8	80	0.45	10	4	30	144	5.52
Pwr +++	2014	A+	High Desert	312	51	94	15	49	301	351	519	870	7	80	0.39	9	2	40	218	6.11
BAvg +++	2014	AA	Jackson	32	3	8	2	2	250	333	500	833	11	69	0.40	0	1	50	250	6.09
Spd ++	2015	A+	Bakersfield	148	17	32	5	20	216	275	365	640	8	76	0.34	2	1	34	149	3.25
Def ++	2015	AA	Jackson	178	15	46	3	12	258	298	393	691	5	83	0.32	0	0	37	135	3.96

Offensive-minded backstop who has athleticism to improve behind plate. Receiving needs attention, but getting better. Has average, accurate arm that is enhanced by quick release. Was better in AA by simplifying approach and allowing natural bat speed to take over. Makes good contact and uses entire field.

Marrero,Deven — 456 — Boston

EXP MLB DEBUT: 2015 | H/W: 6-1 195 | FUT: Starting SS | 7C

Bats R Age 25	Year	Lev	Team	AB	R	H	HR	RBI	Avg	OB	Slg	OPS	bb%	ct%	Eye	SB	CS	x/h%	Iso	RC/G
2012 (1) Arizona St	2013	AA	Portland	72	7	17	0	5	236	329	236	565	12	78	0.63	6	0	0	0	2.60
Pwr ++	2014	AA	Portland	268	42	78	5	39	291	371	433	804	11	79	0.60	12	7	33	142	5.69
BAvg ++	2014	AAA	Pawtucket	186	23	39	1	20	210	258	285	543	6	80	0.32	4	1	31	75	2.16
Spd ++++	2015	AAA	Pawtucket	375	49	96	6	29	256	316	344	660	8	77	0.38	12	5	21	88	3.60
Def ++++	2015	MLB	Boston	53	8	12	1	3	226	268	283	551	5	64	0.16	2	1	8	57	1.89

Rangy INF who is a pure SS, but getting experience at other spots to add to versatility. Is an elite defender with plus range to both sides and great instincts. Goes gap to gap in approach, though set high in HR. Will never hit for much long ball pop due to level swing path. Needs to get on base more to use plus speed.

Martin,Jason — 7 — Houston

EXP MLB DEBUT: 2018 | H/W: 5-10 190 | FUT: Starting OF | 7D

Bats L Age 20	Year	Lev	Team	AB	R	H	HR	RBI	Avg	OB	Slg	OPS	bb%	ct%	Eye	SB	CS	x/h%	Iso	RC/G
2013 (8) HS (CA)																				
Pwr ++	2013	Rk	GCL Astros	179	35	45	0	17	251	356	341	697	14	83	0.94	11	7	27	89	4.61
BAvg +++	2014	Rk	Greeneville	164	32	45	0	21	274	367	415	782	13	82	0.80	8	6	38	140	5.66
Spd +++	2014	A-	Tri City	81	7	18	1	2	222	284	321	605	8	84	0.54	5	3	28	99	3.10
Def ++	2015	A	Quad Cities	396	65	107	8	57	270	348	396	744	11	81	0.64	14	15	25	126	4.86

Undersized OF who enjoyed first full season as pro. Compact swing and advanced bat control provide BA potential and pure, hard contact. Goes gap to gap with line drives, but doesn't have loft or backspin to produce pop requisite of corner OF. Runs well underway which enhances substandard routes and reads in LF.

Martin,Richie — 6 — Oakland

EXP MLB DEBUT: 2018 | H/W: 6-0 190 | FUT: Starting SS | 8C

Bats R Age 21	Year	Lev	Team	AB	R	H	HR	RBI	Avg	OB	Slg	OPS	bb%	ct%	Eye	SB	CS	x/h%	Iso	RC/G
2015 (1) Florida																				
Pwr ++																				
BAvg +++																				
Spd +++	2015	NCAA	Florida	265	63	77	6	36	291	373	430	804	12	87	1.00	20	8	27	140	5.68
Def ++++	2015	A-	Vermont	190	31	45	2	16	237	326	342	668	12	75	0.53	7	7	27	105	3.95

Nimble, athletic INF who can hit hard line drives to all fields and stands out with glove. Plays plus defense with range to both sides and strong, accurate arm. Shows quick, smooth actions and can make difficult plays look easy. Not a sure thing with bat, but has strong swing with selective eye. Power not part of game, but should hit doubles.

Martinez,Eddy — 8 — Chicago (N)

EXP MLB DEBUT: 2018 | H/W: 6-0 195 | FUT: Starting CF | 7C

Bats R Age 21	Year	Lev	Team	AB	R	H	HR	RBI	Avg	OB	Slg	OPS	bb%	ct%	Eye	SB	CS	x/h%	Iso	RC/G
2015 FA (CU)																				
Pwr ++																				
BAvg +++																				
Spd +++																				
Def ++++	2015		*Did not play in minors*																	

Strong, athletic Cuban OF signed by Cubs for $3 million. Has plus bat speed and should be able to hit for average with moderate power. Runs well and is a plus defender with an avg arm. Should be able to stick in CF. Looked a bit stiff at the plate during pre-signing workouts, but has good size and athleticism and could move up quickly.

Marzilli,Evan — 789 — Arizona

EXP MLB DEBUT: 2016 | H/W: 6-0 187 | FUT: Reserve OF | 6C

Bats L Age 25	Year	Lev	Team	AB	R	H	HR	RBI	Avg	OB	Slg	OPS	bb%	ct%	Eye	SB	CS	x/h%	Iso	RC/G
2012 (8) South Carolina	2014	A+	Visalia	176	30	43	5	18	244	357	409	767	15	69	0.57	7	4	37	165	5.46
Pwr ++	2014	AA	Mobile	285	33	70	3	35	246	317	361	679	10	76	0.45	8	5	30	116	4.02
BAvg ++	2015	Rk	Azl DBacks	22	5	9	0	1	409	552	500	1052	24	64	0.88	3	0	11	91	10.97
Spd +++	2015	AA	Mobile	122	17	30	1	8	246	352	344	696	14	77	0.71	6	4	27	98	4.47
Def +++	2015	AAA	Reno	30	4	9	0	2	300	300	400	700	0	77	0.00	1	2	22	100	3.83

Solid, unspectacular OF lost time in '15 due to an ugly ankle injury. Has shown ability to get on-base throughout every level. Makes consistent contact and has flashed pull-side power prior to injury. Can play all OF positions well. Suited for longtime bench role in MLB.

Mateo,Jorge — 6 — New York (A)

EXP MLB DEBUT: 2017 | H/W: 6-0 188 | FUT: Starting SS | 8C

Bats R Age 20	Year	Lev	Team	AB	R	H	HR	RBI	Avg	OB	Slg	OPS	bb%	ct%	Eye	SB	CS	x/h%	Iso	RC/G
2012 FA (DR)																				
Pwr ++	2013	Rk	DSL Yankees	258	50	74	7	26	287	370	450	819	12	80	0.65	49	10	30	163	5.85
BAvg +++	2014	Rk	GCL Yankees	58	14	16	0	1	276	354	397	750	11	71	0.41	11	1	38	121	5.24
Spd +++++	2015	A	Charleston (Sc)	365	51	98	2	33	268	334	378	712	9	78	0.45	71	15	29	110	4.47
Def +++	2015	A+	Tampa	84	15	27	0	7	321	374	452	826	8	79	0.39	11	2	30	131	5.92

Quick, advanced INF who led minors in SB. Held own in High-A and has exciting, aggressive style of play. Has incredible speed and some power potential. Hits hard line drives to gaps and makes acceptable contact. Swing can get long and could stand to be more patient at plate. Has very high upside and should stick at SS with plus arm.

Mathias,Mark — 4 — Cleveland

EXP MLB DEBUT: 2018 | H/W: 6-0 200 | FUT: Starting 2B | 7C

Bats R Age 21	Year	Lev	Team	AB	R	H	HR	RBI	Avg	OB	Slg	OPS	bb%	ct%	Eye	SB	CS	x/h%	Iso	RC/G
2015 (3) Cal Poly																				
Pwr ++																				
BAvg ++++																				
Spd ++	2015	NCAA	Cal Poly	202	42	72	1	28	356	422	436	858	10	91	1.21	9	4	15	79	6.30
Def ++	2015	A-	Mahoning Val	245	38	69	2	32	282	371	408	780	13	85	0.97	5	4	35	127	5.55

Natural-hitting INF with ideal approach to get on base. Recognizes pitches like seasoned pro and has sound hand-eye coordination. Power is of the gap variety, but can turn on good fastballs at times. Needs to hit to have value as speed and defense are currently below average.

Mathisen,Wyatt — 5 — Pittsburgh

EXP MLB DEBUT: 2016 | H/W: 6-1 225 | FUT: Backup 3B | 6C

Bats R Age 22	Year	Lev	Team	AB	R	H	HR	RBI	Avg	OB	Slg	OPS	bb%	ct%	Eye	SB	CS	x/h%	Iso	RC/G
2012 (2) HS (TX)	2013	Rk	GCL Pirates	22	5	9	0	3	409	552	455	1006	24	91	3.50	0	0	11	45	9.08
Pwr ++	2013	A-	Jamestown	26	4	7	0	3	269	387	269	656	16	73	0.71	1	0	0	0	3.93
BAvg +++	2013	A	West Virginia	119	13	22	0	9	185	242	210	452	7	82	0.41	1	0	14	25	1.12
Spd ++	2014	A	West Virginia	375	48	105	3	42	280	338	360	698	8	86	0.61	6	2	21	80	4.24
Def ++	2015	A+	Bradenton	403	46	106	4	34	263	334	342	677	10	82	0.60	0	1	20	79	4.00

Good approach at the plate and makes consistent contact. Has a good understanding of the strike zone and has good raw power. That power has yet to show up in game action and will need to develop to have value at 3B. Move to 3B is a work in progress where his footwork and range are below-average. Needs to show more power to have value.

Maxwell,Bruce — 2 — Oakland

EXP MLB DEBUT: 2016 | H/W: 6-2 235 | FUT: Starting C | 7E

Bats L Age 25	Year	Lev	Team	AB	R	H	HR	RBI	Avg	OB	Slg	OPS	bb%	ct%	Eye	SB	CS	x/h%	Iso	RC/G
2012 (2) Birmingham-Southern	2013	A	Beloit	199	25	57	2	28	286	363	387	750	11	85	0.83	0	0	28	101	5.04
Pwr ++	2013	A+	Stockton	175	19	46	5	21	263	335	394	729	10	81	0.56	0	0	28	131	4.55
BAvg ++	2014	A+	Stockton	289	33	79	6	35	273	364	381	744	12	80	0.71	0	1	23	107	4.92
Spd +	2014	AA	Midland	85	8	12	0	2	141	223	176	400	10	62	0.28	0	1	25	35	-0.21
Def +++	2015	AA	Midland	338	32	82	2	48	243	321	308	629	10	84	0.72	0	1	22	65	3.52

Big, strong catcher who hasn't yet tapped into natural power, but has improved with receiving and agility. Controls running game with average arm and solid release. Could be backup without better offense. Swings quick bat and has strength, but has contact approach with level path to ball. Still hope that power emerges.

May,Jacob — 8 — Chicago (A)

EXP MLB DEBUT: 2016 | H/W: 5-11 180 | FUT: Starting OF | 7D

Bats B Age 24	Year	Lev	Team	AB	R	H	HR	RBI	Avg	OB	Slg	OPS	bb%	ct%	Eye	SB	CS	x/h%	Iso	RC/G
2013 (3) Coastal Carolina	2013	Rk	Great Falls	45	5	17	0	7	378	462	444	906	13	87	1.17	5	1	12	67	7.10
Pwr +	2013	A	Kannapolis	206	36	59	8	28	286	338	461	799	7	79	0.37	19	5	29	175	5.25
BAvg +++	2014	A+	Winston-Salem	415	66	107	2	27	258	326	395	721	9	83	0.59	37	8	40	137	4.67
Spd ++++	2015	Rk	Azl White Sox	16	4	4	0	3	250	294	313	607	6	81	0.33	1	0	25	63	2.98
Def +++	2015	AA	Birmingham	389	47	107	2	32	275	325	334	660	7	81	0.40	37	17	17	59	3.63

Very fast OF who finished 2nd in SL in SB despite missing time with concussion. Focuses on contact in basic approach and has some power potential. Better as RHH, but can get pull conscious at times. At his best when he uses whole field and uses speed to his advantage. True CF with plus range, though below average arm strength.

Mazara,Nomar — 79 — Texas

EXP MLB DEBUT: 2016 | H/W: 6-4 195 | FUT: Starting OF | 8C

Bats L Age 20	Year	Lev	Team	AB	R	H	HR	RBI	Avg	OB	Slg	OPS	bb%	ct%	Eye	SB	CS	x/h%	Iso	RC/G
2011 FA (DR)	2013	A	Hickory	453	48	107	13	62	236	304	382	686	9	71	0.34	1	2	36	146	3.98
Pwr ++++	2014	A	Hickory	398	68	105	19	73	264	356	470	826	13	75	0.58	4	3	40	206	5.92
BAvg +++	2014	AA	Frisco	85	10	26	3	16	306	372	518	890	10	74	0.41	0	0	42	212	6.80
Spd ++	2015	AA	Frisco	409	57	116	13	56	284	357	443	800	10	78	0.51	2	0	32	159	5.50
Def ++	2015	AAA	Round Rock	81	11	29	1	13	358	395	444	840	6	88	0.50	0	0	17	86	5.69

Tall, lean OF who is quickly developing and reached AAA in August. Draws walks and makes acceptable contact for power profile. Learning to use entire field and has hand-eye coordination and barrel awareness to hit for BA and HR. Needs to hang in better against LHP and limited range may relegate him to corner. Strong arm is playable in RF.

McBroom,Ryan — 37 — Toronto

EXP MLB DEBUT: 2018 | H/W: 6-3 230 | FUT: Starting 1B | 7D

Bats R Age 23	Year	Lev	Team	AB	R	H	HR	RBI	Avg	OB	Slg	OPS	bb%	ct%	Eye	SB	CS	x/h%	Iso	RC/G
2014 (15) West Virginia	2012	NCAA	West Virginia	205	37	62	6	41	302	359	463	822	8	88	0.72	3	1	34	161	5.64
Pwr +++	2013	NCAA	West Virginia	220	39	59	12	48	268	306	518	824	5	84	0.33	5	2	53	250	5.40
BAvg +++	2014	NCAA	West Virginia	211	32	72	8	49	341	403	512	915	9	83	0.63	1	1	28	171	6.77
Spd +	2014	A-	Vancouver	273	37	81	11	59	297	329	502	831	5	81	0.25	1	0	42	205	5.50
Def ++	2015	A	Lansing	461	72	145	12	90	315	380	482	862	10	79	0.51	5	4	36	167	6.29

Consistent hitter who was MVP of MWL after finishing 2nd in BA. Uses entire field and makes consistent, hard contact. Has been doubles machine, though only projects to average long ball pop. Displays little athleticism and trial run in LF may not work long-term. Value all tied to bat and he swings it hard.

McCarthy,Joe — 7 — Tampa Bay

EXP MLB DEBUT: 2018 | H/W: 6-3 220 | FUT: Starting OF | 8D

Bats L Age 22	Year	Lev	Team	AB	R	H	HR	RBI	Avg	OB	Slg	OPS	bb%	ct%	Eye	SB	CS	x/h%	Iso	RC/G
2015 (5) Virginia																				
Pwr ++																				
BAvg +++																				
Spd ++++	2015	NCAA	Virginia	112	19	22	2	11	196	338	277	615	18	82	1.20	3	0	23	80	3.59
Def +++	2015	A-	Hudson Valley	184	24	51	0	21	277	342	337	679	9	88	0.78	18	3	18	60	4.15

Polished OF who has good size, but relies more on plate discipline and speed. Could add more muscle to frame, though has sufficient bat speed generated from compact stroke. Puts bat to ball and uses plus speed effectively on base. Has limited arm strength, though is good defender in LF with range and routes. Upside based on power development.

McGuire,Reese — 2 — Pittsburgh

EXP MLB DEBUT: 2018 | H/W: 6-0 181 | FUT: Starting C | 8D

Bats L Age 21	Year	Lev	Team	AB	R	H	HR	RBI	Avg	OB	Slg	OPS	bb%	ct%	Eye	SB	CS	x/h%	Iso	RC/G
2013 (1) HS (WA)																				
Pwr ++	2013	Rk	GCL Pirates	176	30	58	0	21	330	382	392	774	8	90	0.83	5	1	19	63	5.20
BAvg +++	2013	A-	Jamestown	16	3	4	0	0	250	294	250	544	6	94	1.00	1	0	0	0	2.62
Spd +++	2014	A	West Virginia	389	46	102	3	45	262	305	334	639	6	89	0.55	7	2	18	72	3.50
Def ++++	2015	A+	Bradenton	374	32	95	0	34	254	303	294	597	7	90	0.67	14	7	16	40	3.11

Athletic 1st rounder has been slow to develop. Blocks and receives the ball well and has a strong arm. Good understanding of the strike zone and makes good contact. Also has raw power, but it has yet to show up in game action, where he had just 15 extra-base hits. Has above-average speed.

McKenna,Ryan — 8 — Baltimore

EXP MLB DEBUT: 2019 | H/W: 5-11 185 | FUT: Starting OF | 8E

Bats R Age 19	Year	Lev	Team	AB	R	H	HR	RBI	Avg	OB	Slg	OPS	bb%	ct%	Eye	SB	CS	x/h%	Iso	RC/G
2015 (4) HS (NH)																				
Pwr ++																				
BAvg ++																				
Spd +++																				
Def +++	2015	Rk	GCL Orioles	34	5	9	0	3	265	375	324	699	15	82	1.00	1	1	11	59	4.64

Short, speedy OF who could evolve into impact player. Possesses raw skills at present, but is sound CF who exhibits quality reads off bat. Tracks down balls in gaps and speed allows for plus range. May not tap into raw power until he recognizes pitches better and adds leverage to short, quick stroke. May need to tweak swing to drive ball.

McKinney,Billy — 9 — Chicago (N)

EXP MLB DEBUT: 2016 | H/W: 6-1 205 | FUT: Starting LF | 8B

Bats L Age 21	Year	Lev	Team	AB	R	H	HR	RBI	Avg	OB	Slg	OPS	bb%	ct%	Eye	SB	CS	x/h%	Iso	RC/G
2013 (1) HS (TX)	2013	A-	Vermont	34	5	12	1	6	353	405	559	964	8	88	0.75	1	1	33	206	7.32
Pwr +++	2014	A+	Daytona	176	30	53	1	36	301	388	432	820	12	76	0.60	1	0	32	131	6.11
BAvg ++++	2014	A+	Stockton	290	42	70	10	33	241	325	400	725	11	80	0.62	5	3	34	159	4.56
Spd ++	2015	A+	Myrtle Beach	103	19	35	4	25	340	433	544	977	14	87	1.31	0	2	31	204	7.83
Def ++	2015	AA	Tennessee	274	29	78	3	39	285	349	420	769	9	83	0.57	0	0	38	135	5.17

Good all-around offensive potential. Has above average bat speed and makes consistent contact. Advanced understanding of strike zone gives him to potential to be a .300 hitter. Sweet LH stroke is easy to repeat and a power spike should come soon, as he launched 26 doubles at AA. Shoulder injury limited him to 377 AB, but should be healthy in 2016.

McMahon,Ryan — 5 — Colorado

EXP MLB DEBUT: 2017 | H/W: 6-2 185 | FUT: Starting 3B | 9C

Bats L Age 21	Year	Lev	Team	AB	R	H	HR	RBI	Avg	OB	Slg	OPS	bb%	ct%	Eye	SB	CS	x/h%	Iso	RC/G
2013 (2) HS (CA)																				
Pwr ++++																				
BAvg +++	2013	Rk	Grand Junction	218	42	70	11	52	321	398	583	981	11	73	0.47	4	6	46	261	8.13
Spd ++	2014	A	Asheville	482	93	136	18	102	282	354	502	857	10	70	0.38	8	5	49	220	6.52
Def +++	2015	A+	Modesto	496	85	149	18	75	300	363	520	883	9	69	0.32	6	13	45	220	6.94

Continued to excel and was one of the youngest players in the CAL. Has a quick LH stroke and plus raw power. Makes decent contact and has a good understanding of the strike zone, though there is some swing-and-miss. He's an average runner, but has soft hands, good range, and a strong arm. Has the tools to be a fantasy stud.

McNeil,Jeff — 456 — New York (N)

EXP MLB DEBUT: 2017 | H/W: 6-1 165 | FUT: Utility Player | 6D

Bats L Age 23	Year	Lev	Team	AB	R	H	HR	RBI	Avg	OB	Slg	OPS	bb%	ct%	Eye	SB	CS	x/h%	Iso	RC/G
2013 (12) Long Beach St	2013	Rk	Kingsport	164	26	54	0	18	329	392	409	801	9	91	1.21	11	2	20	79	5.66
Pwr +	2013	A	Savannah	232	38	77	2	38	332	385	461	846	8	85	0.59	15	3	31	129	6.02
BAvg +++	2014	A+	St. Lucie	207	31	51	1	13	246	319	319	638	10	88	0.88	2	2	22	72	3.72
Spd +++	2015	A+	St. Lucie	468	80	146	1	40	312	360	382	742	7	87	0.59	16	5	17	71	4.74
Def ++	2015	AA	Binghamton	15	0	3	0	0	200	250	200	450	6	87	0.50	0	1	0	0	1.26

Slap hitting utility infielder who has advanced further than anyone imagined. Finished 2nd in FSL in BA. Tremendous bat control, will slap balls through holes across the infield. Slight build won't allow for power to develop. Will get most XBHs down the foul lines. Solid defensively across the INF. Athlete with plus foot speed; could play in OF.

Meadows,Austin — 8 — Pittsburgh

EXP MLB DEBUT: 2017 | H/W: 6-2 200 | FUT: Starting LF | 9D

Bats L Age 20	Year	Lev	Team	AB	R	H	HR	RBI	Avg	OB	Slg	OPS	bb%	ct%	Eye	SB	CS	x/h%	Iso	RC/G
2013 (1) HS (GA)	2014	Rk	Bristol	14	2	1	0	0	71	235	71	307	18	79	1.00	0	0	0	0	-0.55
Pwr ++++	2014	Rk	GCL Pirates	4	1	4	0	1	1000		2000	3000	33	100		0	0	75	1000	32.64
BAvg ++++	2014	A	West Virginia	146	18	47	3	15	322	381	486	868	9	79	0.47	2	3	36	164	6.35
Spd +++	2015	A+	Bradenton	508	72	156	7	54	307	359	407	766	7	84	0.52	20	7	21	100	4.96
Def ++	2015	AA	Altoona	25	5	9	0	1	360	407	680	1087	7	80	0.40	1	0	56	320	9.46

Strong, athletic OF has a simple, compact LH stroke and the ball jumps off his bat. He's a plus runner and did swipe a career-best 21 bases. He covers ground in CF, but a below average arm could result in a shift to LF, where his power profiles well. Shows good patience at the plate and makes consistent contact.

Meija,Erick — 46 — Seattle
EXP MLB DEBUT: 2018 | H/W: 5-11 155 | FUT: Starting 2B/SS | 7D

Bats B Age 21 — 2012 FA (DR)

Pwr + | BAvg +++ | Spd +++ | Def ++

Year	Lev	Team	AB	R	H	HR	RBI	Avg	OB	Slg	OPS	bb%	ct%	Eye	SB	CS	x/h%	Iso	RC/G
2014	Rk	Azl Mariners	127	23	36	1	13	283	364	425	789	11	80	0.64	13	2	28	142	5.59
2015	Rk	Azl Mariners	12	4	5	0	2	417	462	500	962	8	83	0.50	2	1	20	83	7.38
2015	A-	Everett	131	24	37	0	11	282	361	336	696	11	83	0.73	18	0	16	53	4.38
2015	A	Clinton	26	5	7	0	3	269	269	346	615	0	85	0.00	0	0	14	77	2.82
2015	AAA	Tacoma	5	1	0	0	0	0	0	0	0	0	40	0.00	0	0		0	-8.89

Small-framed INF with decent all-around skills, but no plus tool. Can play either middle INF spot effectively with decent range and strong arm. Has instincts for game that allow tools to play up. Makes contact with compact stroke and offers some strength, though not much pop.

Mejia,Francisco — 2 — Cleveland
EXP MLB DEBUT: 2018 | H/W: 5-10 175 | FUT: Starting C | 8D

Bats B Age 20 — 2012 FA (DR)

Pwr +++ | BAvg ++ | Spd ++ | Def ++

Year	Lev	Team	AB	R	H	HR	RBI	Avg	OB	Slg	OPS	bb%	ct%	Eye	SB	CS	x/h%	Iso	RC/G
2013	Rk	AZL Indians	105	16	32	4	24	305	336	524	860	5	83	0.28	3	1	44	219	5.88
2014	A-	Mahoning Val	248	32	70	2	36	282	331	407	738	7	81	0.38	2	4	33	125	4.67
2015	A	Lake County	391	45	95	9	53	243	310	345	655	9	80	0.49	4	1	23	102	3.58

Emerging backstop who started slow, but ended strong. Showed off improved power and feel for hitting from both sides. Puts bat to ball easily and controls strike zone. Drives to all fields and should continue to add pop. Can swing aggressively early in count. Unrefined defender, but has very strong arm and quick release.

Mejia,Gabriel — 8 — Cleveland
EXP MLB DEBUT: 2019 | H/W: 5-11 160 | FUT: Starting OF | 8E

Bats B Age 20 — 2013 FA (DR)

Pwr + | BAvg ++++ | Spd ++++ | Def ++

Year	Lev	Team	AB	R	H	HR	RBI	Avg	OB	Slg	OPS	bb%	ct%	Eye	SB	CS	x/h%	Iso	RC/G
2015	Rk	AZL Indians	168	41	60	0	18	357	429	417	845	11	88	1.05	34	10	15	60	6.21
2015	A-	Mahoning Val	56	9	17	0	4	304	316	321	637	2	86	0.13	6	1	6	18	3.08

Lean and fast OF who had standout 1st season in U.S. Possesses clean stroke from both sides and knows value in keeping ball on ground to use plus speed. Led AZL in SB and 2nd in BA. Body needs more strength, but will never be HR guy. Unrefined instincts make him below average CF now, but exhibits good range and will stay there long-term.

Mercado,Oscar — 6 — St. Louis
EXP MLB DEBUT: 2018 | H/W: 6-2 175 | FUT: Utility player | 6B

Bats R Age 21 — 2013 (2) HS (FL)

Pwr + | BAvg ++ | Spd ++++ | Def ++++

Year	Lev	Team	AB	R	H	HR	RBI	Avg	OB	Slg	OPS	bb%	ct%	Eye	SB	CS	x/h%	Iso	RC/G
2013	Rk	GCL Cardinals	163	18	34	1	14	209	283	307	590	9	76	0.44	12	4	29	98	2.87
2014	Rk	Johnson City	245	41	55	3	25	224	283	306	589	8	85	0.54	26	7	24	82	2.89
2015	A	Peoria	472	70	120	4	44	254	289	341	630	5	87	0.38	50	19	25	87	3.29

Slick-fielding SS with plus speed has yet to prove he can hit as a pro. Does have a good line-drive approach that is geared more towards gap power and makes decent contact, but doesn't hit the ball with enough authority. Pitch recognition needs to improve. Solid defender with good instincts and good range.

Michalczewski,Trey — 5 — Chicago (A)
EXP MLB DEBUT: 2017 | H/W: 6-3 210 | FUT: Starting 1B/3B | 8D

Bats B Age 21 — 2013 (7) HS (OK)

Pwr +++ | BAvg +++ | Spd ++ | Def +++

Year	Lev	Team	AB	R	H	HR	RBI	Avg	OB	Slg	OPS	bb%	ct%	Eye	SB	CS	x/h%	Iso	RC/G
2013	Rk	Bristol	195	25	46	3	21	236	317	328	645	11	71	0.41	2	0	22	92	3.51
2014	A	Kannapolis	432	57	118	10	70	273	342	433	775	9	68	0.32	6	3	36	160	5.47
2014	A+	Winston-Salem	72	5	14	0	5	194	284	222	506	11	71	0.43	1	0	14	28	1.61
2015	A+	Winston-Salem	474	59	123	7	75	259	330	395	725	10	76	0.44	4	3	37	135	4.62

Big and strong INF whose shortened stroke and improved pitch selection resulted in more consistent contact. Hits lots of doubles which should evolve into HR with more AB. Works counts to advantage, but still strikes out too often. Possesses enough agility and arm strength to be capable defender, but could move to 1B or LF in future.

Mieses,Johan — 8 — Los Angeles (N)
EXP MLB DEBUT: 2020 | H/W: 6-2 185 | FUT: Starting CF | 8E

Bats R Age 20 — 2013 FA (DR)

Pwr +++ | BAvg +++ | Spd +++ | Def +++

Year	Lev	Team	AB	R	H	HR	RBI	Avg	OB	Slg	OPS	bb%	ct%	Eye	SB	CS	x/h%	Iso	RC/G
2015	A	Great Lakes	166	16	46	5	20	277	322	440	762	6	81	0.35	7	4	35	163	4.79
2015	A+	RanchoCuca	196	35	48	6	19	245	292	439	731	6	71	0.23	3	1	52	194	4.58

Tall Dominican OF finally made his state-side debut. Fared well in the MWL, earning a mid-season promotion to High-A. Toolsy, instinctual player with plus raw power and good bat speed. Needs to develop a better understanding of the strike zone and whiffed 88 times in 362 AB, but also launched 28 doubles and 11 HR as a 19-year old.

Miller,Anderson — 89 — Kansas City
EXP MLB DEBUT: 2018 | H/W: 6-3 205 | FUT: Starting OF | 8D

Bats L Age 21 — 2015 (3) Wstrn Kentucky

Pwr +++ | BAvg +++ | Spd +++ | Def +++

Year	Lev	Team	AB	R	H	HR	RBI	Avg	OB	Slg	OPS	bb%	ct%	Eye	SB	CS	x/h%	Iso	RC/G
2015	NCAA	Wstrn Kentucky	193	47	57	12	35	295	419	560	978	18	77	0.93	5	4	42	264	8.12
2015	Rk	Burlington	38	6	13	2	7	342	342	579	921	0	82	0.00	3	0	38	237	6.20
2015	A	Lexington	169	15	44	2	21	260	317	355	672	8	83	0.50	0	1	25	95	3.86

Emerging prospect with interesting tools and performance to boot. Power evolving from doubles to HR and should continue to grow. Has become more selective at plate with discerning eye and covers plate with quick bat. Draws walks and uses above average speed well. Split time between CF and RF, though likely profiles best in the corner.

Miller,Ian — 8 — Seattle
EXP MLB DEBUT: 2017 | H/W: 6-0 175 | FUT: Fourth OF | 6B

Bats L Age 24 — 2013 (14) Wagner

Pwr + | BAvg +++ | Spd ++++ | Def +++

Year	Lev	Team	AB	R	H	HR	RBI	Avg	OB	Slg	OPS	bb%	ct%	Eye	SB	CS	x/h%	Iso	RC/G
2013	Rk	Pulaski	155	30	46	1	13	297	363	348	711	9	81	0.55	14	6	13	52	4.38
2013	A-	Everett	42	7	14	0	1	333	391	333	725	9	86	0.67	3	1	0	0	4.53
2014	A	Clinton	166	33	45	0	13	271	335	349	685	9	79	0.46	16	2	20	78	4.10
2015	A+	Bakersfield	159	20	47	0	6	296	337	352	689	6	79	0.29	21	5	15	57	3.95
2015	AA	Jackson	347	40	88	0	23	254	311	320	631	8	85	0.55	29	13	20	66	3.47

Speedy CF who used wheels to set high in SB. Lacks power (1 career HR), but knows speed and contact are his best tools. Puts bat to ball in simple approach and has shown ability to hit LHP. Could get on base more, but has disciplined eye. Good defensive CF with great range and average arm.

Miller,Jalen — 6 — San Francisco
EXP MLB DEBUT: 2019 | H/W: 5-10 175 | FUT: Starting SS | 8E

Bats R Age 19 — 2015 (3) HS (GA)

Pwr ++ | BAvg +++ | Spd ++++ | Def ++++

Year	Lev	Team	AB	R	H	HR	RBI	Avg	OB	Slg	OPS	bb%	ct%	Eye	SB	CS	x/h%	Iso	RC/G
2015	Rk	Azl Giants	174	28	38	0	13	218	288	259	547	9	76	0.40	11	2	16	40	2.22

Glove-first SS has wiry, athletic build. Plus athletic ability and first-step quickness will give him SB upside; soft hands, good range and decent arm project his glove at SS long-term. Has quick load and good bat speed required for BA, but will need to exhibit more patience. With added muscle, raw power could be fringe-average down the road.

Minier,Amaurys — 3 — Minnesota
EXP MLB DEBUT: 2019 | H/W: 6-2 190 | FUT: Starting 1B | 8E

Bats B Age 20 — 2012 FA (DR)

Pwr ++++ | BAvg ++ | Spd + | Def +

Year	Lev	Team	AB	R	H	HR	RBI	Avg	OB	Slg	OPS	bb%	ct%	Eye	SB	CS	x/h%	Iso	RC/G
2013	Rk	GCL Twins	112	10	24	6	17	214	254	455	710	5	74	0.21	1	1	54	241	4.05
2014	Rk	GCL Twins	171	25	50	8	33	292	395	520	915	15	70	0.56	2	2	42	228	7.53
2015	Rk	Elizabethton	175	19	34	2	21	194	269	280	549	9	62	0.27	0	1	32	86	2.15
2015	Rk	GCL Twins	6	1	2	0	0	333	333	333	667	0	67	0.00	0	0	0	0	3.37

Large-framed prospect who transitioned to 1B full-time. Owns plus power from both sides, though hasn't translated well to game action. Swings hard with plus bat speed, but isn't selective and lacks hand-eye coordination for contact. All or nothing approach hinders BA. Bat-only prospect as defense and speed are liabilities.

Molina,Leonardo — 89 — New York (A)
EXP MLB DEBUT: 2019 | H/W: 6-2 180 | FUT: Starting OF | 9E

Bats R Age 18 — 2013 FA (DR)

Pwr ++ | BAvg ++ | Spd +++ | Def +++

Year	Lev	Team	AB	R	H	HR	RBI	Avg	OB	Slg	OPS	bb%	ct%	Eye	SB	CS	x/h%	Iso	RC/G
2014	Rk	GCL Yankees	192	18	37	1	21	193	265	260	526	9	73	0.37	6	1	30	68	1.89
2015	Rk	GCL Yankees	162	15	40	2	17	247	291	364	655	6	77	0.27	6	5	33	117	3.51

Projectable OF with high ceiling. Spent repeat year in rookie ball, but still young and raw. Possesses loud tools and should add power as he matures into body. Bat speed is impressive and should hit for BA as he finds consistent stroke. Has good speed that allows him to steal bases and range well in CF. Long ways away, but is major sleeper.

Moncada,Yoan

4 | **Boston** | EXP MLB DEBUT: 2017 | H/W: 6-2 205 | FUT: Starting 2B | **9C**

Bats B Age 20
2015 FA (CU)

- Pwr +++
- BAvg ++++
- Spd ++++
- Def ++

Year	Lev	Team	AB	R	H	HR	RBI	Avg	OB	Slg	OPS	bb%	ct%	Eye	SB	CS	x/h%	Iso	RC/G
2015	A	Greenville	306	61	85	8	38	278	365	438	803	12	73	0.51	49	3	35	160	5.78

Elite prospect who had outstanding debut season. Should hit for easy high BA due to bat speed, instincts, and swing mechanics. Has plus raw power that could develop in time. Aggressively runs bases with plus speed. Hasn't been a strong defender at 2B, but has the tools to be above average. Has potential to be middle-of-order hitter.

Mondesi,Raul A.

46 | **Kansas City** | EXP MLB DEBUT: 2016 | H/W: 6-1 185 | FUT: Starting SS | **9C**

Bats B Age 20
2011 FA (DR)

- Pwr +++
- BAvg ++++
- Spd ++++
- Def +++++

Year	Lev	Team	AB	R	H	HR	RBI	Avg	OB	Slg	OPS	bb%	ct%	Eye	SB	CS	x/h%	Iso	RC/G
2012	Rk	Idaho Falls	207	35	60	3	30	290	350	386	736	8	69	0.29	11	2	20	97	4.79
2013	A	Lexington	482	61	126	7	47	261	310	361	671	7	76	0.29	24	10	21	100	3.70
2014	A+	Wilmington	435	54	92	8	33	211	253	354	607	5	72	0.20	17	4	37	143	2.84
2015	AA	NW Arkansas	304	36	74	6	33	243	283	372	655	5	71	0.19	19	6	30	128	3.47

Exciting prospect who can impact game on many levels. Stands out with glove with all requisite tools. Quick actions and smooth feet give him ample range and has strong, accurate arm. Hasn't put together great offensive year, but has plus bat speed and plus-plus wheels. Needs to tame free-swinging ways. Should reach double figures in HR at peak.

Moran,Colin

5 | **Houston** | EXP MLB DEBUT: 2016 | H/W: 6-3 215 | FUT: Starting 3B | **7B**

Bats L Age 23
2013 (1) North Carolina

- Pwr ++
- BAvg ++++
- Spd +
- Def +++

Year	Lev	Team	AB	R	H	HR	RBI	Avg	OB	Slg	OPS	bb%	ct%	Eye	SB	CS	x/h%	Iso	RC/G
2013	NCAA	North Carolina	281	76	97	13	91	345	465	544	1010	18	91	2.52	1	0	28	199	8.43
2013	A	Greensboro	154	19	46	4	23	299	361	442	803	9	84	0.60	1	0	28	143	5.44
2014	A+	Jupiter	361	34	106	5	33	294	344	393	738	7	85	0.53	1	2	25	100	4.62
2014	AA	Corpus Christi	112	12	34	2	22	304	355	411	766	7	79	0.39	0	1	24	107	4.93
2015	AA	Corpus Christi	366	47	112	9	67	306	379	459	838	11	78	0.54	1	0	32	153	6.05

Natural-hitting INF with advanced approach and ability to bat .300+. Missed time with fractured jaw, but continued to hit when healthy. All HR came late in season and could see power spike with added loft in stroke. Knows strike zone and will get on base. Lacks foot speed for SB, but lack of quickness doesn't hinder him with glove.

Morgan,Gareth

789 | **Seattle** | EXP MLB DEBUT: 2018 | H/W: 6-4 220 | FUT: Starting OF | **8E**

Bats R Age 19
2014 (2) HS (ON)

- Pwr ++++
- BAvg +
- Spd ++
- Def ++

Year	Lev	Team	AB	R	H	HR	RBI	Avg	OB	Slg	OPS	bb%	ct%	Eye	SB	CS	x/h%	Iso	RC/G
2014	Rk	Azl Mariners	155	15	23	2	12	148	228	252	480	9	53	0.22	4	1	48	103	1.20
2015	Rk	Azl Mariners	222	31	50	5	30	225	265	383	648	5	60	0.13	5	1	42	158	3.78

High-risk OF with potential high reward. Returned to rookie ball and only slightly better. Has ideal frame for RF power prospect, but cannot put bat to ball. Draws few walks in all-or-nothing approach and fails to read spin. Natural power may be best in org and has strength in wrists and forearms to make hard contact. Will take time to develop.

Morgan,Josh

56 | **Texas** | EXP MLB DEBUT: 2018 | H/W: 5-11 185 | FUT: Starting SS/3B | **7C**

Bats R Age 20
2014 (3) HS (CA)

- Pwr ++
- BAvg +++
- Spd +++
- Def +++

Year	Lev	Team	AB	R	H	HR	RBI	Avg	OB	Slg	OPS	bb%	ct%	Eye	SB	CS	x/h%	Iso	RC/G
2014	Rk	Azl Rangers	113	26	38	0	10	336	432	372	803	14	88	1.46	2	2	8	35	5.95
2014	A-	Spokane	89	11	27	0	9	303	374	315	688	10	89	1.00	1	1	4	11	4.30
2015	A	Hickory	351	59	101	3	36	288	369	362	731	11	85	0.85	9	4	19	74	4.81

Athletic INF who had missed time after July due to injury. All-around player who gets on base with patient approach and has easy feel for contact. Recognizes spin well and hits hard line drives to all fields. Power is not part of his equation, but he offers above average speed. Split time between SS and 3B and has feet, range, and arm for both.

Moroff,Max

4 | **Pittsburgh** | EXP MLB DEBUT: 2017 | H/W: 5-11 175 | FUT: Utility player | **6B**

Bats B Age 22
2012 (16) HS (FL)

- Pwr ++
- BAvg +++
- Spd ++
- Def +++

Year	Lev	Team	AB	R	H	HR	RBI	Avg	OB	Slg	OPS	bb%	ct%	Eye	SB	CS	x/h%	Iso	RC/G
2012	Rk	GCL Pirates	67	17	23	1	7	343	476	433	909	20	84	1.55	7	3	17	90	7.51
2013	A	West Virginia	429	75	100	8	48	233	334	345	679	13	76	0.64	8	8	29	112	4.11
2014	A+	Bradenton	467	57	114	1	50	244	322	340	663	10	72	0.42	21	15	32	96	3.90
2015	AA	Altoona	523	79	153	7	51	293	376	409	785	12	79	0.63	17	13	27	117	5.49

Small, athletic infielder was moved from SS to 2B. Nice breakout season at the plate. Good hand-eye coordination and understanding of the strike zone allows him to make solid contact. Has moderate power and is at his best when he hits the ball in the gaps. Solid defender with good range. Profiles as a solid UT player.

Mountcastle,Ryan

6 | **Baltimore** | EXP MLB DEBUT: 2019 | H/W: 6-3 195 | FUT: Starting 3B/LF | **8D**

Bats R Age 19
2015 (1) HS (FL)

- Pwr +++
- BAvg +++
- Spd ++
- Def ++

Year	Lev	Team	AB	R	H	HR	RBI	Avg	OB	Slg	OPS	bb%	ct%	Eye	SB	CS	x/h%	Iso	RC/G
2015	Rk	GCL Orioles	163	21	51	3	14	313	349	411	760	5	78	0.25	10	4	20	98	4.70
2015	A-	Aberdeen	33	2	7	1	5	212	212	303	515	0	70	0.00	0	1	14	91	1.13

Advanced hitter who makes hard, consistent contact with above average bat speed. Has feel for barrel and leverage in swing could result in plus power down the line. Has tendency to chase pitches, but catches up to good FB. Plays SS at present, though projects better at 3B or LF. Fringy arm and lacks ideal quickness for MIF.

Moya,Steven

79 | **Detroit** | EXP MLB DEBUT: 2014 | H/W: 6-6 260 | FUT: Starting OF | **8D**

Bats L Age 24
2008 FA (DR)

- Pwr +++++
- BAvg ++
- Spd ++
- Def +++

Year	Lev	Team	AB	R	H	HR	RBI	Avg	OB	Slg	OPS	bb%	ct%	Eye	SB	CS	x/h%	Iso	RC/G
2014	AA	Erie	515	81	142	35	105	276	307	555	862	4	69	0.14	16	4	50	280	6.22
2014	MLB	Detroit	8	2	3	0	0	375	375	375	750	0	75	0.00	0	0	0	0	4.24
2015	A+	Lakeland	40	3	11	3	8	275	293	575	868	2	68	0.08	0	0	55	300	6.28
2015	AAA	Toledo	500	53	120	20	74	240	279	420	699	5	68	0.17	5	4	42	180	4.06
2015	MLB	Detroit	22	1	4	0	0	182	280	273	553	12	55	0.30	0	0	25	91	2.62

Tall OF who finished 3rd in IL in both HR and Ks. Covers plate well with long arms, but has holes in swing that result in Ks. Likes to swing stick early in count and will be fed a lot of breaking balls. Runs well for size and has improved corner OF routes and reads. Uses entire field, but lack of contact may hinder plus-plus all-fields power.

Munoz,Carlos

3 | **Pittsburgh** | EXP MLB DEBUT: 2019 | H/W: 5-11 225 | FUT: Backup 1B | **6A**

Bats L Age 21
2011 FA (MX)

- Pwr +++
- BAvg +++
- Spd +
- Def ++

Year	Lev	Team	AB	R	H	HR	RBI	Avg	OB	Slg	OPS	bb%	ct%	Eye	SB	CS	x/h%	Iso	RC/G
2013	Rk	DSL Pirates	207	40	66	3	36	319	460	459	919	21	87	2.00	0	1	32	140	7.72
2014	Rk	GCL Pirates	197	20	56	4	38	284	379	421	800	13	92	1.88	0	2	34	137	5.86
2015	Rk	Bristol	206	35	67	11	39	325	421	587	1008	14	90	1.62	2	0	48	262	8.13
2015	A-	West Virginia	20	7	3	1	3	150	370	350	720	26	65	1.00	0	0	67	200	4.85

Short, stocky 1B had a breakout season, hitting .325/.427/.587 and was named Appy MVP, though he was old for the level. Uses a nice LH stroke to barrel the ball consistently with excellent strike zone judgment. Good power and had a career-high 11 HR in 206 AB. Lack of athleticism limits him and the Pirates didn't move him up.

Munoz,Yairo

6 | **Oakland** | EXP MLB DEBUT: 2017 | H/W: 6-1 165 | FUT: Starting SS | **7B**

Bats R Age 21
2012 FA (DR)

- Pwr +++
- BAvg +++
- Spd ++
- Def +++

Year	Lev	Team	AB	R	H	HR	RBI	Avg	OB	Slg	OPS	bb%	ct%	Eye	SB	CS	x/h%	Iso	RC/G
2013	Rk	Azl Athletics	67	8	13	1	5	194	270	284	554	9	84	0.64	1	0	31	90	2.53
2014	A-	Vermont	252	29	75	5	20	298	317	448	765	3	83	0.17	14	6	33	151	4.67
2015	A	Beloit	369	48	87	9	48	236	279	363	642	6	83	0.35	10	2	30	127	3.33
2015	A+	Stockton	150	21	48	4	26	320	366	480	846	7	87	0.55	1	1	33	160	5.84

Young, quick INF who was better in High-A than Low-A in breakout season. Set highs in doubles and HR while improving consistency in glovework. Still can be erratic in field, but has range and arm to stick at SS. Impressive batting tools and could hit for both BA and power. Makes easy contact, though has fringy speed.

Murphy,Tanner

2 | **Atlanta** | EXP MLB DEBUT: 2020 | H/W: 6-1 215 | FUT: Reserve C | **6D**

Bats R Age 21
2013 (4) HS (MO)

- Pwr ++
- BAvg +
- Spd +
- Def +++

Year	Lev	Team	AB	R	H	HR	RBI	Avg	OB	Slg	OPS	bb%	ct%	Eye	SB	CS	x/h%	Iso	RC/G
2013	Rk	GCL Braves	97	7	22	0	8	227	312	258	570	11	65	0.35	5	0	14	31	2.50
2014	Rk	Danville	157	21	38	5	19	242	364	389	752	16	76	0.79	2	1	34	146	5.15
2015	A	Rome	337	33	65	7	35	193	275	312	586	10	73	0.42	0	0	38	119	2.69

Defense-first catcher struggled mightily at the plate during his full-season debut. Has raw power but bat speed lags behind due to elongation. Struggles reading pitches out of the pitchers hands. Good enough bat control to keep K numbers down. Behind the plate, he moves well, has solid presentation skills and a plus arm.

Murphy,Tom — 2 — Colorado

EXP MLB DEBUT: 2015 | H/W: 6-1 220 | FUT: Starting C | 7C

Bats R Age 25 — 2012 (3) Buffalo

Pwr +++ | BAvg ++ | Spd ++ | Def ++

Year	Lev	Team	AB	R	H	HR	RBI	Avg	OB	Slg	OPS	bb%	ct%	Eye	SB	CS	x/h%	Iso	RC/G
2013	AA	Tulsa	69	9	20	3	9	290	329	493	822	5	77	0.25	0	0	40	203	5.49
2014	AA	Tulsa	94	16	20	5	15	213	315	415	730	13	71	0.52	0	0	45	202	4.61
2015	AA	New Britain	265	36	66	13	44	249	309	468	777	8	70	0.29	5	2	47	219	5.20
2015	AAA	Albuquerque	129	19	35	7	19	271	299	535	833	4	67	0.12	0	1	51	264	6.04
2015	MLB	Colorado	35	5	9	3	9	257	333	543	876	10	71	0.40	0	0	44	286	6.37

Strong backstop started the year at AA and made his MLB debut before a 2nd shoulder injury. Has a good approach at the plate that generates above-average power. Has good bat speed, but struggles to make contact, making him a .250 hitter unless he adjusts. Moves well behind the plate with a strong arm.

Naquin,Tyler — 8 — Cleveland

EXP MLB DEBUT: 2016 | H/W: 6-2 190 | FUT: Starting OF | 7B

Bats L Age 24 — 2012 (1) Texas A&M

Pwr ++ | BAvg +++ | Spd +++ | Def +++

Year	Lev	Team	AB	R	H	HR	RBI	Avg	OB	Slg	OPS	bb%	ct%	Eye	SB	CS	x/h%	Iso	RC/G
2013	A+	Carolina	448	69	124	9	42	277	337	424	762	8	75	0.37	14	7	34	147	5.02
2013	AA	Akron	80	9	18	1	6	225	271	300	571	6	73	0.23	1	3	22	75	2.29
2014	AA	Akron	304	54	95	4	30	313	372	424	797	9	77	0.41	14	3	22	112	5.48
2015	AA	Akron	139	15	47	1	10	338	399	453	852	9	83	0.58	6	1	28	115	6.18
2015	AAA	Columbus	186	34	49	6	17	263	351	430	781	12	74	0.51	6	2	39	167	5.39

Injury-prone OF who opened season late due to quad issue. When healthy, has tools to be contributor. May lack ideal power, but brings disciplined approach to plate and his hard line drives to all fields. Makes easy contact and uses speed well on base and in OF. Strong arm and instincts make him solid average CF.

Nay,Mitch — 5 — Toronto

EXP MLB DEBUT: 2017 | H/W: 6-3 200 | FUT: Starting 3B | 7C

Bats R Age 22 — 2012 (1) HS (AZ)

Pwr +++ | BAvg +++ | Spd + | Def +++

Year	Lev	Team	AB	R	H	HR	RBI	Avg	OB	Slg	OPS	bb%	ct%	Eye	SB	CS	x/h%	Iso	RC/G
2013	Rk	Bluefield	230	41	69	6	42	300	369	426	795	10	85	0.71	0	1	25	126	5.39
2014	A	Lansing	473	57	135	3	59	285	340	389	729	8	83	0.49	6	2	30	104	4.60
2014	A+	Dunedin	37	2	7	0	1	189	250	216	466	8	76	0.33	0	0	14	27	1.08
2015	A+	Dunedin	391	32	95	5	42	243	300	353	653	8	81	0.43	0	1	29	110	3.60

Strong INF who has yet to tap into impressive raw power, but continues to make decent contact. Long swing can be exploited as he doesn't cover plate well. Needs to add power to repertoire in order to have value as 3B. Lacks quickness at 3B, but has improved hands and footwork. Owns strong, accurate arm.

Naylor,Josh — 3 — Miami

EXP MLB DEBUT: 2020 | H/W: 6-0 225 | FUT: Starting 1B | 9D

Bats L Age 18 — 2015 (1) HS (ON)

Pwr ++++ | BAvg +++ | Spd ++ | Def ++

Year	Lev	Team	AB	R	H	HR	RBI	Avg	OB	Slg	OPS	bb%	ct%	Eye	SB	CS	x/h%	Iso	RC/G
2015	Rk	GCL Marlins	98	8	32	1	16	327	353	418	771	4	89	0.36	1	0	19	92	4.83

Plus-plus raw power; won several showcase HR competitions in HS. Huge player moves well for his size, but is a below-avg runner. Has a thick frame and can crush pitches with a powerful LH stroke. Makes consistent contact by staying behind the ball and uses the entire field. Could develop into a Kyle Schwarber-type.

Neuhaus,Tucker — 46 — Milwaukee

EXP MLB DEBUT: 2018 | H/W: 6-3 190 | FUT: Backup INF | 6C

Bats L Age 20 — 2013 (2) HS (FL)

Pwr +++ | BAvg ++ | Spd +++ | Def +++

Year	Lev	Team	AB	R	H	HR	RBI	Avg	OB	Slg	OPS	bb%	ct%	Eye	SB	CS	x/h%	Iso	RC/G
2013	Rk	Azl Brewers	195	29	45	0	24	231	312	303	614	11	71	0.41	6	3	29	72	3.21
2014	Rk	Helena	232	31	54	3	21	233	294	328	621	8	67	0.26	9	2	30	95	3.15
2015	A	Wisconsin	369	32	92	4	40	249	311	355	666	8	79	0.43	0	2	29	106	3.79

Former 2nd rounder's growth has been incremental, albeit rather slow. Strong build and good bat speed foretell of future solid average power, but poor discipline and contact skills vs. LHPs limit his BA/OBP ceiling. Switched from 3B to primarily 2B last year, where his soft hands, glove-work and speed could be best utilized defensively long-term.

Nevin,Tyler — 5 — Colorado

EXP MLB DEBUT: 2019 | H/W: 6-4 200 | FUT: Starting 3B | 7B

Bats R Age 18 — 2015 (1) HS (CA)

Pwr ++++ | BAvg ++++ | Spd ++ | Def ++

Year	Lev	Team	AB	R	H	HR	RBI	Avg	OB	Slg	OPS	bb%	ct%	Eye	SB	CS	x/h%	Iso	RC/G
2015	Rk	Grand Junction	189	29	50	2	18	265	362	386	749	13	78	0.69	3	7	36	122	5.14

Advanced hitter is son of former big leaguer Phil Nevin. Plus raw power and good bat speed should translate well and gives him the potential to move up quickly. Avg runner will have to work hard to stick at 3B. Had TJS in '13, but is now healthy. Has an avg arm with good hands, but scouts are mixed on his future position.

Newman,Kevin — 6 — Pittsburgh

EXP MLB DEBUT: 2019 | H/W: 6-1 180 | FUT: Starting 2B | 7B

Bats R Age 22 — 2015 (1) Arizona

Pwr ++ | BAvg ++++ | Spd +++ | Def +++

Year	Lev	Team	AB	R	H	HR	RBI	Avg	OB	Slg	OPS	bb%	ct%	Eye	SB	CS	x/h%	Iso	RC/G
2015	NCAA	Arizona	227	53	84	2	36	370	421	489	910	8	93	1.33	22	3	26	119	6.75
2015	A-	West Virginia	159	25	36	2	9	226	272	340	612	6	86	0.45	7	1	36	113	3.15
2015	A	West Virginia	98	14	30	0	8	306	364	367	732	8	92	1.13	6	1	17	61	4.82

Was one of the best pure hitters in the draft and twice won the Cape Cod league batting title. Plus hand-eye coordination and strike zone judgment allow him to make consistent contact and he should hit for BA as he moves up, but with below-average power. Good range with an average arm, but scouts are mixed on ability to stick at SS.

Ngoepe,Gift — 6 — Pittsburgh

EXP MLB DEBUT: 2016 | H/W: 5-8 200 | FUT: Utility player | 6C

Bats R Age 26 — 2008 FA (SA)

Pwr + | BAvg ++ | Spd +++ | Def ++++

Year	Lev	Team	AB	R	H	HR	RBI	Avg	OB	Slg	OPS	bb%	ct%	Eye	SB	CS	x/h%	Iso	RC/G
2013	A+	Bradenton	96	17	28	0	6	292	419	427	846	18	64	0.60	7	1	36	135	7.35
2013	AA	Altoona	220	29	39	3	16	177	270	282	552	11	63	0.34	10	3	38	105	2.24
2014	AA	Altoona	437	58	104	9	52	238	318	380	697	10	69	0.38	13	8	34	142	4.33
2015	AA	Altoona	246	31	64	3	25	260	326	362	688	9	73	0.36	3	6	27	102	4.08
2015	AAA	Indianapolis	61	5	15	0	1	246	313	311	625	9	75	0.40	1	2	27	66	3.29

Athletic INF spent most of the season playing SS, but profiles as a utility-type. Gave up switch hitting and had a solid season at the plate. Struggles to make consistent contact and has yet to prove he can hit a breaking ball. Runs well but is not a base-stealing threat. Plus defense and position flexibility will be his ticket to the majors.

Nimmo,Brandon — 789 — New York (N)

EXP MLB DEBUT: 2016 | H/W: 6-3 205 | FUT: Platoon OF | 7B

Bats L Age 23 — 2011 (1) HS (WY)

Pwr ++ | BAvg ++++ | Spd +++ | Def +++

Year	Lev	Team	AB	R	H	HR	RBI	Avg	OB	Slg	OPS	bb%	ct%	Eye	SB	CS	x/h%	Iso	RC/G
2014	A+	St. Lucie	227	59	73	4	25	322	444	458	902	18	78	0.98	9	3	25	137	7.39
2014	AA	Binghamton	240	38	57	6	26	238	337	396	733	13	78	0.67	5	1	39	158	4.83
2015	A+	St. Lucie	16	3	2	0	2	125	300	188	488	20	81	1.33	0	0	50	63	2.15
2015	AA	Binghamton	269	26	75	2	16	279	342	368	710	9	80	0.47	0	2	23	89	4.38
2015	AAA	Las Vegas	91	19	24	3	8	264	385	418	803	17	78	0.90	5	4	29	154	5.84

Fmr 1st rd pick falling short on lofty expectations. Borderline-plus hit tool is aided by advanced approach. Almost too patient for his own good. Has cut down on swing length and susceptibility to strikeouts. Added strength hasn't translated to higher HR totals. Generates too much topspin off bat to be real power threat. A league-average OF.

Nottingham,Jacob — 23 — Oakland

EXP MLB DEBUT: 2018 | H/W: 6-3 230 | FUT: Starting C | 8C

Bats R Age 21 — 2013 (6) HS (CA)

Pwr +++ | BAvg +++ | Spd + | Def ++

Year	Lev	Team	AB	R	H	HR	RBI	Avg	OB	Slg	OPS	bb%	ct%	Eye	SB	CS	x/h%	Iso	RC/G
2013	Rk	GCL Astros	146	23	36	1	20	247	341	363	704	13	74	0.55	4	2	36	116	4.55
2014	Rk	Greeneville	174	25	40	5	28	230	302	385	687	9	69	0.33	3	2	40	155	4.08
2015	A	Quad Cities	230	34	75	10	46	326	375	543	918	7	78	0.35	1	2	39	217	6.82
2015	A+	Lancaster	71	14	23	4	14	324	351	606	957	4	86	0.30	0	0	48	282	6.87
2015	A+	Stockton	164	25	49	3	22	299	347	409	755	7	77	0.32	1	0	24	110	4.77

Strong backstop who put himself on radar in first full season with developing pop and surprising BA. Moved to High-A in June and continued to hit. Takes vicious hacks, yet can shorten stroke at times. Needs to develop better selectivity. Has physical frame behind plate and also saw time at 1B. Needs time to smooth out release.

Nunez,Dom — 2 — Colorado

EXP MLB DEBUT: 2018 | H/W: 6-0 175 | FUT: Starting C | 7C

Bats L Age 21 — 2013 (6) HS (CA)

Pwr ++ | BAvg +++ | Spd ++ | Def +++

Year	Lev	Team	AB	R	H	HR	RBI	Avg	OB	Slg	OPS	bb%	ct%	Eye	SB	CS	x/h%	Iso	RC/G
2013	Rk	Grand Junction	195	24	39	3	23	200	268	323	591	8	83	0.53	11	8	44	123	2.94
2014	Rk	Grand Junction	176	30	55	8	40	313	386	517	903	11	84	0.75	5	7	36	205	6.68
2015	A	Asheville	373	61	105	13	53	282	371	448	819	12	85	0.96	7	7	34	166	5.83

Converted backstop continues to make strides behind the plate. Has a strong, accurate arm with a quick release. Good approach at the plate with a compact LH stroke that is geared towards making contact. Swing does generate some loft with above-avg power. Started slowly, but stroked the ball after that, hitting .335/.444/.607 in the 2nd half.

Nunez,Renato — 35 — Oakland

EXP MLB DEBUT: 2016 | H/W: 6-1 200 | FUT: Starting 3B | 8B

Bats R Age 22	Year	Lev	Team	AB	R	H	HR	RBI	Avg	OB	Slg	OPS	bb%	ct%	Eye	SB	CS	x/h%	Iso	RC/G
2010 FA (VZ)																				
Pwr ++++	2012	Rk	Azl Athletics	160	31	52	4	42	325	390	550	940	10	80	0.53	4	0	48	225	7.36
BAvg +++	2013	A	Beloit	508	69	131	19	85	258	297	423	720	5	73	0.21	2	2	35	165	4.20
Spd ++	2014	A+	Stockton	509	75	142	29	96	279	324	517	841	6	78	0.30	2	0	42	238	5.69
Def +	2015	AA	Midland	381	62	106	18	61	278	328	480	808	7	83	0.42	1	0	39	202	5.29

Improving prospect who got better as season progressed. Finished 2nd in TL in HR while showing more consistent, hard contact. Destroys LHP and can catch up to any FB. Swings hard at all times and has tendency to get pull happy. Most of time spent at 3B, but also played 1B. Defense isn't forte, but bat can carry him.

O'Brien,Peter — 379 — Arizona

EXP MLB DEBUT: 2015 | H/W: 6-4 235 | FUT: Starting OF | 8C

Bats R Age 25	Year	Lev	Team	AB	R	H	HR	RBI	Avg	OB	Slg	OPS	bb%	ct%	Eye	SB	CS	x/h%	Iso	RC/G
2012 (2) Miami	2014	A+	Tampa	112	19	36	10	19	321	345	688	1032	3	74	0.14	0	0	56	366	8.11
Pwr ++++	2014	AA	Mobile	13	1	5	1	4	385	429	615	1044	7	62	0.20	0	0	20	231	9.59
BAvg ++	2014	AA	Trenton	274	47	67	23	51	245	286	555	841	6	72	0.21	0	0	57	310	5.72
Spd +	2015	AAA	Reno	490	77	139	26	107	284	326	551	877	6	75	0.25	1	3	50	267	6.34
Def +	2015	MLB	Arizona	10	1	4	1	3	400	500	800	1300	17	50	0.40	0	0	50	400	17.39

Power-hitting former C without defensive position. Made MLB debut in 2015. 2nd in PCL in HR with 26. Could be 30-HR bat with better hit tool. Susceptible to breaking balls. Doesn't adjust approach to count. Likely a .240 MLB hitter. 30-grade runner & fielder. Would benefit with a trade to an AL team.

O'Conner,Justin — 2 — Tampa Bay

EXP MLB DEBUT: 2016 | H/W: 6-0 190 | FUT: Starting C | 8D

Bats R Age 24	Year	Lev	Team	AB	R	H	HR	RBI	Avg	OB	Slg	OPS	bb%	ct%	Eye	SB	CS	x/h%	Iso	RC/G
2010 (1) HS (IN)	2012	A-	Hudson Valley	238	39	53	5	29	223	277	370	647	7	69	0.25	2	0	45	147	3.48
Pwr +++	2013	A	Bowling Green	399	49	93	14	56	233	288	381	669	7	72	0.28	5	0	33	148	3.61
BAvg ++	2014	A+	Charlotte	319	40	90	10	44	282	314	486	800	4	76	0.19	0	0	48	204	5.31
Spd ++	2014	AA	Montgomery	80	9	21	2	3	263	272	388	659	1	75	0.05	0	0	29	125	3.22
Def ++++	2015	AA	Montgomery	429	50	99	9	53	231	253	371	624	3	70	0.10	10	2	39	140	2.97

Excellent defensive C with incredible arm strength and neutralizer of running game. Impacts game behind plate and has good power to all fields. Breaking balls are problematic for him and he lacks patience to get on base. Strikes out often and BA ability in question. When makes contact, he can hit ball a long way.

O'Hearn,Ryan — 3 — Kansas City

EXP MLB DEBUT: 2017 | H/W: 6-2 200 | FUT: Starting 1B | 7C

Bats L Age 22	Year	Lev	Team	AB	R	H	HR	RBI	Avg	OB	Slg	OPS	bb%	ct%	Eye	SB	CS	x/h%	Iso	RC/G
2014 (8) Sam Houston St	2013	NCAA	Sam Houston St	183	19	48	1	25	262	345	361	705	11	77	0.55	0	1	25	98	4.47
Pwr ++++	2014	NCAA	Sam Houston St	257	37	75	8	44	292	348	451	799	8	79	0.42	1	1	29	160	5.34
BAvg ++	2014	Rk	Idaho Falls	249	61	90	13	54	361	448	590	1038	14	76	0.66	3	2	33	229	8.77
Spd +	2015	A	Lexington	314	44	87	19	56	277	351	494	845	10	72	0.41	7	2	34	217	6.04
Def ++	2015	A+	Wilmington	161	14	38	8	21	236	317	447	764	11	66	0.35	0	0	47	211	5.21

Patient, powerful INF who led SAL in HR despite moving to High-A in July. Struggled upon promotion, but showcased plus power while maintaining disciplined eye at plate. Can be pull-happy and has shown struggles with LHP. Will likely hit for either BA or HR, but not both. Average defender with clean hands, but doesn't range well.

Ohlman,Mike — 2 — St. Louis

EXP MLB DEBUT: 2018 | H/W: 6-4 215 | FUT: Backup C | 6C

Bats R Age 25	Year	Lev	Team	AB	R	H	HR	RBI	Avg	OB	Slg	OPS	bb%	ct%	Eye	SB	CS	x/h%	Iso	RC/G
2009 (11) HS (FL)	2012	Rk	GCL Orioles	29	5	8	1	3	276	323	483	805	6	66	0.20	1	0	50	207	5.90
Pwr ++	2012	A	Delmarva	171	27	52	2	28	304	417	456	873	16	84	1.22	0	1	38	152	6.90
BAvg ++	2013	A+	Frederick	361	61	113	13	53	313	405	524	929	13	74	0.60	5	0	41	211	7.52
Spd ++	2014	AA	Bowie	403	40	95	2	33	236	309	318	627	10	79	0.50	0	0	29	82	3.38
Def +	2015	AA	Springfield	366	53	100	12	69	273	354	418	772	11	79	0.60	0	1	29	145	5.15

Huge backstop came over from the Orioles for cash considerations. Has a decent bat with moderate raw power and a good understanding of the strike zone. Will have to work hard to stick behind the plate. He has a strong arm, but struggles blocking the ball and is slow in his actions—not surprising given his size. Profiles as a backup catcher.

Olivera,Hector — 57 — Atlanta

EXP MLB DEBUT: 2015 | H/W: 6-2 220 | FUT: Starting 3B/LF | 8B

Bats R Age 31	Year	Lev	Team	AB	R	H	HR	RBI	Avg	OB	Slg	OPS	bb%	ct%	Eye	SB	CS	x/h%	Iso	RC/G
2015 FA (CU)	2015	A	Rome	12	1	1	0	0	83	214	83	298	14	92	2.00	0	0	0	0	0.32
Pwr +++	2015	AA	Tulsa	22	3	7	1	6	318	400	455	855	12	77	0.60	0	0	14	136	6.14
BAvg +++	2015	AAA	Gwinnett	39	5	9	0	3	231	268	308	576	5	90	0.50	0	0	33	77	2.85
Spd ++	2015	AAA	Oklahoma City	31	5	12	1	1	387	387	581	968	0	90	0.00	0	0	25	194	6.64
Def +++	2015	MLB	Atlanta	79	4	20	2	11	253	298	405	703	6	85	0.42	0	0	35	152	4.12

Rusty after a two-yr layoff, struggled to stay on the field. Made MLB debut after trade from LA at deadline. Flashed above-average to plus hit tool. Long progression in swing path. Strong hands and quick wrists lead to solid bat speed. Has 15-20 HR in swing, but was never power hitter in Cuba. Former 2B, spent last season at 3B. Moved to LF in winter ball.

Olson,Matt — 39 — Oakland

EXP MLB DEBUT: 2016 | H/W: 6-4 230 | FUT: Starting 1B | 8B

Bats L Age 22	Year	Lev	Team	AB	R	H	HR	RBI	Avg	OB	Slg	OPS	bb%	ct%	Eye	SB	CS	x/h%	Iso	RC/G
2012 (1) HS (GA)	2012	Rk	Azl Athletics	177	29	50	8	41	282	342	520	862	8	74	0.35	0	0	50	237	6.30
Pwr ++++	2012	A-	Vermont	11	3	3	1	4	273	429	545	974	21	64	0.75	0	0	33	273	8.67
BAvg ++	2013	A	Beloit	481	69	108	23	93	225	325	435	760	13	69	0.49	4	3	51	210	5.16
Spd +	2014	A+	Stockton	512	111	134	37	97	262	399	543	942	19	73	0.85	2	0	51	281	7.72
Def ++	2015	AA	Midland	466	82	116	17	75	249	387	438	825	18	70	0.76	5	1	47	189	6.37

Mammoth slugger who has walked 100+ times in each of past two seasons while hitting for plus power. Covers plate with simple stroke and has leverage and loft for consistent pop. Knows strike zone and can go opposite way. Struggles with LHP (.216) and will always swing and miss. Split time between 1B and RF and doesn't run well.

O'Neill,Tyler — 79 — Seattle

EXP MLB DEBUT: 2017 | H/W: 5-11 210 | FUT: Starting OF | 7B

Bats R Age 20	Year	Lev	Team	AB	R	H	HR	RBI	Avg	OB	Slg	OPS	bb%	ct%	Eye	SB	CS	x/h%	Iso	RC/G
2013 (3) HS (BC)	2013	Rk	Azl Mariners	100	12	31	1	15	310	384	450	834	11	73	0.44	2	4	29	140	6.26
Pwr ++++	2014	Rk	Azl Mariners	2	0	0	0	0	0	0	0	0	0	50	0.00	0	0		0	-7.85
BAvg +++	2014	A-	Everett	10	2	4	0	2	400	455	600	1055	9	50	0.20	0	0	50	200	13.24
Spd +++	2014	A	Clinton	219	31	54	13	38	247	310	466	775	8	64	0.25	5	0	41	219	5.36
Def ++	2015	A+	Bakersfield	407	68	106	32	87	260	310	558	867	7	66	0.21	16	5	52	297	6.49

Short, compact OF who led CAL in HR and set highs in HR and SB. Has bat speed to catch up to any FB and uses simple swing with leverage to drive ball. Likes to swing early in count and needs to address breaking balls. Owns average speed and is smart baserunner. Raw OF play should get better with more reps and has playable arm.

Orimoloye,Demi — 79 — Milwaukee

EXP MLB DEBUT: 2019 | H/W: 6-4 225 | FUT: Starting OF | 8E

Bats R Age 19	Year	Lev	Team	AB	R	H	HR	RBI	Avg	OB	Slg	OPS	bb%	ct%	Eye	SB	CS	x/h%	Iso	RC/G
2015 (4) HS (ON)																				
Pwr ++++																				
BAvg +++																				
Spd ++++																				
Def +++	2015	Rk	Azl Brewers	137	23	40	6	26	292	307	518	825	2	72	0.08	19	6	43	226	5.59

Raw, gifted athlete. Standout tool is speed, which plays well on the bases and allows for plus range in the OF. Strong arm likely lands him in RF long-term. Aggressive, pull-oriented approach will need fine tuning and swing shortening, but bat speed and leverage foretell of future plus raw power.

Ortiz,Jhailyn — 37 — Philadelphia

EXP MLB DEBUT: 2022 | H/W: 6-3 240 | FUT: Starting 1B | 9E

Bats R Age 17	Year	Lev	Team	AB	R	H	HR	RBI	Avg	OB	Slg	OPS	bb%	ct%	Eye	SB	CS	x/h%	Iso	RC/G
2015 FA (DR)																				
Pwr ++++																				
BAvg ++																				
Spd +																				
Def ++	2015			*Did not play in minors*																

Big-bodied already, teenager had best raw power in 2015 international class with combination of bat speed and strength. But tons of risk with high strikeout rates, including current ineptitude against breaking stuff. Will need to keep his body type in check as he matures, and could limit him to 1B in the future.

Padlo,Kevin — 5 — Colorado

EXP MLB DEBUT: 2018 | H/W: 6-2 200 | FUT: Starting 3B | 8D

Bats R Age 19	Year	Lev	Team	AB	R	H	HR	RBI	Avg	OB	Slg	OPS	bb%	ct%	Eye	SB	CS	x/h%	Iso	RC/G
2014 (5) HS (CA)																				
Pwr +++																				
BAvg +++	2014	Rk	Grand Junction	160	32	48	8	44	300	414	594	1007	16	76	0.82	6	1	56	294	8.64
Spd +++	2015	A-	Boise	255	44	75	9	46	294	400	502	902	15	76	0.73	33	5	44	208	7.19
Def +++	2015	A	Asheville	83	11	12	2	7	145	268	277	545	14	69	0.54	2	1	58	133	2.15

Struggled in his full-season debut, before being sent to short-season ball where he turned things around. Flashes a quick bat and above-average power to go along with good strike zone judgment. Struggles with off-speed stuff. Moves well defensively with good hands and a strong arm, but remains raw at 3B. A player to keep an eye on.

Palacios,Jermaine — 6 — Minnesota

EXP MLB DEBUT: 2019 | H/W: 6-0 145 | FUT: Starting 2B/SS | 7C

Bats R Age 19
2013 FA (VZ)
- Pwr ++
- BAvg ++++
- Spd +++
- Def ++

Year	Lev	Team	AB	R	H	HR	RBI	Avg	OB	Slg	OPS	bb%	ct%	Eye	SB	CS	x/h%	Iso	RC/G
2015	Rk	Elizabethton	140	23	47	2	23	336	350	507	857	2	86	0.15	5	2	38	171	5.75
2015	Rk	GCL Twins	95	13	40	1	14	421	471	589	1061	9	88	0.82	4	2	30	168	8.54

Well-rounded player who dominated rookie ball in first year in U.S. Played mostly SS, but committed too many errors despite range and arm. Hits to all fields and controls bat with simple approach. Smashes line drives to both gaps and can jerk balls out to pull side. Destroys LHP, but will need to be selective to maintain high BA at higher levels.

Palka,Daniel — 379 — Minnesota

EXP MLB DEBUT: 2017 | H/W: 6-2 220 | FUT: Starting LF/RF | 7D

Bats L Age 24
2013 (3) Georgia Tech
- Pwr ++++
- BAvg ++
- Spd ++
- Def ++

Year	Lev	Team	AB	R	H	HR	RBI	Avg	OB	Slg	OPS	bb%	ct%	Eye	SB	CS	x/h%	Iso	RC/G
2013	NCAA	Georgia Tech	237	55	81	17	66	342	418	637	1055	12	75	0.52	6	0	41	295	8.89
2013	Rk	Missoula	205	36	62	7	38	302	389	502	891	12	78	0.64	2	2	44	200	6.84
2013	A-	Hillsboro	47	10	16	2	10	340	426	574	1000	13	66	0.44	1	0	31	234	9.07
2014	A	South Bend	455	63	113	22	82	248	331	466	797	11	72	0.43	9	3	44	218	5.55
2015	A+	Visalia	511	95	143	29	90	280	351	532	883	10	68	0.34	24	7	48	252	6.89

Powerful slugger who owns plus power to all fields, but swing and miss may make pop irrelevant. Moved to OF corners after serving as 1B and could become average despite limited wheels. Steals bases more on instincts than speed, though SB likely to fall dramatically. Will draw walks, but long swing can be exploited.

Papi,Mike — 379 — Cleveland

EXP MLB DEBUT: 2017 | H/W: 6-2 190 | FUT: Starting OF | 8E

Bats L Age 23
2014 (1) Virginia
- Pwr ++
- BAvg ++
- Spd ++
- Def +++

Year	Lev	Team	AB	R	H	HR	RBI	Avg	OB	Slg	OPS	bb%	ct%	Eye	SB	CS	x/h%	Iso	RC/G
2013	NCAA	Virginia	176	57	67	7	57	381	507	619	1126	20	86	1.80	6	2	37	239	10.12
2014	NCAA	Virginia	244	55	75	11	56	307	446	488	934	20	81	1.33	8	3	29	180	7.64
2014	A-	Mahoning Val	9	2	2	0	3	222	222	222	444	0	100		0	0	0	0	1.56
2014	A	Lake County	135	21	24	3	15	178	311	274	585	16	76	0.81	2	0	29	96	2.91
2015	A+	Lynchburg	416	53	98	4	45	236	360	356	716	16	72	0.69	6	7	41	120	4.86

Selective hitter who had thumb surgery in Sept 2014 and struggled to get on track in 2015. Draws walks and has strength and bat speed for power. LHP give him problems, especially with breaking balls. Can play OF corner with strong arm, but is offense-first prospect. Ideal candidate for a rebound season.

Park,Hoy Jun — 6 — New York (A)

EXP MLB DEBUT: 2019 | H/W: 6-1 175 | FUT: Starting SS | 8E

Bats L Age 19
2014 FA (SK)
- Pwr ++
- BAvg +++
- Spd +++
- Def +++

Year	Lev	Team	AB	R	H	HR	RBI	Avg	OB	Slg	OPS	bb%	ct%	Eye	SB	CS	x/h%	Iso	RC/G
2015	Rk	Pulaski	222	48	53	5	30	239	340	383	723	13	77	0.68	12	7	36	144	4.72

Lean, quick INF who spent first year in US and showed impressive skills. Has room to add strength and struck out more than expected. Brings patient approach to plate and has quick stroke to shoot gaps with line drives. Can go to opposite field in situations. Owns good range and quick feet to stay at SS, but needs to clean up errors.

Paroubeck,Jordan — 7 — Los Angeles (N)

EXP MLB DEBUT: 2018 | H/W: 6-2 190 | FUT: Starting LF | 8D

Bats B Age 21
2013 (2) HS (CA)
- Pwr +++
- BAvg +++
- Spd +++
- Def +++

Year	Lev	Team	AB	R	H	HR	RBI	Avg	OB	Slg	OPS	bb%	ct%	Eye	SB	CS	x/h%	Iso	RC/G
2014	Rk	Azl Padres	140	26	40	4	24	286	346	457	804	8	70	0.31	4	2	35	171	5.71
2015	Rk	Azl Dodgers	49	11	12	1	8	245	327	429	756	11	73	0.46	0	0	50	184	5.16
2015	Rk	Ogden	87	21	33	4	20	379	455	621	1075	12	69	0.44	1	1	36	241	9.83

Tall OF was traded from SD to ATL and then to LA. Hamstring injury limited him to 35 games, but he raked when on the field—.331/.409/.551. Has plus bat speed and above-avg power. Showed some contact issues in his debut. Plus speed and above-avg arm means he could play either corner slot. Should add power as he fills out.

Patterson,Jordan — 9 — Colorado

EXP MLB DEBUT: 2017 | H/W: 6-4 215 | FUT: Starting RF/1B | 7B

Bats L Age 24
2013 (4) South Alabama
- Pwr +++
- BAvg ++
- Spd ++++
- Def +++

Year	Lev	Team	AB	R	H	HR	RBI	Avg	OB	Slg	OPS	bb%	ct%	Eye	SB	CS	x/h%	Iso	RC/G
2013	NCAA	South Alabama	233	69	82	4	49	352	449	519	968	15	85	1.17	4	2	37	167	7.95
2013	Rk	Grand Junction	206	44	60	10	37	291	351	495	846	8	82	0.51	10	6	37	204	5.85
2014	A	Asheville	453	69	126	14	66	278	345	430	775	9	74	0.39	25	8	33	152	5.17
2015	A+	Modesto	303	62	92	10	43	304	345	568	912	6	71	0.22	9	6	52	264	7.21
2015	AA	New Britain	185	26	53	7	32	286	327	503	829	6	77	0.26	9	4	49	216	5.66

OF continues to impress, hitting .297 with 17 HR and 18 SB. Has good raw LH power but needs to prove that he can make enough contact to hit. Has a direct approach to the ball and plus bat speed so the power is legit. Good range and a plus arm should allow him to stick in RF or switch to 1B.

Paulino,Dorssys — 7 — Cleveland

EXP MLB DEBUT: 2017 | H/W: 6-0 175 | FUT: Starting OF | 7D

Bats R Age 21
2011 FA (DR)
- Pwr ++
- BAvg +++
- Spd ++
- Def ++

Year	Lev	Team	AB	R	H	HR	RBI	Avg	OB	Slg	OPS	bb%	ct%	Eye	SB	CS	x/h%	Iso	RC/G
2012	A-	Mahoning Val	59	5	16	1	8	271	306	407	713	5	76	0.21	2	1	38	136	4.20
2013	A	Lake County	476	56	117	5	46	246	291	349	639	6	81	0.33	12	7	31	103	3.35
2014	A	Lake County	427	51	107	3	35	251	304	354	658	7	76	0.33	5	6	31	103	3.64
2015	A	Lake County	313	38	80	6	39	256	304	364	669	7	81	0.36	11	5	25	109	3.67
2015	A+	Lynchburg	154	27	47	4	30	305	374	526	900	10	81	0.57	5	2	43	221	6.86

Compact OF who is starting to emerge after 2 1/2 years in Low-A. Set career high in HR while also showing more consistent, hard contact. Tweaked swing to keep bat head in zone longer and uses quick wrists to generate gap power. Moved to OF in '14 and still lacks instincts for routes and jumps. Offers fringy speed.

Pentecost,Max — 2 — Toronto

EXP MLB DEBUT: 2017 | H/W: 6-2 191 | FUT: Starting C | 8C

Bats R Age 23
2014 (1) Kennesaw St
- Pwr ++
- BAvg +++
- Spd +++
- Def +++

Year	Lev	Team	AB	R	H	HR	RBI	Avg	OB	Slg	OPS	bb%	ct%	Eye	SB	CS	x/h%	Iso	RC/G
2013	NCAA	Kennesaw St	212	36	64	3	30	302	368	410	778	9	87	0.81	4	0	27	108	5.27
2014	NCAA	Kennesaw St	268	59	113	9	61	422	480	627	1107	10	90	1.15	17	0	31	205	8.99
2014	Rk	GCL Blue Jays	22	2	8	0	3	364	364	455	818	0	86	0.00	0	1	25	91	5.11
2014	A-	Vancouver	83	15	26	0	9	313	329	410	739	2	78	0.11	2	1	19	96	4.43
2015		*Did not play; injured*																	

Premium athlete who missed entire season after shoulder surgery. Has agility and mobility behind plate and has exemplary receiving skills. Needs to get better, but has chance to be solid C. Swings fast bat and sprays line drives to all fields. Should grow into at least average power as doubles evolve into HR.

Peraza,Jose — 4 — Cincinnati

EXP MLB DEBUT: 2015 | H/W: 6-0 180 | FUT: Starting 2B | 8B

Bats R Age 21
2010 FA (VZ)
- Pwr +
- BAvg +++
- Spd ++++
- Def +++

Year	Lev	Team	AB	R	H	HR	RBI	Avg	OB	Slg	OPS	bb%	ct%	Eye	SB	CS	x/h%	Iso	RC/G
2014	A+	Lynchburg	284	44	97	1	27	342	364	454	818	3	89	0.31	35	7	23	113	5.40
2014	AA	Mississippi	185	35	62	1	17	335	359	422	781	4	92	0.47	25	8	18	86	4.99
2015	AAA	Gwinnett	391	52	115	3	37	294	320	379	699	4	91	0.43	26	7	17	84	4.08
2015	AAA	Oklahoma City	90	11	26	1	5	289	304	378	682	2	89	0.20	7	0	19	89	3.72
2015	MLB	LA Dodgers	22	3	4	0	1	182	250	318	568	8	91	1.00	3	0	50	136	3.13

High-energy 2B was traded from LA to ATL as part of the Todd Frazier trade. Top-of-the-order hitter handles the bat well with a short compact stroke and makes consistent contact. Plus runner swiped 33 bases after stealing 60 in '14. Smart player gets the most of his abilities. Continues to improve on defense.

Perez,Arvicent — 2 — Detroit

EXP MLB DEBUT: 2018 | H/W: 5-10 180 | FUT: Starting C | 7E

Bats R Age 22
2011 FA (VZ)
- Pwr ++
- BAvg ++
- Spd +
- Def +++

Year	Lev	Team	AB	R	H	HR	RBI	Avg	OB	Slg	OPS	bb%	ct%	Eye	SB	CS	x/h%	Iso	RC/G
2014	Rk	GCL Tigers	81	14	25	3	20	309	317	519	836	1	91	0.14	3	0	40	210	5.34
2014	A	West Michigan	46	7	16	0	6	348	362	391	753	2	89	0.20	1	1	13	43	4.49
2015	A-	Connecticut	19	3	5	0	1	263	263	316	579	0	89	0.00	0	1	20	53	2.50
2015	A	West Michigan	118	7	27	0	5	229	248	263	511	2	83	0.15	1	0	15	34	1.64

Stocky catcher with solid defensive attributes, though missed time with variety of injuries. Is an advanced blocker and receiver with strong, accurate arm. Focuses on contact and can put bat to ball with plus plate coverage. Rarely draws walks and can be free swinger due to easy contact. Shows gap power with line drive approach.

Perez,Fernando — 4 — San Diego

EXP MLB DEBUT: 2017 | H/W: 6-0 210 | FUT: Starting 2B | 7C

Bats L Age 22
2012 (3) Central Arizona
- Pwr +++
- BAvg ++
- Spd ++
- Def ++

Year	Lev	Team	AB	R	H	HR	RBI	Avg	OB	Slg	OPS	bb%	ct%	Eye	SB	CS	x/h%	Iso	RC/G
2012	Rk	Azl Padres	55	6	15	2	16	273	298	455	753	4	69	0.12	1	0	33	182	4.74
2013	Rk	Azl Padres	12	3	5	1	4	417	462	750	1212	8	83	0.50	0	0	40	333	10.04
2013	A-	Eugene	211	15	45	3	27	213	265	308	574	7	68	0.22	0	1	29	95	2.38
2014	A	Fort Wayne	469	69	133	18	95	284	320	454	774	5	77	0.24	3	2	32	171	4.83
2015	A+	Lake Elsinore	446	46	100	10	53	224	287	352	639	8	74	0.34	1	1	34	128	3.32

Powerful INF who had drop off from '14, but has tools that could be cultivated. Exhibits power to all fields, though inability to hit LHP (.118) and free-swinging approach need to be tamed. Has showed signs of shortening swing when behind in count. Defense has gotten better despite lack of quickness and instincts. Could become offensive-minded 2B.

Perkins,Blake

8 | Washington | EXP MLB DEBUT: 2019 | H/W: 6-1 165 | FUT: Starting CF | 7D

Bats B Age 19	Year	Lev	Team	AB	R	H	HR	RBI	Avg	OB	Slg	OPS	bb%	ct%	Eye	SB	CS	x/h%	Iso	RC/G
2015 (2) HS (AZ)																				
Pwr ++																				
BAvg ++																				
Spd ++++																				
Def ++++	2015	Rk	GCL Nationals	166	21	35	1	12	211	268	283	551	7	78	0.36	4	5	23	72	2.27

Fluid athlete who makes everything seem easy. Picked up switch-hitting in instructional league, which should capitalize on his plus-plus speed. Strong wrists get the bat through the zone quickly, though jury is out on whether average power manifests. Glides to balls in CF with plus range and average arm.

Peter,Jake

4 | Chicago (A) | EXP MLB DEBUT: 2017 | H/W: 6-0 185 | FUT: Starting 2B | 7C

Bats L Age 23	Year	Lev	Team	AB	R	H	HR	RBI	Avg	OB	Slg	OPS	bb%	ct%	Eye	SB	CS	x/h%	Iso	RC/G
2014 (7) Creighton	2013	NCAA	Creighton	203	33	71	1	35	350	408	463	871	9	90	0.95	8	2	23	113	6.40
Pwr +	2014	NCAA	Creighton	197	43	59	4	37	299	367	431	798	10	91	1.24	4	4	25	132	5.57
BAvg ++	2014	Rk	Great Falls	152	26	59	2	21	388	436	579	1015	8	91	1.00	1	1	32	191	7.94
Spd +++	2014	A+	Winston-Salem	89	8	21	0	5	236	269	303	572	4	85	0.31	1	0	24	67	2.60
Def ++++	2015	A+	Winston-Salem	497	76	129	3	57	260	331	348	679	10	82	0.60	23	3	26	89	4.08

Instinctual and savvy INF who works counts, gets on base, and steals bases with average speed. Owns hand-eye coordination and makes contact with short stroke. Doesn't project to much power, but can shoot gaps and leg out doubles. Has arm strength to play any infield spot. An under the radar prospect.

Peterson,D.J.

35 | Seattle | EXP MLB DEBUT: 2016 | H/W: 6-1 210 | FUT: Starting 1B | 8C

Bats R Age 24	Year	Lev	Team	AB	R	H	HR	RBI	Avg	OB	Slg	OPS	bb%	ct%	Eye	SB	CS	x/h%	Iso	RC/G
2013 (1) New Mexico	2013	A	Clinton	99	16	29	7	20	293	340	576	915	7	76	0.29	1	0	45	283	6.68
Pwr ++++	2014	A+	High Desert	273	51	89	18	73	326	378	615	994	8	76	0.35	6	0	47	289	7.81
BAvg +++	2014	AA	Jackson	222	32	58	13	38	261	328	473	801	9	77	0.43	1	1	36	212	5.28
Spd ++	2015	AA	Jackson	358	39	80	7	44	223	285	346	632	8	75	0.34	5	0	35	123	3.25
Def ++	2015	AAA	Tacoma	14	0	3	0	0	214	214	286	500	0	79	0.00	0	1	33	71	1.33

Stocky, strong INF who had big drop-off from '14 and started to turn it around with positive July. Played mostly 1B and has bat to match, but needs to work on approach. Can get pull happy and has tendency to be free swinger. Plus bat speed results in plus, natural power and has pitch recognition to hit for BA. Doesn't run well, but not a clogger.

Peterson,Dustin

7 | Atlanta | EXP MLB DEBUT: 2017 | H/W: 6-2 180 | FUT: Starting LF | 7C

Bats R Age 21	Year	Lev	Team	AB	R	H	HR	RBI	Avg	OB	Slg	OPS	bb%	ct%	Eye	SB	CS	x/h%	Iso	RC/G
2013 (2) HS (AZ)																				
Pwr +++																				
BAvg ++	2013	Rk	Azl Padres	157	20	46	0	18	293	331	344	675	5	79	0.27	3	0	17	51	3.74
Spd ++	2014	A	Fort Wayne	527	64	123	10	79	233	268	361	629	5	74	0.18	1	3	36	127	3.06
Def ++	2015	A+	Carolina	446	58	112	8	62	251	318	348	666	9	80	0.48	6	3	22	96	3.75

Acquired by ATL in trade last offseason, the Braves moved him to LF, now his fulltime home. Hasn't tapped into raw power yet but shows solid loft against live pitching, especially on balls middle in. He's a patient hitter but lacks the hit tool to be anything more than a solid contributor. Bat will dictate where he plays.

Phillips,Brett

89 | Milwaukee | EXP MLB DEBUT: 2017 | H/W: 6-0 180 | FUT: Starting OF | 9D

Bats L Age 21	Year	Lev	Team	AB	R	H	HR	RBI	Avg	OB	Slg	OPS	bb%	ct%	Eye	SB	CS	x/h%	Iso	RC/G
2012 (6) HS (FL)	2014	A	Quad Cities	384	68	116	13	58	302	362	521	883	9	80	0.47	18	10	40	219	6.49
Pwr +++	2014	A+	Lancaster	109	19	37	4	10	339	415	560	974	11	82	0.70	5	4	38	220	7.74
BAvg +++	2015	A+	Lancaster	291	68	93	15	53	320	367	588	955	7	78	0.34	8	6	44	268	7.29
Spd +++	2015	AA	Biloxi	80	14	20	0	6	250	362	413	774	15	63	0.47	2	1	50	163	6.21
Def +++	2015	AA	Corpus Christi	134	22	43	1	18	321	359	463	822	6	81	0.31	7	2	30	142	5.65

Athletic OF features promising skills blend. Selective with solid contact ability, Phillips's HR pop surged in '14 through swing change, allowing him to smoke pitches to all fields. Above aveage instincts give him a chance to steal bases and stay in CF; could switch to RF with plus arm. At his peak, future 20 HR/20 SB candidate atop MLB lineup.

Pierre,Nicolas

789 | Milwaukee | EXP MLB DEBUT: 2019 | H/W: 6-3 170 | FUT: Starting OF | 7D

Bats R Age 19	Year	Lev	Team	AB	R	H	HR	RBI	Avg	OB	Slg	OPS	bb%	ct%	Eye	SB	CS	x/h%	Iso	RC/G
2013 FA (DR)																				
Pwr +++																				
BAvg +++																				
Spd +++																				
Def +++	2015	Rk	Azl Brewers	145	20	29	0	8	200	227	234	461	3	76	0.14	3	3	14	34	0.85

Dominican OF struggled to hit for much average or power in stateside debut, but has promising attributes. At 6'3", has athletic ability to cover ground in CF and could stick there long term. Employs level swing and quick bat for intriguing raw pop, but aggressive approach often leads to swing-and-miss.

Pimentel,Sandber

3 | Oakland | EXP MLB DEBUT: 2018 | H/W: 6-3 220 | FUT: Starting 1B | 9E

Bats L Age 21	Year	Lev	Team	AB	R	H	HR	RBI	Avg	OB	Slg	OPS	bb%	ct%	Eye	SB	CS	x/h%	Iso	RC/G
2011 FA (DR)																				
Pwr ++++																				
BAvg ++																				
Spd +																				
Def ++	2015	A	Beloit	411	50	100	13	41	243	325	380	705	11	75	0.48	1	2	30	136	4.26

Promising prospect who faded down stretch in first full year in U.S. Has very disciplined approach and feel for bat that could lead to moderate BA. Exemplifies ideal power for 1B with strong, fast bat and natural strength. Has long arms that result in exploitable swing and will fan frequently. Very poor runner who lacks mobility and agility.

Pinder,Chad

6 | Oakland | EXP MLB DEBUT: 2016 | H/W: 6-2 190 | FUT: Starting 2B/SS | 7B

Bats R Age 24	Year	Lev	Team	AB	R	H	HR	RBI	Avg	OB	Slg	OPS	bb%	ct%	Eye	SB	CS	x/h%	Iso	RC/G
2013 (2) Virginia Tech	2012	NCAA	Virginia Tech	212	36	69	7	37	325	367	538	905	6	80	0.33	6	5	43	212	6.61
Pwr +++	2013	NCAA	Virginia Tech	240	49	77	8	50	321	375	483	859	8	84	0.55	5	4	29	163	6.02
BAvg ++++	2013	A-	Vermont	140	14	28	3	8	200	263	293	556	8	71	0.29	1	0	25	93	2.10
Spd ++	2014	A+	Stockton	403	61	116	13	55	288	325	489	814	5	75	0.22	12	9	43	201	5.51
Def ++	2015	AA	Midland	477	71	151	15	86	317	354	486	841	6	78	0.27	7	5	32	170	5.74

MVP of Texas League who finished 2nd in BA and moved back to SS. Doubles machine who has added slight loft to swing to exhibit average HR pop. Swings quick bat, but free-swinging ways need to be tamed. Needs to be more selective at plate. Has strong arm with quick hands, but has a slow release.

Plummer,Nick

7 | St. Louis | EXP MLB DEBUT: 2020 | H/W: 5-10 200 | FUT: Starting LF | 8D

Bats L Age 19	Year	Lev	Team	AB	R	H	HR	RBI	Avg	OB	Slg	OPS	bb%	ct%	Eye	SB	CS	x/h%	Iso	RC/G
2015 (1) HS (MI)																				
Pwr +++																				
BAvg +++																				
Spd +++																				
Def +++	2015	Rk	GCL Cardinals	180	43	41	1	22	228	365	344	710	18	69	0.70	8	6	34	117	4.89

Showed an advanced feel for hitting with the potential for above average power. Quick LH stroke with a gap-to-gap approach. Average runner who reads the ball well off the bat, but scouts are mixed on his ability to stick in CF. Struggled tremendously in his debut, hitting just .228 with 56 K in 180 AB.

Polanco,Jorge

46 | Minnesota | EXP MLB DEBUT: 2014 | H/W: 5-11 200 | FUT: Starting 2B/SS | 7B

Bats B Age 22	Year	Lev	Team	AB	R	H	HR	RBI	Avg	OB	Slg	OPS	bb%	ct%	Eye	SB	CS	x/h%	Iso	RC/G
2009 FA (DR)	2014	AA	New Britain	146	13	41	1	16	281	323	342	665	6	81	0.32	7	3	17	62	3.61
Pwr ++	2014	MLB	Minnesota	6	2	2	0	3	333	500	833	1333	25	67	1.00	0	0	100	500	15.61
BAvg +++	2015	AA	Chattanooga	394	55	114	6	47	289	347	393	741	8	84	0.56	18	10	23	104	4.70
Spd +++	2015	AAA	Rochester	88	7	25	0	6	284	315	352	667	4	89	0.40	1	0	24	68	3.76
Def ++	2015	MLB	Minnesota	10	1	3	0	1	300	417	300	717	17	90	2.00	1	0	0	0	5.10

Advanced INF who has added strength to become a competent producer with bat and glove. Played SS in '15, though may be better at 2B due to average quickness and range. Has bat speed from both sides and uses entire field in approach. Drives ball for extra base hits and should hit for moderately high BA. Runs well, but gets caught stealing frequently.

Polo,Tito

8 | Pittsburgh | EXP MLB DEBUT: 2019 | H/W: 5-9 184 | FUT: Starting CF | 7D

Bats R Age 21	Year	Lev	Team	AB	R	H	HR	RBI	Avg	OB	Slg	OPS	bb%	ct%	Eye	SB	CS	x/h%	Iso	RC/G
2012 FA (CB)																				
Pwr ++																				
BAvg ++	2013	Rk	DSL Pirates	160	29	44	2	16	275	337	369	706	9	74	0.37	22	5	18	94	4.28
Spd ++++	2014	Rk	GCL Pirates	158	30	46	3	25	291	360	475	835	10	78	0.50	8	4	37	184	6.07
Def ++++	2015	A	West Virginia	360	51	85	3	26	236	291	328	619	7	79	0.36	46	13	29	92	3.14

Fleet-footed CF from Columbia has some of the best speed in the system. Stole 46 bags in 2015 at Low-A W. Virginia, but struggled to make consistent contact and hit just .236, but fared well in GCL in 2014 and is worth keeping an eye on. Has the speed, range, and arm and range to stick in CF.

Powell,Boog — 789 — Seattle

EXP MLB DEBUT: 2016 | H/W: 5-10 185 | FUT: Fourth OF | 6B

Bats L Age 23
2012 (20) Orange Coast

Pwr + | BAvg + + + | Spd + + + + | Def + +

Year	Lev	Team	AB	R	H	HR	RBI	Avg	OB	Slg	OPS	bb%	ct%	Eye	SB	CS	x/h%	Iso	RC/G
2013	A-	Vermont	212	30	60	0	14	283	361	344	706	11	84	0.76	14	6	17	61	4.52
2014	A	Beloit	254	43	85	3	17	335	450	429	879	17	81	1.08	16	13	16	94	6.99
2014	A+	Stockton	61	11	23	0	11	377	449	459	908	12	93	2.00	0	2	17	82	7.03
2015	AA	Montgomery	238	44	78	1	22	328	401	416	817	11	84	0.76	11	8	17	88	5.85
2015	AAA	Durham	206	22	53	2	18	257	357	364	721	13	80	0.78	7	6	28	107	4.79

Fundamentally-sound OF who is tough out by working counts and getting on base. Has simple approach to make easy contact, yet has strength to drive gaps. Won't produce much HR pop and tools are short. Can play any OF spot with plus speed and could steal more bases if given green light.

Prime,Correlle — 3 — Colorado

EXP MLB DEBUT: 2019 | H/W: 6-5 220 | FUT: Backup 1B | 6C

Bats R Age 22
2012 (12) HS (FL)

Pwr + + + | BAvg + + | Spd + + | Def + +

Year	Lev	Team	AB	R	H	HR	RBI	Avg	OB	Slg	OPS	bb%	ct%	Eye	SB	CS	x/h%	Iso	RC/G
2012	Rk	Grand Junction	127	17	36	1	11	283	372	362	735	12	73	0.53	0	0	22	79	4.89
2013	Rk	Grand Junction	224	30	63	7	39	281	315	446	761	5	75	0.20	11	2	33	165	4.74
2014	A	Asheville	508	84	148	21	102	291	338	520	858	7	74	0.27	8	2	48	228	6.18
2015	A+	Modesto	518	64	124	12	72	239	272	375	646	4	70	0.15	8	4	36	135	3.30

Strong 1B prospect regressed, hitting just .239. Is overly aggressive searching for power and walked just 23 times, striking out 156. Below average in every other aspect of the game, which means he has to hit to move up and have value and that didn't happen. Should get another crack at the CAL in '16.

Pruitt,Reggie — 8 — Toronto

EXP MLB DEBUT: 2019 | H/W: 6-0 169 | FUT: Starting OF | 7D

Bats R Age 18
2015 (24) HS (GA)

Pwr + | BAvg + + | Spd + + + + | Def + + +

Year	Lev	Team	AB	R	H	HR	RBI	Avg	OB	Slg	OPS	bb%	ct%	Eye	SB	CS	x/h%	Iso	RC/G
2015	Rk	GCL Blue Jays	121	23	27	0	12	223	293	289	582	9	69	0.32	15	2	26	66	2.69

Lean OF who has exceptional speed. Will never hit for power as his choppy stroke isn't conducive to driving ball. Keeps ball on ground, but needs to learn to bunt and make more consistent contact. Has leadoff type skills and is willing to work counts. Profiles as true CF with significant range and sufficient arm strength.

Pujols,Jose — 9 — Philadelphia

EXP MLB DEBUT: 2019 | H/W: 6-3 175 | FUT: Starting RF | 8D

Bats R Age 20
2012 FA (DR)

Pwr + + + + | BAvg + + | Spd + + (4.50) | Def + + +

Year	Lev	Team	AB	R	H	HR	RBI	Avg	OB	Slg	OPS	bb%	ct%	Eye	SB	CS	x/h%	Iso	RC/G
2013	Rk	GCL Phillies	160	27	30	6	18	188	274	369	642	11	65	0.34	1	3	50	181	3.49
2014	Rk	GCL Phillies	151	21	35	5	28	232	288	411	699	7	64	0.22	1	2	43	179	4.35
2014	A-	Williamsport	61	3	13	0	5	213	213	295	508	0	66	0.00	0	0	38	82	1.36
2015	A-	Williamsport	256	43	61	4	30	238	306	359	665	9	68	0.31	5	4	34	121	3.83

Plenty of raw power, but comes from quick wrists/bat speed more than strength. Struggles with contact, especially off-speed, which limits current in-game power. Elite RF arm; though overall defense needs to improve. Though lanky now, has frame to add bulk, but is below-average runner. Two loud tools with promise seeking considerable refinement.

Quinn,Roman — 8 — Philadelphia

EXP MLB DEBUT: 2017 | H/W: 5-10 170 | FUT: Starting CF | 8C

Bats B Age 22
2011 (2) HS (FL)

Pwr + + + | BAvg + + + | Spd + + + + + | Def + + +

Year	Lev	Team	AB	R	H	HR	RBI	Avg	OB	Slg	OPS	bb%	ct%	Eye	SB	CS	x/h%	Iso	RC/G
2012	A-	Williamsport	267	56	75	1	23	281	349	408	757	9	77	0.46	30	6	28	127	5.13
2013	A	Lakewood	260	37	62	5	21	238	310	346	656	9	75	0.42	32	9	24	108	3.62
2014	A+	Clearwater	327	51	84	7	36	257	331	370	701	10	76	0.45	32	12	24	113	4.21
2015	AA	Reading	232	44	71	4	15	306	356	435	791	7	82	0.43	29	10	23	129	5.26

An exciting table-setter with top-shelf speed, injuries have cut into development time. But when healthy, is a disruptive force on the bases. Also has a discerning eye at the plate. Small but strong, has surprising sting in his bat, especially as LHH, where he shoots the gaps and takes extra bases. Progressing with better reads/routes in CF.

Ragira,Brian — 39 — San Francisco

EXP MLB DEBUT: 2017 | H/W: 6-2 185 | FUT: Starting RF | 7D

Bats R Age 24
2013 (4) Stanford

Pwr + + + | BAvg + + | Spd + | Def + + +

Year	Lev	Team	AB	R	H	HR	RBI	Avg	OB	Slg	OPS	bb%	ct%	Eye	SB	CS	x/h%	Iso	RC/G
2013	NCAA	Stanford	222	34	71	8	42	320	360	482	842	6	89	0.58	4	1	27	162	5.67
2013	Rk	Azl Giants	28	4	10	0	6	357	379	464	844	3	79	0.17	0	0	20	107	5.81
2013	A-	Salem-Kaizer	179	29	47	3	36	263	356	391	747	13	70	0.48	1	1	34	128	5.14
2014	A+	San Jose	457	58	119	20	82	260	316	444	760	7	72	0.29	2	2	37	184	4.85
2015	A+	San Jose	391	44	98	10	58	251	309	391	700	8	72	0.31	0	2	35	141	4.14

Stanford product has strong, mature build with solid-avg power produced from loose, easy swing. Fails to make consistent enough contact against quality breaking pitches, which is the main reason he has yet to crack AA-ball. Enough range and arm strength to profile well in RF, where he could produce 20-25 HR if everything comes together.

Ramirez,Harold — 8 — Pittsburgh

EXP MLB DEBUT: 2017 | H/W: 5-11 210 | FUT: Starting CF | 8D

Bats R Age 21
2011 FA (CB)

Pwr + + + | BAvg + + | Spd + + + + | Def + + +

Year	Lev	Team	AB	R	H	HR	RBI	Avg	OB	Slg	OPS	bb%	ct%	Eye	SB	CS	x/h%	Iso	RC/G
2012	Rk	GCL Pirates	135	18	35	1	12	259	291	333	624	4	85	0.30	9	5	20	74	3.13
2013	A-	Jamestown	274	42	78	5	40	285	340	409	749	8	81	0.44	23	11	26	124	4.76
2014	A	West Virginia	204	30	63	1	24	309	344	402	746	5	83	0.31	12	3	25	93	4.63
2015	A+	Bradenton	306	45	103	4	47	337	387	458	844	8	84	0.52	22	15	22	121	5.92

Started the season on the DL, but impressed once on the field. Strong and mature, he has an aggressive approach with good pop and plus speed on the bases. Can be overly aggressive, but makes consistent, hard contact. Good raw power that has yet to translate into game action, but could take off if he can learn to be more selective.

Ramirez,Nick — 3 — Milwaukee

EXP MLB DEBUT: 2016 | H/W: 6-3 225 | FUT: Backup 1B | 6C

Bats L Age 26
2011 (4) Cal St Fullerton

Pwr + + + | BAvg + + | Spd + | Def + +

Year	Lev	Team	AB	R	H	HR	RBI	Avg	OB	Slg	OPS	bb%	ct%	Eye	SB	CS	x/h%	Iso	RC/G
2011	A	Wisconsin	137	11	27	3	23	197	247	350	597	6	74	0.25	0	0	56	153	2.74
2012	A	Wisconsin	383	46	95	16	70	248	296	446	742	6	62	0.18	0	0	46	198	5.04
2013	A+	Brevard County	500	70	129	19	81	258	330	438	768	10	66	0.32	5	0	38	180	5.35
2014	AA	Huntsville	490	71	113	19	82	231	308	410	718	10	69	0.36	1	4	40	180	4.50
2015	AA	Biloxi	432	63	105	14	63	243	341	391	732	13	73	0.56	2	0	34	148	4.74

Strong 1B owns solid average power, having tallied at least 10 HR in each of his five years in the system. Trouble is making enough contact for that power to flourish, as he routinely struggles to hit quality secondary offerings. Range hampered by poor athletic ability, which could further limit his ability to contribute to a big-league roster.

Ramos,Henry — 79 — Boston

EXP MLB DEBUT: 2016 | H/W: 6-2 190 | FUT: Starting OF | 7D

Bats B Age 23
2010 (5) HS (PR)

Pwr + + | BAvg + + | Spd + + + | Def + + + +

Year	Lev	Team	AB	R	H	HR	RBI	Avg	OB	Slg	OPS	bb%	ct%	Eye	SB	CS	x/h%	Iso	RC/G
2013	A+	Salem	469	69	118	12	55	252	330	416	746	10	79	0.55	11	12	39	164	4.88
2014	AA	Portland	181	26	59	2	23	326	365	431	796	6	79	0.29	2	4	22	105	5.25
2015	Rk	GCL Red Sox	24	4	7	0	2	292	414	292	705	17	88	1.67	2	0	0	0	4.92
2015	A-	Lowell	12	1	4	0	1	333	333	333	667	0	67	0.00	0	0	0	0	3.37
2015	AA	Portland	131	8	32	0	8	244	317	359	676	10	80	0.54	0	0	41	115	4.12

Athletic OF who repeated AA, though missed time with torn meniscus. Improving pitch recognition aids offense, but needs AB to realize power potential. Inconsistent swing and aggressive nature hamper contact. Could evolve into ideal RF with power and arm strength, though far from reaching potential. Slowing down as injuries have taken toll.

Ramos,Milton — 46 — New York (N)

EXP MLB DEBUT: 2019 | H/W: 5-11 158 | FUT: Starting SS | 8E

Bats R Age 20
2014 (3) HS (FL)

Pwr + | BAvg + + | Spd + + + + | Def + + + +

Year	Lev	Team	AB	R	H	HR	RBI	Avg	OB	Slg	OPS	bb%	ct%	Eye	SB	CS	x/h%	Iso	RC/G
2014	Rk	GCL Mets	166	20	40	0	29	241	300	355	655	8	80	0.41	6	6	35	114	3.76
2015	Rk	GCL Mets	36	3	7	0	3	194	216	222	438	3	75	0.11	1	2	14	28	0.49
2015	Rk	Kingsport	164	22	52	1	24	317	345	415	760	4	82	0.23	3	6	25	98	4.72

Plus SS who made tremendous strides at the plate since making pro debut. Was best defender taken in 2014 draft; stock fell due to swing concerns. Has displayed a solid line drive approach but lacks plate discipline. Doesn't have power in frame. Plus speed hasn't translated to base paths. Best defensive SS in system full of MLB quality SS.

Ramsey,James — 789 — Cleveland

EXP MLB DEBUT: 2016 | H/W: 5-11 200 | FUT: Starting OF | 7C

Bats L Age 26
2012 (1) Florida St

Pwr + + + | BAvg + + + | Spd + + + | Def + + +

Year	Lev	Team	AB	R	H	HR	RBI	Avg	OB	Slg	OPS	bb%	ct%	Eye	SB	CS	x/h%	Iso	RC/G
2013	AA	Springfield	347	61	87	15	44	251	350	424	774	13	69	0.49	8	4	32	173	5.36
2013	AAA	Memphis	3	0	0	0	0	0	0	0	0	0	67	0.00	0	0		0	-6.12
2014	AA	Springfield	243	47	73	13	36	300	380	527	906	11	73	0.47	4	2	38	226	7.01
2014	AAA	Columbus	109	17	31	3	16	284	361	468	829	11	69	0.38	1	0	42	183	6.26
2015	AAA	Columbus	440	46	107	12	42	243	325	382	706	11	71	0.41	3	4	33	139	4.36

Consistent and well-rounded OF who lacks a standout tool. Can play all OF spots with enough instincts to play CF. Runs well to enhance defense, but doesn't steal many bags. Brings mature approach to plate, though could make better contact if not selling out for pop. Power is mostly of pull variety and can spray ball to all fields.

Randolph,Corneilus — 7 — Philadelphia
EXP MLB DEBUT: 2019 | H/W: 5-11 205 | FUT: Starting LF | 9D

Bats L Age 18
2015 (1) HS (GA)
Pwr +++
BAvg ++++
Spd ++
Def ++

Year	Lev	Team	AB	R	H	HR	RBI	Avg	OB	Slg	OPS	bb%	ct%	Eye	SB	CS	x/h%	Iso	RC/G
2015	Rk	GCL Phillies	172	35	52	1	24	302	412	442	854	16	81	1.00	7	5	37	140	6.68

Best pure hitter in the 2015 high school class. Has an enviable combination of elite bat speed, balanced approach and excellent plate discipline. Already uses entire field has good pitch recognition skills; home-run power is expected to develop as he matures. Doesn't run well, and average arm limits him to LF, but the bat will carry him.

Ravelo,Rangel — 3 — Oakland
EXP MLB DEBUT: 2016 | H/W: 6-2 220 | FUT: Starting 1B | 7C

Bats R Age 23
2010 (6) HS (FL)
Pwr +++
BAvg +++
Spd +
Def +++

Year	Lev	Team	AB	R	H	HR	RBI	Avg	OB	Slg	OPS	bb%	ct%	Eye	SB	CS	x/h%	Iso	RC/G
2013	A+	Winston-Salem	301	43	94	4	53	312	393	455	848	12	85	0.87	4	1	35	143	6.29
2014	AA	Birmingham	476	72	147	11	66	309	382	473	854	11	84	0.73	10	6	35	164	6.23
2015	Rk	Azl Athletics	25	7	9	0	7	360	500	560	1060	22	88	2.33	1	0	44	200	9.69
2015	AA	Midland	88	13	28	2	17	318	381	477	859	9	81	0.53	0	1	32	159	6.23
2015	AAA	Nashville	101	10	28	1	18	277	324	376	700	6	78	0.32	0	0	25	99	4.11

Advanced hitter who began '15 late due to wrist injury. Continues to hit with above average bat control and plate coverage. High BA hitter with easy, hard contact. Has average power potential, but prefers to use whole field. Big frame results in sub-par speed and isn't quickest or most agile 1B. Has good glove, though, with average arm.

Read,Raudy — 2 — Washington
EXP MLB DEBUT: 2018 | H/W: 6-0 170 | FUT: Starting C | 7C

Bats R Age 22
2011 FA (DR)
Pwr +++
BAvg ++
Spd +
Def +++

Year	Lev	Team	AB	R	H	HR	RBI	Avg	OB	Slg	OPS	bb%	ct%	Eye	SB	CS	x/h%	Iso	RC/G
2013	Rk	GCL Nationals	147	9	37	2	17	252	281	327	608	4	88	0.35	2	6	19	75	2.97
2014	A-	Auburn	210	27	59	6	35	281	326	462	788	6	82	0.38	0	3	44	181	5.15
2015	A	Hagerstown	295	38	72	5	36	244	303	369	673	8	83	0.50	4	3	36	125	3.88
2015	A+	Potomac	18	1	7	0	5	389	450	500	950	10	83	0.67	0	0	29	111	7.47

Shows a knack for hitting and exhibits a good approach. Has plus raw power that has yet to fully manifest in game action. Favors his pull side, but continues to work on using the entire field. Cuts down runners with elite arm and is a solid receiver, though still working on in-game management.

Reed,A.J. — 3 — Houston
EXP MLB DEBUT: 2016 | H/W: 6-4 240 | FUT: Starting 1B | 8C

Bats L Age 22
2014 (2) Kentucky
Pwr ++++
BAvg +++
Spd +
Def ++

Year	Lev	Team	AB	R	H	HR	RBI	Avg	OB	Slg	OPS	bb%	ct%	Eye	SB	CS	x/h%	Iso	RC/G
2013	NCAA	Kentucky	214	30	60	13	52	280	358	519	877	11	81	0.63	1	1	38	238	6.33
2014	A-	Tri City	124	22	38	5	30	306	411	516	927	15	82	1.00	2	0	42	210	7.33
2014	A	Quad Cities	125	21	34	7	24	272	316	528	844	6	74	0.25	0	0	50	256	5.86
2015	A+	Lancaster	318	75	110	23	81	346	448	638	1087	16	77	0.81	0	0	39	292	9.41
2015	AA	Corpus Christi	205	38	68	1	46	332	409	424	834	12	76	0.55	0	0	24	93	6.19

Strong 1B who was CAL MVP after leading minors in HR and OPS. Demonstrates all-fields pop with vicious stroke. Very selective hitter who recognizes pitches and will draw walks. Swing is long and will strike out, but makes consistent contact for slugger. Needs to improve approach against LHP. Does not run well and has limited range.

Reed,Michael — 79 — Milwaukee
EXP MLB DEBUT: 2015 | H/W: 6-0 190 | FUT: Starting RF | 7C

Bats R Age 23
2011 (5) HS (TX)
Pwr ++
BAvg +++
Spd ++++
Def +++

Year	Lev	Team	AB	R	H	HR	RBI	Avg	OB	Slg	OPS	bb%	ct%	Eye	SB	CS	x/h%	Iso	RC/G
2013	A	Wisconsin	455	68	130	1	40	286	382	400	782	13	76	0.66	26	10	28	114	5.67
2014	A+	Brevard County	365	50	93	5	47	255	386	378	764	18	78	0.99	33	13	32	123	5.53
2015	AA	Biloxi	313	43	87	5	49	278	383	422	804	14	74	0.66	25	7	34	144	5.96
2015	AAA	Colorado Springs	126	19	31	0	21	246	349	381	730	14	75	0.65	1	0	48	135	5.05
2015	MLB	Milwaukee	6	2	2	0	0	333	333	500	833	0	50	0.00	0	0	50	167	8.60

Strong, athletic OF with solid blend of tools. Instincts and first-step quickness help him nab bases at a respectable clip. Plus arm and good reads project him best at RF. Works deep into counts and has advanced strike-zone judgment to draw walks. Line-drive swing helps him expose gaps; raw pop is below average. BA tied to his ability to hit off-speed.

Reetz,Jakson — 2 — Washington
EXP MLB DEBUT: 2019 | H/W: 6-1 195 | FUT: Starting C | 8D

Bats R Age 20
2014 (3) HS (NE)
Pwr +++
BAvg +++
Spd +
Def +++

Year	Lev	Team	AB	R	H	HR	RBI	Avg	OB	Slg	OPS	bb%	ct%	Eye	SB	CS	x/h%	Iso	RC/G
2014	Rk	GCL Nationals	117	20	32	1	15	274	406	368	773	18	74	0.87	6	3	25	94	5.70
2015	A-	Auburn	113	18	24	0	5	212	294	248	541	10	67	0.35	3	0	17	35	2.06

Disappointing year at the plate, but team still believes in his long-term potential. Has gap power now, with more waiting to be unlocked via his short stroke. Has tools behind the plate, also has a plus arm and above average receiving skills. Patience required as he's likely to move slowly for now, but receives accolades for being a smart, heady player.

Refsnyder,Rob — 4 — New York (A)
EXP MLB DEBUT: 2015 | H/W: 6-0 205 | FUT: Starting 2B | 7B

Bats R Age 25
2012 (5) Arizona
Pwr ++
BAvg ++++
Spd +++
Def ++

Year	Lev	Team	AB	R	H	HR	RBI	Avg	OB	Slg	OPS	bb%	ct%	Eye	SB	CS	x/h%	Iso	RC/G
2013	A+	Tampa	413	66	117	6	51	283	397	404	802	16	83	1.11	16	6	31	121	5.93
2014	AA	Trenton	228	35	78	6	30	342	380	548	928	6	83	0.37	5	5	38	206	6.84
2014	AAA	Scranton/WB	287	47	86	8	33	300	387	456	844	13	77	0.61	4	4	33	157	6.24
2015	AAA	Scranton/WB	450	66	122	9	56	271	352	402	754	11	84	0.77	12	2	32	131	5.04
2015	MLB	NY Yankees	43	3	13	2	5	302	348	512	859	7	84	0.43	2	0	38	209	5.90

Natural-hitting INF who has solid all-around game. Has plate discipline and bat control to draw walks and put bat to ball. Making harder contact and some of line drives could evolve into HR. Quick hands and hand-eye coordination lead to fine BA. Not a strong defender, but makes do with soft hands. Footwork could be better, but not a liability.

Rei,Austin — 2 — Boston
EXP MLB DEBUT: 2018 | H/W: 6-0 185 | FUT: Starting C | 7D

Bats R Age 22
2015 (3) Washington
Pwr ++
BAvg +++
Spd ++
Def +++

Year	Lev	Team	AB	R	H	HR	RBI	Avg	OB	Slg	OPS	bb%	ct%	Eye	SB	CS	x/h%	Iso	RC/G
2015	NCAA	Washington	91	14	30	7	20	330	408	681	1089	12	69	0.43	0	0	57	352	9.85
2015	A-	Lowell	112	14	20	2	12	179	252	295	547	9	65	0.28	1	0	40	116	2.07

Fundamentally-sound backstop with chance to be solid player with bat and glove. Owns bat speed and will see pitches, but strikes out too often and can sell out for power. Has been a good defender who receives and blocks well. Arm strength is evident and enhanced by quick release. Has relatively low ceiling, but also fairly high floor.

Reinheimer,Jack — 46 — Arizona
EXP MLB DEBUT: 2016 | H/W: 6-0 185 | FUT: Starting 2B/SS | 7B

Bats R Age 23
2013 (5) East Carolina
Pwr ++
BAvg +++
Spd +++
Def +++

Year	Lev	Team	AB	R	H	HR	RBI	Avg	OB	Slg	OPS	bb%	ct%	Eye	SB	CS	x/h%	Iso	RC/G
2013	A-	Everett	249	39	67	2	30	269	352	325	678	11	80	0.63	18	5	13	56	4.05
2014	A	Clinton	436	69	115	2	46	264	324	335	659	8	83	0.51	34	9	20	71	3.75
2014	A+	High Desert	85	15	29	1	12	341	371	459	830	4	86	0.33	5	2	24	118	5.54
2015	AA	Jackson	202	25	56	1	16	277	324	351	676	6	81	0.36	12	1	21	74	3.82
2015	AA	Mobile	283	39	75	4	26	265	350	371	721	12	81	0.69	9	5	27	106	4.65

Acquired by ARI in mid-season trade with SEA. Solid, unspectacular middle infield prospect. Can play SS but defensive profile plays better at 2B. Makes consistent contact and showed an improved eye at the plate late in the season. Balls find holes off bat. Has room on frame to build muscle. Stronger body will aid power projection.

Renda,Tony — 4 — Cincinnati
EXP MLB DEBUT: 2016 | H/W: 5-8 175 | FUT: Utility INF | 6A

Bats R Age 25
2012 (2) California
Pwr +
BAvg +++
Spd +++
Def ++

Year	Lev	Team	AB	R	H	HR	RBI	Avg	OB	Slg	OPS	bb%	ct%	Eye	SB	CS	x/h%	Iso	RC/G
2012	A-	Auburn	295	47	78	0	32	264	334	295	629	10	89	0.94	15	3	12	31	3.63
2013	A	Hagerstown	521	99	153	3	51	294	375	405	780	12	88	1.05	30	6	32	111	5.52
2014	A+	Potomac	414	75	127	0	47	307	372	377	749	9	86	0.73	19	5	20	70	4.97
2015	AA	Harrisburg	206	31	55	1	23	267	329	340	669	8	93	1.27	13	3	22	73	4.15
2015	AA	Trenton	274	42	74	2	21	270	329	372	701	8	91	1.00	10	3	31	102	4.46

Under-the-radar prospect who makes extreme contact and has skills to stick. Draws walks with discerning eye and rarely fans. Hits line drives to both gaps and has enough speed to be effective on base. Lacks size and won't hit for much pop nor does he project well. Handles 2B, but not a standout. Ranges well and arm strength is OK.

Renfroe,Hunter — 9 — San Diego
EXP MLB DEBUT: 2016 | H/W: 6-2 215 | FUT: Starting RF | 8B

Bats R Age 24
2013 (1) Mississippi St
Pwr ++++
BAvg +++
Spd ++
Def +++

Year	Lev	Team	AB	R	H	HR	RBI	Avg	OB	Slg	OPS	bb%	ct%	Eye	SB	CS	x/h%	Iso	RC/G
2013	A	Fort Wayne	66	6	14	2	7	212	257	379	636	6	65	0.17	0	0	50	167	3.31
2014	A+	Lake Elsinore	278	46	82	16	52	295	359	565	924	9	71	0.35	9	3	49	270	7.29
2014	AA	San Antonio	224	17	52	5	23	232	309	353	662	10	76	0.47	2	1	33	121	3.72
2015	AA	San Antonio	421	50	109	14	54	259	313	425	738	7	73	0.29	4	1	36	166	4.59
2015	AAA	El Paso	90	15	30	6	24	333	362	633	995	4	78	0.20	1	0	43	300	7.54

Strong OF who has some holes in game, but projects to be slugging RF. Owns plus power to all fields with vicious uppercut stroke and bat speed. Brings patience to plate, but swung and missed frequently in '15. Can get pull happy at times, though shortened swing late in season. Exhibits plus arm strength and good range.

Reyes,Franmil — 9 — San Diego

EXP MLB DEBUT: 2018 | H/W: 6-4 240 | FUT: Starting OF | 8E

Bats R Age 20 — 2011 FA (DR)

Pwr +++ / BAvg ++ / Spd ++ / Def ++

Year	Lev	Team	AB	R	H	HR	RBI	Avg	OB	Slg	OPS	bb%	ct%	Eye	SB	CS	x/h%	Iso	RC/G
2013	Rk	Azl Padres	165	24	52	3	30	315	389	467	856	11	76	0.51	5	5	33	152	6.40
2013	A-	Eugene	44	4	9	1	4	205	222	295	518	2	77	0.10	0	0	22	91	1.45
2014	A	Fort Wayne	508	67	126	11	59	248	300	368	668	7	77	0.32	1	5	29	120	3.66
2015	A	Fort Wayne	455	52	116	8	62	255	323	393	717	9	80	0.51	10	5	34	138	4.48

Large-framed prospect who repeated Low-A and made more consistent contact, but still has little feel for hitting. Drew more walks and has patience, but doesn't recognize spin and long swing can be exploited. Owns good power to all fields, though doesn't have much projection. Relegated to 1B with below average agility and quickness.

Reyes,Jomar — 5 — Baltimore

EXP MLB DEBUT: 2018 | H/W: 6-3 220 | FUT: Starting 3B/1B | 8C

Bats R Age 19 — 2014 FA (DR)

Pwr ++++ / BAvg +++ / Spd + / Def ++

Year	Lev	Team	AB	R	H	HR	RBI	Avg	OB	Slg	OPS	bb%	ct%	Eye	SB	CS	x/h%	Iso	RC/G
2014	Rk	GCL Orioles	186	23	53	4	29	285	338	425	763	7	80	0.39	1	0	30	140	4.92
2015	Rk	GCL Orioles	16	2	4	0	4	250	333	375	708	11	69	0.40	1	0	50	125	4.71
2015	A	Delmarva	309	36	86	5	44	278	318	440	758	6	76	0.25	1	0	42	162	4.87

Talented hitter with high ceiling predicated on strength and brute power. Swings fast bat and can catch up to plus velocity, yet can shorten swing for contact. Still needs work with pitch recognition which could elevate power output. Smokes doubles to gaps, though below average speed limits him. Not much range at 3B and could move across diamond.

Reyes,Victor — 789 — Arizona

EXP MLB DEBUT: 2018 | H/W: 6-3 170 | FUT: Reserve OF | 6B

Bats L Age 21 — 2011 FA (VZ)

Pwr + / BAvg +++ / Spd ++ / Def ++

Year	Lev	Team	AB	R	H	HR	RBI	Avg	OB	Slg	OPS	bb%	ct%	Eye	SB	CS	x/h%	Iso	RC/G
2013	Rk	GCL Braves	112	22	40	0	21	357	419	446	866	10	82	0.60	5	1	23	89	6.41
2013	Rk	Danville	81	12	26	0	4	321	345	358	703	4	89	0.33	0	0	12	37	4.04
2014	A	Rome	332	32	86	0	34	259	309	298	607	7	83	0.41	12	7	15	39	3.02
2015	A	Kane County	424	57	132	2	59	311	345	389	734	5	86	0.38	13	4	18	78	4.48

Contact-hitting OF posted positive results repeating Single-A. Tremendous hand-eye coordination. Can put bat on ball anywhere it's pitched. Struggles managing strike zone, resulting in few walks. Little to no current power; zero signs of it in BP or in-game. Poor arm projects him as utility outfielder.

Reynolds,Matt — 456 — New York (N)

EXP MLB DEBUT: 2016 | H/W: 6-1 205 | FUT: Starting IF | 7B

Bats R Age 25 — 2012 (2) Arkansas

Pwr ++ / BAvg +++ / Spd ++ / Def +++

Year	Lev	Team	AB	R	H	HR	RBI	Avg	OB	Slg	OPS	bb%	ct%	Eye	SB	CS	x/h%	Iso	RC/G
2013	AA	Binghamton	3	0	0	0	0	0	0	0	0	0	100		0	0		0	-2.66
2014	AA	Binghamton	211	33	75	1	21	355	433	422	855	12	81	0.71	6	3	12	66	6.38
2014	AAA	Las Vegas	267	54	89	5	40	333	382	479	861	7	78	0.35	14	4	28	146	6.21
2015	Rk	GCL Mets	5	1	2	0	1	400	500	400	900	17	80	1.00	0	0	0	0	7.22
2015	AAA	Las Vegas	445	70	119	6	65	267	317	402	719	7	79	0.35	13	4	36	135	4.39

Versatile MIF who should be a solid major leaguer. Contact hitter with gap power. Short, compact swing aids line-drive approach. An 8-12 HR hitter at full projection. Defensively, better suited for 2B and 3B. Instincts and soft hands help play up limitations at SS. Was on MLB playoff roster but did not appear in games.

Riddle,J.T. — 6 — Miami

EXP MLB DEBUT: 2016 | H/W: 6-3 175 | FUT: Utility player | 6B

Bats L Age 24 — 2013 (13) Kentucky

Pwr + / BAvg +++ / Spd +++ / Def +++

Year	Lev	Team	AB	R	H	HR	RBI	Avg	OB	Slg	OPS	bb%	ct%	Eye	SB	CS	x/h%	Iso	RC/G
2013	A-	Batavia	222	38	54	2	18	243	276	315	591	4	87	0.36	6	1	22	72	2.81
2014	A	Greensboro	435	65	122	9	60	280	321	400	721	6	87	0.47	5	1	25	120	4.33
2015	A+	Jupiter	185	30	50	0	9	270	311	314	625	6	84	0.38	7	3	14	43	3.21
2015	AA	Jacksonville	173	26	50	5	20	289	320	422	742	4	86	0.33	0	0	24	133	4.43
2015	AAA	New Orleans	3	2	2	0	0	667	800	667	1467	40	100		0	0	0	0	15.92

Gritty, no nonsense player gets the most of his abilities. Aggressive approach at the plate and uses a short, compact stroke. Played at three different levels, hitting .283/.323/.368. Contact oriented approach doesn't generate power and had just 19 extra base hits. Marlins hope he can stick at SS where he has a plus arm, good hands, and solid range.

Rijo,Wendell — 4 — Boston

EXP MLB DEBUT: 2018 | H/W: 5-11 170 | FUT: Starting 2B | 7C

Bats R Age 20 — 2012 FA (DR)

Pwr ++ / BAvg +++ / Spd +++ / Def ++

Year	Lev	Team	AB	R	H	HR	RBI	Avg	OB	Slg	OPS	bb%	ct%	Eye	SB	CS	x/h%	Iso	RC/G
2013	Rk	GCL Red Sox	170	28	46	0	20	271	354	359	713	11	83	0.76	15	5	33	88	4.67
2013	A-	Lowell	14	1	5	0	0	357	357	571	929	0	79	0.00	0	1	40	214	6.85
2014	A	Greenville	409	56	104	9	46	254	344	416	760	12	75	0.54	16	6	40	161	5.19
2015	A+	Salem	404	47	105	6	47	260	317	381	699	8	77	0.36	15	7	33	121	4.16

Polished INF who was youngest player in CAR and held his own. Understands game and exhibits keen hand-eye coordination for BA potential. Power limited to doubles, but can overswing at meaty pitches. Could stand to get on base more to use average wheels. Has OK hands and feet for 2B, but is fringy defender.

Riley,Austin — 5 — Atlanta

EXP MLB DEBUT: 2019 | H/W: 6-2 220 | FUT: Starting 3B | 8D

Bats R Age 19 — 2015 (1) HS (MS)

Pwr ++++ / BAvg +++ / Spd ++ / Def +++

Year	Lev	Team	AB	R	H	HR	RBI	Avg	OB	Slg	OPS	bb%	ct%	Eye	SB	CS	x/h%	Iso	RC/G
2015	Rk	Danville	111	18	39	5	19	351	424	586	1010	11	75	0.50	0	1	38	234	8.41
2015	Rk	GCL Braves	106	18	27	7	21	255	331	500	831	10	65	0.32	2	1	44	245	6.17

Strong, tall 3B was talk of the GCL & Appy this summer, slugging 12 HRs in 217 ABs. Could be steal of '15 draft at 41st pick. Generates backspin and loft naturally and should hit for plus power. Questions about bat speed may cause prospect status to fall some. Body is at full projection and may battle weight issues throughout career.

Rivera,T.J. — 456 — New York (N)

EXP MLB DEBUT: 2016 | H/W: 6-0 190 | FUT: Utility INF | 6B

Bats R Age 27 — 2011 (NDFA) Troy

Pwr + / BAvg +++ / Spd ++ / Def ++

Year	Lev	Team	AB	R	H	HR	RBI	Avg	OB	Slg	OPS	bb%	ct%	Eye	SB	CS	x/h%	Iso	RC/G
2013	A+	St. Lucie	502	76	145	2	51	289	334	351	685	6	85	0.47	6	2	18	62	3.97
2014	A+	St. Lucie	252	42	86	4	47	341	376	452	828	5	85	0.38	2	1	23	111	5.53
2014	AA	Binghamton	201	28	72	1	28	358	392	438	829	5	87	0.41	1	0	19	80	5.57
2015	AA	Binghamton	220	37	75	5	27	341	375	455	830	5	90	0.55	1	1	20	114	5.50
2015	AAA	Las Vegas	183	26	56	2	21	306	332	443	774	4	86	0.28	0	0	36	137	4.90

Scrappy, 27 yr old middle INF continues to defy odds as a NDFA out of college. Hit .325/.364/.449 between Double-A & Triple-A. Short, quick swing leads to consistent contact. Has power to pull-side and hits the gaps with line drives. Useful piece with ability to play all INF positions.

Rivera,Yadiel — 6 — Milwaukee

EXP MLB DEBUT: 2015 | H/W: 6-2 180 | FUT: Backup SS | 6B

Bats R Age 23 — 2010 (9) HS (PR)

Pwr ++ / BAvg ++ / Spd +++ / Def +++++

Year	Lev	Team	AB	R	H	HR	RBI	Avg	OB	Slg	OPS	bb%	ct%	Eye	SB	CS	x/h%	Iso	RC/G
2014	A+	Brevard County	231	35	59	3	17	255	304	346	650	6	78	0.32	5	3	22	91	3.43
2014	AA	Huntsville	183	31	48	2	13	262	301	410	710	5	80	0.28	5	2	35	148	4.25
2015	AA	Biloxi	184	23	51	1	16	277	338	375	713	8	84	0.57	8	7	25	98	4.47
2015	AAA	Colorado Springs	290	32	69	1	28	238	263	303	567	3	82	0.19	4	3	19	66	2.34
2015	MLB	Milwaukee	14	0	1	0	0	71	71	71	143	0	71	0.00	0	0	0	0	-3.73

Features some of the best defensive skills in the minors, wielding a plus throwing arm, premium range, footwork and instincts. Bat is another story. Aggressive approach limits walks and stolen base chances. Showed nice gap power in AFL action, but raw pop not a real factor. With only average contact skills, his BA upside is limited.

Roache,Victor — 7 — Milwaukee

EXP MLB DEBUT: 2017 | H/W: 6-1 225 | FUT: Starting LF | 8D

Bats R Age 24 — 2012 (1) Georgia Southern

Pwr ++++ / BAvg ++ / Spd ++ / Def ++

Year	Lev	Team	AB	R	H	HR	RBI	Avg	OB	Slg	OPS	bb%	ct%	Eye	SB	CS	x/h%	Iso	RC/G
2012	NCAA	Georgia Southern	17	6	7	2	5	412	583	765	1348	29	94	7.00	0	0	29	353	12.67
2013	A	Wisconsin	459	62	114	22	74	248	317	440	757	9	70	0.34	6	2	35	192	4.90
2014	A+	Brevard County	433	46	98	18	54	226	287	400	687	8	68	0.27	11	4	38	173	3.93
2015	A+	Brevard County	239	23	62	10	36	259	319	448	767	8	61	0.22	3	3	37	188	5.58
2015	AA	Biloxi	223	23	55	8	35	247	317	430	748	9	71	0.36	2	1	40	184	4.87

Former 1st-round pick with plus raw power but suspect contact skills. Has leverage and bat speed to eclipse 30 HR down the road, but long swing often leaves him exposed to breaking balls in the dirt, which will limit his BA upside. Speed no longer a factor to his game. Average arm and fringy range means his future could be limited to LF.

Robertson,Daniel — 6 — Tampa Bay

EXP MLB DEBUT: 2016 | H/W: 6-0 205 | FUT: Starting SS | 8C

Bats R Age 22 — 2012 (1) HS (CA)

Pwr +++ / BAvg +++ / Spd ++ / Def +++

Year	Lev	Team	AB	R	H	HR	RBI	Avg	OB	Slg	OPS	bb%	ct%	Eye	SB	CS	x/h%	Iso	RC/G
2012	A-	Vermont	94	9	17	1	8	181	238	234	472	7	67	0.23	1	1	18	53	0.85
2013	A	Beloit	401	59	111	9	46	277	344	401	745	9	80	0.52	1	7	28	125	4.77
2014	A+	Stockton	548	110	170	15	60	310	390	471	861	12	83	0.77	4	4	32	161	6.34
2015	Rk	GCL Devil Rays	8	2	1	0	0	125	364	125	489	27	75	1.50	1	0	0	0	1.95
2015	AA	Montgomery	299	49	82	4	41	274	346	415	761	10	81	0.57	2	3	35	140	5.12

Natural-hitting INF who missed time with broken hand. Knows how to hit and reads pitches well. Finds pitches he can drive and has strength and quick bat for BA and average pop. Will expand zone at times in hopes for power. Not the fleetest afoot, but has good instincts on base. Fundamental defender with quick hands and arm.

Robinson,Drew | 46 | Texas | EXP MLB DEBUT: 2016 | H/W: 6-1 200 | FUT: Starting 2B | 7D

Bats L Age 23	Year	Lev	Team	AB	R	H	HR	RBI	Avg	OB	Slg	OPS	bb%	ct%	Eye	SB	CS	x/h%	Iso	RC/G
2010 (4) HS (NV)	2013	A+	Myrtle Beach	436	62	112	8	70	257	362	404	766	14	72	0.58	10	2	37	147	5.44
Pwr +++	2014	AA	Frisco	331	41	63	11	40	190	272	366	637	10	62	0.30	6	5	49	175	3.51
BAvg ++	2014	AAA	Round Rock	23	3	7	1	5	304	448	522	970	21	70	0.86	3	0	43	217	8.63
Spd ++	2015	AA	Frisco	432	78	100	21	64	231	355	454	809	16	68	0.60	14	8	49	222	6.05
Def ++	2015	AAA	Round Rock	23	4	7	0	2	304	407	391	799	15	83	1.00	2	1	29	87	5.92

Patient INF who led TL in HR and 2nd in Ks. Has clean stroke and likes to use entire field. Power potential is only average, but has strength to pull balls out. Can be too passive at plate and let hittable pitches go by. Limited contact hinders BA and has below average speed despite SB. Mostly played 2B, but can play SS and OF with strong arm.

Robles,Victor | 8 | Washington | EXP MLB DEBUT: 2018 | H/W: 6-0 185 | FUT: Starting CF | 9C

Bats R Age 18	Year	Lev	Team	AB	R	H	HR	RBI	Avg	OB	Slg	OPS	bb%	ct%	Eye	SB	CS	x/h%	Iso	RC/G
2013 FA (DR)																				
Pwr +++																				
BAvg ++++																				
Spd ++++	2015	Rk	GCL Nationals	73	19	27	2	11	370	446	562	1007	12	84	0.83	12	1	33	192	8.18
Def ++++	2015	A-	Auburn	140	29	48	2	16	343	378	479	857	5	85	0.38	12	4	23	136	5.93

Destroyed rookie and short-season ball as 18 year old. Premium hit tool via advanced approach and top-shelf bat speed result in hard line drives. As he adds strength and some loft to his swing, power will come naturally. Likewise, speed disrupts the game on bases and in the field; takes excellent routes and has a strong arm. A baby, but superstar potential.

Rodgers,Brendan | 6 | Colorado | EXP MLB DEBUT: 2019 | H/W: 6-0 180 | FUT: Starting SS | 9C

Bats R Age 19	Year	Lev	Team	AB	R	H	HR	RBI	Avg	OB	Slg	OPS	bb%	ct%	Eye	SB	CS	x/h%	Iso	RC/G
2015 (1) HS (FL)																				
Pwr ++++																				
BAvg +++																				
Spd +++																				
Def +++	2015	Rk	Grand Junction	143	22	39	3	20	273	342	420	761	9	74	0.41	4	3	33	147	5.08

Has plus raw power, good bat speed, and a solid understanding of the strike zone. Should continue to add power as he matures and moves up. Above-average runner with good range, soft hands, and a strong arm that gives him a chance to stick at SS, though he has the power to be an asset at any position.

Rodriguez,Carlos | 37 | St. Louis | EXP MLB DEBUT: 2020 | H/W: 6-2 215 | FUT: Starting 1B/LF | 7D

Bats R Age 19	Year	Lev	Team	AB	R	H	HR	RBI	Avg	OB	Slg	OPS	bb%	ct%	Eye	SB	CS	x/h%	Iso	RC/G
2014 FA (DR)																				
Pwr +++																				
BAvg +++																				
Spd ++																				
Def ++	2015			*Did not play in U.S.*																

Strong, powerful 1B prospect has yet to make his state-side debut and spent the year in the DSL. Rodriguez stroked the ball hitting .311/.366/.497 as an 18-year-old. Moves well defensively with soft hands and a good feel for 1B.

Rodriguez,David | 2 | Tampa Bay | EXP MLB DEBUT: 2019 | H/W: 5-11 200 | FUT: Starting C | 8E

Bats R Age 20	Year	Lev	Team	AB	R	H	HR	RBI	Avg	OB	Slg	OPS	bb%	ct%	Eye	SB	CS	x/h%	Iso	RC/G
2012 FA (VZ)																				
Pwr ++																				
BAvg ++																				
Spd ++	2014	Rk	GCL Devil Rays	128	15	35	0	23	273	321	383	704	7	76	0.29	3	0	34	109	4.29
Def +++	2015	Rk	Princeton	178	20	46	4	27	258	316	376	692	8	78	0.38	1	1	26	118	4.00

Short, stocky C with chance to be standout with glove. Footwork is a bit crude, but has strong arm with quick release. Calls a good game and has advanced receiving skills. Has a lot of work to do with bat. Sees pitches and covers plate with nice stroke. Offers some pop, but value mostly tied to BA and OBP.

Rodriguez,Luigi | 789 | Cleveland | EXP MLB DEBUT: 2017 | H/W: 5-11 160 | FUT: Starting OF | 7D

Bats B Age 23	Year	Lev	Team	AB	R	H	HR	RBI	Avg	OB	Slg	OPS	bb%	ct%	Eye	SB	CS	x/h%	Iso	RC/G
2009 FA (DR)	2012	A	Lake County	463	75	124	11	48	268	339	406	745	10	71	0.38	24	9	30	138	4.89
Pwr ++	2013	A	Lake County	76	14	20	1	9	263	349	329	678	12	67	0.40	5	3	15	66	4.06
BAvg +++	2013	A+	Carolina	113	16	32	0	11	283	382	398	780	14	68	0.50	3	4	38	115	5.88
Spd +++	2014	A+	Carolina	336	50	84	6	30	250	347	366	713	13	74	0.57	15	8	27	116	4.58
Def +++	2015	A+	Lynchburg	372	59	109	12	49	293	336	492	828	6	78	0.29	24	8	39	199	5.68

Speedy OF who will miss 80 games due to PED suspension. Set career high in HR and showed improvement, though hasn't made it past High-A. Uses smooth, level swing to produce gap power and has good speed and instincts. Expands K zone and can sell out for power. Doesn't draw walks and needs to be more selective. Has average arm to play all OF spots.

Rodriguez,Nelson | 3 | Cleveland | EXP MLB DEBUT: 2017 | H/W: 6-2 250 | FUT: Starting 1B | 7D

Bats R Age 21	Year	Lev	Team	AB	R	H	HR	RBI	Avg	OB	Slg	OPS	bb%	ct%	Eye	SB	CS	x/h%	Iso	RC/G
2012 (15) HS (NY)	2013	A-	Mahoning Val	261	32	75	9	37	287	359	452	811	10	77	0.48	0	2	33	165	5.62
Pwr ++++	2013	A	Lake County	160	18	31	1	13	194	306	256	563	14	67	0.49	0	0	26	63	2.46
BAvg ++	2014	A	Lake County	485	67	130	22	88	268	349	482	831	11	71	0.42	0	0	44	214	6.09
Spd +	2015	A+	Lynchburg	396	65	109	17	84	275	358	495	853	11	69	0.42	1	0	47	220	6.53
Def ++	2015	AA	Akron	93	7	11	4	14	118	196	269	465	9	60	0.24	0	0	55	151	0.55

Large-framed 1B who offers ton of power at plate, though inability to make consistent contact may mute pop at higher levels. Covers plate with long arms, but can be beaten inside with good FB. Willing to work counts and draw walks and has feel for breaking balls. Secondary skills are far behind. Very poor runner with sub-par hands at 1B.

Rodriguez,Ronny | 4 | Cleveland | EXP MLB DEBUT: 2016 | H/W: 6-0 170 | FUT: Starting 2B | 7D

Bats R Age 23	Year	Lev	Team	AB	R	H	HR	RBI	Avg	OB	Slg	OPS	bb%	ct%	Eye	SB	CS	x/h%	Iso	RC/G
2010 FA (DR)	2011	A	Lake County	370	41	91	11	42	246	272	449	720	3	78	0.16	10	7	51	203	4.22
Pwr ++	2012	A+	Carolina	454	67	120	19	66	264	294	452	745	4	81	0.22	7	7	36	187	4.40
BAvg +++	2013	AA	Akron	468	62	124	5	52	265	289	376	665	3	84	0.21	12	3	29	111	3.56
Spd ++	2014	AA	Akron	413	52	94	5	34	228	272	324	596	6	78	0.27	4	5	32	97	2.73
Def +++	2015	AA	Akron	269	34	77	11	29	286	312	491	803	4	78	0.17	4	5	38	204	5.15

Very athletic and wiry strong INF who missed all of April and May and split time between 1B and 2B. Power starting to return, though big swing can be exploited. Shows little selectivity or patience and not willing to draw walks. Spent 3rd year in AA and continues to show quality defensive tools. Has good skills, but little feel for game.

Rodriguez,Yorman | 89 | Cincinnati | EXP MLB DEBUT: 2014 | H/W: 6-3 210 | FUT: Starting CF | 7C

Bats R Age 23	Year	Lev	Team	AB	R	H	HR	RBI	Avg	OB	Slg	OPS	bb%	ct%	Eye	SB	CS	x/h%	Iso	RC/G
2008 FA (VZ)	2013	A+	Bakersfield	251	41	63	9	35	251	311	470	781	8	69	0.29	6	3	52	219	5.43
Pwr +++	2013	AA	Pensacola	262	30	70	4	31	267	331	385	717	9	71	0.33	4	0	30	118	4.50
BAvg ++	2014	AA	Pensacola	450	69	118	9	40	262	332	389	721	9	74	0.40	12	5	29	127	4.51
Spd +++	2014	MLB	Cincinnati	27	3	6	0	2	222	250	222	472	4	56	0.08	0	1	0	0	0.85
Def ++++	2015	AAA	Louisville	308	42	83	10	41	269	308	429	736	5	74	0.21	4	1	31	159	4.44

Raw despite September '14 call-up. Has the potential to hit .260 with 20 plus HRs. Pitch recognition skills will hamper bat from reaching potential. Reached double-digits in HRs for 1st time in career. Runs well but struggled with calf injury, depressing his '15 SB numbers. Solid CF with solid 1st step and average range is aided by 70-grade arm.

Romero,Avery | 4 | Miami | EXP MLB DEBUT: 2017 | H/W: 5-11 195 | FUT: Starting 2B | 7C

Bats R Age 22	Year	Lev	Team	AB	R	H	HR	RBI	Avg	OB	Slg	OPS	bb%	ct%	Eye	SB	CS	x/h%	Iso	RC/G
2012 (3) HS (FL)	2013	A-	Batavia	209	27	62	2	30	297	344	411	755	7	84	0.44	3	4	32	115	4.84
Pwr ++	2013	A	Greensboro	34	5	5	1	5	147	237	265	502	11	85	0.80	0	0	40	118	1.95
BAvg +++	2014	A	Greensboro	366	51	117	5	46	320	363	429	792	6	87	0.53	6	4	25	109	5.22
Spd ++	2014	A+	Jupiter	100	12	32	0	10	320	364	400	764	7	87	0.54	4	1	25	80	4.99
Def ++	2015	A+	Jupiter	455	47	118	3	42	259	316	314	631	8	84	0.54	3	4	15	55	3.38

Strong hands and quick wrists generate above average bat speed that allows him to go gap-to-gap. Barrels the ball consistently and relies on contact-orientated approach. Is a tick below avg runner, but has athleticism. Moves well on D with good actions and a strong arm. The move from SS to 2B a success and he now profiles as at least an average defender.

Rondon,Adrian | 6 | Tampa Bay | EXP MLB DEBUT: 2020 | H/W: 6-1 190 | FUT: Starting SS | 9E

Bats R Age 17	Year	Lev	Team	AB	R	H	HR	RBI	Avg	OB	Slg	OPS	bb%	ct%	Eye	SB	CS	x/h%	Iso	RC/G
2014 FA (DR)																				
Pwr ++																				
BAvg ++																				
Spd +++																				
Def +++	2015	Rk	GCL Devil Rays	145	3	24	0	11	166	253	234	488	10	61	0.30	0	2	38	69	1.28

Athletic INF who hit under .200 each month, but has sky-high ceiling. Should be able to stick at SS with strong arm, clean hands, and good footwork. Has potential to be middle-of-order run producer with at least average pop and BA. Can be fooled by breaking balls and swing mechanics need to be modified. Runs well and should be able to steal bases.

Rondon,Jose — 6 — San Diego

EXP MLB DEBUT: 2017 | H/W: 6-1 160 | FUT: Starting SS | 7C

Bats R | Age 22 | 2011 FA (CU)

Pwr + | BAvg +++ | Spd ++ | Def +++

Year	Lev	Team	AB	R	H	HR	RBI	Avg	OB	Slg	OPS	bb%	ct%	Eye	SB	CS	x/h%	Iso	RC/G
2014	Rk	Azl Angels	8	3	1	0	0	125	222	125	347	11	100		2	1	0	0	1.36
2014	A+	Inland Empire	297	40	97	0	24	327	363	418	781	5	83	0.34	8	6	23	91	5.09
2014	A+	Lake Elsinore	136	18	41	1	12	301	362	390	752	9	83	0.57	3	1	24	88	4.91
2015	A+	Lake Elsinore	237	50	71	3	22	300	357	414	770	8	84	0.55	17	6	25	114	5.08
2015	AA	San Antonio	100	6	19	0	9	190	221	230	451	4	85	0.27	1	3	16	40	1.13

Lean INF who ended season in July with broken elbow. Makes easy, consistent contact with plus bat control and short stroke. Can be tough out, but doesn't have enough strength to hit HR. Possesses below average speed, but runs bases well for SB. Needs to hit for BA to have value, but offers good SS glove with nimble actions.

Rosario,Amed — 6 — New York (N)

EXP MLB DEBUT: 2017 | H/W: 6-2 170 | FUT: Starting SS | 9C

Bats R | Age 20 | 2012 FA (DR)

Pwr +++ | BAvg +++ | Spd ++++ | Def ++++

Year	Lev	Team	AB	R	H	HR	RBI	Avg	OB	Slg	OPS	bb%	ct%	Eye	SB	CS	x/h%	Iso	RC/G
2013	Rk	Kingsport	212	22	51	3	23	241	278	358	637	5	80	0.26	2	6	29	118	3.24
2014	A-	Brooklyn	266	39	77	1	23	289	332	380	712	6	82	0.36	7	3	22	90	4.28
2014	A	Savannah	30	2	4	1	4	133	161	300	461	3	63	0.09	0	0	50	167	0.60
2015	A+	St. Lucie	385	41	99	0	25	257	299	335	634	6	81	0.32	12	4	25	78	3.32
2015	AA	Binghamton	10	1	1	0	1	100	100	100	200	0	50	0.00	1	0	0	0	-4.05

NYM has been aggressively challenging Rosario. Held his own in FSL as 19-year-old against much older competition. Quick bat with line drive approach to RCF. Barreling baseballs at greater rate. Liners are showing more carry as he ages. Likely no more than a 10-15 HR threat. Has plus speed. Rangy at SS with soft hands and a strong throwing arm.

Ruiz,Rio — 5 — Atlanta

EXP MLB DEBUT: 2017 | H/W: 6-1 215 | FUT: Starting 3B | 8E

Bats L | Age 21 | 2012 (4) HS (CA)

Pwr +++ | BAvg ++ | Spd + | Def ++

Year	Lev	Team	AB	R	H	HR	RBI	Avg	OB	Slg	OPS	bb%	ct%	Eye	SB	CS	x/h%	Iso	RC/G
2012	Rk	GCL Astros	85	13	23	0	11	271	361	412	773	12	74	0.55	2	0	43	141	5.58
2012	Rk	Greeneville	50	8	11	1	7	220	278	380	658	7	80	0.40	0	0	45	160	3.67
2013	A	Quad Cities	416	46	108	12	63	260	339	430	769	11	78	0.54	12	3	43	171	5.17
2014	A+	Lancaster	516	76	151	11	77	293	390	436	826	14	82	0.90	4	4	33	143	6.07
2015	AA	Mississippi	420	48	98	5	46	233	333	324	657	13	78	0.67	2	2	28	90	3.87

Took a step back with a disappointing '15 season. Shows solid hit and power tools in BP but struggles barreling baseballs against live pitching. Has a good idea of the strike zone, working counts and taking walks. Bat will carry his glove at 3B.

Sanchez,Ali — 2 — New York (N)

EXP MLB DEBUT: 2019 | H/W: 6-0 175 | FUT: Starting C | 8E

Bats R | Age 19 | 2013 FA (VZ)

Pwr ++ | BAvg +++ | Spd ++ | Def ++++

Year	Lev	Team	AB	R	H	HR	RBI	Avg	OB	Slg	OPS	bb%	ct%	Eye	SB	CS	x/h%	Iso	RC/G
2015	Rk	GCL Mets	162	20	45	0	17	278	328	315	642	7	84	0.46	2	0	13	37	3.48
2015	Rk	Kingsport	11	2	2	0	3	182	182	182	364	0	82	0.00	0	0	0	0	-0.33

Young, athletic catcher has an idea with the bat. Showcased ability to barrel the ball and hit to all fields in GCL stint. Has some untapped raw power but will be slow to develop. Possesses advanced pitch presentation skills. Solid throwing arm is depressed by poor throwing mechanics.

Sanchez,Gary — 2 — New York (A)

EXP MLB DEBUT: 2015 | H/W: 6-2 230 | FUT: Starting C | 8C

Bats R | Age 23 | 2009 FA (DR)

Pwr ++++ | BAvg +++ | Spd ++ | Def ++

Year	Lev	Team	AB	R	H	HR	RBI	Avg	OB	Slg	OPS	bb%	ct%	Eye	SB	CS	x/h%	Iso	RC/G
2013	AA	Trenton	92	12	23	2	10	250	343	380	723	12	83	0.81	0	0	35	130	4.71
2014	AA	Trenton	429	48	116	13	65	270	337	406	742	9	79	0.47	1	1	28	135	4.66
2015	AA	Trenton	233	33	61	12	36	262	315	476	791	7	79	0.36	6	0	43	215	5.11
2015	AAA	Scranton/WB	132	17	39	6	26	295	350	500	850	8	79	0.39	1	2	38	205	5.91
2015	MLB	NY Yankees	2	0	0	0	0	0	0	0	0	0	50	0.00	0	0		0	-7.85

Bat-first backstop who tied career high in HR and was Sept call-up. Possesses plus power that could evolve into more and has instincts and swing to hit for moderate BA. Tends to get pull happy and doesn't run well, though he can steal a base. Defense is still in question, though no dispute about arm strength. NYY showing trust in his future at C.

Sanchez,Manny — 79 — Tampa Bay

EXP MLB DEBUT: 2019 | H/W: 6-2 220 | FUT: Starting OF | 8E

Bats R | Age 20 | 2013 FA (DR)

Pwr +++ | BAvg ++ | Spd +++ | Def ++

Year	Lev	Team	AB	R	H	HR	RBI	Avg	OB	Slg	OPS	bb%	ct%	Eye	SB	CS	x/h%	Iso	RC/G
2013	Rk	DSL Devil Rays	251	47	62	13	52	247	341	466	808	13	81	0.77	8	1	45	219	5.61
2014	Rk	Princeton	208	21	50	3	17	240	291	361	652	7	65	0.21	2	0	34	120	3.65
2015	A-	Hudson Valley	209	28	57	5	22	273	339	426	765	9	67	0.31	5	0	37	153	5.30

Tall, strong OF who has yet to play in full-season ball. Lot of swing and miss and will need to find cleaner swing and more patience at plate. Has plus power potential predicated on bat speed and natural strength in wrists. Fits best in RF where rocket arm is an asset. Lots of polish needed, but TAM will be patient.

Sandberg,Cord — 7 — Philadelphia

EXP MLB DEBUT: 2018 | H/W: 6-3 215 | FUT: Starting LF | 7D

Bats L | Age 21 | 2013 (3) HS (FL)

Pwr +++ | BAvg ++ | Spd ++ | Def ++

Year	Lev	Team	AB	R	H	HR	RBI	Avg	OB	Slg	OPS	bb%	ct%	Eye	SB	CS	x/h%	Iso	RC/G
2013	Rk	GCL Phillies	169	23	35	2	14	207	306	272	578	12	79	0.67	4	3	17	65	2.79
2014	A-	Williamsport	264	33	62	6	24	235	265	345	610	4	79	0.20	8	3	23	110	2.76
2015	A	Lakewood	499	53	127	5	59	255	295	345	640	5	82	0.33	5	7	27	90	3.34

Present inconsistent swing mechanics damper overall profile. When working, swing looks easy; sprays hard line drives. When not, its mechanical and pull happy. Though walk and strikeout rates improved, still has trouble tracking breaking balls. Has the build for power, but will need incorporate loft. Defensive limitations will keep him in LF.

Sanger,Brendon — 79 — Los Angeles (A)

EXP MLB DEBUT: 2018 | H/W: 6-0 190 | FUT: Starting OF | 7D

Bats L | Age 22 | 2015 (4) Florida Atlantic

Pwr ++ | BAvg +++ | Spd ++ | Def ++

Year	Lev	Team	AB	R	H	HR	RBI	Avg	OB	Slg	OPS	bb%	ct%	Eye	SB	CS	x/h%	Iso	RC/G
2015	NCAA	Florida Atlantic	230	57	85	7	48	370	493	583	1076	20	87	1.87	2	0	36	213	9.48
2015	Rk	Orem	217	45	65	4	29	300	420	456	876	17	82	1.15	13	3	38	157	6.95

Disciplined OF who draws walks and gets on base, but has limited offensive utility. Possesses feel for bat control and knows strike zone. Lacks power for corner OF, though can smash doubles to all fields. Can overswing at times and doesn't have natural bat speed for power projection. Runs OK and may not have enough speed for CF. Tweener prospect.

Schales,Brian — 5 — Miami

EXP MLB DEBUT: 2020 | H/W: 6-1 170 | FUT: Starting 3B | 7D

Bats R | Age 20 | 2014 (4) HS (CA)

Pwr +++ | BAvg ++ | Spd + | Def +++

Year	Lev	Team	AB	R	H	HR	RBI	Avg	OB	Slg	OPS	bb%	ct%	Eye	SB	CS	x/h%	Iso	RC/G
2014	Rk	GCL Marlins	173	24	42	1	23	243	307	306	613	8	84	0.57	2	5	21	64	3.22
2015	A	Greensboro	443	59	115	4	45	260	318	348	666	8	83	0.50	3	2	24	88	3.80

Has average tools other than speed. Good bat speed and the ability to barrel the ball should allow him to hit for BA. Has above-avg raw power, but hit just 4 HR. Moves well at 3B with decent range, good hands, and a plus arm. Should be able to stick at 3B as he moves up, but will need power to develop for him to have fantasy value.

Schebler,Scott — 7 — Cincinnati

EXP MLB DEBUT: 2015 | H/W: 6-0 225 | FUT: Starting OF | 7B

Bats L | Age 25 | 2010 (26) DesMoinesAreaCC

Pwr +++ | BAvg ++ | Spd ++ | Def ++

Year	Lev	Team	AB	R	H	HR	RBI	Avg	OB	Slg	OPS	bb%	ct%	Eye	SB	CS	x/h%	Iso	RC/G
2012	A	Great Lakes	515	67	134	6	67	260	301	388	689	6	81	0.30	17	11	34	128	3.97
2013	A+	RanchoCuca	477	95	141	27	91	296	344	581	924	7	71	0.25	16	5	49	285	7.23
2014	AA	Chattanooga	489	82	137	28	73	280	341	556	897	8	78	0.41	10	4	47	276	6.61
2015	AAA	Oklahoma City	432	57	104	13	50	241	305	410	715	8	78	0.43	15	2	37	169	4.34
2015	MLB	LA Dodgers	36	6	9	3	4	250	308	500	808	8	64	0.23	2	1	33	250	5.62

Thick-bodied OF failed to duplicate his breakout of '14, but did manage to make his MLB debut. Has good raw power with good bat speed and makes consistent, hard contact. An average runner and defender, he is likely limited to LF in the majors. Can be overly aggressive, which causes his swing to get big.

Schrock,Max — 4 — Washington

EXP MLB DEBUT: 2019 | H/W: 5-8 180 | FUT: Starting 2B | 7C

Bats L | Age 21 | 2015 (13) South Carolina

Pwr +++ | BAvg ++++ | Spd ++ | Def ++

Year	Lev	Team	AB	R	H	HR	RBI	Avg	OB	Slg	OPS	bb%	ct%	Eye	SB	CS	x/h%	Iso	RC/G
2015	NCAA	South Carolina	192	44	63	6	34	328	424	500	924	14	91	1.78	8	2	30	172	7.25
2015	A-	Auburn	172	31	53	2	14	308	357	448	804	7	91	0.81	2	1	30	140	5.52

Hit the ground running as a pro, showcasing exquisite bat-to-ball skills and plate discipline that points to a plus BA. Has enough bat speed for average power. Opinions diverge on his defense; poor footspeed and average arm could move him to LF, where bat might not be enough. Ultimate upside (staying at 2B) is a Neil Walker-type player.

Seager,Corey — 6 — Los Angeles (N)

EXP MLB DEBUT: 2015 | H/W: 6-4 215 | FUT: Starting SS/3B | 9A

Bats L Age 21 | 2012 (1) HS (NC)

Pwr ++++ | BAvg ++++ | Spd ++ | Def +++

Year	Lev	Team	AB	R	H	HR	RBI	Avg	OB	Slg	OPS	bb%	ct%	Eye	SB	CS	x/h%	Iso	RC/G
2014	A+	RanchoCuca	327	61	115	18	70	352	406	633	1039	8	77	0.39	5	1	47	281	8.50
2014	AA	Chattanooga	148	28	51	2	27	345	386	534	920	6	74	0.26	1	1	41	189	7.21
2015	AA	Tulsa	80	17	30	5	15	375	412	675	1087	6	86	0.45	1	1	43	300	8.45
2015	AAA	Oklahoma City	421	64	117	13	61	278	329	451	780	7	85	0.49	3	0	38	173	5.08
2015	MLB	LA Dodgers	98	17	33	4	17	337	420	561	981	13	81	0.74	2	0	39	224	7.89

Dynamic player more than held his own in big league debut. Has plus bat speed that allows him to make hard contact with leverage. Just starting to tap into his raw power. Moves well for his size and saw extended action at SS in the majors, but long-term his size and power profile better at 3B where his range and plus arm play well.

Severino,Pedro — 2 — Washington

EXP MLB DEBUT: 2015 | H/W: 6-2 200 | FUT: Backup C | 7C

Bats R Age 22 | 2010 FA (DR)

Pwr + | BAvg ++ | Spd ++ | Def ++++

Year	Lev	Team	AB	R	H	HR	RBI	Avg	OB	Slg	OPS	bb%	ct%	Eye	SB	CS	x/h%	Iso	RC/G
2012	Rk	GCL Nationals	109	9	24	0	8	220	280	266	546	8	92	1.00	0	0	17	46	2.74
2013	A	Hagerstown	282	28	68	1	45	241	275	333	608	4	81	0.24	1	0	32	92	2.93
2014	A+	Potomac	291	41	72	9	36	247	298	399	697	7	80	0.37	2	0	35	151	3.99
2015	AA	Harrisburg	329	33	81	5	34	246	287	331	619	5	84	0.37	1	2	22	85	3.08
2015	MLB	Washington	4	1	1	0	0	250	250	500	750	0	75	0.00	0	0	100	250	4.87

Athletic and agile catcher shines behind the plate, with advanced receiving skills plus a rocket arm and quick release. He still struggles with a bat in his hand, as poor pitch recognition and below-average bat speed sap his offensive potential. There's still time, but without improvement, he'll only be an asset on defense.

Seymour,Anfernee — 6 — Miami

EXP MLB DEBUT: 2020 | H/W: 5-11 165 | FUT: Starting SS | 8D

Bats B Age 20 | 2014 (7) HS (FL)

Pwr ++ | BAvg +++ | Spd +++++ | Def ++

Year	Lev	Team	AB	R	H	HR	RBI	Avg	OB	Slg	OPS	bb%	ct%	Eye	SB	CS	x/h%	Iso	RC/G
2014	Rk	GCL Marlins	98	24	24	0	3	245	327	265	593	11	72	0.44	11	2	4	20	2.83
2015	A-	Batavia	238	39	65	0	14	273	329	349	678	8	78	0.38	29	6	22	76	3.96

Speedster remains raw in many aspects. Has 80 grade speed and stole 29 bases in 64 games. Short, quick stroke is designed more for contact than power, but should enable him to use his speed and hit for BA. Is a work in progress on defense, but shows plus range, a good arm, and good instincts at SS.

Shaffer,Richie — 35 — Tampa Bay

EXP MLB DEBUT: 2015 | H/W: 6-2 220 | FUT: Starting 3B/1B | 8C

Bats R Age 25 | 2012 (1) Clemson

Pwr ++++ | BAvg ++ | Spd ++ | Def ++

Year	Lev	Team	AB	R	H	HR	RBI	Avg	OB	Slg	OPS	bb%	ct%	Eye	SB	CS	x/h%	Iso	RC/G
2013	A+	Charlotte	469	55	119	11	73	254	306	399	704	7	77	0.33	6	0	38	145	4.15
2014	AA	Montgomery	427	58	95	19	64	222	313	440	753	12	72	0.47	4	0	54	218	4.99
2015	AA	Montgomery	149	22	39	7	27	262	360	470	830	13	67	0.47	3	0	44	208	6.31
2015	AAA	Durham	244	42	66	19	45	270	353	582	935	11	70	0.42	1	1	56	311	7.47
2015	MLB	Tampa Bay	74	11	14	4	6	189	286	392	678	12	57	0.31	0	1	50	203	4.29

Strong INF who rebounded from poor '14 and figures into TAM plans. Set easy high in HR while showcasing plus bat speed and all-fields pop. Swing can get long and will rack up Ks, especially against good breaking balls. All about offense as he has poor foot speed. Has plus arm that could work at 3B or possibly RF. Needs to hit to play every day.

Shaw,Christopher — 3 — San Francisco

EXP MLB DEBUT: 2018 | H/W: 6-4 255 | FUT: Starting 1B | 8C

Bats L Age 22 | 2015 (1) Boston College

Pwr ++++ | BAvg +++ | Spd + | Def ++

Year	Lev	Team	AB	R	H	HR	RBI	Avg	OB	Slg	OPS	bb%	ct%	Eye	SB	CS	x/h%	Iso	RC/G
2015	NCAA	Boston College	144	25	46	11	43	319	402	611	1014	12	82	0.77	0	0	43	292	8.02
2015	A-	Salem-Kaizer	178	22	51	12	30	287	355	551	906	10	77	0.46	0	0	45	264	6.68

Tall, hulking 1st rounder who led NWL in HR and ISO (min. 200 PA). Has plus raw power to all fields and generates good bat speed through quick, accentuated swing. Solid barrel control, decent contact skills project BA as average tool. Can get aggressive, but willing to walk. Has range and hands to stick at 1B long-term.

Shepherd,Zach — 5 — Detroit

EXP MLB DEBUT: 2018 | H/W: 6-3 185 | FUT: Starting 3B | 8E

Bats R Age 20 | 2012 FA (AU)

Pwr ++ | BAvg +++ | Spd ++ | Def +++

Year	Lev	Team	AB	R	H	HR	RBI	Avg	OB	Slg	OPS	bb%	ct%	Eye	SB	CS	x/h%	Iso	RC/G
2014	Rk	GCL Tigers	173	34	52	4	29	301	376	497	873	11	75	0.48	5	1	40	197	6.72
2015	A	West Michigan	383	48	94	5	51	245	328	339	667	11	69	0.40	4	3	26	94	3.89

Balanced hitter who possesses intriguing tools. Didn't hit for much power and struggled with contact, but has pretty, quick stroke. Power projects to at least average as he has strong wrists. Gets on base consistently, but doesn't have much speed for SB. Has the skills to be a solid defender with soft hands and strong arm. Breakout candidate.

Sierra,Magneuris — 8 — St. Louis

EXP MLB DEBUT: 2019 | H/W: 5-11 160 | FUT: Starting CF | 8C

Bats L Age 19 | 2012 FA (DR)

Pwr ++ | BAvg +++ | Spd ++++ | Def ++++

Year	Lev	Team	AB	R	H	HR	RBI	Avg	OB	Slg	OPS	bb%	ct%	Eye	SB	CS	x/h%	Iso	RC/G
2013	Rk	DSL Cardinals	212	44	57	1	21	269	357	340	696	12	84	0.88	15	7	18	71	4.46
2014	Rk	GCL Cardinals	202	42	78	2	30	386	431	505	936	7	85	0.53	13	3	22	119	6.99
2015	Rk	Johnson City	216	38	68	3	15	315	370	394	764	8	81	0.45	15	2	16	79	4.92
2015	A	Peoria	178	19	34	1	7	191	222	247	469	4	71	0.13	4	5	15	56	0.83

Struggled in the MWL, but rebounded nicely when demoted back to APPY. Quick LH stroke that barrels the ball, but breaking balls down in the zone give him fits. Above average speed led to a career-high 19 SB. Doesn't project to have more than average power, but has the speed and arm strength to stick in CF.

Sierra,Miguelangel — 6 — Houston

EXP MLB DEBUT: 2020 | H/W: 5-11 165 | FUT: Starting SS | 7E

Bats R Age 18 | 2014 FA (VZ)

Pwr + | BAvg ++ | Spd +++ | Def +++

Year	Lev	Team	AB	R	H	HR	RBI	Avg	OB	Slg	OPS	bb%	ct%	Eye	SB	CS	x/h%	Iso	RC/G
2015	Rk	DSL Astros	169	31	51	3	19	302	376	479	855	11	72	0.42	8	5	43	178	6.59
2015	Rk	GCL Astros	75	6	12	0	1	160	241	213	454	10	56	0.24	4	3	25	53	0.71

Lean, quick INF who struggled with bat in first year in US, but more than makes up for with excellent glove. Nimble feet and smooth actions highlight defense along with good range and hands. Can make spectacular plays. Not much strength in frame and can't catch up to velocity. Gets on base to use average speed, but needs significant work with bat.

Sisco,Chance — 2 — Baltimore

EXP MLB DEBUT: 2017 | H/W: 6-2 193 | FUT: Starting C | 7B

Bats L Age 21 | 2013 (2) HS (CA)

Pwr ++ | BAvg ++++ | Spd ++ | Def ++

Year	Lev	Team	AB	R	H	HR	RBI	Avg	OB	Slg	OPS	bb%	ct%	Eye	SB	CS	x/h%	Iso	RC/G
2013	Rk	GCL Orioles	97	15	36	1	11	371	465	464	929	15	78	0.81	1	1	17	93	7.54
2013	A-	Aberdeen	5	1	1	0	0	200	333	200	533	17	60	0.50	0	0	0	0	1.98
2014	A	Delmarva	426	56	145	5	63	340	400	448	848	9	81	0.53	1	2	23	108	6.08
2015	A+	Frederick	263	30	81	4	26	308	385	422	807	11	84	0.80	8	1	23	114	5.70
2015	AA	Bowie	74	9	19	2	8	257	337	392	729	11	81	0.64	0	1	32	135	4.64

Balanced hitter who missed time with injuries, but ascending up ladder. Draws walks with mature approach and level swing allows him to use entire field. Needs to pull more to tap into raw power, but hits for high BA. Defense needs work, though getting better with receiving and blocking. Owns nice arm, but iffy footwork negates strength.

Skole,Matt — 35 — Washington

EXP MLB DEBUT: 2016 | H/W: 6-4 225 | FUT: Backup 1B/3B | 6A

Bats L Age 26 | 2011 (5) Georgia Tech

Pwr +++ | BAvg ++ | Spd ++ | Def +

Year	Lev	Team	AB	R	H	HR	RBI	Avg	OB	Slg	OPS	bb%	ct%	Eye	SB	CS	x/h%	Iso	RC/G
2012	A+	Potomac	70	11	22	0	12	314	360	486	846	7	76	0.29	1	0	50	171	6.26
2013	AA	Harrisburg	5	1	1	0	2	200	429	400	829	29	60	1.00	0	0	100	200	7.54
2014	AA	Harrisburg	461	58	111	14	68	241	351	399	750	14	72	0.61	3	1	40	158	5.10
2015	AA	Harrisburg	314	34	73	12	56	232	327	398	725	12	71	0.48	3	1	37	166	4.62
2015	AAA	Syracuse	151	21	36	8	26	238	358	457	814	16	77	0.80	0	1	47	219	5.86

Has proven patience and power, but not a lot else. Lots of strikeouts damper his plus raw power, though bounced back from a 2013 arm injury and, given his slight improvement at Triple-A, seems ready to contribute off an MLB bench. Below-average defense at both COR IF spots keeps him from a full-time profile.

Slater,Austin — 479 — San Francisco

EXP MLB DEBUT: 2017 | H/W: 6-2 215 | FUT: Starting 2B | 7C

Bats R Age 23 | 2014 (8) Stanford

Pwr ++ | BAvg +++ | Spd +++ | Def +++

Year	Lev	Team	AB	R	H	HR	RBI	Avg	OB	Slg	OPS	bb%	ct%	Eye	SB	CS	x/h%	Iso	RC/G
2014	NCAA	Stanford	229	39	78	2	40	341	384	493	877	7	87	0.55	6	1	32	153	6.31
2014	Rk	Azl Giants	9	2	3	0	2	333	333	556	889	0	78	0.00	0	0	33	222	6.42
2014	A-	Salem-Kaizer	118	21	41	2	23	347	398	449	848	8	86	0.59	7	1	20	102	5.91
2015	A+	San Jose	250	25	73	3	34	292	319	396	715	4	82	0.23	4	3	26	104	4.14
2015	AA	Richmond	199	21	59	0	13	296	343	362	705	7	76	0.29	1	1	20	65	4.21

Stanford product has a short, line-drive swing that should allow for solid-avg ct% and BA skills. Raw power is lacking, but has size and strength to max out at 10-15 HR. Works the count and has good OB skills, though don't bank on many SB. Versatile defender whose home could be at 2B, as he has enough athletic ability and the arm to stick.

Smith,Chad

789 | **Texas** | EXP MLB DEBUT: 2020 | H/W: 6-2 200 | FUT: Starting OF | **8E**

Bats L Age 18
2015 (5) HS (GA)
Pwr ++
BAvg ++
Spd +++
Def +++

Year	Lev	Team	AB	R	H	HR	RBI	Avg	OB	Slg	OPS	bb%	ct%	Eye	SB	CS	x/h%	Iso	RC/G
2015	Rk	Azl Rangers	165	13	36	1	23	218	254	315	569	5	66	0.14	3	4	31	97	2.37

Raw OF who has impressive tools, but struggles to make consistent contact due to free swinging ways. Can play all OF spots and profiles as RF with average raw power and strong arm. Has chance to hit for BA due to short, quick stroke. Runs well underway and should be able to steal bases as he gains experience.

Smith,Dominic

3 | **New York (N)** | EXP MLB DEBUT: 2017 | H/W: 6-0 185 | FUT: Starting 1B | **9D**

Bats L Age 20
2013 (1) HS (CA)
Pwr +++
BAvg ++++
Spd ++
Def +++

Year	Lev	Team	AB	R	H	HR	RBI	Avg	OB	Slg	OPS	bb%	ct%	Eye	SB	CS	x/h%	Iso	RC/G
2013	Rk	Kingsport	6	2	4	0	4	667	750	1333	2083	25	100		0	0	100	667	21.29
2013	Rk	GCL Mets	167	23	48	3	22	287	377	407	784	13	78	0.65	2	4	27	120	5.49
2014	A	Savannah	461	52	125	1	44	271	344	338	682	10	83	0.66	5	4	22	67	4.16
2015	A+	St. Lucie	456	58	139	6	79	305	354	417	771	7	84	0.47	2	1	28	112	5.02

Strong, stocky 1B took a step forward in development in the pitcher-friendly FSL. Hit tool is exceptional. Ball explodes off of bat with moderate uppercut plane. Hits the ball where it's pitched. Doesn't try to do too much. Hasn't learned how to generate backspin and lift off the bat. May never hit for big power. Solid defensively.

Smith,Dwight

79 | **Toronto** | EXP MLB DEBUT: 2016 | H/W: 5-11 195 | FUT: Starting OF | **7B**

Bats L Age 23
2011 (1) HS (GA)
Pwr ++
BAvg +++
Spd +++
Def +++

Year	Lev	Team	AB	R	H	HR	RBI	Avg	OB	Slg	OPS	bb%	ct%	Eye	SB	CS	x/h%	Iso	RC/G
2012	Rk	Bluefield	159	20	36	4	21	226	276	340	616	6	86	0.50	1	1	28	113	3.12
2012	A-	Vancouver	63	5	11	0	8	175	246	254	500	9	83	0.55	0	0	36	79	1.93
2013	A	Lansing	423	57	120	7	46	284	362	388	750	11	81	0.63	25	5	23	104	4.94
2014	A+	Dunedin	472	83	134	12	60	284	362	453	816	11	85	0.84	15	4	36	169	5.79
2015	AA	New Hampshire	460	74	122	7	44	265	333	376	709	9	86	0.73	4	3	29	111	4.45

Pure-hitting OF who was seeing action at 2B in AFL. Makes extreme contact with direct path to ball and hits line drives to opp field. Offers some pull side power, but will be fringe-average at best. Can be tough out with willingness to see pitches and understanding of K zone. Likely best suited in LF where average speed and arm are good enough.

Smith,Mallex

8 | **Atlanta** | EXP MLB DEBUT: 2016 | H/W: 5-9 170 | FUT: Starting CF | **8C**

Bats L Age 22
2012 (5) Santa Fe JC
Pwr +
BAvg +++
Spd +++++
Def +++

Year	Lev	Team	AB	R	H	HR	RBI	Avg	OB	Slg	OPS	bb%	ct%	Eye	SB	CS	x/h%	Iso	RC/G
2013	A	Fort Wayne	424	81	111	4	29	262	352	340	692	12	80	0.70	64	16	21	78	4.31
2014	A	Fort Wayne	254	56	75	0	15	295	387	394	781	13	78	0.69	48	16	25	98	5.60
2014	A+	Lake Elsinore	223	43	73	5	16	327	409	475	885	12	78	0.65	40	10	30	148	6.76
2015	AA	Mississippi	206	35	70	2	22	340	416	413	829	12	80	0.66	23	6	13	73	5.99
2015	AAA	Gwinnett	278	49	78	0	13	281	338	367	705	8	84	0.55	34	7	23	86	4.37

Speedy CF who showed '14 breakout was no fluke. Hit .306 between AA & AAA, cooling off as the season came to a close. Patient at plate. Quick swing stays balanced. Takes what the pitcher gives him. 80-grade speed his best asset. Future lead-off hitter.

Soltis,Casey

8 | **Miami** | EXP MLB DEBUT: 2019 | H/W: 6-1 185 | FUT: Starting CF | **7D**

Bats L Age 20
2014 (5) HS (CA)
Pwr ++
BAvg ++
Spd +++
Def +++

Year	Lev	Team	AB	R	H	HR	RBI	Avg	OB	Slg	OPS	bb%	ct%	Eye	SB	CS	x/h%	Iso	RC/G
2014	Rk	GCL Marlins	121	13	32	0	8	264	341	289	630	10	73	0.42	2	1	9	25	3.33
2015	A	Greensboro	55	5	10	0	2	182	250	200	450	8	58	0.22	2	0	10	18	0.52

5th round pick was limited to 55 AB due to an elbow injury. When healthy has good raw power, but that hasn't translated to game action. Has a short, compact stroke, but struggles to make consistent contact. Moves well with good range and arm strength, but it might not be enough to stick in CF and his power might not be enough for a corner spot.

Sosa,Edmundo

6 | **St. Louis** | EXP MLB DEBUT: 2019 | H/W: 5-11 170 | FUT: Starting SS | **8D**

Bats R Age 20
2012 FA (PN)
Pwr ++
BAvg +++
Spd +++
Def ++++

Year	Lev	Team	AB	R	H	HR	RBI	Avg	OB	Slg	OPS	bb%	ct%	Eye	SB	CS	x/h%	Iso	RC/G
2013	Rk	DSL Cardinals	169	33	53	3	27	314	393	450	842	12	91	1.47	7	5	26	136	6.21
2014	Rk	GCL Cardinals	207	37	57	1	23	275	333	377	710	8	86	0.62	8	5	25	101	4.45
2014	A-	State College	5	0	1	0	0	200	200	200	400	0	60	0.00	0	0	0	0	-0.49
2015	Rk	Johnson City	200	30	60	7	16	300	352	485	837	7	81	0.42	6	2	32	185	5.77

Good all-around skills and understands how to play. Has advanced feel for hitting, showing patience and an knack for barreling the ball. Not likely to hit for power, but has good gap ability and the swing for more pop as he matures. Quick on D with good hands and range, but a below average arm.

Soto,Isael

8 | **Miami** | EXP MLB DEBUT: 2018 | H/W: 6-0 190 | FUT: Starting CF | **8E**

Bats L Age 19
2013 FA (DR)
Pwr ++++
BAvg +++
Spd ++
Def ++

Year	Lev	Team	AB	R	H	HR	RBI	Avg	OB	Slg	OPS	bb%	ct%	Eye	SB	CS	x/h%	Iso	RC/G
2014	Rk	GCL Marlins	183	26	46	7	23	251	290	426	716	5	74	0.21	1	2	37	175	4.15
2015	Rk	GCL Marlins	26	3	9	1	5	346	452	615	1067	16	77	0.83	0	1	44	269	9.48
2015	A-	Batavia	21	1	2	0	0	95	136	95	232	5	52	0.10	0	0	0	0	-3.48
2015	A	Greensboro	64	2	8	0	1	125	164	141	305	4	58	0.11	0	0	13	16	-1.96

Athletic OF suffered a season ending knee injury and was limited to 111 AB. Has a strong frame and shows plus raw power with plus bat speed. Is a free swinger and can be overly aggressive, striking out 27 times with just 3 walks. Average to below-avg speed with a good arm and should settle in as a corner OF.

Soto,Juan

7 | **Washington** | EXP MLB DEBUT: 2020 | H/W: 6-3 180 | FUT: Starting OF | **8E**

Bats L Age 17
2015 FA (DR)
Pwr +++
BAvg +++
Spd +
Def ++

Year	Lev	Team	AB	R	H	HR	RBI	Avg	OB	Slg	OPS	bb%	ct%	Eye	SB	CS	x/h%	Iso	RC/G
2015			*Did not play in minors*																

Seen as one of the top all-around hitters in the 2015 international draft class due to advanced approach and superior contact skills. Still needs to grow into his power, but has the size and the acumen to adjust. Likely limited to an OF corner spot due to below-average arm and speed. Far away, but one to dream on.

Sparks,Taylor

5 | **Cincinnati** | EXP MLB DEBUT: 2017 | H/W: 6-3 200 | FUT: Starting 3B | **7E**

Bats R Age 23
2014 (2) UC-Irvine
Pwr +++
BAvg +
Spd +++
Def ++++

Year	Lev	Team	AB	R	H	HR	RBI	Avg	OB	Slg	OPS	bb%	ct%	Eye	SB	CS	x/h%	Iso	RC/G
2012	NCAA	UC Irvine	124	20	25	3	12	202	267	363	630	8	65	0.25	2	1	44	161	3.36
2013	NCAA	UC Irvine	222	38	80	10	50	360	377	581	958	3	82	0.15	7	3	31	221	6.85
2014	NCAA	UC Irvine	253	45	78	5	37	308	375	506	881	10	72	0.39	8	8	40	198	6.89
2014	Rk	Billings	198	41	46	10	30	232	336	490	826	14	58	0.37	14	1	52	258	7.03
2015	A+	Daytona	446	68	110	13	54	247	294	401	695	6	64	0.19	14	4	35	155	4.27

Power hitter held back due to contact issues. Struck out 162 times in 446 AB. Hitchy swing with lot of length. Tends to get under balls when he makes contact. Puts on show during BP, translating to 13 HRs against live pitching. Average speed and plus defense completes package. Hit tool will determine whether he makes it to the Show.

Starling,Bubba

8 | **Kansas City** | EXP MLB DEBUT: 2016 | H/W: 6-4 210 | FUT: Starting OF | **8D**

Bats R Age 23
2011 (1) HS (KS)
Pwr +++
BAvg ++
Spd +++
Def ++++

Year	Lev	Team	AB	R	H	HR	RBI	Avg	OB	Slg	OPS	bb%	ct%	Eye	SB	CS	x/h%	Iso	RC/G
2012	Rk	Burlington	200	35	55	10	33	275	364	485	849	12	65	0.40	10	1	36	210	6.65
2013	A	Lexington	435	51	105	13	63	241	324	398	721	11	71	0.41	22	3	36	156	4.59
2014	A+	Wilmington	482	67	105	9	54	218	290	338	628	9	69	0.33	17	2	34	120	3.26
2015	A+	Wilmington	44	6	17	2	12	386	471	614	1084	14	61	0.41	2	1	35	227	10.97
2015	AA	NW Arkansas	331	51	84	10	32	254	316	426	742	8	73	0.33	4	5	39	172	4.75

Athletic OF who had best season as pro and starting to realize vast potential. Has size and strength to be asset with both bat and glove. Improving approach has enhanced natural power and continues to exhibit excellent speed despite drop in SB. Pitch recognition and hand-eye coordination not ideal for BA. Excellent defender with plus range and arm.

Stassi,Max

2 | **Houston** | EXP MLB DEBUT: 2013 | H/W: 5-10 200 | FUT: Starting C | **7C**

Bats R Age 25
2009 (4) HS (CA)
Pwr +++
BAvg ++
Spd ++
Def +++

Year	Lev	Team	AB	R	H	HR	RBI	Avg	OB	Slg	OPS	bb%	ct%	Eye	SB	CS	x/h%	Iso	RC/G
2013	MLB	Houston	7	0	2	0	1	286	286	286	571	0	71	0.00	0	0	0	0	1.97
2014	AAA	Oklahoma City	392	49	97	9	45	247	287	378	665	5	74	0.21	1	0	32	130	3.54
2014	MLB	Houston	20	2	7	0	4	350	350	450	800	0	70	0.00	0	0	29	100	5.34
2015	AAA	Fresno	294	37	62	13	43	211	275	384	659	8	68	0.28	1	1	37	173	3.51
2015	MLB	Houston	15	4	6	1	2	400	438	600	1038	6	67	0.20	0	0	17	200	8.85

Short, strong backstop who is still waiting for chance to stick in HOU. Owns average tools behind plate and continues to be solid receiver and blocker. Arm strength is fringy, but enhanced by good footwork and quick release. Doesn't hit for BA as swing tends to get long, but has natural strength and quick wrists to inject power to all fields.

Staton,Allen | 456 | St. Louis

EXP MLB DEBUT: 2019 | H/W: 5-10 190 | FUT: Utility player | 6B

Bats R Age 23 — 2015 FA (US)

Pwr + + + | BAvg + + | Spd + + | Def + +

Year	Lev	Team	AB	R	H	HR	RBI	Avg	OB	Slg	OPS	bb%	ct%	Eye	SB	CS	x/h%	Iso	RC/G
2015	Rk	Johnson City	163	25	50	9	44	307	339	571	910	5	77	0.21	2	0	46	264	6.58
2015	Rk	GCL Cardinals	40	4	12	1	8	300	391	500	891	13	90	1.50	2	0	42	200	6.88
2015	A+	Palm Beach	27	3	5	0	1	185	313	185	498	16	78	0.83	0	1	0	0	1.87

NDFA had an impressive pro debut. Hard-nosed player who gets the most of his abilities. Shows sure hands on defense with a strong arm and split time between 3B, 2B, and SS. Gets surprising pop from his short RH stroke with above-average raw power. Will need to prove this was no fluke as he struggled when moved up to A+.

Stephenson,Tyler | 2 | Cincinnati

EXP MLB DEBUT: 2020 | H/W: 6-4 225 | FUT: Starting C | 9E

Bats R Age 19 — 2015 (1) HS (GA)

Pwr + + + + | BAvg + + | Spd + + | Def + + + +

Year	Lev	Team	AB	R	H	HR	RBI	Avg	OB	Slg	OPS	bb%	ct%	Eye	SB	CS	x/h%	Iso	RC/G
2015	Rk	Billings	194	28	52	1	16	268	343	361	703	10	78	0.52	0	2	31	93	4.39

High 2015 draftee skyrocketed up draft boards. Tons of raw power that has yet to develop. Needs work on swing mechanics. Length of swing and sweeping actions cause projection of hit tool to fall. A MLB catcher with easy movements for a large-framed receiver. Blocks off daylight and has a plus throwing arm.

Stevenson,Andrew | 8 | Washington

EXP MLB DEBUT: 2017 | H/W: 6-0 185 | FUT: Starting CF | 8C

Bats L Age 21 — 2015 (2) Louisiana St

Pwr + | BAvg + + + | Spd + + + + | Def + + + +

Year	Lev	Team	AB	R	H	HR	RBI	Avg	OB	Slg	OPS	bb%	ct%	Eye	SB	CS	x/h%	Iso	RC/G
2015	NCAA	LSU	247	53	86	1	24	348	388	453	841	6	88	0.55	26	7	22	105	5.83
2015	Rk	GCL Nationals	5	1	1	0	0	200	333	200	533	17	60	0.50	0	0	0	0	1.98
2015	A-	Auburn	72	11	26	0	9	361	418	431	848	9	83	0.58	7	3	12	69	6.10
2015	A	Hagerstown	137	28	39	1	16	285	324	358	682	6	88	0.50	16	4	15	73	3.94

Advanced college hitter most known for highlight-reel catches in CF. Great reads/jumps, and plus-plus speed enhances range, though arm strength is below average. Noisy LH swing at present, more oriented towards up-the-middle contact than power. Could end up as leadoff type and has high SB potential.

Stewart,Christin | 7 | Detroit

EXP MLB DEBUT: 2017 | H/W: 6-0 205 | FUT: Starting OF | 8D

Bats L Age 22 — 2015 (1) Tennessee

Pwr + + + + | BAvg + + + | Spd + + | Def + +

Year	Lev	Team	AB	R	H	HR	RBI	Avg	OB	Slg	OPS	bb%	ct%	Eye	SB	CS	x/h%	Iso	RC/G
2015	NCAA	Tennessee	177	39	55	15	47	311	405	633	1038	14	79	0.74	4	5	45	322	8.50
2015	Rk	GCL Tigers	22	5	8	1	2	364	440	682	1122	12	77	0.60	2	1	50	318	9.93
2015	A-	Connecticut	49	7	12	2	11	245	315	490	805	9	63	0.28	0	0	50	245	6.16
2015	A	West Michigan	185	29	53	7	31	286	350	492	842	9	76	0.40	3	2	38	205	6.03

Strong, physical OF who is all about offensive production. Dominated low levels with plus bat speed and power. Could stand to shorten stroke at times and can bail out against LHP. Relegated to LF with limited speed and below average arm strength, but with his power, profiles as middle-of-the-order hitter.

Stewart,D.J. | 7 | Baltimore

EXP MLB DEBUT: 2018 | H/W: 6-0 230 | FUT: Starting OF | 8D

Bats L Age 22 — 2015 (1) Florida St

Pwr + + + | BAvg + + + | Spd + + | Def + + +

Year	Lev	Team	AB	R	H	HR	RBI	Avg	OB	Slg	OPS	bb%	ct%	Eye	SB	CS	x/h%	Iso	RC/G
2015	NCAA	Florida St	214	62	68	15	59	318	484	593	1078	24	78	1.47	12	3	40	276	9.74
2015	A-	Aberdeen	238	25	52	6	24	218	287	345	632	9	78	0.44	4	1	31	126	3.28

Short, strong OF with plus strength and impressive raw power. May need to tweak swing to realize pop potential. Knows strike zone and willing to work counts to find good pitch to hit. Has instincts to be natural hitter, but hits too many groundballs. Possesses decent athleticism to serve him well in OF, but weak arm limits him to LF.

Stokes,Troy | 78 | Milwaukee

EXP MLB DEBUT: 2018 | H/W: 5-8 182 | FUT: Starting LF | 7D

Bats R Age 20 — 2014 (4) HS (MD)

Pwr + + | BAvg + + + | Spd + + + + | Def + +

Year	Lev	Team	AB	R	H	HR	RBI	Avg	OB	Slg	OPS	bb%	ct%	Eye	SB	CS	x/h%	Iso	RC/G
2014	Rk	Azl Brewers	172	29	45	0	18	262	352	331	683	12	73	0.51	19	3	24	70	4.24
2015	Rk	Helena	226	51	61	5	27	270	363	407	770	13	78	0.66	26	6	31	137	5.30

Small, athletic OF followed up debut with solid stint in the Pioneer League. Exhibits nice approach and gets on base at a premium clip, making him a future SB asset. Employs quick, line-drive swing to all fields. Raw power not there yet, but showed pull-side pop in '15 and has room for more muscle. Good reads, range should allow him to stick in CF.

Story,Trevor | 6 | Colorado

EXP MLB DEBUT: 2016 | H/W: 6-1 180 | FUT: Starting SS | 8C

Bats R Age 23 — 2011 (1) HS (TX)

Pwr + + + | BAvg + + + | Spd + + + | Def + + +

Year	Lev	Team	AB	R	H	HR	RBI	Avg	OB	Slg	OPS	bb%	ct%	Eye	SB	CS	x/h%	Iso	RC/G
2014	A-	Tri-City	7	2	2	0	0	286	375	429	804	13	57	0.33	0	0	50	143	7.08
2014	A+	Modesto	184	38	61	5	28	332	428	582	1009	14	68	0.53	20	4	48	250	9.30
2014	AA	Tulsa	205	29	41	9	20	200	296	380	677	12	60	0.34	3	1	44	180	4.16
2015	AA	New Britain	256	46	72	10	40	281	368	523	891	12	71	0.48	15	2	50	242	7.07
2015	AAA	Albuquerque	256	37	71	10	40	277	320	504	824	6	73	0.24	7	1	48	227	5.73

Impressed at both AA and AAA. Can be overly aggressive as he hunts for power, but he does draw a decent number of BB and has plus bat speed. Pitch recognition continues to be an issue. Solid defender with decent range, good hands, and a plus arm.

Stuart,Champ | 8 | New York (N)

EXP MLB DEBUT: 2018 | H/W: 6-0 175 | FUT: Starting CF | 7E

Bats R Age 23 — 2013 (6) Brevard College

Pwr + + | BAvg + | Spd + + + + | Def + + +

Year	Lev	Team	AB	R	H	HR	RBI	Avg	OB	Slg	OPS	bb%	ct%	Eye	SB	CS	x/h%	Iso	RC/G
2012	NCAA	Brevard	148	43	62	6	34	419	500	622	1122	14	80	0.83	14	3	27	203	9.75
2013	NCAA	Brevard	140	47	42	5	13	300	424	479	902	18	74	0.81	39	3	33	179	7.35
2013	Rk	Kingsport	150	26	36	1	14	240	380	353	734	18	61	0.59	11	2	33	113	5.51
2014	A	Savannah	285	50	73	3	28	256	340	340	680	11	66	0.37	29	4	18	84	4.17
2015	A+	St. Lucie	330	43	58	4	17	176	265	242	507	11	57	0.28	21	3	22	67	1.50

Raw, athletic OF had an atrocious '15 with the bat after making significant strides the previous 2 seasons. Swings wildly and in parts. Cannot pick up spin of breaking ball. Elevates instead of using plus-plus foot speed to outrun the baseball. Struck out 43% in '15. Has continued to show improvement in the field and on the bases.

Suchy,Michael | 9 | Pittsburgh

EXP MLB DEBUT: 2019 | H/W: 6-3 228 | FUT: Starting RF | 7C

Bats R Age 22 — 2014 (5) FloridaGulfCoast

Pwr + + + | BAvg + + + | Spd + + | Def + +

Year	Lev	Team	AB	R	H	HR	RBI	Avg	OB	Slg	OPS	bb%	ct%	Eye	SB	CS	x/h%	Iso	RC/G
2012	NCAA	FloridaGulfCoast	123	17	24	0	6	195	283	228	510	11	66	0.36	5	0	17	33	1.59
2013	NCAA	FloridaGulfCoast	226	37	71	9	46	314	378	473	851	9	80	0.51	7	4	24	159	5.97
2014	NCAA	FloridaGulfCoast	239	54	76	8	49	318	371	519	889	8	80	0.43	10	6	37	201	6.49
2014	A-	Jamestown	237	35	56	1	17	236	312	333	645	10	78	0.49	7	9	27	97	3.64
2015	A	West Virginia	447	74	123	10	76	275	353	441	794	11	77	0.52	6	3	40	166	5.56

Strong, two-sport high school player was a 5th round pick in 2014. Has plus bat speed and turned in a solid performance at Low-A. Started slow, but hit .294/.363/.478 in the 2nd half and was more aggressive at the plate. Strikes out a lot, but also drew 54 BB. Jump in power is legit and makes him an interesting long-term prospect.

Survance,Kyle | 8 | Los Angeles (A)

EXP MLB DEBUT: 2018 | H/W: 6-1 190 | FUT: Starting OF | 7D

Bats L Age 22 — 2015 (8) Houston

Pwr + + | BAvg + + + | Spd + + + + | Def + +

Year	Lev	Team	AB	R	H	HR	RBI	Avg	OB	Slg	OPS	bb%	ct%	Eye	SB	CS	x/h%	Iso	RC/G
2015	NCAA	Houston	246	51	73	2	34	297	375	402	778	11	79	0.60	31	8	22	106	5.39
2015	Rk	Orem	124	27	45	2	21	363	432	484	916	11	81	0.65	17	5	22	121	7.01

Speedy OF who surprised in pro debut with offensive performance. Has contact-oriented stroke and simple approach to get on base. Plays the game hard and has plus speed to maximize SB. Controls bat and can use entire field. Will likely never be HR guy. Defense needs attention as he doesn't get good jumps or take efficient routes to balls.

Swanson,Dansby | 6 | Atlanta

EXP MLB DEBUT: 2018 | H/W: 6-0 190 | FUT: Starting SS | 9B

Bats R Age 22 — 2015 (1) Vanderbilt

Pwr + + + | BAvg + + + + | Spd + + + + | Def + + +

Year	Lev	Team	AB	R	H	HR	RBI	Avg	OB	Slg	OPS	bb%	ct%	Eye	SB	CS	x/h%	Iso	RC/G
2015	NCAA	Vanderbilt	281	76	94	15	64	335	423	623	1046	13	81	0.80	16	2	48	288	8.73
2015	A-	Hillsboro	83	19	24	1	11	289	392	482	874	14	83	1.00	0	0	46	193	6.86

Acquired in the Shelby Miller trade this off-season, this physical specimen has glove and arm to stay at SS long-term. Patient approach at the plate maximizes hit tool to potentially plus-plus levels. Will never be significant power threat. Should take advantage of gaps to accumulate bundles of extra base hits. Footspeed will turn doubles into triples.

Sweeney,Darnell — 48 — Philadelphia

EXP MLB DEBUT: 2015 | H/W: 6-1 195 | FUT: Utility player | **7C**

Bats B Age 25	Year	Lev	Team	AB	R	H	HR	RBI	Avg	OB	Slg	OPS	bb%	ct%	Eye	SB	CS	x/h%	Iso	RC/G
2012 (13) Central Florida	2012	A	Great Lakes	199	34	58	5	23	291	368	447	815	11	79	0.59	17	4	29	156	5.76
Pwr +++	2013	A+	RanchoCuca	552	79	152	11	77	275	328	455	782	7	73	0.28	48	20	40	179	5.37
BAvg +++	2014	AA	Chattanooga	490	88	141	14	57	288	384	463	848	14	76	0.66	15	16	38	176	6.39
Spd +++	2015	AAA	Oklahoma City	472	69	128	9	49	271	331	409	740	8	75	0.36	32	13	34	138	4.71
Def ++	2015	MLB	Philadelphia	85	9	15	3	11	176	286	353	639	13	68	0.48	0	2	53	176	3.47

Classic tweener prospect without a standout tool, but fringe-average in several. Speed to steal bases, but gets caught a lot. Power has developed by incorporating lower half and will take a walk, but still Ks far too often. 2B is best position; can also handle CF, but glove and arm lack consistency. In all, a bat-first utility player.

Tapia,Raimel — 8 — Colorado

EXP MLB DEBUT: 2016 | H/W: 6-2 160 | FUT: Starting LF | **8C**

Bats L Age 22	Year	Lev	Team	AB	R	H	HR	RBI	Avg	OB	Slg	OPS	bb%	ct%	Eye	SB	CS	x/h%	Iso	RC/G
2010 FA (DR)																				
Pwr +++																				
BAvg +++	2013	Rk	Grand Junction	258	53	92	7	47	357	392	562	954	5	88	0.48	10	9	36	205	7.02
Spd ++++	2014	A	Asheville	481	93	157	9	72	326	372	453	825	7	81	0.39	33	16	27	127	5.63
Def ++	2015	A+	Modesto	544	74	166	12	71	305	335	467	801	4	81	0.23	26	10	33	162	5.21

Plus athlete continues to impress in OF and had a solid season. Has a good, contact-oriented approach at the plate. Good strike zone judgment and a quick LH bat. Power continues to develop and he stroked 34 doubles, 12 HR, and 26 SB. Has enough speed to stick in CF, though he needs to be more consistent.

Taveras,Leody — 8 — Texas

EXP MLB DEBUT: 2021 | H/W: 6-1 160 | FUT: Starting OF | **9E**

Bats B Age 17	Year	Lev	Team	AB	R	H	HR	RBI	Avg	OB	Slg	OPS	bb%	ct%	Eye	SB	CS	x/h%	Iso	RC/G
2015 FA (DR)																				
Pwr ++																				
BAvg +++																				
Spd +++																				
Def +++	2015		*Did not play in U.S.*																	

All-around prospect who has vast ceiling due to plentiful tools and athleticism. Has clean, quick stroke from both sides and could grow into plus power once he adds strengths. Has crude approach at plate and needs to shorten swing when applicable. Exhibits above average speed and arm to make him viable CF candidate. Will need patience.

Taylor,Tyrone — 89 — Milwaukee

EXP MLB DEBUT: 2016 | H/W: 6-0 185 | FUT: Starting OF | **8D**

Bats R Age 22	Year	Lev	Team	AB	R	H	HR	RBI	Avg	OB	Slg	OPS	bb%	ct%	Eye	SB	CS	x/h%	Iso	RC/G
2012 (2) HS (CA)	2012	Rk	Azl Brewers	36	11	14	0	6	389	405	694	1100	3	92	0.33	3	1	57	306	8.72
Pwr +++	2013	A	Wisconsin	485	69	133	8	57	274	323	400	723	7	87	0.56	19	8	32	126	4.47
BAvg +++	2014	A+	Brevard County	507	69	141	6	68	278	330	396	726	7	89	0.67	22	6	32	118	4.59
Spd ++++	2014	AA	Huntsville	13	0	1	0	0	77	143	77	220	7	62	0.20	1	0	0	0	-3.22
Def +++	2015	AA	Biloxi	454	48	118	3	43	260	307	337	644	6	88	0.56	10	6	22	77	3.58

Stock fell after a pedestrian SL debut (.649 OPS), but still has promising tools. Plus speed, instincts help defensive ability in CF and prowess on the bases. Has quick stroke, makes sharp contact to all fields and shows decent discipline. Raw pop isn't there yet, but could be an average tool. Power/speed guy to keep tabs on.

Telis,Tomas — 2 — Miami

EXP MLB DEBUT: 2014 | H/W: 5-8 215 | FUT: Backup C | **6C**

Bats B Age 24	Year	Lev	Team	AB	R	H	HR	RBI	Avg	OB	Slg	OPS	bb%	ct%	Eye	SB	CS	x/h%	Iso	RC/G
2007 FA (VZ)	2014	MLB	Texas	68	7	17	0	8	250	261	279	540	1	85	0.10	0	0	12	29	1.98
Pwr ++	2015	AAA	New Orleans	48	3	16	0	4	333	396	333	730	9	88	0.83	2	0	0	0	4.67
BAvg +++	2015	AAA	Round Rock	282	43	82	5	25	291	324	404	729	5	89	0.45	1	2	26	113	4.40
Spd +	2015	MLB	Miami	27	1	4	0	0	148	179	148	327	4	89	0.33	0	0	0	0	-0.12
Def ++	2015	MLB	Texas	11	1	2	0	2	182	182	182	364	0	91	0.00	0	0	0	0	0.19

Short, stocky backstop came over from the Rangers in the Sam Dyson deal. Has a solid approach at the plate and makes consistent contact shooting line-drives to all fields. Had TJS in 2010 so has an average arm behind the plate, but has worked hard in other areas and is now a solid defender. Profiles as backup backstop who can hit for BA.

Tellez,Rowdy — 3 — Toronto

EXP MLB DEBUT: 2018 | H/W: 6-4 245 | FUT: Starting 1B | **8D**

Bats L Age 21	Year	Lev	Team	AB	R	H	HR	RBI	Avg	OB	Slg	OPS	bb%	ct%	Eye	SB	CS	x/h%	Iso	RC/G
2013 (30) HS (CA)	2013	Rk	GCL Blue Jays	124	10	29	2	20	234	317	371	688	11	79	0.58	1	0	34	137	4.20
Pwr ++++	2014	Rk	Bluefield	191	26	56	4	36	293	357	424	781	9	86	0.70	3	2	29	131	5.24
BAvg ++	2014	A	Lansing	42	6	15	2	7	357	449	500	949	14	76	0.70	0	0	13	143	7.54
Spd +	2015	A	Lansing	270	36	80	7	49	296	354	444	798	8	79	0.43	2	2	33	148	5.37
Def ++	2015	A+	Dunedin	131	17	36	7	28	275	345	473	818	10	79	0.50	3	0	33	198	5.54

Huge-framed slugger who has good feel for bat control and contact despite typical power profile. Has plus-plus pop to all fields and should get better as he tames aggressive approach. Has plenty of loft in stroke, though can be pull-conscious. Doesn't display much agility or quickness at 1B and lacks foot speed.

Thomas,Lane — 4 — Toronto

EXP MLB DEBUT: 2019 | H/W: 6-1 210 | FUT: Starting 2B | **7E**

Bats R Age 20	Year	Lev	Team	AB	R	H	HR	RBI	Avg	OB	Slg	OPS	bb%	ct%	Eye	SB	CS	x/h%	Iso	RC/G
2014 (5) HS (TN)																				
Pwr ++	2014	Rk	Bluefield	65	10	21	1	8	323	380	431	811	8	75	0.38	2	0	24	108	5.64
BAvg ++	2014	Rk	GCL Blue Jays	131	21	34	0	11	260	362	382	744	14	75	0.64	7	3	35	122	5.22
Spd ++	2015	A-	Vancouver	169	20	38	5	33	225	260	391	650	5	80	0.24	5	4	47	166	3.34
Def ++	2015	A	Lansing	35	1	4	0	2	114	184	171	356	8	71	0.30	1	0	50	57	-0.51

Athletic, quick prospect who converted to 2B in '15. Has soft hands and quick feet to profile well at that position. Arm strength is only fringe average. Uses fast bat and barrel awareness to make decent contact and has nice BA potential. Offers raw power, but mostly gap power at present.

Thompson,David — 35 — New York (N)

EXP MLB DEBUT: 2018 | H/W: 6-1 220 | FUT: Backup 3B | **6C**

Bats R Age 22	Year	Lev	Team	AB	R	H	HR	RBI	Avg	OB	Slg	OPS	bb%	ct%	Eye	SB	CS	x/h%	Iso	RC/G
2015 (4) Miami																				
Pwr ++++																				
BAvg +																				
Spd ++	2015	NCAA	Miami	253	59	83	19	90	328	426	640	1066	15	89	1.48	1	3	47	312	8.71
Def +	2015	A-	Brooklyn	206	22	45	3	22	218	258	320	578	5	79	0.25	3	0	31	102	2.48

Collegiate 3B with enormous and rare all-fields power potential. Lead NCAA in HRs in 2015. Has solid approach at plate but elongated swing hampers hit tool. Questions surround ability to barrel balls using wood bat. Defensively, his weak throwing arm depresses positional projection. A move to 1B likely occurs this spring.

Thompson,Trayce — 789 — Los Angeles (N)

EXP MLB DEBUT: 2015 | H/W: 6-3 210 | FUT: Starting OF | **8D**

Bats R Age 25	Year	Lev	Team	AB	R	H	HR	RBI	Avg	OB	Slg	OPS	bb%	ct%	Eye	SB	CS	x/h%	Iso	RC/G
2009 (2) HS (CA)	2012	AAA	Charlotte	18	1	3	0	0	167	250	278	528	10	67	0.33	1	0	67	111	2.00
Pwr ++++	2013	AA	Birmingham	507	78	116	15	73	229	310	383	693	11	73	0.43	25	8	37	154	4.15
BAvg ++	2014	AA	Birmingham	518	86	123	16	59	237	322	419	741	11	71	0.43	20	5	46	181	4.91
Spd +++	2015	AAA	Charlotte	388	53	101	13	39	260	302	441	742	6	80	0.29	11	5	40	180	4.52
Def +++	2015	MLB	Chi White Sox	122	17	36	5	16	295	363	533	896	10	79	0.50	1	0	44	238	6.72

Tall and powerful, he stood out in his big league trial. Exhibits plenty of pop and destroys LHP. Has body and tools to be full-time player, but lacks feel for hitting and plate approach. Contact will be an issue due to long swing. Runs well underway, but SB output has fallen. Can play any OF spot and projects well in RF with arm and plus range.

Tilson,Charlie — 7 — St. Louis

EXP MLB DEBUT: 2016 | H/W: 5-11 175 | FUT: Starting OF | **7A**

Bats L Age 23	Year	Lev	Team	AB	R	H	HR	RBI	Avg	OB	Slg	OPS	bb%	ct%	Eye	SB	CS	x/h%	Iso	RC/G
2011 (2) HS (IL)	2013	A	Peoria	376	49	114	4	30	303	347	388	735	6	85	0.43	15	6	16	85	4.52
Pwr ++	2013	A+	Palm Beach	34	1	9	0	0	265	359	353	712	13	82	0.83	0	0	22	88	4.73
BAvg +++	2014	A+	Palm Beach	370	54	114	5	36	308	350	414	764	6	79	0.32	10	7	18	105	4.85
Spd ++++	2014	AA	Springfield	139	19	33	2	17	237	269	324	593	4	80	0.21	2	3	21	86	2.60
Def +++	2015	AA	Springfield	539	85	159	4	32	295	350	388	738	8	87	0.64	46	19	21	93	4.73

High-energy player with a smooth compact LH stroke and is willing to drive the ball the other way. Ideal top-of-the-order hitter who puts the ball into play and uses his above average speed. Can be aggressive at the plate as shown by inconsistent walk rates. Not likely to hit for power, but has good speed and is a good defender in CF.

Tocci,Carlos — 8 — Philadelphia

EXP MLB DEBUT: 2018 | H/W: 6-2 160 | FUT: Starting CF | **7C**

Bats R Age 20	Year	Lev	Team	AB	R	H	HR	RBI	Avg	OB	Slg	OPS	bb%	ct%	Eye	SB	CS	x/h%	Iso	RC/G
2011 FA (VZ)	2012	Rk	GCL Phillies	97	13	27	0	9	278	320	299	619	6	81	0.33	9	2	7	21	3.05
Pwr ++	2013	A	Lakewood	421	40	88	0	26	209	248	249	498	5	82	0.29	6	7	19	40	1.60
BAvg +++	2014	A	Lakewood	487	59	118	2	30	242	279	324	604	5	80	0.26	10	11	24	82	2.87
Spd ++++	2015	A	Lakewood	234	35	75	2	25	321	374	423	797	8	87	0.65	14	2	24	103	5.41
Def ++++	2015	A+	Clearwater	275	31	71	2	18	258	289	313	602	4	81	0.23	3	9	15	55	2.74

Finally showed some improvement in third year in Low-A, where bat speed and balanced swing turned into doubles. Unlikely to ever hit for big power, he still needs to add strength to his skinny frame. His plus speed more evident in the field, where he's a plus defender, than on bases. Arm is accurate and strong.

Torrens,Luis | 2 | **New York (A)** | EXP MLB DEBUT: 2019 | H/W: 6-0 175 | FUT: Starting C | **8D**

Bats R Age 19	Year	Lev	Team	AB	R	H	HR	RBI	Avg	OB	Slg	OPS	bb%	ct%	Eye	SB	CS	x/h%	Iso	RC/G
2012 FA (VZ)	2013	Rk	GCL Yankees 2	174	17	42	1	14	241	343	299	642	13	77	0.68	2	0	19	57	3.69
Pwr ++	2014	Rk	GCL Yankees	16	1	4	0	1	250	250	313	563	0	88	0.00	0	0	25	63	2.28
BAvg +++	2014	A-	Stn Island	185	27	50	2	18	270	322	405	727	7	78	0.34	1	2	36	135	4.54
Spd ++	2014	A	Charleston (Sc)	26	4	4	1	3	154	313	269	582	19	73	0.86	0	0	25	115	2.72
Def +++	2015		*Did not play; injured*																	

Advanced backstop who missed entire season after shoulder surgery in March. Still very young and should return to normal. Is a solid defender with strong, accurate arm and receiving should only get better. Has both BA and power potential, but needs at bats. Can shoot gaps with strong stroke and has feel to hit breaking balls.

Torres,Gleyber | 6 | **Chicago (N)** | EXP MLB DEBUT: 2017 | H/W: 6-1 175 | FUT: Starting SS | **8B**

Bats R Age 19	Year	Lev	Team	AB	R	H	HR	RBI	Avg	OB	Slg	OPS	bb%	ct%	Eye	SB	CS	x/h%	Iso	RC/G
2013 FA (VZ)																				
Pwr +++	2014	Rk	Azl Cubs	154	33	43	1	29	279	380	377	757	14	79	0.76	8	7	23	97	5.28
BAvg +++	2014	A-	Boise	28	4	11	1	4	393	469	786	1254	13	75	0.57	2	0	55	393	12.14
Spd +++	2015	A	South Bend	464	53	136	3	62	293	353	386	739	8	77	0.40	22	13	24	93	4.74
Def ++++	2015	A+	Myrtle Beach	23	1	4	0	2	174	208	174	382	4	70	0.14	0	1	0	0	-0.46

Top prospect in the system. Takes a short, compact stroke and above average bat speed with a solid understanding of the strike zone. Power is starting to develop and he stroked a career-high 24 doubles. Should settle in as a 10-15 HR guy once he matures. Has good range at short, with soft hands, and a strong, accurate arm.

Torres,Nick | 79 | **San Diego** | EXP MLB DEBUT: 2017 | H/W: 6-1 220 | FUT: Starting OF | **7D**

Bats R Age 22	Year	Lev	Team	AB	R	H	HR	RBI	Avg	OB	Slg	OPS	bb%	ct%	Eye	SB	CS	x/h%	Iso	RC/G
2014 (4) Cal Poly	2014	NCAA	Cal Poly	242	39	78	6	52	322	357	483	840	5	90	0.52	4	4	32	161	5.68
Pwr ++	2014	Rk	Azl Padres	1	1	0	0	0	0	500	0	500	50	100		0	0		0	4.75
BAvg +++	2014	A-	Eugene	169	20	43	3	23	254	284	373	657	4	75	0.17	2	2	33	118	3.39
Spd ++	2015	A	Fort Wayne	288	45	94	2	40	326	366	462	828	6	82	0.35	4	1	35	135	5.71
Def ++	2015	A+	Lake Elsinore	211	21	58	3	30	275	305	408	712	4	79	0.20	5	1	34	133	4.15

Instinctual OF who hit .300+ each month from April thru July. Bat control and pitch recognition are best attributes and easy contact leads to swings early in count and few walks. Hasn't realized raw power potential and may not have enough pop for corner OF. Lacks speed and average arm limits him.

Trahan,Blake | 46 | **Cincinnati** | EXP MLB DEBUT: 2018 | H/W: 5-9 180 | FUT: Starting SS | **8C**

Bats R Age 22	Year	Lev	Team	AB	R	H	HR	RBI	Avg	OB	Slg	OPS	bb%	ct%	Eye	SB	CS	x/h%	Iso	RC/G
2015 (3) LA-Lafayette																				
Pwr +																				
BAvg +++	2015	NCAA	LA-Lafayette	254	51	80	2	29	315	404	406	810	13	87	1.19	17	0	23	91	5.91
Spd ++++	2015	Rk	Billings	186	32	58	1	15	312	393	403	797	12	90	1.32	10	3	21	91	5.74
Def +++	2015	A+	Daytona	35	1	4	0	0	114	114	114	229	0	86	0.00	0	0	0	0	-1.61

Collegian still learning how to play to strengths. Gets under balls trying to drive towards the gaps. Doesn't take full advantage of his plus foot speed by keeping the ball on the ground. Has good actions at SS and plenty of arm to stay at the position. Should be a solid contributor at SS at full projection.

Trahan,Stryker | 29 | **Arizona** | EXP MLB DEBUT: 2018 | H/W: 6-0 230 | FUT: Reserve C | **7E**

Bats L Age 21	Year	Lev	Team	AB	R	H	HR	RBI	Avg	OB	Slg	OPS	bb%	ct%	Eye	SB	CS	x/h%	Iso	RC/G
2012 (1) HS (LA)	2014	A-	Hillsboro	113	15	29	6	22	257	344	496	839	12	80	0.65	2	2	48	239	5.99
Pwr +++	2014	A	South Bend	368	47	73	13	52	198	259	367	626	8	60	0.21	3	0	48	168	3.32
BAvg +	2015	A-	Hillsboro	35	4	5	1	2	143	211	314	525	8	74	0.33	0	0	80	171	1.83
Spd ++	2015	A	Kane County	208	31	49	11	42	236	287	481	768	7	68	0.22	1	0	57	245	5.12
Def ++	2015	A+	Visalia	130	6	18	5	16	138	206	285	490	8	52	0.18	1	0	50	146	1.19

Former high pick has struggled immensely ever since ARI started tinkering with defensive position. Back to catcher mostly in '15, had terrible yr between 3 levels. Bat has slowed considerably as pro. Struck out 37% of time in '15. Plus power held back by poor hit tool. Could stick as an offensive catcher if hit tool improves.

Travis,Sam | 3 | **Boston** | EXP MLB DEBUT: 2017 | H/W: 6-0 195 | FUT: Starting 1B | **7B**

Bats R Age 22	Year	Lev	Team	AB	R	H	HR	RBI	Avg	OB	Slg	OPS	bb%	ct%	Eye	SB	CS	x/h%	Iso	RC/G
2014 (2) Indiana	2014	NCAA	Indiana	245	55	85	12	58	347	407	576	983	9	89	0.96	8	5	35	229	7.47
Pwr +++	2014	A-	Lowell	165	28	55	4	30	333	349	448	798	2	89	0.22	5	1	18	115	4.92
BAvg ++++	2014	A	Greenville	107	12	31	3	14	290	333	495	829	6	87	0.50	0	1	48	206	5.67
Spd ++	2015	A+	Salem	246	35	77	5	40	313	379	467	846	10	83	0.60	10	6	31	154	6.09
Def ++	2015	AA	Portland	243	35	73	4	38	300	384	436	820	12	86	0.97	9	6	32	136	5.94

Advanced, consistent hitter who has plus hand-eye coordination and professional approach. Puts bat to ball with ease and draws walks with selectivity. Has potential to turn doubles into HR, but may need to tweak approach to realize. Limited speed, but is savvy baserunner. Has athleticism, but has work to do on defense.

Trevino,Jose | 2 | **Texas** | EXP MLB DEBUT: 2017 | H/W: 5-11 195 | FUT: Starting C | **7D**

Bats R Age 23	Year	Lev	Team	AB	R	H	HR	RBI	Avg	OB	Slg	OPS	bb%	ct%	Eye	SB	CS	x/h%	Iso	RC/G
2014 (6) Oral Roberts	2012	NCAA	Oral Roberts	246	44	78	13	57	317	361	573	934	6	86	0.50	3	0	44	256	6.76
Pwr +++	2013	NCAA	Oral Roberts	195	32	47	8	37	241	321	410	731	11	85	0.79	0	0	36	169	4.63
BAvg ++	2014	NCAA	Oral Roberts	230	37	70	10	43	304	360	491	851	8	89	0.80	4	0	31	187	5.90
Spd +	2014	A-	Spokane	288	58	74	9	49	257	312	448	760	7	83	0.46	2	0	46	191	4.88
Def ++	2015	A	Hickory	424	62	111	14	63	262	292	415	707	4	86	0.30	1	4	32	153	4.00

Strong backstop who has taken well to catching, but needs to improve blocking and receiving. Makes easy contact with simple stroke and has strength to project to at least average pop. Whips bat through zone, but can be pull-conscious. Owns plus arm, but long release leaves him vulnerable to SB. Has quick feet and should improve with glove.

Tucker,Cole | 6 | **Pittsburgh** | EXP MLB DEBUT: 2018 | H/W: 6-3 185 | FUT: Starting SS | **8D**

Bats B Age 19	Year	Lev	Team	AB	R	H	HR	RBI	Avg	OB	Slg	OPS	bb%	ct%	Eye	SB	CS	x/h%	Iso	RC/G
2014 (1) HS (AZ)																				
Pwr ++																				
BAvg +++																				
Spd +++	2014	Rk	GCL Pirates	180	39	48	2	13	267	359	356	715	13	79	0.68	13	5	21	89	4.61
Def +++	2015	A	West Virginia	300	46	88	2	25	293	329	377	706	5	84	0.33	25	6	20	83	4.12

Tall and wiry, he was having a nice season, but injured his shoulder in July and missed the rest of the season. Switch-hitter has some projection left and could add power as he matures. Has good range, a strong arm, and has good instincts. Swing can get a bit long, but he barrels the ball and is a smart, athletic player.

Tucker,Kyle | 9 | **Houston** | EXP MLB DEBUT: 2019 | H/W: 6-4 190 | FUT: Starting OF | **9D**

Bats L Age 19	Year	Lev	Team	AB	R	H	HR	RBI	Avg	OB	Slg	OPS	bb%	ct%	Eye	SB	CS	x/h%	Iso	RC/G
2015 (1) HS (FL)																				
Pwr +++																				
BAvg ++																				
Spd +++	2015	Rk	Greeneville	112	11	32	1	20	286	328	393	721	6	87	0.47	14	2	31	107	4.41
Def +++	2015	Rk	GCL Astros	119	18	25	2	13	210	260	319	579	6	88	0.57	4	2	28	109	2.84

Lean, athletic OF who has chance to become impact player. Balanced approach at plate allows for contact and OBP while possessing plus power potential. May need to revise swing to handle velocity and should improve against LHP. Exhibits plus instincts for game, especially on defense. Runs well and takes direct routes to balls. Ideal RF profile.

Turner,Stuart | 2 | **Minnesota** | EXP MLB DEBUT: 2016 | H/W: 6-2 230 | FUT: Platoon C | **6B**

Bats R Age 24	Year	Lev	Team	AB	R	H	HR	RBI	Avg	OB	Slg	OPS	bb%	ct%	Eye	SB	CS	x/h%	Iso	RC/G
2013 (3) Mississippi	2013	NCAA	Mississippi	222	44	83	5	51	374	444	518	962	11	83	0.76	2	4	25	144	7.55
Pwr ++	2013	Rk	Elizabethton	121	15	32	3	19	264	331	380	711	9	82	0.55	0	1	25	116	4.30
BAvg ++	2013	AA	New Britain	4	1	2	0	0	500	500	500	1000	0	75	0.00	0	0	0	0	7.40
Spd ++	2014	A+	Fort Myers	325	49	81	7	40	249	315	375	690	9	81	0.51	7	0	31	126	4.07
Def ++++	2015	AA	Chattanooga	327	40	73	4	37	223	317	306	623	12	79	0.65	5	2	25	83	3.39

Excellent defender who should reach majors by glove alone. Has ideal catch-and-throw skills to mute SB and is sound receiver. Makes OK contact with short, line drive stroke, but lacks bat speed for much power. Has good pitch recognition skills and works counts to get on base. Lacks feel for hitting and profiles as bottom of order hitter.

Turner,Trea | 6 | **Washington** | EXP MLB DEBUT: 2015 | H/W: 6-1 175 | FUT: Starting SS | **8A**

Bats R Age 22	Year	Lev	Team	AB	R	H	HR	RBI	Avg	OB	Slg	OPS	bb%	ct%	Eye	SB	CS	x/h%	Iso	RC/G
2014 (1) NC State	2014	A	Fort Wayne	187	31	69	4	22	369	441	529	970	11	74	0.50	14	3	29	160	8.02
Pwr ++	2014	AA	Harrisburg	39	6	14	0	4	359	375	513	888	3	79	0.13	4	0	36	154	6.36
BAvg +++	2015	AA	San Antonio	227	31	73	5	35	322	386	471	858	10	79	0.50	11	4	29	150	6.25
Spd ++++	2015	AAA	Syracuse	188	31	59	3	15	314	358	431	789	6	78	0.32	14	2	22	117	5.20
Def +++	2015	MLB	Washington	40	5	9	1	1	225	295	325	620	9	70	0.33	2	2	22	100	3.03

With strong forearms and wrists, he gets surprising punch out of his smallish frame. Though his swing can get long and he has a tendency to strike out, he's hit for a high BA since turning pro. Possesses excellent speed and uses it well on the bases. Enough range at SS, but with only an average arm, could end up at 2B long-term.

Twine,Justin — 6 — Miami

EXP MLB DEBUT: 2019 | H/W: 5-11 205 | FUT: Starting SS | 8E

Bats R Age 20 — 2014 (2) HS (TX)

Pwr ++ | BAvg ++ | Spd ++++ | Def +++

Year	Lev	Team	AB	R	H	HR	RBI	Avg	OB	Slg	OPS	bb%	ct%	Eye	SB	CS	x/h%	Iso	RC/G
2014	Rk	GCL Marlins	166	19	38	1	16	229	256	355	611	3	69	0.12	5	1	37	127	2.96
2015	A	Greensboro	451	44	93	7	39	206	217	310	527	1	76	0.06	8	4	32	104	1.60

2nd round pick has yet to hit as a pro and after two seasons has a slash line of .212/.248/.323. He has plus speed, good bat speed, and excellent raw strength, but is overly aggressive and his swing can be long. Range and hands are fringy but for now the Marlins continue to see him as a SS.

Unroe,Riley — 4 — Tampa Bay

EXP MLB DEBUT: 2018 | H/W: 5-11 180 | FUT: Starting SS | 7D

Bats B Age 20 — 2013 (2) HS (LA)

Pwr ++ | BAvg ++ | Spd +++ | Def +++

Year	Lev	Team	AB	R	H	HR	RBI	Avg	OB	Slg	OPS	bb%	ct%	Eye	SB	CS	x/h%	Iso	RC/G
2013	Rk	GCL Devil Rays	167	34	41	1	15	246	370	341	711	17	74	0.77	7	2	27	96	4.79
2014	Rk	Princeton	243	32	55	3	19	226	309	325	634	11	81	0.62	7	5	29	99	3.52
2015	A	Bowling Green	439	45	112	4	35	255	333	321	654	10	77	0.52	13	9	17	66	3.67

Fundamentally-sound INF who works counts and uses gap approach to have value. Runs bases with plus speed and can hit for BA, particularly from left side. Offers enough pop to keep defenses honest, but plays contact-oriented, gap-to-gap game. Soft hands are best assets at 2B where his average arm is playable.

Urena,Jhoan — 5 — New York (N)

EXP MLB DEBUT: 2018 | H/W: 6-1 200 | FUT: Starting 3B | 8E

Bats B Age 21 — 2013 FA (DR)

Pwr +++ | BAvg +++ | Spd ++ | Def +++

Year	Lev	Team	AB	R	H	HR	RBI	Avg	OB	Slg	OPS	bb%	ct%	Eye	SB	CS	x/h%	Iso	RC/G
2013	Rk	GCL Mets	157	19	47	0	20	299	353	376	729	8	78	0.38	4	1	19	76	4.59
2014	A-	Brooklyn	283	30	85	5	47	300	361	431	792	9	80	0.47	7	9	31	131	5.38
2015	Rk	GCL Mets	15	4	5	2	2	333	474	800	1274	21	100		1	0	60	467	11.09
2015	A+	St. Lucie	210	15	45	0	18	214	253	267	520	5	81	0.28	2	0	18	52	1.86

Young, switch hitting 3B with hit and power tool to be solid contributor. Lost 2 months to wrist injury. Weak wrist sapped bat's quickness. BB rate decreased after aggressive promotion to High-A. Raw BP power hasn't materialized playing in pitcher's parks. Has soft hands and good reactions at third. Plenty of arm to stick.

Urena,Richard — 6 — Toronto

EXP MLB DEBUT: 2018 | H/W: 6-1 170 | FUT: Starting SS | 8C

Bats L Age 20 — 2012 FA (DR)

Pwr +++ | BAvg +++ | Spd +++ | Def +++

Year	Lev	Team	AB	R	H	HR	RBI	Avg	OB	Slg	OPS	bb%	ct%	Eye	SB	CS	x/h%	Iso	RC/G
2013	Rk	DSL Blue Jays	243	45	72	1	35	296	374	403	777	11	82	0.70	9	5	31	107	5.41
2014	Rk	Bluefield	217	35	69	2	20	318	365	433	798	7	76	0.31	5	4	28	115	5.43
2014	A-	Vancouver	33	3	8	0	5	242	306	364	669	8	85	0.60	1	0	38	121	4.05
2015	A	Lansing	384	62	102	15	58	266	290	438	727	3	78	0.15	5	5	31	172	4.13
2015	A+	Dunedin	124	9	31	1	8	250	268	315	582	2	79	0.12	3	1	16	65	2.37

Young, athletic SS who finished 3rd in MWL in HR. Has defensive attributes to remain at SS. Exhibits quick, smooth actions and has soft hands and plus range. Is a free swinger and aggressive approach needs to be polished. Has surprising pop in lean frame and offers average speed. Should improve in BA department.

Urias,Luis — 456 — San Diego

EXP MLB DEBUT: 2019 | H/W: 5-9 160 | FUT: Starting 2B | 7E

Bats R Age 18 — 2013 FA (MX)

Pwr + | BAvg ++ | Spd +++ | Def +++

Year	Lev	Team	AB	R	H	HR	RBI	Avg	OB	Slg	OPS	bb%	ct%	Eye	SB	CS	x/h%	Iso	RC/G
2014	Rk	Azl Padres	155	29	48	0	14	310	382	355	736	10	92	1.38	10	6	13	45	4.99
2014	Rk	DSL Padres	10	1	1	0	0	100	182	100	282	9	90	1.00	0	0	0	0	-0.24
2015	A-	Tri-City	31	6	11	0	1	355	444	387	832	14	97	5.00	3	3	9	32	6.40
2015	A	Fort Wayne	193	28	56	0	16	290	344	326	671	8	91	0.89	5	10	11	36	4.03

Diminutive INF who showed advanced contact skills in aggressive assignment. Showcased versatility by playing multiple positions and has hands and arm to be asset at any spot. Not much punch in level stroke and is only singles hitter at present. Not much power projection in slight frame and will need to become better situational hitter.

Valera,Beryvic — 4 — St. Louis

EXP MLB DEBUT: 2016 | H/W: 5-11 160 | FUT: Starting 2B | 7C

Bats B Age 23 — 2010 FA (PN)

Pwr + | BAvg ++++ | Spd +++ | Def +++

Year	Lev	Team	AB	R	H	HR	RBI	Avg	OB	Slg	OPS	bb%	ct%	Eye	SB	CS	x/h%	Iso	RC/G
2013	A	Peoria	515	71	159	0	48	309	359	367	726	7	94	1.33	13	7	15	58	4.73
2014	A+	Palm Beach	294	35	98	0	37	333	386	388	773	8	96	1.92	13	10	12	54	5.31
2014	AA	Springfield	227	31	65	0	20	286	331	339	670	6	90	0.68	4	5	15	53	3.94
2015	A+	Palm Beach	51	9	18	0	7	353	468	451	919	18	96	5.50	0	3	22	98	7.69
2015	AA	Springfield	360	37	85	3	31	236	302	297	599	9	93	1.26	2	4	16	61	3.37

Versatile switch-hitting infielder started the season well, hitting .353 in 51 AB at A+, but struggled to adjust when moved up to AA. Hits well from both sides of the plate and uses the whole field. Doesn't have much power, but has good speed. Solid range and actions and can play multiple positions. Saw action at every position but 1B and CA in '15.

Vallot,Chase — 2 — Kansas City

EXP MLB DEBUT: 2019 | H/W: 6-0 215 | FUT: Starting C | 8E

Bats R Age 19 — 2014 (1) HS (LA)

Pwr ++++ | BAvg ++ | Spd ++ | Def +

Year	Lev	Team	AB	R	H	HR	RBI	Avg	OB	Slg	OPS	bb%	ct%	Eye	SB	CS	x/h%	Iso	RC/G
2014	Rk	Burlington	186	29	40	7	27	215	311	403	715	12	56	0.32	0	1	53	188	5.16
2015	A	Lexington	279	46	61	13	40	219	319	427	745	13	62	0.39	1	0	48	208	5.21

Short, strong C with immense power potential. Struggles to hit for BA due to inability to make consistent contact. Swings hard and lunges at times, but has shown improving batting eye. Bat speed and natural strength are best attributes. Throws with power and accuracy, though needs to clean up footwork. Receiving needs major work to stay at catcher.

Van Gansen,Peter — 6 — San Diego

EXP MLB DEBUT: 2018 | H/W: 5-8 165 | FUT: Starting SS | 7E

Bats L Age 22 — 2015 (12) Cal Poly

Pwr ++ | BAvg ++ | Spd ++ | Def ++++

Year	Lev	Team	AB	R	H	HR	RBI	Avg	OB	Slg	OPS	bb%	ct%	Eye	SB	CS	x/h%	Iso	RC/G
2015	A-	Tri-City	270	45	72	2	30	267	349	352	701	11	85	0.85	6	1	21	85	4.47

Steady defender who can impact game with glove. Flashes quick hands and feet and can make plays to both sides. Doesn't make many errors and showcases strong, accurate arm. Offers patient approach with discerning eye, but projects to hit at bottom of order. Lacks punch in controlled swing and can't hit LHP.

Van Hoosier,Evan — 4 — Texas

EXP MLB DEBUT: 2018 | H/W: 5-11 185 | FUT: Utility player | 6B

Bats R Age 22 — 2013 (8) So Nevada

Pwr ++ | BAvg +++ | Spd +++ | Def ++

Year	Lev	Team	AB	R	H	HR	RBI	Avg	OB	Slg	OPS	bb%	ct%	Eye	SB	CS	x/h%	Iso	RC/G
2013	NCAA	So Nevada	176	52	65	5	33	369	434	608	1042	10	91	1.33	16	5	32	239	8.36
2013	A-	Spokane	169	21	42	2	9	249	314	361	674	9	82	0.52	3	1	31	112	3.95
2014	A	Hickory	437	79	117	11	58	268	335	442	776	9	81	0.52	14	2	39	174	5.21
2015	Rk	Azl Rangers	28	5	8	0	1	286	333	393	726	7	79	0.33	2	0	38	107	4.56
2015	A+	High Desert	257	40	85	2	33	331	375	494	869	7	78	0.32	5	3	33	163	6.39

Fundamentally-sound INF who missed time with hamstring injury and facing 50 game suspension for drugs. Offers quickness at 2B, but lacks range and arm for any other spot. Grinds out at bats and has feel for contact. Goes gap to gap in order to use speed effectively. HR output dropped despite home park, but knows game is about contact and speed.

Vasquez,Danry — 7 — Houston

EXP MLB DEBUT: 2016 | H/W: 6-3 169 | FUT: Starting OF | 7D

Bats L Age 22 — 2010 FA (VZ)

Pwr ++ | BAvg +++ | Spd ++ | Def ++

Year	Lev	Team	AB	R	H	HR	RBI	Avg	OB	Slg	OPS	bb%	ct%	Eye	SB	CS	x/h%	Iso	RC/G
2013	A	Quad Cities	118	12	34	3	20	288	323	398	721	5	87	0.40	2	0	18	110	4.22
2013	A	West Michigan	375	47	106	6	40	283	337	400	737	8	85	0.55	9	8	25	117	4.66
2014	A+	Lancaster	423	67	123	5	47	291	352	407	759	9	84	0.59	1	2	30	116	4.99
2015	A+	Lancaster	168	21	53	3	21	315	365	470	835	7	86	0.54	6	4	34	155	5.80
2015	AA	Corpus Christi	277	30	68	0	19	245	287	300	586	5	85	0.38	3	7	21	54	2.79

Slender OF who struggled in 1st taste of AA. Has been high upside prospect for years, but looking likely he will never realize power potential. Focuses on bat control and contact with solid understanding of strike zone. Has positive feel for hitting, but bat speed is too short for pop. Doesn't run well and below average range will keep him in LF.

Velazquez,Andrew — 456 — Tampa Bay

EXP MLB DEBUT: 2017 | H/W: 5-8 175 | FUT: Utility player | 6A

Bats B Age 21 — 2012 (7) HS (NY)

Pwr ++ | BAvg ++++ | Spd +++ | Def +++

Year	Lev	Team	AB	R	H	HR	RBI	Avg	OB	Slg	OPS	bb%	ct%	Eye	SB	CS	x/h%	Iso	RC/G
2012	Rk	Azl DBacks	116	33	37	1	20	319	410	500	910	13	70	0.51	20	3	38	181	7.73
2013	A	South Bend	235	23	61	0	16	260	320	336	656	8	75	0.36	7	2	23	77	3.69
2014	A	South Bend	544	94	158	9	56	290	363	428	791	10	75	0.46	50	15	27	138	5.54
2015	Rk	GCL Devil Rays	13	2	3	0	2	231	333	231	564	13	54	0.33	0	0	0	0	2.66
2015	A+	Charlotte	186	29	54	0	10	290	343	360	703	7	72	0.28	5	8	20	70	4.31

Short, versatile INF who missed time with fractured hand. Split time between 2B, SS, and 3B and has feel for glove. Owns nimble footwork and quick hands to make routine plays. Strikes out far too often for lack of pop, though has barrel control and balanced swing to hit for BA. Could reach seats, but prefers to use middle of field.

Verdugo,Alex — 8 — Los Angeles (N) — EXP MLB DEBUT: 2018 — H/W: 6-0 205 — FUT: Starting RF — 8C

	Year	Lev	Team	AB	R	H	HR	RBI	Avg	OB	Slg	OPS	bb%	ct%	Eye	SB	CS	x/h%	Iso	RC/G
Bats L Age 19																				
2014 (2) HS (AZ)																				
Pwr ++	2014	Rk	Ogden	20	3	8	0	8	400	400	450	850	0	80	0.00	3	0	13	50	5.47
BAvg +++	2014	Rk	Azl Dodgers	170	28	59	3	33	347	416	518	933	11	92	1.43	8	0	34	171	7.19
Spd +++	2015	A	Great Lakes	421	50	124	5	42	295	322	394	716	4	87	0.32	13	5	24	100	4.20
Def +++	2015	A+	RanchoCuca	91	20	35	4	19	385	411	659	1070	4	87	0.33	1	0	43	275	8.22

Polished hitter uses a short, compact stroke and has good bat speed. Makes consistent contact, but can be overly aggressive. Has a line-drive approach, but he could develop average power once he learns to hit with more backspin and loft. Average speed with a plus arm, make RF the most likely destination.

Vielma,Engelb — 6 — Minnesota — EXP MLB DEBUT: 2018 — H/W: 5-11 150 — FUT: Starting SS — 7D

	Year	Lev	Team	AB	R	H	HR	RBI	Avg	OB	Slg	OPS	bb%	ct%	Eye	SB	CS	x/h%	Iso	RC/G
Bats B Age 21																				
2011 FA (VZ)																				
Pwr +	2013	Rk	Elizabethton	23	7	5	0	1	217	250	217	467	4	70	0.14	1	0	0	0	0.73
BAvg +++	2013	Rk	GCL Twins	131	20	31	0	11	237	315	260	575	10	82	0.65	7	3	10	23	2.80
Spd +++	2014	A	Cedar Rapids	418	63	111	1	33	266	312	323	635	6	83	0.39	10	6	16	57	3.34
Def ++++	2015	A+	Fort Myers	441	49	119	1	29	270	324	306	630	7	84	0.49	35	12	10	36	3.33

Smooth, quick SS who started slow, but finished hot. Is excellent defender with above average hands, range, and arm. Possesses instincts and positioning, though can be careless at times. Rarely hits for power as he focuses on contact and using opposite field. Runs fairly well and can steal bases with polished instincts. Good bunter for base hits.

Villalona,Angel — 3 — San Francisco — EXP MLB DEBUT: 2016 — H/W: 6-3 255 — FUT: Backup 1B — 6C

	Year	Lev	Team	AB	R	H	HR	RBI	Avg	OB	Slg	OPS	bb%	ct%	Eye	SB	CS	x/h%	Iso	RC/G
Bats R Age 25																				
2006 FA (DR)	2013	AA	Richmond	196	23	46	8	28	235	265	413	678	4	69	0.13	0	0	41	179	3.65
Pwr +++	2014	Rk	Azl Giants	22	4	6	0	3	273	273	409	682	0	86	0.00	0	0	50	136	3.72
BAvg ++	2014	AA	Richmond	365	35	83	10	54	227	273	381	654	6	74	0.24	1	1	39	153	3.43
Spd +	2015	A+	San Jose	257	29	64	13	48	249	323	447	770	10	75	0.44	0	0	39	198	5.00
Def +	2015	AA	Richmond	56	3	8	0	6	143	186	179	365	5	70	0.18	0	0	25	36	-0.58

Previously heralded 1B prospect has yet to crack AAA ball. Owns plus raw power with natural loft in his swing, but contact woes prevent in-game pop from flourishing; BA skills suffer as a result. Poor range and athleticism limit his glove to 1B. Future value almost exclusively tied into HR power.

Villanueva,Christian — 5 — Chicago (N) — EXP MLB DEBUT: 2016 — H/W: 5-11 210 — FUT: Backup 3B — 6B

	Year	Lev	Team	AB	R	H	HR	RBI	Avg	OB	Slg	OPS	bb%	ct%	Eye	SB	CS	x/h%	Iso	RC/G
Bats R Age 24																				
2008 FA (MX)	2013	AA	Tennessee	490	60	128	19	72	261	309	469	779	6	76	0.29	5	7	48	208	5.06
Pwr ++++	2014	AA	Tennessee	234	31	58	4	32	248	304	385	689	8	82	0.45	0	1	41	137	4.06
BAvg ++	2014	AAA	Iowa	223	22	47	6	26	211	279	372	651	9	71	0.33	2	1	51	161	3.54
Spd ++	2015	AA	Tennessee	24	5	5	2	7	208	321	458	780	14	79	0.80	0	0	40	250	5.09
Def ++++	2015	AAA	Iowa	455	56	118	18	88	259	312	437	750	7	82	0.44	2	3	36	178	4.64

Short, thick-bodied 3B has plus power, but hasn't develop as anticipated. Uses a short, compact stroke and good bat speed to launch impressive blasts. Also makes consistent contact, but has never developed much selectivity, which cuts into BA. Plus defender with good hands, range, and strong, accurate arm, but is now buried at 3B with the Cubs.

Vogelbach,Dan — 3 — Chicago (N) — EXP MLB DEBUT: 2017 — H/W: 6-0 250 — FUT: Starting 1B — 7D

	Year	Lev	Team	AB	R	H	HR	RBI	Avg	OB	Slg	OPS	bb%	ct%	Eye	SB	CS	x/h%	Iso	RC/G
Bats L Age 23																				
2011 (2) HS (FL)	2013	A	Kane County	433	55	123	17	71	284	367	450	818	12	82	0.75	4	4	31	166	5.72
Pwr ++++	2013	A+	Daytona	50	13	14	2	5	280	455	440	895	24	74	1.23	1	0	29	160	7.47
BAvg +++	2014	A+	Daytona	482	71	129	16	76	268	356	429	785	12	81	0.73	4	4	35	162	5.39
Spd +	2015	Rk	Azl Cubs	11	4	5	0	0	455	647	636	1283	35	91	6.00	0	0	40	182	13.39
Def +	2015	AA	Tennessee	254	41	69	7	39	272	405	425	830	18	76	0.93	1	1	35	154	6.37

Thick-bodied with plus raw power, but has seen his HR output drop over last three years. Shows a good understanding of the strike zone, but can be too patient and needs to hunt for pitches he can drive. Has a short, compact stroke. Is well below average defensively, with limited range and stiff hands. He is likely best suited as a DH.

Wade,LaMonte — 78 — Minnesota — EXP MLB DEBUT: 2018 — H/W: 6-1 189 — FUT: Starting OF — 8D

	Year	Lev	Team	AB	R	H	HR	RBI	Avg	OB	Slg	OPS	bb%	ct%	Eye	SB	CS	x/h%	Iso	RC/G
Bats L Age 22																				
2015 (9) Maryland																				
Pwr +++																				
BAvg +++	2015	NCAA	Maryland	158	30	53	4	32	335	441	468	910	16	87	1.50	7	2	23	133	7.19
Spd +++	2015	Rk	Elizabethton	231	36	72	9	44	312	426	506	932	17	85	1.35	12	1	31	195	7.46
Def ++	2015	A	Cedar Rapids	14	1	2	0	1	143	200	143	343	7	86	0.50	0	0	0	0	0.01

Developing OF who surprised org with hitting ability upon signing. Swings quick bat and puts ball in play, even against LHP. Draws walks in mature approach and has strength for at least average power. Can be fooled by good breaking balls. Defensive instincts aren't polished and may move to OF corner, but shows average speed and range to get better.

Wade,Tyler — 46 — New York (A) — EXP MLB DEBUT: 2017 — H/W: 6-1 180 — FUT: Starting 2B/SS — 7C

	Year	Lev	Team	AB	R	H	HR	RBI	Avg	OB	Slg	OPS	bb%	ct%	Eye	SB	CS	x/h%	Iso	RC/G
Bats L Age 21																				
2013 (4) HS (CA)	2013	Rk	GCL Yankees	162	37	50	0	12	309	423	370	793	16	74	0.76	11	1	20	62	5.95
Pwr +	2013	A-	Stn Island	13	0	1	0	1	77	200	77	277	13	69	0.50	0	0	0	0	-1.77
BAvg +++	2014	A	Charleston (Sc)	507	77	138	1	51	272	346	349	695	10	77	0.48	22	13	22	77	4.28
Spd ++++	2015	A+	Tampa	368	51	103	2	28	280	349	353	702	10	82	0.60	31	15	17	73	4.34
Def +++	2015	AA	Trenton	113	6	23	1	3	204	217	265	483	2	79	0.08	2	1	22	62	1.11

Smooth INF who is emerging with both bat and glove. Blitzed High-A with clean, level stroke before succumbing to AA pitching. Swings hard and grinds out at bats. Draws walks and is able to use plus speed on base. Exhibits instincts for all facets of game, including defense. Owns average arm, but has clean, quick hands.

Wakamatsu,Luke — 6 — Cleveland — EXP MLB DEBUT: 2020 — H/W: 6-3 185 — FUT: Starting SS — 8E

	Year	Lev	Team	AB	R	H	HR	RBI	Avg	OB	Slg	OPS	bb%	ct%	Eye	SB	CS	x/h%	Iso	RC/G
Bats B Age 19																				
2015 (20) HS (TX)																				
Pwr +																				
BAvg ++																				
Spd +++																				
Def +++	2015	Rk	AZL Indians	105	8	28	1	12	267	336	400	736	9	62	0.28	4	2	32	133	5.30

Tall, instinctual INF who is standout with glove. May move off SS if he continues to grow, but has great hands, quick feet, and strong arm. Brings mature approach to plate, but needs work with bat. Below average strength limits ability to drive ball and too much swing and miss in game. Has average power potential, but will take time.

Waldrop,Kyle — 379 — Cincinnati — EXP MLB DEBUT: 2015 — H/W: 6-3 215 — FUT: Platoon OF — 6B

	Year	Lev	Team	AB	R	H	HR	RBI	Avg	OB	Slg	OPS	bb%	ct%	Eye	SB	CS	x/h%	Iso	RC/G
Bats L Age 24																				
2010 (12) HS (FL)	2014	A+	Bakersfield	256	54	92	6	32	359	410	516	926	8	78	0.39	11	2	29	156	7.02
Pwr +++	2014	AA	Pensacola	232	27	73	8	35	315	361	517	879	7	81	0.39	3	4	38	203	6.28
BAvg ++	2015	AA	Pensacola	242	21	67	6	31	277	311	430	741	5	75	0.20	2	2	33	153	4.53
Spd ++	2015	AAA	Louisville	205	8	38	1	13	185	212	229	442	3	74	0.13	0	1	18	44	0.50
Def ++	2015	MLB	Cincinnati	1	0	0	0	0	0	0	0	0	0	0	0.00	0	0		0	

Made MLB debut in '15 despite sideways results. Has only showed glimpses of raw power against live pitching. Length in swing was exposed by advanced pitching. Swing tends to sweep at baseballs instead of gliding to the point of contact. He can play 1B, LF & RF adequately. Long term future is a power bat off the bench.

Walker,Adam Brett — 7 — Minnesota — EXP MLB DEBUT: 2016 — H/W: 6-5 225 — FUT: Starting OF — 8D

	Year	Lev	Team	AB	R	H	HR	RBI	Avg	OB	Slg	OPS	bb%	ct%	Eye	SB	CS	x/h%	Iso	RC/G
Bats R Age 24																				
2012 (3) Jacksonville	2012	NCAA	Jacksonville	210	44	72	12	42	343	423	581	1004	12	78	0.62	19	1	36	238	8.13
Pwr +++++	2012	Rk	Elizabethton	232	44	58	14	45	250	307	496	802	8	67	0.25	4	0	43	246	5.60
BAvg ++	2013	A	Cedar Rapids	508	83	141	27	109	278	319	526	845	6	77	0.27	10	0	46	248	5.78
Spd +++	2014	A+	Fort Myers	505	78	124	25	94	246	306	436	742	8	69	0.28	9	5	36	190	4.65
Def ++	2015	AA	Chattanooga	502	75	120	31	106	239	309	498	807	9	61	0.26	13	4	54	259	6.15

Strong OF who has elite power from right side and has at least 25 HR in each full season as pro. Set high in HR and SB, though somewhat muted by high K totals. Led SL in HR and Ks. Exhibits good speed and instincts in OF, but game is all about pop. Will have to live with low BA, however.

Walker,Christian — 3 — Baltimore — EXP MLB DEBUT: 2014 — H/W: 6-0 220 — FUT: Starting 1B — 7C

	Year	Lev	Team	AB	R	H	HR	RBI	Avg	OB	Slg	OPS	bb%	ct%	Eye	SB	CS	x/h%	Iso	RC/G
Bats R Age 25																				
2012 (4) South Carolina	2014	AA	Bowie	366	58	110	20	77	301	366	516	883	9	77	0.46	2	1	34	216	6.40
Pwr +++	2014	AAA	Norfolk	166	15	43	6	19	259	332	428	759	10	70	0.37	0	0	37	169	5.04
BAvg +++	2014	MLB	Baltimore	18	1	3	1	1	167	211	389	599	5	50	0.11	0	0	67	222	3.47
Spd +	2015	AAA	Norfolk	534	68	137	18	74	257	319	423	742	8	75	0.36	1	3	38	167	4.68
Def ++	2015	MLB	Baltimore	9	0	1	0	0	111	333	111	444	25	56	0.75	0	0	0	0	0.23

Stocky 1B who continues to hit for power after tinkering with swing. Has strength and bat speed to produce pop to all fields and recognizes pitches. Approach can be erratic and often swings at pitches he can't drive. Despite higher HR totals, has seen BA decline. Not a polished defender, but not a liability. Lacks quick feet, but can scoop balls.

Wall,Forrest

4 | **Colorado** | EXP MLB DEBUT: 2018 | H/W: 6-0 176 | FUT: Starting 2B | **8D**

Bats L Age 20
2014 (1) HS (FL)

Pwr + +
BAvg + + + +
Spd + + +
Def + + +

Year	Lev	Team	AB	R	H	HR	RBI	Avg	OB	Slg	OPS	bb%	ct%	Eye	SB	CS	x/h%	Iso	RC/G
2014	Rk	Grand Junction	157	48	50	3	24	318	418	490	909	15	80	0.84	18	5	30	172	7.27
2015	A-	Boise	10	4	5	0	1	500	688	500	1188	38	80	3.00	2	2	0	0	12.68
2015	A	Asheville	361	57	101	7	46	280	353	438	791	10	80	0.57	23	9	33	158	5.48

Solid full-season debut. Quick, compact LH stroke generates good bat speed and average power. Spreads out at the plate with a moderate leg kick to trigger swing. Stays back and balanced even against off-speed stuff, which allows him to make good contact. Currently has more of a line-drive approach, but has the size and swing for more pop.

Wallach,Chad

23 | **Cincinnati** | EXP MLB DEBUT: 2017 | H/W: 6-3 215 | FUT: Reserve C | **6C**

Bats R Age 24
2013 (5) Cal St Fullerton

Pwr + +
BAvg + +
Spd + +
Def + +

Year	Lev	Team	AB	R	H	HR	RBI	Avg	OB	Slg	OPS	bb%	ct%	Eye	SB	CS	x/h%	Iso	RC/G
2013	NCAA	Cal St Fullerton	162	24	50	2	32	309	367	444	812	8	90	0.88	2	2	34	136	5.67
2013	A-	Batavia	146	19	33	0	13	226	280	267	547	7	82	0.41	0	0	18	41	2.30
2014	A	Greensboro	271	50	87	7	49	321	427	476	903	16	86	1.28	3	0	31	155	7.10
2014	A+	Jupiter	64	4	21	0	8	328	434	375	809	16	89	1.71	0	0	14	47	6.14
2015	A+	Daytona	370	41	91	3	32	246	318	351	669	10	79	0.51	2	3	35	105	3.92

Son of former MLB 3B Tim Wallach. Regressed with bat after breaking out in '14. Got away from line drive approach, causing production to drop significantly. BBs decreased while Ks increased. Solid but unspectacular behind the plate. Aided by a plus arm behind the dish.

Ward,Drew

5 | **Washington** | EXP MLB DEBUT: 2018 | H/W: 6-3 215 | FUT: Starting 3B/1B | **7C**

Bats L Age 21
2013 (3) HS (OK)

Pwr + + +
BAvg + + +
4.44 Spd + +
Def + +

Year	Lev	Team	AB	R	H	HR	RBI	Avg	OB	Slg	OPS	bb%	ct%	Eye	SB	CS	x/h%	Iso	RC/G
2013	Rk	GCL Nationals	168	24	49	1	28	292	383	387	770	13	74	0.57	2	4	29	95	5.45
2014	A	Hagerstown	431	45	116	10	73	269	334	413	747	9	72	0.35	2	2	34	144	4.88
2015	Rk	GCL Nationals	13	2	2	1	2	154	313	385	697	19	38	0.38	0	0	50	231	6.64
2015	A+	Potomac	377	47	94	6	47	249	320	358	678	9	71	0.35	2	1	29	109	3.96

Still young for his level, repeated his 2014 output against higher competition. Balanced LH swing, but can get long and has not yet unlocked the power his frame would suggest. Strikes out frequently. Slow reactions and limited range in the field point to a future move to 1B; where he might not have the bat necessary to be a starter.

Ward,Taylor

2 | **Los Angeles (A)** | EXP MLB DEBUT: 2018 | H/W: 6-2 190 | FUT: Starting C | **7B**

Bats R Age 22
2015 (1) Fresno St

Pwr + +
BAvg + + +
Spd + +
Def + + +

Year	Lev	Team	AB	R	H	HR	RBI	Avg	OB	Slg	OPS	bb%	ct%	Eye	SB	CS	x/h%	Iso	RC/G
2015	NCAA	Fresno St	214	39	65	7	42	304	402	486	888	14	84	1.03	7	0	35	182	6.80
2015	Rk	Orem	109	20	38	2	19	349	486	459	944	21	93	3.63	5	2	18	110	8.03
2015	A	Burlington	92	10	32	1	12	348	412	413	825	10	84	0.67	1	1	13	65	5.78

Compact, athletic backstop who isn't blessed with plus tools, but gets job done with simple approach and contact-oriented stroke. Discerning eye at plate is best current attribute and gets on base consistently. Can drive ball to gaps and shows some pull power. Exhibits terrific arm strength with accuracy, though needs polish with receiving.

Wendle,Joey

4 | **Oakland** | EXP MLB DEBUT: 2016 | H/W: 6-1 190 | FUT: Starting 2B | **7C**

Bats L Age 25
2012 (6) West Chester

Pwr + +
BAvg + + +
Spd + + +
Def + + +

Year	Lev	Team	AB	R	H	HR	RBI	Avg	OB	Slg	OPS	bb%	ct%	Eye	SB	CS	x/h%	Iso	RC/G
2012	A-	Mahoning Val	245	32	80	4	37	327	365	469	835	6	90	0.60	4	1	29	143	5.71
2013	A+	Carolina	413	73	122	16	64	295	363	513	877	10	81	0.56	10	2	43	218	6.42
2014	Rk	AZL Indians	22	8	10	0	4	455	538	591	1129	15	82	1.00	1	1	20	136	10.17
2014	AA	Akron	336	46	85	8	50	253	307	414	720	7	83	0.46	4	2	39	161	4.41
2015	AAA	Nashville	577	80	167	10	57	289	316	442	757	4	80	0.19	12	2	36	153	4.68

Instinctual INF who continues to produce despite limited tools. Increased K rate as he can sell out for pop, but smokes line drives to all fields and uses average speed to get doubles. Walk rate declined and could be tougher out with better discipline. Played season at 2B where arm and range most suitable.

Westbrook,Jamie

4 | **Arizona** | EXP MLB DEBUT: 2017 | H/W: 5-9 170 | FUT: Starting 2B | **8D**

Bats R Age 20
2013 (5) HS (AZ)

Pwr + +
BAvg + + +
Spd + + +
Def + + +

Year	Lev	Team	AB	R	H	HR	RBI	Avg	OB	Slg	OPS	bb%	ct%	Eye	SB	CS	x/h%	Iso	RC/G
2013	Rk	Missoula	67	12	17	1	13	254	315	343	658	8	70	0.30	1	0	24	90	3.62
2013	Rk	Azl DBacks	154	31	45	1	20	292	363	468	830	10	86	0.81	3	3	38	175	6.07
2014	A	South Bend	509	69	132	8	49	259	311	375	686	7	81	0.39	6	3	30	116	3.95
2015	A+	Visalia	480	75	153	17	72	319	351	510	862	5	86	0.35	14	4	35	192	5.85

Had breakout season in hitter friendly CAL. Hit 17 HR but likely won't carry totals to upper levels. Advanced skill against off-speed pitches. Inside-out swing propels balls to RCF gap regularly. 55-grade runner and fielder. Limited to 2B due to poor weak throwing arm.

White,Isaiah

8 | **Miami** | EXP MLB DEBUT: 2017 | H/W: 6-0 170 | FUT: Starting CF | **8E**

Bats R Age 19
2015 (3) HS (NC)

Pwr + +
BAvg + + +
Spd + + + + +
Def + + + +

Year	Lev	Team	AB	R	H	HR	RBI	Avg	OB	Slg	OPS	bb%	ct%	Eye	SB	CS	x/h%	Iso	RC/G
2015	Rk	GCL Marlins	126	19	37	0	8	294	310	381	691	2	65	0.07	13	0	24	87	4.15

3rd round pick had a solid pro debut, but can be extremely aggressive at the plate (3BB/44K). He does have impressive raw tools and some of the best speed in the system, but he needs to prove he can make enough contact to hit for BA. Plus-plus runner covers ground well and is a true CF. Raw, but tons of upside.

White,Mikey

56 | **Oakland** | EXP MLB DEBUT: 2018 | H/W: 6-1 200 | FUT: Starting SS/3B | **7D**

Bats R Age 22
2015 (2) Alabama

Pwr + +
BAvg + + +
Spd + +
Def + + +

Year	Lev	Team	AB	R	H	HR	RBI	Avg	OB	Slg	OPS	bb%	ct%	Eye	SB	CS	x/h%	Iso	RC/G
2015	NCAA	Alabama	218	48	74	4	35	339	422	537	958	12	78	0.66	8	1	39	197	7.85
2015	A-	Vermont	111	18	35	2	16	315	392	459	851	11	74	0.48	0	2	34	144	6.42
2015	A	Beloit	130	16	26	1	12	200	257	262	519	7	77	0.33	0	1	23	62	1.77

Reliable INF who can play multiple positions with excellent hands and strong arm. Maximizes average tools with feel for game. Likes to work deep counts, but lacks bat speed to catch up to good velocity. Struggles with breaking balls. Hope is that he makes more consistent, hard contact and lets natural ability take over. Not much upside.

White,Tyler

35 | **Houston** | EXP MLB DEBUT: 2016 | H/W: 5-10 225 | FUT: Reserve INF | **6B**

Bats R Age 25
2013 (33) Westrn Carolina

Pwr + +
BAvg + + +
Spd +
Def + +

Year	Lev	Team	AB	R	H	HR	RBI	Avg	OB	Slg	OPS	bb%	ct%	Eye	SB	CS	x/h%	Iso	RC/G
2013	A-	Tri City	112	19	32	3	25	286	360	384	744	10	92	1.44	1	0	16	98	4.94
2014	A	Quad Cities	239	41	73	7	41	305	394	485	880	13	83	0.88	0	1	38	180	6.65
2014	A+	Lancaster	150	28	40	8	23	267	382	527	909	16	82	1.04	0	0	55	260	7.09
2015	AA	Corpus Christi	190	33	54	7	40	284	414	426	840	18	82	1.20	1	0	24	142	6.36
2015	AAA	Fresno	213	37	77	7	59	362	467	559	1025	16	82	1.11	0	1	35	197	8.71

Pure hitting INF with career BA of .311. Advancing quickly solely on bat production. Draws ton of walks with grinding approach and not afraid to shorten swing with two strikes and make contact. Owns LHP and hangs in against breaking balls. Exhibits below average pop and lacks foot speed. Split time between 1B and 3B, but below average at both.

Whitley,Garrett

8 | **Tampa Bay** | EXP MLB DEBUT: 2019 | H/W: 6-0 200 | FUT: Starting OF | **9D**

Bats R Age 19
2015 (1) HS (NY)

Pwr + + + +
BAvg + +
Spd + + + +
Def + + +

Year	Lev	Team	AB	R	H	HR	RBI	Avg	OB	Slg	OPS	bb%	ct%	Eye	SB	CS	x/h%	Iso	RC/G
2015	Rk	GCL Devil Rays	96	12	18	3	13	188	304	365	668	14	74	0.64	5	4	50	177	3.97
2015	A-	Hudson Valley	42	3	6	0	4	143	234	190	425	11	71	0.42	3	1	17	48	0.51

Exciting prospect with very high ceiling. Has potential to hit for high BA and significant power. Has strong, athletic frame and current plus speed. Plate approach and swing mechanics can be inconsistent and may struggle to make contact at times. Plays CF now, though may move to LF due to weak arm. Covers a lot of ground.

Williams,Justin

9 | **Tampa Bay** | EXP MLB DEBUT: 2018 | H/W: 6-2 215 | FUT: Starting OF | **8D**

Bats L Age 20
2013 (2) HS (LA)

Pwr + + +
BAvg + + +
Spd + +
Def + +

Year	Lev	Team	AB	R	H	HR	RBI	Avg	OB	Slg	OPS	bb%	ct%	Eye	SB	CS	x/h%	Iso	RC/G
2013	A	South Bend	9	3	1	0	0	111	273	111	384	18	78	1.00	0	0	0	0	0.44
2014	Rk	Missoula	189	31	73	2	23	386	437	471	908	8	77	0.39	1	1	14	85	6.85
2014	A	South Bend	102	16	29	2	23	284	330	461	791	6	77	0.30	0	1	38	176	5.32
2015	A	Bowling Green	387	43	110	7	42	284	308	413	721	3	80	0.17	3	1	31	129	4.16
2015	A+	Charlotte	83	8	20	0	6	241	250	301	551	1	83	0.07	3	1	25	60	2.09

Aggressive hitter who looks part of top prospect and has intriguing tools. Has strength and bat speed that projects to above average power and should hit for BA despite free-swinging ways. Has hand-eye coordination, though will struggle with offspeed stuff. Improving defender with average arm and will likely slot in at RF full-time.

Williams,Mason | 78 | **New York (A)** | EXP MLB DEBUT: 2015 | H/W: 6-0 185 | FUT: Starting OF | **7C**

Bats L Age 24	Year	Lev	Team	AB	R	H	HR	RBI	Avg	OB	Slg	OPS	bb%	ct%	Eye	SB	CS	x/h%	Iso	RC/G
2010 (4) HS (FL)	2013	AA	Trenton	72	7	11	1	4	153	164	264	428	1	75	0.06	0	0	45	111	0.36
Pwr ++	2014	AA	Trenton	507	67	113	5	40	223	289	304	593	8	87	0.69	21	8	24	81	3.07
BAvg +++	2015	AA	Trenton	120	14	38	0	11	317	410	375	785	14	86	1.12	11	6	18	58	5.67
Spd +++	2015	AAA	Scranton/WB	81	12	26	0	11	321	382	432	814	9	93	1.33	2	1	31	111	5.85
Def ++++	2015	MLB	NY Yankees	21	3	6	1	3	286	318	571	890	5	86	0.33	0	0	67	286	6.23

Athletic, fast OF who rebounded from poor '14 and is back in NYY plans. Underwent shoulder surgery in August, but should be fine. Reached majors mostly with defense, but starting to swing consistently. Gets on base at high clip and makes easy contact despite vicious cuts. Power not part of his game, though has strength to reach seats.

Williams,Nick | 78 | **Philadelphia** | EXP MLB DEBUT: 2016 | H/W: 6-3 195 | FUT: Starting LF | **8B**

Bats L Age 22	Year	Lev	Team	AB	R	H	HR	RBI	Avg	OB	Slg	OPS	bb%	ct%	Eye	SB	CS	x/h%	Iso	RC/G
2012 (2) HS (TX)	2014	Rk	Azl Rangers	13	3	4	0	2	308	357	462	819	7	85	0.50	0	0	25	154	5.77
Pwr +++	2014	A+	Myrtle Beach	377	61	110	13	68	292	326	491	816	5	69	0.16	5	7	41	199	5.76
BAvg +++	2014	AA	Frisco	62	4	14	0	4	226	250	290	540	3	66	0.10	1	1	21	65	1.88
Spd +++	2015	AA	Frisco	378	56	113	13	45	299	354	479	832	8	80	0.42	10	8	34	180	5.72
Def +++	2015	AA	Reading	97	21	31	4	10	320	340	536	876	3	79	0.15	3	0	35	216	6.00

Quick hands and exceptional bat speed are the hallmarks of his high BA and above-average power. Tamed his aggressive, swing-at-everything approach and became complete hitter in 2015, which raises his ceiling and HR potential a tick. Speed shows up in the field chasing down flyballs and on basepaths.

Williamson,Mac | 9 | **San Francisco** | EXP MLB DEBUT: 2015 | H/W: 6-4 240 | FUT: Starting RF | **8D**

Bats R Age 25	Year	Lev	Team	AB	R	H	HR	RBI	Avg	OB	Slg	OPS	bb%	ct%	Eye	SB	CS	x/h%	Iso	RC/G
2012 (3) Wake Forest	2013	A+	San Jose	520	94	152	25	89	292	356	504	859	9	75	0.39	10	1	38	212	6.20
Pwr ++++	2014	A+	San Jose	85	16	27	3	11	318	408	506	914	13	84	0.93	6	1	37	188	7.06
BAvg ++	2015	AA	Richmond	259	41	76	5	42	293	356	429	784	9	80	0.47	3	1	30	135	5.27
Spd +++	2015	AAA	Sacramento	189	35	47	8	31	249	340	439	779	12	71	0.47	1	0	43	190	5.37
Def ++	2015	MLB	SF Giants	32	2	7	0	1	219	219	281	500	0	75	0.00	1	0	14	63	1.23

Tall, strong OF had quality AFL stint after MLB debut in Sept. Has strong wrists and employs good stretch in load, allowing for plus bat speed and power. Struggles with ct% vs. off-speed, which will hinder his BA upside, but is willing to walk. Strong arm plays well in RF and has enough range to stick there long-term.

Wilson,Austin | 89 | **Seattle** | EXP MLB DEBUT: 2016 | H/W: 6-4 245 | FUT: Starting OF | **8D**

Bats R Age 24	Year	Lev	Team	AB	R	H	HR	RBI	Avg	OB	Slg	OPS	bb%	ct%	Eye	SB	CS	x/h%	Iso	RC/G
2013 (2) Stanford	2013	NCAA	Stanford	118	26	34	5	26	288	359	475	833	10	85	0.72	5	2	35	186	5.81
Pwr +++	2013	A-	Everett	203	22	49	6	27	241	300	414	714	8	79	0.40	2	4	41	172	4.31
BAvg ++	2014	Rk	Azl Mariners	8	3	5	1	1	625	667	1375	2042	11	75	0.50	1	0	60	750	22.33
Spd +++	2014	A	Clinton	261	38	76	12	54	291	355	517	873	9	75	0.40	1	1	42	226	6.42
Def +++	2015	A+	Bakersfield	380	51	91	10	48	239	297	374	671	8	70	0.27	8	7	32	134	3.74

Muscular OF who is more about tools than production. Had solid last 2 months and could be ready for breakout. Revised swing mechanics early to take advantage of bat speed and natural power. Swing can get long at times and can be jammed inside with quality FB. Minor injuries haven't helped. Fits profile of RF with strong arm and average range.

Wilson,D.J. | 8 | **Chicago (N)** | EXP MLB DEBUT: 2019 | H/W: 5-8 177 | FUT: Starting CF | **7C**

Bats R Age 19	Year	Lev	Team	AB	R	H	HR	RBI	Avg	OB	Slg	OPS	bb%	ct%	Eye	SB	CS	x/h%	Iso	RC/G
2015 (4) HS (OH)																				
Pwr +																				
BAvg +++																				
Spd ++++																				
Def ++++	2015	Rk	Azl Cubs	79	12	21	0	6	266	318	354	672	7	81	0.40	5	1	24	89	3.89

Short, fleet-footed OF was signed to an over-slot $1.3 million. Short, compact LH stroke and a good understanding of the strike zone should allow him to hit for BA but with below-average power. Covers ground well in CF with an avg arm and is plus defender. Solid debut in the AZL and is a player to watch. Similar to Ben Revere and Adam Eaton.

Wilson,Jacob | 457 | **St. Louis** | EXP MLB DEBUT: 2016 | H/W: 6-0 180 | FUT: Utility Infielder | **6C**

Bats R Age 25	Year	Lev	Team	AB	R	H	HR	RBI	Avg	OB	Slg	OPS	bb%	ct%	Eye	SB	CS	x/h%	Iso	RC/G
2012 (10) Memphis	2013	A+	Palm Beach	117	12	21	3	10	179	284	291	574	13	83	0.85	0	1	33	111	2.85
Pwr ++	2014	A+	Palm Beach	121	18	36	0	20	298	361	397	758	9	80	0.50	0	0	33	99	5.07
BAvg ++	2014	AA	Springfield	131	15	40	5	21	305	359	519	878	8	82	0.48	3	1	45	214	6.30
Spd ++	2015	AA	Springfield	120	18	27	7	21	225	321	450	771	12	79	0.68	0	2	48	225	5.09
Def +++	2015	AAA	Memphis	307	41	71	11	56	231	285	391	676	7	78	0.34	2	1	37	160	3.70

Was fully recovered from a knee injury that shut him down, but he struggled at the plate, hitting just .230 between AA/AAA. Works hard to get the most of his abilities. Has good bat speed and raw power and launched 18 HR, but can be overly aggressive at the plate. Profiles as a super utility type and split time between 3B, 2B, and LF.

Wilson,Marcus | 789 | **Arizona** | EXP MLB DEBUT: 2019 | H/W: 6-3 175 | FUT: Starting CF | **8E**

Bats R Age 19	Year	Lev	Team	AB	R	H	HR	RBI	Avg	OB	Slg	OPS	bb%	ct%	Eye	SB	CS	x/h%	Iso	RC/G
2014 (2) HS (CA)																				
Pwr ++																				
BAvg ++																				
Spd +++++	2014	Rk	Azl DBacks	131	15	27	1	22	206	293	275	567	11	69	0.40	4	2	19	69	2.46
Def ++++	2015	Rk	Missoula	213	42	55	1	22	258	358	338	696	13	71	0.54	7	4	25	80	4.45

A raw, athletic OF type that baseball usually loses to other sports, made strides cutting down swing length and improving eye at the plate. Has room to add 25 lbs of muscle without compromising speed. A project both at the plate and on the bases. Only stole 7 bases despite plus-plus run tool. Will stick in CF.

Winker,Jesse | 7 | **Cincinnati** | EXP MLB DEBUT: 2016 | H/W: 6-3 210 | FUT: Starting LF | **9C**

Bats L Age 22	Year	Lev	Team	AB	R	H	HR	RBI	Avg	OB	Slg	OPS	bb%	ct%	Eye	SB	CS	x/h%	Iso	RC/G
2012 (1) HS (FL)	2012	Rk	Billings	228	42	77	5	35	338	437	500	937	15	78	0.80	1	3	31	162	7.64
Pwr ++++	2013	A	Dayton	417	73	117	16	76	281	375	463	838	13	82	0.84	6	1	33	182	6.09
BAvg ++++	2014	A+	Bakersfield	205	42	65	13	49	317	429	580	1009	16	78	0.87	5	1	43	263	8.43
Spd ++	2014	AA	Pensacola	77	15	16	2	8	208	330	351	680	15	71	0.64	0	0	44	143	4.18
Def ++	2015	AA	Pensacola	443	69	125	13	55	282	385	433	818	14	81	0.89	8	4	31	151	5.95

Had an incredible 2nd half after a so-so start. Has 70-grade raw power along with disciplined approach. Line drive hitter capable of bombarding doubles, but swing elongates at times. Prone to get under pitches. A below-average defender, LF is only defensive option.

Wisdom,Patrick | 5 | **St. Louis** | EXP MLB DEBUT: 2016 | H/W: 6-2 210 | FUT: Starting 3B | **7C**

Bats R Age 24	Year	Lev	Team	AB	R	H	HR	RBI	Avg	OB	Slg	OPS	bb%	ct%	Eye	SB	CS	x/h%	Iso	RC/G
2012 (1) St. Mary's	2012	A-	Batavia	241	40	68	6	32	282	364	465	829	11	76	0.53	2	1	40	183	6.07
Pwr +++	2013	A	Peoria	372	54	86	13	62	231	309	411	720	10	69	0.37	4	1	43	180	4.56
BAvg ++	2013	A+	Palm Beach	92	8	23	2	11	250	317	359	676	9	75	0.39	1	0	26	109	3.82
Spd ++	2014	AA	Springfield	452	49	97	14	53	215	277	367	644	8	67	0.26	5	1	38	153	3.41
Def +++	2015	AA	Springfield	414	51	98	14	61	237	296	406	702	8	74	0.33	11	3	39	169	4.12

1st round pick has failed to live up to expectations and now has a career slash line of .237/.307/.402. Has avg bat speed, moderate power, but his approach has not developed and is simply too aggressive. Has good athleticism and handles 3B well with good hands. range, and a plus arm. Below avg speed limits him to 3B or LF. The clock is ticking...

Wise,Carl | 5 | **Toronto** | EXP MLB DEBUT: 2018 | H/W: 6-2 215 | FUT: Starting 3B | **7D**

Bats R Age 21	Year	Lev	Team	AB	R	H	HR	RBI	Avg	OB	Slg	OPS	bb%	ct%	Eye	SB	CS	x/h%	Iso	RC/G
2015 (4) Charleston																				
Pwr +++																				
BAvg ++	2015	NCAA	Charleston	246	64	77	12	70	313	381	557	938	10	85	0.71	3	0	43	244	7.07
Spd +	2015	Rk	Bluefield	31	7	8	0	5	258	303	323	626	6	81	0.33	0	0	25	65	3.21
Def ++	2015	A-	Vancouver	182	18	42	1	26	231	263	308	571	4	76	0.19	0	0	26	77	2.34

Offensive-oriented INF with potential to hit for above average power. Has work to do with swing-happy approach and glovework. Understands strike zone, but has issues with breaking balls and can be pull conscious. Needs to find defensive home. Lacks quickness to be solid 3B, though arm strength is solid. May eventually move to 1B.

Wiseman,Rhett | 7 | **Washington** | EXP MLB DEBUT: 2019 | H/W: 5-11 200 | FUT: Starting OF | **7C**

Bats L Age 21	Year	Lev	Team	AB	R	H	HR	RBI	Avg	OB	Slg	OPS	bb%	ct%	Eye	SB	CS	x/h%	Iso	RC/G
2015 (3) Vanderbilt																				
Pwr +++																				
BAvg ++																				
Spd ++	2015	NCAA	Vanderbilt	290	70	92	15	49	317	400	566	966	12	75	0.55	12	2	41	248	7.82
Def ++	2015	A-	Auburn	210	25	52	5	35	248	307	376	683	8	75	0.35	6	2	33	129	3.89

Focused on power in his final college year; has strength/bat speed for it. But sacrificed contact in the process, and strikeouts now a hurdle to his approach. A heady, tough player who runs good routes in the OF and will take a walk at the plate, but will need to even out the contact/power disparity to make his mark.

Wong,Kean — 4 — Tampa Bay

EXP MLB DEBUT: 2018 | H/W: 5-11 190 | FUT: Starting 2B | 7B

Bats L Age 20	Year	Lev	Team	AB	R	H	HR	RBI	Avg	OB	Slg	OPS	bb%	ct%	Eye	SB	CS	x/h%	Iso	RC/G
2013 (4) HS (HI)																				
Pwr +																				
BAvg ++++	2013	Rk	GCL Devil Rays	177	27	58	0	22	328	367	390	757	6	88	0.50	7	1	16	62	4.83
Spd ++	2014	A	Bowling Green	422	56	129	2	24	306	347	370	717	6	83	0.37	13	7	16	64	4.29
Def +++	2015	A+	Charlotte	394	46	108	1	36	274	324	332	656	7	84	0.45	15	6	17	58	3.65

Compact INF with limited power, but solid offensive package. Can hit LHP and makes simple contact with clean swing. Has level swing path for hard line drives and has enough speed to be threat. Reads spin out of hand and is tough out. Lack of arm strength keeps him at 2B and has average arm and hands.

Wren,Kyle — 78 — Milwaukee

EXP MLB DEBUT: 2016 | H/W: 5-10 175 | FUT: Starting CF | 7C

Bats L Age 24	Year	Lev	Team	AB	R	H	HR	RBI	Avg	OB	Slg	OPS	bb%	ct%	Eye	SB	CS	x/h%	Iso	RC/G
2013 (8) Georgia Tech	2013	A+	Lynchburg	1	0	0	0	0	0	500	0	500	50	100		0	1		0	4.75
Pwr +	2014	A+	Lynchburg	291	46	86	0	27	296	361	357	719	9	87	0.77	33	9	16	62	4.62
BAvg +++	2014	AA	Mississippi	205	28	58	0	16	283	335	376	710	7	80	0.40	13	5	26	93	4.37
Spd +++++	2015	AA	Biloxi	227	26	68	0	13	300	367	326	693	10	87	0.83	20	9	9	26	4.29
Def +++	2015	AAA	Colorado Springs	291	33	73	1	26	251	297	320	616	6	85	0.42	16	4	21	69	3.17

Short, agile OF has ingredients of future lead-off type. Doesn't hit for much power, but quick stroke, contact and speed make his hit tool solid average. Patient, disciplined approach help him reach base, where he has track record for SB success. Gets good reads and takes quality routs in CF, the position in which he profiles best long-term.

Yacinich,Jake — 46 — Los Angeles (A)

EXP MLB DEBUT: 2018 | H/W: 6-2 195 | FUT: Utility player | 6B

Bats L Age 23	Year	Lev	Team	AB	R	H	HR	RBI	Avg	OB	Slg	OPS	bb%	ct%	Eye	SB	CS	x/h%	Iso	RC/G
2014 (8) Iowa	2013	NCAA	Iowa	154	22	44	0	24	286	325	312	637	6	86	0.41	4	3	9	26	3.35
Pwr +	2014	NCAA	Iowa	208	45	76	1	32	365	419	447	866	8	86	0.63	25	4	14	82	6.23
BAvg ++	2014	Rk	Orem	17	5	3	0	2	176	333	235	569	19	65	0.67	1	0	33	59	2.71
Spd ++	2015	A	Burlington	328	49	88	2	26	268	308	335	644	5	83	0.35	6	3	16	67	3.39
Def +++	2015	A+	Inland Empire	27	5	7	0	3	259	286	370	656	4	78	0.17	1	0	43	111	3.52

Long, lean INF who missed time with separated shoulder. Draws rave reviews for steady defense as he exhibits quick actions and clean, soft hands. Arm and range good enough to stick at SS. May not hit enough to warrant every day role. Makes contact with slap approach, but doesn't drive ball and can be free swinger. Owns well below average pop.

Yarbrough,Alex — 4 — Los Angeles (A)

EXP MLB DEBUT: 2016 | H/W: 6-0 200 | FUT: Starting 2B | 7D

Bats B Age 25	Year	Lev	Team	AB	R	H	HR	RBI	Avg	OB	Slg	OPS	bb%	ct%	Eye	SB	CS	x/h%	Iso	RC/G
2012 (4) Mississippi	2012	A	Cedar Rapids	244	35	70	0	27	287	315	410	725	4	92	0.50	9	2	30	123	4.53
Pwr ++	2012	AA	Arkansas	18	1	2	0	0	111	111	167	278	0	83	0.00	0	0	50	56	-1.10
BAvg ++	2013	A+	Inland Empire	582	77	182	11	80	313	343	459	802	4	82	0.25	14	4	29	146	5.22
Spd ++	2014	AA	Arkansas	544	66	155	5	77	285	326	397	723	6	77	0.27	6	6	30	112	4.39
Def ++	2015	AAA	Salt Lake	500	56	118	3	48	236	274	324	598	5	73	0.19	1	1	30	88	2.72

Pure hitting INF who struggled all season, but has chance to become offensive 2B. Has natural strength and bat speed to produce doubles, though HR not part of game. BA in decline as Ks have increased. Doesn't run much and lack of quickness mutes glovework where range most suitable for 2B. Needs to regain BA to have chance as big league starter.

Yastrzemski,Mike — 789 — Baltimore

EXP MLB DEBUT: 2016 | H/W: 5-11 180 | FUT: Fourth OF | 6B

Bats L Age 25	Year	Lev	Team	AB	R	H	HR	RBI	Avg	OB	Slg	OPS	bb%	ct%	Eye	SB	CS	x/h%	Iso	RC/G
2013 (14) Vanderbilt																				
Pwr ++	2014	A	Delmarva	258	52	79	10	44	306	354	554	908	7	75	0.30	12	4	43	248	6.88
BAvg +++	2014	A+	Frederick	93	21	29	1	19	312	366	462	829	8	83	0.50	5	0	34	151	5.85
Spd +++	2014	AA	Bowie	184	23	46	3	12	250	303	413	716	7	82	0.41	1	2	43	163	4.42
Def +++	2015	AA	Bowie	476	63	117	6	59	246	308	372	680	8	79	0.43	8	7	36	126	3.99

Fundamentally-sound OF who plays game hard despite limited tools. Can make contact and use entire field with ideal bat control. Possesses mostly doubles power, though can jerk ball out. Runs fairly well, though not a burner and is smart on base. Plays all OF positions, though not a master at any. Has average speed and throws with accuracy.

Ynfante,Wadye — 8 — St. Louis

EXP MLB DEBUT: 2020 | H/W: 6-0 160 | FUT: Starting CF | 8D

Bats R Age 18	Year	Lev	Team	AB	R	H	HR	RBI	Avg	OB	Slg	OPS	bb%	ct%	Eye	SB	CS	x/h%	Iso	RC/G
2014 FA (DR)																				
Pwr +++																				
BAvg +++																				
Spd +++																				
Def +++	2015			*Did not play in U.S.*																

Wiry, athletic OF from the DR was one of the Cards most impressive players in the DSL hitting .311/.362/.458. Moves well defensively with good range and a decent arm. Has a good approach at the plate with plus bat speed and impressive raw power. Still raw in some aspects of his game and should make his state-side debut in rookie ball in 2016.

Young,Chesny — 46 — Chicago (N)

EXP MLB DEBUT: 2018 | H/W: 6-0 170 | FUT: Utility player | 7D

Bats R Age 23	Year	Lev	Team	AB	R	H	HR	RBI	Avg	OB	Slg	OPS	bb%	ct%	Eye	SB	CS	x/h%	Iso	RC/G
2014 (14) Mercer	2014	Rk	Azl Cubs	6	0	1	0	0	167	286	167	452	14	67	0.50	0	0	0	0	0.74
Pwr +	2014	A-	Boise	48	13	17	0	9	354	446	417	863	14	83	1.00	1	0	18	63	6.65
BAvg ++++	2014	A	Kane County	105	14	34	0	9	324	355	419	774	5	79	0.23	2	1	24	95	4.99
Spd ++	2015	A	South Bend	108	23	34	0	14	315	383	380	763	10	94	1.71	9	3	18	65	5.33
Def +++	2015	A+	Myrtle Beach	402	65	129	1	30	321	389	388	777	10	89	1.02	12	5	17	67	5.37

Has done nothing but hit as a pro. Uses a compact stroke to shoot line-drives to all fields and has some of the best bat control in the minors. Won the CAR batting title and career slash line is now .321/.390/.392. Is a jack of all trades on defense and played 2B, SS, 3B, LF, 1B, RF, and DH. Below avg speed and almost no power limit his potential.

Yrizarri,Yeyson — 6 — Texas

EXP MLB DEBUT: 2019 | H/W: 6-0 175 | FUT: Starting SS | 7C

Bats R Age 19	Year	Lev	Team	AB	R	H	HR	RBI	Avg	OB	Slg	OPS	bb%	ct%	Eye	SB	CS	x/h%	Iso	RC/G
2013 FA (VZ)																				
Pwr ++	2014	Rk	DSL Rangers	43	7	13	0	6	302	348	419	766	7	91	0.75	1	1	31	116	5.13
BAvg ++	2014	Rk	Azl Rangers	190	23	45	1	19	237	271	332	603	5	81	0.25	5	3	33	95	2.87
Spd +++	2015	A-	Spokane	245	27	65	2	29	265	283	339	622	2	81	0.13	8	6	20	73	2.90
Def +++	2015	AAA	Round Rock	33	2	9	0	4	273	294	364	658	3	85	0.20	0	1	22	91	3.52

Lean, quick INF whose glove is ahead of bat at this stage. Incredible arm strength is best tool and could slide over to 3B if offense develops. Projects to average power due to quick, short stroke and makes acceptable contact. Rarely draws walks which mutes average speed on base. Struggles with spin.

Zagunis,Mark — 9 — Chicago (N)

EXP MLB DEBUT: 2017 | H/W: 6-0 205 | FUT: Starting RF | 7B

Bats R Age 23	Year	Lev	Team	AB	R	H	HR	RBI	Avg	OB	Slg	OPS	bb%	ct%	Eye	SB	CS	x/h%	Iso	RC/G
2014 (3) Virginia Tech	2014	NCAA	Virginia Tech	209	44	69	2	39	330	419	426	845	13	90	1.60	16	3	20	96	6.37
Pwr ++	2014	Rk	Azl Cubs	8	1	1	0	1	125	222	250	472	11	75	0.50	0	0	100	125	1.45
BAvg +++	2014	A-	Boise	154	32	46	2	27	299	416	422	838	17	80	1.00	11	2	28	123	6.47
Spd +++	2014	A	Kane County	50	11	14	0	4	280	400	440	840	17	82	1.11	5	0	50	160	6.64
Def +++	2015	A+	Myrtle Beach	413	78	112	8	54	271	389	412	801	16	79	0.93	12	10	33	140	5.92

Moved from behind the plate to OF and continued to rake. Mature approach at the plate. Compact line-drive stroke and good plate discipline give him the tools to hit for BA. Should develop average power, but won't be a masher. Walked almost as often as he struck out and now has a career .411 OB%.

Zangari,Corey — 3 — Chicago (A)

EXP MLB DEBUT: 2019 | H/W: 6-4 240 | FUT: Starting 1B | 9E

Bats R Age 18	Year	Lev	Team	AB	R	H	HR	RBI	Avg	OB	Slg	OPS	bb%	ct%	Eye	SB	CS	x/h%	Iso	RC/G
2015 (6) HS (OK)																				
Pwr ++++																				
BAvg ++																				
Spd +	2015	Rk	Azl White Sox	195	29	63	6	40	323	359	492	852	5	75	0.22	1	0	32	169	5.97
Def +	2015	Rk	Great Falls	17	0	4	0	1	235	350	353	703	15	82	1.00	0	0	50	118	4.78

Gargantuan slugger who will rack up Ks, but has bat speed and power to project to well above average pop. Leveraged stroke can be exploited, but can drive ball to all fields. Secondary skills are very limited and will need to gain reps at 1B, which is a new position. Plus arm is best tool outside of power. Lacks quickness and speed.

Zimmer,Bradley — 89 — Cleveland

EXP MLB DEBUT: 2016 | H/W: 6-4 185 | FUT: Starting OF | 8A

Bats L Age 23	Year	Lev	Team	AB	R	H	HR	RBI	Avg	OB	Slg	OPS	bb%	ct%	Eye	SB	CS	x/h%	Iso	RC/G
2014 (1) San Francisco	2014	NCAA	San Francisco	220	42	81	7	31	368	446	573	1019	12	85	0.91	21	11	30	205	8.30
Pwr +++	2014	A-	Mahoning Val	168	32	51	4	30	304	374	464	839	10	82	0.63	11	4	33	161	6.01
BAvg +++	2014	A	Lake County	11	4	3	2	2	273	385	909	1294	15	73	0.67	1	0	100	636	11.97
Spd +++	2015	A+	Lynchburg	285	59	87	10	38	305	385	488	873	11	73	0.48	32	5	33	182	6.66
Def +++	2015	AA	Akron	187	24	41	6	24	219	288	374	662	9	71	0.33	12	2	39	155	3.63

All-around prospect who showcased all five tools in stellar season. Gets on base due to mature approach and smooth swing that results in both BA and power. Not a blazer, but runs well underway and is smart on base. Has lanky frame that could add strength. Can play CF, but may move to corner if he slows down.

Pitchers are classified as Starters (SP) or Relievers (RP).

THROWS: Handedness — right (RH) or left (LH).

AGE: Pitcher's age, as of April 1, 2016.

DRAFTED: The year, round, and school that the pitcher performed at as an amateur if drafted, or the year and country where the player was signed from, if a free agent.

EXP MLB DEBUT: The year a player is expected to debut in the major leagues.

H/W: The player's height and weight.

FUT: The role that the pitcher is expected to have for the majority of his major league career, not necessarily his greatest upside.

PITCHES: Each pitch that a pitcher throws is graded and designated with a "+", indicating the quality of the pitch, taking into context the pitcher's age and level pitched. Pitches are graded for their velocity, movement, and command. An average pitch will receive three "+" marks. If known, a pitcher's velocity for each pitch is indicated.

FB	fastball
CB	curveball
SP	split-fingered fastball
SL	slider
CU	change-up
CT	cut-fastball
KC	knuckle-curve
KB	knuckle-ball
SC	screwball
SU	slurve

PLAYER STAT LINES: Pitchers receive statistics for the last five teams that they played for (if applicable), including college and the major leagues.

TEAM DESIGNATIONS: Each team that the pitcher performed for during a given year is included.

LEVEL DESIGNATIONS: The level for each team a player performed is included. "AAA" means Triple-A, "AA" means Double-A, "A+" means high Class-A, "A-" means low Class-A and "Rk" means rookie level.

SABERMETRIC CATEGORIES: Descriptions of all the sabermetric categories appear in the glossary.

CAPSULE COMMENTARIES: For each pitcher, a brief analysis of their skills/statistics, and their future potential is provided.

ELIGIBILITY: Eligibility for inclusion is the standard for which Major League Baseball adheres to; 50 innings pitched or 45 days on the 25-man roster, not including the month of September.

POTENTIAL RATINGS: The Potential Ratings are a two-part system in which a player is assigned a number rating based on his upside potential (1-10) and a letter rating based on the probability of reaching that potential (A-E).

Potential

10:	Hall of Famer	5:	MLB reserve
9:	Elite player	4:	Top minor leaguer
8:	Solid regular	3:	Average minor leaguer
7:	Average regular	2:	Minor league reserve
6:	Platoon player	1:	Minor league roster filler

Probability Rating

A:	90% probability of reaching potential
B:	70% probability of reaching potential
C:	50% probability of reaching potential
D:	30% probability of reaching potential
E:	10% probability of reaching potential

FASTBALL: Scouts grade a fastball in terms of both velocity and movement. Movement of a pitch is purely subjective, but one can always watch the hitter to see how he reacts to a pitch or if he swings and misses. Pitchers throw four types of fastballs with varying movement. A two-seam fastball is often referred to as a sinker. A four-seam fastball appears to maintain its plane at high velocities. A cutter can move in different directions and is caused by the pitcher both cutting-off his extension out front and by varying the grip. A split-fingered fastball (forkball) is thrown with the fingers spread apart against the seams and demonstrates violent downward movement. Velocity is often graded on the 20-80 scale and is indicated by the chart below.

Scout Grade	Velocity (mph)
80	96+
70	94-95
60	92-93
50 (avg)	89-91
40	87-88
30	85-86
20	82-84

PITCHER RELEASE TIMES: The speed (in seconds) that a pitcher releases a pitch from the stretch is extremely important in terms of halting the running game and establishing good pitching mechanics. Pitchers are timed from the movement of the front leg until the baseball reaches the catcher's mitt. The phrases "slow to the plate" or "quick to the plate" may appear in the capsule commentary box.

1.0-1.2	+
1.3-1.4	MLB average
1.5+	−

Abreu,Albert

SP | Houston | EXP MLB DEBUT: 2019 | H/W: 6-2 175 | FUT: #3 starter | 8E

Thrws R Age 20
2013 FA (DR)

92-96	FB	++++
74-77	CB	+++
82-85	SL	+
82-86	CU	++

Year	Lev	Team	W	L	Sv	IP	K	ERA	WHIP	BF/G	OBA	H%	S%	xERA	Ctl	Dom	Cmd	hr/9	BPV
2015	Rk	Greeneville	2	3	1	46	51	2.53	1.21	14.3	212	29	80	2.56	4.1	9.9	2.4	0.4	86

Athletic pitcher who split time between SP and RP in first season in US. Was better as RP as he touches high 90s with FB. Clean arm action produces easy velocity, but lacks stamina to pitch deep into games. Control is erratic from outing to outing and will need to change speeds to stick as SP. When on, is tough to make hard contact against.

Acevedo,Domingo

SP | New York (A) | EXP MLB DEBUT: 2017 | H/W: 6-7 225 | FUT: #2 starter | 9D

Thrws R Age 21
2012 FA (DR)

94-99	FB	+++++
82-85	SL	++
85-87	CU	+++

Year	Lev	Team	W	L	Sv	IP	K	ERA	WHIP	BF/G	OBA	H%	S%	xERA	Ctl	Dom	Cmd	hr/9	BPV
2013	Rk	DSL Yankees	1	2	0	41	43	2.63	1.29	15.3	266	37	77	3.11	2.4	9.4	3.9	0.0	123
2014	Rk	GCL Yankees 2	0	1	0	15	21	4.17	1.46	12.9	273	43	68	3.59	3.6	12.5	3.5	0.0	147
2015	A-	Staten Island	3	0	0	48	53	1.69	1.08	17.0	215	30	86	2.26	2.8	9.9	3.5	0.4	121
2015	A	Charleston (Sc)	0	0	0	1	1	7.50	2.50	6.4	371	46	67	7.88	7.5	7.5	1.0	0.0	-50

Very tall SP who can reach triple digits with double-plus FB. Can be guilty of overthrowing which impacts FB command, but is very tough to hit. Gets groundballs and Ks with FB and improving SL, though development of firm CU has been key. Needs to repeat delivery more consistently for better pitch location.

Adam,Jason

SP | Minnesota | EXP MLB DEBUT: 2017 | H/W: 6-4 225 | FUT: #4 starter | 7D

Thrws R Age 24
2010 (5) HS (KS)

88-95	FB	+++
80-82	SL	+++
82-85	CU	++

Year	Lev	Team	W	L	Sv	IP	K	ERA	WHIP	BF/G	OBA	H%	S%	xERA	Ctl	Dom	Cmd	hr/9	BPV
2012	A+	Wilmington	7	12	0	158		3.53	1.16	23.3	249	29	73	3.55	2.1	7.0	3.4	1.0	89
2013	AA	NW Arkansas	8	11	0	144	126	5.19	1.44	23.6	274	33	64	4.30	3.4	7.9	2.3	0.8	69
2014	AA	New Britain	0	0	0	7	3	5.14	1.71	15.9	336	37	67	5.30	2.6	3.9	1.5	0.0	18
2014	AA	NW Arkansas	4	8	0	98	89	5.05	1.40	21.8	279	34	64	4.34	2.8	8.2	3.0	0.8	91
2014	AAA	Omaha	1	1	0	15	11	2.38	1.39	7.9	285	35	81	3.66	2.4	6.6	2.8	0.0	72

Big-framed pitcher who did not pitch in '15 after surgery to clean up stress fracture in elbow. Has big FB and average SL to be potent, but can't seem to develop effective CU. Slows arm speed and has been hit hard by LHH. K rate low despite velocity and break on SL, but doesn't beat himself by walking hitters.

Adams,Chance

RP | New York (A) | EXP MLB DEBUT: 2017 | H/W: 6-0 215 | FUT: Setup reliever | 7C

Thrws R Age 21
2015 (5) Dallas Baptist

92-96	FB	++++
81-83	SL	+++
	CU	+

Year	Lev	Team	W	L	Sv	IP	K	ERA	WHIP	BF/G	OBA	H%	S%	xERA	Ctl	Dom	Cmd	hr/9	BPV
2015	NCAA	Dallas Baptist	7	1	2	59	83	1.98	0.92	9.6	198	31	80	1.69	2.0	12.7	6.4	0.5	192
2015	A-	Staten Island	1	0	0	9	13	0.98	0.87	8.5	162	28	88	0.74	2.9	12.7	4.3	0.0	168
2015	A	Charleston (Sc)	1	1	0	11	16	3.21	0.98	8.5	181	31	64	1.24	3.2	12.9	4.0	0.0	163
2015	A+	Tampa	1	0	0	14	16	1.29	1.00	10.7	233	34	86	1.92	1.3	10.3	8.0	0.0	168

Short, powerful RP who has chance to get to majors quickly with dynamic FB/SL duo. Racks up ton of Ks with both pitches and FB is difficult for hitters to get into air. Commands FB and SL well despite max effort delivery. Throws consistent strikes and won't beat himself, though doesn't have legitimate weapon to combat LHH.

Adams,Spencer

SP | Chicago (A) | EXP MLB DEBUT: 2018 | H/W: 6-3 171 | FUT: #3 starter | 8C

Thrws R Age 19
2014 (2) HS (GA)

89-94	FB	+++
80-83	SL	+++
82-84	CU	+++

Year	Lev	Team	W	L	Sv	IP	K	ERA	WHIP	BF/G	OBA	H%	S%	xERA	Ctl	Dom	Cmd	hr/9	BPV
2014	Rk	Azl White Sox	3	3	0	41	59	3.71	1.29	16.9	297	44	73	4.32	0.9	12.9	14.8	0.9	226
2015	A	Kannapolis	9	5	0	100	73	3.24	1.22	21.3	282	33	75	3.78	1.0	6.6	6.6	0.6	110
2015	A+	Winston-Salem	3	0	0	29	23	2.16	1.31	24.0	274	34	84	3.57	2.2	7.1	3.3	0.3	88

Projectable SP with solid pitch mix, but velocity wavered and was very hittable. Locates pitches impeccably to all quadrants and can change speeds well. FB has late life and sink while SL is swing-and-miss pitch. Can slow arm on CU, but has good feel for art of pitching. Has upside, but needs to regain velocity to reach his ceiling.

Agosta,Martin

SP | San Francisco | EXP MLB DEBUT: 2017 | H/W: 6-1 180 | FUT: #4 starter | 7C

Thrws R Age 25
2012 (2) St. Mary's

89-92	FB	+++
78-80	SL	+++
80-83	CU	+++

Year	Lev	Team	W	L	Sv	IP	K	ERA	WHIP	BF/G	OBA	H%	S%	xERA	Ctl	Dom	Cmd	hr/9	BPV
2012	Rk	Azl Giants	0	0	0	10	19	4.41	1.67	9.2	218	45	71	3.34	7.9	16.8	2.1	0.0	105
2013	A	Augusta	9	3	0	91	109	2.07	1.10	19.8	181	26	82	1.92	4.2	10.8	2.5	0.4	97
2014	Rk	Azl Giants	1	0	0	14	19	4.50	1.29	14.4	288	44	61	3.38	1.3	12.2	9.5	0.0	203
2014	A+	San Jose	3	3	0	39	25	9.23	2.18	17.7	317	35	56	7.22	7.8	5.8	0.7	1.2	-90
2015	A+	San Jose	5	9	0	106	125	4.25	1.29	16.8	271	36	71	4.36	2.2	10.6	4.8	1.3	149

Former 2nd-round pick who led the CAL in Dom. Employs a sinking FB that operates at 89-92 mph, SL with average late break and decent CU. Has made command strides as an SP, which will help him stay in the rotation as a #4 in best-case scenario. Lacks a plus pitch and doesn't miss many bats, so expect his Dom to fade a bit at the next level.

Aiken,Brady

SP | Cleveland | EXP MLB DEBUT: 2019 | H/W: 6-4 205 | FUT: #1 starter | 9D

Thrws L Age 19
2015 (1) IMG Academy

91-97	FB	++++
77-80	CB	++++
	CU	+++

Year	Lev	Team	W	L	Sv	IP	K	ERA	WHIP	BF/G	OBA	H%	S%	xERA	Ctl	Dom	Cmd	hr/9	BPV
2015		*Did not pitch; injured*																	

Long and athletic SP was #1 overall pick in '14, but didn't sign and then underwent TJ surgery in March '15. When healthy, has dazzling pitch mix that could front rotation. Throws hard, but has ability to change speeds. Clean delivery and quick arm give potential to add to good command. Can use CB to throw for strikes or get hitters to chase.

Alcantara,Raul

SP | Oakland | EXP MLB DEBUT: 2017 | H/W: 6-3 205 | FUT: #4 starter | 7C

Thrws R Age 23
2009 FA (DR)

90-94	FB	+++
80-84	SL	++
77-80	CB	++
80-83	CU	+++

Year	Lev	Team	W	L	Sv	IP	K	ERA	WHIP	BF/G	OBA	H%	S%	xERA	Ctl	Dom	Cmd	hr/9	BPV
2012	A	Burlington	6	11	0	102	57	5.11	1.54	16.5	292	32	68	5.14	3.3	5.0	1.5	1.1	18
2013	A	Beloit	7	1	0	77	58	2.45	1.18	23.7	279	34	80	3.36	0.8	6.8	8.3	0.4	118
2013	A+	Stockton	5	5	0	79	66	3.76	1.14	22.3	247	29	70	3.34	1.9	7.5	3.9	0.9	101
2014	AA	Midland	2	0	0	19	10	2.34	1.15	25.4	239	28	77	2.42	2.3	4.7	2.0	0.0	39
2015	A+	Stockton	0	2	0	48	29	3.92	1.29	13.2	284	32	69	3.92	1.5	5.4	3.6	0.6	75

Tall SP who returned in June after TJ surgery. Performed at High-A and was on strict pitch count. Uses smooth, repeatable delivery and generates velocity with ideal arm speed. Throws strikes, though can live in fat part of plate. CU has fading action and is nice weapon against LHH. K rate is disappointing, but could improve.

Alcantara,Sandy

SP | St. Louis | EXP MLB DEBUT: 2020 | H/W: 6-4 170 | FUT: #2 starter | 9D

Thrws R Age 20
2013 FA (DR)

94-98	FB	+++++
	CB	++
	CU	++

Year	Lev	Team	W	L	Sv	IP	K	ERA	WHIP	BF/G	OBA	H%	S%	xERA	Ctl	Dom	Cmd	hr/9	BPV
2015	Rk	GCL Cardinals	4	4	0	64	51	3.23	1.23	21.6	246	30	74	3.10	2.8	7.2	2.6	0.4	71

Added size and strength and now owns a plus 94-98 mph FB that tops out at 102 mph. Mixes in a CU that is raw but shows potential and has some feel for a CB. Made his U.S. debut and more than held his own in the GCL. Lots of projection left.

Alcantara,Victor

SP | Los Angeles (A) | EXP MLB DEBUT: 2017 | H/W: 6-2 190 | FUT: #3 SP / Setup RP | 8E

Thrws R Age 23
2011 FA (DR)

93-96	FB	+++
84-88	SL	+++
84-87	CU	+++

Year	Lev	Team	W	L	Sv	IP	K	ERA	WHIP	BF/G	OBA	H%	S%	xERA	Ctl	Dom	Cmd	hr/9	BPV
2013	Rk	Orem	2	5	0	59	48	7.47	1.83	16.1	305	35	60	6.49	5.3	7.3	1.4	1.5	6
2014	A	Burlington	7	6	1	125	117	3.81	1.26	18.9	217	28	69	2.81	4.3	8.4	2.0	0.4	53
2015	A+	Inland Empire	7	12	0	136	125	5.63	1.54	22.0	284	35	63	4.63	3.8	8.3	2.2	0.7	63

Durable arm who struggled after April, but has pitch mix and arm strength to be potent prospect. Registers groundballs and Ks with electric FB featuring velocity and plus sink. Has difficulty commanding FB, but should get better as he finds consistent release point. Hard SL tough to control, but serves as another K pitch. Has tendency to aim ball.

Alexander,Tyler

SP | Detroit | EXP MLB DEBUT: 2017 | H/W: 6-2 200 | FUT: #4 starter | 7C

Thrws L Age 21
2015 (2) Texas Christian

88-91	FB	+++
77-80	SL	+++
81-82	CU	++

Year	Lev	Team	W	L	Sv	IP	K	ERA	WHIP	BF/G	OBA	H%	S%	xERA	Ctl	Dom	Cmd	hr/9	BPV
2015	NCAA	Texas Christian	6	3	0	93	72	3.09	1.09	21.5	259	31	74	3.17	1.0	7.0	7.2	0.7	117
2015	A-	Connecticut	0	2	0	37	33	0.97	0.59	10.5	140	16	95	0.55	1.2	8.0	6.6	0.7	130

Durable SP who had one of the best pro debuts after draft. Exhibits pinpoint command of three offerings and showcases feel for changing speeds and sequencing. Works both sides of plate and keeps ball down. K rate will likely fall as he advances, so key will be to induce weak contact and limit walks.

Allard,Kolby — SP — Atlanta

EXP MLB DEBUT: 2019 | H/W: 6-1 180 | FUT: #1 starter | **10D**

Thrws L Age 18 — 2015 (1) HS (CA)

Velo	Pitch	Grade
92-94	FB	++++
79-80	CB	++++
	CU	++

Year	Lev	Team	W	L	Sv	IP	K	ERA	WHIP	BF/G	OBA	H%	S%	xERA	Ctl	Dom	Cmd	hr/9	BPV
2015	Rk	GCL Braves	0	0	0	6	12	0.00	0.17	6.0	56	17	100		0.0	18.0		0.0	342

Dubbed by some the best pitcher in the '15 draft, the tall, lean LH fell to ATL at #14 due to a stress reaction in his back. Underwent off-season surgery. Features 3 potential plus pitches. His best pitch is a 12-6 CB with two-plane break. FB plays faster than radar gun velocity. Has a feel for a deceptive, sinking CU.

Allen,Logan — SP — San Diego

EXP MLB DEBUT: 2019 | H/W: 6-3 200 | FUT: #3 starter | **8E**

Thrws L Age 18 — 2015 (8) HS (FL)

Velo	Pitch	Grade
88-94	FB	+++
77-79	CB	+++
79-81	SL	++
	CU	++

Year	Lev	Team	W	L	Sv	IP	K	ERA	WHIP	BF/G	OBA	H%	S%	xERA	Ctl	Dom	Cmd	hr/9	BPV
2015	Rk	GCL Red Sox	0	0	0	20	24	0.90	0.65	9.9	175	27	85	0.35	0.5	10.8	24.0	0.0	200
2015	A-	Lowell	0	0	0	4	2	2.20	1.46	17.6	342	39	83	4.76	0.0	4.4		0.0	97

Tall, durable pitcher with impressive pitch mix for age. Tough on LHH with big-breaking CB that exhibits power and FB that could add more velocity as he cleans up mechanics. Has advanced control and command at present, but lacks true out pitch. Needs to repeat arm speed on CU to make it weapon against RHH.

Almonte,Miguel — SP — Kansas City

EXP MLB DEBUT: 2015 | H/W: 6-2 180 | FUT: #3 starter / Closer | **8C**

Thrws R Age 23 — 2010 FA (DR)

Velo	Pitch	Grade
91-96	FB	++++
76-79	CB	++
83-87	CU	++++

Year	Lev	Team	W	L	Sv	IP	K	ERA	WHIP	BF/G	OBA	H%	S%	xERA	Ctl	Dom	Cmd	hr/9	BPV
2013	A	Lexington	6	9	0	130		3.11	1.16	20.7	239	32	73	2.80	2.5	9.1	3.7	0.4	115
2014	A+	Wilmington	6	8	0	110	101	4.50	1.26	19.5	256	32	65	3.60	2.6	8.3	3.2	0.7	96
2015	AA	NW Arkansas	4	4	0	67	55	4.03	1.37	16.5	256	31	70	3.70	3.6	7.4	2.0	0.5	53
2015	AAA	Omaha	2	2	0	36	41	5.47	1.33	13.6	244	33	58	3.59	3.7	10.2	2.7	0.7	101
2015	MLB	KC Royals	0	2	0	8	10	6.59	1.71	4.1	232	19	80	7.82	7.7	11.0	1.4	4.4	8

Power-armed hurler who moved to pen in AAA in prep for big league callup. Owns excellent FB/CU combo while erratic, slurvy CB keeps him from reaching vast potential. Posted higher K rate as RP, but has too good of an arm to convert full-time. Needs to sequence better and throw more strikes, but pure stuff is too good to ignore.

Almonte,Yency — SP — Colorado

EXP MLB DEBUT: 2017 | H/W: 6-3 205 | FUT: #3 starter | **8D**

Thrws R Age 21 — 2012 (17) HS (FL)

Velo	Pitch	Grade
90-95	FB	+++
80-82	SL	+++
	CU	++

Year	Lev	Team	W	L	Sv	IP	K	ERA	WHIP	BF/G	OBA	H%	S%	xERA	Ctl	Dom	Cmd	hr/9	BPV
2013	Rk	Orem	3	3	0	53	35	6.95	1.64	18.2	306	35	56	5.40	3.6	5.9	1.7	0.8	29
2014	Rk	Azl Angels	0	1	0	3	5	19.69	2.50	8.5	437	63	13	9.20	2.8	14.1	5.0	0.0	195
2014	A	Burlington	2	5	0	42	32	4.93	1.29	19.2	252	29	63	3.94	3.0	6.9	2.3	1.1	60
2015	A	Kannapolis	8	4	0	92	71	3.90	1.28	22.2	261	31	71	3.77	2.5	6.9	2.7	0.8	74
2015	A+	Winston-Salem	3	3	0	44	39	2.44	0.90	23.5	183	24	72	1.30	2.4	7.9	3.3	0.2	95

Sleeper prospect who had breakout campaign. Threw FB with conviction early in count which allowed his hard SL to play up. Repeats delivery well and owns clean arm action to add late movement. Will need to enhance CU which can be telegraphed with slower arm speed. Could be intriguing RP if CU doesn't improve.

Altavilla,Dan — SP — Seattle

EXP MLB DEBUT: 2017 | H/W: 5-11 200 | FUT: #4 SP / Setup RP | **7D**

Thrws R Age 23 — 2014 (5) Mercyhurst

Velo	Pitch	Grade
90-94	FB	+++
82-84	SL	+++
81-82	CU	++

Year	Lev	Team	W	L	Sv	IP	K	ERA	WHIP	BF/G	OBA	H%	S%	xERA	Ctl	Dom	Cmd	hr/9	BPV
2014	A-	Everett	5	3	0	66	66	4.36	1.61	20.9	284	36	75	5.06	4.4	9.0	2.1	1.0	62
2015	A+	Bakersfield	6	12	0	148	134	4.07	1.29	21.7	248	31	69	3.50	3.2	8.1	2.5	0.7	78

Short, durable, and consistent SP with solid stuff, but likely to end up in pen due to max effort delivery. Has trouble with below average CU that can be too firm. FB features late action and hard SL can miss bats. Flyball tendencies may harm him eventually and lack of height doesn't help.

Alvarez,Dario — RP — New York (N)

EXP MLB DEBUT: 2014 | H/W: 6-1 170 | FUT: Setup reliever | **6B**

Thrws L Age 27 — 2007 FA (DR)

Velo	Pitch	Grade
89-92	FB	++
78-82	SL	+++
86-87	CT	+

Year	Lev	Team	W	L	Sv	IP	K	ERA	WHIP	BF/G	OBA	H%	S%	xERA	Ctl	Dom	Cmd	hr/9	BPV
2014	AA	Binghamton	1	0	1	5	9	0.00	0.77	3.7	214	41	100	1.06	0.0	15.6		0.0	298
2014	MLB	NY Mets	0	0	0	1	1	16.36	3.64	1.8	563	59	67	23.66	0.0	8.2		8.2	165
2015	AA	Binghamton	1	1	0	31	43	3.19	1.19	3.9	194	30	74	2.46	4.6	12.5	2.7	0.6	117
2015	AAA	Las Vegas	2	1	0	11	19	2.45	1.00	2.6	162	33	73	1.04	4.1	15.5	3.8	0.0	187
2015	MLB	NY Mets	1	0	0	3	2	14.06	1.88	2.5	357	30	25	11.33	2.8	5.6	2.0	5.6	43

Late blooming, side-armed RP has enjoyed cups of coffee with the big league club. SL flashes plus but lacks consistency to get MLB hitters out. FB has sinking action but struggles generating swings and misses. Struggles against RH hitters with no out pitch. Introduced cutter to arsenal in 2015 to combat RHs with mixed results.

Alvarez,R.J. — RP — Oakland

EXP MLB DEBUT: 2014 | H/W: 6-2 215 | FUT: Setup reliever | **7C**

Thrws R Age 24 — 2012 (3) Florida Atlantic

Velo	Pitch	Grade
93-97	FB	++++
83-86	SL	+++
	CU	+

Year	Lev	Team	W	L	Sv	IP	K	ERA	WHIP	BF/G	OBA	H%	S%	xERA	Ctl	Dom	Cmd	hr/9	BPV
2014	AA	Arkansas	0	0	1	27	38	0.33	0.85	4.7	146	25	96	0.53	3.3	12.7	3.8	0.0	156
2014	AA	San Antonio	0	1	6	16	23	2.80	1.18	3.8	261	42	74	2.71	1.7	12.9	7.7	0.0	204
2014	MLB	San Diego	0	0	0	8	9	1.13	1.00	3.1	117	18	88	0.64	5.6	10.1	1.8	0.0	48
2015	AAA	Nashville	3	3	5	35	41	4.11	1.51	4.9	267	37	73	4.15	4.4	10.5	2.4	0.5	90
2015	MLB	Oakland	0	0	0	20	23	9.90	2.00	4.6	324	37	55	8.71	5.9	10.4	1.8	3.2	46

Hard-throwing RP who uses max-effort delivery to blow FB by hitters. Tough delivery to repeat and struggles to throw strikes. Has stuff to pitch in late innings and can dominate RHH. K rate remains high as he uses FB and hard SL to advantage. Rarely changes speeds and will need to have FB command to retire quality big league hitters.

Alvarez,Yadier — SP — Los Angeles (N)

EXP MLB DEBUT: 2020 | H/W: 6-3 175 | FUT: #2 starter | **9D**

Thrws R Age 20 — 2015 FA (CU)

Velo	Pitch	Grade
92-97	FB	++++
	SL	+++
	CU	++

Year	Lev	Team	W	L	Sv	IP	K	ERA	WHIP	BF/G	OBA	H%	S%	xERA	Ctl	Dom	Cmd	hr/9	BPV
2015		*Did not pitch in U.S.*																	

Long, lean, projectable Cuban hurler was given $16 million bonus. Widely regarded as the best international FA. Flashed a plus 92-97 mph FB during workouts and mixes in a potentially plus SL and has the makings of a decent CU. Mechanics are solid, but needs to work on developing a consistent release point and command is a significant issue.

Anderson,Chris — SP — Los Angeles (N)

EXP MLB DEBUT: 2016 | H/W: 6-3 235 | FUT: #3 starter | **7D**

Thrws R Age 23 — 2013 (1) Jacksonville

Velo	Pitch	Grade
92-94	FB	++++
82-85	SL	+++
80-83	CB	+++

Year	Lev	Team	W	L	Sv	IP	K	ERA	WHIP	BF/G	OBA	H%	S%	xERA	Ctl	Dom	Cmd	hr/9	BPV
2013	NCAA	Jacksonville	7	5	0	104	101	2.50	1.12	29.3	234	31	79	2.67	2.3	8.7	3.7	0.4	112
2013	A	Great Lakes	3	0	0	46	50	1.96	1.22	15.5	198	29	82	2.05	4.7	9.8	2.1	0.0	67
2014	A+	RanchoCuca	7	7	0	134	146	4.63	1.57	21.8	280	37	71	4.68	4.2	9.8	2.3	0.7	80
2015	AA	Tulsa	9	7	0	126	98	4.06	1.44	23.4	257	30	74	4.19	4.2	7.0	1.7	0.9	30
2015	AAA	Oklahoma City	0	3	0	6	2	19.18	3.77	13.4	449	44	48	15.57	13.3	3.0	0.2	3.0	-287

Big, durable hurler gets good downhill tilt. Pounds the strike zone with a solid three-pitch mix. Best offering is an above-average 92-94 mph FB that tops out at 98 mph. Mixes in a quality SL with an average CU. Control continues to be an issue and he walked 68 in 133 IP and saw his Dom drop from 9.8 to 6.8.

Appel,Mark — SP — Philadelphia

EXP MLB DEBUT: 2016 | H/W: 6-5 220 | FUT: #2 starter | **9D**

Thrws R Age 24 — 2013 (1) Stanford

Velo	Pitch	Grade
92-98	FB	+++
83-87	SL	+++
80-83	CU	+++

Year	Lev	Team	W	L	Sv	IP	K	ERA	WHIP	BF/G	OBA	H%	S%	xERA	Ctl	Dom	Cmd	hr/9	BPV
2013	A	Quad Cities	3	1	0	33	27	3.82	1.18	16.5	244	30	68	3.06	2.5	7.4	3.0	0.5	84
2014	A+	Lancaster	2	5	0	44	40	9.80	1.93	17.4	373	44	49	8.19	2.2	8.2	3.6	1.8	104
2014	AA	Corpus Christi	1	2	0	39	38	3.69	1.23	22.6	241	31	70	3.06	3.0	8.8	2.9	0.5	95
2015	AA	Corpus Christi	5	1	0	63	49	4.28	1.44	20.7	276	32	73	4.59	3.3	7.0	2.1	1.0	55
2015	AAA	Fresno	5	2	0	68	61	4.49	1.40	23.9	259	32	69	4.02	3.7	8.1	2.2	0.8	63

Tall, durable SP with raw ingredients and power to be top of rotation guy. Has yet to find consistency in arsenal despite three average to plus pitches. Uses height to pitch downhill and keep ball on ground. Uses FB and power SL to register Ks. CU shows flashes, but can telegraph pitch by slowing arm. Still has upside.

Araujo,Pedro — RP — Chicago (N)

EXP MLB DEBUT: 2018 | H/W: 6-3 214 | FUT: Setup reliever | **7C**

Thrws R Age 22 — 2011 FA (DR)

Velo	Pitch	Grade
90-93	FB	++++
	CB	++
	CU	++

Year	Lev	Team	W	L	Sv	IP	K	ERA	WHIP	BF/G	OBA	H%	S%	xERA	Ctl	Dom	Cmd	hr/9	BPV
2013	Rk	DSL Cubs	6	0	0	25	31	1.07	0.71	11.1	174	26	88	0.84	1.1	11.1	10.3	0.4	188
2014	Rk	DSL Cubs	2	1	0	20	14	1.35	1.15	19.9	232	29	87	2.32	2.7	6.3	2.3	0.0	59
2014	Rk	Azl Cubs	0	0	1	16	27	2.80	1.24	6.5	209	37	79	2.71	4.5	15.1	3.4	0.6	169
2015	A-	Eugene	0	2	1	50	70	2.69	1.04	9.2	233	37	73	2.17	1.6	12.6	7.8	0.2	201

Tall, strong-bodied reliever signed out of the Dominican Republic for $100,000 in 2011. The 22-year-old has been slow to develop, but had his best season yet. Improved command has been key. Move to relief simplified his arsenal and gives him a chance at the next level.

Armstrong,Shawn — RP — Cleveland

EXP MLB DEBUT: 2015 | H/W: 6-2 225 | FUT: Middle reliever | 6B

Thrws R Age 25
2011 (18) East Carolina
90-94 FB +++
82-85 SL +++
81-83 CU ++

Year	Lev	Team	W	L	Sv	IP	K	ERA	WHIP	BF/G	OBA	H%	S%	xERA	Ctl	Dom	Cmd	hr/9	BPV
2013	AA	Akron	2	3	0	33	43	4.09	1.61	4.9	256	37	75	4.25	5.7	11.7	2.0	0.5	74
2014	AA	Akron	6	2	15	51	68	2.12	1.14	4.6	213	32	84	2.50	3.4	12.0	3.6	0.5	143
2014	AAA	Columbus	0	0	0	5	4	5.40	1.40	4.2	221	23	67	4.50	5.4	7.2	1.3	1.8	2
2015	AAA	Columbus	1	2	16	49	80	2.38	1.28	4.4	211	39	79	2.31	4.8	14.6	3.1	0.0	153
2015	MLB	Cleveland	0	0	0	8	11	2.25	0.88	3.7	181	26	83	2.03	2.3	12.4	5.5	1.1	180

RP has been healthy last two years and served as closer. Posts high K rate and low oppBA based on potent sinker/SL combo. Can cut FB to give movement while SL used as K pitch when ahead in count. Control comes and goes and will need to be cleaned up in order to earn big league role. Has only allowed 7 HR in pro career.

Aro,Jonathan — RP — Seattle

EXP MLB DEBUT: 2015 | H/W: 6-1 175 | FUT: Middle reliever | 6B

Thrws R Age 25
2011 FA (DR)
89-93 FB +++
81-84 SL +++
81-83 CU +

Year	Lev	Team	W	L	Sv	IP	K	ERA	WHIP	BF/G	OBA	H%	S%	xERA	Ctl	Dom	Cmd	hr/9	BPV
2014	A	Greenville	1	3	7	67	74	2.28	1.10	10.5	216	30	80	2.35	3.0	9.9	3.4	0.4	117
2014	A+	Salem	2	0	1	20	24	1.80	0.95	10.8	175	25	83	1.53	3.2	10.8	3.4	0.5	127
2015	AA	Portland	3	2	0	22	19	2.85	1.04	10.7	194	26	70	1.58	3.3	7.7	2.4	0.0	69
2015	AAA	Pawtucket	0	1	2	51	53	3.16	1.04	7.6	229	31	69	2.31	1.8	9.3	5.3	0.4	138
2015	MLB	Boston	0	1	0	10	8	7.13	1.88	7.9	345	39	65	7.52	3.6	7.1	2.0	1.8	50

Short pitcher who made rapid ascent to majors. Keeps ball on ground and doesn't beat himself with walks. Has deceptive delivery and slot that makes FB look sneaky quick. Only possesses average velocity at best, but commands FB well and locates to both sides. Hard SL can miss bats, but doesn't have change-of-pace pitch.

Asher,Alec — SP — Philadelphia

EXP MLB DEBUT: 2015 | H/W: 6-4 215 | FUT: #5 starter | 6A

Thrws R Age 24
2012 (4) Polk County JC
91-93 FB +++
84-86 SL +++
82-84 CU ++
78-81 CB ++

Year	Lev	Team	W	L	Sv	IP	K	ERA	WHIP	BF/G	OBA	H%	S%	xERA	Ctl	Dom	Cmd	hr/9	BPV
2014	AA	Frisco	11	11	0	154		3.80	1.11	21.6	242	28	69	3.34	1.9	7.1	3.8	1.1	96
2015	AA	Frisco	1	4	0	43	43	3.98	1.33	22.3	243	32	70	3.48	3.8	9.0	2.4	0.6	78
2015	AAA	Lehigh Valley	2	0	0	26	12	2.08	1.15	25.8	269	28	89	3.83	1.0	4.2	4.0	1.0	65
2015	AAA	Round Rock	3	6	0	64	54	4.77	1.40	22.6	282	30	76	5.73	2.7	7.6	2.8	2.2	82
2015	MLB	Philadelphia	0	6	0	29	16	9.31	1.79	19.1	339	34	50	7.88	3.1	5.0	1.6	2.5	24

Though has an innings-eater frame, stuff took a minor step back in 2015 and was hit hard in MLB debut. Gets downhill plane on FB, which he can locate, but is also straight and hittable. A previously plus SL lost some depth and other secondaries (CU, CB) couldn't compensate. Generally around the plate, but needs a reliable offspeed out pitch.

Baker,Dylan — SP — Cleveland

EXP MLB DEBUT: 2017 | H/W: 6-2 215 | FUT: #4 SP / Setup RP | 7C

Thrws R Age 24
2012 (5) Wstrn Nevada
90-95 FB +++
83-86 SL +++
78-82 CB ++
80-84 CU ++

Year	Lev	Team	W	L	Sv	IP	K	ERA	WHIP	BF/G	OBA	H%	S%	xERA	Ctl	Dom	Cmd	hr/9	BPV
2012	Rk	AZL Indians	0	1	0	24	30	4.13	1.63	13.3	262	38	74	4.22	5.6	11.3	2.0	0.4	69
2013	A	Lake County	7	6	0	143	117	3.65	1.30	21.8	235	30	70	2.91	3.9	7.4	1.9	0.2	45
2014	Rk	AZL Indians	0	0	0	5	13	1.73	0.58	5.9	120	38	100	1.11	1.7	22.5	13.0	1.7	376
2014	A+	Carolina	3	3	0	46	28	4.09	1.36	21.5	257	29	70	3.75	3.5	5.5	1.6	0.6	22
2015	A+	Lynchburg	1	0	0	5	9	0.00	0.20	15.1	0	0	100		1.8	16.2	9.0	0.0	261

Physical SP who pitched 5 no-hit innings before succumbing to TJ surgery in May. Has the frame and stuff to be either SP or RP. Electric FB is best pitch and mixes in hard SL and CB to keep hitters at bay. CU can be too loose, but can succeed with just FB/SL combo. Has effort in delivery, but doesn't have major command problems.

Ball,Trey — SP — Boston

EXP MLB DEBUT: 2017 | H/W: 6-5 185 | FUT: #3 starter | 8D

Thrws L Age 21
2013 (1) HS (IN)
91-95 FB +++
74-78 CB ++
78-82 CU +++

Year	Lev	Team	W	L	Sv	IP	K	ERA	WHIP	BF/G	OBA	H%	S%	xERA	Ctl	Dom	Cmd	hr/9	BPV
2013	Rk	GCL Red Sox	0	1	0	7	5	6.43	2.29	7.1	336	38	73	7.93	7.7	6.4	0.8	1.3	-75
2014	A	Greenville	5	10	0	100	68	4.68	1.50	19.6	282	32	70	4.66	3.5	6.1	1.7	0.8	33
2015	A+	Salem	9	13	0	129	77	4.74	1.46	22.1	262	28	70	4.57	4.2	5.4	1.3	1.1	2

Raw, lean SP is all about projection. Faltered late in season and performance doesn't match stuff. Uses height to throw downhill which keeps FB low. Repeats athletic delivery, but struggles to command plate. Leaves improving CB up in zone often and can be hit hard. CU may be best pitch and gives him weapon against LHH.

Balog,Alex — SP — Colorado

EXP MLB DEBUT: 2017 | H/W: 6-5 210 | FUT: #4 starter | 7C

Thrws R Age 23
2013 (2) San Francisco
90-93 FB +++
78-80 CB ++
84-86 SL +++
78-80 CU ++

Year	Lev	Team	W	L	Sv	IP	K	ERA	WHIP	BF/G	OBA	H%	S%	xERA	Ctl	Dom	Cmd	hr/9	BPV
2012	NCAA	San Francisco	4	4	0	78	57	3.45	1.19	20.9	219	26	71	2.70	3.6	6.6	1.8	0.5	40
2013	NCAA	San Francisco	3	4	0	91	67	3.65	1.39	27.4	268	31	75	4.06	3.3	6.6	2.0	0.7	49
2013	Rk	Grand Junction	1	4	0	30	17	9.30	1.97	20.5	376	39	54	8.62	2.4	5.1	2.1	2.1	45
2014	A	Asheville	8	5	1	150	114	3.96	1.33	23.0	272	32	71	3.97	2.5	6.8	2.8	0.7	75
2015	A+	Modesto	3	8	0	97	72	3.71	1.15	24.1	254	30	67	3.05	1.8	6.7	3.8	0.5	91

Righty has a nice 4-pitch mix. FB sits at 90-93 mph with sinking action and mixes in a power CB and a hard SL. Low Dom is due to underdeveloped CU that needs to improve. Is not overpowering, but has a good understanding of how to change speeds and keep hitters off-balance. Survived a full season in the CAL, walking just 19 in 97 IP.

Banda,Anthony — SP — Arizona

EXP MLB DEBUT: 2017 | H/W: 6-2 190 | FUT: #4 starter | 7C

Thrws L Age 22
2012 (10) San Jacinto JC
88-91 FB +++
77-79 CB +++
CU ++

Year	Lev	Team	W	L	Sv	IP	K	ERA	WHIP	BF/G	OBA	H%	S%	xERA	Ctl	Dom	Cmd	hr/9	BPV
2012	Rk	Azl Brewers	2	3	0	41	43	5.90	1.89	13.9	317	41	68	6.00	5.2	9.4	1.8	0.7	46
2013	Rk	Helena	3	4	0	60	45	4.49	1.48	18.5	274	31	72	4.69	3.7	6.7	1.8	1.0	38
2014	A	South Bend	3	0	0	35	34	1.54	1.11	23.0	245	32	89	2.86	1.8	8.7	4.9	0.5	127
2014	A	Wisconsin	6	6	2	83	83	3.68	1.47	17.8	264	35	75	3.92	4.1	9.0	2.2	0.4	69
2015	A+	Visalia	8	8	0	151	152	3.33	1.25	22.0	260	34	73	3.37	2.3	9.0	3.9	0.5	118

LH starter showed consistency for 1st time in pro career. Gained confidence after '14 trade to ARI. Touches 94 with FB but works 88-91. Throws a hard 12-6 CB. Changes eye levels to keep hitters off-balance. Feel for CU is improving as he moves through pro ball.

Banuelos,Manny — SP — Atlanta

EXP MLB DEBUT: 2015 | H/W: 5-10 205 | FUT: #3 starter | 7B

Thrws L Age 25
2008 FA (MX)
88-92 FB +++
78-80 CU ++++
73-75 CB +++
80-83 SL ++

Year	Lev	Team	W	L	Sv	IP	K	ERA	WHIP	BF/G	OBA	H%	S%	xERA	Ctl	Dom	Cmd	hr/9	BPV
2014	AA	Trenton	1	3	0	49	44	4.59	1.20	11.6	224	25	67	3.73	3.5	8.1	2.3	1.5	69
2014	AAA	Scranton/WB	1	0	0	15	13	3.60	1.60	16.6	249	29	82	4.79	6.0	7.8	1.3	1.2	-4
2015	Rk	GCL Braves	0	0	0	2	3	0.00	2.00	9.6	262	43	100	4.79	9.0	13.5	1.5	0.0	18
2015	AAA	Gwinnett	6	2	0	84	69	2.24	1.24	21.3	212	27	81	2.49	4.3	7.4	1.7	0.2	35
2015	MLB	Atlanta	1	4	0	26	19	5.17	1.61	16.5	290	32	71	5.57	4.1	6.6	1.6	1.4	24

Made MLB debut in '15; struggled to stay healthy with additional arm issues. FB velocity returned to pre-TJS levels but command is lacking. Missed up in the zone and was beat by MLB hitters. Best pitch is a plus CU with solid deception, drop & speed differential off the FB. Could ditch loopy SL and still be an effective SP.

Barbato,Johnny — RP — New York (A)

EXP MLB DEBUT: 2016 | H/W: 6-2 230 | FUT: Setup reliever | 7D

Thrws R Age 23
2010 (6) HS (FL)
92-96 FB +++
76-79 CB +++
81-82 CU +

Year	Lev	Team	W	L	Sv	IP	K	ERA	WHIP	BF/G	OBA	H%	S%	xERA	Ctl	Dom	Cmd	hr/9	BPV
2012	A	Fort Wayne	6	1	3	73	84	1.85	1.14	6.0	201	28	86	2.34	3.8	10.3	2.7	0.5	101
2013	A+	Lake Elsinore	3	6	14	88	89	5.01	1.40	7.6	266	34	64	4.15	3.4	9.1	2.7	0.8	91
2014	AA	San Antonio	2	2	16	31	33	2.89	1.16	4.6	229	30	79	3.09	2.9	9.5	3.3	0.9	112
2015	AA	Trenton	2	2	0	42	44	4.06	1.33	6.7	261	34	71	3.94	3.0	9.4	3.1	0.9	107
2015	AAA	Scranton/WB	4	0	3	25	26	0.36	0.96	6.8	156	21	100	1.27	4.0	9.4	2.4	0.4	80

Dynamic RP who has big body and hard FB to match. Likes to throw hard and effort in delivery best served in short stints. Stuff can still be raw and has tendency to pitch up in zone. FB exhibits late movement and sink while hard CB shows good breaking action. Has good durability and stamina.

Barlow,Scott — SP — Los Angeles (N)

EXP MLB DEBUT: 2017 | H/W: 6-3 170 | FUT: #5 starter/reliever | 7D

Thrws R Age 23
2011 (6) HS (CA)
89-93 FB +++
80-83 SL +++
75-78 CB ++
83-85 CU ++

Year	Lev	Team	W	L	Sv	IP	K	ERA	WHIP	BF/G	OBA	H%	S%	xERA	Ctl	Dom	Cmd	hr/9	BPV
2014	A	Great Lakes	6	7	1	106	104	4.50	1.40	19.4	274	34	69	4.37	3.0	8.8	3.0	0.9	97
2015	Rk	Azl Dodgers	0	1	0	9	11	4.00	1.33	12.5	240	33	73	3.78	4.0	11.0	2.8	1.0	108
2015	A	Great Lakes	0	1	0	4	1	6.43	2.14	20.8	403	36	86	11.69	2.1	2.1	1.0	4.3	-1
2015	A+	RanchoCuca	8	3	0	71	64	2.53	1.31	21.0	233	29	82	3.20	4.1	8.1	2.0	0.5	54
2015	AAA	Oklahoma City	0	1	0	3	3	16.88	3.13	19.0	437	54	40	10.83	8.4	8.4	1.0	0.0	-58

Tall, lanky RHP survived an extended stint in the CAL. Comes after hitters from a high 3/4 arm slot and has a decent low-90s FB with some good arm-side run. Mixes in a quality SL that is a true swing-and-miss offering. CB and CU have chance to play average. Improved Cmd and Dom hint at the potential.

Barrett,Jake — RP — Arizona

EXP MLB DEBUT: 2016 | H/W: 6-3 220 | FUT: Setup reliever | 8D

Thrws R Age 24
2012 (3) Arizona St
94-96 FB ++++
86-87 SL +++
78-80 +

Year	Lev	Team	W	L	Sv	IP	K	ERA	WHIP	BF/G	OBA	H%	S%	xERA	Ctl	Dom	Cmd	hr/9	BPV
2013	AA	Mobile	1	1	14	24	22	0.37	0.87	3.7	209	26	105	2.01	1.1	8.2	7.3	0.7	135
2014	AA	Mobile	1	2	12	26	24	2.41	1.42	4.4	254	34	81	3.26	4.1	8.3	2.0	0.0	55
2014	AAA	Reno	1	0	16	29	23	3.72	1.28	4.0	212	24	74	3.26	4.7	7.1	1.5	0.9	21
2015	AA	Mobile	3	0	4	30	30	4.20	1.50	5.2	287	37	72	4.49	3.3	9.0	2.7	0.6	91
2015	AAA	Reno	1	3	11	23	21	5.09	1.70	4.7	294	37	68	4.91	4.7	8.2	1.8	0.4	39

Hard-throwing reliever struggled with command throughout 2015. Lost control of mid-90s FB. Thrown downhill, pitch has solid arm-side run. SL has potential to be MLB out pitch with 2 plane break. Should be effective against LH hitters. Rarely thrown CU is remedial at best.

Barrios,Yhonathan — RP — Milwaukee

EXP MLB DEBUT: 2015 | H/W: 5-11 200 | FUT: Closer | 8E

Thrws R Age 24 — 2009 FA (CB)

- 94-97 FB ++++
- 83-86 CU +++
- 82-84 SL ++

Year	Lev	Team	W	L	Sv	IP	K	ERA	WHIP	BF/G	OBA	H%	S%	xERA	Ctl	Dom	Cmd	hr/9	BPV
2014	A+	Bradenton	0	1	11	20	12	2.25	0.95	5.0	175	20	78	1.59	3.2	5.4	1.7	0.5	30
2015	AA	Altoona	0	1	10	24	12	1.49	1.07	4.7	199	22	88	2.11	3.3	4.5	1.3	0.4	8
2015	AA	Biloxi	3	2	6	20	16	3.15	1.35	5.2	281	34	77	3.90	2.3	7.2	3.2	0.5	87
2015	AAA	Indianapolis	1	2	1	15	9	4.74	1.78	5.4	307	36	70	4.97	4.7	5.3	1.1	0.0	-14
2015	MLB	Milwaukee	0	0	0	6	7	0.00	0.48	4.1	146	22	100		0.0	10.2		0.0	201

Converted INF is still a project on mound, but opened eyes in callup. FB is plus, touching 100 and settling 94-97 with sink for grounders. Has good feel for solid CU; SL is raw, but has decent late break. Easy delivery and arm action from 3/4 slot. Short build, but tons of mileage left in his arm. Future value as closer with more refinement.

Beck,Chris — SP — Chicago (A)

EXP MLB DEBUT: 2015 | H/W: 6-3 225 | FUT: #4 starter | 7C

Thrws R Age 25 — 2012 (2) Georgia Southern

- 90-94 FB +++
- 81-84 SL +++
- 77-79 CB ++
- 81-85 CU +++

Year	Lev	Team	W	L	Sv	IP	K	ERA	WHIP	BF/G	OBA	H%	S%	xERA	Ctl	Dom	Cmd	hr/9	BPV
2013	AA	Birmingham	2	2	0	28	22	2.89	1.04	21.6	248	31	69	2.23	1.0	7.1	7.3	0.0	119
2014	AA	Birmingham	5	8	0	116	57	3.41	1.27	23.7	261	29	74	3.53	2.4	4.4	1.8	0.5	33
2014	AAA	Charlotte	1	3	0	33	28	4.08	1.48	20.3	278	35	71	4.03	3.5	7.6	2.2	0.3	60
2015	AAA	Charlotte	3	2	0	54	40	3.16	1.18	21.7	247	29	74	3.07	2.3	6.7	2.9	0.5	75
2015	MLB	Chi White Sox	0	1	0	6	3	6.00	2.33	30.9	371	42	71	7.49	6.0	4.5	0.8	0.0	-63

Strong and durable, season ended in June due to elbow. Made MLB debut and has talent and repertoire to be dependable SP. Owns 4 fringy-to-average pitches led by hard sinker. Lacks true put away pitch, but can get hitters to chase CB. CU remains best secondary pitch, though SL has lost luster. Can be tough to hit when he's mixing well.

Beede,Tyler — SP — San Francisco

EXP MLB DEBUT: 2017 | H/W: 6-4 200 | FUT: #2 starter | 9C

Thrws R Age 22 — 2014 (1) Vanderbilt

- 92-95 FB ++++
- 82-84 CB +++
- 82-86 CU +++

Year	Lev	Team	W	L	Sv	IP	K	ERA	WHIP	BF/G	OBA	H%	S%	xERA	Ctl	Dom	Cmd	hr/9	BPV
2014	NCAA	Vanderbilt	8	8	0	113		4.06	1.28	24.4	224	30	67	2.83	4.2	9.2	2.2	0.3	70
2014	Rk	Azl Giants	0	1	0	8	11	3.29	1.46	8.8	257	40	75	3.39	4.4	12.1	2.8	0.0	117
2014	A-	Salem-Kaizer	0	0	0	6	7	2.90	1.77	14.2	314	43	82	5.03	4.4	10.2	2.3	0.0	83
2015	A+	San Jose	2	2	0	52	37	2.25	1.15	23.0	258	31	81	2.99	1.6	6.4	4.1	0.3	91
2015	AA	Richmond	3	8	0	72	49	5.24	1.35	23.1	234	27	59	3.31	4.4	6.1	1.4	0.5	10

Tall RH scuffled after jump to AA, but still has front-line stuff. FB is plus, sitting 92-95 T97 with life. Replicates arm speed for effective CU to keep hitters honest; CB has nice 11-5 action and should be avg pitch. Works down in zone for ground balls. Ctl issues persist, but chalk those up to mechanical tweaks. With refinement, a solid #2.

Berrios,Jose — SP — Minnesota

EXP MLB DEBUT: 2016 | H/W: 6-0 185 | FUT: #3 starter | 8B

Thrws R Age 21 — 2012 (1) HS (PR)

- 91-96 FB ++++
- 80-83 SL +++
- 80-82 CU +++

Year	Lev	Team	W	L	Sv	IP	K	ERA	WHIP	BF/G	OBA	H%	S%	xERA	Ctl	Dom	Cmd	hr/9	BPV
2014	A+	Fort Myers	9	3	0	96	109	1.97	1.05	23.3	223	31	82	2.28	2.2	10.2	4.7	0.4	144
2014	AA	New Britain	3	4	0	40	28	3.58	1.12	19.8	225	27	67	2.59	2.7	6.3	2.3	0.4	58
2014	AAA	Rochester	0	1	0	3	3	18.00	3.33	18.5	453	56	40	11.74	9.0	9.0	1.0	0.0	-63
2015	AA	Chattanooga	8	3	0	90	92	3.09	1.12	23.7	232	30	74	2.79	2.4	9.2	3.8	0.6	119
2015	AAA	Rochester	6	2	0	75	83	2.63	0.97	23.8	218	29	76	2.33	1.7	9.9	5.9	0.7	152

Plus athlete who is on verge of big leagues with three average-to-plus offerings and advanced control. Varies speed on breaking ball while keeping hitters off-balance with deceptive CU. Repeats easy delivery well and uses three pitches to miss bats. Posts low oppBA by excellent sequencing.

Berry,Tim — SP — Miami

EXP MLB DEBUT: 2014 | H/W: 6-2 180 | FUT: #4 starter | 7C

Thrws L Age 25 — 2009 (50) HS (CA)

- 89-94 FB +++
- 75-79 SL ++
- 80-82 CU +++

Year	Lev	Team	W	L	Sv	IP	K	ERA	WHIP	BF/G	OBA	H%	S%	xERA	Ctl	Dom	Cmd	hr/9	BPV
2012	A+	Frederick	5	5	0	75	61	4.32	1.37	21.0	282	34	69	4.23	2.4	7.3	3.1	0.7	85
2012	AA	Bowie	0	1	0	1	4	52.50	7.50	12.4	674	110	22	31.32	15.0	30.0	2.0	0.0	153
2013	A+	Frederick	11	7	0	152	119	3.85	1.29	23.1	267	32	72	3.86	2.4	7.0	3.0	0.8	81
2014	AA	Bowie	6	7	0	133	108	3.52	1.25	23.6	245	29	74	3.52	3.0	7.3	2.4	0.8	67
2015	AA	Bowie	2	7	0	82	57	7.34	1.72	16.2	316	36	56	5.78	3.7	6.2	1.7	0.9	30

Loose-armed pitcher who repeated AA to disastrous results. Moved to pen in July before being shut down in August due to sprained knee. Walk rate rose while K rate fell. Pitches in lower half of zone with FB that has late action. Slurvy SL needs to be crisper to be potent. CU may be best offering, but not an out pitch.

Biagini,Joe — SP — Toronto

EXP MLB DEBUT: 2016 | H/W: 6-4 215 | FUT: #5 starter | 7C

Thrws R Age 25 — 2011 (26) UC-Davis

- 91-94 FB ++++
- 78-80 CB ++
- 80-84 CU +++

Year	Lev	Team	W	L	Sv	IP	K	ERA	WHIP	BF/G	OBA	H%	S%	xERA	Ctl	Dom	Cmd	hr/9	BPV
2012	A-	Salem-Kaizer	2	4	0	59	63	4.27	1.22	17.0	245	32	66	3.36	2.7	9.6	3.5	0.8	117
2012	A	Augusta	0	4	0	34	36	7.41	1.91	17.9	273	35	61	5.76	7.7	9.5	1.2	1.1	-18
2013	A	Augusta	7	6	0	96	79	5.05	1.50	20.8	273	34	65	4.18	3.9	7.4	1.9	0.5	45
2014	A+	San Jose	10	9	0	128	103	4.01	1.40	23.5	269	33	70	3.77	3.2	7.2	2.2	0.4	61
2015	AA	Richmond	10	7	0	130	84	2.42	1.12	22.3	234	27	79	2.61	2.4	5.8	2.5	0.3	59

Taken from SF in Rule 5. Works from overhand slot and can run FB up to 96 mph, though it sits in the low-90s. CU is a good pace-changer with solid velo separation; CB flashes potential as a decent third. Command has improved noticeably, which helps his bid to stay in rotation. Doesn't miss many bats, so Dom upside is limited.

Bickford,Phil — SP — San Francisco

EXP MLB DEBUT: 2018 | H/W: 6-4 200 | FUT: #3 starter | 9D

Thrws R Age 20 — 2015 (1) JC of So Nevada

- 92-95 FB ++++
- 78-81 SL +++
- CU ++

Year	Lev	Team	W	L	Sv	IP	K	ERA	WHIP	BF/G	OBA	H%	S%	xERA	Ctl	Dom	Cmd	hr/9	BPV
2015	Rk	Azl Giants	0	1	0	22	32	2.04	0.86	8.1	173	30	74	0.83	2.4	13.0	5.3	0.0	187

Tall, projectable RH who had a terrific pro debut. FB touches 97 mph and sits 92-95; mixes in lively 2-seamer in low-90s with good command. SL has plus 11/5 tilt from 3/4 slot, but lacks consistency; CU still raw. Drives off mound with good torque. Some effort to delivery, but room to pack on muscle. With refined SL/CU, has #2 SP upside.

Biddle,Jesse — SP — Philadelphia

EXP MLB DEBUT: 2017 | H/W: 6-4 235 | FUT: #4 starter | 7C

Thrws L Age 24 — 2010 (1) HS (PA)

- 90-92 FB +++
- 73-76 CB ++
- 83-85 SL +++
- 82-84 CU +++

Year	Lev	Team	W	L	Sv	IP	K	ERA	WHIP	BF/G	OBA	H%	S%	xERA	Ctl	Dom	Cmd	hr/9	BPV
2014	Rk	GCL Phillies	0	0	0	2	3	4.50	1.00	7.6	151	0	100	5.17	4.5	13.5	3.0	4.5	140
2014	A+	Clearwater	2	0	0	10	9	0.90	0.90	18.6	96	14	89	0.21	5.4	8.1	1.5	0.0	18
2014	AA	Reading	3	10	0	82	80	5.04	1.49	22.1	252	31	68	4.54	4.8	8.8	1.8	1.2	46
2015	AA	Reading	7	2	0	80	57	4.26	1.55	23.3	285	33	74	4.78	3.8	6.4	1.7	0.8	30
2015	AAA	Lehigh Valley	2	4	0	44	32	6.31	1.90	23.2	314	36	66	6.14	5.5	6.5	1.2	0.8	-13

Has been a disappointment in high minors; maneuvered through injury, inconsistency and bad luck. Has a starter's body and now a four-pitch mix, but seems like he's often working out of trouble. Shaky control and no real put-away pitch continue to be steep hurdles. Had Tommy John surgery in the fall, so on the shelf until 2017.

Binford,Christian — SP — Kansas City

EXP MLB DEBUT: 2016 | H/W: 6-6 220 | FUT: #4 starter | 7D

Thrws R Age 23 — 2011 (30) HS (PA)

- 89-91 FB +++
- 79-82 SL ++
- 74-77 CB +++
- 75-80 CU ++

Year	Lev	Team	W	L	Sv	IP	K	ERA	WHIP	BF/G	OBA	H%	S%	xERA	Ctl	Dom	Cmd	hr/9	BPV
2014	A+	Wilmington	5	4	0	82	92	2.41	1.01	22.5	237	33	75	2.21	1.2	10.1	8.4	0.2	167
2014	AA	NW Arkansas	3	2	0	48	38	3.19	1.06	23.3	250	28	77	3.56	1.1	7.1	6.3	1.3	116
2014	AAA	Omaha	0	1	0	10	9	5.40	2.10	12.3	362	44	75	7.54	4.5	8.1	1.8	0.9	42
2015	AA	NW Arkansas	4	7	0	91	60	5.04	1.55	24.9	315	36	67	5.07	2.3	5.9	2.6	0.6	63
2015	AAA	Omaha	1	4	0	27	9	5.96	1.69	20.5	288	29	67	5.73	5.0	3.0	0.6	1.3	-62

Tall SP who was poor at AAA and AA in '15. Showed less aptitude for strike throwing and struggled to locate FB to corners. Gets good pitch movement due to arm action and uses height to pitch downhill and get grounders. Has proven to be too hittable and low K rate is major concern. Lacks out pitch, though changes speeds and keeps hitters off guard.

Bird,Zachary — SP — Atlanta

EXP MLB DEBUT: 2017 | H/W: 6-3 205 | FUT: #4 starter | 7C

Thrws R Age 21 — 2012 (9) HS (MS)

- 91-93 FB +++
- 70-73 CB +
- 83-86 SL +++
- 83-84 CU +

Year	Lev	Team	W	L	Sv	IP	K	ERA	WHIP	BF/G	OBA	H%	S%	xERA	Ctl	Dom	Cmd	hr/9	BPV
2013	Rk	Ogden	2	4	0	43	44	5.83	1.44	20.4	261	34	58	3.99	4.0	9.2	2.3	0.6	76
2013	A	Great Lakes	2	5	0	60	50	5.10	1.68	14.2	249	30	70	4.58	6.8	7.5	1.1	0.8	-29
2014	A	Great Lakes	6	17	0	118	110	4.26	1.46	19.5	261	33	71	4.13	4.2	8.4	2.0	0.7	56
2015	A+	RanchoCuca	5	7	0	89	95	4.75	1.37	19.6	228	30	65	3.37	4.9	9.6	2.0	0.6	60
2015	AA	Mississippi	1	1	0	12	8	4.43	1.64	18.1	189	23	70	3.04	8.9	5.9	0.7	0.0	-115

Athletic hurler acquired by ATL in a trade sending playoff pieces to LA. FB velocity ticked up and overall command improved throughout the season. Transitioning from a thrower to a pitcher. Breaking pitches have shown improvement but still have a ways to go to becoming effective pitches. A poor CU may cause projection to drop.

Blach,Ty — SP — San Francisco

EXP MLB DEBUT: 2016 | H/W: 6-1 200 | FUT: #5 starter | 7A

Thrws L Age 25 — 2012 (5) Creighton

- 89-92 FB +++
- 78-81 SL +++
- 80-82 CU +++

Year	Lev	Team	W	L	Sv	IP	K	ERA	WHIP	BF/G	OBA	H%	S%	xERA	Ctl	Dom	Cmd	hr/9	BPV
2011	NCAA	Creighton	10	3	0	102	100	2.65	1.21	21.6	246	33	78	2.88	2.6	8.8	3.4	0.3	108
2012	NCAA	Creighton	6	6	0	120	83	2.70	1.02	21.9	217	26	74	2.16	2.1	6.2	3.0	0.4	73
2013	A+	San Jose	12	4	0	130	117	2.91	1.09	23.1	253	32	75	2.95	1.2	8.1	6.5	0.6	130
2014	AA	Richmond	8	8	0	141	91	3.13	1.28	23.1	263	30	76	3.56	2.5	5.8	2.3	0.5	55
2015	AAA	Sacramento	11	12	0	165	93	4.47	1.33	25.4	289	32	68	4.40	1.7	5.1	3.0	0.9	64

Durable LH brings plus command and good pitchability to the table, but lacks a plus offering. Works low in zone with sinking low-90s FB for groundball contact. CU gets nice velo separation with depth and drops slurvy CB to both sides of plate. Poor Dom limits his upside, but projects to have quality Cmd as average back-end SP at next level.

Black,Corey

RP | Chicago (N) | EXP MLB DEBUT: 2016 | H/W: 5-11 175 | FUT: Setup reliever | 7B

Thrws R Age 24
2012 (4) Faulkner

Velo	Pitch	Grade
94-96	FB	++++
85-88	SL	++
80-83	CU	++
76-78	CB	++

Year	Lev	Team	W	L	Sv	IP	K	ERA	WHIP	BF/G	OBA	H%	S%	xERA	Ctl	Dom	Cmd	hr/9	BPV
2012	A	Charleston (Sc)	2	2	0	23	29	3.88	0.99	17.7	216	33	57	1.68	1.9	11.3	5.8	0.0	168
2013	A+	Daytona	4	0	0	25	28	2.88	1.28	20.5	238	31	83	3.71	3.6	10.1	2.8	1.1	102
2013	A+	Tampa	3	8	0	82	88	4.27	1.51	18.7	254	35	70	3.69	4.9	9.6	2.0	0.2	58
2014	AA	Tennessee	6	7	0	124	119	3.48	1.38	20.0	222	27	78	3.64	5.1	8.6	1.7	0.9	34
2015	AA	Tennessee	3	5	0	86	101	4.92	1.41	9.8	234	32	65	3.64	4.9	10.6	2.1	0.7	75

Short, hard-throwing RHP worked mostly in relief in 2015 with mixed results. Has some of the best velocity in the system, but continues to struggle with control. FB sits at 94-96 and tops out at 100. Also throws a SL, CB, and CU. The move to relief seems likely to stick and should allow him to simplify his approach.

Black,Ray

RP | San Francisco | EXP MLB DEBUT: 2017 | H/W: 6-4 225 | FUT: Closer | 9E

Thrws R Age 25
2011 (7) Pittsburgh

Velo	Pitch	Grade
96-99	FB	+++++
85-89	SL	++++

Year	Lev	Team	W	L	Sv	IP	K	ERA	WHIP	BF/G	OBA	H%	S%	xERA	Ctl	Dom	Cmd	hr/9	BPV
2010	NCAA	Pittsburgh	0	3	1	16	15	17.22	2.65	7.4	380	42	32	11.56	8.3	8.3	1.0	3.3	-57
2011	NCAA	Pittsburgh	1	1	4	20	33	6.30	2.35	5.7	271	47	70	5.79	11.7	14.9	1.3	0.0	-31
2014	A	Augusta	1	3	1	31	64	3.76	0.96	3.6	154	39	59	1.11	4.1	18.5	4.6	0.3	242
2014	A+	San Jose	1	0	0	4	7	2.25	0.75	3.6	81	19	67		4.5	15.8	3.5	0.0	180
2015	A+	San Jose	2	1	0	25	51	2.88	1.52	5.4	156	36	83	2.93	9.0	18.4	2.0	0.7	105

Hardest thrower in the minors comes with tremendous injury risk, but elite upside is undeniable. FB has touched 103 mph and sits an easy 96-99. Complements with wicked, powerful 11-5 SL for more whiffs. Violent arm action says he'll always struggle with command, but with that Dom profile, it might not matter all too much.

Blackburn,Clayton

SP | San Francisco | EXP MLB DEBUT: 2016 | H/W: 6-4 230 | FUT: #4 starter | 8C

Thrws R Age 23
2011 (16) HS (OK)

Velo	Pitch	Grade
88-91	FB	+++
72-74	CB	++++
78-80	SL	++
80-82	CU	+++

Year	Lev	Team	W	L	Sv	IP	K	ERA	WHIP	BF/G	OBA	H%	S%	xERA	Ctl	Dom	Cmd	hr/9	BPV
2012	A	Augusta	8	4	0	131		2.54	1.02	22.9	239	33	74	2.25	1.2	9.8	7.9	0.2	161
2013	A+	San Jose	7	5	0	133	138	3.65	1.10	22.7	228	29	69	2.88	2.4	9.3	3.9	0.8	122
2014	Rk	Azl Giants	0	1	0	5	9	3.60	0.80	9.1	221	44	50	1.21	0.0	16.2		0.0	310
2014	AA	Richmond	5	6	0	93	85	3.29	1.23	20.9	264	34	71	3.01	1.9	8.2	4.3	0.1	114
2015	AAA	Sacramento	10	4	0	123	99	2.85	1.29	22.0	268	33	78	3.57	2.3	7.2	3.1	0.4	85

Big, sturdy RH who led the PCL in ERA. Easy delivery with clean, repeatable 3/4 arm slot and good command of four-pitch mix. FB sits 88-91 mph with sink; CB is plus with 11/5 bite; SL/CU are fringy, but has good feel for both. Pounds low in of zone for ground balls and has decent SwK history. Velo isn't sexy, but will get job done as back-end SP.

Blair,Aaron

SP | Atlanta | EXP MLB DEBUT: 2016 | H/W: 6-4 230 | FUT: #2 starter | 8B

Thrws R Age 23
2013 (1) Marshall

Velo	Pitch	Grade
92-95	FB	++++
83-86	CU	++++
77-79	CB	+++

Year	Lev	Team	W	L	Sv	IP	K	ERA	WHIP	BF/G	OBA	H%	S%	xERA	Ctl	Dom	Cmd	hr/9	BPV
2014	A	South Bend	1	2	0	35	44	4.09	1.11	23.0	201	29	62	2.28	3.6	11.3	3.1	0.5	124
2014	A+	Visalia	4	2	0	72	81	4.37	1.26	22.6	256	34	66	3.59	2.6	10.1	3.9	0.7	129
2014	AA	Mobile	4	1	0	46	46	1.95	1.00	22.0	187	24	86	2.12	3.1	9.0	2.9	0.8	95
2015	AA	Mobile	6	3	0	83	64	2.71	1.12	25.2	230	27	80	3.03	2.5	6.9	2.8	0.9	76
2015	AAA	Reno	7	2	0	77	56	3.16	1.22	23.9	236	28	75	3.10	3.2	6.5	2.1	0.6	51

Acquired in the Shelby Miller deal by ATL this offseason, this RH is close to making his MLB debut. Goes after hitters with mid-90s running FB. CU is potentially plus offering with good deception and arm-side bore. CB is solid, used to change the eye levels of hitters. Close to #2 starter ceiling now.

Bleeker,Derrick

RP | Baltimore | EXP MLB DEBUT: 2017 | H/W: 6-5 220 | FUT: Setup reliever | 7D

Thrws R Age 25
2012 (37) Arkansas

Velo	Pitch	Grade
92-97	FB	++++
82-86	SL	++

Year	Lev	Team	W	L	Sv	IP	K	ERA	WHIP	BF/G	OBA	H%	S%	xERA	Ctl	Dom	Cmd	hr/9	BPV
2012	NCAA	Arkansas	0	0	0	1	3	0.00	0.91	2.1	244	91	100	1.69	0.0	24.5		0.0	460
2013	Rk	GCL Orioles	0	0	0	3	4	0.00	0.67	3.5	106	18	100		3.0	12.0	4.0	0.0	153
2014	A-	Aberdeen	1	2	2	23	23	3.12	1.21	7.2	269	36	71	2.95	1.6	9.0	5.8	0.0	137
2014	A	Delmarva	0	0	1	12	14	2.23	0.66	7.0	190	26	71	1.25	0.0	10.4		0.7	205
2015	A	Delmarva	1	2	2	20	18	6.68	1.29	8.3	313	38	46	4.65	0.0	8.0		0.9	162

Strong RP who ended season in May after elbow injury. Only 59 career IP and needs to stay healthy. Has pure arm strength and electric FB that he locates impeccably. Uses high 3/4 slot that makes him imposing to hit. Hard SL can be dynamite at times, but throws mostly FB. Has raw mechanics and may need overhaul.

Blewett,Scott

SP | Kansas City | EXP MLB DEBUT: 2018 | H/W: 6-6 210 | FUT: #2 starter | 8D

Thrws R Age 19
2014 (2) HS (NY)

Velo	Pitch	Grade
90-93	FB	+++
75-78	CB	+++
83-85	CU	++

Year	Lev	Team	W	L	Sv	IP	K	ERA	WHIP	BF/G	OBA	H%	S%	xERA	Ctl	Dom	Cmd	hr/9	BPV
2014	Rk	Burlington	1	2	0	28	29	4.82	1.50	15.1	255	32	69	4.38	4.8	9.3	1.9	1.0	56
2015	A	Lexington	3	5	0	81	60	5.22	1.38	18.9	278	33	61	4.15	2.7	6.7	2.5	0.7	66

Physical, tall SP who faded down stretch. Stamina is present concern, but should be ironed out with more experience. Uses height and arm angle effectively by locating FB down in zone. Improving CB has evolved into out pitch while CU is distant third. Tends to rush delivery and leave balls up. Could return to Low-A for '16 and CU will be key.

Blueberg,Colby

RP | San Diego | EXP MLB DEBUT: 2017 | H/W: 6-0 185 | FUT: Setup reliever | 6B

Thrws R Age 22
2014 (24) Nevada

Velo	Pitch	Grade
91-94	FB	+++
80-82	SL	+++
	CU	++

Year	Lev	Team	W	L	Sv	IP	K	ERA	WHIP	BF/G	OBA	H%	S%	xERA	Ctl	Dom	Cmd	hr/9	BPV
2014	NCAA	Nevada	4	2	2	51	46	1.23	1.04	5.6	200	27	87	1.62	3.0	8.1	2.7	0.0	83
2014	A-	Eugene	2	0	1	32	37	0.56	0.93	6.7	209	31	93	1.45	1.7	10.3	6.2	0.0	159
2014	A	Fort Wayne	1	0	0	3	3	0.00	1.67	6.7	262	35	100	4.00	6.0	9.0	1.5	0.0	18
2015	A	Fort Wayne	4	1	21	58	62	1.08	0.82	5.2	167	24	85	0.72	2.3	9.6	4.1	0.0	128
2015	A+	Lake Elsinore	0	0	0	1	2	30.00	3.33	7.4	470	59	0	19.17	7.5	15.0	2.0	7.5	86

Short RP who served as closer and had outstanding season. Posted low oppBA due to deceptive delivery that has moving parts and effort. Locates FB to all parts of strike zone and rarely misses up. Did not allow HR, but will need to live down in zone as he doesn't have plus velocity. SL is reliable and can use as chaser or for strikes.

Bonilla,Lisalverto

RP | Los Angeles (N) | EXP MLB DEBUT: 2014 | H/W: 6-0 225 | FUT: Setup reliever | 7C

Thrws R Age 25
2008 FA (DR)

Velo	Pitch	Grade
90-95	FB	+++
78-81	SL	++
82-84	CU	++++

Year	Lev	Team	W	L	Sv	IP	K	ERA	WHIP	BF/G	OBA	H%	S%	xERA	Ctl	Dom	Cmd	hr/9	BPV
2013	AA	Frisco	2	0	6	30	50	0.30	0.83	5.2	159	31	96	0.58	2.7	15.0	5.6	0.0	214
2013	AAA	Round Rock	5	5	0	43	56	7.95	1.77	7.6	300	40	56	6.35	5.0	11.7	2.3	1.7	93
2014	AAA	Round Rock	4	2	1	74	92	4.12	1.32	7.9	259	35	72	4.08	3.0	11.2	3.7	1.1	137
2014	MLB	Texas	3	0	0	20	17	3.12	1.24	16.4	186	22	78	2.82	5.3	7.6	1.4	0.9	10
2015	MLB	Texas	*Did not pitch; injured*																

Short and strong pitcher who underwent TJ surgery in April '15. Showed promise as SP in spot starts with TEX in '14, but fits best in pen. Plus CU is best pitch and gets Ks while FB has good velocity and run. FB can be straight at higher velocities. SL lacks ideal break and remains below average. Throws strikes despite effort in delivery.

Booser,Cameron

RP | Minnesota | EXP MLB DEBUT: 2017 | H/W: 6-3 225 | FUT: Setup reliever | 7D

Thrws L Age 23
2013 Central Arizona CC

Velo	Pitch	Grade
92-96	FB	++++
82-85	SL	++
	CU	+

Year	Lev	Team	W	L	Sv	IP	K	ERA	WHIP	BF/G	OBA	H%	S%	xERA	Ctl	Dom	Cmd	hr/9	BPV
2013	Rk	GCL Twins	0	0	0	3	3	2.81	0.94	4.0	250	33	67	2.00	0.0	8.4		0.0	170
2014	Rk	Elizabethton	1	5	2	31	42	2.03	1.35	6.8	242	38	83	2.90	4.1	12.2	3.0	0.0	127
2015	A	Cedar Rapids	1	2	10	46	64	3.72	1.54	6.3	193	31	74	2.97	7.8	12.5	1.6	0.2	32

Big, strong pitcher who could play prominent role in bullpen, but struggles to hit strike zone consistently. Dominates LHH (.148 oppBA) and registers Ks and induces groundballs with vicious, sinking FB. SL developing into average offering and will need against RHH. Has durability to pitch multiple innings.

Borucki,Ryan

SP | Toronto | EXP MLB DEBUT: 2018 | H/W: 6-4 175 | FUT: #3 starter | 8E

Thrws L Age 22
2012 (15) HS (IL)

Velo	Pitch	Grade
88-94	FB	+++
75-79	CB	++
80-83	CU	+++

Year	Lev	Team	W	L	Sv	IP	K	ERA	WHIP	BF/G	OBA	H%	S%	xERA	Ctl	Dom	Cmd	hr/9	BPV
2012	Rk	GCL Blue Jays	1	0	0	6	10	3.00	0.67	5.2	191	30	67	1.94	0.0	15.0		1.5	288
2014	Rk	Bluefield	2	1	0	33	30	2.72	0.97	15.7	218	27	73	2.18	1.6	8.2	5.0	0.5	121
2014	A-	Vancouver	1	1	1	23	22	1.94	0.69	16.3	166	22	73	0.73	1.2	8.5	7.3	0.4	140
2015	Rk	GCL Blue Jays	0	0	0	1	1	0.00	1.00	3.8	262	35	100	2.32	0.0	9.0		0.0	180
2015	A-	Vancouver	0	1	0	4	6	4.29	2.14	10.4	336	51	78	6.29	6.4	12.9	2.0	0.0	76

Tall, quick-armed SP who missed most of season with sore elbow. Underwent TJ surgery in past and injuries are concern. When healthy, throws with loose arm to generate velocity and pitch movement. No pitch comes out straight. Exhibits feel for potential plus CU, though CB needs work. Limits walks and will get Ks.

Bostick,Akeem

SP | Houston | EXP MLB DEBUT: 2017 | H/W: 6-6 215 | FUT: #4 starter | 7C

Thrws R Age 20
2013 (2) HS (SC)

Velo	Pitch	Grade
88-93	FB	+++
80-82	SL	++
80-83	CU	+++

Year	Lev	Team	W	L	Sv	IP	K	ERA	WHIP	BF/G	OBA	H%	S%	xERA	Ctl	Dom	Cmd	hr/9	BPV
2013	Rk	Azl Rangers	4	1	1	41	33	2.85	1.31	12.1	266	34	76	3.18	2.6	7.2	2.8	0.0	77
2014	A	Hickory	5	6	0	92	64	5.18	1.37	18.4	274	31	63	4.36	2.7	6.3	2.3	1.0	57
2015	A	Quad Cities	3	1	1	42	33	1.50	0.76	18.8	197	23	86	1.52	0.6	7.1	11.0	0.6	128
2015	A+	Lancaster	6	4	0	64	48	5.90	1.48	21.2	299	35	60	5.01	2.5	6.7	2.7	1.0	71

Lean, athletic SP who repeats delivery well and throws consistent strikes. Has some projection remaining, but may not develop plus velocity. Drives ball downhill with height and arm slot and has plus athleticism. Not many Ks as he pitches to contact. Improving SL thrown for strikes, but not much of chase pitch. Sinking CU is best current offering.

Bowman,Matt	SP	St. Louis	EXP MLB DEBUT: 2016	H/W: 6-0 165	FUT: #4 starter	7C

Thrws R Age 24	Year	Lev	Team	W	L	Sv	IP	K	ERA	WHIP	BF/G	OBA	H%	S%	xERA	Ctl	Dom	Cmd	hr/9	BPV
2012 (13) Princeton	2013	A	Savannah	4	0	0	30	26	2.68	1.06	23.4	247	32	72	2.28	1.2	7.7	6.5	0.0	125
89-92 FB +++	2013	A+	St. Lucie	6	4	0	96	90	3.18	1.19	24.1	234	29	75	3.13	2.9	8.4	2.9	0.7	91
78-80 CU +++	2014	AA	Binghamton	7	6	0	98	92	3.12	1.31	23.9	269	34	78	3.82	2.5	8.4	3.4	0.6	103
72-74 CB +++	2014	AAA	Las Vegas	3	2	0	36	32	3.49	1.30	21.3	272	35	72	3.46	2.2	8.0	3.6	0.2	101
85-86 SL ++	2015	AAA	Las Vegas	7	16	0	140	77	5.53	1.68	22.5	318	35	68	5.81	3.3	5.0	1.5	1.0	19

Selected from NYM in Rule 5. Four-pitch RHP without flash. Fringe-average FB/CB/CU. Until 2015, was viewed as a command/control type a la Dillon Gee. Was hit hard in the PCL due to FB left up in zone and increased usage of SL. SL is below average, one-plane offering and could be dropped by STL.

Bradley,Archie	SP	Arizona	EXP MLB DEBUT: 2015	H/W: 6-4 230	FUT: #2 starter	9E

Thrws R Age 23	Year	Lev	Team	W	L	Sv	IP	K	ERA	WHIP	BF/G	OBA	H%	S%	xERA	Ctl	Dom	Cmd	hr/9	BPV
2011 (1) HS (OK)	2014	AAA	Reno	1	4	0	24	23	5.23	1.58	21.2	277	37	63	3.98	4.5	8.6	1.9	0.0	52
91-95 FB ++++	2015	Rk	Azl DBacks	0	0	0	4	6	0.00	1.25	16.3	151	27	100	1.57	6.8	13.5	2.0	0.0	79
79-82 CB ++++	2015	A+	Visalia	0	0	0	4	6	4.50	1.25	16.3	210	16	100	6.47	4.5	13.5	3.0	4.5	140
84-85 CU ++	2015	AAA	Reno	1	0	0	21	20	2.99	1.47	22.6	304	37	86	5.32	2.1	8.5	4.0	1.3	114
	2015	MLB	Arizona	2	3	0	35	23	5.88	1.65	19.7	266	30	64	4.76	5.6	5.9	1.0	0.8	-28

Struggled with injuries for a second straight season. Made MLB debut but season ended due to shoulder tightness. Stuff is still evident. Plus FB and CB complement each other. Depth of CB has improved. Continues to progress with CU grip. Deception has improved tremendously over past 3 seasons.

Bradley,Jed	RP	Milwaukee	EXP MLB DEBUT: 2016	H/W: 6-4 225	FUT: Setup reliever	7C

Thrws L Age 25	Year	Lev	Team	W	L	Sv	IP	K	ERA	WHIP	BF/G	OBA	H%	S%	xERA	Ctl	Dom	Cmd	hr/9	BPV
2011 (1) Georgia Tech	2013	A+	Brevard County	4	4	0	78		4.15	1.54	21.3	269	32	74	4.44	4.5	6.7	1.5	0.7	17
89-93 FB +++	2014	A+	Brevard County	5	2	0	60	53	3.00	1.06	23.3	242	30	73	2.78	1.5	7.9	5.3	0.6	120
83-85 SL ++	2014	AA	Huntsville	5	8	0	87	71	4.55	1.63	22.8	302	36	73	5.28	3.7	7.3	2.0	0.8	50
80-83 CU +++	2015	AA	Biloxi	1	1	0	32	31	3.35	1.21	5.6	242	32	71	2.85	2.8	8.7	3.1	0.3	98
	2015	AAA	Colorado Springs	2	4	0	26	15	9.00	2.12	6.4	380	43	54	7.43	3.5	5.2	1.5	0.3	18

Former college SP stud started well in his first year out of the 'pen, but stumbled when promoted to AAA mid-season. Still sits low-90s with FB, but often leaves it up in the zone for hard contact. CU flashes plus potential with good fade; SL still grades as fringe-avg offering. Will need time to adjust to new role, but low K rate limits his value.

Brady,Sean	SP	Cleveland	EXP MLB DEBUT: 2018	H/W: 6-0 175	FUT: #4 starter	7D

Thrws L Age 21	Year	Lev	Team	W	L	Sv	IP	K	ERA	WHIP	BF/G	OBA	H%	S%	xERA	Ctl	Dom	Cmd	hr/9	BPV
2013 (5) HS (FL)																				
87-92 FB +++	2013	Rk	AZL Indians	0	1	0	32	30	1.97	0.94	12.0	210	27	82	2.03	1.7	8.4	5.0	0.6	124
77-80 CB +++	2014	A-	Mahoning Val	2	4	0	71	44	2.79	1.34	21.1	254	30	78	3.33	3.4	5.6	1.6	0.3	26
80-82 CU +++	2014	A	Lake County	0	1	0	2	2	16.36	3.64	14.2	492	49	67	21.24	8.2	8.2	1.0	8.2	-56
	2015	A	Lake County	7	12	0	146	118	3.82	1.23	22.8	268	32	73	3.87	1.8	7.3	4.1	0.9	101

Command-oriented SP who was consistent from month to month. Doesn't exhibit velocity or projection, but keeps ball low and is tough on LHH. Spots FB to both sides of plate and mixes in average CB with big bend. CU shows late movement, though not enough power to deceive RHH. Allowed high oppBA as he doesn't own true K pitch.

Brault,Steven	SP	Pittsburgh	EXP MLB DEBUT: 2017	H/W: 6-1 175	FUT: #4 starter	7C

Thrws L Age 23	Year	Lev	Team	W	L	Sv	IP	K	ERA	WHIP	BF/G	OBA	H%	S%	xERA	Ctl	Dom	Cmd	hr/9	BPV
2013 (11) Regis	2013	A-	Aberdeen	1	2	0	43	38	2.09	1.09	14.0	224	29	80	2.26	2.5	8.0	3.2	0.2	93
90-93 FB +++	2014	A	Delmarva	9	8	0	130	115	3.05	1.04	22.8	226	29	69	2.21	1.9	8.0	4.1	0.3	109
SL +++	2014	A+	Frederick	2	0	0	16	9	0.56	0.56	18.1	134	16	89		1.1	5.0	4.5	0.0	78
CU +++	2015	A+	Bradenton	4	1	0	65	45	3.04	1.27	20.5	252	30	76	3.29	2.9	6.2	2.1	0.4	52
	2015	AA	Altoona	9	3	0	90	80	2.00	1.01	23.0	221	29	79	1.92	1.9	8.0	4.2	0.1	111

Athletic LHP isn't overpowering and comes after hitters with an avg low-90 FB that has good late sink. Mixes in an improved SL and a decent CU. Succeeds by keeping hitters off-balance and working the edges of the strike zone with above-avg control. Simple, repeatable mechanics allow him to thrive.

Brennan,Brandon	SP	Chicago (A)	EXP MLB DEBUT: 2017	H/W: 6-4 220	FUT: #4 SP / Setup RP	7C

Thrws R Age 24	Year	Lev	Team	W	L	Sv	IP	K	ERA	WHIP	BF/G	OBA	H%	S%	xERA	Ctl	Dom	Cmd	hr/9	BPV
2012 (4) Orange Coast JC	2013	A	Kannapolis	4	9	0	81	54	5.55	1.55	23.6	302	34	64	5.06	3.0	6.0	2.0	0.8	45
91-95 FB ++++	2014	Rk	Great Falls	1	1	0	19	12	3.28	1.25	15.6	239	26	77	3.56	3.3	5.6	1.7	0.9	31
81-83 SL ++	2014	A	Kannapolis	2	0	0	17	15	2.62	0.99	21.8	185	25	71	1.34	3.1	7.8	2.5	0.0	75
82-84 CU ++	2014	A+	Winston-Salem	2	0	0	30	22	2.98	1.46	21.5	273	33	79	3.93	3.6	6.6	1.8	0.3	39
	2015	A+	Winston-Salem	3	4	0	58	39	3.56	1.36	20.2	251	30	73	3.40	3.7	6.0	1.6	0.3	26

Tall SP who missed most of season with sprained neck. Dom is low despite natural stuff. Plus sinker produces ton of ground balls, and has athleticism to repeat clean delivery. Throws downhill and uses SL as out pitch. Lacks feel for changing speeds and needs to sequence pitches better.

Brentz,Jake	SP	Seattle	EXP MLB DEBUT: 2019	H/W: 6-2 195	FUT: #3 starter	8E

Thrws L Age 21	Year	Lev	Team	W	L	Sv	IP	K	ERA	WHIP	BF/G	OBA	H%	S%	xERA	Ctl	Dom	Cmd	hr/9	BPV
2013 (11) HS (MO)																				
90-94 FB +++	2013	Rk	GCL Blue Jays	0	0	0	7	8	11.25	2.36	4.1	198	25	50	6.10	15.0	10.0	0.7	1.3	-207
74-76 CB ++	2014	Rk	GCL Blue Jays	1	3	2	39	34	4.13	1.43	13.9	213	27	69	3.00	6.0	7.8	1.3	0.2	-3
83-85 CU ++	2015	Rk	Bluefield	0	1	0	22	16	4.09	1.64	16.3	287	33	76	5.07	4.5	6.5	1.5	0.8	14
	2015	A-	Everett	1	1	1	14	14	3.86	1.21	11.3	186	26	65	1.91	5.1	9.0	1.8	0.0	41

Quick-armed pitcher with high upside based upon projection and clean delivery. Lacks feel and has limited innings in 3 pro years. All pitches exhibit good movement, but has difficulty commanding sinking FB. Needs to add ticks to slow CB to make true power offering, though CU continues to improve. Keeps ball low in zone.

Brice,Austin	SP	Miami	EXP MLB DEBUT: 2017	H/W: 6-4 205	FUT: Setup reliever	7D

Thrws R Age 23	Year	Lev	Team	W	L	Sv	IP	K	ERA	WHIP	BF/G	OBA	H%	S%	xERA	Ctl	Dom	Cmd	hr/9	BPV
2010 (9) HS (NC)	2011	Rk	GCL Marlins	6	0	0	48	55	2.99	1.35	18.3	191	27	78	2.64	6.2	10.3	1.7	0.4	36
92-95 FB ++++	2012	A	Greensboro	8	6	3	109	122	4.37	1.50	18.9	238	31	74	4.26	5.6	10.1	1.8	1.1	48
80-82 CB +++	2013	A	Greensboro	8	11	0	113	111	5.73	1.77	19.9	270	34	68	5.20	6.5	8.8	1.4	0.9	1
CU ++	2014	A+	Jupiter	8	9	0	127	109	3.61	1.33	21.1	241	30	72	3.22	3.9	7.7	2.0	0.4	52
	2015	AA	Jacksonville	6	9	0	125	127	4.68	1.46	21.4	244	31	69	3.99	5.0	9.1	1.8	0.8	48

Tall, projectable RHP works with a 92-94 FB. His CB can be plus and a mixes in a show-me CU that projects as average. Raw stuff is good, but inconsistent mechanics result in below-avg control and he walked 69 in 125.1 at AA. A move to relief seems likely.

Briceno,Endrys	SP	Detroit	EXP MLB DEBUT: 2018	H/W: 6-5 175	FUT: #3 starter	8E

Thrws R Age 24	Year	Lev	Team	W	L	Sv	IP	K	ERA	WHIP	BF/G	OBA	H%	S%	xERA	Ctl	Dom	Cmd	hr/9	BPV
2009 FA (VZ)	2012	A-	Connecticut	4	3	0	57	30	5.19	1.43	20.3	271	30	62	4.02	3.5	4.7	1.4	0.5	10
90-95 FB ++++	2013	A	West Michigan	7	9	0	116	65	4.49	1.51	20.1	275	31	69	4.17	4.0	5.0	1.3	0.4	2
78-82 CB ++	2014	A+	Lakeland	0	0	0	16	7	3.38	1.19	21.4	262	28	72	3.37	1.7	3.9	2.3	0.6	43
80-83 CU ++	2015	Rk	GCL Tigers	0	1	0	11	16	1.62	0.90	10.3	223	37	80	1.52	0.8	13.0	16.0	0.0	230
	2015	A+	Lakeland	2	3	0	33	16	4.09	1.61	18.3	295	32	75	4.88	3.8	4.4	1.1	0.5	-7

Tall, slender SP who missed most of '14 (TJ surgery) and returned to full-season in July. Has very projectable arm and delivery. Throws downhill with quick arm and gets late run and sink on plus FB. K rate disappointing for stuff and size, but exhibits good control and pitch location. Lacks reliable out pitch, though CB ahead of CU.

Bridwell,Parker	SP	Baltimore	EXP MLB DEBUT: 2016	H/W: 6-4 190	FUT: #3 starter	7C

Thrws R Age 24	Year	Lev	Team	W	L	Sv	IP	K	ERA	WHIP	BF/G	OBA	H%	S%	xERA	Ctl	Dom	Cmd	hr/9	BPV
2010 (9) HS (TX)	2011	A	Delmarva	0	3	0	21	13	7.22	1.70	19.2	278	33	53	4.33	5.5	5.5	1.0	0.0	-32
87-94 FB +++	2012	A	Delmarva	5	9	0	114	71	5.99	1.62	22.0	275	30	64	5.21	5.0	5.6	1.1	1.2	-15
78-83 SL +++	2013	A	Delmarva	8	9	0	142	144	4.75	1.41	23.1	260	34	65	3.85	3.7	9.1	2.4	0.6	81
78-82 CU +++	2014	A+	Frederick	7	10	0	141	142	4.46	1.37	22.7	236	30	68	3.56	4.5	9.1	2.0	0.7	60
	2015	AA	Bowie	4	5	0	97	93	3.99	1.38	22.6	260	33	72	3.86	3.5	8.6	2.4	0.6	78

Tall, lanky SP who ended 1st year in AA in July due to elbow. Possesses impressive arsenal, though inconsistent command, due to inability to repeat delivery, has held him back. Has above average sinking FB that induces groundballs and quality breaking ball at disposal. CU has evolved into average pitch and could get better.

Brigham,Jeff	SP	Miami	EXP MLB DEBUT: 2018	H/W: 6-0 200	FUT: #5 starter/reliever	6C

Thrws R Age 24	Year	Lev	Team	W	L	Sv	IP	K	ERA	WHIP	BF/G	OBA	H%	S%	xERA	Ctl	Dom	Cmd	hr/9	BPV
2014 (4) Washington	2014	NCAA	Washington	7	4	0	90	45	2.90	1.13	22.2	237	27	74	2.65	2.3	4.5	2.0	0.3	37
90-94 FB +++	2014	Rk	Ogden	0	3	0	32	33	3.63	1.49	12.6	261	34	76	4.06	4.5	9.2	2.1	0.6	63
80-82 SL +	2015	A	Great Lakes	2	0	0	7	11	1.29	0.71	12.4	132	26	80	0.03	2.6	14.1	5.5	0.0	203
CU +	2015	A+	Jupiter	2	2	0	33	22	1.90	1.30	22.8	266	32	84	3.15	2.4	6.0	2.4	0.0	59
	2015	A+	RanchoCuca	4	5	0	68	64	5.96	1.68	18.0	289	35	65	5.41	4.8	8.5	1.8	1.1	42

Short, stocky reliever was traded as part of the Mat Latos deal. Has a good 90-94 mph FB but throws with some effort and can rush his delivery, resulting in below-avg control. Career Ctl is now 4.0. Flashes a decent SL with good late break and a below-avg CU. Profiles as a back-end guy or long reliever.

Brown,Mitch | SP | Cleveland | EXP MLB DEBUT: 2017 | H/W: 6-1 195 | FUT: #4 starter | 7D

Thrws R Age 21	Year	Lev	Team	W	L	Sv	IP	K	ERA	WHIP	BF/G	OBA	H%	S%	xERA	Ctl	Dom	Cmd	hr/9	BPV
2012 (2) HS (MN)	2012	Rk	AZL Indians	2	0	0	27	26	3.64	1.10	13.3	207	25	70	2.81	3.3	8.6	2.6	1.0	84
89-95 FB +++	2013	Rk	AZL Indians	2	4	0	52	48	5.37	1.65	19.4	280	36	65	4.55	5.0	8.3	1.7	0.3	32
82-85 SL ++	2013	A	Lake County	1	1	0	15	18	11.84	2.11	15.0	329	41	43	8.32	6.5	10.7	1.6	2.4	34
77-79 CB +++	2014	A	Lake County	8	8	0	138	127	3.32	1.22	20.7	225	29	72	2.75	3.6	8.3	2.3	0.4	70
81-84 CU ++	2015	A+	Lynchburg	9	12	0	141	109	5.16	1.59	23.0	270	31	68	4.82	4.9	6.9	1.4	1.0	11

Durable SP who repeats athletic delivery, but saw regression across board. Walk rate rose while K rate fell as hard CB proved inconsistent. Throws quality cut FB, but needs 2nd pitch to emerge. May need to ditch a breaking ball while also repeating arm speed on CU. Has stuff to be decent and will be given time.

Buehler,Walker | SP | Los Angeles (N) | EXP MLB DEBUT: 2019 | H/W: 6-2 175 | FUT: #3 starter | 7C

Thrws R Age 21	Year	Lev	Team	W	L	Sv	IP	K	ERA	WHIP	BF/G	OBA	H%	S%	xERA	Ctl	Dom	Cmd	hr/9	BPV
2015 (1) Vanderbilt																				
90-95 FB ++++																				
80-85 SL +++																				
76-80 CB +++																				
CU +++	2015	NCAA	Vanderbilt	5	2	0	88	92	2.96	1.31	22.7	255	34	79	3.56	3.1	9.4	3.1	0.6	104

Elbow injury and inconsistent production caused slide to the Dodgers at #24 and he had TJS in August. When he's right has a four-pitch mix that includes a plus 92-95 mph FB, CB and SL. Shows an ability to spin the ball, but too often his breaking balls are inconsistent. Max effort delivery will need to be refined.

Bundy,Dylan | SP | Baltimore | EXP MLB DEBUT: 2012 | H/W: 6-1 200 | FUT: #1 starter | 9C

Thrws R Age 23	Year	Lev	Team	W	L	Sv	IP	K	ERA	WHIP	BF/G	OBA	H%	S%	xERA	Ctl	Dom	Cmd	hr/9	BPV
2011 (1) HS (OK)	2012	AA	Bowie	2	0	0	16		3.33	1.36	22.6	235	28	76	3.40	4.4	7.2	1.6	0.6	28
91-95 FB ++++	2012	MLB	Baltimore	0	0	0	1	0	0.00	1.67	2.7	228	23	100	3.64	7.5	0.0	0.0	0.0	-185
77-82 CB ++++	2014	A-	Aberdeen	0	1	0	15	22	0.60	0.87	18.4	191	33	92	1.05	1.8	13.2	7.3	0.0	207
81-85 CU +++	2014	A+	Frederick	1	2	0	26	15	4.83	1.57	19.1	276	32	66	3.99	4.5	5.2	1.2	0.0	-10
	2015	AA	Bowie	0	3	0	22	25	3.68	1.18	11.0	253	36	65	2.64	2.0	10.2	5.0	0.0	147

Advanced, athletic arm that can't stay healthy. Ended season in May after shoulder pain and was making progress prior to injury. Only 63 IP in 3 years, but stuff is electric when on mound. Has makings of ace with plus FB and terrific CB. Has clean arm action and ability to spot pitches low in zone. Throws strikes and changes speeds.

Burdi,Nick | RP | Minnesota | EXP MLB DEBUT: 2016 | H/W: 6-5 215 | FUT: Closer | 8D

Thrws R Age 23	Year	Lev	Team	W	L	Sv	IP	K	ERA	WHIP	BF/G	OBA	H%	S%	xERA	Ctl	Dom	Cmd	hr/9	BPV
2014 (2) Louisville	2014	NCAA	Louisville	3	1	18	37	65	0.49	0.76	4.1	147	30	96	0.50	2.4	15.8	6.5	0.2	237
93-98 FB ++++	2014	A	Cedar Rapids	0	0	4	13	26	4.15	1.23	4.1	179	43	63	1.79	5.5	18.0	3.3	0.0	192
85-88 SL +++	2014	A+	Fort Myers	2	0	1	7	12	0.00	0.99	3.9	200	38	100	1.43	2.5	15.2	6.0	0.0	223
	2015	A+	Fort Myers	2	2	2	20	29	2.25	0.75	5.5	175	29	71	1.01	1.4	13.1	9.7	0.5	216
	2015	AA	Chattanooga	3	4	2	43	54	4.58	1.67	6.5	247	35	72	4.36	6.7	11.3	1.7	0.6	41

Aggressive RP who was lit up at start of year in AA, went back to High-A, before returning and faring much better. Very tough to hit with plus FB that exhibits late sink and run. Counters with SL that flashes plus. Can get on side of SL and leave up in zone. Can make quick work of hitters when throwing strikes, but command needs polish.

Burr,Ryan | RP | Arizona | EXP MLB DEBUT: 2017 | H/W: 6-4 225 | FUT: Setup reliever | 8D

Thrws R Age 21	Year	Lev	Team	W	L	Sv	IP	K	ERA	WHIP	BF/G	OBA	H%	S%	xERA	Ctl	Dom	Cmd	hr/9	BPV
2015 (5) Arizona St																				
95-97 FB ++++																				
SL ++	2015	NCAA	Arizona St	8	2	14	46	74	2.93	1.50	6.0	253	43	81	3.76	4.9	14.4	3.0	0.4	146
CU +	2015	A-	Hillsboro	3	0	3	14	21	1.91	0.85	4.0	150	24	82	1.16	3.2	13.4	4.2	0.6	173
	2015	A	Kane County	1	0	0	19	28	0.47	0.94	5.5	181	31	94	1.12	2.8	13.1	4.7	0.0	178

Strong-armed, nasty RHP with tools to be effective late-inning reliever. Was the closer at Arizona State. Features blow-away velocity with FB. Has late movement and can be effective up or down. SL is a few steps behind FB. Slurvy at times, SL has shown flashes of becoming plus. Throws a CU to keep LH hitters honest. Needs work on pitch.

Burrows,Beau | SP | Detroit | EXP MLB DEBUT: 2019 | H/W: 6-2 200 | FUT: #3 starter | 8C

Thrws R Age 19	Year	Lev	Team	W	L	Sv	IP	K	ERA	WHIP	BF/G	OBA	H%	S%	xERA	Ctl	Dom	Cmd	hr/9	BPV
2015 (1) HS (TX)																				
91-96 FB ++++																				
76-79 CB +++																				
84-86 CU ++																				
	2015	Rk	GCL Tigers	1	0	0	28	33	1.61	1.04	10.8	186	28	83	1.44	3.5	10.6	3.0	0.0	113

Broad SP who may not have textbook delivery, but thrives with plus FB and CB that flashes plus. Has strength to maintain velocity and exhibits decent control despite age. Pitches consistently down in strike zone and induces groundball outs. Lacks projection in frame and arm action, but has enough in the tank to be mid-rotation guy.

Butler,Ryan | SP | San Diego | EXP MLB DEBUT: 2017 | H/W: 6-4 225 | FUT: #4 SP / Closer | 7D

Thrws R Age 24	Year	Lev	Team	W	L	Sv	IP	K	ERA	WHIP	BF/G	OBA	H%	S%	xERA	Ctl	Dom	Cmd	hr/9	BPV
2014 (7) Charlotte	2014	A-	Eugene	0	0	1	7	6	8.75	2.08	7.1	371	46	53	6.83	3.8	7.5	2.0	0.0	52
93-97 FB ++++	2014	A	Fort Wayne	1	1	10	21	30	0.85	1.08	4.6	221	36	91	1.97	2.5	12.7	5.0	0.0	178
81-83 SL ++	2015	Rk	Azl Padres	0	0	0	1	2	0.00	1.00	3.8	262	55	100	2.23	0.0	18.0		0.0	342
84-85 CU ++	2015	A+	Lake Elsinore	3	2	0	46	31	3.70	1.43	16.4	285	33	73	4.12	2.7	6.0	2.2	0.4	53
	2015	AA	San Antonio	0	3	0	17	7	4.76	1.47	24.3	250	28	64	3.40	4.8	3.7	0.8	0.0	-44

Tall pitcher who missed much of season with injuries as he converted to SP. May move back to pen where he can dominate with plus FB that features heavy sink. Hitters rarely elevate FB, but can tee off on hanging SL and rudimentary CU. Dom surprisingly low despite velocity and delivery likely best suited for RP. Fills up zone with strikes.

Buttrey,Ty | SP | Boston | EXP MLB DEBUT: 2017 | H/W: 6-6 235 | FUT: #4 starter | 7C

Thrws R Age 23	Year	Lev	Team	W	L	Sv	IP	K	ERA	WHIP	BF/G	OBA	H%	S%	xERA	Ctl	Dom	Cmd	hr/9	BPV
2012 (4) HS (NC)	2014	Rk	GCL Red Sox	0	0	0	5	4	1.80	0.60	8.6	124	17	67		1.8	7.2	4.0	0.0	99
90-95 FB +++	2014	A-	Lowell	0	0	0	11	12	3.21	1.61	16.5	258	36	78	3.79	5.6	9.6	1.7	0.0	40
77-80 CB +++	2014	A	Greenville	0	5	0	46	40	6.85	1.80	19.3	313	38	62	6.02	4.7	7.8	1.7	1.0	32
80-82 CU ++	2015	A	Greenville	1	0	0	22	22	2.45	0.91	20.5	215	27	78	2.25	1.2	9.0	7.3	0.8	147
	2015	A+	Salem	8	10	0	115	81	4.22	1.41	23.2	265	31	69	3.77	3.5	6.3	1.8	0.4	37

Angular SP who revised delivery over past two seasons to use height and gain extension. Commands plate well with FB that he throws on downhill plane, but often slows arm speed on CU. CB can be good with sufficient break, but doesn't throw for strikes consistently. Lacks stamina despite size and FB can be straight.

Cabrera,Mauricio | RP | Atlanta | EXP MLB DEBUT: 2017 | H/W: 6-3 230 | FUT: Setup RP / Closer | 8E

Thrws R Age 22	Year	Lev	Team	W	L	Sv	IP	K	ERA	WHIP	BF/G	OBA	H%	S%	xERA	Ctl	Dom	Cmd	hr/9	BPV
2010 FA (DR)	2013	A	Rome	3	8	0	131	107	4.19	1.44	23.3	242	30	69	3.37	4.9	7.3	1.5	0.2	19
95-98 FB +++++	2014	Rk	GCL Braves	0	0	0	4	3	6.75	1.25	5.4	210	27	40	2.30	4.5	6.8	1.5	0.0	18
87-89 SL +++	2014	A+	Lynchburg	1	1	0	29	28	5.59	1.48	6.6	227	30	60	3.37	5.9	8.7	1.5	0.3	15
90-91 CU +	2015	A+	Carolina	2	2	1	31	28	5.52	1.52	5.8	255	33	61	3.81	4.9	8.1	1.6	0.3	31
	2015	AA	Mississippi	0	1	0	17	25	5.79	1.75	6.0	199	32	66	3.88	9.5	13.2	1.4	0.5	-1

Converted to RP in '15. Plus-plus FB is his trademark. Has hit triple digits throughout his professional career. Falls in love with velocity at times, compromising movement and command. SL is an above-average offering with 2-plane break. SL plays up when FB command is sound. Stuff projects to the late innings.

Casadilla,Franyel | SP | St. Louis | EXP MLB DEBUT: 2021 | H/W: 6-3 175 | FUT: #3 starter | 8D

Thrws R Age 19	Year	Lev	Team	W	L	Sv	IP	K	ERA	WHIP	BF/G	OBA	H%	S%	xERA	Ctl	Dom	Cmd	hr/9	BPV
2015 FA (VZ)																				
93-95 FB +++																				
CB ++																				
CU ++																				
	2015			*Did not pitch in U.S.*																

Long and lean Dominican hurler features a potentially plus 93-95 mph FB. Mixes in a CB and CU that show potential, but need refinement. Casadilla impressed in the DSL, going 4-3 with a 2.16 ERA and walking just 11 in 79 IP. Shows good command for such a young player and should make his U.S. debut in 2016.

Cash,Ralston | RP | Los Angeles (N) | EXP MLB DEBUT: 2016 | H/W: 6-3 215 | FUT: Middle reliever | 6C

Thrws R Age 24	Year	Lev	Team	W	L	Sv	IP	K	ERA	WHIP	BF/G	OBA	H%	S%	xERA	Ctl	Dom	Cmd	hr/9	BPV
2010 (2) HS (GA)	2013	A	Great Lakes	4	3	0	53	56	3.21	1.37	13.9	210	28	78	3.23	5.6	9.5	1.7	0.7	38
88-92 FB ++	2014	A	Great Lakes	3	1	1	50	62	2.87	1.10	6.8	189	29	72	1.79	3.9	11.1	2.8	0.2	112
75-77 CB +++	2014	AA	Chattanooga	0	0	0	8	10	3.33	1.36	5.6	180	28	73	2.18	6.7	11.1	1.7	0.0	38
83-85 SL ++	2015	AA	Tulsa	2	6	3	57	56	3.47	1.21	4.7	207	25	76	3.19	4.3	8.8	2.1	1.1	62
	2015	AAA	Oklahoma City	0	0	0	1	2	0.00	3.00	5.8	415	71	100	9.92	9.0	18.0	2.0	0.0	99

Tall, lanky reliever. Comes after hitters from a high 3/4 arm slot and has a decent low-90s FB with some good arm-side run. Mixes in a quality SL that can be swing-and-miss. Scrapped the CU when he moved to relief and CB has chance to play average. FB command continues to be an issue and he walked 4.3/9 in 2015.

Castellani,Ryan — SP — Colorado

EXP MLB DEBUT: 2019 | H/W: 6-4 195 | FUT: #3 starter | 7C

Thrws R Age 20
2014 (2) HS (AZ)

- 88-92 FB +++
- 73-75 CB ++
- 79-83 CU ++
- 77-80 SL ++

Year	Lev	Team	W	L	Sv	IP	K	ERA	WHIP	BF/G	OBA	H%	S%	xERA	Ctl	Dom	Cmd	hr/9	BPV
2014	A-	Tri-City	1	2	0	37	25	3.65	1.19	14.8	251	29	69	3.13	2.2	6.1	2.8	0.5	68
2015	A	Asheville	2	7	0	113	94	4.46	1.44	17.8	296	36	68	4.31	2.3	7.5	3.2	0.4	90

Durable RHP has a sinking FB that sits at 88-92 mph. Has a lean, projectable frame and could add velo as he matures. Does a good job of throwing downhill, keeping the ball on the ground and in the park. Mixes in a CB, SL, and CU, but none project as above-average. He does pound the strike zone and should develop into a solid #3 starter.

Castillo,Jose — SP — San Diego

EXP MLB DEBUT: 2019 | H/W: 6-4 200 | FUT: #3 starter | 8E

Thrws L Age 20
2012 FA (VZ)

- 90-95 FB +++
- 82-85 SL +++
- 80-83 CU ++

Year	Lev	Team	W	L	Sv	IP	K	ERA	WHIP	BF/G	OBA	H%	S%	xERA	Ctl	Dom	Cmd	hr/9	BPV
2013	Rk	GCL Devil Rays	2	2	0	30	25	5.96	1.39	10.6	285	35	54	3.93	2.4	7.5	3.1	0.3	88
2014	Rk	GCL Devil Rays	0	0	0	4	4	4.29	1.19	5.6	202	28	60	2.04	4.3	8.6	2.0	0.0	57
2015	A-	Tri-City	3	1	0	52	35	3.63	1.34	16.7	269	32	71	3.47	2.8	6.0	2.2	0.2	52
2015	A	Fort Wayne	1	1	0	27	16	4.00	1.52	19.5	247	28	74	4.09	5.3	5.3	1.0	0.7	-30

Raw, tall SP who exhibits athleticism and solid arsenal. Has limited experience in U.S. and could be one to watch. Throws with little effort, but has tendency to aim ball and not let natural movement take over. Has difficulty repeating delivery which impacts command. Hard SL serves as K pitch and has ability to improve CU with repeatable arm speed.

Castro,Miguel — RP — Colorado

EXP MLB DEBUT: 2015 | H/W: 6-5 190 | FUT: Closer | 8D

Thrws R Age 21
2012 FA (DR)

- 92-97 FB ++++
- 80-83 SL ++
- 82-84 CU ++

Year	Lev	Team	W	L	Sv	IP	K	ERA	WHIP	BF/G	OBA	H%	S%	xERA	Ctl	Dom	Cmd	hr/9	BPV
2015	A+	Dunedin	0	0	0	5		0.00	0.20	5.0	0	0	100		1.8	12.6	7.0	0.0	196
2015	AAA	Albuquerque	2	0	0	13	10	1.36	0.98	4.6	139	18	85	0.85	4.8	6.8	1.4	0.0	12
2015	AAA	Buffalo	1	3	0	19	21	4.69	1.98	7.1	324	40	82	7.48	5.6	9.8	1.8	1.9	43
2015	MLB	Colorado	0	1	0	5	6	10.59	1.96	4.9	294	32	50	8.51	7.1	10.6	1.5	3.5	18
2015	MLB	Toronto	0	2	4	12	12	4.46	1.74	4.2	305	37	79	6.20	4.5	8.9	2.0	1.5	58

Tall, wiry hurler repeats his mechanics well and uses a clean delivery to pump in a plus 92-97 mph FB. FB tops out at 99 mph with good sinking action. SL is a work in progress, but can get swings and misses. Pitched in relief in '15 and managed to get in 18 G in the majors.

Cease,Dylan — SP — Chicago (N)

EXP MLB DEBUT: 2019 | H/W: 6-1 175 | FUT: #2 starter | 9D

Thrws R Age 20
2014 (6) HS (GA)

- 94-96 FB ++++
- 80-83 CB +++
- 80-83 CU ++

Year	Lev	Team	W	L	Sv	IP	K	ERA	WHIP	BF/G	OBA	H%	S%	xERA	Ctl	Dom	Cmd	hr/9	BPV
2015	Rk	Azl Cubs	1	2	0	24	25	2.63	1.17	8.7	151	22	75	1.40	6.0	9.4	1.6	0.0	25

Elbow injury eventually led to TJS in 2014. Made a quick recovery and was solid in pro debut. Velocity was back to pre-draft levels and his FB now sits at 94-96 mph with plus late movement. Power CB gives him a 2nd plus offering and CU shows potential. Control was not all the way back, but the long-term potential is exciting.

Cederoth,Michael — SP — Minnesota

EXP MLB DEBUT: 2017 | H/W: 6-6 195 | FUT: #3 SP / Setup RP | 8E

Thrws R Age 23
2014 (3) San Diego St

- 92-95 FB ++++
- 81-83 SL +++
- 76-78 CB ++
- 83-86 CU +

Year	Lev	Team	W	L	Sv	IP	K	ERA	WHIP	BF/G	OBA	H%	S%	xERA	Ctl	Dom	Cmd	hr/9	BPV
2012	NCAA	San Diego St	4	4	0	67	62	4.16	1.56	19.6	231	30	73	3.72	6.4	8.3	1.3	0.4	-6
2013	NCAA	San Diego St	3	9	0	95	109	4.26	1.26	25.9	212	30	65	2.67	4.5	10.3	2.3	0.4	81
2014	NCAA	San Diego St	6	2	20	51	55	2.29	1.25	6.5	200	28	82	2.49	4.9	9.7	2.0	0.4	59
2014	Rk	Elizabethton	4	2	0	45	42	3.58	1.31	17.0	243	32	71	3.03	3.6	8.4	2.3	0.2	72
2015	A	Cedar Rapids	1	4	0	35	37	4.10	1.45	13.6	250	33	71	3.77	4.6	9.5	2.1	0.5	64

Tall SP who ended season in June due to undisclosed illness. Uses plus FB with run and sink to intimidate hitters and has SL that serves as out pitch. Has trouble repeating delivery that features moving parts. High 3/4 slot gives him tough angle to plate and can get Ks. Needs CU to stick as SP, but arm action provides little deception.

Cessa,Luis — SP — New York (A)

EXP MLB DEBUT: 2016 | H/W: 6-3 190 | FUT: #4 starter | 7C

Thrws R Age 23
2008 FA (MX)

- 90-94 FB +++
- 83-85 SL ++
- 83-85 CU +++

Year	Lev	Team	W	L	Sv	IP	K	ERA	WHIP	BF/G	OBA	H%	S%	xERA	Ctl	Dom	Cmd	hr/9	BPV
2014	A+	St. Lucie	7	8	0	114	83	4.02	1.20	23.0	255	30	66	3.26	2.1	6.5	3.1	0.6	78
2014	AA	Binghamton	0	1	0	3	3	14.06	2.81	18.0	437	45	57	15.33	5.6	8.4	1.5	5.6	18
2015	AA	Binghamton	7	4	0	77	61	2.57	1.22	24.0	262	32	78	3.10	2.0	7.1	3.6	0.2	93
2015	AAA	Las Vegas	0	3	0	24	24	8.59	1.83	22.4	371	46	51	7.20	1.5	9.0	6.0	1.1	139
2015	AAA	Toledo	1	3	0	37	34	6.05	1.64	23.7	305	38	61	5.02	3.6	8.2	2.3	0.5	68

Intriguing SP who struggled in AAA, but still raw after converting from OF in '10. Controls plate with average stuff and has chance to be big league SP if SL improves. Likes to use FB early and use solid CU as neutralizer. Is able to repeat his athletic delivery, arm speed and slot. Ability to get swings and misses is in doubt.

Chalmers,Dakota — SP — Oakland

EXP MLB DEBUT: 2020 | H/W: 6-3 175 | FUT: #1 starter | 9E

Thrws R Age 19
2015 (3) HS (GA)

- 90-96 FB +++
- 75-78 CB ++
- 82-86 SL ++
- CU ++

Year	Lev	Team	W	L	Sv	IP	K	ERA	WHIP	BF/G	OBA	H%	S%	xERA	Ctl	Dom	Cmd	hr/9	BPV
2015	Rk	Azl Athletics	0	1	0	20	18	2.69	1.59	8.1	209	28	81	3.14	7.6	8.1	1.1	0.0	-42

Very projectable SP with ceiling to match. Throws hard now and should add a few ticks with cleaner mechanics and more strength. Has rough delivery that is tough to repeat and command suffers. Has two breaking balls that show glimpses of promise and CU could become dynamite. Needs to throw more strikes.

Chargois,J.T. — RP — Minnesota

EXP MLB DEBUT: 2016 | H/W: 6-3 200 | FUT: Closer | 7B

Thrws R Age 25
2012 (2) Rice

- 94-99 FB ++++
- 81-84 SL +++
- CU +

Year	Lev	Team	W	L	Sv	IP	K	ERA	WHIP	BF/G	OBA	H%	S%	xERA	Ctl	Dom	Cmd	hr/9	BPV
2015	A+	Fort Myers	1	0	4	15	19	2.40	1.13	3.7	221	34	76	2.10	3.0	11.4	3.8	0.0	142
2015	AA	Chattanooga	1	1	11	33	34	2.73	1.39	4.3	218	30	80	3.00	5.5	9.3	1.7	0.3	38

Strong-framed RP who returned after missing 2 seasons after TJ surgery. Served as closer and has knockout stuff. Registers Ks and groundballs with plus FB and complements with slurvy SL that he uses as chase pitch. Erratic control byproduct of complicated, max-effort delivery, but short arm action gives him deception.

Clarke,Taylor — RP — Arizona

EXP MLB DEBUT: 2018 | H/W: 6-4 195 | FUT: Setup reliever | 7D

Thrws R Age 22
2015 (3) Charleston

- 91-94 FB +++
- 78-79 SL ++
- CU ++

Year	Lev	Team	W	L	Sv	IP	K	ERA	WHIP	BF/G	OBA	H%	S%	xERA	Ctl	Dom	Cmd	hr/9	BPV
2015	NCAA	Charleston	13	1	1	114	143	1.74	0.79	24.2	191	28	82	1.39	1.1	11.3	10.2	0.6	191
2015	A-	Hillsboro	0	0	3	21	27	0.00	0.57	5.5	119	20	100		1.7	11.6	6.8	0.0	180

Over-the-top, strike throwing reliever. Commands low 90s FB to both sides of plate. Generates significant downhill plane due to overhand delivery. Ill-suited to throw SL; will never be aveage offering. Should toy with CB grips. Has feel for CU, but doesn't throw it enough.

Clarkin,Ian — SP — New York (A)

EXP MLB DEBUT: 2018 | H/W: 6-2 190 | FUT: #3 starter | 8D

Thrws L Age 21
2013 (1) HS (CA)

- 90-94 FB +++
- 70-73 CB +++
- 88-90 CT +++
- 80-83 CU +++

Year	Lev	Team	W	L	Sv	IP	K	ERA	WHIP	BF/G	OBA	H%	S%	xERA	Ctl	Dom	Cmd	hr/9	BPV
2013	Rk	GCL Yankees	0	2	0	5	4	10.80	1.80	7.7	262	23	43	7.73	7.2	7.2	1.0	3.6	-47
2014	A	Charleston (Sc)	3	3	0	70	71	3.21	1.23	17.7	245	31	76	3.39	2.8	9.1	3.2	0.8	106
2014	A+	Tampa	1	0	0	5	4	1.80	1.60	22.1	332	41	88	4.91	1.8	7.2	4.0	0.0	99
2015	A+	Tampa																	

Tall, lean SP who did not pitch in '15 due to elbow inflammation. Has injury history and lack of pro experience. When healthy, gets great pitch movement and can cut FB at will. Has enough velocity and life to work off FB while mixing in slow CB and plus CU. Has deception in clean delivery and does nice job of repeating slot and release point.

Cleavinger,Garrett — RP — Baltimore

EXP MLB DEBUT: 2017 | H/W: 6-1 210 | FUT: Setup reliever | 7D

Thrws L Age 21
2015 (3) Oregon

- 91-94 FB +++
- 78-80 CB +++
- CU +

Year	Lev	Team	W	L	Sv	IP	K	ERA	WHIP	BF/G	OBA	H%	S%	xERA	Ctl	Dom	Cmd	hr/9	BPV
2015	NCAA	Oregon	6	2	9	40	66	1.58	0.93	4.0	151	28	86	1.16	3.8	14.9	3.9	0.5	182
2015	A-	Aberdeen	6	1	1	25	32	2.16	1.28	5.4	166	24	87	2.50	6.5	11.5	1.8	0.7	50

Strong, aggressive RP who misses bats with lively FB and power CB. Very tough on LHH with big-breaking CB and could get to majors quickly as situational guy. Has potential to be more, but needs to control plate and command FB. Doesn't change speeds much, but attacking nature is his strength. Held LHH to .138 oppBA.

Clevinger,Michael

SP | Cleveland | EXP MLB DEBUT: 2016 | H/W: 6-4 220 | FUT: #3 starter | 8C

Thrws R Age 25	Year	Lev	Team	W	L	Sv	IP	K	ERA	WHIP	BF/G	OBA	H%	S%	xERA	Ctl	Dom	Cmd	hr/9	BPV
2011 (4) Seminole State JC	2013	Rk	Azl Angels	0	0	0	3	3	3.00	1.33	6.2	191	27	75	2.27	6.0	9.0	1.5	0.0	18
91-95 FB +++	2014	A	Burlington	3	0	0	24	27	1.88	0.88	17.7	191	26	84	1.81	1.9	10.1	5.4	0.8	150
81-83 SL +++	2014	A+	Carolina	0	1	0	20	15	4.90	1.53	17.6	260	31	67	4.08	4.9	6.7	1.4	0.4	6
81-84 CU +++	2014	A+	Inland Empire	1	3	0	55	58	5.39	1.54	18.5	272	34	68	5.05	4.4	9.5	2.1	1.3	69
	2015	AA	Akron	9	8	0	158	145	2.73	1.06	22.7	222	28	75	2.37	2.3	8.3	3.6	0.5	105

Big, strong SP who modified delivery and arm slot while remaining healthy in breakout season. Showed much improved control and command and limited hard contact. Pitches aggressively with FB and can use as K pitch along with SL. Keeps ball low in zone and doesn't allow many HR.

Clifton,Trevor

SP | Chicago (N) | EXP MLB DEBUT: 2018 | H/W: 6-4 170 | FUT: #4 starter | 7D

Thrws R Age 20	Year	Lev	Team	W	L	Sv	IP	K	ERA	WHIP	BF/G	OBA	H%	S%	xERA	Ctl	Dom	Cmd	hr/9	BPV
2013 (12) HS (TN)																				
92-94 FB ++++																				
80-83 CB ++	2013	Rk	Azl Cubs	0	0	0	10	15	7.13	2.08	6.2	313	49	62	5.75	7.1	13.4	1.9	0.0	66
CU ++	2014	A-	Boise	4	2	0	61	54	3.69	1.46	20.1	255	32	74	3.81	4.4	8.0	1.8	0.4	42
	2015	A	South Bend	8	10	0	108	103	3.99	1.28	19.3	230	29	69	3.14	3.9	8.6	2.2	0.6	67

Projectable RHP has added size and velocity since being drafted in the 12th round in 2013. FB sits at 92-94, topping out at 97 mph. Scrapped his SL in favor of a hard low-80s CB. Held his own as a 20-yr-old in the MWL. If CU improves he could settle in as a solid #3-4 starter.

Cochran-Gill,Trey

RP | Oakland | EXP MLB DEBUT: 2016 | H/W: 5-10 190 | FUT: Setup reliever | 6B

Thrws R Age 23	Year	Lev	Team	W	L	Sv	IP	K	ERA	WHIP	BF/G	OBA	H%	S%	xERA	Ctl	Dom	Cmd	hr/9	BPV
2014 (17) Auburn	2014	Rk	Pulaski	3	0	8	25		0.36	0.67	4.9	165	27	94	0.29	1.1	11.8	11.0	0.0	201
88-93 FB +++	2014	A-	Everett	2	0	4	10	11	0.00	1.18	5.8	218	31	100	2.18	3.5	9.7	2.8	0.0	97
81-85 SL +++	2015	A+	Bakersfield	2	1	2	19	18	1.41	0.57	6.5	129	18	73		1.4	8.4	6.0	0.0	132
CU +	2015	AA	Jackson	4	3	4	53	30	5.43	1.72	7.1	283	33	65	4.46	5.4	5.1	0.9	0.0	-37
	2015	AAA	Tacoma	0	1	0	2	3	0.00	2.27	11.2	326	48	100	6.46	8.2	12.3	1.5	0.0	18

Short, quick-armed RP who has yet to allow HR in pro career. Uses average FB with vicious sink to live in lower half zone. Primarily uses FB early in count and has solid SL in arsenal. Isn't afraid to pitch to contact. Erratic control limits upside as he fails to repeat compact delivery. Long arm action isn't deceptive.

Cole,A.J.

SP | Washington | EXP MLB DEBUT: 2015 | H/W: 6-5 200 | FUT: #3 starter | 7A

Thrws R Age 24	Year	Lev	Team	W	L	Sv	IP	K	ERA	WHIP	BF/G	OBA	H%	S%	xERA	Ctl	Dom	Cmd	hr/9	BPV
2010 (4) HS (FL)	2013	AA	Harrisburg	4	2	0	45	49	2.20	0.91	24.0	196	26	79	1.81	2.0	9.8	4.9	0.6	140
90-93 FB ++++	2014	AA	Harrisburg	6	3	0	71	61	2.92	1.32	21.0	283	36	76	3.56	1.9	7.7	4.1	0.1	106
80-84 SL ++	2014	AAA	Syracuse	7	0	0	63	50	3.43	1.37	24.0	280	32	81	4.72	2.4	7.1	2.9	1.3	81
81-83 CU +++	2015	AAA	Syracuse	5	6	0	105	76	3.17	1.19	20.1	235	27	76	3.18	2.9	6.5	2.2	0.8	56
CB ++	2015	MLB	Washington	0	0	1	9	9	5.93	1.65	13.6	353	44	64	6.31	1.0	8.9	9.0	1.0	152

Well-proportioned starter with clean, repeatable mechanics that lead to good control. Has a quick arm and athletic delivery. Is able to spot and work off his fastball. Change-up is his best secondary; both breaking pitches presently inconsistent. Offerings can find too much of the barrel at times.

Cole,Taylor

SP | Toronto | EXP MLB DEBUT: 2016 | H/W: 6-1 190 | FUT: #5 starter | 6B

Thrws R Age 26	Year	Lev	Team	W	L	Sv	IP	K	ERA	WHIP	BF/G	OBA	H%	S%	xERA	Ctl	Dom	Cmd	hr/9	BPV
2011 (29) Brigham Young	2013	A	Lansing	7	11	0	132	101	4.02	1.52	22.0	275	33	72	4.14	4.0	6.9	1.7	0.3	33
89-92 FB +++	2013	A+	Dunedin	0	1	0	5	2	1.80	1.60	22.1	299	33	88	4.41	3.6	3.6	1.0	0.0	-14
80-83 SL ++	2014	A+	Dunedin	8	9	0	132	171	3.07	1.16	21.9	234	35	72	2.58	2.7	11.7	4.4	0.3	156
81-83 CU +++	2014	AA	New Hampshire	0	2	0	12	10	7.44	1.57	26.6	260	31	50	4.44	5.2	7.4	1.4	0.7	11
	2015	AA	New Hampshire	7	10	0	164	128	4.06	1.40	24.7	273	32	73	4.42	3.0	7.0	2.3	1.0	63

Command-oriented SP who got better as season progressed. Spots FB to all quadrants of strike zone and has one of best CU in org. Repeats simple, compact delivery. Needs pitch to battle LHH (.302 oppBA) and FB has tendency to be too straight. Not an overpowering guy and can be hittable. Fall in K rate a definite concern.

Cooney,Tim

SP | St. Louis | EXP MLB DEBUT: 2015 | H/W: 6-2 196 | FUT: #3 starter | 7A

Thrws L Age 25	Year	Lev	Team	W	L	Sv	IP	K	ERA	WHIP	BF/G	OBA	H%	S%	xERA	Ctl	Dom	Cmd	hr/9	BPV
2012 (3) Wake Forest	2013	A+	Palm Beach	3	3	0	36	23	2.75	1.17	23.9	272	32	76	3.15	1.0	5.8	5.8	0.3	95
89-93 FB +++	2013	AA	Springfield	7	10	0	118	125	3.81	1.27	24.2	284	37	70	3.88	1.4	9.5	6.9	0.6	152
74-77 CB +++	2014	AAA	Memphis	14	6	0	158	119	3.47	1.30	25.0	262	30	78	4.21	2.7	6.8	2.5	1.2	68
SL +++	2015	AAA	Memphis	6	4	0	88	63	2.76	0.87	23.3	197	22	74	2.07	1.6	6.4	3.9	0.9	90
CU ++	2015	MLB	St. Louis	1	0	0	31	29	3.18	1.22	21.0	242	30	77	3.43	2.9	8.4	2.9	0.9	91

Finesse LHP from has a good feel for pitching. Keeps hitters off balance with four average offerings. FB sits at 89-93 with late life. Mixes in a mid-70s CB, as well as SL/CT and CU. Locates all four well and does a good job of changing speeds. Held his own in MLB debut before being shut down with appendicitis.

Coonrod,Samuel

SP | San Francisco | EXP MLB DEBUT: 2017 | H/W: 6-2 225 | FUT: #4 starter | 8C

Thrws R Age 23	Year	Lev	Team	W	L	Sv	IP	K	ERA	WHIP	BF/G	OBA	H%	S%	xERA	Ctl	Dom	Cmd	hr/9	BPV
2014 (5) So Illinois	2012	NCAA	So Illinois	3	5	0	64	54	4.64	1.25	14.5	250	30	64	3.59	2.8	7.6	2.7	0.8	79
91-95 FB ++++	2013	NCAA	So Illinois	3	6	0	79	68	4.32	1.62	23.4	261	34	70	3.87	5.6	7.7	1.4	0.0	7
79-83 SL +++	2014	NCAA	So Illinois	2	6	0	84	77	2.89	1.39	23.6	228	29	79	3.16	5.0	8.2	1.6	0.3	31
82-84 CU ++	2014	Rk	Azl Giants	1	0	0	27	25	3.97	1.40	7.6	294	38	68	3.79	2.0	8.3	4.2	0.0	113
	2015	A	Augusta	7	5	0	111	114	3.16	1.23	19.6	247	33	73	2.93	2.8	9.2	3.4	0.2	110

Strong, durable RH who led the SAL in Dom and features good control of three-pitch mix. FB settles in low 90s but can reach back for 96. Tight SL is effective bat-misser vs. RHH. CU lacks depth, but gets good velo separation. Smooth, calculated delivery sans much effort from 3/4 slot should help him maintain velo long-term.

Coshow,Cale

RP | New York (A) | EXP MLB DEBUT: 2016 | H/W: 6-5 260 | FUT: #4 SP / Setup RP | 7C

Thrws R Age 23	Year	Lev	Team	W	L	Sv	IP	K	ERA	WHIP	BF/G	OBA	H%	S%	xERA	Ctl	Dom	Cmd	hr/9	BPV
2013 (13) Oklahoma Christian	2014	A-	Staten Island	0	0	0	3	3	0.00	0.67	10.5	191	27	100	0.59	0.0	9.0		0.0	180
91-96 FB +++	2014	A	Charleston (Sc)	1	1	0	8	13	5.49	1.83	6.4	377	58	67	6.23	1.1	14.3	13.0	0.0	245
77-80 CB ++	2015	A	Charleston (Sc)	0	0	7	16	20	1.13	0.88	5.4	181	28	86	0.98	2.3	11.3	5.0	0.0	160
82-85 SL +++	2015	A+	Tampa	7	2	1	64	56	2.24	0.89	14.9	203	26	75	1.55	1.5	7.9	5.1	0.3	118
CU ++	2015	AA	Trenton	2	3	0	33	21	3.53	1.27	22.6	237	28	71	2.95	3.5	5.7	1.6	0.3	25

Large-framed pitcher who is advancing quickly and was put in rotation in AA in August. FB features both velocity and late life and induces high amount of groundballs. Looking for consistency with secondary pitches with CB lagging behind. SL is quality pitch, but CU needs upgrade.

Cotton,Jharel

SP | Los Angeles (N) | EXP MLB DEBUT: 2016 | H/W: 5-11 195 | FUT: #3 starter/reliever | 8D

Thrws R Age 24	Year	Lev	Team	W	L	Sv	IP	K	ERA	WHIP	BF/G	OBA	H%	S%	xERA	Ctl	Dom	Cmd	hr/9	BPV
2012 (20) East Carolina	2014	A+	RanchoCuca	6	10	0	126	138	4.06	1.16	20.1	241	30	70	3.65	2.4	9.8	4.1	1.3	130
92-95 FB ++++	2015	A	Great Lakes	0	0	0	3	6	5.81	1.61	13.7	314	59	60	4.55	2.9	17.4	6.0	0.0	253
80-83 CU +++	2015	A+	RanchoCuca	1	0	0	22	28	1.63	0.95	20.8	183	27	85	1.58	2.9	11.4	4.0	0.4	146
73-75 CB ++	2015	AA	Tulsa	5	2	0	62	71	2.32	1.13	22.3	218	30	82	2.60	3.0	10.3	3.4	0.6	121
	2015	AAA	Oklahoma City	0	0	0	7	9	5.07	1.55	6.2	310	45	64	4.39	2.5	11.4	4.5	0.0	155

Pitched at four different levels, working both as a starter and in relief. FB velocity has jumped from 88-91 mph to 92-95 mph and mixes in a plus late, breaking CU that gives him a deadly 1-2 punch. Lack of size and a quality breaking ball could push him into relief full-time, but either way he should make an impact in the majors.

Covey,Dylan

SP | Oakland | EXP MLB DEBUT: 2017 | H/W: 6-2 195 | FUT: #4 starter | 7C

Thrws R Age 24	Year	Lev	Team	W	L	Sv	IP	K	ERA	WHIP	BF/G	OBA	H%	S%	xERA	Ctl	Dom	Cmd	hr/9	BPV
2013 (4) San Diego	2013	A-	Vermont	0	0	0	12	15	0.00	0.83	11.0	210	32	100	1.21	0.8	11.3	15.0	0.0	200
88-93 FB +++	2013	A	Beloit	1	1	0	47	31	4.78	1.72	21.4	325	37	73	5.83	3.2	5.9	1.8	0.8	37
79-81 CB +++	2014	A	Beloit	4	9	0	101	70	4.81	1.24	22.8	258	31	58	3.14	2.3	6.2	2.7	0.3	68
81-83 SL ++	2014	A+	Stockton	3	5	0	39	22	7.15	1.64	21.7	308	35	53	5.08	3.5	5.1	1.5	0.5	16
81-83 CU +++	2015	A+	Stockton	8	9	0	140	100	3.60	1.27	22.0	255	29	74	3.71	2.8	6.4	2.3	0.8	59

Athletic SP who finished 3rd in ERA in CAL in best year to date. Keeps ball low in zone to induce grounders, though fails to get swings and misses with average repertoire. FB features cutting action and is rarely straight while hard CB is best secondary. Needs to have better command to succeed at upper levels.

Cravy,Tyler

SP | Milwaukee | EXP MLB DEBUT: 2015 | H/W: 6-2 210 | FUT: #4 SP / Middle RP | 7C

Thrws R Age 26	Year	Lev	Team	W	L	Sv	IP	K	ERA	WHIP	BF/G	OBA	H%	S%	xERA	Ctl	Dom	Cmd	hr/9	BPV
2009 (17) Napa Valley CC	2014	Rk	Azl Brewers	0	1	0	6	8	0.00	0.67	10.5	106	18	100		3.0	12.0	4.0	0.0	153
89-92 FB +++	2014	AA	Huntsville	8	1	0	73	64	1.72	0.85	19.2	186	22	87	1.81	1.8	7.9	4.3	0.9	110
83-86 SL +++	2014	AAA	Nashville	0	0	0	3	4	2.90	1.94	14.7	255	39	83	4.56	8.7	11.6	1.3	0.0	-8
83-86 CU ++	2015	AAA	Colorado Springs	7	7	0	95	75	3.97	1.29	23.0	255	31	69	3.52	2.9	7.1	2.4	0.6	67
76-81 CB ++	2015	MLB	Milwaukee	0	8	0	42	35	5.76	1.64	13.4	283	33	66	5.24	4.7	7.5	1.6	1.1	26

Mature RH survives on command, mixing speeds and movement to compensate for lack of a plus offering. Spots low-90s FB well for ground balls and mixes in an average CT; CB and SL are fringe-average at best; CU has well below-average action. Hides the ball well for deception, allowing stuff to play up in spurts. Profiles as a middle-inning reliever long-term.

Crawford,Jonathon — SP — Cincinnati

EXP MLB DEBUT: 2018 | H/W: 6-2 205 | FUT: Setup reliever | 8D

Thrws R Age 24
2013 (1) Florida

Velo	Pitch	Grade
92-95	FB	+++
82-85	SL	+++
	CU	++

Year	Lev	Team	W	L	Sv	IP	K	ERA	WHIP	BF/G	OBA	H%	S%	xERA	Ctl	Dom	Cmd	hr/9	BPV
2013	NCAA	Florida	3	6	0	86	69	3.86	1.36	24.0	248	30	71	3.43	3.9	7.2	1.9	0.4	43
2013	A-	Connecticut	0	2	0	19	21	1.89	1.26	9.7	219	32	83	2.41	4.3	9.9	2.3	0.0	82
2014	A	West Michigan	8	3	0	123	85	2.85	1.16	21.3	211	26	74	2.31	3.7	6.2	1.7	0.2	31
2015	Rk	AZL Reds	0	0	0	8	8	4.44	1.11	10.6	259	35	56	2.56	1.1	8.9	8.0	0.0	148
2015	A+	Daytona	0	1	0	5	6	8.82	1.57	11.2	258	37	38	3.68	5.3	10.6	2.0	0.0	66

Missed action due to shoulder tendinitis. Has stuff to start but shoulder health & effort in his delivery likely have him slated for pen. FB is best pitch. Movement causes weak contact. SL has two-plane break & could become plus if thrown harder. CU is a workable pitch but FB/SL combination is likely enough to be successful as RP.

Crawford,Leonardo — SP — Los Angeles (N)

EXP MLB DEBUT: 2020 | H/W: 6-0 180 | FUT: #3 starter | 7C

Thrws L Age 19
2015 FA (NI)

Velo	Pitch	Grade
90-92	FB	+++
	CB	++
	CU	++

Year	Lev	Team	W	L	Sv	IP	K	ERA	WHIP	BF/G	OBA	H%	S%	xERA	Ctl	Dom	Cmd	hr/9	BPV

Did not pitch in U.S.

Lefty has yet to make his U.S. debut, but was impressive in the DSL, posting a 1.41 ERA and a 10.4 Dom. Uses a high leg kick to drive home a good low-90 FB and has the arm strength for more as he matures. Also mixes in a CB and a CU; both show potential. Should make his state-side debut in '16.

Crick,Kyle — SP — San Francisco

EXP MLB DEBUT: 2017 | H/W: 6-4 220 | FUT: #2 SP / Setup RP | 9D

Thrws R Age 23
2011 (1) HS (TX)

Velo	Pitch	Grade
93-97	FB	++++
82-84	SL	+++
87-89	CU	++
88-91	CT	++

Year	Lev	Team	W	L	Sv	IP	K	ERA	WHIP	BF/G	OBA	H%	S%	xERA	Ctl	Dom	Cmd	hr/9	BPV
2011	Rk	Azl Giants	1	0	0	7		6.43	2.43	5.2	313	43	71	6.66	10.3	10.3	1.0	0.0	-75
2012	A	Augusta	7	6	0	111	128	2.51	1.28	19.8	193	29	79	2.22	5.4	10.4	1.9	0.1	58
2013	A+	San Jose	3	1	0	68	95	1.58	1.28	20.0	200	33	87	2.31	5.1	12.5	2.4	0.1	105
2014	AA	Richmond	6	7	0	90	111	3.80	1.54	17.1	235	33	77	3.96	6.1	11.1	1.8	0.7	53
2015	AA	Richmond	3	4	0	63	73	3.29	1.79	8.1	209	30	81	3.90	9.4	10.4	1.1	0.3	-49

Strong, quick-armed RH switched to the pen after poor Ctl plagued SP production. FB still electric 93-97 mph (T99) with great sink; hard SL/CT misses bats; CU flashes nice fade; mixes in CB with 12-6 depth. Struggles to work ahead and delivery is often sloppy. Still time to sort out mechanics to stay in rotation, but future might now be as RP.

Danish,Tyler — SP — Chicago (A)

EXP MLB DEBUT: 2016 | H/W: 6-0 205 | FUT: #4 starter | 7B

Thrws R Age 21
2013 (2) HS (FL)

Velo	Pitch	Grade
88-93	FB	+++
78-82	SL	+++
79-82	CU	+++

Year	Lev	Team	W	L	Sv	IP	K	ERA	WHIP	BF/G	OBA	H%	S%	xERA	Ctl	Dom	Cmd	hr/9	BPV
2013	Rk	Bristol	1	0	0	26	22	1.38	0.77	7.2	170	21	84	0.95	1.7	7.6	4.4	0.3	108
2013	A	Kannapolis	0	0	0	4	6	0.00	0.50	6.6	151	27	100		0.0	13.5		0.0	261
2014	A	Kannapolis	3	0	0	38	25	0.71	1.00	20.7	207	25	92	1.65	2.4	5.9	2.5	0.0	61
2014	A+	Winston-Salem	5	3	0	91	78	2.66	1.21	20.4	253	31	81	3.37	2.3	7.7	3.4	0.7	95
2015	AA	Birmingham	8	12	0	142	90	4.50	1.65	24.4	304	34	74	5.39	3.8	5.7	1.5	0.8	18

Enjoyed breakout in '14, but struggled in '15, as he became hittable and his walk rate elevated. Despite poor numbers, has solid average arsenal with pitches that exhibit great movement. Uses low arm slot to keep ball down, and has very good CU to combat LHH. Ceiling isn't high, but has good chance to be dependable back-end guy.

Davies,Zach — SP — Milwaukee

EXP MLB DEBUT: 2015 | H/W: 6-0 160 | FUT: #4 starter | 7A

Thrws R Age 23
2011 (26) HS (AZ)

Velo	Pitch	Grade
88-91	FB	+++
78-82	CU	++++
73-75	CB	+++
79-82	SL	++

Year	Lev	Team	W	L	Sv	IP	K	ERA	WHIP	BF/G	OBA	H%	S%	xERA	Ctl	Dom	Cmd	hr/9	BPV
2013	A+	Frederick	7	9	0	148	132	3.70	1.23	23.1	258	32	71	3.43	2.3	8.0	3.5	0.6	100
2014	AA	Bowie	10	7	0	110	109	3.35	1.25	21.3	255	33	75	3.48	2.6	8.9	3.4	0.7	108
2015	AAA	Colorado Springs	1	2	0	27	21	5.00	1.85	25.2	333	39	73	6.19	4.0	7.0	1.8	0.7	36
2015	AAA	Norfolk	5	6	0	101	81	2.85	1.23	21.5	242	30	77	2.97	2.9	7.2	2.5	0.4	68
2015	MLB	Milwaukee	3	2	0	34	24	3.71	1.21	22.8	213	25	69	2.73	4.0	6.4	1.6	0.5	25

Short, slender right-hander who succeeds with pitchability over velo. Commands FB down well for worm-burners; plus CU gets whiffs with arm speed/repeatable delivery; SL/CB show average movement. Working on a cutter. Pitches with a plan and has great feel for everything. Track record for durability. Will gobble quality innings at the next level.

Davila,Garrett — SP — Kansas City

EXP MLB DEBUT: 2020 | H/W: 6-2 180 | FUT: #4 starter | 7D

Thrws L Age 19
2015 (4) HS (NC)

Velo	Pitch	Grade
87-92	FB	++
75-77	CB	+++
81-84	CU	++

Year	Lev	Team	W	L	Sv	IP	K	ERA	WHIP	BF/G	OBA	H%	S%	xERA	Ctl	Dom	Cmd	hr/9	BPV
2015		*Did not pitch*																	

Projectable SP who will take time to develop, but payoff could be immense. Only has average velocity now, but could add extra ticks as he cleans up delivery and adds strength to thin frame. Slow CB exhibits big bend and could grow into plus offering. Command comes and goes and can have tendency to aim ball.

Davis,Rookie — SP — Cincinnati

EXP MLB DEBUT: 2016 | H/W: 6-5 245 | FUT: #3 starter | 8D

Thrws R Age 22
2011 (14) HS (NC)

Velo	Pitch	Grade
90-95	FB	++++
77-81	CB	+++
81-84	CU	++

Year	Lev	Team	W	L	Sv	IP	K	ERA	WHIP	BF/G	OBA	H%	S%	xERA	Ctl	Dom	Cmd	hr/9	BPV
2013	A-	Staten Island	2	4	0	42	39	2.36	1.40	16.1	280	36	83	3.80	2.8	8.4	3.0	0.2	93
2013	A	Charleston (Sc)	0	0	0	10	8	0.00	0.90	18.6	242	31	100	1.82	0.0	7.2		0.0	148
2014	A	Charleston (Sc)	7	8	0	126	106	4.93	1.40	19.7	274	34	63	3.97	3.0	7.6	2.5	0.5	73
2015	A+	Tampa	6	6	0	97	105	3.71	1.15	20.3	256	35	67	2.96	1.7	9.7	5.8	0.4	148
2015	AA	Trenton	2	1	0	33	24	4.35	1.39	23.2	289	35	67	3.97	2.2	6.5	3.0	0.3	77

Tall, large SP who is emerging as legitimate prospect. Has physical frame with improving stuff across board. FB has evolved into plus pitch with cutting action and late drop. Hard CB serves as wipeout offering while using same arm speed on CU. Hittable when in middle of plate.

Dawson,Shane — SP — Toronto

EXP MLB DEBUT: 2017 | H/W: 6-1 200 | FUT: #4 starter | 7C

Thrws L Age 22
2012 (17) Lethbridge JC

Velo	Pitch	Grade
86-92	FB	+++
75-78	CB	+++
81-84	SL	++
81-82	CU	+++

Year	Lev	Team	W	L	Sv	IP	K	ERA	WHIP	BF/G	OBA	H%	S%	xERA	Ctl	Dom	Cmd	hr/9	BPV
2013	Rk	Bluefield	1	3	2	27	35	3.32	0.85	14.2	182	28	59	1.23	2.0	11.6	5.8	0.3	173
2013	A-	Vancouver	1	1	0	18	26	2.97	1.15	18.1	249	40	71	2.49	2.0	12.9	6.5	0.0	196
2014	A	Lansing	3	5	0	56	46	3.38	1.41	16.9	258	31	77	3.92	3.9	7.4	1.9	0.6	47
2015	A	Lansing	12	4	0	101	98	3.02	1.18	21.3	250	32	76	3.18	2.1	8.7	4.1	0.6	117
2015	A+	Dunedin	3	2	0	26	22	3.12	1.08	20.3	214	26	73	2.56	2.8	7.6	2.8	0.7	80

Finesse pitcher who has spent most of past 2 seasons in Low-A and had breakout campaign. All about control and pitch location as he lacks plus pitch. Sequences 4 pitches and throws to both sides of plate. Slow CB is best offering and can negate LHH. Keeps ball in yard and limits walks. Has chance to become back-end guy.

De La Cruz,Oscar — SP — Chicago (N)

EXP MLB DEBUT: 2019 | H/W: 6-4 200 | FUT: #3 starter | 8D

Thrws R Age 21
2012 FA (DR)

Velo	Pitch	Grade
92-94	FB	++++
80-82	CB	+++
	CU	++

Year	Lev	Team	W	L	Sv	IP	K	ERA	WHIP	BF/G	OBA	H%	S%	xERA	Ctl	Dom	Cmd	hr/9	BPV
2015	A-	Eugene	6	3	0	73	73	2.84	1.00	21.5	214	28	72	2.16	2.1	9.0	4.3	0.5	123

Tall, lanky hurler was lights-outs in his US debut. Fastball is already at 92-94 mph with room for more. Power CB and CU show potential, but need refinement. Uses his size to pitch downhill and showed solid command.

De Leon,Jose — SP — Los Angeles (N)

EXP MLB DEBUT: 2017 | H/W: 6-2 185 | FUT: #2 starter | 9D

Thrws R Age 23
2013 (24) Southern

Velo	Pitch	Grade
91-94	FB	++++
83-85	SL	+++
83-85	CU	+++

Year	Lev	Team	W	L	Sv	IP	K	ERA	WHIP	BF/G	OBA	H%	S%	xERA	Ctl	Dom	Cmd	hr/9	BPV
2013	Rk	Azl Dodgers	2	3	0	33	35	4.07	1.51	16.0	255	35	71	3.74	4.9	9.5	1.9	0.3	57
2014	Rk	Ogden	5	0	0	54	77	2.66	1.16	21.6	224	36	77	2.51	3.2	12.8	4.1	0.3	163
2014	A	Great Lakes	2	0	0	22	42	1.22	0.72	19.7	183	39	87	0.93	0.8	17.0	21.0	0.4	303
2015	A+	RanchoCuca	4	1	0	37	58	1.69	0.91	19.8	199	35	82	1.48	1.9	14.0	7.3	0.2	218
2015	AA	Tulsa	2	6	0	76	105	3.66	1.18	19.1	221	31	75	3.43	3.4	12.4	3.6	1.3	149

24th rounder continues to impress. Attacks hitters with a good 91-94 mph FB that hits 96. Also shows a good 83-85 mph SL and an improved CU. Ability to miss bats while attacking the strike zone is plus as his 37 BB/163 K ratio demonstrates. Tends to pitch up in the zone, but velocity, late life, and deception allow him to stay out of trouble.

de los Santos,Abel — RP — Washington

EXP MLB DEBUT: 2015 | H/W: 6-2 200 | FUT: Setup reliever | 7C

Thrws R Age 23
2010 FA (DR)

Velo	Pitch	Grade
93-96	FB	+++
77-79	CB	++
84-87	CU	+++

Year	Lev	Team	W	L	Sv	IP	K	ERA	WHIP	BF/G	OBA	H%	S%	xERA	Ctl	Dom	Cmd	hr/9	BPV
2013	A-	Spokane	4	1	1	41	48	3.50	1.12	8.1	222	30	71	2.90	2.8	10.5	3.7	0.9	130
2014	A	Hickory	0	1	0	10	12	1.76	0.78	4.6	196	26	86	1.75	0.9	10.6	12.0	0.9	185
2014	A+	Myrtle Beach	5	2	8	45	53	1.99	1.02	5.3	185	27	80	1.58	3.4	10.6	3.1	0.2	117
2015	AA	Harrisburg	4	4	8	57	55	3.46	1.14	5.8	247	31	73	3.35	1.9	8.7	4.6	0.9	123
2015	MLB	Washington	0	0	0	1	3	7.50	2.50	3.2	371	72	100	14.78	7.5	22.5	3.0	7.5	221

Quick-armed prospect whose velocity ticked up with a move to the bullpen. Still lacks a top-notch out pitch, but gets good separation between FB and CB, and sprinkles in CU to keep lefties at bay. Good control despite rough mechanics. Will find his way into MLB bullpen soon, but unlikely to have a big impact.

de los Santos,Enyel — SP — San Diego

EXP MLB DEBUT: 2019 | H/W: 6-3 170 | FUT: #3 starter | 8D

Thrws R Age 20 — 2014 FA (DR)

Velo	Pitch	Grade
91-95	FB	+++
77-79	CB	+++
	CU	+++

Year	Lev	Team	W	L	Sv	IP	K	ERA	WHIP	BF/G	OBA	H%	S%	xERA	Ctl	Dom	Cmd	hr/9	BPV
2015	Rk	AZL Mariners	3	0	0	24	29	2.60	1.20	19.4	260	37	79	3.12	1.9	10.8	5.8	0.4	162
2015	A-	Everett	3	0	0	37	42	4.11	1.34	19.4	261	36	69	3.61	3.1	10.2	3.2	0.5	116

Athletic SP who is major sleeper. Showing consistent improvement with arm action and repeatable delivery. Generates easy velocity despite lean frame and can locate potential plus FB to both sides. Can throw too many strikes and command needs polish. Has two solid secondary pitches in CB and CU; CU being better of two.

De Paula,Rafael — SP — San Diego

EXP MLB DEBUT: 2018 | H/W: 6-2 215 | FUT: #3 SP / Setup RP | 8E

Thrws R Age 25 — 2010 FA (DR)

Velo	Pitch	Grade
91-96	FB	++++
82-86	SL	++
	CU	++

Year	Lev	Team	W	L	Sv	IP	K	ERA	WHIP	BF/G	OBA	H%	S%	xERA	Ctl	Dom	Cmd	hr/9	BPV
2013	A	Charleston (Sc)	6	2	0	64	96	2.95	1.03	19.0	192	32	71	1.87	3.2	13.5	4.2	0.4	173
2013	A+	Tampa	1	3	0	49	50	6.06	1.71	20.2	281	36	65	5.25	5.5	9.2	1.7	0.9	35
2014	A+	Lake Elsinore	2	4	0	42	41	6.61	1.52	22.9	283	34	58	5.32	3.6	8.7	2.4	1.5	78
2014	A+	Tampa	6	5	0	89	104	4.15	1.42	18.8	260	36	70	3.79	3.8	10.5	2.7	0.5	104
2015	A+	Lake Elsinore	5	9	0	120	129	5.02	1.43	14.6	270	35	66	4.49	3.5	9.7	2.7	1.0	97

Big, strong pitcher who moved to pen in late July and showed better results. Spent 2 1/2 years in A+ and still struggles with poor command and flyball tendencies. Has plus FB, but tends to overuse whether ahead or behind in count. SL has moments and can register Ks when on. Lacks offspeed pitch, but can dominate with heavy sinking FB.

Degano,Jeff — SP — New York (A)

EXP MLB DEBUT: 2018 | H/W: 6-4 215 | FUT: #4 starter | 7C

Thrws L Age 23 — 2015 (2) Indiana St

Velo	Pitch	Grade
90-94	FB	+++
78-83	SL	++++
79-83	CU	++

Year	Lev	Team	W	L	Sv	IP	K	ERA	WHIP	BF/G	OBA	H%	S%	xERA	Ctl	Dom	Cmd	hr/9	BPV
2015	NCAA	Indiana St	8	3	0	99	126	2.36	1.07	25.7	218	33	78	2.16	2.5	11.5	4.5	0.3	155
2015	Rk	GCL Yankees 2	0	4	0	9	7	5.87	1.96	7.3	350	41	71	7.05	3.9	6.8	1.8	1.0	36
2015	A-	Staten Island	0	0	0	10	14	2.65	1.47	10.9	258	40	80	3.42	4.4	12.4	2.8	0.0	121

Tall SP who is intriguing due to size and glimpses of plus breaking ball. Does nice job of changing velocity and bend in SL while FB has enough velocity to keep hitters honest. FB often lacks movement and CU is far behind other two offerings. Uses height well in delivery.

DeJong,Chase — SP — Los Angeles (N)

EXP MLB DEBUT: 2018 | H/W: 6-4 205 | FUT: #4 starter | 6B

Thrws R Age 22 — 2012 (2) HS (CA)

Velo	Pitch	Grade
88-92	FB	+++
75-78	CB	++++
	CU	++

Year	Lev	Team	W	L	Sv	IP	K	ERA	WHIP	BF/G	OBA	H%	S%	xERA	Ctl	Dom	Cmd	hr/9	BPV
2012	Rk	GCL Blue Jays	1	0	0	12	15	1.50	0.67	7.0	171	27	75	0.35	0.8	11.3	15.0	0.0	200
2013	Rk	Bluefield	2	3	0	56	66	3.05	1.21	17.4	269	38	74	3.24	1.6	10.6	6.6	0.3	166
2014	A	Lansing	1	6	0	97	73	4.82	1.39	17.8	292	33	67	4.81	2.0	6.8	3.3	1.1	85
2015	A	Lansing	7	4	0	86	77	3.14	1.08	24.0	236	28	75	3.07	1.9	8.0	4.3	0.9	112
2015	A+	RanchoCuca	4	3	0	50	52	3.96	1.18	18.2	238	30	70	3.46	2.7	9.4	3.5	1.1	114

Came over from the Jays in exchange for Int. signing slots. Spike in Dom (6.7 in '14 vs. 8.5 in '15) fueled a breakout. Is not overpowering with a FB that sits at 88-91 mph, but has good location and mixes in a plus CB and improved CU. Delivery is stiff and he isn't particularly athletic, but knows how to pitch and could be a #4 starter.

Del Pozo,Miguel — RP — Miami

EXP MLB DEBUT: 2019 | H/W: 6-1 180 | FUT: Setup reliever | 6C

Thrws L Age 23 — 2010 FA (DR)

Velo	Pitch	Grade
90-93	FB	+++
	CB	+
	CU	+

Year	Lev	Team	W	L	Sv	IP	K	ERA	WHIP	BF/G	OBA	H%	S%	xERA	Ctl	Dom	Cmd	hr/9	BPV
2012	Rk	GCL Marlins	1	2	1	31	32	4.05	1.61	7.7	235	32	73	3.77	6.7	9.3	1.4	0.3	5
2013	A-	Batavia	2	1	0	24	36	4.85	1.70	6.4	261	42	70	4.38	6.3	13.4	2.1	0.4	89
2013	A+	Jupiter	0	0	0	2	0	0.00	1.50	4.3	151	15	100	2.34	9.0	0.0	0.0	0.0	-225
2014	A	Greensboro	2	6	4	66	85	4.91	1.18	6.4	241	35	58	3.11	2.6	11.6	4.5	0.7	157
2015	A+	Jupiter	2	5	0	59	55	4.26	1.57	9.6	305	39	71	4.53	3.0	8.4	2.8	0.2	87

Short, stocky Dominican lefty worked mostly in relief with mixed results. Has a good FB/CB combo that keeps the ball down in the zone and hitters off-balance. He gave up just 1 HR in 59.1 IP, but lack of CU is problematic and FSL hitters batted .300 against him.

Devenski,Chris — SP — Houston

EXP MLB DEBUT: 2016 | H/W: 6-3 195 | FUT: #4 starter | 7D

Thrws R Age 25 — 2011 (25) Cal St Fullerton

Velo	Pitch	Grade
89-93	FB	+++
78-80	CB	++
82-83	CU	+++

Year	Lev	Team	W	L	Sv	IP	K	ERA	WHIP	BF/G	OBA	H%	S%	xERA	Ctl	Dom	Cmd	hr/9	BPV
2013	A	Quad Cities	4	3	0	43	32	4.39	1.60	23.8	331	39	73	5.48	1.9	6.7	3.6	0.6	88
2013	A+	Lancaster	4	2	1	75	65	7.91	1.82	16.6	334	39	57	6.96	3.7	7.8	2.1	1.6	58
2014	A+	Lancaster	5	5	2	76	77	4.13	1.08	17.5	246	31	64	3.18	1.4	9.1	6.4	0.9	143
2014	AA	Corpus Christi	5	3	0	41	37	3.94	1.24	16.7	222	25	75	3.85	3.9	8.1	2.1	1.5	57
2015	AA	Corpus Christi	7	4	2	119	104	3.02	1.26	20.3	258	31	80	3.78	2.5	7.9	3.2	0.9	92

Command-oriented SP who started season with 27 scoreless IP and finished 2nd in ERA. Can spot pitches and isn't afraid to waste pitch in order to deceive hitters. Likes to go to FB early in count and wipe out hitters with CU. Posted reverse splits in '15 and could stand to add power to CB. Won't beat himself, but can leave balls high in zone.

Diaz,Edwin — SP — Seattle

EXP MLB DEBUT: 2017 | H/W: 6-3 165 | FUT: #3 starter | 8C

Thrws R Age 22 — 2012 (3) HS (PR)

Velo	Pitch	Grade
90-94	FB	++++
81-84	SL	+++
82-85	CU	++

Year	Lev	Team	W	L	Sv	IP	K	ERA	WHIP	BF/G	OBA	H%	S%	xERA	Ctl	Dom	Cmd	hr/9	BPV
2012	Rk	Azl Mariners	2	1	0	19	20	5.21	1.53	9.2	183	23	67	3.55	8.1	9.5	1.2	0.9	-29
2013	Rk	Pulaski	5	2	0	69	79	1.43	0.91	19.8	188	26	90	1.77	2.3	10.3	4.4	0.7	140
2014	A	Clinton	6	8	0	116	111	3.33	1.19	19.4	227	30	71	2.70	3.3	8.6	2.6	0.4	85
2015	A+	Bakersfield	2	0	0	37	42	1.70	0.81	19.2	168	22	85	1.36	2.2	10.2	4.7	0.7	143
2015	AA	Jackson	5	10	0	104	103	4.58	1.34	21.6	258	34	64	3.51	3.2	8.9	2.8	0.4	92

Tall, thin SP who is adding strength to frame and producing at high level. Struggled in initial taste of AA, but should get better. Plus FB highlights arsenal and thrown from low 3/4 slot. Locates it well despite natural movement. Can rush delivery which impacts CU, but has average potential. Throws strikes with all pitches and can miss bats.

Diaz,Jairo — RP — Colorado

EXP MLB DEBUT: 2014 | H/W: 6-0 200 | FUT: Closer | 7B

Thrws R Age 24 — 2007 FA (VZ)

Velo	Pitch	Grade
97-98	FB	++++
87-90	SL	++

Year	Lev	Team	W	L	Sv	IP	K	ERA	WHIP	BF/G	OBA	H%	S%	xERA	Ctl	Dom	Cmd	hr/9	BPV
2014	A+	Inland Empire	2	3	4	32	37	4.78	1.28	4.5	256	35	62	3.46	2.8	10.4	3.7	0.6	129
2014	AA	Arkansas	2	1	11	32	48	2.24	1.24	4.8	248	40	84	3.23	2.8	13.4	4.8	0.6	184
2014	MLB	LA Angels	0	0	0	5	8	3.46	1.35	4.3	214	38	71	2.53	5.2	13.8	2.7	0.0	127
2015	AAA	Albuquerque	3	5	8	55	50	4.58	1.60	5.2	247	30	73	4.57	6.1	8.2	1.4	1.0	2
2015	MLB	Colorado	0	1	0	19	18	2.37	1.16	3.6	230	28	85	3.19	2.8	8.5	3.0	0.9	95

Came over as part of the Josh Rutledge deal and profiles as a possible closer. The 24-year-old has a plus-plus FB that sits at 97-98 and tops out at 100 mph. He struggled with control in the past, but was solid in '15, walking just 6 in 19 innings for the Rockies. Avg SL keeps hitters honest and gives him the potential to succeed in the majors.

Diaz,Miguel — SP — Milwaukee

EXP MLB DEBUT: 2019 | H/W: 6-1 175 | FUT: #3 SP / Setup RP | 7C

Thrws R Age 21 — 2011 FA (DR)

Velo	Pitch	Grade
94-96	FB	++++
75-77	SL	++
	CU	++

Year	Lev	Team	W	L	Sv	IP	K	ERA	WHIP	BF/G	OBA	H%	S%	xERA	Ctl	Dom	Cmd	hr/9	BPV
2013	Rk	DSL Brewers	3	2	0	48	34	2.43	1.18	17.5	209	26	77	2.13	3.9	6.3	1.6	0.0	26
2014	Rk	Azl Brewers	4	2	0	47	53	4.21	1.32	15.0	241	33	68	3.37	3.8	10.1	2.7	0.6	97
2015	Rk	Azl Brewers	0	3	0	20	23	2.24	1.24	11.7	261	36	83	3.32	2.2	10.3	4.6	0.4	143

Raw, projectable RH who sat out first half of '15 with elbow fracture. Sits mid-90s with late arm-side run to plus FB, which misses bats regularly. Action on sharp, mid-70s SL is inconsistent but flashes potential; ditto for CU. Simplified delivery has helped control; athleticism should allow for command growth. Hard to dislike his stuff as RP.

Diplan,Marcos — SP — Milwaukee

EXP MLB DEBUT: 2019 | H/W: 6-0 160 | FUT: #3 starter | 8E

Thrws R Age 19 — 2013 FA (DR)

Velo	Pitch	Grade
90-95	FB	++++
77-79	CB	+++
83-86	CU	++

Year	Lev	Team	W	L	Sv	IP	K	ERA	WHIP	BF/G	OBA	H%	S%	xERA	Ctl	Dom	Cmd	hr/9	BPV
2015	Rk	Helena	2	2	2	50	54	3.77	1.36	16.1	250	33	73	3.72	3.8	9.7	2.6	0.7	91

Slightly undersized RH has raw but intriguing three-pitch mix. FB sits low-90s, but touches 96 regularly and has improved his control. CB flashes good 11-5 action. Athleticism should help with feel for unrefined, often firm CU. Some effort in delivery, but room to pack on muscle, which will help him pitch deeper into games and reduce wear and tear.

Duff,Jimmy — RP — New York (N)

EXP MLB DEBUT: 2018 | H/W: 6-6 200 | FUT: Setup reliever | 6D

Thrws R Age 22 — 2014 (20) Stonehill

Velo	Pitch	Grade
87-89	FB	++
	CU	+++
73-74	SL	++

Year	Lev	Team	W	L	Sv	IP	K	ERA	WHIP	BF/G	OBA	H%	S%	xERA	Ctl	Dom	Cmd	hr/9	BPV
2014	Rk	Kingsport	3	1	0	34	24	1.85	1.00	10.0	219	26	82	2.03	1.8	6.3	3.4	0.3	82
2015	A	Savannah	2	2	12	41	44	3.50	1.17	4.7	257	35	68	2.87	1.8	9.6	5.5	0.2	144
2015	A+	St. Lucie	1	0	1	18	13	1.98	0.93	5.7	238	28	81	2.32	0.5	6.4	13.0	0.5	120

Tall, strike-throwing reliever who creates deception by folding his body into a compact cube. FB is fringy at best. Command and control help it play up. CU is best pitch. Deceptive with tremendous sink. SL is extremely blah.

Dull,Ryan

RP | **Oakland** | EXP MLB DEBUT: 2015 | H/W: 5-10 175 | FUT: Setup reliever | **6B**

Thrws R Age 26
2012 (32) UNC-Asheville

Velo	Pitch	Grade
87-92	FB	+ + +
79-82	SL	+ + +
	CU	+ +

Year	Lev	Team	W	L	Sv	IP	K	ERA	WHIP	BF/G	OBA	H%	S%	xERA	Ctl	Dom	Cmd	hr/9	BPV
2013	AA	Midland	0	1	1	11	12	4.82	1.61	5.0	322	40	75	6.25	2.4	9.6	4.0	1.6	126
2014	AA	Midland	5	5	6	56	61	2.89	1.19	5.6	247	32	80	3.51	2.4	9.8	4.1	1.0	129
2015	AA	Midland	3	1	12	45	52	0.60	0.93	4.8	186	27	95	1.38	2.6	10.4	4.0	0.2	135
2015	AAA	Nashville	0	1	0	16	21	1.13	0.81	4.8	181	27	92	1.35	1.7	11.8	7.0	0.6	185
2015	MLB	Oakland	1	2	1	17	16	4.24	1.06	5.1	200	20	71	3.68	3.2	8.5	2.7	2.1	85

Short RP who had breakout campaign and reached OAK as September call-up. Has confidence to use any pitch and has significant deception in delivery. Pitch movement makes it difficult for hitters to make hard contact against. FB is only average and has very good SL and passable CU. Not as good as stats suggest.

Dykxhoorn,Brock

SP | **Houston** | EXP MLB DEBUT: 2018 | H/W: 6-8 250 | FUT: #5 starter | **6B**

Thrws R Age 21
2014 (6) Central Arizona JC

Velo	Pitch	Grade
88-91	FB	+ + +
81-83	SL	+ +
83-85	CU	+ +

Year	Lev	Team	W	L	Sv	IP	K	ERA	WHIP	BF/G	OBA	H%	S%	xERA	Ctl	Dom	Cmd	hr/9	BPV
2014	Rk	Greeneville	3	3	0	31	36	4.34	1.22	10.5	255	35	64	3.31	2.3	10.4	4.5	0.6	143
2015	A	Quad Cities	8	5	0	109	94	3.88	1.16	19.7	245	30	67	3.12	2.1	7.8	3.6	0.7	100

Long-limbed, large SP who succeeds with angle to plate. No pitch is above average and is far from overpowering. Gives hitter difficult looks with slot and can throw strikes with all pitches. FB barely touches 90 and SL often lacks movement. Repeats arm speed on CU, but can be thrown too hard and lacks separation from FB.

Edwards,C.J.

RP | **Chicago (N)** | EXP MLB DEBUT: 2015 | H/W: 6-2 170 | FUT: Closer | **8E**

Thrws R Age 24
2011 (48) HS (SC)

Velo	Pitch	Grade
92-95	FB	+ + + +
75-78	CB	+ + +
80-83	SL	+ +
82-85	CU	+ + + +

Year	Lev	Team	W	L	Sv	IP	K	ERA	WHIP	BF/G	OBA	H%	S%	xERA	Ctl	Dom	Cmd	hr/9	BPV
2014	Rk	Azl Cubs	0	0	0	5		1.73	1.15	10.3	120	23	83	1.02	6.9	13.8	2.0	0.0	80
2014	AA	Tennessee	1	2	0	48	46	2.44	1.06	18.6	181	25	76	1.66	3.9	8.6	2.2	0.2	67
2015	AA	Tennessee	2	2	4	23	36	2.72	1.21	7.2	144	25	78	1.76	6.6	14.0	2.1	0.4	91
2015	AAA	Iowa	3	1	2	31	39	2.88	1.25	5.5	146	23	74	1.54	6.9	11.3	1.6	0.0	34
2015	MLB	Chi Cubs	0	0	0	4	4	4.29	1.43	3.6	202	28	67	2.64	6.4	8.6	1.3	0.0	-1

Was moved to relief to keep him healthy. FB sits at 92-95 mph, topping out at 97 mph with good late cutting action. Complements the FB with a quality, 12-6 CB and an above-average CU. Control remains an issue, as he walked 41 in 55.1 IP. He also gets plenty of swings-and-misses and held minor league hitters to a .139 oppBAA.

Edwards,Jon

RP | **San Diego** | EXP MLB DEBUT: 2014 | H/W: 6-5 235 | FUT: Setup reliever | **6B**

Thrws R Age 28
2006 (14) HS (TX)

Velo	Pitch	Grade
92-96	FB	+ + +
84-87	SL	+ + +
77-79	CB	+ +

Year	Lev	Team	W	L	Sv	IP	K	ERA	WHIP	BF/G	OBA	H%	S%	xERA	Ctl	Dom	Cmd	hr/9	BPV
2014	MLB	Texas	0	0	0	8	9	4.44	2.22	4.5	363	48	78	6.99	5.6	10.0	1.8	0.0	48
2015	AAA	El Paso	0	0	3	4	7	0.00	1.50	3.5	210	41	100	2.84	6.8	15.8	2.3	0.0	119
2015	AAA	Round Rock	2	1	20	31	44	1.44	0.83	3.6	170	28	84	1.01	2.3	12.7	5.5	0.3	184
2015	MLB	San Diego	0	0	0	10	16	3.53	1.37	3.9	173	19	91	4.60	7.1	14.1	2.0	2.6	82
2015	MLB	Texas	0	0	0	6	6	6.00	2.33	2.8	262	31	77	7.09	12.0	9.0	0.8	1.5	-144

Large-framed RP who was up and down between AAA and majors. Served as closer in TEX org and has size and arm strength to pump high-octane FB into zone. Improved control was key to solid campaign and is tough to hit when FB and hard SL working in tandem. Doesn't change speeds often and has tendency to leave balls up in strike zone.

Eflin,Zach

SP | **Philadelphia** | EXP MLB DEBUT: 2016 | H/W: 6-4 200 | FUT: #3 starter | **7C**

Thrws R Age 21
2012 (1) HS (FL)

Velo	Pitch	Grade
92-94	FB	+ + +
81-83	SL	+ +
73-76	CB	+ +
81-83	CU	+ + +

Year	Lev	Team	W	L	Sv	IP	K	ERA	WHIP	BF/G	OBA	H%	S%	xERA	Ctl	Dom	Cmd	hr/9	BPV
2012	Rk	Azl Padres	0	1	0	7	4	7.71	1.71	7.9	313	36	50	4.91	3.9	5.1	1.3	0.0	6
2013	A	Fort Wayne	7	6	0	118	86	2.74	1.19	21.6	248	29	78	3.14	2.4	6.5	2.8	0.5	72
2014	A+	Lake Elsinore	10	7	0	128	93	3.80	1.32	22.1	277	32	72	3.95	2.2	6.5	3.0	0.6	77
2015	AA	Reading	8	6	0	131	68	3.70	1.21	23.0	269	29	71	3.76	1.6	4.7	3.0	0.8	59

Generates grounders with heavy 2-seam FB best when it stays down in the zone. CU is next-best pitch, with good feel and drop. A reliable breaking ball is a work-in-progress; cutter-slider was replaced by mid-70s CB later in the season. He'll need one of them to get to average to fulfill his #3 ceiling.

Ellington,Brian

RP | **Miami** | EXP MLB DEBUT: 2015 | H/W: 6-4 195 | FUT: Setup reliever | **7A**

Thrws R Age 25
2012 (16) West Florida

Velo	Pitch	Grade
94-97	FB	+ + + +
	CB	+ +
	SL	+ +

Year	Lev	Team	W	L	Sv	IP	K	ERA	WHIP	BF/G	OBA	H%	S%	xERA	Ctl	Dom	Cmd	hr/9	BPV
2013	A	Greensboro	3	2	0	42	27	4.69	1.49	11.4	252	29	68	4.05	4.9	5.8	1.2	0.6	-11
2014	A+	Jupiter	2	2	0	47	56	4.78	1.59	5.9	277	39	68	4.37	4.6	10.7	2.3	0.4	87
2015	AA	Jacksonville	4	1	0	43	47	2.51	0.95	6.5	188	27	71	1.26	2.7	9.8	3.6	0.0	122
2015	AAA	New Orleans	0	0	0	1	1	0.00	0.00	3.1	0	0			0.0	8.2		0.0	165
2015	MLB	Miami	2	1	0	25	18	2.88	1.20	4.4	194	23	76	2.33	4.7	6.5	1.4	0.4	8

Strong-armed reliever comes after hitters from a high 3/4 arm slot. Was lights-out at AA and for the Marlins and has a plus 94-97 mph FB that tops out at 98. FB lacks movement due to arm slot and he mixes in a power CB and a below-avg SL. Commands all three offerings and limited opposing hitters to a .193 BA.

Ellis,Christopher

SP | **Atlanta** | EXP MLB DEBUT: 2016 | H/W: 6-4 220 | FUT: #4 starter | **7C**

Thrws R Age 23
2014 (3) Mississippi

Velo	Pitch	Grade
90-92	FB	+ + +
83-85	CB	+ +
81-83	CU	+ + +

Year	Lev	Team	W	L	Sv	IP	K	ERA	WHIP	BF/G	OBA	H%	S%	xERA	Ctl	Dom	Cmd	hr/9	BPV
2013	NCAA	Mississippi	1	2	0	21	16	5.57	2.00	7.8	344	40	73	6.93	4.7	6.9	1.5	0.9	14
2014	NCAA	Mississippi	10	3	0	116	67	2.56	1.32	25.3	253	29	82	3.55	3.3	5.2	1.6	0.5	24
2014	Rk	Orem	0	1	0	15	16	7.11	1.64	7.5	284	36	57	5.36	4.7	9.5	2.0	1.2	61
2015	A+	Inland Empire	4	5	0	62	70	3.91	1.17	22.6	232	31	69	3.16	2.9	10.1	3.5	0.9	122
2015	AA	Arkansas	7	4	0	78	62	3.92	1.54	22.7	259	30	77	4.63	5.0	7.2	1.4	1.0	13

Downhill thrower creates deception from height and arm slot. FB is an average offering with tendency of hanging up in the zone. Can manipulate FB with various angles. Has established a solid CU w/ good deception but lacks the movement of FB. CB is inconsistent and may hold projection back.

Erwin,Zack

SP | **Oakland** | EXP MLB DEBUT: 2018 | H/W: 6-5 195 | FUT: #4 starter | **7D**

Thrws L Age 22
2015 (4) Clemson

Velo	Pitch	Grade
87-92	FB	+ + +
76-78	CB	+ + +
	CU	+ +

Year	Lev	Team	W	L	Sv	IP	K	ERA	WHIP	BF/G	OBA	H%	S%	xERA	Ctl	Dom	Cmd	hr/9	BPV
2015	NCAA	Clemson	7	4	0	106	92	3.05	1.17	24.9	265	33	75	3.35	1.4	7.8	5.8	0.6	122
2015	Rk	Great Falls	2	0	0	21	15	0.85	0.95	9.9	222	28	90	1.69	1.3	6.4	5.0	0.0	99
2015	A	Kannapolis	0	2	0	19	15	1.89	1.00	10.4	219	28	79	1.78	1.9	7.1	3.8	0.0	95

Athletic, angular SP who is more about feel than natural stuff. Lacks legitimate out pitch, though CU could evolve into weapon against hitters from both sides. Locates FB to all parts of strike zone and at best when spotted low for groundballs. Goes to CB against LHP and exhibits quality break and velocity.

Escobar,Edwin

SP | **Boston** | EXP MLB DEBUT: 2014 | H/W: 6-2 225 | FUT: #4 SP / Setup RP | **7C**

Thrws L Age 23
2008 FA (VZ)

Velo	Pitch	Grade
90-95	FB	+ + +
81-84	SL	+ + +
83-85	CU	+ +

Year	Lev	Team	W	L	Sv	IP	K	ERA	WHIP	BF/G	OBA	H%	S%	xERA	Ctl	Dom	Cmd	hr/9	BPV
2014	AAA	Fresno	3	8	0	111	96	5.11	1.49	23.9	290	34	68	5.18	3.0	7.8	2.6	1.3	77
2014	MLB	Boston	0	0	0	2	2	4.50	0.50	3.3	151	22	0		0.0	9.0		0.0	180
2015	A	Greenville	0	0	0	1	0	0.00	0.00	2.8	0	0			0.0	0.0		0.0	18
2015	AAA	Pawtucket	3	3	0	49	24	5.12	1.57	11.4	273	28	71	5.31	4.6	4.4	1.0	1.5	-26

Versatile, deceptive pitcher who began season late due to shoulder injury. Began season in pen before moving to SP. Has two average to plus offerings in FB and SL. Both can register Ks when healthy. SL has nasty bite while FB exhibits late movement. Only needs better CU to stick as SP.

Eshelman,Thomas

SP | **Philadelphia** | EXP MLB DEBUT: 2017 | H/W: 6-3 210 | FUT: #4 starter | **7C**

Thrws R Age 21
2015 (2) Cal St Fullerton

Velo	Pitch	Grade
86-91	FB	+ + +
75-77	CB	+ +
	CU	+ +

Year	Lev	Team	W	L	Sv	IP	K	ERA	WHIP	BF/G	OBA	H%	S%	xERA	Ctl	Dom	Cmd	hr/9	BPV
2015	NCAA	Cal St Fullerton	8	5	1	137	139	1.58	0.82	26.2	214	29	82	1.54	0.5	9.1	19.9	0.3	170
2015	Rk	GCL Astros	0	1	0	4	3	4.50	1.25	8.1	210	27	60	2.30	4.5	6.8	1.5	0.0	18
2015	A	Quad Cities	0	0	0	6	5	4.43	1.97	14.6	343	42	75	6.03	4.4	7.4	1.7	0.0	31

Efficient SP with average stuff, but has double plus command and pitch location. Uses pinpoint control and moves ball effectively in and out of zone to keep hitters off guard. FB lacks ideal velocity and sub-par CB won't miss many bats. CU could become weapon against LHH. Needs to continue plus sequencing to carve out long career.

Espada,Jose

SP | **Toronto** | EXP MLB DEBUT: 2019 | H/W: 6-0 170 | FUT: #3 starter | **8E**

Thrws R Age 19
2015 (5) HS (PR)

Velo	Pitch	Grade
86-92	FB	+ + +
77-79	CB	+ + +
	CU	+

Year	Lev	Team	W	L	Sv	IP	K	ERA	WHIP	BF/G	OBA	H%	S%	xERA	Ctl	Dom	Cmd	hr/9	BPV
2015	Rk	GCL Blue Jays	0	2	0	34	31	3.43	0.97	12.9	206	25	67	2.28	2.1	8.2	3.9	0.8	108

Small, aggressive SP who has advanced pitchability and moxie, yet still has projection remaining. Won't be a top-of-the-rotation guy as he lacks size and strength, but he can sequence pitches and live in lower half of strike zone. Solid CB is best current offering and will need to drastically improve CU.

Espinoza,Anderson	SP	Boston	EXP MLB DEBUT: 2018	H/W: 6-0 160	FUT: #1 starter	9D

Thrws R Age 18
2014 FA (VZ)

Velo	Pitch	Grade	Year	Lev	Team	W	L	Sv	IP	K	ERA	WHIP	BF/G	OBA	H%	S%	xERA	Ctl	Dom	Cmd	hr/9	BPV
93-98	FB	++++																				
78-80	CB	+++	2015	Rk	DSL Red Sox 2	0	0	0	15	21	1.20	1.07	14.6	235	38	88	2.09	1.8	12.6	7.0	0.0	196
83-86	CU	+++	2015	Rk	GCL Red Sox	0	1	0	40	40	0.68	0.83	14.6	175	25	91	0.81	2.0	9.0	4.4	0.0	125
			2015	A	Greenville	0	1	0	3	4	8.71	1.94	14.7	314	46	50	5.42	5.8	11.6	2.0	0.0	70

Slight-framed SP with very high ceiling and advanced command for age. Very tough to make hard contact against with very fast arm and easy velocity. Has potential for three plus to double-plus offerings, highlighted by sharp CB. Outstanding feel for changing speeds and fools with hitters with varying depth on pitches. Could be let loose in '16.

Evans,Jacob	RP	St. Louis	EXP MLB DEBUT: 2018	H/W: 6-2 215	FUT: Middle reliever	6C

Thrws L Age 22
2015 (6) Oklahoma

Velo	Pitch	Grade	Year	Lev	Team	W	L	Sv	IP	K	ERA	WHIP	BF/G	OBA	H%	S%	xERA	Ctl	Dom	Cmd	hr/9	BPV
88-91	FB	++																				
	CB	+++																				
	CU	++	2015	NCAA	Oklahoma	6	1	8	43	53	1.67	1.07	6.0	229	34	84	2.23	2.1	11.1	5.3	0.2	161
			2015	A-	State College	4	3	1	49	42	3.11	0.98	11.7	228	29	66	2.00	1.3	7.7	6.0	0.2	122

Collegiate LH reliever was a 6th round pick after a standout Jr. season as closer for Oklahoma. Nice three-pitch mix that includes an average FB in 88-91 mph range, a CB, and a CU that needs work. Was used mostly in relief in his pro debut, where he showed excellent command, walking just 7 in 49.2 IP.

Faria,Jacob	SP	Tampa Bay	EXP MLB DEBUT: 2016	H/W: 6-4 200	FUT: #4 starter	7C

Thrws R Age 22
2011 (10) HS (CA)

Velo	Pitch	Grade	Year	Lev	Team	W	L	Sv	IP	K	ERA	WHIP	BF/G	OBA	H%	S%	xERA	Ctl	Dom	Cmd	hr/9	BPV
			2012	Rk	Princeton	3	4	0	42		5.14	1.26	13.2	271	31	62	4.33	1.9	7.3	3.8	1.3	97
90-94	FB	+++	2013	Rk	Princeton	3	3	0	62	71	2.03	1.00	19.8	232	33	80	2.18	1.3	10.3	7.9	0.3	168
78-80	CB	+++	2014	A	Bowling Green	7	9	0	119	107	3.47	1.22	20.9	252	31	73	3.37	2.4	8.1	3.3	0.7	98
	CU	++	2015	A+	Charlotte	10	1	0	74	63	1.34	0.99	23.5	196	26	86	1.58	2.7	7.7	2.9	0.1	84
			2015	AA	Montgomery	7	3	0	75	96	2.52	1.09	22.6	197	29	79	2.27	3.6	11.5	3.2	0.6	128

Consistent SP who led minors in wins. Owns impressive repertoire and added new cut FB to give him another weapon. CU showing improvement while FB has consistent velocity and sink. Moves ball around plate and repeats arm speed and slot. May not have good enough breaking ball to register Ks at higher levels.

Fasola,John	RP	Texas	EXP MLB DEBUT: 2017	H/W: 6-2 195	FUT: Setup reliever	7D

Thrws R Age 24
2014 (31) Kent State

Velo	Pitch	Grade	Year	Lev	Team	W	L	Sv	IP	K	ERA	WHIP	BF/G	OBA	H%	S%	xERA	Ctl	Dom	Cmd	hr/9	BPV
91-94	FB	+++	2014	NCAA	Kent St	2	2	3	29	28	4.66	1.31	5.7	268	35	62	3.48	2.5	8.7	3.5	0.3	107
83-85	SL	++++	2014	A-	Spokane	0	1	5	26	40	2.07	1.00	5.2	222	37	80	2.06	1.7	13.8	8.0	0.3	220
	CU	++	2015	A	Hickory	1	1	13	26	34	1.72	0.80	5.0	188	30	76	0.87	1.4	11.7	8.5	0.0	192
			2015	A+	High Desert	3	2	6	29	30	5.28	1.38	5.3	275	33	68	5.20	2.8	9.3	3.3	1.9	110

Tall, quick-armed RP who was dominant in Low-A before getting hit hard in High-A. FB features late sink and can be solid-average, though command needs work. Best pitch is hard SL that misses bats. He controls it well and is effective against hitters from both sides. CU is work in progress, though doesn't need in short stints.

Faulkner,Andrew	RP	Texas	EXP MLB DEBUT: 2015	H/W: 6-3 200	FUT: #4 SP / Setup RP	7C

Thrws L Age 23
2011 (14) HS (SC)

Velo	Pitch	Grade	Year	Lev	Team	W	L	Sv	IP	K	ERA	WHIP	BF/G	OBA	H%	S%	xERA	Ctl	Dom	Cmd	hr/9	BPV
			2014	A+	Myrtle Beach	10	1	1	104	100	2.07	1.12	19.6	227	31	80	2.25	2.7	8.6	3.2	0.1	101
91-94	FB	+++	2014	AA	Frisco	2	4	0	30	33	5.07	1.39	18.2	247	32	64	3.94	4.2	9.8	2.4	0.9	82
78-82	SL	++	2015	AA	Frisco	7	4	1	92	90	4.20	1.42	14.0	244	31	72	3.97	4.6	8.8	1.9	0.9	52
82-85	CU	+++	2015	AAA	Round Rock	0	0	0	8	13	0.00	0.38	4.3	81	17	100		1.1	14.6	13.0	0.0	251
			2015	MLB	Texas	0	0	0	9	10	2.93	1.20	3.4	236	27	89	4.29	2.9	9.8	3.3	2.0	115

Versatile LHP who is advancing rapidly and earned big league time. Aggressively combats hitters with three pitches. Shows good FB that he locates low in zone and average CU has excellent sink. Has difficulty maintaining delivery and command suffers. Very tough on LHH. Needs better SL to return as SP.

Fedde,Erick	SP	Washington	EXP MLB DEBUT: 2018	H/W: 6-3 180	FUT: #2 starter	9D

Thrws R Age 23
2014 (1) UNLV

Velo	Pitch	Grade	Year	Lev	Team	W	L	Sv	IP	K	ERA	WHIP	BF/G	OBA	H%	S%	xERA	Ctl	Dom	Cmd	hr/9	BPV
91-93	FB	++++																				
81-83	SL	++++																				
	CU	+++	2015	A-	Auburn	4	1	0	35	36	2.57	1.31	18.1	278	37	80	3.57	2.1	9.3	4.5	0.3	129
			2015	A	Hagerstown	1	2	0	29	23	4.34	1.10	19.0	227	28	58	2.43	2.5	7.1	2.9	0.3	79

Drafted right after TJS in 2014, it was a win to have him back on the mound in late 2015. Stuff wasn't all the way back, but before surgery his heavy mid-90s sinker and hard SL both graded as plus pitches. CU is improving, and could eventually also be a plus pitch. A smooth delivery and solid frame round out the package.

Feigl,Brady	RP	Atlanta	EXP MLB DEBUT: 2017	H/W: 6-4 195	FUT: Setup reliever	7C

Thrws L Age 25
2013 Mount St. Mary's

Velo	Pitch	Grade	Year	Lev	Team	W	L	Sv	IP	K	ERA	WHIP	BF/G	OBA	H%	S%	xERA	Ctl	Dom	Cmd	hr/9	BPV
			2010	NCAA	Mount St. Mary's	2	7	0	51	55	8.29	1.90	18.5	346	44	54	6.71	3.7	9.7	2.6	0.9	93
91-93	FB	+++	2012	NCAA	Mount St. Mary's	2	5	0	46	30	4.50	1.54	22.3	282	32	72	4.74	3.9	5.9	1.5	0.8	18
77-79	SL	+++	2014	A	Rome	2	3	0	43	37	3.54	1.34	7.2	287	36	73	3.94	1.9	7.7	4.1	0.4	106
			2014	A+	Lynchburg	3	2	1	22	23	2.05	0.68	5.9	151	22	67	0.18	1.6	9.4	5.8	0.0	143
			2015	AAA	Gwinnett	0	0	0	0	0	0.00	15.00	3.6	639	64	100	48.31	90.0	0.0	0.0	0.0	-2412

Former NDFA moving rapidly through the organization. Was a viable option to make his MLB debut early in 15' before TJS ended his season in April. Two-pitch pitcher. Commands FB low in the zone with average velocity & solid downward run. Movement will induce GB contact. Slider has potential to be plus offering.

Feliz,Michael	SP	Houston	EXP MLB DEBUT: 2015	H/W: 6-4 225	FUT: #3 starter / Closer	8C

Thrws R Age 22
2010 FA (DR)

Velo	Pitch	Grade	Year	Lev	Team	W	L	Sv	IP	K	ERA	WHIP	BF/G	OBA	H%	S%	xERA	Ctl	Dom	Cmd	hr/9	BPV
			2013	A-	Tri City	4	2	1	69	78	1.96	0.96	18.6	214	30	80	1.82	1.7	10.2	6.0	0.3	155
90-96	FB	++++	2014	A	Quad Cities	8	6	0	102	111	4.05	1.38	17.2	265	36	70	3.81	3.3	9.8	3.0	0.5	106
84-87	SL	+++	2015	A+	Lancaster	1	1	0	32	33	4.47	1.30	16.6	248	33	65	3.42	3.4	9.2	2.8	0.6	93
79-83	CU	++	2015	AA	Corpus Christi	6	3	1	78	70	2.19	0.92	19.5	191	24	79	1.78	2.3	8.1	3.5	0.6	101
			2015	MLB	Houston	0	0	0	8	7	7.88	1.63	7.1	285	31	55	6.35	4.5	7.9	1.8	2.3	38

Big-framed pitcher who reached HOU as RP, but still expected to return to rotation. Electric FB is best pitch and exhibits late movement. Mixes in SL that can be plus at times and features sharp breaking action. Uses clean, quick delivery and adds a hint of deception. Improved control has been key and only needs to develop CU.

Fenter,Gray	SP	Baltimore	EXP MLB DEBUT: 2019	H/W: 6-1 200	FUT: #3 SP / Setup RP	8E

Thrws R Age 20
2015 (7) HS (AR)

Velo	Pitch	Grade	Year	Lev	Team	W	L	Sv	IP	K	ERA	WHIP	BF/G	OBA	H%	S%	xERA	Ctl	Dom	Cmd	hr/9	BPV
88-94	FB	+++																				
75-80	CB	++																				
81-84	CU	++																				
			2015	Rk	GCL Orioles	0	0	0	21	18	1.70	0.99	9.0	201	26	81	1.53	2.5	7.6	3.0	0.0	87

Strong-framed pitcher who has decent arsenal, though quite inconsistent. Can spot sinking FB low in zone and counter with CB that shows hard, nasty break. Has tendency to leave CB and CU up in zone and can be hit hard. Frame lacks projection and no more velocity may be forthcoming. Must rely on development of secondaries to have future.

Fernandez,Junior	SP	St. Louis	EXP MLB DEBUT: 2019	H/W: 6-1 180	FUT: #3 starter	9D

Thrws R Age 19
2014 FA (DR)

Velo	Pitch	Grade	Year	Lev	Team	W	L	Sv	IP	K	ERA	WHIP	BF/G	OBA	H%	S%	xERA	Ctl	Dom	Cmd	hr/9	BPV
94-98	FB	++++																				
85-88	SL	++																				
78-81	CU	+++	2015	Rk	GCL Cardinals	3	2	0	51	58	3.88	1.35	19.3	273	39	68	3.35	2.6	10.2	3.9	0.0	131
			2015	A+	Palm Beach	0	0	0	6	5	1.45	1.61	13.7	314	39	90	4.65	2.9	7.3	2.5	0.0	70

FB now sits at 94-98 mph FB, topping out at 100 mph. Ditched his CB for a potentially plus hard SL and mixes in a plus CU. There were concerns about his control, but filled the zone in '15, walking just 17 in 57.2 IP while striking out 63. Improved velocity upgrades his potential.

Fernandez,Pablo	SP	Los Angeles (N)	EXP MLB DEBUT: 2018	H/W: 6-1 185	FUT: #4 starter	7D

Thrws R Age 26
2014 FA (CU)

Velo	Pitch	Grade	Year	Lev	Team	W	L	Sv	IP	K	ERA	WHIP	BF/G	OBA	H%	S%	xERA	Ctl	Dom	Cmd	hr/9	BPV
88-92	FB	+++																				
	SL	++	2015	Rk	AZL Dodgers	0	0	0	4	7	2.14	0.71	7.4	202	29	100	2.79	0.0	15.0		2.1	288
	CB	++	2015	A	Great Lakes	1	1	0	17	16	5.76	1.16	17.1	292	27	75	7.10	0.0	8.4		4.2	169
	CU	++	2015	A+	RanchoCuca	2	1	0	21	18	4.27	1.42	22.4	304	36	74	5.21	1.7	7.7	4.5	1.3	110

Cuban hurler comes after hitters with a decent four-pitch mix that includes a FB, CB, SL, and CU. Uses a variety of arm angles to create deception and get movement. Was solid in his debut, going 3-2 with a 3.92 ERA at three stops. Was used primarily as a reliever in Cuba but for now the Dodgers see him as a starter.

Fernandez,Pedro | SP | Kansas City | EXP MLB DEBUT: 2017 | H/W: 6-0 175 | FUT: #4 SP / Setup RP | 7C

Thrws R Age 21	Year	Lev	Team	W	L	Sv	IP	K	ERA	WHIP	BF/G	OBA	H%	S%	xERA	Ctl	Dom	Cmd	hr/9	BPV
2011 FA (DR)	2013	Rk	Azl Royals	0	1	0	34	38	1.84	1.05	16.6	225	30	88	2.70	2.1	10.0	4.8	0.8	141
90-95 FB ++++	2013	Rk	DSL Royals	0	0	0	12	15	0.75	0.67	10.5	129	21	88		2.3	11.3	5.0	0.0	160
82-84 SL +++	2014	A	Lexington	1	8	3	61	60	5.01	1.36	16.0	225	28	64	3.57	4.9	8.8	1.8	0.9	46
81-84 CU ++	2015	A	Lexington	6	2	0	78	89	3.12	1.03	16.7	194	28	68	1.73	3.1	10.3	3.3	0.2	119
	2015	A+	Wilmington	0	6	0	32	25	8.94	1.99	22.1	381	45	52	7.31	2.2	7.0	3.1	0.6	83

Short, stocky pitcher who can either start or relieve. Could stick as SP if he locates pitches better. Repeats complex delivery and maintained slot better. Uses SL as true out pitch, though long arm action mutes impact of fringy CU. Doesn't allow many HR despite flyball tendencies. Could be an intriguing power arm in bullpen.

Ferrell,Jeff | RP | Detroit | EXP MLB DEBUT: 2015 | H/W: 6-3 185 | FUT: Setup reliever | 6B

Thrws R Age 25	Year	Lev	Team	W	L	Sv	IP	K	ERA	WHIP	BF/G	OBA	H%	S%	xERA	Ctl	Dom	Cmd	hr/9	BPV
2010 (26) Pitt CC	2013	A+	Lakeland	6	6	0	119	77	4.01	1.32	19.7	265	29	73	4.26	2.7	5.8	2.1	1.1	49
90-95 FB +++	2014	AA	Erie	10	9	0	138	92	5.54	1.54	24.0	309	35	65	5.43	2.5	6.0	2.4	1.1	59
77-78 CB ++	2015	AA	Erie	0	0	12	27	35	1.67	0.93	5.9	216	29	95	2.77	1.3	11.7	8.8	1.3	192
83-85 CU +++	2015	AAA	Toledo	0	1	4	11	10	4.86	1.17	4.0	204	19	70	4.30	4.1	8.1	2.0	2.4	54
	2015	MLB	Detroit	0	0	0	11	6	6.49	1.44	5.3	277	26	62	5.97	3.2	4.9	1.5	2.4	18

Strong RP who repeated level after struggles as SP in '14. Was dynamite all year that culminated in trip to DET. FB ticked up in velocity while keeping same, late sink and run. Can leave ball up, but mixes in fringy CB and solid-average CU. Served as closer in Double-A, but doesn't have the demeanor or repertoire to close in majors.

Ferrell,Riley | SP | Houston | EXP MLB DEBUT: 2017 | H/W: 6-2 200 | FUT: Setup reliever | 7C

Thrws R Age 22	Year	Lev	Team	W	L	Sv	IP	K	ERA	WHIP	BF/G	OBA	H%	S%	xERA	Ctl	Dom	Cmd	hr/9	BPV
2015 (3) Texas Christian																				
92-96 FB +++																				
83-87 SL +++																				
CU ++	2015	NCAA	Texas Christian	1	3	14	31	53	2.60	0.96	3.7	102	19	75	0.89	5.8	15.3	2.7	0.6	137
	2015	A	Quad Cities	0	0	1	16	17	1.11	1.42	5.7	180	26	91	2.35	7.2	9.4	1.3	0.0	-7

Quick-armed RP who could get to majors quickly on basis of FB/SL combo. All pitches feature velocity and life, though control problems may mute effectiveness. Owns clean arm action, but has effort in delivery. Keeps ball on ground and can dominate hitters with potential plus SL. Mixes in CU occasionally, though not weapon.

Finley,Drew | SP | New York (A) | EXP MLB DEBUT: 2019 | H/W: 6-3 200 | FUT: #3 starter | 8E

Thrws R Age 19	Year	Lev	Team	W	L	Sv	IP	K	ERA	WHIP	BF/G	OBA	H%	S%	xERA	Ctl	Dom	Cmd	hr/9	BPV
2015 (3) HS (CA)																				
88-91 FB +++																				
77-79 CB +++																				
82-84 CU ++																				
	2015	Rk	Pulaski	0	1	0	32	41	3.94	1.63	11.9	268	33	88	6.33	5.3	11.5	2.2	2.5	81

Tall SP with advanced delivery. Thrives with deceptive mechanics that make it difficult for hitters to read. Has fringy velocity now, but could grow into more. Inconsistent CB could become top offering. Spots FB well to all quadrants of strike zone and shows mature sequencing abilities. Despite pitch movement, allows high amount of HR.

Flaherty,Jack | SP | St. Louis | EXP MLB DEBUT: 2019 | H/W: 6-4 205 | FUT: #3 starter | 8C

Thrws R Age 20	Year	Lev	Team	W	L	Sv	IP	K	ERA	WHIP	BF/G	OBA	H%	S%	xERA	Ctl	Dom	Cmd	hr/9	BPV
2014 (1) HS (CA)																				
88-92 FB +++																				
73-75 CB ++																				
77-80 SL +++	2014	Rk	GCL Cardinals	1	1	0	22	28	1.62	0.99	10.6	223	33	86	2.15	1.6	11.4	7.0	0.4	179
80-83 CU +++	2015	A	Peoria	9	3	0	95	97	2.84	1.29	21.7	256	34	77	3.15	2.9	9.2	3.1	0.2	104

Polished hurler has a good four-pitch mix and was lights-out in the MWL, but some scouts wonder about his long-term projection. FB sits a 88-92 and throws a SL, CB, and CU, all of which have the potential to be average. Has easy athleticism and repeatable mechanics. Fills up the strike zone and knows how to pitch.

Flexen,Chris | SP | New York (N) | EXP MLB DEBUT: 2018 | H/W: 6-3 215 | FUT: #3 starter | 7D

Thrws R Age 21	Year	Lev	Team	W	L	Sv	IP	K	ERA	WHIP	BF/G	OBA	H%	S%	xERA	Ctl	Dom	Cmd	hr/9	BPV
2012 (14) HS (CA)	2013	Rk	Kingsport	8	1	0	69	62	2.09	0.94	23.6	214	26	83	2.30	1.6	8.1	5.2	0.8	121
91-93 FB +++	2014	A	Savannah	3	5	0	69	46	4.83	1.62	23.6	278	32	70	4.76	4.8	6.0	1.2	0.7	-4
75-77 CB +++	2015	Rk	GCL Mets	0	0	0	6	5	0.00	0.50	6.6	106	14	100		1.5	7.5	5.0	0.0	113
CU ++	2015	A-	Brooklyn	0	2	0	12	13	5.21	1.90	19.0	305	42	70	5.21	6.0	9.7	1.6	0.0	31
SL +	2015	A	Savannah	4	0	0	33	33	1.90	1.05	21.4	230	32	80	2.04	1.9	8.9	4.7	0.0	128

Returned from TJS mid-season to post impressive results in SAL. Evident NYM worked on cleaning up cross-fire delivery during time off. FB velocity came back after surgery. Touched 95 in last start. CB is best secondary. Classic 12-6 drop. Needs to work on CU and possibly scrap SL to reach projection.

Flores,Kendry | SP | Miami | EXP MLB DEBUT: 2015 | H/W: 6-2 175 | FUT: #4 starter | 7B

Thrws R Age 24	Year	Lev	Team	W	L	Sv	IP	K	ERA	WHIP	BF/G	OBA	H%	S%	xERA	Ctl	Dom	Cmd	hr/9	BPV
2009 FA (DR)	2014	A+	San Jose	4	6	0	105	112	4.11	1.26	21.5	254	32	71	3.99	2.7	9.6	3.5	1.2	117
88-91 FB +++	2015	A+	Jupiter	0	0	0	2	1	0.00	0.45	3.6	139	16	100		0.0	4.1		0.0	92
CB ++	2015	AA	Jacksonville	3	3	0	56	42	2.08	0.85	22.9	172	20	78	1.33	2.4	6.7	2.8	0.5	74
SL ++	2015	AAA	New Orleans	3	2	0	58	42	2.63	1.08	22.7	230	27	77	2.56	2.2	6.5	3.0	0.5	76
CU ++	2015	MLB	Miami	1	2	0	12	9	5.16	1.64	7.8	317	39	65	4.78	3.0	6.6	2.3	0.0	58

Has some of the best control in the system and a nice four-pitch mix. FB sits 88-91 mph and is backed up by a CU, SL, and CB all of which project as average or above. Knows how to pitch and keeps hitters off balance with location and changing speeds. Shoulder injury cost him the last month of the season, but he should be fine in '16.

Flynn,Brian | SP | Kansas City | EXP MLB DEBUT: 2013 | H/W: 6-7 250 | FUT: #5 starter | 6B

Thrws L Age 25	Year	Lev	Team	W	L	Sv	IP	K	ERA	WHIP	BF/G	OBA	H%	S%	xERA	Ctl	Dom	Cmd	hr/9	BPV
2011 (7) Wichita St	2013	MLB	Miami	0	2	0	18	15	8.50	2.22	22.7	347	39	64	8.62	6.5	7.5	1.2	2.0	-23
89-93 FB +++	2014	AAA	New Orleans	8	10	0	139	104	4.07	1.57	24.5	301	35	76	5.14	3.2	6.7	2.1	0.8	52
75-79 CB ++	2014	MLB	Miami	0	1	0	7	6	9.00	2.14	17.4	378	47	53	7.10	3.9	7.7	2.0	0.0	53
81-83 SL ++	2015	AAA	Omaha	0	0	0	0	1	0.00	5.00	1.6	639	177	100	22.66	0.0	45.0		0.0	828
CU +++	2015	MLB	KC Royals	Did not pitch in majors - injured																

Tall, hulking SP who tore lat muscle in April and missed rest of season. Fits back-end profile due to limited stuff, but has good pitchability and moxie. Throws with angle to plate and adds sink to average FB. Commands CU quite well and repeats arm slot and speed. Uses two breaking balls, but both fall short of average.

Freeland,Kyle | SP | Colorado | EXP MLB DEBUT: 2017 | H/W: 6-3 170 | FUT: #3 starter | 8C

Thrws L Age 22	Year	Lev	Team	W	L	Sv	IP	K	ERA	WHIP	BF/G	OBA	H%	S%	xERA	Ctl	Dom	Cmd	hr/9	BPV
2014 (1) Evansville	2014	NCAA	Evansville	10	2	0	99	128	1.91	0.93	26.6	220	34	77	1.57	1.2	11.6	9.8	0.0	195
92-95 FB +++	2014	Rk	Grand Junction	1	0	0	17	15	1.58	1.05	13.2	249	33	83	2.29	1.1	7.9	7.5	0.0	132
80-83 SL +++	2014	A	Asheville	2	0	0	21	18	0.85	0.85	15.6	190	24	94	1.45	1.7	7.6	4.5	0.4	110
CT +++	2015	Rk	Grand Junction	0	0	0	7	9	0.00	0.57	11.9	92	16	100		2.6	11.6	4.5	0.0	157
CU ++	2015	A+	Modesto	3	2	0	39	19	4.82	1.43	23.8	303	32	69	5.12	1.8	4.4	2.4	1.1	47

Missed time due to shoulder and elbow injuries and was limited to 46.2 IP. Looked rusty when he returned in High-A. When healthy has a deep repertoire and a fast arm that generates low 90s velocity. Mixes in a CT, hard SL, and a good CU to keep hitters at bay. Spots FB to all parts of the plate and has a high pitching IQ.

Fried,Max | SP | Atlanta | EXP MLB DEBUT: 2018 | H/W: 6-4 185 | FUT: #2 starter | 8D

Thrws L Age 22	Year	Lev	Team	W	L	Sv	IP	K	ERA	WHIP	BF/G	OBA	H%	S%	xERA	Ctl	Dom	Cmd	hr/9	BPV
2012 (1) HS (CA)																				
90-94 FB +++	2012	Rk	Azl Padres	0	1	0	17	17	3.66	1.16	6.9	224	29	68	2.72	3.1	8.9	2.8	0.5	93
74-78 CB ++++	2013	A	Fort Wayne	6	7	0	118	100	3.50	1.38	21.6	243	30	75	3.53	4.3	7.6	1.8	0.5	40
80-83 CU ++	2014	Rk	Azl Padres	0	0	0	5	8	5.40	2.20	8.4	362	57	73	6.88	5.4	14.4	2.7	0.0	131
	2014	A	Fort Wayne	0	1	0	5	2	5.19	1.73	11.8	323	32	75	6.76	3.5	3.5	1.0	1.7	-13

Acquired by ATL in the Justin Upton trade. Spent '15 rehabbing from TJS in August '14. His best pitch is a 12-6 hard CB that he can throw in any count. FB flashes plus with solid arm-side run. He lived up in the zone due to poor FB command prior to surgery. A return to health should eventually remedy command issues. Has slight feel of CU.

Fry,Jace | SP | Chicago (A) | EXP MLB DEBUT: 2017 | H/W: 6-1 190 | FUT: #5 SP / Long RP | 6B

Thrws L Age 22	Year	Lev	Team	W	L	Sv	IP	K	ERA	WHIP	BF/G	OBA	H%	S%	xERA	Ctl	Dom	Cmd	hr/9	BPV
2014 (3) Oregon St	2012	NCAA	Oregon St	5	3	0	88	53	2.45	1.17	27.0	215	26	77	2.27	3.6	5.4	1.5	0.1	19
88-93 FB +++	2013	NCAA	Oregon St	0	1	0	7	2	5.00	1.11	4.7	228	25	50	2.22	2.5	2.5	1.0	0.0	-5
80-83 SL +++	2014	NCAA	Oregon St	11	2	0	120	98	1.80	0.94	28.2	197	25	80	1.50	2.2	7.3	3.3	0.1	89
75-78 CB ++	2014	Rk	Great Falls	1	0	0	9	10	2.93	1.09	5.1	212	31	70	1.89	2.9	9.8	3.3	0.0	115
81-83 CU ++	2015	A+	Winston-Salem	1	8	0	52	39	3.63	1.38	22.4	290	35	74	4.12	2.9	6.8	2.3	0.2	60

Lean, athletic SP who ended season in May after second TJ surgery. Aggressively placed in High-A and showed progress with command. Pitches in lower half of strike zone with solid-average FB from low arm slot. Repeats delivery that has hint of deception. Throws all pitches for strikes, though doesn't miss many bats.

Fulenchek,Garrett

SP | Tampa Bay | EXP MLB DEBUT: 2019 | H/W: 6-4 205 | FUT: #3 starter | 8E

Thrws R Age 19
2014 (2) HS (TX)

88-95	FB	+++
83-86	SL	++
	CU	++

Year	Lev	Team	W	L	Sv	IP	K	ERA	WHIP	BF/G	OBA	H%	S%	xERA	Ctl	Dom	Cmd	hr/9	BPV
2014	Rk	GCL Braves	0	7	0	37	29	4.84	1.51	13.4	245	30	67	3.83	5.3	7.0	1.3	0.5	1
2015	Rk	Princeton	1	0	0	13	15	5.54	2.69	7.2	262	38	77	6.57	15.2	10.4	0.7	0.0	-206
2015	Rk	Danville	0	1	0	4	4	8.57	3.10	12.4	297	39	69	8.11	17.1	8.6	0.5	0.0	-291

Quick-armed SP who has difficulty repeating delivery and shows horrendous control as a result. Has good athleticism and body control, but can't find plate with any pitch. Throws from high 3/4 slot which allows heavy FB to play up, but can't command hard-breaking SL. CU is distant third pitch. Has high ceiling, but will take time to develop.

Fulmer,Carson

SP | Chicago (A) | EXP MLB DEBUT: 2017 | H/W: 6-1 190 | FUT: #2 starter | 9D

Thrws R Age 22
2015 (1) Vanderbilt

91-96	FB	++++
77-80	CB	++++
82-84	CU	++

Year	Lev	Team	W	L	Sv	IP	K	ERA	WHIP	BF/G	OBA	H%	S%	xERA	Ctl	Dom	Cmd	hr/9	BPV
2015	NCAA	Vanderbilt	14	2	0	127	167	1.84	1.03	25.8	184	28	85	1.86	3.5	11.8	3.3	0.5	135
2015	Rk	Azl White Sox	0	0	0	1	1	0.00	1.00	3.8	262	35	100	2.32	0.0	9.0		0.0	180
2015	A+	Winston-Salem	0	0	0	22	25	2.05	1.14	10.9	205	27	87	2.69	3.7	10.2	2.8	0.8	103

Short and max-effort pitcher with deep, powerful arsenal who maintains velocity deep into games. Delivery has moving parts, but spots plus FB down in zone. Has trouble commanding hard CB due to vicious late break. Has ideal build and mechanics for RP, but pitch mix is valuable as a SP.

Fulmer,Michael

SP | Detroit | EXP MLB DEBUT: 2016 | H/W: 6-3 200 | FUT: #3 starter | 8C

Thrws R Age 23
2011 (1) HS (OK)

91-95	FB	++++
83-85	SL	+++
	CU	++

Year	Lev	Team	W	L	Sv	IP	K	ERA	WHIP	BF/G	OBA	H%	S%	xERA	Ctl	Dom	Cmd	hr/9	BPV
2014	A+	St. Lucie	6	10	0	95		3.97	1.50	21.6	295	37	74	4.69	2.9	8.1	2.8	0.7	85
2014	AA	Binghamton	0	1	0	3	1	17.42	2.90	17.7	407	39	38	12.38	8.7	2.9	0.3	2.9	-165
2015	A+	St. Lucie	0	0	0	7	9	3.86	0.57	23.7	168	22	33	1.28	0.0	11.6		1.3	226
2015	AA	Binghamton	6	2	0	86	83	1.88	1.12	22.6	231	30	84	2.50	2.4	8.7	3.6	0.3	109
2015	AA	Erie	4	1	0	31	33	2.88	1.09	20.3	235	29	80	3.26	2.0	9.5	4.7	1.2	135

Tall, strong hurler who led EL in ERA in career year. Results starting to match stuff thanks to improved control and increasing K rate. Added velocity and location to heavy FB and hard SL can be plus at times. CU also getting better with time. Pitches don't indicate a top-of-rotation guy, but is a keeper.

Gant,John

SP | Atlanta | EXP MLB DEBUT: 2016 | H/W: 6-5 205 | FUT: #4 starter | 7C

Thrws R Age 23
2011 (21) HS (FL)

88-91	FB	+++
78-79	CB	++
80-82	CU	+++

Year	Lev	Team	W	L	Sv	IP	K	ERA	WHIP	BF/G	OBA	H%	S%	xERA	Ctl	Dom	Cmd	hr/9	BPV
2013	A-	Brooklyn	6	4	0	71	81	2.91	1.14	21.7	209	30	73	2.09	3.5	10.2	2.9	0.1	107
2014	A	Savannah	11	5	0	123	114	2.56	1.20	23.5	236	30	79	2.81	2.9	8.3	2.9	0.4	89
2015	A+	St. Lucie	2	0	0	40	48	1.80	0.92	25.0	193	26	88	2.08	2.2	10.8	4.8	0.9	151
2015	AA	Binghamton	4	5	0	59	43	4.72	1.57	23.6	287	34	68	4.43	4.0	6.5	1.7	0.3	29
2015	AA	Mississippi	4	0	0	40	43	2.01	1.04	22.2	198	28	80	1.83	3.1	9.6	3.1	0.2	107

Acquired by ATL in a trade sending playoff pieces to NYM. Best pitch is a 2-seam FB with sinking action and bore into RHH. Best secondary pitch is a 12-6 hard CB that he can throw for strikes. Feel for the CU lags behind in development but showed improvement throughout '15. Floor is a middle RP.

Garabito,Gerson

SP | Kansas City | EXP MLB DEBUT: 2019 | H/W: 6-0 160 | FUT: #4 starter | 7E

Thrws R Age 20
2012 FA (DR)

89-95	FB	++++
77-79	CB	++
81-82	CU	++

Year	Lev	Team	W	L	Sv	IP	K	ERA	WHIP	BF/G	OBA	H%	S%	xERA	Ctl	Dom	Cmd	hr/9	BPV
2013	Rk	DSL Royals	1	0	0	26	17	3.09	1.53	9.5	237	29	78	3.35	5.8	5.8	1.0	0.0	-35
2014	Rk	DSL Royals	2	1	0	49	61	1.28	1.04	14.6	148	23	88	1.21	4.9	11.2	2.3	0.2	86
2015	Rk	Azl Royals	3	2	0	57	42	4.11	1.25	16.6	244	30	65	3.02	3.0	6.6	2.2	0.3	56

Quick-armed SP who flashed plus, smooth delivery in first year in US. Has average velocity now and could grow into high-90s. Has frame to add strength, though lack of height is concern. Has feel for spin and CB has shown drastic improvement. Throws strikes, but command within zone could be better. Needs better CU for LHH.

Garcia,Elniery

SP | Philadelphia | EXP MLB DEBUT: 2019 | H/W: 6-0 155 | FUT: #4 starter | 7D

Thrws L Age 21
2011 FA (DR)

89-91	FB	+++
72-75	CB	+++
82-84	CU	++

Year	Lev	Team	W	L	Sv	IP	K	ERA	WHIP	BF/G	OBA	H%	S%	xERA	Ctl	Dom	Cmd	hr/9	BPV
2013	Rk	GCL Phillies	1	3	0	36	31	5.22	1.57	17.7	296	37	64	4.51	3.5	7.7	2.2	0.2	63
2014	Rk	GCL Phillies	2	2	0	26	23	2.08	1.15	14.8	262	34	80	2.71	1.4	8.0	5.8	0.0	124
2014	A-	Williamsport	0	0	0	4	5	6.43	1.90	5.0	336	42	71	7.73	4.3	10.7	2.5	2.1	95
2015	A	Lakewood	8	9	0	120	66	3.23	1.34	23.8	270	30	77	3.82	2.7	5.0	1.8	0.5	34

Slightly-built southpaw makes up for average stuff with advanced feel for pitching. FB is high 80s/low 90s, but could end up with plus command. Tight CB exhibits sharp break and is best secondary pitch. CU also has potential. Easy motion, but more consistent release point would allow pitches to play up. Needs consistent "out" pitch; has time.

Garcia,Jarlin

SP | Miami | EXP MLB DEBUT: 2016 | H/W: 6-2 170 | FUT: #3 starter | 8D

Thrws L Age 23
2010 FA (DR)

90-95	FB	+++
	CB	++++
	SL	++
80-83	CU	+++

Year	Lev	Team	W	L	Sv	IP	K	ERA	WHIP	BF/G	OBA	H%	S%	xERA	Ctl	Dom	Cmd	hr/9	BPV
2012	Rk	GCL Marlins	1	3	0	40	32	3.60	1.30	13.7	252	31	72	3.38	3.2	7.2	2.3	0.5	63
2013	A-	Batavia	2	3	0	69	74	3.12	1.10	18.1	229	30	75	2.98	2.3	9.6	4.1	0.9	128
2014	A	Greensboro	10	5	0	133	111	4.39	1.30	21.9	288	34	68	4.28	1.4	7.5	5.3	0.9	115
2015	A+	Jupiter	3	5	0	97	69	3.06	1.23	21.8	260	31	75	3.23	2.1	6.4	3.0	0.4	76
2015	AA	Jacksonville	1	3	0	36	35	4.97	1.52	22.4	271	34	69	4.69	4.2	8.7	2.1	1.0	61

Dominican lefty has a FB that sits a 90-93 mph, topping out at 95 mph. Backs up the heater with a decent CU, CB, and a power SL. CB is his 2nd best offering, but needs to be more consistent and FB is relatively straight. Still has some projection left and he does pound the strike zone.

Garcia,Jason

RP | Baltimore | EXP MLB DEBUT: 2015 | H/W: 6-0 185 | FUT: Closer | 7C

Thrws R Age 23
2010 (17) HS (FL)

92-98	FB	++++
82-87	SL	+++
	CU	+

Year	Lev	Team	W	L	Sv	IP	K	ERA	WHIP	BF/G	OBA	H%	S%	xERA	Ctl	Dom	Cmd	hr/9	BPV
2013	A	Greenville	2	2	1	36	36	4.24	1.36	16.8	245	31	70	3.69	4.0	9.0	2.3	0.7	72
2014	A-	Lowell	1	1	0	20	22	3.56	1.29	16.6	250	35	69	2.87	3.1	9.8	3.1	0.0	110
2014	A	Greenville	2	1	3	35	37	3.84	1.36	16.4	238	33	69	2.91	4.3	9.5	2.2	0.0	71
2015	AA	Bowie	1	2	0	15	14	4.20	1.40	7.0	221	26	74	3.93	5.4	8.4	1.6	1.2	23
2015	MLB	Baltimore	1	0	0	29	22	4.32	1.44	5.9	233	27	72	3.93	5.2	6.8	1.3	0.9	-1

Power-armed RP who moved to pen full-time in '15 and missed time with shoulder injury. Has electric FB that features vicious, late life, though has difficulty controlling it. Struggles with LHH as he has below average CU, but has two out pitches in FB and hard SL. Has closer stuff, though command continues to waver. Injury history is concern.

Garcia,Onelki

RP | Chicago (A) | EXP MLB DEBUT: 2013 | H/W: 6-3 225 | FUT: Setup reliever | 6B

Thrws L Age 26
2012 (3) HS (CU)

92-95	FB	++++
81-84	SL	+++
74-78	CB	++
	CU	+

Year	Lev	Team	W	L	Sv	IP	K	ERA	WHIP	BF/G	OBA	H%	S%	xERA	Ctl	Dom	Cmd	hr/9	BPV
2013	AAA	Albuquerque	0	1	0	9	14	3.91	0.98	3.5	188	33	56	1.29	2.9	13.7	4.7	0.0	185
2013	MLB	LA Dodgers	0	0	0	1	1	16.36	4.55	2.7	244	0	75	18.71	32.7	8.2	0.3	8.2	-718
2014	A+	RanchoCuca	0	1	0	0	0	90.00	15.00	3.6	780	78	33	61.58	45.0	0.0	0.0	0.0	-1197
2015	AA	Birmingham	1	0	0	17	24	5.23	1.51	5.7	281	44	62	3.85	3.7	12.6	3.4	0.0	145
2015	AAA	Charlotte	0	1	3	38	48	4.72	1.76	7.0	295	41	73	5.35	5.2	11.3	2.2	0.7	82

Physical RP who has impressive K rate. Could be poised for role in CHW pen as he uses deliberate delivery and power stuff to fool with hitters. Hasn't been able to consistently throw strikes and can aim ball at times. FB can be too straight and could benefit from sequencing more efficiently. Has chance to pop with better control.

Garcia,Yeudy

SP | Pittsburgh | EXP MLB DEBUT: 2019 | H/W: 6-3 185 | FUT: #3 starter | 8D

Thrws R Age 23
2013 FA (DR)

93-95	FB	++++
83-86	SL	++
85-87	CU	++

Year	Lev	Team	W	L	Sv	IP	K	ERA	WHIP	BF/G	OBA	H%	S%	xERA	Ctl	Dom	Cmd	hr/9	BPV
2015	A	West Virginia	12	5	1	124	112	2.10	1.07	16.1	208	27	81	2.09	3.0	8.1	2.7	0.3	84

Dominican righty didn't sign as a pro until he was 20. Had a breakout season and dominated SAL hitters with a plus 93-96 mph that tops out at 98 mph. Pitches effectively off the FB and keeps hitters honest with an above-avg SL and CU. Struggled with control, but missed plenty of bat and limited the opposition to a .204 BA.

Garrett,Amir

SP | Cincinnati | EXP MLB DEBUT: 2017 | H/W: 6-5 210 | FUT: #3 starter | 8C

Thrws L Age 23
2011 (22) HS (NV)

92-94	FB	++++
84-86	SL	+++
80-82	CU	++

Year	Lev	Team	W	L	Sv	IP	K	ERA	WHIP	BF/G	OBA	H%	S%	xERA	Ctl	Dom	Cmd	hr/9	BPV
2012	Rk	AZL Reds	0	2	0	14	13	5.79	1.86	9.4	262	33	68	5.09	7.7	8.4	1.1	0.6	-40
2013	Rk	Billings	1	1	0	23	17	2.72	1.38	19.5	252	31	78	3.16	3.9	6.6	1.7	0.0	32
2013	A	Dayton	1	3	0	34	15	6.88	1.65	19.0	294	31	58	5.46	4.2	4.0	0.9	1.1	-25
2014	A	Dayton	7	8	0	133	127	3.65	1.25	20.0	235	30	72	3.28	3.4	8.6	2.5	0.7	79
2015	A+	Daytona	9	7	0	140	133	2.44	1.23	21.8	228	30	80	2.70	3.5	8.5	2.4	0.3	76

Former 2-sport star who gave up basketball to concentrate on pitching in '14. Made tremendous strides in 2nd full-time season. Repeating mechanics is a pitch-by-pitch struggle but doesn't affect command of FB. SL took a big step up, becoming 2nd best secondary. Adding additional depth could push pitch to plus.

Gatto,Joe — SP — Los Angeles (A)

EXP MLB DEBUT: 2018 | H/W: 6-3 204 | FUT: #4 starter | **7C**

Thrws R Age 20
2014 (2) HS (NJ)

Velo	Pitch	Grade
89-94	FB	+++
77-80	CB	+++
81-85	CU	++

Year	Lev	Team	W	L	Sv	IP	K	ERA	WHIP	BF/G	OBA	H%	S%	xERA	Ctl	Dom	Cmd	hr/9	BPV
2014	Rk	Azl Angels	2	1	0	25	15	5.40	1.68	11.3	319	37	66	5.25	3.2	5.4	1.7	0.4	28
2014	Rk	Orem	0	0	0	2	1	4.50	1.50	8.6	347	30	100	9.18	0.0	4.5		4.5	99
2015	Rk	Orem	2	3	0	54	38	4.33	1.66	20.2	324	38	74	5.57	2.8	6.3	2.2	0.7	55

Athletic, smooth SP who has ideal frame to add velocity while improving command and control. Has yet to pitch in full-season ball and should get opportunity. Has solid present pitches that can get better, particularly CB and CU. FB has plus sink that hitters cannot elevate. Proven hittable with pitch-to-contact approach at present.

German,Domingo — SP — New York (A)

EXP MLB DEBUT: 2018 | H/W: 6-2 175 | FUT: #3 starter | **8D**

Thrws R Age 23
2009 FA (DR)

Velo	Pitch	Grade
90-96	FB	++++
79-82	CB	++
80-83	CU	+++

Year	Lev	Team	W	L	Sv	IP	K	ERA	WHIP	BF/G	OBA	H%	S%	xERA	Ctl	Dom	Cmd	hr/9	BPV
2013	Rk	GCL Marlins	3	0	0	26	27	1.38	0.77	18.7	170	23	84	0.93	1.7	9.3	5.4	0.3	140
2013	A-	Batavia	2	3	0	41	34	1.76	0.93	19.2	222	29	79	1.63	1.1	7.5	6.8	0.0	123
2014	A	Greensboro	9	3	0	123	113	2.49	1.15	19.5	250	32	79	2.95	1.8	8.3	4.5	0.4	117
2015	A+	Tampa	*Did not pitch - injured*																

Live-armed SP who missed entire season after TJ surgery in April. Throws consistent strikes with easy delivery and velocity despite heavy sink on plus FB. More thrower than pitcher at this point and needs to upgrade CB to have chance. Pitches low in zone and has effective CU against LHH. Looked to build upon '14 breakout.

Gibson,Daniel — RP — Arizona

EXP MLB DEBUT: 2016 | H/W: 6-2 220 | FUT: Setup reliever | **7B**

Thrws L Age 24
2013 (7) Florida

Velo	Pitch	Grade
92-95	FB	++++
83-86	SL	+++

Year	Lev	Team	W	L	Sv	IP	K	ERA	WHIP	BF/G	OBA	H%	S%	xERA	Ctl	Dom	Cmd	hr/9	BPV
2013	A	South Bend	0	1	0	8		1.11	0.99	5.1	208	25	88	1.63	2.2	5.6	2.5	0.0	58
2014	A	South Bend	3	2	3	36	45	1.99	1.14	3.9	210	31	83	2.20	3.5	11.2	3.2	0.2	126
2014	A+	Visalia	4	3	0	22	22	9.32	1.94	5.0	331	41	50	6.87	4.9	8.9	1.8	1.2	47
2015	A+	Visalia	2	1	1	28	38	1.61	0.82	3.8	168	27	82	1.00	2.3	12.2	5.4	0.3	177
2015	AA	Mobile	1	0	2	24	20	1.50	1.33	3.8	210	27	88	2.51	5.3	7.5	1.4	0.0	11

Lefty reliever took huge step up in development. Commands plus FB with ease. FB is hard to square up due to late movement. SL showed signs of becoming a weapon in '15. 2-plane movement became effective pitch against RH & LH hitters. No longer just a LOOGY. Capable of getting hitters out in any situation.

Gilbert,Tyler — SP — Philadelphia

EXP MLB DEBUT: 2019 | H/W: 6-3 190 | FUT: #4 starter | **7D**

Thrws L Age 22
2015 (6) USC

Velo	Pitch	Grade
89-92	FB	++
75-77	CB	+++
80-82	CU	++

Year	Lev	Team	W	L	Sv	IP	K	ERA	WHIP	BF/G	OBA	H%	S%	xERA	Ctl	Dom	Cmd	hr/9	BPV
2015	NCAA	USC	5	2	2	67	66	2.81	1.38	12.8	264	34	81	3.82	3.3	8.8	2.6	0.5	87
2015	A-	Williamsport	4	3	0	42	44	2.79	1.14	16.6	262	36	73	2.67	1.3	9.4	7.3	0.0	153

Potential for two plus pitches. CB is best at present, lacks bite but at 75-77 mph has good shape. FB (89-92) has some armside run to it, and could project a tick or two upwards with more strength and repetitions. A touch of deception with a torso turn in his delivery, but control is not a problem. Also flashes a CU with some fade vs. RHH.

Giolito,Lucas — SP — Washington

EXP MLB DEBUT: 2016 | H/W: 6-6 255 | FUT: #1 starter | **10C**

Thrws R Age 21
2012 (1) HS (CA)

Velo	Pitch	Grade
93-96	FB	+++++
79-82	CB	++++
81-83	CU	+++

Year	Lev	Team	W	L	Sv	IP	K	ERA	WHIP	BF/G	OBA	H%	S%	xERA	Ctl	Dom	Cmd	hr/9	BPV
2013	Rk	GCL Nationals	1	1	0	22	25	2.84	1.31	11.5	233	34	76	2.69	4.1	10.1	2.5	0.0	91
2013	A-	Auburn	1	0	0	14	14	0.64	0.93	17.5	186	24	100	1.79	2.6	9.0	3.5	0.6	111
2014	A	Hagerstown	10	2	0	98	110	2.20	1.00	18.7	202	27	81	2.15	2.6	10.1	3.9	0.6	130
2015	A+	Potomac	3	5	0	69	86	2.73	1.23	21.5	250	37	76	2.83	2.6	11.2	4.3	0.1	149
2015	AA	Harrisburg	4	2	0	47	45	3.82	1.38	24.7	265	34	71	3.69	3.2	8.6	2.6	0.4	85

Likely has the best two-pitch combination in the minors: a heavy and lively mid-90s FB and a sharp two-plane curveball. Both have plus-plus potential. Add in an improved, sinking CU, a clean and repeatable delivery, ability to pitch downhill, and an appropriate mean streak? This is what an ace pitching prospect looks like.

Givens,Mychal — RP — Baltimore

EXP MLB DEBUT: 2015 | H/W: 6-0 210 | FUT: Closer | **7B**

Thrws R Age 25
2009 (2) HS (FL)

Velo	Pitch	Grade
92-96	FB	++++
82-85	SL	+++
84-88	CU	++

Year	Lev	Team	W	L	Sv	IP	K	ERA	WHIP	BF/G	OBA	H%	S%	xERA	Ctl	Dom	Cmd	hr/9	BPV
2013	A	Delmarva	2	3	3	42	36	4.27	1.26	6.1	222	28	63	2.66	4.1	7.7	1.9	0.2	47
2014	A+	Frederick	1	2	3	33	27	3.26	1.12	7.2	184	22	71	2.17	4.4	7.3	1.7	0.5	33
2014	AA	Bowie	0	0	0	25	28	3.94	1.67	6.3	212	31	74	3.36	8.2	10.0	1.2	0.0	-24
2015	AA	Bowie	4	2	15	57	79	1.73	0.95	6.1	191	31	81	1.40	2.5	12.5	4.9	0.2	174
2015	MLB	Baltimore	2	0	0	30	38	1.80	0.87	5.0	191	29	80	1.35	1.8	11.4	6.3	0.3	175

Very athletic RP who broke through on basis of much improved command and control. Converted from SS in '13 and has excellent feel for three offerings. Lively, sinking FB is best pitch and thrown from low 3/4 slot that also makes SL better than advertised. Hitters either fan or bury ball into ground.

Glasnow,Tyler — SP — Pittsburgh

EXP MLB DEBUT: 2016 | H/W: 6-8 225 | FUT: #1 starter | **9C**

Thrws R Age 22
2011 (5) HS (CA)

Velo	Pitch	Grade
93-95	FB	+++++
75-78	CB	+++
85-87	CU	+++

Year	Lev	Team	W	L	Sv	IP	K	ERA	WHIP	BF/G	OBA	H%	S%	xERA	Ctl	Dom	Cmd	hr/9	BPV
2013	A	West Virginia	9	3	0	111	164	2.19	1.04	17.8	147	23	83	1.68	4.9	13.3	2.7	0.7	124
2014	A+	Bradenton	12	5	0	124	157	1.74	1.06	20.9	175	27	84	1.56	4.1	11.4	2.8	0.2	111
2015	A-	West Virginia	0	1	0	5	6	3.53	0.98	9.7	173	26	60	1.16	3.5	10.6	3.0	0.0	113
2015	AA	Altoona	5	3	0	63	82	2.43	0.95	19.8	188	29	74	1.51	2.7	11.7	4.3	0.3	156
2015	AAA	Indianapolis	2	1	0	41	48	2.20	1.34	21.3	222	32	83	2.85	4.8	10.5	2.2	0.2	77

Tall RHP continues to impress. Dominates with a plus-plus 93-95 mph FB that tops out 98 mph. Gets good downhill tilt and has late life on his heater with nice arm-side run. His upper-70s CB is now above-average and flashes plus at times. CU remains a work in progress, but has potential. Control is the only red flag.

Goforth,David — RP — Milwaukee

EXP MLB DEBUT: 2015 | H/W: 5-10 205 | FUT: Setup reliever | **7C**

Thrws R Age 27
2011 (7) Mississippi

Velo	Pitch	Grade
93-96	FB	++++
88-91	SL	+++
76-79	CB	++

Year	Lev	Team	W	L	Sv	IP	K	ERA	WHIP	BF/G	OBA	H%	S%	xERA	Ctl	Dom	Cmd	hr/9	BPV
2013	A+	Brevard County	7	5	0	78	58	3.11	1.22	22.5	233	28	75	2.94	3.2	6.7	2.1	0.5	51
2013	AA	Huntsville	4	3	5	46	36	3.31	1.08	9.0	197	25	67	1.91	3.5	7.0	2.0	0.2	50
2014	AA	Huntsville	5	4	27	64	46	3.79	1.39	5.0	249	30	71	3.40	4.1	6.4	1.6	0.3	24
2015	AAA	Colorado Springs	0	4	4	47	34	2.68	1.34	5.1	214	26	80	2.94	5.2	6.5	1.3	0.4	-4
2015	MLB	Milwaukee	1	0	0	24	24	4.09	1.65	5.4	319	39	81	6.22	3.0	8.9	3.0	1.5	98

Small, hard-throwing RH lives in the mid-90s with his straight FB. Complements it with hard 88-91 SL that gets ground balls. Mixes in CB at times, but is a well below-average offering. Has fringe-average command and doesn't miss as many bats as velo would suggest. Future looks to be in setup role.

Gohara,Luiz — SP — Seattle

EXP MLB DEBUT: 2019 | H/W: 6-3 210 | FUT: #3 starter | **8D**

Thrws L Age 19
2012 FA (BR)

Velo	Pitch	Grade
91-95	FB	++++
81-84	SL	+++
81-85	CU	++

Year	Lev	Team	W	L	Sv	IP	K	ERA	WHIP	BF/G	OBA	H%	S%	xERA	Ctl	Dom	Cmd	hr/9	BPV
2013	Rk	Pulaski	1	2	0	21	27	4.25	1.46	15.1	269	39	70	3.95	3.8	11.5	3.0	0.4	121
2014	Rk	Azl Mariners	1	1	0	12	16	2.21	1.07	23.7	242	37	77	2.19	1.5	11.8	8.0	0.0	191
2014	A-	Everett	0	6	0	37	37	8.25	1.89	15.9	305	37	56	6.56	5.8	9.0	1.5	1.5	22
2015	A-	Everett	3	7	0	53	62	6.26	1.86	17.8	309	42	65	5.79	5.4	10.5	1.9	0.7	61
2015	A	Clinton	0	1	0	9	5	1.96	1.74	21.0	278	32	88	4.45	5.9	4.9	0.8	0.0	-52

Young, powerful SP who repeated NWL and showed flashes of being dominant, frontline guy. Uses height to throw on downhill plane and will induce high amount of groundballs. Can blow ball by hitters up in zone with plus FB. Has solid-average SL that could evolve into plus and only needs to repeat arm speed to make CU more effective.

Gomber,Austin — SP — St. Louis

EXP MLB DEBUT: 2019 | H/W: 6-5 205 | FUT: #4 starter | **7D**

Thrws L Age 22
2014 (4) Florida Atlantic

Velo	Pitch	Grade
90-92	FB	++
74-77	CB	++
	CU	+++

Year	Lev	Team	W	L	Sv	IP	K	ERA	WHIP	BF/G	OBA	H%	S%	xERA	Ctl	Dom	Cmd	hr/9	BPV
2012	NCAA	Florida Atlantic	3	4	0	61	63	3.83	1.49	18.8	252	34	73	3.69	4.9	9.3	1.9	0.3	54
2013	NCAA	Florida Atlantic	8	4	0	106	103	2.97	1.16	23.4	241	30	78	3.24	2.4	8.7	3.7	0.8	111
2014	NCAA	Florida Atlantic	3	6	0	77	72	3.27	1.21	25.9	264	34	73	3.31	1.8	8.4	4.8	0.5	122
2014	A-	State College	2	2	0	47	36	2.30	1.55	18.7	293	35	87	4.72	3.4	6.9	2.0	0.6	49
2015	A	Peoria	15	3	0	135	140	2.67	0.97	23.3	203	27	75	2.12	2.3	9.3	4.1	0.7	125

6-5 college LHP has a decent three-pitch mix that includes an avg 90-92 mph FB, CB, and CU. CB was slow, sweeping variety in college, but was better as a pro and shows above-average potential. CU is also an average pitch and he commands the strike zone well. Has a bit of deception in his delivery, but understands how to pitch and keep hitters off-balance.

Gonsalves,Stephen — SP — Minnesota

EXP MLB DEBUT: 2017 | H/W: 6-5 190 | FUT: #4 starter | **7B**

Thrws L Age 21
2013 (4) HS (CA)

Velo	Pitch	Grade
90-93	FB	+++
77-80	CB	+++
81-83	SL	+++
81-83	CU	+++

Year	Lev	Team	W	L	Sv	IP	K	ERA	WHIP	BF/G	OBA	H%	S%	xERA	Ctl	Dom	Cmd	hr/9	BPV
2013	Rk	Elizabethton	1	1	0	14	21	1.29	1.00	17.8	202	35	86	1.51	2.6	13.5	5.3	0.0	192
2014	Rk	Elizabethton	2	0	0	29	26	2.79	1.14	19.1	220	28	75	2.41	3.1	8.1	2.6	0.3	79
2014	A	Cedar Rapids	2	3	0	36	44	3.23	1.16	18.0	233	34	71	2.55	2.7	10.9	4.0	0.2	141
2015	A	Cedar Rapids	6	1	0	55	77	1.15	0.80	22.1	158	26	88	0.83	2.5	12.6	5.1	0.3	179
2015	A+	Fort Myers	7	2	0	79	55	2.62	1.31	21.8	228	28	79	2.91	4.3	6.3	1.4	0.2	14

Long, athletic SP who had breakout season. Dominated Low-A with solid four pitch arsenal. No pitch stands out, but can throw strikes with all and exhibits feel for changing speeds. Uses tough angle to plate which allows spike CB to play up. Deceptive CU may be best offering and battles RHH. May not add more velocity as projected.

Gonzales,Marco

SP | St. Louis | EXP MLB DEBUT: 2014 | H/W: 6-1 195 | FUT: #4 starter | 8C

Thrws L Age 24
2013 (1) Gonzaga

Velo	Pitch	Grade
88-92	FB	+++
75-77	CB	++
	CU	++++
77-79	SL	++

Year	Lev	Team	W	L	Sv	IP	K	ERA	WHIP	BF/G	OBA	H%	S%	xERA	Ctl	Dom	Cmd	hr/9	BPV
2014	MLB	St. Louis	4	2	0	34	31	4.21	1.55	14.9	249	30	76	4.53	5.5	8.2	1.5	1.1	16
2015	A+	Palm Beach	0	0	0	4	4	0.00	1.19	8.4	297	39	100	3.31	0.0	8.6		0.0	172
2015	AA	Springfield	0	0	0	6	6	0.00	0.97	11.7	255	34	100	2.15	0.0	8.7		0.0	175
2015	AAA	Memphis	1	5	0	69	51	5.47	1.66	22.1	318	36	70	6.08	3.1	6.6	2.1	1.3	53
2015	MLB	St. Louis	0	0	0	2	1	16.36	3.64	14.2	530	54	57	18.65	4.1	4.1	1.0	4.1	-19

Has a fluid delivery that leads to plus command of his four-pitch mix. FB lacks premium velocity and sits at 88-92 mph, but with good location. Best offering is a plus CU that he will throw in any count. Also mixes in an inconsistent CB and a seldom used SL. Got lit up in the PCL and will need to rebound in '16.

Gossett,Daniel

SP | Oakland | EXP MLB DEBUT: 2017 | H/W: 6-2 185 | FUT: #4 starter | 7D

Thrws R Age 23
2014 (2) Clemson

Velo	Pitch	Grade
90-94	FB	+++
81-83	SL	++
79-82	CU	++

Year	Lev	Team	W	L	Sv	IP	K	ERA	WHIP	BF/G	OBA	H%	S%	xERA	Ctl	Dom	Cmd	hr/9	BPV
2012	NCAA	Clemson	6	3	2	77	87	4.32	1.31	16.7	222	31	66	3.01	4.6	10.2	2.2	0.5	78
2013	NCAA	Clemson	10	4	0	98	91	2.57	1.18	24.5	220	28	81	2.84	3.5	8.3	2.4	0.6	74
2014	NCAA	Clemson	7	2	0	107	107	1.93	1.01	27.3	205	28	82	1.93	2.5	9.0	3.6	0.3	112
2014	A-	Vermont	1	0	0	24	25	2.25	0.71	7.1	191	26	69	1.04	0.4	9.4	25.0	0.4	177
2015	A	Beloit	5	13	0	144	112	4.74	1.41	22.6	271	31	68	4.43	3.2	7.0	2.2	1.0	56

Tall, lean SP who gets by with fringy pitches and some projection remaining due to quick arm action. All pitches show potential, but needs to add strength. FB can be straight while decent SL exhibits inconsistent break. Repeats arm speed on CU which has been somewhat effective against LHH. Stamina has been concern as he loses velocity.

Graves,Brett

SP | Oakland | EXP MLB DEBUT: 2017 | H/W: 6-1 170 | FUT: #4 starter | 7E

Thrws R Age 23
2014 (3) Missouri

Velo	Pitch	Grade
89-93	FB	++
78-80	CB	++
81-83	CU	+++

Year	Lev	Team	W	L	Sv	IP	K	ERA	WHIP	BF/G	OBA	H%	S%	xERA	Ctl	Dom	Cmd	hr/9	BPV
2013	NCAA	Missouri	2	5	0	71		3.80	1.39	21.4	280	29	77	4.69	2.7	4.1	1.5	1.1	19
2014	NCAA	Missouri	3	6	0	93	64	3.87	1.25	27.0	272	32	68	3.47	1.7	6.2	3.6	0.4	82
2014	Rk	Azl Athletics	0	0	0	1	1	0.00	1.00	3.8	0	0	100		9.0	9.0	1.0	0.0	-63
2014	A-	Vermont	3	2	0	21	18	6.86	1.43	11.2	288	36	48	4.19	2.6	7.7	3.0	0.4	87
2015	A	Beloit	12	8	0	142	91	5.38	1.49	21.9	295	33	64	4.96	2.8	5.8	2.1	0.9	46

Underperforming SP who was poor all year and could move to pen. Declining velocity a concern and lacks pitch movement with long arm action. Limits walks by repeating delivery and has good angle to plate despite lack of height. Shows feel for changing speeds, but struggles with LHH (.345 oppBA). CB is below average.

Gray,Jon

SP | Colorado | EXP MLB DEBUT: 2015 | H/W: 6-4 235 | FUT: #2 starter | 9D

Thrws R Age 24
2013 (1) Oklahoma

Velo	Pitch	Grade
94-96	FB	++++
85-88	SL	++++
81-84	CU	++

Year	Lev	Team	W	L	Sv	IP	K	ERA	WHIP	BF/G	OBA	H%	S%	xERA	Ctl	Dom	Cmd	hr/9	BPV
2013	Rk	Grand Junction	0	0	0	13	15	4.12	1.30	13.5	289	41	65	3.44	1.4	10.3	7.5	0.0	166
2013	A+	Modesto	4	0	0	24	36	0.75	0.67	16.7	129	24	88		2.3	13.5	6.0	0.0	200
2014	AA	Tulsa	10	5	0	124	113	3.92	1.19	20.7	234	29	68	3.12	3.0	8.2	2.8	0.7	85
2015	AAA	Albuquerque	6	6	0	114	110	4.34	1.49	23.4	286	36	71	4.57	3.2	8.7	2.7	0.7	87
2015	MLB	Colorado	0	2	0	40	40	5.60	1.64	19.9	314	40	66	5.55	3.1	9.0	2.9	0.9	95

Attacks hitters with a plus 95-96 mph FB that tops out at 98. Holds velocity well and commands his FB to both sides of the plate. ERA is not indicative of long-term potential. SL is a true swing-and-miss pitch with good late break. CU continues to improve, but still needs work. Look for better results in '16, but there will be bumps in the road.

Green,Chad

SP | New York (A) | EXP MLB DEBUT: 2016 | H/W: 6-3 210 | FUT: #4 starter | 7D

Thrws R Age 24
2013 (11) Louisville

Velo	Pitch	Grade
90-94	FB	+++
80-82	SL	++
81-84	CU	++

Year	Lev	Team	W	L	Sv	IP	K	ERA	WHIP	BF/G	OBA	H%	S%	xERA	Ctl	Dom	Cmd	hr/9	BPV
2013	NCAA	Louisville	10	4	0	104	74	2.42	1.19	23.2	248	30	79	2.89	2.3	6.4	2.7	0.3	70
2013	Rk	GCL Tigers	1	0	0	3	6	3.00	1.00	5.7	262	45	100	5.05	0.0	18.0		3.0	342
2013	A+	Lakeland	3	0	1	17	10	3.68	1.29	7.0	249	30	68	2.90	3.2	5.3	1.7	0.0	27
2014	A	West Michigan	6	4	0	130	125	3.11	1.15	22.4	248	32	74	3.02	1.9	8.6	4.5	0.6	121
2015	AA	Erie	5	14	0	148	137	3.95	1.44	23.4	289	36	73	4.33	2.6	8.3	3.2	0.5	97

Sleeper prospect who bypassed High-A and was outstanding from July on. Commands plate with easily locatable FB despite late sink and run. Knows how to pitch and attacks hitters with all pitches. SL and CU need work, but play up due to repeatable arm speed and slot. Doesn't have the stuff to dominate, but limits walks and HR.

Green,Hunter

SP | Los Angeles (A) | EXP MLB DEBUT: 2019 | H/W: 6-4 175 | FUT: #3 starter | 8E

Thrws L Age 20
2013 (2) HS (KY)

Velo	Pitch	Grade
85-93	FB	+++
76-79	CB	+++
78-80	CU	++

Year	Lev	Team	W	L	Sv	IP	K	ERA	WHIP	BF/G	OBA	H%	S%	xERA	Ctl	Dom	Cmd	hr/9	BPV
2015			*Did not pitch - injured*																

Injury-laden pitcher who hasn't pitched in two seasons due to back and fractured elbow. When healthy, throws with clean delivery and arm action to produce good velocity. Has projectable frame and will need to add strength. Uses CB as K pitch and needs to improve feel for changing speeds. High ceiling, but needs to be on mound.

Greene,Conner

SP | Toronto | EXP MLB DEBUT: 2017 | H/W: 6-3 165 | FUT: #3 starter | 8D

Thrws R Age 21
2013 (7) HS (CA)

Velo	Pitch	Grade
88-94	FB	+++
78-81	CB	++
84-89	SP	+++

Year	Lev	Team	W	L	Sv	IP	K	ERA	WHIP	BF/G	OBA	H%	S%	xERA	Ctl	Dom	Cmd	hr/9	BPV
2014	Rk	Bluefield	1	2	0	27	21	4.30	1.40	19.1	253	31	68	3.53	4.0	6.9	1.8	0.3	36
2014	Rk	GCL Blue Jays	1	2	0	31	30	2.02	0.99	17.0	221	28	83	2.32	1.7	8.7	5.0	0.6	127
2015	A	Lansing	7	3	0	67	65	3.89	1.40	20.2	284	36	72	4.14	2.5	8.7	3.4	0.5	106
2015	A+	Dunedin	2	3	0	40	35	2.25	1.10	22.4	242	31	79	2.52	1.8	7.9	4.4	0.2	111
2015	AA	New Hampshire	3	1	0	25	15	4.68	1.48	21.5	262	30	67	3.90	4.3	5.4	1.3	0.4	-1

Long, thin SP who modified delivery to take advantage of arm action and speed. FB added a few mph and could evolve into plus pitch. Does nice job of repeating arm speed on CU which gives it boost. CB is below average at present and exhibits inconsistent break. Has great angle to plate with release point and still has projection remaining.

Gregorio,Joan

SP | San Francisco | EXP MLB DEBUT: 2017 | H/W: 6-7 180 | FUT: #4 starter | 7D

Thrws R Age 24
2010 FA (DR)

Velo	Pitch	Grade
91-95	FB	++++
82-85	SL	+++
84-86	CU	++

Year	Lev	Team	W	L	Sv	IP	K	ERA	WHIP	BF/G	OBA	H%	S%	xERA	Ctl	Dom	Cmd	hr/9	BPV
2012	A-	Salem-Kaizer	7	7	0	76	69	5.56	1.42	20.2	284	34	62	4.69	2.7	8.2	3.0	1.1	91
2013	A	Augusta	6	3	0	69	84	4.03	1.18	19.8	250	36	65	2.97	2.2	10.9	4.9	0.4	155
2014	A	Augusta	2	7	1	68	65	3.57	1.13	20.7	207	27	67	2.20	3.6	8.6	2.4	0.3	76
2014	A+	San Jose	2	2	0	22	27	6.89	1.80	17.1	301	41	61	5.65	5.3	10.9	2.1	0.8	73
2015	AA	Richmond	3	2	1	78	72	3.11	1.23	8.6	225	28	77	3.06	3.7	8.3	2.3	0.7	68

Dominican LH features a lean 6'7" frame and long limbs that often lead to delivery and Ctl issues. Still has solid swing-and-miss ability, starting with 91-95 mph FB that peaks at 97. SL action is inconsistent, but flashes good tilt when on; CU may never fully develop. Finished '15 as SP, but two-pitch mix could play better as RP long-term.

Griffin,Foster

SP | Kansas City | EXP MLB DEBUT: 2018 | H/W: 6-3 200 | FUT: #3 starter | 8D

Thrws L Age 20
2014 (1) HS (FL)

Velo	Pitch	Grade
89-93	FB	+++
75-79	CB	++
79-82	CU	+++

Year	Lev	Team	W	L	Sv	IP	K	ERA	WHIP	BF/G	OBA	H%	S%	xERA	Ctl	Dom	Cmd	hr/9	BPV
2014	Rk	Burlington	0	2	0	28	19	3.21	1.11	10.0	194	22	72	2.36	3.9	6.1	1.6	0.6	24
2015	A	Lexington	4	6	0	102	71	5.46	1.55	20.3	299	35	64	4.92	3.1	6.3	2.0	0.7	47

Tall, lanky SP who had poor beginning of season, but has intriguing upside. Will be project, but could be worth wait due to potential for three above average pitches. Uses athletic delivery to command plate and has deceptive arm speed on CU. Modest K rate is a concern. CB lacks consistency and bite, though can change speeds effectively.

Gsellman,Robert

SP | New York (N) | EXP MLB DEBUT: 2017 | H/W: 6-4 200 | FUT: #4 starter | 7B

Thrws R Age 22
2011 (13) HS (CA)

Velo	Pitch	Grade
89-92	FB	+++
76-78	CB	+++
80-82	CU	+++

Year	Lev	Team	W	L	Sv	IP	K	ERA	WHIP	BF/G	OBA	H%	S%	xERA	Ctl	Dom	Cmd	hr/9	BPV
2013	A-	Brooklyn	3	3	0	70	64	2.06	1.01	22.4	230	30	80	2.18	1.5	8.2	5.3	0.3	124
2013	A	Savannah	2	3	0	29	14	3.72	1.41	24.6	300	33	74	4.54	1.9	4.3	2.3	0.6	46
2014	A	Savannah	10	6	0	116	92	2.56	1.34	24.2	271	34	80	3.48	2.6	7.1	2.7	0.2	75
2015	A+	St. Lucie	6	0	0	51	37	1.76	0.94	24.0	205	25	81	1.63	1.9	6.5	3.4	0.2	83
2015	AA	Binghamton	7	7	0	92	49	3.52	1.25	23.4	255	29	71	3.26	2.5	4.8	1.9	0.4	36

High floor RHP who has developed into solid prospect. Each of three pitches should be MLB average at full projection. Pitches downhill and generates a ton of ground balls with sinking FB. SL and CU are servicable pitches. CU has good deception and more bore than FB. Simply doesn't elicit swings and misses with stuff.

Guaipe,Mayckol

RP | Seattle | EXP MLB DEBUT: 2015 | H/W: 6-4 235 | FUT: Setup reliever | 6B

Thrws R Age 25
2006 FA (VZ)

Velo	Pitch	Grade
90-94	FB	+++
81-83	SL	+++
	CU	+

Year	Lev	Team	W	L	Sv	IP	K	ERA	WHIP	BF/G	OBA	H%	S%	xERA	Ctl	Dom	Cmd	hr/9	BPV
2012	A	Clinton	5	0	0	58	34	3.41	1.29	21.7	268	30	75	3.75	2.3	5.3	2.3	0.6	50
2013	A+	High Desert	3	4	5	59	57	5.64	1.49	7.3	262	33	61	4.27	4.4	8.7	2.0	0.8	55
2014	AA	Jackson	1	3	12	56	56	2.89	0.96	5.3	222	29	72	2.31	1.4	9.0	6.2	0.6	141
2015	AAA	Tacoma	0	4	5	47	36	2.87	1.26	5.0	270	32	79	3.63	1.9	6.9	3.6	0.6	90
2015	MLB	Seattle	0	3	0	26	22	5.50	1.79	5.8	315	36	74	6.73	4.5	7.6	1.7	1.7	33

Thick, strong RP who took long route to majors, but has chance to stick. Has been RP since '13 and has arm strength and FB/SL to pitch high-leverage innings. Repeats smooth delivery and exhibits command. Can struggle with LHH as he lacks offspeed pitch. K rate could be better.

Guduan,Reymin — RP — Houston

EXP MLB DEBUT: 2016 | H/W: 6-4 205 | FUT: Closer | **8E**

Thrws L Age 24
2009 FA (DR)

Velo	Pitch	Grade
93-97	FB	++++
83-86	SL	+++
	CU	+

Year	Lev	Team	W	L	Sv	IP	K	ERA	WHIP	BF/G	OBA	H%	S%	xERA	Ctl	Dom	Cmd	hr/9	BPV
2013	AAA	Oklahoma City	0	0	0	2	4	4.29	1.90	9.9	144	34	75	3.12	12.9	17.1	1.3	0.0	-21
2014	Rk	Greeneville	2	5	0	44	58	4.49	1.81	15.7	299	43	74	5.26	5.5	11.8	2.1	0.4	82
2015	A	Quad Cities	3	0	0	12	15	0.75	0.75	7.1	151	24	89	0.34	2.3	11.3	5.0	0.0	160
2015	A+	Lancaster	0	3	4	17	25	3.16	1.35	5.5	199	34	74	2.35	5.8	13.2	2.3	0.0	99
2015	AA	Corpus Christi	1	3	0	16	19	11.74	2.42	5.3	306	39	50	8.10	10.6	10.6	1.0	1.7	-78

Tall, lean hurler who moved to RP in '15 and dominated before getting hit hard in AA. Power FB and SL ideal for late innings role and can wipe out hitters with high, hard stuff or get them to chase SL out of zone. Quick arm adds deception and pitch movement, though needs to throw strikes. Induces lots of groundballs and is tough to hit.

Guerrero,Jordan A. — SP — Chicago (A)

EXP MLB DEBUT: 2017 | H/W: 6-3 190 | FUT: #4 starter | **7C**

Thrws L Age 21
2012 (15) HS (CA)

Velo	Pitch	Grade
89-93	FB	+++
77-78	CB	++
81-83	CU	+++

Year	Lev	Team	W	L	Sv	IP	K	ERA	WHIP	BF/G	OBA	H%	S%	xERA	Ctl	Dom	Cmd	hr/9	BPV
2012	Rk	Bristol	0	1	0	9	6	3.00	1.56	5.6	283	34	79	4.04	4.0	6.0	1.5	0.0	18
2013	Rk	Bristol	0	3	0	25	15	4.30	1.43	21.4	305	33	75	5.42	1.8	5.4	3.0	1.4	66
2014	A	Kannapolis	6	2	0	78	80	3.46	1.38	12.1	269	35	76	3.93	3.1	9.2	3.0	0.6	100
2015	A	Kannapolis	6	1	0	55	60	2.29	0.94	23.0	213	30	75	1.69	1.6	9.8	6.0	0.2	150
2015	A+	Winston-Salem	7	3	0	93	88	3.57	1.11	22.9	238	30	68	2.81	2.0	8.5	4.2	0.6	116

Breakout pitcher in org as he mastered Low-A en route to High-A, as short arm action and pitch movement kept hitters off balance. FB cuts and is rarely straight. Impressive arm speed on CU leads to deception, though CB lacks bite. Unlikely to be a high K pitcher; will need to hit spots and keep ball down.

Guerrero,Jordan M. — RP — San Diego

EXP MLB DEBUT: 2019 | H/W: 6-5 260 | FUT: Setup reliever | **7D**

Thrws R Age 19
2015 (6) Polk St JC

Velo	Pitch	Grade
91-96	FB	+++
84-85	SL	++

Year	Lev	Team	W	L	Sv	IP	K	ERA	WHIP	BF/G	OBA	H%	S%	xERA	Ctl	Dom	Cmd	hr/9	BPV
2015	Rk	Azl Padres	3	1	1	27	27	4.30	1.62	9.3	288	38	72	4.55	4.3	8.9	2.1	0.3	63

Huge-framed hurler who is all about arm strength, but needs a lot of seasoning and polish. Relies on FB and SL and has no feel for changing speeds or sequencing. FB can be straight, but he throws with tough angle to plate. SL could become plus pitch in time, but can get on side of it and telegraph it. Some upside, but only as RP.

Guerrero,Tayron — RP — San Diego

EXP MLB DEBUT: 2016 | H/W: 6-7 215 | FUT: Setup reliever | **7C**

Thrws R Age 25
2009 FA (CL)

Velo	Pitch	Grade
92-97	FB	++++
81-84	SL	+++
	CU	+

Year	Lev	Team	W	L	Sv	IP	K	ERA	WHIP	BF/G	OBA	H%	S%	xERA	Ctl	Dom	Cmd	hr/9	BPV
2014	A	Fort Wayne	6	1	1	36	42	1.00	0.94	5.4	178	25	94	1.60	3.0	10.5	3.5	0.5	126
2014	A+	Lake Elsinore	0	0	3	13	14	2.73	1.36	3.9	212	28	82	3.22	5.5	9.5	1.8	0.7	43
2015	AA	San Antonio	1	5	13	42	46	2.78	1.26	4.6	218	29	80	2.99	4.3	9.8	2.3	0.6	80
2015	AAA	El Paso	0	0	1	13	15	4.09	1.44	5.1	177	26	68	2.36	7.5	10.2	1.4	0.0	0

Very tall, deceptive RP who only needs to find consistency in control to earn high-leverage innings in SD. Generates easy velocity to plus FB that is tough to elevate. Can rely too much on FB, but good enough to be one-pitch guy. SL flashes plus, but rarely throws for strikes. Deceptive delivery and angle make him stingy.

Guerrieri,Taylor — SP — Tampa Bay

EXP MLB DEBUT: 2016 | H/W: 6-3 195 | FUT: #2 starter | **9D**

Thrws R Age 23
2011 (1) HS (SC)

Velo	Pitch	Grade
90-95	FB	++++
77-81	CB	++++
80-83	CU	++

Year	Lev	Team	W	L	Sv	IP	K	ERA	WHIP	BF/G	OBA	H%	S%	xERA	Ctl	Dom	Cmd	hr/9	BPV
2012	A-	Hudson Valley	1	2	0	52	45	1.04	0.77	15.6	193	26	85	0.88	0.9	7.8	9.0	0.0	135
2013	A	Bowling Green	6	2	0	67	51	2.01	0.99	18.2	222	26	84	2.42	1.6	6.9	4.3	0.7	98
2014	Rk	GCL Devil Rays	0	0	0	9	10	0.00	0.99	6.9	214	31	100	1.67	2.0	9.9	5.0	0.0	143
2015	A+	Charlotte	2	2	0	42	44	2.14	1.14	13.9	238	33	79	2.35	2.4	9.4	4.0	0.0	124
2015	AA	Montgomery	3	1	0	36	28	1.50	1.00	17.2	216	26	88	2.22	2.0	7.0	3.5	0.5	90

Lean-framed SP who returned from TJ surgery with surprising dominance. Has electric arm that peppers plus FB in lower half of strike zone and can use CB as out pitch. Pitches efficiently to both sides of plate and shows feel for improving CU. Can be power pitcher, but also can take a few ticks off for more movement.

Gunkel,Joe — SP — Baltimore

EXP MLB DEBUT: 2016 | H/W: 6-5 225 | FUT: #5 SP / Middle RP | **6B**

Thrws R Age 24
2013 (18) West Chester

Velo	Pitch	Grade
89-93	FB	+++
79-84	SL	+++
80-82	CU	++

Year	Lev	Team	W	L	Sv	IP	K	ERA	WHIP	BF/G	OBA	H%	S%	xERA	Ctl	Dom	Cmd	hr/9	BPV
2014	A	Greenville	3	0	2	51	62	2.29	0.72	10.7	153	22	71	0.79	1.9	10.9	5.6	0.5	162
2014	A+	Salem	3	5	0	52	39	4.66	1.44	22.2	297	35	67	4.44	2.2	6.7	3.0	0.5	79
2015	A+	Salem	1	1	2	22	22	2.05	0.91	10.3	205	26	83	2.13	1.6	9.0	5.5	0.8	136
2015	AA	Bowie	8	4	0	104	69	2.59	0.96	23.2	225	26	75	2.33	1.3	6.0	4.6	0.6	90
2015	AA	Portland	2	1	0	18	22	3.98	1.88	21.3	337	46	79	6.14	4.0	10.9	2.8	0.5	108

Tall pitcher who throws with low 3/4 slot that may be more conducive to bullpen work. Has command of FB that exhibits vicious, late life and gets inordinate number of groundballs. Sweeping SL can be tough on RHH, but needs better offspeed pitch against LHH. Has posted stellar numbers, more due to delivery and slot than natural stuff.

Gustave,Jandel — RP — Houston

EXP MLB DEBUT: 2016 | H/W: 6-2 160 | FUT: Closer | **8E**

Thrws R Age 23
2010 FA (DR)

Velo	Pitch	Grade
92-98	FB	++++
84-88	SL	++
	CU	++

Year	Lev	Team	W	L	Sv	IP	K	ERA	WHIP	BF/G	OBA	H%	S%	xERA	Ctl	Dom	Cmd	hr/9	BPV
2012	Rk	GCL Astros	2	1	0	28	22	5.79	1.82	13.0	233	30	65	4.03	8.7	7.1	0.8	0.0	-89
2013	Rk	Greeneville	2	3	0	43	49	2.71	1.41	18.3	238	33	81	3.41	4.8	10.2	2.1	0.4	72
2014	A	Quad Cities	5	5	2	79	82	5.01	1.56	15.0	297	39	66	4.54	3.3	9.3	2.8	0.3	97
2015	AA	Corpus Christi	5	2	20	58	49	2.16	1.31	5.2	237	30	84	3.06	3.9	7.6	2.0	0.3	50

Long, lean RP who bypassed A+ and finished 2nd in TL in saves. Moved to RP in '15 and stuff played up in short stints. Can reach triple digits with plus FB and has electric arm speed. Lacks reliable second pitch, though can dominate with lively FB alone. Inconsistent slot hampers command and tends to fall behind in count too often.

Hader,Josh — SP — Milwaukee

EXP MLB DEBUT: 2016 | H/W: 6-3 160 | FUT: #4 starter | **7B**

Thrws L Age 22
2012 (19) HS (MD)

Velo	Pitch	Grade
90-94	FB	++++
75-78	CB	+++
83-85	CU	+++

Year	Lev	Team	W	L	Sv	IP	K	ERA	WHIP	BF/G	OBA	H%	S%	xERA	Ctl	Dom	Cmd	hr/9	BPV
2013	A	Delmarva	3	6	0	85	79	2.65	1.28	20.5	218	28	80	2.87	4.4	8.4	1.9	0.4	48
2014	A+	Lancaster	9	2	2	103	112	2.71	1.11	18.4	207	27	79	2.61	3.3	9.8	2.9	0.8	104
2014	AA	Corpus Christi	1	1	0	20	24	6.30	1.60	17.7	221	30	60	4.12	7.2	10.8	1.5	0.9	18
2015	AA	Biloxi	1	4	0	38	50	2.83	0.99	20.8	200	29	74	2.16	2.6	11.8	4.5	0.7	160
2015	AA	Corpus Christi	3	3	1	65	69	3.18	1.29	15.7	246	32	77	3.48	3.3	9.5	2.9	0.7	100

Tall, lanky southpaw opened eyes in AFL. Plus FB sits 90-94 but can elevate at 97-98 for whiffs; CB has late bite; CU has made strides. Deceptive delivery, unorthodox low 3/4 slot keep hitters off balance. Command has shown signs of growth. Seemed destined for the 'pen, but continues to prove he has makeup for the rotation long-term.

Hall,Cody — RP — San Francisco

EXP MLB DEBUT: 2015 | H/W: 6-4 220 | FUT: Setup reliever | **7C**

Thrws R Age 28
2011 (19) Southern

Velo	Pitch	Grade
94-97	FB	++++
83-85	SL	+++
85-87	CU	++

Year	Lev	Team	W	L	Sv	IP	K	ERA	WHIP	BF/G	OBA	H%	S%	xERA	Ctl	Dom	Cmd	hr/9	BPV
2013	A+	San Jose	2	0	2	33	48	1.36	0.66	4.4	138	22	85	0.48	1.9	13.0	6.9	0.5	201
2013	AA	Richmond	2	2	8	26	27	2.41	0.96	4.9	188	22	86	2.58	2.8	9.3	3.4	1.4	111
2014	AA	Richmond	1	4	11	51	57	3.16	1.09	4.3	225	31	72	2.56	2.5	10.0	4.1	0.5	132
2015	AAA	Sacramento	1	3	3	67	55	3.48	1.38	6.6	261	32	74	3.67	3.5	7.4	2.1	0.4	57
2015	MLB	SF Giants	0	0	0	8	7	6.67	1.73	5.3	304	36	62	5.83	4.4	7.8	1.8	1.1	38

Big, strong RH can reach back for 98 mph with his straight FB, but sits mid-90s. Backs it up with a hard SL that has average tilt and can get left up in the zone. CU gets decent velo separation, but overall depth is poor. Employs short arm action with effort in delivery, often leading to control issues. At 27, prospect status is dwindling.

Hancock,Justin — SP — San Diego

EXP MLB DEBUT: 2016 | H/W: 6-4 185 | FUT: #5 SP / Middle RP | **7D**

Thrws R Age 25
2011 (9) Lincoln Trail CC

Velo	Pitch	Grade
89-94	FB	+++
74-78	CB	++
81-82	CU	+++

Year	Lev	Team	W	L	Sv	IP	K	ERA	WHIP	BF/G	OBA	H%	S%	xERA	Ctl	Dom	Cmd	hr/9	BPV
2014	Rk	Azl Padres	0	0	0	3	0	0.00	1.33	6.2	321	32	100	4.13	0.0	0.0		0.0	18
2014	AA	San Antonio	3	2	0	59	41	4.12	1.56	19.9	293	34	75	4.92	3.5	6.3	1.8	0.8	36
2015	AA	San Antonio	7	6	0	120	92	3.60	1.47	23.4	273	33	76	4.23	3.7	6.9	1.9	0.6	43
2015	AAA	El Paso	1	0	0	10	5	2.67	1.88	23.7	345	37	89	6.71	3.6	4.5	1.3	0.9	2

Tall, lean pitcher who uses quick arm to generate ample pitch movement. Keeps ball in yard by using height and angle to pitch low in zone. Doesn't own true out offering and will be subject to high oppBA. Heavy FB is best pitch and slow CB not up to snuff. Can change speeds, but needs to exhibit better control to stick as SP.

Harris,Jonathan — SP — Toronto

EXP MLB DEBUT: 2017 | H/W: 6-4 175 | FUT: #3 starter | **8C**

Thrws R Age 22
2015 (1) Missouri St

Velo	Pitch	Grade
90-95	FB	++++
83-85	SL	+++
78-82	CB	+++
82-87	CU	++

Year	Lev	Team	W	L	Sv	IP	K	ERA	WHIP	BF/G	OBA	H%	S%	xERA	Ctl	Dom	Cmd	hr/9	BPV
2015	NCAA	Missouri St	8	2	0	103	116	2.45	1.08	26.8	205	29	76	1.94	3.1	10.1	3.2	0.2	116
2015	A-	Vancouver	0	5	0	36	32	6.75	1.92	14.2	321	40	62	5.76	5.3	8.0	1.5	0.3	20

Thin, yet physical SP who can dominate with deep, powerful pitch mix. Establishes plate with plus FB and can vary speed and shape of two breaking balls. Lets FB rip with great arm speed which adds late movement. Holds velocity deep into games and has excellent angle to plate. Has to improve CU and should be able to improve control.

Harvey,Hunter — SP — Baltimore

EXP MLB DEBUT: 2018 | H/W: 6-3 175 | FUT: #2 starter | 8C

Thrws R Age 21
2013 (1) HS (NC)

Velo	Pitch	Grade
91-95	FB	++++
72-78	CB	++++
81-84	CU	++

Year	Lev	Team	W	L	Sv	IP	K	ERA	WHIP	BF/G	OBA	H%	S%	xERA	Ctl	Dom	Cmd	hr/9	BPV
2013	Rk	GCL Orioles	0	0	0	13	18	1.37	0.92	9.8	213	35	83	1.44	1.4	12.4	9.0	0.0	203
2013	A-	Aberdeen	0	1	0	12	15	2.25	1.25	16.3	245	37	80	2.70	3.0	11.3	3.8	0.0	140
2014	A	Delmarva	7	5	0	87	106	3.20	1.14	20.3	212	30	72	2.48	3.4	10.9	3.2	0.5	123
2015		*Did not pitch - injured*																	

Tall, thin SP who missed season due to forearm and elbow discomfort. Has not undergone surgery and appears to be ready for Spring. When healthy, has nice pitch mix highlighted by plus FB and slow CB. Throws across body which limits CU, but has feel for changing speeds and pitch movement. Could move quickly when he proves health.

Helsley,Ryan — SP — St. Louis

EXP MLB DEBUT: 2019 | H/W: 6-1 195 | FUT: #4 starter | 6C

Thrws R Age 21
2015 (5) Northeastern St

Velo	Pitch	Grade
90-94	FB	++++
	CB	++
	CU	++

Year	Lev	Team	W	L	Sv	IP	K	ERA	WHIP	BF/G	OBA	H%	S%	xERA	Ctl	Dom	Cmd	hr/9	BPV
2015	Rk	Johnson City	1	1	0	40	35	2.02	1.30	15.0	226	29	84	2.82	4.3	7.9	1.8	0.2	44

Short, hard-throwing RHP was the Cardinals 5th round pick. Best offering is a good 90-94 mph FB, topping out at 97 mph that he throws up in the zone. Mixes in a fringy CB and CU, both of which need work for him to remain a starter as a Pro. Control is an issue and he walked 4.2/9 in his debut. Could be moved to relief down the road.

Heredia,Luis — SP — Pittsburgh

EXP MLB DEBUT: 2018 | H/W: 6-6 205 | FUT: Setup reliever | 8E

Thrws R Age 21
2010 FA (MX)

Velo	Pitch	Grade
90-93	FB	+++
75-78	CB	++
83-85	SL	++
	CU	++

Year	Lev	Team	W	L	Sv	IP	K	ERA	WHIP	BF/G	OBA	H%	S%	xERA	Ctl	Dom	Cmd	hr/9	BPV
2011	Rk	GCL Pirates	1	2	0	30		4.78	1.56	11.0	248	29	70	4.41	5.7	6.9	1.2	0.9	-12
2012	A-	State College	4	2	0	66	40	2.72	1.10	18.5	221	26	75	2.34	2.7	5.4	2.0	0.3	43
2013	A	West Virginia	7	3	0	65	55	3.05	1.37	19.5	221	27	80	3.38	5.1	7.6	1.5	0.7	17
2014	A	West Virginia	2	4	0	89	43	4.15	1.35	20.6	257	27	71	4.04	3.3	4.3	1.3	0.9	6
2015	A+	Bradenton	5	6	0	86	54	5.44	1.73	18.6	302	35	66	5.08	4.6	5.7	1.2	0.3	-5

Continues to underwhelm. Came into camp out of shape and was limited to 86 IP. Has a good 90-93 mph FB, but it lacks the zip it once had. His CB, SL, and CU are avg or below-average offerings. Mechanics have become inconsistent, leading to struggles with control and a lack of dominance. At this point a move to relief seems in order.

Hernandez,Jonathan — SP — Texas

EXP MLB DEBUT: 2020 | H/W: 6-2 150 | FUT: #4 starter | 7E

Thrws R Age 19
2013 FA (DR)

Velo	Pitch	Grade
88-92	FB	++++
80-83	SL	++
	CU	+

Year	Lev	Team	W	L	Sv	IP	K	ERA	WHIP	BF/G	OBA	H%	S%	xERA	Ctl	Dom	Cmd	hr/9	BPV
2015	Rk	Azl Rangers	1	1	0	45	33	3.00	1.27	16.7	262	32	74	3.01	2.4	6.6	2.8	0.0	72

Very thin SP who spent first year in US. FB may lack plus velocity, but has outstanding, late movement that is tough to elevate. Keeps ball low in zone and rarely allows flyballs. Could add more ticks to FB, but has fringy SL and poor CU. Needs strength to solidify secondary pitches to have future.

Hess,David — SP — Baltimore

EXP MLB DEBUT: 2017 | H/W: 6-1 180 | FUT: #4 starter | 7C

Thrws R Age 22
2014 (5) Tennessee Tech

Velo	Pitch	Grade
89-94	FB	+++
78-82	SL	+++
73-76	CB	++
80-85	CU	+++

Year	Lev	Team	W	L	Sv	IP	K	ERA	WHIP	BF/G	OBA	H%	S%	xERA	Ctl	Dom	Cmd	hr/9	BPV
2014	A-	Aberdeen	2	1	0	25	24	3.23	1.20	12.6	237	31	72	2.82	2.9	8.6	3.0	0.4	95
2014	A-	Delmarva	0	0	0	8	12	3.38	0.88	14.8	237	27	100	4.80	0.0	13.5		3.4	261
2015	A+	Frederick	9	4	0	133	110	3.58	1.24	19.3	230	28	71	3.02	3.6	7.4	2.1	0.5	55
2015	AA	Bowie	1	1	0	10	12	4.50	1.40	21.1	262	38	64	3.31	3.6	10.8	3.0	0.0	115

Savvy pitcher who is moving quickly and could be dynamic RP if he makes conversion. Throws good strikes with four pitches despite effort in complicated delivery. Has two breaking balls of varying speeds and bend. SL ahead of CB, but both pale in comparison to FB and CU. More of a flyball pitcher, but doesn't allow many HR.

Hildenberger,Trevor — RP — Minnesota

EXP MLB DEBUT: 2016 | H/W: 6-2 200 | FUT: Setup reliever | 6A

Thrws R Age 25
2014 (22) California

Velo	Pitch	Grade
87-92	FB	+++
77-81	SL	++
	CU	++

Year	Lev	Team	W	L	Sv	IP	K	ERA	WHIP	BF/G	OBA	H%	S%	xERA	Ctl	Dom	Cmd	hr/9	BPV
2014	NCAA	California	3	3	10	47	48	2.86	1.10	6.6	235	32	73	2.40	2.1	9.2	4.4	0.2	126
2014	Rk	Elizabethton	0	0	0	1	2	0.00	0.00	2.8	0	0			0.0	18.0		0.0	342
2014	Rk	GCL Twins	1	4	10	28	30	2.57	1.14	4.8	255	35	77	2.88	1.6	9.6	6.0	0.3	148
2015	A	Cedar Rapids	2	1	14	45	59	0.80	0.64	5.6	159	26	86	0.15	1.0	11.8	11.8	0.0	203
2015	A+	Fort Myers	1	1	3	19	21	3.32	0.89	5.4	219	32	59	1.48	0.9	9.9	10.5	0.0	171

Sidearmer who served as closer and had standout season. Keeps hitters off balance with arm slot and delivery that he consistently repeats. Not much velocity, but lives in lower quarter of strike zone and hitters rarely elevate average FB. Has good arm speed on CU, but succeeds more due to mechanics than natural stuff.

Hill,David — SP — Colorado

EXP MLB DEBUT: 2018 | H/W: 6-2 195 | FUT: #3 starter | 8D

Thrws R Age 21
2015 (4) San Diego

Velo	Pitch	Grade
92-94	FB	+++
	SL	+++
	CU	++

Year	Lev	Team	W	L	Sv	IP	K	ERA	WHIP	BF/G	OBA	H%	S%	xERA	Ctl	Dom	Cmd	hr/9	BPV
2015	NCAA	San Diego	9	3	0	100	115	2.34	1.01	27.4	190	27	77	1.67	3.1	10.3	3.3	0.3	119
2015	A-	Boise	0	0	0	23	23	3.12	1.26	11.8	235	31	75	2.97	3.5	9.0	2.6	0.4	85

4th round pick had a solid debut. Has a good 92-94 mph sinking FB that comes out of a low 3/4 arm slot. Release point leads to solid action and arm-side run, but below avg Cmd. Breaking ball comes out of the same arm slot and shows plus potential, but will need to be more consistent. CU is a work in progress. This is an arm worth watching.

Hillman,Juan — SP — Cleveland

EXP MLB DEBUT: 2019 | H/W: 6-2 183 | FUT: #3 starter | 8E

Thrws L Age 18
2015 (2) HS (FL)

Velo	Pitch	Grade
86-92	FB	++
75-78	CB	+++
79-82	CU	++++

Year	Lev	Team	W	L	Sv	IP	K	ERA	WHIP	BF/G	OBA	H%	S%	xERA	Ctl	Dom	Cmd	hr/9	BPV
2015	Rk	AZL Indians	0	2	0	24	20	4.13	1.29	12.3	278	35	65	3.29	1.9	7.5	4.0	0.0	102

Quick-armed pitcher who hits spots and has above average command despite youth. FB has chance to add ticks, but secondary pitches show relative polish. Adds movement to all offerings and CU can be out pitch. Key to future will depend on development of FB which can be too straight at times.

Hinsz,Gage — SP — Pittsburgh

EXP MLB DEBUT: 2019 | H/W: 6-4 210 | FUT: #3 starter | 7D

Thrws R Age 19
2014 (11) HS (MT)

Velo	Pitch	Grade
90-93	FB	+++
	CB	++
	CU	++

Year	Lev	Team	W	L	Sv	IP	K	ERA	WHIP	BF/G	OBA	H%	S%	xERA	Ctl	Dom	Cmd	hr/9	BPV
2014	Rk	GCL Pirates	0	0	0	8	7	3.38	1.50	11.5	262	34	75	3.59	4.5	7.9	1.8	0.0	38
2015	Rk	Bristol	3	4	0	38	24	3.79	1.58	16.7	257	30	75	3.96	5.4	5.7	1.0	0.2	-27

6-4 RHP has good size and some nice projection left. Already saw his velo jump from the mid-80s to 90-93 mph prior to the draft. Has an easy high 3/4 arm slot and throws downhill, keeping the ball low in the zone. Breaking ball and change-up need work but show decent potential.

Hoffman,Jeff — SP — Colorado

EXP MLB DEBUT: 2017 | H/W: 6-4 185 | FUT: #2 starter | 9D

Thrws R Age 23
2014 (1) East Carolina

Velo	Pitch	Grade
91-96	FB	++++
80-82	CB	++++
83-85	SL	+++
84-87	CU	+++

Year	Lev	Team	W	L	Sv	IP	K	ERA	WHIP	BF/G	OBA	H%	S%	xERA	Ctl	Dom	Cmd	hr/9	BPV
2015	A+	Dunedin	3	3	0	56	38	3.21	1.32	21.1	272	31	77	3.90	2.4	6.1	2.5	0.6	63
2015	AA	New Britain	2	2	0	36	29	3.24	1.02	19.8	210	25	71	2.43	2.5	7.2	2.9	0.7	81
2015	AA	New Hampshire	0	0	0	11	8	1.61	0.98	21.3	222	28	82	1.77	1.6	6.4	4.0	0.0	90

Was traded as part of the Tulowitzki deal and had TJS in '14. Has a dominant 91-96 mph FB and mixes in a SL and an improved CU. Best offering is a plus-plus power CB that is his out pitch. FB velocity was back in the mid-to-upper 90s. Command comes and goes and may take a while to improve.

Holdzkom,John — SP — Pittsburgh

EXP MLB DEBUT: 2014 | H/W: 6-9 245 | FUT: Setup reliever | 7D

Thrws R Age 28
2006 (4) Salt Lake CC

Velo	Pitch	Grade
94-96	FB	++++
85-88	SL	+++

Year	Lev	Team	W	L	Sv	IP	K	ERA	WHIP	BF/G	OBA	H%	S%	xERA	Ctl	Dom	Cmd	hr/9	BPV
2014	AA	Altoona	1	0	0	6	10	0.00	0.50	5.0	56	13	100		3.0	15.0	5.0	0.0	207
2014	AAA	Indianapolis	2	0	2	21	27	2.55	1.13	4.7	190	28	78	2.12	4.2	11.5	2.7	0.4	110
2014	MLB	Pittsburgh	1	0	1	9	14	2.00	0.67	3.5	136	21	80	0.89	2.0	14.0	7.0	1.0	216
2015	A-	West Virginia	0	0	0	2	3	0.00	0.00	2.8	0	0			0.0	13.5		0.0	261
2015	AAA	Indianapolis	2	0	2	22	27	3.26	1.49	4.5	204	31	76	2.81	6.9	11.0	1.6	0.0	29

Late-blooming flamethrower. Had TJ surgery in '08 and struggles with control landed him in independent ball for several years. Can be untouchable at times with 94-96 FB that tops out at 100 mph and a nasty SL. But still hasn't figured out how to throw strikes consistently.

Hollon, Clinton — SP — Toronto

EXP MLB DEBUT: 2018 | H/W: 6-1 195 | FUT: #4 starter | 7D

Thrws R Age 21
2013 (2) HS (KY)

90-95	FB	+++		
81-84	SL	+++		
75-78	CB	++		
	CU	++		

Year	Lev	Team	W	L	Sv	IP	K	ERA	WHIP	BF/G	OBA	H%	S%	xERA	Ctl	Dom	Cmd	hr/9	BPV
2015	A-	Vancouver	2	2	0	45	40	3.19	1.15	19.9	225	29	71	2.42	3.0	8.0	2.7	0.2	81
2015	A	Lansing	1	1	0	13	5	4.12	1.37	18.3	229	26	67	2.89	4.8	3.4	0.7	0.0	-50

Athletic, quick-armed SP who did not pitch in '14 and had '15 season end early due to drug suspension. Has strength to pepper strike zone with darting FB with late, heavy sink. Mixes in SL that shows plus potential and middling CB and CU. Mechanics can get out of whack and can overthrow.

Holmes, Clay — SP — Pittsburgh

EXP MLB DEBUT: 2018 | H/W: 6-5 230 | FUT: #4 starter | 7D

Thrws R Age 23
2011 (9) HS (AL)

90-93	FB	++++		
80-83	CB	++		
	CU	++		

Year	Lev	Team	W	L	Sv	IP	K	ERA	WHIP	BF/G	OBA	H%	S%	xERA	Ctl	Dom	Cmd	hr/9	BPV
2015	Rk	GCL Pirates	1	0	0	13	10	2.06	1.07	17.0	260	33	79	2.49	0.7	6.9	10.0	0.0	123
2015	A+	Bradenton	0	2	0	23	16	2.74	1.09	15.0	217	27	72	1.98	2.7	6.3	2.3	0.0	57

Tall RHP had TJS and missed all of '14 and did not return until mid-June. When he did, the results were encouraging. Has a good 90-93 mph FB that has good downhill tilt and generates plenty of ground-ball outs—1.7 gb/fb ratio in his career. Scrapped his SL in favor or a more consistently effective CB and a CU that needs works.

Holmes, Grant — SP — Los Angeles (N)

EXP MLB DEBUT: 2019 | H/W: 6-1 215 | FUT: #2 starter | 9D

Thrws R Age 20
2014 (1) HS (SC)

92-95	FB	++++		
83-85	CB	++++		
	CU	++		

Year	Lev	Team	W	L	Sv	IP	K	ERA	WHIP	BF/G	OBA	H%	S%	xERA	Ctl	Dom	Cmd	hr/9	BPV
2014	Rk	Ogden	1	1	0	18	25	4.97	1.38	19.0	271	41	63	3.84	3.0	12.4	4.2	0.5	161
2014	Rk	Azl Dodgers	1	2	0	30	33	3.00	0.90	15.9	191	26	68	1.73	2.1	9.9	4.7	0.6	140
2015	A	Great Lakes	6	4	0	103	117	3.14	1.36	17.9	228	32	78	3.26	4.7	10.2	2.2	0.5	75

Strong bodied hurler attacks hitters with a plus 92-95 mph FB. Also has a plus power CB that is his best offering and a CU that shows potential. Showed impressive FB command in his pro debut, which bodes well for his development. FB velo is down significantly from HS, but the total package remains very good.

Honeywell, Brent — SP — Tampa Bay

EXP MLB DEBUT: 2017 | H/W: 6-2 180 | FUT: #3 starter | 8B

Thrws R Age 21
2014 (2) Walters St CC

89-94	FB	+++		
81-84	SL	+++		
75-79	CB	++		
81-85	CU	+++		

Year	Lev	Team	W	L	Sv	IP	K	ERA	WHIP	BF/G	OBA	H%	S%	xERA	Ctl	Dom	Cmd	hr/9	BPV
2014	Rk	Princeton	2	1	0	33	40	1.08	0.75	13.2	169	25	88	0.79	1.6	10.8	6.7	0.3	169
2015	A	Bowling Green	4	4	0	65	76	2.91	1.00	20.7	224	32	71	2.20	1.7	10.5	6.3	0.4	163
2015	A+	Charlotte	5	2	0	65	53	3.46	1.11	21.3	237	30	67	2.53	2.1	7.3	3.5	0.3	94

Athletic, projectable SP who has excellent velocity, command, and feel for pitching. Aggressively pitches inside and and uses multiple breaking balls as outs pitches. Repeats deceptive delivery which enhances CU that could become plus offering. Can be very tough to hit, especially when he uses screwball. High upside and floor.

Houser, Adrian — SP — Milwaukee

EXP MLB DEBUT: 2015 | H/W: 6-4 230 | FUT: #4 starter | 7C

Thrws R Age 23
2011 (2) HS (OK)

90-94	FB	+++		
74-77	CB	+++		
79-83	CU	++		

Year	Lev	Team	W	L	Sv	IP	K	ERA	WHIP	BF/G	OBA	H%	S%	xERA	Ctl	Dom	Cmd	hr/9	BPV
2014	A	Quad Cities	5	6	0	108	93	4.16	1.26	17.6	245	31	66	3.14	3.1	7.7	2.5	0.4	74
2015	A+	Lancaster	2	2	0	49	45	4.39	1.38	17.2	257	35	68	3.72	3.7	10.1	2.8	0.5	100
2015	AA	Biloxi	4	1	0	37	32	2.92	1.05	20.5	240	29	77	3.09	1.5	7.8	5.3	1.0	119
2015	AA	Corpus Christi	1	2	0	33	23	6.25	1.63	21.0	295	32	65	5.94	4.1	6.3	1.5	1.6	20
2015	MLB	Milwaukee	0	0	0	2	0	0.00	1.50	4.3	151	15	100	2.34	9.0	0.0	0.0	0.0	-225

Tall, mature RH got a late cup of coffee after impressive SL debut. FB settles 90-94, but touches 96 with arm-side run. CB shows good 11-5 bite and is bat-misser vs. RHH. Repeatable arm slot has helped CU, but still only so-so. Has physical qualities of back-end SP, but quality FB/CB mix could make him valuable in the 'pen.

Howard, Nick — RP — Cincinnati

EXP MLB DEBUT: 2017 | H/W: 6-4 215 | FUT: Setup reliever | 7D

Thrws R Age 23
2014 (1) Virginia

91-94	FB	+++		
82-85	SL	+++		
85-86	CU	++		

Year	Lev	Team	W	L	Sv	IP	K	ERA	WHIP	BF/G	OBA	H%	S%	xERA	Ctl	Dom	Cmd	hr/9	BPV
2012	NCAA	Virginia	3	0	0	41	37	2.84	1.12	8.5	226	29	73	2.36	2.6	8.1	3.1	0.2	93
2013	NCAA	Virginia	6	4	0	61	52	3.39	1.34	19.6	280	35	74	3.72	2.2	7.7	3.5	0.3	96
2014	NCAA	Virginia	2	2	20	37	60	1.94	0.99	4.6	180	31	85	1.92	3.4	14.5	4.3	0.7	188
2014	A	Dayton	2	1	0	33	23	3.80	1.17	12.1	230	25	71	3.39	3.0	6.2	2.1	1.1	50
2015	A+	Daytona	3	2	2	38	31	6.63	2.21	8.0	241	31	67	5.10	11.8	7.3	0.6	0.0	-170

Taken in the 1st Rd of the '14 draft. CIN has toyed with converting to SP but best work remains in the bullpen. FB is a borderline plus-plus pitch. Sitting in the mid-to-high 90s as a RP, late movement makes it impossible to hit. Struggles with command, which has contributed to his struggles as a professional. SL has good depth.

Hoyt, James — RP — Houston

EXP MLB DEBUT: 2016 | H/W: 6-5 220 | FUT: Setup reliever | 6B

Thrws R Age 29
2011 FA Centenary

93-96	FB	+++		
82-85	SL	+++		
	CU	+		

Year	Lev	Team	W	L	Sv	IP	K	ERA	WHIP	BF/G	OBA	H%	S%	xERA	Ctl	Dom	Cmd	hr/9	BPV
2013	A+	Lynchburg	3	2	0	49	72	4.94	1.30	11.9	219	35	61	3.00	4.6	13.2	2.9	0.5	132
2013	AA	Mississippi	0	1	1	32	33	2.52	0.93	5.5	158	22	72	1.15	3.6	9.2	2.5	0.3	86
2014	AA	Mississippi	2	2	6	31	43	1.15	0.93	4.2	178	29	89	1.34	2.9	12.4	4.3	0.3	163
2014	AAA	Gwinnett	1	1	1	28	34	5.46	1.86	5.5	325	43	73	6.61	4.5	10.9	2.4	1.3	93
2015	AAA	Fresno	0	1	9	49	66	3.49	1.20	4.2	258	39	69	2.92	2.0	12.1	6.0	0.2	182

Hard-throwing RP who was dominant from July on. Spent entire career in pen and has vastly improved control. Posts high K rate on impressive FB/SL combo. Likes to use SL as chase pitch, but can drop in zone for strikes. FB can be straight at higher velocities and has flyball tendencies. Fairly old for prospect, but took circuitous route.

Hu, Chih-Wei — SP — Tampa Bay

EXP MLB DEBUT: 2018 | H/W: 6-1 230 | FUT: #4 starter | 7D

Thrws R Age 22
2012 FA (TW)

89-92	FB	+++		
82-84	SL	++		
	CU	+++		

Year	Lev	Team	W	L	Sv	IP	K	ERA	WHIP	BF/G	OBA	H%	S%	xERA	Ctl	Dom	Cmd	hr/9	BPV
2014	Rk	Elizabethton	1	0	0	16	16	1.69	0.56	18.0	134	19	67		1.1	9.0	8.0	0.0	150
2014	A	Cedar Rapids	7	2	0	55	48	2.29	0.96	20.8	205	27	74	1.51	2.1	7.9	3.7	0.0	102
2015	A+	Charlotte	0	3	1	18	20	7.46	1.71	16.4	311	41	53	5.29	4.0	9.9	2.5	0.5	90
2015	A+	Fort Myers	5	3	0	84	73	2.46	1.16	22.4	250	31	81	3.08	2.0	7.8	3.8	0.5	104
2015	AAA	Rochester	1	0	0	6	6	1.50	1.00	22.9	106	15	83	0.55	6.0	9.0	1.5	0.0	18

Thick SP who throws with good command and consistently hits spots. Lacks frontline velocity and doesn't have true out pitch, but shows savvy and moxie on mound. Has advanced control and keeps ball in yard. CU could develop into above average pitch, but won't miss bats. SL is a little short and usually thrown for strikes.

Huang, Wei-Chieh — SP — Arizona

EXP MLB DEBUT: 2018 | H/W: 6-1 170 | FUT: #4 starter | 7B

Thrws R Age 22
2014 FA (TW)

88-92	FB	+++		
72-75	CB	++		
81-84	CU	++++		

Year	Lev	Team	W	L	Sv	IP	K	ERA	WHIP	BF/G	OBA	H%	S%	xERA	Ctl	Dom	Cmd	hr/9	BPV
2015	A	Kane County	7	3	0	76	68	2.01	0.97	19.3	213	28	78	1.73	1.9	8.0	4.3	0.1	112

Undersized command-control RHP pitched effectively in US debut. Has three pitches; commands low-90s 2-seam FB up and down, left and right. Generates only slight arm-side run. CB is slurvy. High 3/4s arm angle better suited for SL. CU is advanced. Plus deception and movement. Polished package.

Hudson, Bryan — SP — Chicago (N)

EXP MLB DEBUT: 2019 | H/W: 6-8 220 | FUT: #2 starter | 8D

Thrws L Age 18
2015 (3) HS (IL)

92-94	FB	++++		
	CB	++++		
	CU	++		

Year	Lev	Team	W	L	Sv	IP	K	ERA	WHIP	BF/G	OBA	H%	S%	xERA	Ctl	Dom	Cmd	hr/9	BPV
2015	Rk	Azl Cubs	0	0	0	6	5	2.90	1.29	5.1	255	32	75	2.98	2.9	7.3	2.5	0.0	70

Huge lefty was the Cubs 3rd round pick. Best offering is a potentially plus hard CB. FB currently sits at 92-94, but he could add more as he fills out. Cold weather hurler is less polished than others, but showed solid command and has huge upside.

Hursh, Jason — RP — Atlanta

EXP MLB DEBUT: 2016 | H/W: 6-3 200 | FUT: Setup reliever | 7B

Thrws R Age 24
2013 (1) Oklahoma St

92-94	FB	+++		
76-78	CB	++		
81-83	CU	++		

Year	Lev	Team	W	L	Sv	IP	K	ERA	WHIP	BF/G	OBA	H%	S%	xERA	Ctl	Dom	Cmd	hr/9	BPV
2013	NCAA	Oklahoma St	6	5	0	106	86	2.80	1.25	27.0	260	32	78	3.26	2.4	7.3	3.1	0.3	85
2013	A	Rome	1	1	0	27	15	0.67	1.11	11.8	208	24	97	2.26	3.3	5.0	1.5	0.3	18
2014	AA	Mississippi	11	7	0	148	83	3.59	1.31	22.7	266	30	71	3.47	2.6	5.0	1.9	0.3	38
2014	AA	Mississippi	3	6	2	82	60	5.15	1.74	15.6	324	39	69	5.45	3.5	6.6	1.9	0.3	42
2015	AAA	Gwinnett	1	0	0	15	5	5.40	1.40	6.3	274	27	63	4.69	3.0	3.0	1.0	1.2	-9

Former 1st rd pick who was converted to the pen after years of mediocre results as SP. FB command has been his Achilles heel throughout professional career. When right, his FB generates ton of grounders. Best secondary pitch is a SL with strong depth and break, effective against hitters from both sides of the plate. CU is a non-factor.

Imhof,Matt	SP	Philadelphia	EXP MLB DEBUT: 2017	H/W: 6-5 220	FUT: #4 starter	7C

Thrws L Age 22
2014 (2) Cal Poly

89-91	FB	+ +
75-80	SL	+ + +
81-83	CU	+ +

Year	Lev	Team	W	L	Sv	IP	K	ERA	WHIP	BF/G	OBA	H%	S%	xERA	Ctl	Dom	Cmd	hr/9	BPV
2014	NCAA	Cal Poly	10	4	0	99	124	2.45	1.09	25.8	189	29	76	1.78	3.9	11.3	2.9	0.2	115
2014	Rk	GCL Phillies	0	0	0	3	2	0.00	1.00	11.5	191	24	100	1.46	3.0	6.0	2.0	0.0	45
2014	A-	Williamsport	1	0	0	12	11	0.75	0.83	14.6	151	21	90	0.58	3.0	8.3	2.8	0.0	86
2014	A	Lakewood	0	2	0	27	27	4.32	1.40	16.3	295	37	71	4.75	2.0	9.0	4.5	1.0	126
2015	A+	Clearwater	8	5	0	77	59	3.96	1.44	18.3	249	29	75	4.14	4.5	6.9	1.5	0.9	19

Biceps injury limited his IP in 2015, but when healthy, uses his long limbs to create downhill plane on his pitches and natural movement on his FB. CB is best pitch, and CU is still work in progress. Has some deception to delivery. Was big strikeout pitcher in college; hasn't yet translated to pros. Control could also use some work.

Jackson,Luke	RP	Texas	EXP MLB DEBUT: 2015	H/W: 6-2 205	FUT: #3 starter / Closer	8D

Thrws R Age 24
2010 (1) HS (FL)

91-97	FB	+ + + +
83-87	SL	+ + +
79-83	CB	+ +
83-85	CU	+ +

Year	Lev	Team	W	L	Sv	IP	K	ERA	WHIP	BF/G	OBA	H%	S%	xERA	Ctl	Dom	Cmd	hr/9	BPV
2013	AA	Frisco	2	0	0	27	30	0.67	0.93	16.9	146	22	92	0.74	4.0	10.0	2.5	0.0	90
2014	AA	Frisco	8	2	1	83	83	3.03	0.99	21.1	198	26	70	1.99	2.6	9.0	3.5	0.5	110
2014	AAA	Round Rock	1	3	0	40	43	10.35	2.10	17.9	332	40	51	8.05	6.3	9.7	1.5	2.0	22
2015	AAA	Round Rock	2	3	0	66	79	4.36	1.47	7.3	250	35	69	3.69	4.8	10.8	2.3	0.4	83
2015	MLB	Texas	0	0	0	6	6	4.43	1.15	3.5	225	26	67	3.60	3.0	8.9	3.0	1.5	98

Tall, durable pitcher who was moved to pen. Earned September callup due to excellent FB/SL combo. Registers Ks with all pitches and also mixes in CB for different look. Keeps ball down consistently, but needs to exhibit better control. Long arm action and inability to change speeds likely to keep him as RP.

Jaime,Juan	RP	Los Angeles (N)	EXP MLB DEBUT: 2014	H/W: 6-2 250	FUT: Setup reliever	8E

Thrws R Age 28
2004 FA (DR)

95-98	FB	+ + + +
	CB	+ +
	CU	+ +

Year	Lev	Team	W	L	Sv	IP	K	ERA	WHIP	BF/G	OBA	H%	S%	xERA	Ctl	Dom	Cmd	hr/9	BPV
2015	AA	Mississippi	0	0	0	1		0.00	4.17	4.2	371	84	100	11.93	22.5	22.5	1.0	0.0	-185
2015	AA	Tulsa	0	2	0	11	20	4.02	1.79	4.7	202	41	75	3.47	9.6	16.1	1.7	0.0	47
2015	AAA	Gwinnett	0	0	0	3	4	11.25	3.13	4.8	307	44	60	8.31	16.9	11.3	0.7	0.0	-235
2015	AAA	Oklahoma City	0	0	0	9	7	1.96	1.41	5.6	278	35	85	3.61	2.9	6.8	2.3	0.0	62
2015	MLB	Atlanta	0	1	0	1	1	8.18	3.64	3.6	0	0	75	6.31	32.7	8.2	0.3	0.0	-718

Traded from ATL to LA as part of the J. Uribe deal and played at 7 different stops. Plus FB sits in the upper-90s and is his best offering to go along with a CB and CU. Can be overpowering, but struggles to find the strike zone and he walked 29 in 37.1 IP. Also struck out 54. Has the stuff to close if he can ever figure things out.

Jay,Tyler	RP	Minnesota	EXP MLB DEBUT: 2017	H/W: 6-1 180	FUT: #3 starter / Closer	8C

Thrws L Age 21
2015 (1) Illinois

91-96	FB	+ + + +
82-84	SL	+ + +
75-77	CB	+ + +
83-87	CU	+ +

Year	Lev	Team	W	L	Sv	IP	K	ERA	WHIP	BF/G	OBA	H%	S%	xERA	Ctl	Dom	Cmd	hr/9	BPV
2015	NCAA	Illinois	5	2	14	66	76	1.09	0.71	7.8	176	26	87	0.78	1.0	10.3	10.9	0.3	178
2015	A+	Fort Myers	0	1	1	18	22	3.98	1.44	4.1	261	38	69	3.38	4.0	10.9	2.8	0.0	108

Served as closer in college, but will likely be tried as SP as pro. Has extremely quick arm that generates plus velocity for LHP and adds hint of deception to make unhittable at times. Wipeout SL used when ahead in counts and registers Ks. Also mixes in slower CB and firm CU. Keeps ball down and has potential to be high K pitcher.

Jaye,Myles	SP	Texas	EXP MLB DEBUT: 2016	H/W: 6-3 170	FUT: #4 SP / Setup RP	7C

Thrws R Age 24
2010 (17) HS (GA)

89-93	FB	+ + +
81-83	SL	+ + +
	CU	+ + +

Year	Lev	Team	W	L	Sv	IP	K	ERA	WHIP	BF/G	OBA	H%	S%	xERA	Ctl	Dom	Cmd	hr/9	BPV
2013	A+	Winston-Salem	9	6	0	118	89	4.12	1.41	25.0	268	32	71	4.02	3.4	6.8	2.0	0.6	50
2013	AA	Birmingham	0	1	0	3	3	19.69	3.13	19.0	470	57	30	11.66	5.6	8.4	1.5	0.0	18
2014	A+	Winston-Salem	3	0	0	29	15	1.55	0.93	27.2	212	23	88	2.13	1.6	4.7	3.0	0.6	60
2014	AA	Birmingham	4	12	0	132	73	5.32	1.51	23.8	282	31	64	4.56	3.6	5.0	1.4	0.7	10
2015	AA	Birmingham	12	9	0	147	104	3.30	1.24	23.0	245	29	74	3.18	2.9	6.4	2.2	0.5	55

Thin and projectable SP who repeated AA and was much better. Establishes plate with aggressive FB and mixes in erratic SL and solid CU. Owns deception in delivery and stuff plays up due to ideal sequencing. May not have a K pitch, but keeps ball in ballpark and has chance to add velocity down the line.

Jenkins,Tyrell	SP	Atlanta	EXP MLB DEBUT: 2016	H/W: 6-4 180	FUT: #3 starter	8C

Thrws R Age 23
2010 (1) HS (TX)

92-95	FB	+ + + +
78-80	CB	+ + +
82-84	CU	+ + +

Year	Lev	Team	W	L	Sv	IP	K	ERA	WHIP	BF/G	OBA	H%	S%	xERA	Ctl	Dom	Cmd	hr/9	BPV
2013	A	Peoria	4	4	0	49	34	4.77	1.53	21.3	269	31	69	4.46	4.4	6.2	1.4	0.7	11
2013	A+	Palm Beach	0	0	0	10	6	4.50	1.40	14.1	316	37	64	4.16	0.9	5.4	6.0	0.0	91
2014	A+	Palm Beach	6	5	0	74	41	3.28	1.31	23.5	262	29	77	3.82	2.8	5.0	1.8	0.7	32
2015	AA	Mississippi	5	5	0	93	59	3.00	1.34	24.2	243	28	77	3.23	4.0	5.7	1.4	0.3	14
2015	AAA	Gwinnett	3	4	0	45	29	3.59	1.40	21.1	253	28	76	3.97	4.0	5.8	1.5	0.8	14

Had his best season as a professional, pitching well enough to earn a mid-season promotion to AAA. Still, arm fatigue cost him the last month of the season. His FB is his pitch but a 1-7 CB has come into its own as an effective out pitch. Previously fringy, his CU is rounding into a MLB pitch. Has the tools to be enter the rotation next season.

Jerez,Williams	RP	Boston	EXP MLB DEBUT: 2017	H/W: 6-4 190	FUT: Setup reliever	7D

Thrws L Age 23
2011 (2) HS (NY)

91-94	FB	+ + +
81-85	SL	+ + +
	CU	+

Year	Lev	Team	W	L	Sv	IP	K	ERA	WHIP	BF/G	OBA	H%	S%	xERA	Ctl	Dom	Cmd	hr/9	BPV
2014	Rk	GCL Red Sox	3	1	1	24	27	2.24	1.04	10.3	227	33	76	1.95	1.9	10.1	5.4	0.0	149
2014	A-	Lowell	1	1	0	10	13	4.50	1.90	9.4	316	46	74	5.35	5.4	11.7	2.2	0.0	83
2015	A-	Greenville	3	1	3	39	43	2.07	1.36	11.7	281	37	88	4.12	2.3	9.9	4.3	0.7	134
2015	A+	Salem	1	0	0	12	12	0.74	1.24	9.8	244	33	93	2.68	3.0	8.9	3.0	0.0	98

Tall and wiry RP who is in 2nd year of pitching after converting from OF. Shows surprising feel for solid FB/SL combo. Can be hittable as he's aronud plate too much, but should get better with more experience. More thrower than pitcher and could evolve with SL that can be plus pitch at times.

Jewell,Jake	SP	Los Angeles (A)	EXP MLB DEBUT: 2018	H/W: 6-3 200	FUT: #4 SP / Setup RP	7C

Thrws R Age 22
2014 (5) Northeastern OK A&M JC

91-94	FB	+ + +
84-86	SL	+ + +
75-78	CU	+ +

Year	Lev	Team	W	L	Sv	IP	K	ERA	WHIP	BF/G	OBA	H%	S%	xERA	Ctl	Dom	Cmd	hr/9	BPV
2014	Rk	Azl Angels	1	0	0	30	26	1.50	1.16	13.3	213	28	86	2.11	3.6	7.8	2.2	0.0	61
2014	Rk	Orem	0	2	0	12	9	8.93	2.15	20.0	392	46	56	8.10	3.0	6.7	2.3	0.7	58
2015	A	Burlington	6	8	2	111	110	4.78	1.27	14.7	260	33	62	3.58	2.5	8.9	3.5	0.6	111

Strong pitcher who was moved to SP mid-year. Faltered late after solid start. Repeats delivery which positively impacts command and offers enough pitch movement to keep hitters at bay despite average velocity. Power SL is true K pitch, though can slow arm speed on CU. Will need to maintain velocity deep into games if he is to remain SP.

Jimenez,Joe	RP	Detroit	EXP MLB DEBUT: 2018	H/W: 6-3 220	FUT: Closer	8D

Thrws R Age 21
2013 FA (PR)

92-97	FB	+ + + +
83-85	SL	+ + +
81-82	CU	+

Year	Lev	Team	W	L	Sv	IP	K	ERA	WHIP	BF/G	OBA	H%	S%	xERA	Ctl	Dom	Cmd	hr/9	BPV
2013	Rk	GCL Tigers	3	0	1	18	24	0.50	0.83	8.2	151	25	93	0.54	3.0	12.0	4.0	0.0	153
2014	A-	Connecticut	3	2	4	26	41	2.75	1.07	4.4	229	39	74	2.33	2.1	14.1	6.8	0.3	216
2015	A	West Michigan	5	1	17	43	61	1.47	0.79	3.9	159	26	84	0.91	2.3	12.8	5.5	0.4	186

Strong RP who pitched in Futures Game in first year of full-season pro ball. Has tenacity and pitch mix of a future closer. Peppers strike zone with electric FB and limits RHH with SL that flashes plus. Effort in delivery will keep him in bullpen, but repeats mechanics well. Should continue high strikeout totals.

Johansen,Jacob	RP	Washington	EXP MLB DEBUT: 2017	H/W: 6-6 235	FUT: Setup reliever	7C

Thrws R Age 25
2013 (2) Dallas Baptist

92-94	FB	+ + +
83-85	SL	+ + +
	CU	+ +

Year	Lev	Team	W	L	Sv	IP	K	ERA	WHIP	BF/G	OBA	H%	S%	xERA	Ctl	Dom	Cmd	hr/9	BPV
2013	A-	Auburn	1	1	0	42		1.07	0.95	15.9	156	22	90	1.12	3.8	9.4	2.4	0.2	83
2013	A-	Hagerstown	0	2	0	9	7	5.93	1.98	21.8	336	39	71	6.87	4.9	6.9	1.4	1.0	9
2014	A	Hagerstown	5	6	0	100	89	5.21	1.75	15.8	298	38	68	4.98	4.9	8.0	1.6	0.3	29
2015	Rk	GCL Nationals	0	1	0	5	3	1.76	0.78	6.1	218	26	75	1.24	0.0	5.3		0.0	113
2015	A+	Potomac	1	7	1	48	48	5.44	1.81	9.3	307	38	72	6.08	5.1	9.0	1.8	1.1	43

Switch to bullpen didn't have desired results; still walked too many and hitters square him up often. FB is lively enough for roughly a K per IP, but he can't command it, which diminishes effectiveness of good SL. Could still contribute if control improves, but age now limits his upside.

Johnson,Brian	SP	Boston	EXP MLB DEBUT: 2015	H/W: 6-4 235	FUT: #4 starter	7A

Thrws L Age 25
2012 (1) Florida

88-94	FB	+ + +
80-83	SL	+ +
73-78	CB	+ + +
83-86	CU	+ + +

Year	Lev	Team	W	L	Sv	IP	K	ERA	WHIP	BF/G	OBA	H%	S%	xERA	Ctl	Dom	Cmd	hr/9	BPV
2013	A+	Salem	1	0	0	11	8	1.64	1.27	22.5	225	28	86	2.54	4.1	6.5	1.6	0.0	25
2014	A+	Salem	3	1	0	25	33	3.93	1.19	20.2	245	38	63	2.54	2.5	11.8	4.7	0.0	163
2014	AA	Portland	10	2	0	118	99	1.75	0.93	22.1	190	24	84	1.69	2.4	7.6	3.1	0.5	88
2015	AAA	Pawtucket	9	6	0	96	90	2.53	1.10	20.9	215	27	79	2.50	3.0	8.4	2.8	0.6	89
2015	MLB	Boston	0	1	0	4	3	8.78	1.71	18.6	206	26	43	3.41	8.8	6.6	0.8	0.0	-101

Deceptive, tall SP who has deep repertoire and uncanny ability to change speeds and move ball around plate. Only 19 IP after June due to elbow, but no surgery needed. Locates pitches with precision and works efficiently with above average control. Lacks out pitch, though is tough to make hard contact against as no pitch is straight.

Johnson,Chase — SP — San Francisco

EXP MLB DEBUT: 2017 | H/W: 6-3 185 | FUT: #4 starter | 7C

Thrws R Age 24 — 2013 (3) Cal Poly

Velo	Pitch	Grade
92-95	FB	++++
	SL	++
	CU	++

Year	Lev	Team	W	L	Sv	IP	K	ERA	WHIP	BF/G	OBA	H%	S%	xERA	Ctl	Dom	Cmd	hr/9	BPV
2013	Rk	Azl Giants	1	0	0	5	7	1.76	1.18	6.8	258	40	83	2.67	1.8	12.4	7.0	0.0	193
2013	A-	Salem-Kaizer	3	2	0	41	37	4.17	1.17	16.4	237	30	64	3.05	2.6	8.1	3.1	0.7	93
2014	A	Augusta	4	7	0	110	94	4.58	1.37	20.1	263	33	65	3.67	3.3	7.7	2.4	0.4	68
2015	A+	San Jose	8	3	0	111	111	2.43	1.16	22.1	233	31	80	2.72	2.8	9.0	3.3	0.4	106
2015	AA	Richmond	1	1	0	13	18	6.14	1.82	20.4	301	45	63	4.91	5.5	12.3	2.3	0.0	92

Converted college closer has a lean frame, smooth delivery and works from high 3/4 slot. FB can peak at 97 mph, but settles in lower-90s. SL flashes late bite at times and CU has average fade, but poor command undermines both. Works low for ground balls and has build/track record for durability. With refinement, chance to be SP.

Johnson,Chris — SP — San Francisco

EXP MLB DEBUT: 2017 | H/W: 6-4 205 | FUT: #5 starter | 7D

Thrws R Age 24 — 2012 (17) Portland

Velo	Pitch	Grade
88-92	FB	++
75-78	CB	+++
	CU	++

Year	Lev	Team	W	L	Sv	IP	K	ERA	WHIP	BF/G	OBA	H%	S%	xERA	Ctl	Dom	Cmd	hr/9	BPV
2012	NCAA	Portland	4	4	0	76	57	3.08	1.34	21.1	274	33	78	3.82	2.5	6.8	2.7	0.5	72
2012	A-	Salem-Kaizer	2	4	0	48	47	6.91	1.39	12.7	292	36	50	4.96	2.1	8.8	4.3	1.3	121
2013	A-	Salem-Kaizer	6	3	0	83	78	2.49	0.88	20.5	217	29	69	1.54	0.9	8.5	9.8	0.1	147
2014	A	Augusta	0	1	0	2	0	9.00	2.50	10.6	347	35	60	7.51	9.0	0.0	0.0	0.0	-225
2015	A	Augusta	1	5	0	67	48	5.36	1.62	21.3	334	39	65	5.38	1.9	6.4	3.4	0.4	83

Tall RH returned from '14 injury with less Dom, but still showed good control and feel for three-pitch mix. FB is below avg, but is effective low in zone with sink. CB is his go-to pitch with two strikes and flashes solid-avg 11-5 tilt; will need to throw CU more vs. LHH. Easy arm action, online delivery. Upside isn't high, but neither is the risk.

Johnson,Hobbs — SP — Milwaukee

EXP MLB DEBUT: 2017 | H/W: 5-11 230 | FUT: #5 starter | 7D

Thrws L Age 24 — 2013 (14) North Carolina

Velo	Pitch	Grade
88-91	FB	+++
	CU	+++
	SL	+

Year	Lev	Team	W	L	Sv	IP	K	ERA	WHIP	BF/G	OBA	H%	S%	xERA	Ctl	Dom	Cmd	hr/9	BPV
2013	Rk	Helena	0	0	0	8	9	1.13	0.88	7.4	237	34	86	1.66	0.0	10.1		0.0	200
2013	A	Wisconsin	0	0	1	13	23	0.69	1.31	7.7	262	49	94	3.02	2.8	15.9	5.8	0.0	230
2014	A+	Brevard County	12	8	0	147	105	2.93	1.09	23.0	221	26	75	2.63	2.6	6.4	2.4	0.6	63
2015	AA	Biloxi	7	8	0	117	94	3.84	1.43	19.9	214	26	72	3.15	5.9	7.2	1.2	0.4	-12

Short, stocky LH who struggled to find plate against advanced hitters. FB sits 88-91 with sink; CU flashes good fade vs. RHH; SL movement subpar and often drops high 3/4 arm slot when thrown. Works downhill with good extension and hides ball, allowing velo to play up. Not ideal SP size, but FB/CU tandem has fared well in the 'pen.

Johnson,Pierce — SP — Chicago (N)

EXP MLB DEBUT: 2016 | H/W: 6-3 200 | FUT: #3 starter | 8C

Thrws R Age 24 — 2012 (1) Missouri St

Velo	Pitch	Grade
91-93	FB	++++
86-88	CT	++++
80-83	CB	+++
82-84	CU	+++

Year	Lev	Team	W	L	Sv	IP	K	ERA	WHIP	BF/G	OBA	H%	S%	xERA	Ctl	Dom	Cmd	hr/9	BPV
2013	A	Kane County	5	5	0	69	74	3.12	1.30	21.9	258	35	77	3.51	2.9	9.6	3.4	0.5	114
2013	A+	Daytona	6	1	0	48	50	2.24	1.29	19.8	232	32	82	2.81	3.9	9.3	2.4	0.2	80
2014	A	Kane County	0	1	0	11	8	2.45	0.64	19.0	114	12	67	0.50	2.5	6.5	2.7	0.8	70
2014	AA	Tennessee	5	4	0	91	91	2.57	1.25	20.6	189	24	83	2.78	5.3	9.0	1.7	0.8	36
2015	AA	Tennessee	6	2	0	95	72	2.08	1.14	23.5	221	27	83	2.51	3.0	6.8	2.3	0.4	59

Comes after hitters with two plus offerings. Starts with a good 91-93 mph FB that has late life and tops out at 95 mph. Hitters have a tough time squaring it up. Also has a plus hard CB that gets swings and misses and an improved CU that has potential. Inconsistent mechanics and release point result in below-average control.

Jones,Zack — RP — Milwaukee

EXP MLB DEBUT: 2016 | H/W: 6-1 185 | FUT: Setup reliever | 7E

Thrws R Age 25 — 2012 (4) San Jose St

Velo	Pitch	Grade
93-97	FB	++++
81-85	SL	++

Year	Lev	Team	W	L	Sv	IP	K	ERA	WHIP	BF/G	OBA	H%	S%	xERA	Ctl	Dom	Cmd	hr/9	BPV
2013	A+	Fort Myers	4	3	14	48	70	1.87	1.16	4.9	171	28	85	1.92	5.2	13.1	2.5	0.4	112
2014	Rk	GCL Twins	0	0	0	5	9	3.53	1.37	3.6	173	36	71	2.09	7.1	15.9	2.3	0.0	113
2014	A+	Fort Myers	0	0	3	5	5	0.00	1.00	3.8	175	25	100	1.25	3.6	9.0	2.5	0.0	83
2015	A+	Fort Myers	2	2	2	24	38	2.23	0.99	5.1	170	32	75	1.12	3.7	14.1	3.8	0.0	172
2015	AA	Chattanooga	3	2	10	27	30	6.00	1.56	4.4	240	31	62	4.35	6.0	10.0	1.7	1.0	36

Flamethrowing RP who was great in A+, but struggled in AA as closer. Has electric FB that he overthrows and overuses; lacks consistent 2nd pitch. Aggressively throws inside with FB that touches triple digits. Strong K rate could get better if SL improves. Has flyball tendencies as and he leaves SL hanging. Selected from MIN in Rule 5.

Jorge,Felix — SP — Minnesota

EXP MLB DEBUT: 2018 | H/W: 6-2 170 | FUT: #4 starter | 7C

Thrws R Age 22 — 2011 FA (DR)

Velo	Pitch	Grade
89-93	FB	+++
78-82	SL	+++
81-84	CU	++

Year	Lev	Team	W	L	Sv	IP	K	ERA	WHIP	BF/G	OBA	H%	S%	xERA	Ctl	Dom	Cmd	hr/9	BPV
2012	Rk	GCL Twins	0	3	1	34	37	2.37	1.23	11.5	237	34	79	2.56	3.2	9.7	3.1	0.0	108
2013	Rk	Elizabethton	2	2	0	61	72	2.95	1.21	20.5	246	35	75	2.90	2.7	10.6	4.0	0.3	138
2014	Rk	Elizabethton	4	2	0	66	61	2.59	1.09	21.5	238	31	76	2.49	1.9	8.3	4.4	0.3	116
2014	A	Cedar Rapids	2	5	0	39	23	9.00	1.97	15.6	341	36	56	7.99	4.6	5.3	1.2	2.1	-11
2015	A	Cedar Rapids	6	7	0	142	114	2.79	1.06	23.9	228	27	76	2.68	2.0	7.2	3.6	0.7	93

Lean SP who returned to Low-A and was much better. Some effort in his loose delivery, but generates velocity, run, and sink with impressive FB. Throws SL for strikes despite vicious break, though CU remains third pitch. Attacks hitters inside and can pitch up in zone. Could use better command, but has requisite tools to stick as SP.

Jurado,Ariel — SP — Texas

EXP MLB DEBUT: 2018 | H/W: 6-1 180 | FUT: #3 starter | 8D

Thrws R Age 20 — 2012 FA (PN)

Velo	Pitch	Grade
90-95	FB	++++
75-78	CB	++
81-82	CU	+++

Year	Lev	Team	W	L	Sv	IP	K	ERA	WHIP	BF/G	OBA	H%	S%	xERA	Ctl	Dom	Cmd	hr/9	BPV
2013	Rk	DSL Rangers	6	0	0	49	47	2.39	1.04	21.0	258	34	76	2.54	0.6	8.6	15.7	0.2	159
2014	Rk	Azl Rangers	2	1	0	38	35	1.65	1.13	10.8	245	32	86	2.64	1.9	8.2	4.4	0.2	116
2015	A	Hickory	12	1	0	99	95	2.45	1.05	17.4	248	32	78	2.69	1.1	8.6	7.9	0.5	144

Sinkerballer who enjoyed success in first full-season assignment. Limits HR by keeping ball down in zone and locates well. Lacks consistent feel for CB and CU, though both have flashes. Can reach back for more velocity and pitch to both sides of plate. Key to development will be CB as he will need swing and miss pitch.

Kahaloa,Ian — SP — Cincinnati

EXP MLB DEBUT: 2020 | H/W: 6-1 185 | FUT: #3 starter | 8E

Thrws R Age 18 — 2015 (5) HS (HI)

Velo	Pitch	Grade
91-94	FB	+++
	SL	++
	CU	+

Year	Lev	Team	W	L	Sv	IP	K	ERA	WHIP	BF/G	OBA	H%	S%	xERA	Ctl	Dom	Cmd	hr/9	BPV
2015	Rk	AZL Reds	0	0	0	24	31	2.25	0.92	11.2	191	29	76	1.55	2.3	11.6	5.2	0.4	167

Extremely raw RHP taken by CIN in the 5th Rd from the state of Hawaii. A late-breaking FB sits in the low 90s. He struggled maintaining velocity through most of his AZL starts. Secondaries are a work in progress. His SL shows potential becoming an above average pitch. Has yet to find a feel for a CU.

Kaminsky,Rob — SP — Cleveland

EXP MLB DEBUT: 2017 | H/W: 5-11 190 | FUT: #4 starter | 7B

Thrws L Age 21 — 2013 (1) HS (NJ)

Velo	Pitch	Grade
88-92	FB	+++
76-79	CB	++++
80-83	CU	+++

Year	Lev	Team	W	L	Sv	IP	K	ERA	WHIP	BF/G	OBA	H%	S%	xERA	Ctl	Dom	Cmd	hr/9	BPV
2013	Rk	GCL Cardinals	0	3	0	22	28	3.68	1.45	11.8	270	39	74	3.94	3.7	11.5	3.1	0.4	125
2014	A	Peoria	8	2	0	100	79	1.89	1.02	21.4	201	25	81	1.77	2.8	7.1	2.5	0.2	71
2015	A+	Palm Beach	6	5	0	94	79	2.10	1.17	22.1	236	31	80	2.41	2.7	7.5	2.8	0.0	82
2015	A+	Lynchburg	0	1	0	9	4	3.91	1.96	22.0	334	37	78	5.87	4.9	3.9	0.8	0.0	-44

Short, compact SP who thrives with moxie and FB/CB combo. Size could be worrisome, but has enough velocity in sinker to induce ton of groundballs. CB is clearly best pitch and exhibits plus break. K rate may fall as he advances, but has potential for three average to plus offerings. Posted severe reverse splits in '15 and did not allow HR.

Kaprielian,James — SP — New York (A)

EXP MLB DEBUT: 2017 | H/W: 6-4 200 | FUT: #3 starter | 8C

Thrws R Age 22 — 2015 (1) UCLA

Velo	Pitch	Grade
89-94	FB	+++
78-82	CB	++++
81-85	SL	++
82-89	CU	+++

Year	Lev	Team	W	L	Sv	IP	K	ERA	WHIP	BF/G	OBA	H%	S%	xERA	Ctl	Dom	Cmd	hr/9	BPV
2015	NCAA	UCLA	10	4	0	106	114	2.03	1.12	24.6	223	30	85	2.66	2.8	9.7	3.5	0.6	116
2015	Rk	GCL Yankees 2	0	0	0	2	2	12.86	1.90	5.0	252	34	25	4.47	8.6	8.6	1.0	0.0	-59
2015	A-	Staten Island	0	1	0	9	12	2.00	1.11	11.8	240	37	80	2.27	2.0	12.0	6.0	0.0	180

Tall, polished SP who has deep pitch mix and capable of dominating. While FB may not be plus pitch, he commands it to both sides of plate. Registers Ks with plus CB that he can drop in zone for strikes or use as chase offering. Mixes in hard SL and very good CU. Delivery tough to repeat due to moving parts, but doesn't impact control.

Keller,Brad — SP — Arizona

EXP MLB DEBUT: 2018 | H/W: 6-5 230 | FUT: #4 starter | 7C

Thrws R Age 20 — 2013 (8) HS (GA)

Velo	Pitch	Grade
89-94	FB	++++
82-83	SL	++
85-86	CU	++

Year	Lev	Team	W	L	Sv	IP	K	ERA	WHIP	BF/G	OBA	H%	S%	xERA	Ctl	Dom	Cmd	hr/9	BPV
2013	Rk	Azl DBacks	7	3	0	56	61	2.24	1.41	18.3	251	34	84	3.48	4.2	9.8	2.3	0.3	81
2014	Rk	Azl DBacks	4	0	0	31	20	2.32	1.25	21.1	255	29	84	3.44	2.6	5.8	2.2	0.6	52
2014	Rk	Missoula	1	4	0	33	30	7.05	2.05	20.2	348	41	68	7.84	4.9	8.1	1.7	1.6	33
2014	A-	Hillsboro	1	0	0	6	8	0.00	0.33	18.9	56	10	100		1.5	12.0	8.0	0.0	194
2015	A	Kane County	8	9	0	142	109	2.60	1.16	21.7	242	30	77	2.66	2.3	6.9	2.9	0.2	79

Big-bodied, strike-throwing RH had a solid full-season debut. FB is best pitch, touches 96. Commands to all quadrants of strike zone. Tinkers with FB grip to get desired movement. Will run pitch in and away. SL only carries one-plane break. Shows a feel for the CU and could develop into an effective MLB pitch.

Keller,Jon — RP — Baltimore

EXP MLB DEBUT: 2016 | H/W: 6-5 210 | FUT: Setup reliever | 7D

Thrws R Age 23
2013 (22) Tampa

Velo	Pitch	Grade
91-96	FB	+++
81-85	SL	+++
	CU	+

Year	Lev	Team	W	L	Sv	IP	K	ERA	WHIP	BF/G	OBA	H%	S%	xERA	Ctl	Dom	Cmd	hr/9	BPV
2013	A-	Aberdeen	1	0	0	3	2	3.00	0.67	10.5	106	13	50		3.0	6.0	2.0	0.0	45
2014	A	Delmarva	3	0	5	56	66	1.60	0.94	8.8	197	29	83	1.49	2.2	10.6	4.7	0.2	148
2014	A+	Frederick	0	0	0	4	5	8.78	3.66	13.3	409	55	73	11.52	15.4	11.0	0.7	0.0	-199
2015	A+	Frederick	3	4	4	63	50	3.84	1.46	9.0	267	33	71	3.69	3.8	7.1	1.9	0.1	42
2015	AA	Bowie	0	0	0	12	8	3.69	1.15	6.9	149	19	64	1.37	5.9	5.9	1.0	0.0	-35

Angular RP who uses size to advantage to throw downhill and deter hitters from elevating stuff. Throws with clean mechanics and hits spots with FB. Has difficulty commanding secondary offerings and below average CU makes him vulnerable to LHH. K rate fell dramatically as SL didn't exhibit same shape or power.

Keller,Mitch — SP — Pittsburgh

EXP MLB DEBUT: 2019 | H/W: 6-3 195 | FUT: #3 starter | 8D

Thrws R Age 20
2014 (2) HS (IA)

Velo	Pitch	Grade
90-94	FB	+++
	CB	+++
	CU	++

Year	Lev	Team	W	L	Sv	IP	K	ERA	WHIP	BF/G	OBA	H%	S%	xERA	Ctl	Dom	Cmd	hr/9	BPV
2014	Rk	GCL Pirates	0	0	0	27	29	1.99	1.18	12.0	199	29	81	1.97	4.3	9.6	2.2	0.0	75
2015	Rk	Bristol	0	3	0	19	25	5.63	2.14	15.9	316	45	73	6.39	7.5	11.7	1.6	0.5	26

Compact, strong-armed RHP is a good athlete with a low-90s FB that tops at 96 mph. Easy arm action and easily repeatable mechanics. Gets good, late life on the FB and keeps it down in the zone. Second best offering is a hard CB that has potential, but lacks consistency. Forearm tightness limited him to 6 ineffective starts in 2015.

Kelly,Casey — SP — Atlanta

EXP MLB DEBUT: 2012 | H/W: 6-3 215 | FUT: #4 starter | 7C

Thrws R Age 26
2008 (1) HS (FL)

Velo	Pitch	Grade
89-94	FB	+++
77-80	CB	+++
82-85	CU	+++

Year	Lev	Team	W	L	Sv	IP	K	ERA	WHIP	BF/G	OBA	H%	S%	xERA	Ctl	Dom	Cmd	hr/9	BPV
2014	A+	Lake Elsinore	0	0	0	8		4.44	1.73	18.4	380	50	71	6.07	0.0	10.0		0.0	198
2014	AA	San Antonio	1	0	0	12	8	0.75	1.00	22.9	245	30	92	2.12	0.8	6.0	8.0	0.0	106
2015	AA	San Antonio	1	8	1	82	60	4.94	1.56	13.3	289	34	69	4.86	3.7	6.6	1.8	0.8	36
2015	AAA	El Paso	1	2	0	15	14	6.51	1.64	17.0	318	41	56	4.79	3.0	8.3	2.8	0.0	87
2015	MLB	San Diego	0	2	0	11	7	8.11	1.98	17.8	378	43	57	7.47	2.4	5.7	2.3	0.8	54

Injury-riddled SP who missed all of '13 and most of '14 after TJ surgery. Brought back slowly and showed better mix as season went along. When healthy, has three average offerings that are tough to elevate. FB may lack velocity, but commands well and has plus sinking action. Big-breaking CB can be tough to hit while CU has flashes of plus.

Kilome,Franklyn — SP — Philadelphia

EXP MLB DEBUT: 2019 | H/W: 6-6 175 | FUT: #2 starter | 9D

Thrws R Age 20
2013 FA (DR)

Velo	Pitch	Grade
92-95	FB	++++
78-80	CB	+++
80-83	CU	++

Year	Lev	Team	W	L	Sv	IP	K	ERA	WHIP	BF/G	OBA	H%	S%	xERA	Ctl	Dom	Cmd	hr/9	BPV
2014	Rk	GCL Phillies	3	1	0	40	25	3.14	1.17	14.6	241	28	73	2.93	2.5	5.6	2.3	0.4	52
2015	A-	Williamsport	3	2	0	49	36	3.30	1.26	18.2	228	28	72	2.74	3.8	6.6	1.7	0.2	33

Pumps considerable velocity out of his large frame, now sitting low-to-mid 90s. Uses leg drive to take pressure off the arm in his clean delivery that he's learning to repeat. Can locate FB to both sides; hard CB with plus potential is best secondary; and is continuing to refine the CU. Has shown the drive to improve at young age. Bright future.

Kime,Dace — SP — Cleveland

EXP MLB DEBUT: 2017 | H/W: 6-4 200 | FUT: #4 SP / Setup RP | 7D

Thrws R Age 24
2013 (3) Louisville

Velo	Pitch	Grade
90-94	FB	+++
81-84	SL	++
78-82	CB	+++
	CU	++

Year	Lev	Team	W	L	Sv	IP	K	ERA	WHIP	BF/G	OBA	H%	S%	xERA	Ctl	Dom	Cmd	hr/9	BPV
2013	NCAA	Louisville	6	1	1	69	83	3.00	1.22	10.3	247	36	73	2.77	2.6	10.8	4.2	0.1	142
2013	A-	Mahoning Val	0	2	0	24	26	2.98	1.45	11.5	218	31	77	2.86	6.0	9.7	1.6	0.0	31
2014	A	Lake County	7	14	0	136	108	5.22	1.50	21.0	278	33	65	4.57	3.7	7.1	1.9	0.8	47
2015	A	Lake County	2	3	0	35	32	3.34	1.11	23.0	251	31	72	3.18	1.5	8.2	5.3	0.8	124
2015	A+	Lynchburg	3	8	0	112	83	4.42	1.46	21.8	277	34	67	3.80	3.5	6.7	1.9	0.1	45

Physical, durable SP who rebounded from poor '14. Exhibited better control as he ironed out rough mechanics. Repeats arm speed on all pitches and can miss bats with solid-average CB. Uses height to throw on downward plane and sequences four pitches well. FB can be too straight at higher velocities and will need better CU.

Kingham,Nick — SP — Pittsburgh

EXP MLB DEBUT: 2017 | H/W: 6-6 225 | FUT: #3 starter | 8D

Thrws R Age 24
2010 (4) HS (NV)

Velo	Pitch	Grade
90-93	FB	++++
83-85	CB	+++
	CU	++

Year	Lev	Team	W	L	Sv	IP	K	ERA	WHIP	BF/G	OBA	H%	S%	xERA	Ctl	Dom	Cmd	hr/9	BPV
2013	A+	Bradenton	6	3	0	70	75	3.09	0.99	20.5	218	29	71	2.43	1.8	9.6	5.4	0.8	143
2013	AA	Altoona	3	3	0	73	69	2.71	1.37	21.9	253	33	79	3.25	3.7	8.5	2.3	0.1	71
2014	AA	Altoona	1	7	0	71	54	3.04	1.35	24.7	262	32	77	3.58	3.2	6.8	2.2	0.4	56
2014	AAA	Indianapolis	5	4	0	88	65	3.58	1.10	24.7	220	26	68	2.63	2.8	6.6	2.4	0.6	63
2015	AAA	Indianapolis	1	2	0	31	32	4.34	1.32	21.5	279	36	68	4.18	2.0	9.3	4.6	0.9	130

Tall RHP hurt his elbow in May and had TJ surgery. FB sits at 90-93 mph tops out at 95 mph with a bit of late arm-side run. His CB is an above-average 11-5 offering and CU showed progress. Stands tall in his delivery, but has consistent mechanics and release point, which lead to decent command. Can sometimes leave fastball up in the zone.

Kirby,Nathan — SP — Milwaukee

EXP MLB DEBUT: 2019 | H/W: 6-2 200 | FUT: #4 starter | 8D

Thrws L Age 22
2015 (1) Virginia

Velo	Pitch	Grade
89-92	FB	+++
80-83	SL	+++
80-84	CU	+++

Year	Lev	Team	W	L	Sv	IP	K	ERA	WHIP	BF/G	OBA	H%	S%	xERA	Ctl	Dom	Cmd	hr/9	BPV
2015	NCAA	Virginia	5	3	1	64	81	2.53	1.36	22.3	234	34	82	3.22	4.5	11.4	2.5	0.4	102
2015	A	Wisconsin	0	1	0	12	7	5.90	1.80	11.3	304	35	64	4.99	5.2	5.2	1.0	0.0	-28

Underwent TJS in Sept. FB sits low-90s and plays up with arm-side tilt; SL flashes plus sweeping action for whiffs; maintains arm speed for passable CU. Delivery and arm slot can vary with high pitch counts, but fills the zone effectively. Athletic build with some room to fill out. Injury a concern, but an intriguing LH arm.

Kivel,Jeremy — RP — Cincinnati

EXP MLB DEBUT: 2017 | H/W: 6-1 200 | FUT: Middle reliever | 8E

Thrws R Age 22
2012 (10) HS (TX)

Velo	Pitch	Grade
94-97	FB	++++
87-88	SL	+++

Year	Lev	Team	W	L	Sv	IP	K	ERA	WHIP	BF/G	OBA	H%	S%	xERA	Ctl	Dom	Cmd	hr/9	BPV
2013	Rk	AZL Reds	0	2	0	50	56	3.94	1.45	16.5	261	35	74	4.11	4.1	10.0	2.4	0.7	87
2014	Rk	Billings	1	4	0	40	44	5.37	1.87	14.5	323	42	72	6.24	4.7	9.9	2.1	0.9	68
2015	A	Dayton	0	1	2	50	55	5.40	1.78	6.2	266	35	70	5.17	6.8	9.9	1.4	0.9	12

Max effort RHP made transition to reliever full time in '15. Mid 90s FB is best pitch. Hitters tend to struggle with its late movement. However, FB tends to straighten out when thrown at max velocity. Hard SL breaks sharply down, and is effective down & away. Has dropped CU.

Kline,Branden — SP — Baltimore

EXP MLB DEBUT: 2017 | H/W: 6-3 210 | FUT: #3 SP / Setup RP | 8E

Thrws R Age 24
2012 (2) Virginia

Velo	Pitch	Grade
90-95	FB	+++
81-84	SL	+++
80-83	CU	++

Year	Lev	Team	W	L	Sv	IP	K	ERA	WHIP	BF/G	OBA	H%	S%	xERA	Ctl	Dom	Cmd	hr/9	BPV
2012	A-	Aberdeen	0	0	0	12	12	4.50	1.33	12.5	262	33	67	3.86	3.0	9.0	3.0	0.8	99
2013	A	Delmarva	1	2	0	35	32	5.90	1.57	22.0	293	36	63	5.16	3.6	8.2	2.3	1.0	69
2014	A+	Frederick	8	6	0	126	95	3.85	1.39	23.1	287	34	73	4.27	2.3	6.8	3.0	0.6	78
2014	AA	Bowie	0	2	0	16	9	6.11	1.79	24.9	283	32	64	5.16	6.1	5.0	0.8	0.6	-57
2015	AA	Bowie	3	3	0	39	27	3.68	1.38	20.5	241	27	76	3.89	4.4	6.2	1.4	0.9	12

Athletic SP who ended season in May, when underwent TJ surgery and will likely be out for all '16. When healthy, has potential dominant stuff, but poor command mutes arsenal. K rate doesn't match stuff and could eventually move to pen. Was adding velocity to FB and cleaning up mechanics prior to injury. SL has chance to be out pitch.

Koch,Brandon — RP — Tampa Bay

EXP MLB DEBUT: 2017 | H/W: 6-1 205 | FUT: Closer | 8D

Thrws R Age 22
2015 (4) Dallas Baptist

Velo	Pitch	Grade
91-96	FB	+++
84-88	SL	++++
	CU	+

Year	Lev	Team	W	L	Sv	IP	K	ERA	WHIP	BF/G	OBA	H%	S%	xERA	Ctl	Dom	Cmd	hr/9	BPV
2015	NCAA	Dallas Baptist	3	2	14	43	76	1.26	1.09	6.5	159	32	91	1.64	5.0	15.9	3.2	0.4	169
2015	A-	Hudson Valley	0	1	6	32	47	3.08	0.90	6.6	210	33	69	2.15	1.4	13.2	9.4	0.8	217

Strong RP who could move quickly as electric bullpen arm. Peppers strike zone with lively, quick FB and devastating SL that features solid shape and depth. All pitches are hard and rarely feels need to change speeds. Showed better control as pro, though can be inconsistent with max effort delivery. Keeps ball down in zone.

Kolek,Tyler — SP — Miami

EXP MLB DEBUT: 2018 | H/W: 6-5 260 | FUT: #2 starter | 9D

Thrws R Age 20
2014 (1) HS (TX)

Velo	Pitch	Grade
92-95	FB	++++
85-87	SL	++
	CB	++
	CU	+

Year	Lev	Team	W	L	Sv	IP	K	ERA	WHIP	BF/G	OBA	H%	S%	xERA	Ctl	Dom	Cmd	hr/9	BPV
2014	Rk	GCL Marlins	0	3	0	22	18	4.50	1.59	10.8	262	33	69	3.82	5.3	7.4	1.4	0.0	7
2015	A	Greensboro	4	10	0	108	81	4.57	1.56	19.0	261	31	70	4.30	5.1	6.7	1.3	0.6	2

Struggled in full-season debut. FB velo was down from 98-100 mph in HS to 91-94 mph, though it did tick back up at times. Backs up heat with power CB and hard SL. CU remains below-average. Mechanics are surprisingly simple and he repeats them well. Control remains an issue and his Dom rate was surprisingly low.

Kopech,Michael — SP — Boston
EXP MLB DEBUT: 2018 | H/W: 6-3 205 | FUT: #2 starter | 9D

Thrws R Age 19
2014 (1) HS (TX)

Velo	Pitch	Grade
94-99	FB	++++
83-86	SL	++
81-86	CU	++

Year	Lev	Team	W	L	Sv	IP	K	ERA	WHIP	BF/G	OBA	H%	S%	xERA	Ctl	Dom	Cmd	hr/9	BPV
2014	Rk	GCL Red Sox	0	1	0	13	16	4.77	1.52	7.2	228	34	65	3.15	6.1	10.9	1.8	0.0	49
2015	A	Greenville	4	5	0	65	70	2.63	1.23	16.5	224	31	78	2.66	3.7	9.7	2.6	0.3	92

Tall SP who was suspended 50 games for PEDs, but was dominant in first full season. Throws with electric velocity and can miss bats with SL that only needs consistency. Has effort in unusual delivery, but generally throws strikes despite pitch movement. Rarely allows HR as he keeps ball low. Needs to hone CU to give third pitch.

Kubitza,Austin — SP — Detroit
EXP MLB DEBUT: 2016 | H/W: 6-5 225 | FUT: #4 starter | 7D

Thrws R Age 24
2013 (4) Rice

Velo	Pitch	Grade
87-91	FB	+++
80-82	SL	++
86-89	CT	+++

Year	Lev	Team	W	L	Sv	IP	K	ERA	WHIP	BF/G	OBA	H%	S%	xERA	Ctl	Dom	Cmd	hr/9	BPV
2013	NCAA	Rice	8	4	0	109	134	2.06	1.09	23.7	188	29	79	1.60	4.0	11.1	2.8	0.0	110
2013	Rk	GCL Tigers	0	0	0	8	5	2.22	0.74	4.8	180	22	67	0.68	1.1	5.6	5.0	0.0	88
2013	A+	Lakeland	0	1	0	17	14	5.82	1.53	9.2	250	32	58	3.51	5.3	7.4	1.4	0.0	8
2014	A	West Michigan	10	2	0	131	140	2.34	1.08	22.2	210	29	79	2.16	3.0	9.6	3.3	0.3	111
2015	AA	Erie	9	13	0	133	96	5.81	1.79	22.8	337	40	66	5.87	3.2	6.5	2.0	0.4	47

Tall SP who skipped High-A, but was hit hard by hitters from both sides. All about groundballs and doesn't allow HR. Hitters rarely elevate solid-average sinker that has vicious late action. Can sink, cut, and change speeds effectively. Doesn't beat himself with walks, but lacks out pitch and SL is subpar.

Kuhl,Chad — SP — Pittsburgh
EXP MLB DEBUT: 2017 | H/W: 6-3 215 | FUT: #4 SP / Setup RP | 7C

Thrws R Age 23
2013 (9) Delaware

Velo	Pitch	Grade
94-97	FB	++++
	SL	+++
	CU	++

Year	Lev	Team	W	L	Sv	IP	K	ERA	WHIP	BF/G	OBA	H%	S%	xERA	Ctl	Dom	Cmd	hr/9	BPV
2012	NCAA	Delaware	5	5	1	77		4.44	1.58	22.6	283	35	72	4.65	4.2	7.5	1.8	0.6	39
2013	NCAA	Delaware	10	2	0	105	76	3.76	1.31	29.0	265	31	73	3.89	2.7	6.5	2.5	0.8	63
2013	A-	Jamestown	3	4	0	55	33	2.12	1.07	16.5	254	30	78	2.43	1.0	5.4	5.5	0.0	89
2014	A+	Bradenton	13	5	0	153	100	3.47	1.20	22.0	246	28	71	3.13	2.5	5.9	2.4	0.5	57
2015	AA	Altoona	11	5	0	152	101	2.48	1.14	23.2	237	27	80	2.93	2.4	6.0	2.5	0.6	60

9th round pick had a breakout season in AA, with improved FB velocity. FB was in the low-90s when drafted, but now tops out at 96-97 mph with good late sinking action. Improved consistency on his SL gives him a second potentially plus offering. CU remains a work in progress, but has potential.

Kurcz,Aaron — RP — Oakland
EXP MLB DEBUT: 2016 | H/W: 6-0 175 | FUT: Setup reliever | 6B

Thrws R Age 25
2010 (10) JC of So Nevada

Velo	Pitch	Grade
92-95	FB	+++
83-85	SL	+++

Year	Lev	Team	W	L	Sv	IP	K	ERA	WHIP	BF/G	OBA	H%	S%	xERA	Ctl	Dom	Cmd	hr/9	BPV
2011	A+	Daytona	5	4	0	82	91	3.29	1.23	10.4	224	30	75	3.02	3.7	10.0	2.7	0.7	97
2012	AA	Portland	3	4	4	50	72	3.05	1.38	7.3	229	35	80	3.47	4.9	12.9	2.7	0.7	120
2014	AA	Portland	3	2	3	42	54	2.14	1.29	5.1	213	33	81	2.38	4.7	11.6	2.5	0.0	99
2015	AAA	Gwinnett	4	3	7	33	38	3.27	1.52	4.6	238	33	79	3.79	5.7	10.4	1.8	0.5	50
2015	AAA	Nashville	2	1	0	26	31	4.15	1.69	6.5	283	39	76	5.00	5.2	10.7	2.1	0.7	71

Short RP who has good enough stuff to pitch in majors, potentially in late innings role. Rears back to fire solid FB and complements with above average SL when on. Throws with a lot of effort and command/control decline as a result. Size affects plane to plate and pitches up too often. Can register Ks with two offerings.

Labourt,Jairo — SP — Detroit
EXP MLB DEBUT: 2017 | H/W: 6-4 205 | FUT: #3 SP / Setup RP | 8D

Thrws L Age 22
2011 FA (DR)

Velo	Pitch	Grade
90-95	FB	+++
83-86	SL	+++
81-83	CU	++

Year	Lev	Team	W	L	Sv	IP	K	ERA	WHIP	BF/G	OBA	H%	S%	xERA	Ctl	Dom	Cmd	hr/9	BPV
2013	Rk	Bluefield	2	2	0	51	45	1.93	1.04	16.4	213	27	84	2.28	2.5	7.9	3.2	0.5	94
2014	A-	Vancouver	5	3	0	71	82	1.77	1.18	19.0	190	28	83	1.86	4.7	10.4	2.2	0.0	78
2014	A	Lansing	0	0	0	14	11	6.43	2.50	12.4	275	33	74	6.91	12.9	7.1	0.6	0.6	-202
2015	A+	Dunedin	2	7	0	80	70	4.61	1.59	19.6	269	33	71	4.53	4.9	7.9	1.6	0.7	26
2015	A+	Lakeland	1	5	0	35	34	6.39	1.70	22.8	312	39	61	5.55	3.8	8.7	2.3	0.8	71

Tall, athletic pitcher was acquired at deadline and has tantalizing upside based on hard stuff. Has significant command issues and lack of dependable CU, but both FB and SL have plus potential. Slows arm speed and can telegraph pitches with varying slot. Needs time to develop, but payoff could be huge.

Lail,Brady — SP — New York (A)
EXP MLB DEBUT: 2016 | H/W: 6-2 205 | FUT: #4 starter | 7C

Thrws R Age 22
2012 (18) HS (UT)

Velo	Pitch	Grade
89-94	FB	+++
79-83	CB	+++
	CU	+++

Year	Lev	Team	W	L	Sv	IP	K	ERA	WHIP	BF/G	OBA	H%	S%	xERA	Ctl	Dom	Cmd	hr/9	BPV
2014	A	Charleston (Sc)	8	4	0	97	95	3.71	1.27	22.0	279	36	71	3.76	1.6	8.8	5.6	0.6	134
2014	A+	Tampa	3	1	0	37	21	3.40	1.05	20.5	223	25	68	2.43	2.2	5.1	2.3	0.5	51
2015	A+	Tampa	1	0	0	5	9	0.00	0.80	18.1	221	44	100	1.21	0.0	16.2		0.0	310
2015	AA	Trenton	6	4	0	106	63	2.46	1.10	20.8	233	27	77	2.39	2.2	5.3	2.4	0.2	55
2015	AAA	Scranton/WB	3	2	0	37	13	4.62	1.70	23.9	306	31	75	5.70	4.1	3.2	0.8	1.0	-37

Advanced SP who reached AAA in August. Adding strength and durability and slots in at back of rotation. Doesn't fan many, but sequences well and uses sharp CB to keep hitters guessing. FB lacks movement, though has enough velocity to pitch up. CU has shown improvement to become average pitch. Keeps ball on ground and in yard.

Lamb,John — SP — Cincinnati
EXP MLB DEBUT: 2015 | H/W: 6-4 205 | FUT: #4 starter | 7B

Thrws L Age 25
2008 (5) HS (CA)

Velo	Pitch	Grade
90-92	FB	+++
76-78	CU	+++
67-71	CB	++

Year	Lev	Team	W	L	Sv	IP	K	ERA	WHIP	BF/G	OBA	H%	S%	xERA	Ctl	Dom	Cmd	hr/9	BPV
2013	AAA	Omaha	1	2	0	16	10	6.75	1.38	22.4	250	29	48	3.66	3.9	5.6	1.4	0.6	13
2014	AAA	Omaha	8	10	0	138	131	3.98	1.48	22.0	260	31	77	4.68	4.4	8.5	1.9	1.2	52
2015	AAA	Louisville	1	1	0	17	21	2.65	1.24	23.0	226	34	76	2.42	3.7	11.1	3.0	0.0	118
2015	AAA	Omaha	9	1	0	94	96	2.68	1.16	22.0	232	30	79	2.94	2.8	9.2	3.3	0.7	108
2015	MLB	Cincinnati	1	5	0	49	58	5.85	1.57	21.6	295	38	65	5.57	3.5	10.6	3.1	1.5	115

Acquired by CIN mid-season in the Johnny Cueto trade and made MLB debut 8/14/15. FB finally regained velocity from '11 TJS. Relies heavily on locating 2-seam FB. Changes eye levels with 4-seam FB. Neutralizes RH hitters with a deceptive CU tailing away. Struggles with release point, especially with his breaking pitches.

Lambert,Peter — SP — Colorado
EXP MLB DEBUT: 2019 | H/W: 6-2 185 | FUT: #3 starter | 7C

Thrws R Age 18
2015 (2) HS (CA)

Velo	Pitch	Grade
90-92	FB	+++
73-75	CB	+++
82-84	CU	+++

Year	Lev	Team	W	L	Sv	IP	K	ERA	WHIP	BF/G	OBA	H%	S%	xERA	Ctl	Dom	Cmd	hr/9	BPV
2015	Rk	Grand Junction	0	4	0	31	26	3.47	1.29	16.0	248	30	76	3.69	3.2	7.5	2.4	0.9	67

2015 2nd round pick out of HS in CA has good raw stuff. FB sits in the low-90s, topping out at 94 mph. Mixes in a 12-6 CB that shows above-avg potential and a solid CU. Not a huge player, but has good athleticism, simple repeatable mechanics, and a live arm. Solid debut in the PIO league and has nice mid-rotation potential.

Lamet,Dinelson — SP — San Diego
EXP MLB DEBUT: 2018 | H/W: 6-4 187 | FUT: #3 starter | 8D

Thrws R Age 23
2014 FA (DR)

Velo	Pitch	Grade
90-94	FB	+++
81-85	SL	+++
	CU	++

Year	Lev	Team	W	L	Sv	IP	K	ERA	WHIP	BF/G	OBA	H%	S%	xERA	Ctl	Dom	Cmd	hr/9	BPV
2015	A	Fort Wayne	5	8	0	105	120	3.00	1.20	16.2	217	29	78	2.94	3.8	10.3	2.7	0.8	101

Sleeper pitcher who enjoyed 1st year in U.S. Lean frame has projection and already throws with little effort. Needs time to develop consistency with SL that exhibits late break. Slows arm on CU and will need to battle LHH. Control should get better with more time, especially with repeatable mechanics. RHH only hit .155 against him.

Landa,Yorman — RP — Minnesota
EXP MLB DEBUT: 2019 | H/W: 6-0 175 | FUT: Setup reliever | 7D

Thrws R Age 21
2010 FA (VZ)

Velo	Pitch	Grade
91-96	FB	+++
75-79	CB	++
83-85	CU	+++

Year	Lev	Team	W	L	Sv	IP	K	ERA	WHIP	BF/G	OBA	H%	S%	xERA	Ctl	Dom	Cmd	hr/9	BPV
2012	Rk	GCL Twins	1	3	0	33	27	2.45	1.30	13.6	198	26	79	2.28	5.4	7.3	1.4	0.0	3
2013	Rk	Elizabethton	3	4	0	55	46	2.78	1.36	19.2	229	29	78	2.97	4.7	7.5	1.6	0.2	25
2014	A	Cedar Rapids	3	1	0	25	30	2.88	1.24	7.8	203	30	77	2.50	4.7	10.8	2.3	0.4	86
2015	Rk	GCL Twins	1	0	1	9	9	0.00	0.56	4.3	106	15	100		2.0	9.0	4.5	0.0	126
2015	A	Cedar Rapids	2	1	0	27	31	1.67	1.19	7.2	191	27	87	2.20	4.7	10.3	2.2	0.3	78

Short, thin pitcher who is working way back slowly after shoulder injury in past. Converted to RP in '14 and thrives with solid-average FB and ability to work down in zone. Improved feel and control as he's cleaned up arm action and showed better break on CB. CU can be go-to pitch, but will likely stay in pen due to durability and stamina concerns.

Law,Derek — SP — San Francisco
EXP MLB DEBUT: 2016 | H/W: 6-2 210 | FUT: Setup reliever | 7B

Thrws R Age 25
2011 (9) Miami-Dade

Velo	Pitch	Grade
90-93	FB	+++
74-76	CB	++++
78-82	SL	+++

Year	Lev	Team	W	L	Sv	IP	K	ERA	WHIP	BF/G	OBA	H%	S%	xERA	Ctl	Dom	Cmd	hr/9	BPV
2013	Rk	Azl Giants	1	0	0	5	9	3.46	0.96	3.9	214	41	60	1.54	1.7	15.6	9.0	0.0	252
2013	A	Augusta	0	3	3	35	48	2.31	1.06	7.1	215	34	78	2.06	2.6	12.3	4.8	0.3	171
2013	A+	San Jose	4	0	11	25	45	2.14	0.83	4.2	220	42	75	1.61	0.4	16.1	45.0	0.4	298
2014	AA	Richmond	2	0	13	28	29	2.57	1.18	4.1	194	26	78	2.21	4.5	9.3	2.1	0.3	64
2015	AA	Richmond	0	1	13	25	32	4.64	1.55	3.9	304	43	68	4.62	2.9	11.4	4.0	0.4	147

RH returned from TJS in June, appearing to have stuff and command back. Sinking FB camps in the low-90s as a quality source of ground balls. Power 12-6 CB is still his calling card for whiffs; will blend in an avg SL. Pounds the zone despite funky delivery, which adds deception to his offerings. Could get a MLB look soon.

Leclerc,Jose | SP | Texas

EXP MLB DEBUT: 2016 | H/W: 6-0 165 | FUT: #4 SP / Setup RP | 7B

Thrws R Age 22
2010 FA (DR)

Velo	Pitch	Grade
91-94	FB	+++
74-76	CB	+++
83-86	CU	+++

Year	Lev	Team	W	L	Sv	IP	K	ERA	WHIP	BF/G	OBA	H%	S%	xERA	Ctl	Dom	Cmd	hr/9	BPV
2013	A	Hickory	3	4	5	59	77	3.36	1.25	6.2	242	36	72	2.95	3.2	11.7	3.7	0.3	143
2014	A+	Myrtle Beach	4	1	14	57	79	3.31	1.33	5.6	195	27	81	3.46	5.8	12.5	2.1	1.3	85
2015	AA	Frisco	6	8	0	103	98	5.77	1.65	17.7	250	32	64	4.46	6.4	8.6	1.3	0.7	0

Short, lean hurler who was inconsistent in first full season as SP. K rate decreased and walk rate rose while showing flyball tendencies. Power stuff has different speeds and shapes. Electric FB is sneaky quick and shows run and sink. Best pitch may be CU with outstanding depth and fade. Still young for level and needs better command.

Lee,Nick | RP | Washington

EXP MLB DEBUT: 2016 | H/W: 5-11 185 | FUT: Setup reliever | 7C

Thrws L Age 25
2011 (18) Weatherford JC

Velo	Pitch	Grade
93-95	FB	+++
	CB	++
	CU	++

Year	Lev	Team	W	L	Sv	IP	K	ERA	WHIP	BF/G	OBA	H%	S%	xERA	Ctl	Dom	Cmd	hr/9	BPV
2014	Rk	GCL Nationals	1	0	0	8	6	6.75	1.63	7.1	285	23	78	8.47	4.5	6.8	1.5	4.5	18
2014	A	Hagerstown	1	0	0	8	6	7.78	2.47	8.6	325	37	68	8.04	10.0	6.7	0.7	1.1	-132
2014	A+	Potomac	0	2	0	14	23	10.21	1.77	13.0	299	50	36	4.75	5.1	14.7	2.9	0.0	144
2015	A+	Potomac	1	1	9	28	28	2.57	1.21	5.6	202	27	79	2.40	4.5	9.0	2.0	0.3	59
2015	AA	Harrisburg	2	0	1	24	29	3.75	1.63	5.3	228	34	74	3.43	7.1	10.9	1.5	0.0	21

Hard-throwing lefty reliever that can retire hitters from both sides. Command can waver, due to a funky high-effort delivery that is tough to repeat. But generates strikeouts with mid-90s heat. CB best off-speed, though his CU keeps RHH at bay. Needs to be more consistent at higher levels.

Lee,Zach | SP | Los Angeles (N)

EXP MLB DEBUT: 2015 | H/W: 6-4 210 | FUT: #4 starter | 7C

Thrws R Age 24
2010 (1) HS (TX)

Velo	Pitch	Grade
89-93	FB	+++
75-78	CB	++
81-84	SL	+++
	CU	+++

Year	Lev	Team	W	L	Sv	IP	K	ERA	WHIP	BF/G	OBA	H%	S%	xERA	Ctl	Dom	Cmd	hr/9	BPV
2014	AAA	Albuquerque	7	13	0	150		5.39	1.54	23.4	295	33	66	5.19	3.2	5.8	1.8	1.1	35
2015	Rk	Azl Dodgers	1	0	0	5	2	0.00	0.00	14.1	0	0			0.0	3.6		0.0	83
2015	A+	RanchoCuca	1	0	0	5	2	3.60	1.00	19.1	221	25	60	1.84	1.8	3.6	2.0	0.0	34
2015	AAA	Oklahoma City	11	6	0	113	81	2.71	1.11	23.4	251	30	76	2.86	1.5	6.4	4.3	0.4	93
2015	MLB	LA Dodgers	0	1	0	4	3	15.00	2.86	23.8	482	53	45	13.33	2.1	6.4	3.0	2.1	76

Rebounded nicely, going 13-6 with a 2.63 ERA. Still has a good low-90s FB that tops out at 95 and a nice four-pitch mix. Low Dom limits his long-term potential, but showed improved Ctl. When he's on FB generates good ground ball rates, and complements it with a SL, CU, and CB that he uses in any count and throws for strikes.

Leibrandt,Brandon | SP | Philadelphia

EXP MLB DEBUT: 2018 | H/W: 6-4 190 | FUT: #4 SP / Setup RP | 7C

Thrws L Age 23
2014 (6) Florida St

Velo	Pitch	Grade
85-88	FB	++
	SL	++
	CU	++++

Year	Lev	Team	W	L	Sv	IP	K	ERA	WHIP	BF/G	OBA	H%	S%	xERA	Ctl	Dom	Cmd	hr/9	BPV
2014	NCAA	Florida St	4	1	0	39	30	1.84	1.02	25.0	219	27	84	2.28	2.1	6.9	3.3	0.5	86
2014	Rk	GCL Phillies	1	2	1	19	22	4.22	1.15	15.2	270	37	62	3.22	0.9	10.3	11.0	0.5	178
2014	A-	Williamsport	2	3	0	41	45	2.20	0.90	21.8	201	28	75	1.49	1.8	9.9	5.6	0.2	148
2015	Rk	GCL Phillies	0	0	0	7	8	0.00	0.57	11.9	168	25	100	0.08	0.0	10.3		0.0	203
2015	A+	Clearwater	7	3	0	101	67	3.12	1.03	22.9	225	26	70	2.44	1.9	6.0	3.2	0.5	75

Attempts to answer the question of "How far does pitchability go?" Good control of a short fastball, a devastating change-up and below-average slider is the arsenal. But mixing pitches, not walking guys and advanced feel for his craft has worked so far in the lower minors. But there's some reason to doubt whether it will play at higher levels.

Lemoine,Jacob | SP | Texas

EXP MLB DEBUT: 2018 | H/W: 6-4 195 | FUT: #3 starter | 8E

Thrws R Age 22
2015 (4) Houston

Velo	Pitch	Grade
90-94	FB	++++
84-85	SL	+++
82-85	CU	+

Year	Lev	Team	W	L	Sv	IP	K	ERA	WHIP	BF/G	OBA	H%	S%	xERA	Ctl	Dom	Cmd	hr/9	BPV
2015		*Did not pitch in minors; injured*																	

Tall SP who did not pitch upon signing due to sore shoulder. Did not need surgery. Owns projection, arm strength, and effective FB/SL mix. Needs to find consistency in secondary offerings, but can dominate with FB. Heater features vicious, late sink and can spot it to all quadrants of zone. Will need time to polish SL.

Lemond,Zech | SP | San Diego

EXP MLB DEBUT: 2017 | H/W: 6-1 170 | FUT: #4 SP / Setup RP | 7D

Thrws R Age 23
2014 (3) Rice

Velo	Pitch	Grade
90-94	FB	+++
80-85	CB	+++
82-84	CU	++

Year	Lev	Team	W	L	Sv	IP	K	ERA	WHIP	BF/G	OBA	H%	S%	xERA	Ctl	Dom	Cmd	hr/9	BPV
2013	NCAA	Rice	7	2	14	75	71	2.03	1.02	9.0	209	28	79	1.81	2.5	8.5	3.4	0.1	103
2014	NCAA	Rice	4	1	3	53	52	1.35	1.05	13.7	210	28	89	2.11	2.7	8.8	3.3	0.3	103
2014	A-	Eugene	2	3	0	38	34	3.79	1.16	13.7	267	34	65	3.01	1.2	8.1	6.8	0.2	131
2014	AA	San Antonio	0	0	0	4	2	0.00	0.25	12.3	81	10	100		0.0	4.5		0.0	99
2015	A+	Lake Elsinore	5	10	0	130	101	5.54	1.68	18.3	323	38	67	5.76	3.0	7.0	2.3	0.8	62

Athletic pitcher who was poor all season and could return to pen. Throws consistent strikes from downhill plane and has nifty CB, but can be hit hard from straight FB. Doesn't have pitch to combat LHH and long arm action provides little deception. Locates FB well to both sides of plate, but has difficulty commanding spike CB.

Lewicki,Artie | SP | Detroit

EXP MLB DEBUT: 2018 | H/W: 6-3 195 | FUT: #4 starter | 7D

Thrws R Age 23
2014 (8) Virginia

Velo	Pitch	Grade
90-94	FB	+++
80-85	SL	+++
75-78	CB	++
81-82	CU	++

Year	Lev	Team	W	L	Sv	IP	K	ERA	WHIP	BF/G	OBA	H%	S%	xERA	Ctl	Dom	Cmd	hr/9	BPV
2013	NCAA	Virginia	0	1	0	2	0	13.50	3.00	5.8	347	35	50	8.77	13.5	0.0	0.0	0.0	-347
2014	NCAA	Virginia	8	1	1	68	57	1.32	0.73	15.1	161	20	85	0.81	1.7	7.5	4.4	0.4	107
2014	Rk	GCL Tigers	0	0	0	2	4	0.00	1.50	4.3	262	55	100	3.49	4.5	18.0	4.0	0.0	221
2014	A	West Michigan	2	2	2	25	22	2.50	1.11	9.9	211	26	81	2.62	3.2	7.9	2.4	0.7	73
2015	A	West Michigan	3	4	0	79	77	3.53	1.42	22.3	281	36	75	4.06	2.8	8.8	3.1	0.5	99

Strong-framed SP who missed most of first two months, but was solid when healthy. Has 4 pitches in deep arsenal, though none are plus offerings. Repeats delivery and arm slot and gives different looks with varying velocity on FB and breaking balls. Always around plate and may eventually move to bullpen to take advantage of arm strength.

Leyer,Robinson | SP | Chicago (A)

EXP MLB DEBUT: 2017 | H/W: 6-2 175 | FUT: #3 SP / Setup RP | 8E

Thrws R Age 23
2011 FA (DR)

Velo	Pitch	Grade
91-95	FB	+++
82-84	SL	++
80-85	CU	++

Year	Lev	Team	W	L	Sv	IP	K	ERA	WHIP	BF/G	OBA	H%	S%	xERA	Ctl	Dom	Cmd	hr/9	BPV
2013	Rk	Bristol	2	7	0	56	38	6.41	1.85	20.2	318	36	65	6.08	4.8	6.1	1.3	0.8	-2
2014	A	Kannapolis	5	9	0	134	86	3.82	1.39	22.6	276	32	73	4.10	2.9	5.8	2.0	0.6	44
2015	A+	Winston-Salem	3	6	0	83	64	4.33	1.26	21.2	252	30	66	3.57	2.8	6.9	2.5	0.8	67
2015	AA	Birmingham	3	1	0	38	30	4.96	1.55	13.9	281	33	68	4.65	4.0	7.1	1.8	0.7	37

Strong-armed pitcher who is advancing quickly as secondary offerings develop. Leaves pitches up often and pitch location needs work. Can generate velocity with effort in delivery, though K rate hasn't risen. CU has chance to become above average as he's repeating slot and arm speed. Could add more power to sweepy SL.

Leyva,Lazaro | RP | Baltimore

EXP MLB DEBUT: 2017 | H/W: 6-2 190 | FUT: Closer | 8D

Thrws R Age 21
2014 FA (CU)

Velo	Pitch	Grade
95-99	FB	++++
77-80	CB	+++

Year	Lev	Team	W	L	Sv	IP	K	ERA	WHIP	BF/G	OBA	H%	S%	xERA	Ctl	Dom	Cmd	hr/9	BPV
2015	Rk	GCL Orioles	0	0	0	2	3	0.00	1.50	8.6	151	27	100	2.20	9.0	13.5	1.5	0.0	18
2015	A-	Aberdeen	0	2	1	40	36	2.92	1.17	10.7	215	29	72	2.16	3.6	8.1	2.3	0.0	66

Athletic, electric-armed pitcher who can succeed on FB alone. Throws with effort, though generates velocity more on arm speed. Keeps ball down and has CB that gets swings and misses. Command needs attention and can be inconsistent with slot and delivery. Has big upside, possibly as RP. Needs time to harness arm.

Light,Pat | RP | Boston

EXP MLB DEBUT: 2016 | H/W: 6-5 195 | FUT: Setup reliever | 7C

Thrws R Age 25
2012 (1) Monmouth

Velo	Pitch	Grade
91-96	FB	++++
81-85	SL	+++
	CU	+

Year	Lev	Team	W	L	Sv	IP	K	ERA	WHIP	BF/G	OBA	H%	S%	xERA	Ctl	Dom	Cmd	hr/9	BPV
2013	A	Greenville	1	4	0	28	28	8.97	2.06	13.7	357	44	56	7.70	4.5	9.0	2.0	1.3	58
2014	A	Greenville	2	0	0	17	19	4.21	1.11	22.4	237	32	61	2.75	2.1	10.0	4.8	0.5	141
2014	A+	Salem	6	6	0	115	57	4.93	1.46	22.4	294	32	66	4.72	2.6	4.5	1.7	0.8	29
2015	AA	Portland	1	1	3	29	32	2.47	0.99	5.3	179	23	81	2.14	3.4	9.9	2.9	0.9	104
2015	AAA	Pawtucket	2	4	2	33	35	5.18	1.73	5.8	250	33	69	4.49	7.1	9.5	1.3	0.5	-2

Tall, strong pitcher who was moved to pen in '15 to great results. K rate increased drastically as he showed consistent plus velocity and use of hard SL. FB is rarely straight and hitters have difficulty elevating it. Control fell apart upon promotion to AAA as he overthrew. Fits mold of setup guy.

Lilek,Brett | SP | Miami

EXP MLB DEBUT: 2018 | H/W: 6-4 220 | FUT: #4 starter | 7C

Thrws L Age 22
2015 (2) Arizona St

Velo	Pitch	Grade
92-94	FB	+++
77-78	CB	+++
	SL	++
80-83	CU	++

Year	Lev	Team	W	L	Sv	IP	K	ERA	WHIP	BF/G	OBA	H%	S%	xERA	Ctl	Dom	Cmd	hr/9	BPV
2015	NCAA	Arizona St	4	2	0	78	66	3.22	1.27	18.8	208	26	75	2.75	4.7	7.6	1.6	0.5	27
2015	A-	Batavia	1	2	0	35	43	3.34	1.06	12.3	233	34	67	2.30	1.8	11.1	6.1	0.3	168

Lefty features a FB that sits at 92-94 mph with some late movement. CB is second best offering and has good late break. SL and CU project as average offerings. Struggled with command in college, but was a strike-throwing machine in the pros, walking just 7 in 35 IP while striking out 43.

Lindgren,Jacob — RP — New York (A)

EXP MLB DEBUT: 2015 | H/W: 5-11 205 | FUT: Closer | 8C

Thrws L Age 23
2014 (2) Mississippi St

- 90-95 FB +++
- 82-86 SL ++++
- 80-83 CU ++

Year	Lev	Team	W	L	Sv	IP	K	ERA	WHIP	BF/G	OBA	H%	S%	xERA	Ctl	Dom	Cmd	hr/9	BPV
2014	A	Charleston (Sc)	1	0	1	5	11	1.80	0.20	3.8	66	24	0		0.0	19.8		0.0	374
2014	A+	Tampa	0	0	0	7	17	0.00	0.99	4.5	130	50	100	0.62	5.1	21.5	4.3	0.0	269
2014	AA	Trenton	1	1	0	11	18	4.02	1.34	5.8	160	31	67	1.88	7.2	14.5	2.0	0.0	83
2015	AAA	Scranton/WB	1	1	3	22	29	1.23	1.18	5.9	205	33	88	2.02	4.1	11.9	2.9	0.0	121
2015	MLB	NY Yankees	0	0	0	7	8	5.14	1.29	4.1	202	15	83	5.89	5.1	10.3	2.0	3.9	64

Short, dominating RP who ended season in June for surgery to remove bone spur in elbow. Posts very high K rates on basis of deceptive, sinking FB and power SL. Stuff can be downright filthy, especially when he works with tempo. Control comes and goes and needs to tidy up delivery. LHH have little chance against him.

Lively,Ben — SP — Philadelphia

EXP MLB DEBUT: 2016 | H/W: 6-4 190 | FUT: #5 SP / Long RP | 6A

Thrws R Age 24
2013 (4) Central Florida

- 89-92 FB +++
- 81-84 SL ++
- 72-74 CB ++
- 82-84 CU +++

Year	Lev	Team	W	L	Sv	IP	K	ERA	WHIP	BF/G	OBA	H%	S%	xERA	Ctl	Dom	Cmd	hr/9	BPV
2013	Rk	Billings	0	3	0	37	49	0.73	0.89	11.4	168	28	91	0.87	2.9	11.9	4.1	0.0	154
2013	A	Dayton	0	1	0	4	7	2.25	0.75	14.3	151	32	67	0.29	2.3	15.8	7.0	0.0	241
2014	A+	Bakersfield	10	1	0	79	95	2.28	0.92	22.8	204	29	79	2.01	1.8	10.8	5.9	0.7	164
2014	AA	Pensacola	3	6	0	72	76	3.88	1.33	23.0	228	29	73	3.53	4.5	9.5	2.1	0.9	68
2015	AA	Reading	8	7	0	143	111	4.15	1.43	24.4	284	33	73	4.56	2.8	7.0	2.5	0.9	67

Throws four pitches with good command, but lacks a standout offering. Strikeout rate in lower minors due to deception in delivery more than stuff, which causes FB to play up a tick. Neither CB nor SL are particularly crisp; can throw both for strikes but unlikely to miss bats at higher levels. Sturdy and durable, but most likely a reliever profile.

Long,Grayson — SP — Los Angeles (A)

EXP MLB DEBUT: 2018 | H/W: 6-5 225 | FUT: #4 starter | 7D

Thrws R Age 21
2015 (3) Texas A&M

- 89-93 FB +++
- 81-83 SL +++
- CU +++

Year	Lev	Team	W	L	Sv	IP	K	ERA	WHIP	BF/G	OBA	H%	S%	xERA	Ctl	Dom	Cmd	hr/9	BPV
2015	NCAA	Texas A&M	9	1	0	95	106	2.84	1.30	23.1	240	34	77	2.96	3.7	10.0	2.7	0.2	99
2015	Rk	Orem	0	0	0	19	22	5.16	1.51	6.4	260	36	64	4.00	4.7	10.3	2.2	0.5	77

Tall SP who may not throw hard, but has three average pitches in arsenal and works in bottom half of strike zone. Locates FB well, but has trouble throwing SL and CU for strikes. Gets hitters to chase SL and CU shows decent depth and drop. Could move quickly, especially if he can find more velocity.

Lopez,Frank — SP — Texas

EXP MLB DEBUT: 2017 | H/W: 6-1 175 | FUT: #4 starter | 7E

Thrws L Age 22
2010 FA (VZ)

- 86-92 FB +++
- 75-79 CB +++
- 81-84 CU +++

Year	Lev	Team	W	L	Sv	IP	K	ERA	WHIP	BF/G	OBA	H%	S%	xERA	Ctl	Dom	Cmd	hr/9	BPV
2013	A	Hickory	3	7	0	73	79	4.80	1.49	19.7	264	36	65	3.81	4.3	9.7	2.3	0.2	77
2014	Rk	Azl Rangers	0	0	0	6	7	1.50	0.50	5.0	106	9	100	0.68	1.5	10.5	7.0	1.5	167
2014	A	Hickory	4	3	0	73	80	2.83	1.26	18.6	251	34	78	3.27	2.8	9.8	3.5	0.5	119
2015	A+	High Desert	4	1	0	42	43	2.99	1.02	23.1	227	29	74	2.71	1.7	9.2	5.4	0.9	137
2015	AA	Frisco	3	7	0	75	58	4.92	1.61	20.8	291	34	71	5.32	4.1	7.0	1.7	1.1	33

Savvy SP who has average pitch mix and relies on mixing and hitting spots. K rate fell while walk rate increased in AA upon promotion in May. Big-breaking CB is top offering, but not true out pitch. Locates FB to both sides of plate, but can't miss up. CU is effective third pitch with sink and fade.

Lopez,Jorge — SP — Milwaukee

EXP MLB DEBUT: 2015 | H/W: 6-3 190 | FUT: #4 starter | 8C

Thrws R Age 23
2011 (2) HS (PR)

- 89-93 FB +++
- 80-84 CB +++
- 86-88 CU +++

Year	Lev	Team	W	L	Sv	IP	K	ERA	WHIP	BF/G	OBA	H%	S%	xERA	Ctl	Dom	Cmd	hr/9	BPV
2012	Rk	Azl Brewers	1	3	2	25	20	5.38	1.55	15.7	276	33	65	4.60	4.3	7.2	1.7	0.7	31
2013	A	Wisconsin	7	8	2	117	92	5.23	1.44	19.9	267	31	65	4.44	3.7	7.1	1.9	1.0	46
2014	A+	Brevard County	10	10	0	137	119	4.59	1.38	23.1	271	33	67	4.17	3.0	7.8	2.6	0.8	77
2015	AA	Biloxi	12	5	0	143	137	2.26	1.10	23.4	206	26	82	2.39	3.3	8.6	2.6	0.6	85
2015	MLB	Milwaukee	1	1	0	10	10	5.40	1.90	23.6	332	43	68	5.65	4.5	9.0	2.0	0.0	59

Drafted raw, development of stuff and smarts culminated in a breakout 2015, finishing in SL's top five in ERA, WHIP, Dom. Fastball velo isn't plus, but commands it down well; curve has nice depth/bite and gets ground balls; change-up lags behind, but shows promise. Projectable build, smooth delivery with repeatable arm slot and mechanics.

Lopez,Reynaldo — SP — Washington

EXP MLB DEBUT: 2017 | H/W: 6-0 185 | FUT: #2 starter | 9C

Thrws R Age 22
2012 FA (DR)

- 95-98 FB ++++
- 78-81 CB +++
- 83-85 CU +++

Year	Lev	Team	W	L	Sv	IP	K	ERA	WHIP	BF/G	OBA	H%	S%	xERA	Ctl	Dom	Cmd	hr/9	BPV
2013	A-	Auburn	0	1	0	1	0	57.27	6.36	10.1	693	69	0	30.16	0.0	0.0		0.0	18
2013	A	Hagerstown	0	0	0	4	4	6.75	2.25	20.3	415	49	75	10.24	2.3	9.0	4.0	2.3	119
2014	A-	Auburn	3	2	0	36	31	0.75	0.83	18.8	129	18	90	0.36	3.8	7.8	2.1	0.0	56
2014	A	Hagerstown	4	1	0	47	39	1.34	0.81	19.0	169	22	84	0.89	2.1	7.5	3.5	0.2	95
2015	A+	Potomac	6	7	0	99	94	4.09	1.22	21.1	250	32	66	3.15	2.5	8.5	3.4	0.5	103

Though ERA took step back, most other aspects of 2015 backed up his breakout 2014. Electric FB can reach triple digits; a hard CB induces swings and misses; CU is improving. Repeats arm speed on all. Still some durability concerns, and delivery can be inconsistent. But filthy when on and ready for the high minors.

Lopez,Yoan — SP — Arizona

EXP MLB DEBUT: 2017 | H/W: 6-3 185 | FUT: #4 starter | 7D

Thrws R Age 23
2015 FA (CU)

- 92-94 FB +++
- 76-78 CB +++
- 81-84 CU ++

Year	Lev	Team	W	L	Sv	IP	K	ERA	WHIP	BF/G	OBA	H%	S%	xERA	Ctl	Dom	Cmd	hr/9	BPV
2015	Rk	Azl DBacks	1	0	0	6	6	0.00	0.50	19.9	151	22	100		0.0	9.0		0.0	180
2015	AA	Mobile	1	6	0	48	32	4.69	1.46	20.5	254	29	68	4.09	4.5	6.0	1.3	0.8	5

Slim RHP, working way into becoming quality starter. Works three pitches up and down, left and right with 2-seam FB. Gets good bit of grounders with heavy bore into RH hitters. Struggles with command. Not many swings and misses. 12-6 CB is effective but wraps wrist, telegraphing pitch. CU lags way behind FB & CB. Flat, very hittable.

Lowry,Thad — SP — Chicago (A)

EXP MLB DEBUT: 2018 | H/W: 6-4 215 | FUT: #4 starter | 7E

Thrws R Age 21
2013 (5) HS (TX)

- 90-94 FB +++
- 81-84 SL +++
- 84-87 CU ++

Year	Lev	Team	W	L	Sv	IP	K	ERA	WHIP	BF/G	OBA	H%	S%	xERA	Ctl	Dom	Cmd	hr/9	BPV
2013	Rk	Bristol	3	5	0	44	30	5.51	1.75	13.4	307	36	67	5.26	4.5	6.1	1.4	0.4	7
2014	A	Kannapolis	4	6	0	87	43	4.76	1.52	22.2	296	33	68	4.64	3.0	4.4	1.5	0.5	17
2015	A	Kannapolis	12	8	0	150	94	4.49	1.32	23.9	272	31	65	3.74	2.4	5.6	2.4	0.5	55

Tall pitcher who repeated Low-A and can be power arm despite low K rate. Exhibited better control and K rate in '15, but still pitches to contact with three offerings. FB can get to mid 90s, though has sink at lower levels. Uses hard SL as chase pitch and can drop CU in zone for strikes. Repeating of delivery would enhance command.

Lugo,Luis — SP — Cleveland

EXP MLB DEBUT: 2017 | H/W: 6-5 200 | FUT: #4 starter | 7C

Thrws L Age 22
2011 FA (VZ)

- 88-94 FB +++
- 74-77 CB ++
- 81-84 SL ++
- 79-82 CU +++

Year	Lev	Team	W	L	Sv	IP	K	ERA	WHIP	BF/G	OBA	H%	S%	xERA	Ctl	Dom	Cmd	hr/9	BPV
2012	Rk	AZL Indians	2	4	0	42	51	4.50	1.40	16.1	243	34	69	3.87	4.5	10.9	2.4	0.9	93
2013	A-	Mahoning Val	1	4	0	50	30	1.98	1.00	17.4	216	25	80	1.93	2.0	5.4	2.7	0.2	62
2013	A	Lake County	0	1	0	14	14	3.83	1.35	19.6	260	34	72	3.77	3.2	8.9	2.8	0.6	93
2014	A	Lake County	10	9	0	126	146	4.92	1.30	19.2	259	34	64	4.09	2.9	10.4	3.7	1.1	128
2015	A+	Lynchburg	8	10	0	125	119	4.17	1.45	21.4	268	34	72	4.27	3.7	8.6	2.3	0.8	71

Tall and athletic SP who finished 3rd in CAR in K. Deceptive delivery and arm action allow average stuff to play up, including sneaky FB. Has chance to add velocity, but delivery may not allow for it. Both SL and CB have moments, but are inconsistent. CU may be best pitch and has confidence to use in any count.

Lugo,Seth — SP — New York (N)

EXP MLB DEBUT: 2016 | H/W: 6-4 185 | FUT: #5 starter | 6B

Thrws R Age 26
2011 (34) Centenary

- 88-91 FB +++
- 74-76 CB +++
- SL ++
- CU +

Year	Lev	Team	W	L	Sv	IP	K	ERA	WHIP	BF/G	OBA	H%	S%	xERA	Ctl	Dom	Cmd	hr/9	BPV
2014	A+	St. Lucie	8	3	3	105	114	4.11	1.31	16.1	252	33	71	3.94	3.3	9.8	3.0	1.0	106
2015	AA	Binghamton	6	5	0	109	97	3.80	1.27	23.4	260	32	71	3.59	2.5	8.0	3.2	0.7	95
2015	AAA	Las Vegas	2	2	0	27	30	4.00	1.19	21.6	262	34	69	3.71	1.7	10.0	6.0	1.0	153

4-pitch RHP who has shot at becoming serviceable reliever. FB is best pitch when not overthrown. Sitting 88-91, it flashes solid arm-side bore. Straightens out reaching back for extra. Stays on top of 12-6 CB to change eye levels and elicit swings and misses. CU has come a long way. Also toying with SL.

Mader,Michael — SP — Miami

EXP MLB DEBUT: 2018 | H/W: 6-2 195 | FUT: #4 starter | 7D

Thrws L Age 22
2014 (3) Chipola JC

- 90-93 FB +++
- CB +++
- 76-79 CU ++

Year	Lev	Team	W	L	Sv	IP	K	ERA	WHIP	BF/G	OBA	H%	S%	xERA	Ctl	Dom	Cmd	hr/9	BPV
2014	A-	Batavia	1	0	0	45	28	2.00	1.04	14.5	196	22	84	2.20	3.2	5.6	1.8	0.6	32
2015	A	Greensboro	6	12	0	140	86	4.75	1.41	22.0	263	30	65	3.89	3.7	5.5	1.5	0.5	19

Strong bodied lefty put up pedestrian numbers in his full-season debut. Best offering is an avg 90-93 mph FB with some late fade and he backs it up with an above-avg power CB and a decent CU. Doesn't miss many bats and when combined with below-avg control it doesn't leave him much margin for error.

Maese,Justin — SP — Toronto

EXP MLB DEBUT: 2020 | H/W: 6-3 190 | FUT: #3 starter | 8D

Thrws R Age 19
2015 (3) HS (TX)

Velo	Pitch	Grade
88-94	FB	+++
83-87	SL	+++
81-82	CU	+

Year	Lev	Team	W	L	Sv	IP	K	ERA	WHIP	BF/G	OBA	H%	S%	xERA	Ctl	Dom	Cmd	hr/9	BPV
2015	Rk	GCL Blue Jays	5	0	0	35	19	1.02	1.08	17.2	244	29	89	2.32	1.5	4.9	3.2	0.0	64

Tall, slender SP who had promising pro debut with improving control and command. Has exemplary arm speed for pitch movement and velocity. Locates FB low in zone to keep ball on ground and can counter with hard SL that serves as wipeout pitch. Has tendency to rush delivery and aim ball. Needs to repeat arm speed on CU.

Mahle,Greg — RP — Los Angeles (A)

EXP MLB DEBUT: 2016 | H/W: 6-2 225 | FUT: Setup reliever | 6A

Thrws L Age 22
2014 (15) UC-Santa Barbara

Velo	Pitch	Grade
86-93	FB	++
76-80	SL	++
78-80	CB	+++
	CU	+++

Year	Lev	Team	W	L	Sv	IP	K	ERA	WHIP	BF/G	OBA	H%	S%	xERA	Ctl	Dom	Cmd	hr/9	BPV
2014	NCAA	UC Santa Barbara	6	5	1	70	42	2.70	1.26	8.9	251	29	77	2.97	2.8	5.4	1.9	0.1	39
2014	Rk	Orem	1	1	1	8	11	0.00	1.00	6.1	181	30	100	1.29	3.4	12.4	3.7	0.0	150
2014	A	Burlington	0	1	1	29	38	3.40	1.10	6.3	196	30	68	2.00	3.7	11.8	3.2	0.3	129
2015	A+	Inland Empire	0	1	9	22	31	3.65	1.31	4.4	293	44	71	3.89	1.2	12.6	10.3	0.4	211
2015	AA	Arkansas	3	3	16	35	36	3.08	1.28	4.6	256	34	75	3.18	2.8	9.2	3.3	0.3	108

Intriguing RP who varies speeds and arm angles to fool hitters. Delivery is unorthodox, but gets job done from either sidearm or high 3/4, depending on pitch. Changes speeds on sinker and gets Ks more on deception than stuff. Finished 3rd in TL in saves, but will likely serve as setup RP at peak. CU is best pitch.

Mahle,Tyler — SP — Cincinnati

EXP MLB DEBUT: 2017 | H/W: 6-4 200 | FUT: #3 starter | 8D

Thrws R Age 21
2013 (7) HS (CA)

Velo	Pitch	Grade
89-91	FB	+++
72-75	CB	+++
81-83	SL	++
81-84	CU	+++

Year	Lev	Team	W	L	Sv	IP	K	ERA	WHIP	BF/G	OBA	H%	S%	xERA	Ctl	Dom	Cmd	hr/9	BPV
2013	Rk	AZL Reds	1	3	0	34	30	2.38	1.17	11.3	250	33	78	2.60	2.1	7.9	3.8	0.0	104
2014	Rk	Billings	5	4	0	76	71	3.90	1.25	20.7	271	34	69	3.63	1.8	8.4	4.7	0.6	121
2015	A	Dayton	13	8	0	152	135	2.43	1.12	22.2	253	32	79	2.89	1.5	8.0	5.4	0.4	122

Command-and-control RHP, made strides with secondary pitches to become more than an org arm in 2015. Walked 25 batters in 152 innings. Low 90s FB is average offering that plays up due to plus command. Changes eye levels better than most. Rarely used in '14, a potentially plus 12-6 CB with solid depth & bend became out pitch.

Manaea,Sean — SP — Oakland

EXP MLB DEBUT: 2016 | H/W: 6-5 235 | FUT: #3 starter | 8B

Thrws L Age 24
2013 (1) Indiana St

Velo	Pitch	Grade
88-95	FB	++++
82-85	SL	+++
84-87	CU	++

Year	Lev	Team	W	L	Sv	IP	K	ERA	WHIP	BF/G	OBA	H%	S%	xERA	Ctl	Dom	Cmd	hr/9	BPV
2013	NCAA	Indiana St	5	4	0	73	93	1.48	1.04	21.7	192	29	88	1.86	3.3	11.5	3.4	0.4	134
2014	A+	Wilmington	7	8	0	121	146	3.12	1.29	19.9	230	33	75	2.95	4.0	10.8	2.7	0.4	105
2015	A+	Wilmington	1	0	0	19	22	3.75	1.35	20.0	289	41	69	3.58	1.9	10.3	5.5	0.0	153
2015	AA	Midland	6	0	0	42	51	1.92	1.16	24.0	222	31	87	2.79	3.2	10.9	3.4	0.6	127
2015	AA	NW Arkansas	0	1	0	7	11	5.14	2.14	17.4	313	48	79	7.11	7.7	14.1	1.8	1.3	64

Strongly-built SP who started in June and dominated when healthy. Lively FB is plus pitch and thrown on downhill plane. Can be tough to elevate when he repeats delivery. SL has potential to be 2nd plus pitch and only needs consistency. Has trouble commanding secondary pitches, including fringy CU. Has high ceiling and floor.

Mantiply,Joe — RP — Detroit

EXP MLB DEBUT: 2016 | H/W: 6-4 215 | FUT: Setup reliever | 6B

Thrws L Age 25
2013 (27) Virginia Tech

Velo	Pitch	Grade
88-92	FB	+++
79-82	SL	++
	CU	+++

Year	Lev	Team	W	L	Sv	IP	K	ERA	WHIP	BF/G	OBA	H%	S%	xERA	Ctl	Dom	Cmd	hr/9	BPV
2013	A-	Connecticut	0	1	0	35	30	2.05	1.17	10.8	238	30	85	2.92	2.6	7.7	3.0	0.5	87
2014	A	West Michigan	6	3	8	71	76	2.41	1.07	7.3	221	31	77	2.19	2.4	9.6	4.0	0.3	126
2014	AA	Erie	0	0	1	10	10	3.53	1.47	5.5	294	37	79	4.80	2.6	8.8	3.3	0.9	105
2015	AA	Erie	2	2	2	53	44	2.54	1.15	6.6	247	30	81	3.14	2.0	7.5	3.7	0.7	97
2015	AAA	Toledo	2	0	1	10	7	0.90	0.70	5.0	175	22	86	0.52	0.9	6.3	7.0	0.0	107

Deceptive RP who is on fast track since conversion to pen in '14. Possesses above average control and ability to keep ball on ground. Retires LHH by pitching inside and showing ability to cut and sink FB. Fringy SL can be average pitch, but mostly uses FB to get ahead. Not enough stuff to be high-leverage guy and may be situational RP.

Marquez,German — SP — Tampa Bay

EXP MLB DEBUT: 2018 | H/W: 6-1 184 | FUT: #4 starter | 7C

Thrws R Age 21
2011 FA (VZ)

Velo	Pitch	Grade
91-94	FB	+++
75-79	CB	+++
82-85	CU	+++

Year	Lev	Team	W	L	Sv	IP	K	ERA	WHIP	BF/G	OBA	H%	S%	xERA	Ctl	Dom	Cmd	hr/9	BPV
2013	Rk	Princeton	2	5	0	53	38	4.07	1.24	18.0	235	28	66	2.92	3.4	6.4	1.9	0.3	42
2014	A	Bowling Green	5	7	0	98	95	3.21	1.14	17.7	231	30	72	2.70	2.7	8.7	3.3	0.5	103
2015	A+	Charlotte	7	13	0	139	104	3.56	1.27	21.8	273	33	71	3.53	1.9	6.7	3.6	0.4	89

Stocky SP who throws with easy arm action and showed revised delivery. FB added a few ticks and still shows late life. Mixes average pitch mix well and often shows above average CB as K pitch. K rate declined and also devolved into flyball pitcher. Needs better CU against LHH. Erratic control could limit role as SP and may move to bullpen.

Marshall,Mac — SP — San Francisco

EXP MLB DEBUT: 2018 | H/W: 6-0 181 | FUT: #4 starter | 8E

Thrws L Age 20
2015 (4) Chipola

Velo	Pitch	Grade
88-91	FB	+++
80-82	SL	+++
78-81	CU	++++

Year	Lev	Team	W	L	Sv	IP	K	ERA	WHIP	BF/G	OBA	H%	S%	xERA	Ctl	Dom	Cmd	hr/9	BPV
2015	Rk	Azl Giants	0	0	0	7	11	2.57	1.43	7.4	202	36	80	2.59	6.4	14.1	2.2	0.0	99
2015	A-	Salem-Kaizer	0	0	1	13	18	6.82	2.12	13.0	326	47	67	6.71	6.8	12.3	1.8	0.7	55

Lean, athletic LH lacks velocity and ideal SP frame, but has pitchability skills and three solid offerings. FB jogs in at 88-91 mph from high 3/4 slot; repeats arm spd on plus CU with fade and nice velo separation; SL/CB mixture project as average. Struggles to maintain velo late in starts and has checkered injury past. Chance to be solid, back-end SP.

Marte,Junior — SP — Chicago (N)

EXP MLB DEBUT: 2020 | H/W: 6-0 170 | FUT: #3 starter | 7D

Thrws R Age 20
2013 FA (DR)

Velo	Pitch	Grade
	FB	+++
	CB	++
	CU	++

Year	Lev	Team	W	L	Sv	IP	K	ERA	WHIP	BF/G	OBA	H%	S%	xERA	Ctl	Dom	Cmd	hr/9	BPV
2015	Rk	Azl Cubs	0	0	0	3	6	3.00	1.67	6.7	262	55	80	3.91	6.0	18.0	3.0	0.0	180

Short, strong-armed Dominican hurler. Was lights out in the DSL, going 4-1 with a 1.29 ERA, walking just 16 while striking out 68 in 55.2 IP. Marte is a bit older than most Dominican prospects, but with interesting upside. Should make his state-side debut in 2016.

Martes,Francis — SP — Houston

EXP MLB DEBUT: 2017 | H/W: 6-1 225 | FUT: #3 starter | 8C

Thrws R Age 20
2012 FA (DR)

Velo	Pitch	Grade
93-95	FB	+++
82-84	CB	++++
80-82	CU	+

Year	Lev	Team	W	L	Sv	IP	K	ERA	WHIP	BF/G	OBA	H%	S%	xERA	Ctl	Dom	Cmd	hr/9	BPV
2014	Rk	GCL Astros	1	1	0	11	12	0.82	0.73	9.8	139	21	88	0.17	2.5	9.8	4.0	0.0	128
2014	Rk	GCL Marlins	2	2	0	33	33	5.18	1.48	17.8	238	33	61	3.22	5.5	9.0	1.7	0.0	33
2015	A	Quad Cities	3	2	2	52	45	1.04	0.88	19.3	184	24	89	1.23	2.3	7.8	3.5	0.2	97
2015	A+	Lancaster	4	1	0	35	37	2.31	1.11	23.0	239	33	79	2.54	2.1	9.5	4.6	0.3	134
2015	AA	Corpus Christi	1	0	0	14	16	5.07	1.83	22.0	322	41	75	6.49	4.4	10.1	2.3	1.3	81

Strong, durable SP who pitched well in 3 levels in first full season as pro. FB features electric life, though can be tough to command due to late action. Hard CB is plus pitch and ideal complement to quick FB. CU has its moments, but far from average pitch. Doesn't allow many HR and repeats delivery consistently. Will need CU to battle LHH.

Martin,Brett — SP — Texas

EXP MLB DEBUT: 2018 | H/W: 6-4 190 | FUT: #3 starter | 8E

Thrws L Age 20
2014 (4) Walters St CC

Velo	Pitch	Grade
89-93	FB	+++
74-78	CB	+++
	CU	++

Year	Lev	Team	W	L	Sv	IP	K	ERA	WHIP	BF/G	OBA	H%	S%	xERA	Ctl	Dom	Cmd	hr/9	BPV
2014	Rk	Azl Rangers	1	4	1	35	39	5.40	1.37	9.8	267	36	60	4.04	3.1	10.0	3.3	0.8	115
2015	A	Hickory	5	6	0	95	72	3.50	1.24	19.3	255	30	72	3.39	2.5	6.8	2.8	0.6	74

Long, athletic SP who thrives with deceptive delivery and pitch movement. Induces groundballs by throwing with downward angle to plate. FB is average pitch, but could grow into plus offering. CB shows nice bending action and is weapon against RHP, but could use more power. Sinking CU has been tough to command, but has potential.

Martinez,Jonathan — SP — Chicago (N)

EXP MLB DEBUT: 2018 | H/W: 6-1 200 | FUT: #4 starter | 7D

Thrws R Age 21
2011 FA (VZ)

Velo	Pitch	Grade
90-94	FB	+++
	SL	++
	CU	++

Year	Lev	Team	W	L	Sv	IP	K	ERA	WHIP	BF/G	OBA	H%	S%	xERA	Ctl	Dom	Cmd	hr/9	BPV
2013	Rk	Ogden	3	1	0	32	11	5.03	1.34	22.3	300	32	61	4.31	1.1	3.1	2.8	0.6	43
2013	A	Great Lakes	3	4	0	66	42	3.53	1.22	17.8	258	30	71	3.25	2.2	5.7	2.6	0.4	62
2014	A	Great Lakes	7	5	0	106	91	3.48	1.22	22.5	269	33	73	3.61	1.6	7.7	4.8	0.7	113
2014	A	Kane County	4	0	0	23	15	2.34	1.04	17.8	252	29	82	3.05	0.8	5.8	7.5	0.8	102
2015	A+	Myrtle Beach	9	2	0	116	66	2.56	0.94	19.0	200	22	77	2.15	2.1	5.1	2.4	0.8	54

Short RHP from Venezuela has a nice three-pitch mix. FB sits at 90-94, but lacks plus movement. Throws his SL for strikes, but lack of movement makes the pitch avg at best. CU is another solid-avg offering. Throws tons of strikes, but a drop in Dom limits long-term potential.

Martinez, Juancito — RP — Miami

EXP MLB DEBUT: 2016 | H/W: 6-1 170 | FUT: Setup reliever | 6B
Thrws R | Age 26 | 2008 FA (DR)

95-98	FB	++++
	SL	++

Year	Lev	Team	W	L	Sv	IP	K	ERA	WHIP	BF/G	OBA	H%	S%	xERA	Ctl	Dom	Cmd	hr/9	BPV
2014	A-	Batavia	2	1	6	28	33	2.55	1.21	5.4	224	33	76	2.33	3.5	10.5	3.0	0.0	113
2015	A+	Jupiter	2	1	6	22	24	1.62	0.86	4.5	172	24	83	1.23	2.4	9.7	4.0	0.4	127
2015	AA	Jacksonville	2	2	7	38	18	5.42	1.41	5.1	182	19	61	3.08	7.1	4.2	0.6	0.7	-97

Short RP from the D.R. was lights-out at High-A, but struggled when moved up. A bit of a late bloomer and converted to pitching in '14. Best offering is a plus upper-90s heater that he uses to great effect. Mostly a one-trick pony and hitters at Double-A refused to chase the FB. Ctl is an issue and he walked 30 in 38 IP at AA.

Matuella, Michael — SP — Texas

EXP MLB DEBUT: 2018 | H/W: 6-6 220 | FUT: #1 starter | 9E
Thrws R | Age 21 | 2015 (3) Duke

91-96	FB	++++
77-79	CB	+++
84-85	SL	+++
83-86	CU	++

Year	Lev	Team	W	L	Sv	IP	K	ERA	WHIP	BF/G	OBA	H%	S%	xERA	Ctl	Dom	Cmd	hr/9	BPV
2015		*Did not pitch; injured*																	

Tall, angular SP who had talent to be #1 pick, but was sidelined by TJ surgery in April. Chronic back condition also dropped him in draft. When healthy, has electric stuff led by dazzling, darting FB and two breaking balls. Has tough angle to plate and weak contact ensues. Needs to prove health, but has frontline stuff.

Matz, Steven — SP — New York (N)

EXP MLB DEBUT: 2015 | H/W: 6-2 200 | FUT: #2 starter | 9B
Thrws L | Age 24 | 2009 (2) HS (NY)

93-96	FB	++++
76-78	CB	++++
86-88	SL	+++
83-85	CU	+++

Year	Lev	Team	W	L	Sv	IP	K	ERA	WHIP	BF/G	OBA	H%	S%	xERA	Ctl	Dom	Cmd	hr/9	BPV
2014	AA	Binghamton	6	5	0	71		2.28	1.13	23.4	248	32	81	2.80	1.8	8.7	4.9	0.4	127
2015	A+	St. Lucie	0	0	0	3	3	5.63	2.50	8.5	437	54	75	9.25	2.8	8.4	3.0	0.0	94
2015	AA	Binghamton	1	0	0	11	10	0.00	0.36	17.7	60	9	100		1.6	8.1	5.0	0.0	120
2015	AAA	Las Vegas	7	4	0	90	94	2.20	1.11	23.6	214	28	83	2.53	3.1	9.4	3.0	0.6	103
2015	MLB	NY Mets	4	0	0	35	34	2.30	1.25	23.9	255	31	88	3.82	2.6	8.7	3.4	1.0	105

Four-pitch LHP who started game 4 of the World Series. FB & CB best pitches. Keeps FB low in zone, setting up big 12-6 CB as out pitch. CU has become solid-average offering. Complements FB with better sink and bore. Added SL late in the year that flashed solid-average in limited exposure.

Mazzoni, Cory — RP — San Diego

EXP MLB DEBUT: 2015 | H/W: 6-1 200 | FUT: Setup reliever | 7C
Thrws R | Age 26 | 2011 (2) North Carolina St

92-96	FB	++++
83-86	SL	+++
	SP	++

Year	Lev	Team	W	L	Sv	IP	K	ERA	WHIP	BF/G	OBA	H%	S%	xERA	Ctl	Dom	Cmd	hr/9	BPV
2014	A+	St. Lucie	0	0	0	9	9	5.00	1.56	19.7	302	40	64	4.31	3.0	9.0	3.0	0.0	99
2014	AA	Binghamton	2	0	0	12	10	4.50	1.17	23.9	228	30	57	2.31	3.0	7.5	2.5	0.0	72
2014	AAA	Las Vegas	5	1	0	52	49	4.67	1.27	23.6	269	33	65	4.08	2.1	8.5	4.1	1.0	115
2015	AAA	El Paso	1	3	5	34	46	3.97	1.09	5.1	207	33	59	1.80	3.2	12.2	3.8	0.0	151
2015	MLB	San Diego	0	0	0	8	8	21.95	3.41	6.4	499	58	31	15.26	5.5	8.8	1.6	2.2	28

Strong pitcher who was converted to RP in '15 to great results. Peppers zone with quality strikes, led by plus FB that he locates well. Registers Ks and induces groundballs with power arsenal and shows feel for third pitch. Arm action and effort in delivery will likely keep him in pen, but has stuff to miss bats. Only needs to stay healthy.

McCurry, Brendan — RP — Houston

EXP MLB DEBUT: 2016 | H/W: 5-10 165 | FUT: Setup reliever | 7E
Thrws R | Age 24 | 2014 (22) Oklahoma St

90-93	FB	+++
77-79	CB	+++
80-82	SL	+++
	CU	++

Year	Lev	Team	W	L	Sv	IP	K	ERA	WHIP	BF/G	OBA	H%	S%	xERA	Ctl	Dom	Cmd	hr/9	BPV
2014	Rk	Azl Athletics	0	0	0	1	2	0.00	1.82	5.1	392	64	100	6.48	0.0	16.4		0.0	313
2014	A	Beloit	2	0	2	26	34	0.34	0.57	5.9	140	22	100	0.11	1.0	11.7	11.3	0.0	201
2014	A+	Stockton	0	0	0	1	1	0.00	0.00	2.8	0	0			0.0	9.0		0.0	180
2015	A+	Stockton	1	2	21	46	56	1.95	0.89	4.8	187	27	82	1.64	2.1	10.9	5.1	0.6	157
2015	AA	Midland	0	1	6	16	26	1.67	0.93	4.3	165	29	86	1.42	3.3	14.4	4.3	0.6	188

Short sinkerballer who served as closer in '15. Posted great stats, but stuff doesn't project well to majors. Establishes plate early with average sinking FB and mixes in two breaking balls with varying slots. Deception keeps hitters off guard which allows CB to play up. Has enough repertoire for pen with outside shot at late innings.

McGowin, Kyle — SP — Los Angeles (A)

EXP MLB DEBUT: 2016 | H/W: 6-3 200 | FUT: #4 starter | 7D
Thrws R | Age 24 | 2013 (5) Savannah St

86-93	FB	+++
82-84	SL	+++
78-80	CU	++

Year	Lev	Team	W	L	Sv	IP	K	ERA	WHIP	BF/G	OBA	H%	S%	xERA	Ctl	Dom	Cmd	hr/9	BPV
2013	Rk	Orem	1	1	0	14	12	6.38	1.21	6.3	232	26	47	3.65	3.2	7.7	2.4	1.3	70
2014	Rk	Azl Angels	0	0	0	2	2	0.00	1.50	8.6	262	35	100	3.58	4.5	9.0	2.0	0.0	59
2014	A+	Inland Empire	1	5	0	58	48	2.94	1.15	23.1	237	29	76	2.97	2.5	7.4	3.0	0.6	85
2014	AA	Arkansas	0	1	0	5	3	5.40	1.20	20.1	299	31	60	5.08	0.0	5.4		1.8	115
2015	AA	Arkansas	9	9	0	154	125	4.38	1.29	23.4	254	30	68	3.83	2.9	7.3	2.5	0.9	71

Durable SP who led TL in K. Doesn't own plus offering in arsenal, but sequences well and has sufficient movement to all pitches. Uses lively FB to get ahead in count and mixes in good SL and average CU. Repeats smooth delivery and throws consistent strikes, though can be hit hard. Doesn't have enough velocity to miss up in zone.

McKenzie, Triston — SP — Cleveland

EXP MLB DEBUT: 2020 | H/W: 6-5 165 | FUT: #2 starter | 9E
Thrws R | Age 18 | 2015 (1) HS (FL)

87-92	FB	++
75-78	CB	+++
	CU	+++

Year	Lev	Team	W	L	Sv	IP	K	ERA	WHIP	BF/G	OBA	H%	S%	xERA	Ctl	Dom	Cmd	hr/9	BPV
2015	Rk	AZL Indians	1	1	0	12	17	0.75	0.58	10.2	106	19	86		2.3	12.8	5.7	0.0	187

Very projectable hurler who has very high ceiling. Will take long time to develop, but has tools to be good. Below average velocity now, but secondary pitches show promise, particularly CB. Shows feel for changing speeds and repeats arm speed on CU. Ultimate key will be whether he can add strength and power.

McWilliams, Sam — SP — Arizona

EXP MLB DEBUT: 2019 | H/W: 6-7 190 | FUT: #3 starter | 7D
Thrws R | Age 20 | 2014 (8) HS (TN)

90-92	FB	+++
	CB	++
	CU	+++
	SL	++

Year	Lev	Team	W	L	Sv	IP	K	ERA	WHIP	BF/G	OBA	H%	S%	xERA	Ctl	Dom	Cmd	hr/9	BPV
2014	Rk	GCL Phillies	2	3	0	25	10	5.40	1.36	11.6	284	31	58	3.93	2.2	3.6	1.7	0.4	24
2015	Rk	GCL Phillies	0	2	0	33	21	3.27	1.03	18.2	238	28	67	2.36	1.4	5.7	4.2	0.3	84

Made big strikes in his second go-round of rookie ball with a cleaner delivery that resulted in improved fastball velocity. Still some room to grow; currently a groundballer who gets good downhill plane due to his size. Change-up is best offspeed pitch; both curve and slider are works in progress. Still a long way off, but intriguing raw elements.

Medeiros, Kodi — SP — Milwaukee

EXP MLB DEBUT: 2019 | H/W: 6-2 180 | FUT: #2 starter | 9D
Thrws L | Age 19 | 2014 (1) HS (HI)

90-93	FB	++++
78-82	SL	++++
	CU	++

Year	Lev	Team	W	L	Sv	IP	K	ERA	WHIP	BF/G	OBA	H%	S%	xERA	Ctl	Dom	Cmd	hr/9	BPV
2014	Rk	Azl Brewers	0	2	1	17	26	7.33	2.15	9.5	331	49	66	7.20	6.8	13.6	2.0	1.0	79
2015	A	Wisconsin	4	5	1	93	94	4.45	1.28	15.3	231	32	61	2.61	3.9	9.1	2.4	0.0	77

Former 12th overall pick spent year in mixed SP/RP roles and excelled in both. Racks up ground balls with plus FB velo and life, misses bats with elite sweeping SL. Gets deception from low 3/4 slot with easy delivery and arm action. Athleticism should allow for CU development and command gains. Smallish frame, but intriguing upside.

Medina, Adonis — SP — Philadelphia

EXP MLB DEBUT: 2020 | H/W: 6-1 185 | FUT: #2 starter | 9E
Thrws R | Age 19 | 2014 FA (DR)

90-94	FB	+++
77-79	CB	++
	CU	++

Year	Lev	Team	W	L	Sv	IP	K	ERA	WHIP	BF/G	OBA	H%	S%	xERA	Ctl	Dom	Cmd	hr/9	BPV
2015	Rk	GCL Phillies	3	2	0	45	35	2.99	1.20	18.1	248	31	74	2.84	2.4	7.0	2.9	0.2	79

As a teenager in GCL, his FB jumped from 89-90 upon signing in 2014 to 91-94 as he physically matured as it quickly became his best pitch. In addition, shows a feel for two secondaries that both have average-to-plus potential: a curveball and a deceptive change-up. Not the prototypical frame, but advanced offerings at his age oozes upside.

Medina, Javier — SP — Colorado

EXP MLB DEBUT: 2019 | H/W: 6-2 190 | FUT: #4 starter | 7D
Thrws R | Age 19 | 2015 (3) HS (AZ)

88-92	FB	+++
	CB	++
	CU	

Year	Lev	Team	W	L	Sv	IP	K	ERA	WHIP	BF/G	OBA	H%	S%	xERA	Ctl	Dom	Cmd	hr/9	BPV
2015	Rk	Grand Junction	1	3	0	34	30	6.86	1.79	17.5	347	40	65	7.37	2.6	7.9	3.0	1.8	89

Rockies 3rd round pick in 2015 is relatively raw after not being able to pitch during his senior year in HS. Flashes a good low-90s FB, which he locates well. Also has a decent feel for a CB and CU. The rust showed in his debut and hitters in the PIO lit him up. Look for better results in 2016.

Meisner,Casey — SP — Oakland

EXP MLB DEBUT: 2017 | H/W: 6-7 190 | FUT: #4 starter | **7D**

Thrws R Age 20
2013 (3) HS (TX)

Velo	Pitch	Grade
89-94	FB	+++
76-79	CB	+++
82-83	CU	++

Year	Lev	Team	W	L	Sv	IP	K	ERA	WHIP	BF/G	OBA	H%	S%	xERA	Ctl	Dom	Cmd	hr/9	BPV
2013	Rk	GCL Mets	1	3	0	35	28	3.08	1.17	14.0	238	30	71	2.45	2.6	7.2	2.8	0.0	78
2014	A-	Brooklyn	5	3	0	62	67	3.77	1.37	20.0	277	37	73	3.99	2.6	9.7	3.7	0.6	122
2015	A	Savannah	7	2	0	76	66	2.13	1.03	24.4	216	26	83	2.47	2.3	7.8	3.5	0.7	98
2015	A+	St. Lucie	3	2	0	35	23	2.83	1.40	24.6	262	29	84	4.32	3.6	5.9	1.6	1.0	27
2015	A+	Stockton	3	1	0	32	24	2.80	1.06	17.8	230	28	73	2.33	2.0	6.7	3.4	0.3	86

Long, lean SP who was excellent all year, even after trade from NYM. Brings difficult angle to plate, throwing on downhill plane. No pitch stands out, but will need better CU to round out arsenal. Spots FB well low in strike zone and can use CB has K pitch or for strikes. Induces high amount of groundballs with moderate K rate potential.

Mejia,Adalberto — SP — San Francisco

EXP MLB DEBUT: 2016 | H/W: 6-3 195 | FUT: #4 starter | **8C**

Thrws L Age 22
2011 FA (DR)

Velo	Pitch	Grade
91-94	FB	++++
81-84	SL	+++
82-85	CU	+++

Year	Lev	Team	W	L	Sv	IP	K	ERA	WHIP	BF/G	OBA	H%	S%	xERA	Ctl	Dom	Cmd	hr/9	BPV
2012	A	Augusta	10	7	0	106	79	3.98	1.35	14.7	289	35	69	3.92	1.8	6.7	3.8	0.3	90
2013	A+	San Jose	7	4	0	87	89	3.31	1.13	21.5	234	29	76	3.34	2.4	9.2	3.9	1.1	119
2013	AAA	Fresno	0	0	0	5	2	3.60	1.40	21.1	262	20	100	6.76	3.6	3.6	1.0	3.6	-14
2014	AA	Richmond	7	9	0	108	82	4.67	1.39	20.7	281	33	67	4.29	2.6	6.8	2.6	0.8	71
2015	AA	Richmond	5	2	0	51	38	2.47	1.10	16.7	209	25	78	2.23	3.2	6.7	2.1	0.4	53

LH served 50-game suspension to start '15, pitched in AFL to make up for lost time. Added muscle helped FB velo, which now sits 91-94 mph with arm-side run. Maintains arm speed for effective CU vs. RHH; SL has nice bite; will mix in fringy CB at times. Strike-thrower with good feel, but command and delivery require more consistency.

Mella,Keury — SP — Cincinnati

EXP MLB DEBUT: 2017 | H/W: 6-2 200 | FUT: #3 starter | **8C**

Thrws R Age 22
2011 FA (DR)

Velo	Pitch	Grade
93-95	FB	++++
76-79	CB	+++
79-81	CU	++

Year	Lev	Team	W	L	Sv	IP	K	ERA	WHIP	BF/G	OBA	H%	S%	xERA	Ctl	Dom	Cmd	hr/9	BPV
2013	Rk	Azl Giants	3	2	0	36		2.25	1.25	14.7	251	36	80	2.79	2.8	10.3	3.7	0.0	128
2014	A-	Salem-Kaizer	1	1	0	19	20	1.88	1.15	12.7	228	32	82	2.24	2.8	9.4	3.3	0.0	111
2014	A	Augusta	3	3	0	66	63	3.95	1.24	22.4	270	36	65	3.17	1.8	8.6	4.8	0.1	125
2015	A+	Daytona	3	1	0	21	23	2.99	1.23	21.4	156	20	79	2.42	6.4	9.8	1.5	0.9	22
2015	A+	San Jose	5	3	0	81	83	3.33	1.13	20.1	224	29	71	2.67	2.9	9.2	3.2	0.6	106

Acquired by CIN mid-season in Leake trade. Changes eye levels with mid-90s FB. At its best, takes advantage of heavy sink low in the zone. Struggles with release point on hard CB, which can be slurvy. Command is an issue due to cross-fire delivery. While creating deception, delivery forces arm to work harder, increasing injury risk.

Melotakis,Mason — RP — Minnesota

EXP MLB DEBUT: 2017 | H/W: 6-2 205 | FUT: Setup reliever | **6B**

Thrws L Age 24
2012 (2) Northwestern St

Velo	Pitch	Grade
92-95	FB	+++
82-85	CB	+++
80-83	CU	+

Year	Lev	Team	W	L	Sv	IP	K	ERA	WHIP	BF/G	OBA	H%	S%	xERA	Ctl	Dom	Cmd	hr/9	BPV
2012	Rk	Elizabethton	1	1	0	6	10	1.45	0.65	3.1	103	21	75		2.9	14.5	5.0	0.0	201
2012	A	Beloit	3	1	1	17	24	2.11	1.11	5.2	237	33	94	3.72	2.1	12.6	6.0	1.6	189
2013	A	Cedar Rapids	11	4	1	111	84	3.16	1.31	19.1	253	30	76	3.45	3.2	6.8	2.2	0.5	55
2014	A+	Fort Myers	3	1	1	47	45	3.45	1.57	8.3	274	35	79	4.48	4.6	8.6	1.9	0.6	49
2014	AA	New Britain	1	0	2	16	17	2.25	1.25	5.0	274	38	80	3.11	1.7	9.6	5.7	0.0	145

Stocky pitcher who missed season after TJ surgery in October '14. Has been SP and RP as pro and likely to stay in pen due to sub-par CU. Short arm action gives him deception and has above average velocity when healthy. Uses high 3/4 slot that allows effective CB to play up. Has tendency to rush delivery which negatively impacts command.

Mendez,Yohander — SP — Texas

EXP MLB DEBUT: 2018 | H/W: 6-4 178 | FUT: #3 starter | **8D**

Thrws L Age 21
2011 FA (VZ)

Velo	Pitch	Grade
88-93	FB	+++
80-82	CB	++
82-84	CU	++++

Year	Lev	Team	W	L	Sv	IP	K	ERA	WHIP	BF/G	OBA	H%	S%	xERA	Ctl	Dom	Cmd	hr/9	BPV
2013	A-	Spokane	1	2	0	33	23	3.81	1.45	17.7	249	28	77	4.33	4.6	6.3	1.4	1.1	6
2014	Rk	Azl Rangers	0	1	0	5	7	5.19	1.92	8.2	353	51	70	6.04	3.5	12.1	3.5	0.0	143
2014	A	Hickory	3	0	0	31	28	2.32	0.90	16.5	229	27	83	2.74	0.6	8.1	14.0	1.2	149
2015	A	Hickory	3	3	3	66	74	2.45	1.09	12.3	234	33	77	2.42	2.0	10.1	4.9	0.3	144

Lean, projectable SP who began season in May and was treated cautiously. Has high upside predicated on lively FB and advanced, plus CU. Keeps LHH at bay by moving ball all around zone and has stuff to miss bats. Keeps ball on ground effectively as he pitches on downward angle to plate. Has chance to add more velocity.

Mengden,Daniel — SP — Oakland

EXP MLB DEBUT: 2017 | H/W: 6-2 190 | FUT: #4 starter | **7D**

Thrws R Age 23
2014 (4) Texas A&M

Velo	Pitch	Grade
88-94	FB	+++
82-84	SL	++
74-79	CB	++
82-84	CU	+++

Year	Lev	Team	W	L	Sv	IP	K	ERA	WHIP	BF/G	OBA	H%	S%	xERA	Ctl	Dom	Cmd	hr/9	BPV
2014	Rk	GCL Astros	0	0	0	6	11	4.43	0.66	5.3	189	39	25	0.46	0.0	16.2		0.0	310
2014	A-	Tri City	0	0	0	4	6	2.14	1.43	8.9	297	46	83	3.86	2.1	12.9	6.0	0.0	192
2015	A	Quad Cities	4	1	0	38	36	1.18	0.99	18.2	218	29	89	1.96	1.9	8.5	4.5	0.2	120
2015	A+	Lancaster	2	1	1	49	48	5.30	1.57	21.6	298	38	66	4.96	3.3	8.8	2.7	0.7	87
2015	A+	Stockton	4	2	0	42	41	4.28	1.16	21.0	247	30	67	3.74	2.1	8.8	4.1	1.3	118

Durable SP who was acquired from HOU in July and offers value with deceptive delivery. May not have knockout pitch, but sequences and moves ball around plate. Solid average CU may be best offering as it has depth. Commands FB in lower half of strike zone to induce groundballs. Needs to enhance one of CB or SL as both tend to flatten.

Merritt,Ryan — SP — Cleveland

EXP MLB DEBUT: 2016 | H/W: 6-0 170 | FUT: #5 starter | **6B**

Thrws L Age 24
2011 (16) McLennan CC

Velo	Pitch	Grade
87-91	FB	+++
74-78	CB	++
79-82	CU	++

Year	Lev	Team	W	L	Sv	IP	K	ERA	WHIP	BF/G	OBA	H%	S%	xERA	Ctl	Dom	Cmd	hr/9	BPV
2013	A	Lake County	6	9	0	126	91	3.43	1.27	21.5	285	33	75	4.02	1.3	6.5	5.1	0.7	100
2013	A+	Carolina	0	0	0	9	6	5.00	0.89	16.7	216	24	43	2.42	1.0	6.0	6.0	1.0	99
2014	A+	Carolina	13	3	0	160	127	2.59	0.96	24.2	221	26	76	2.32	1.4	7.1	5.1	0.7	109
2015	AA	Akron	10	7	0	141	89	3.51	1.14	25.4	267	31	69	3.26	1.0	5.7	5.6	0.5	93
2015	AAA	Columbus	2	0	0	30	16	4.20	1.47	25.7	310	35	70	4.52	1.8	4.8	2.7	0.3	56

Athletic, low-ceiling SP who thrives on pinpoint control and ability to change speeds. None of pitches project to anything more than average, but mixes well and gets ample movement. Subject to big innings due to oppBA, but won't walk batters. Repeats clean delivery and uses same arm speed on all pitches.

Meyer,Alex — RP — Minnesota

EXP MLB DEBUT: 2015 | H/W: 6-9 225 | FUT: #3 starter / Closer | **8D**

Thrws R Age 26
2011 (1) Kentucky

Velo	Pitch	Grade
94-98	FB	++++
83-87	CB	++++
81-83	CU	++

Year	Lev	Team	W	L	Sv	IP	K	ERA	WHIP	BF/G	OBA	H%	S%	xERA	Ctl	Dom	Cmd	hr/9	BPV
2013	Rk	GCL Twins	0	0	0	8	16	1.11	1.23	10.9	235	51	90	2.46	3.3	17.8	5.3	0.0	248
2013	AA	New Britain	4	3	0	70	84	3.21	1.27	22.0	233	33	74	2.96	3.7	10.8	2.9	0.4	112
2014	AAA	Rochester	7	7	0	130	153	3.53	1.38	20.3	240	33	76	3.63	4.4	10.6	2.4	0.7	89
2015	AAA	Rochester	4	5	0	92	100	4.79	1.62	10.7	280	38	69	4.50	4.7	9.8	2.1	0.4	67
2015	MLB	Minnesota	0	0	0	2	3	20.45	3.18	6.6	392	38	40	17.64	12.3	12.3	1.0	8.2	-92

Tall pitcher who was moved to RP in-season after struggling as SP. Showed makings of dominant arm in short stints with plus FB and dynamite CB. FB exhibits sink despite velocity, but has trouble repeating mechanics. Can aim ball at times, making him hittable. Erratic control may keep him in bullpen. FB/CB combo could lead to closer.

Meza,Juan — SP — Toronto

EXP MLB DEBUT: 2020 | H/W: 6-2 172 | FUT: #4 starter | **8E**

Thrws R Age 18
2014 FA (VZ)

Velo	Pitch	Grade
88-93	FB	+++
75-78	CB	++
	CU	++

Year	Lev	Team	W	L	Sv	IP	K	ERA	WHIP	BF/G	OBA	H%	S%	xERA	Ctl	Dom	Cmd	hr/9	BPV
2015	Rk	DSL Blue Jays	0	0	1	25	21	6.79	1.75	16.4	297	37	58	5.05	5.0	7.5	1.5	0.4	18
2015	Rk	GCL Blue Jays	1	0	0	5	8	10.80	2.80	7.0	299	45	62	9.02	14.4	14.4	1.0	1.8	-112

Lean, athletic SP who has projection with clean arm action. Should add velocity as he grows into frame, but has decent FB now. Has smooth delivery that he can repeat, which enhances look and feel of CU. Command of CB comes and goes and needs to throw for strikes. Has long-term upside, but will be major project.

Mills,Alec — SP — Kansas City

EXP MLB DEBUT: 2017 | H/W: 6-4 185 | FUT: #4 starter | **7C**

Thrws R Age 24
2012 (22) Tennessee-Martin

Velo	Pitch	Grade
90-95	FB	+++
79-82	CB	++
81-85	CU	+++

Year	Lev	Team	W	L	Sv	IP	K	ERA	WHIP	BF/G	OBA	H%	S%	xERA	Ctl	Dom	Cmd	hr/9	BPV
2012	Rk	Idaho Falls	1	4	3	50	50	4.66	1.49	12.7	291	36	72	5.15	3.0	9.0	2.9	1.3	97
2013	A	Lexington	2	3	6	45	47	1.60	0.82	9.1	180	25	81	1.04	1.8	9.4	5.2	0.2	138
2014	Rk	Idaho Falls	2	2	0	19	14	4.71	1.26	11.1	271	33	58	3.11	1.9	6.6	3.5	0.0	86
2014	A	Lexington	2	1	0	38	33	1.18	0.92	20.3	189	25	86	1.22	2.4	7.8	3.3	0.0	95
2015	A+	Wilmington	7	7	0	113	111	3.02	1.20	21.7	277	36	74	3.26	1.1	8.8	7.9	0.2	147

Breakout prospect who is gaining strength after TJ surgery in '13. Despite high oppBA, posted very low Ctl while K rate increased. Induces groundballs with solid-average sinker and excellent CU can miss bats. Limited HR by using height and slot to throw downhill. Can lose velocity late in games, but could be byproduct of previous surgery.

Milroy,Matt — SP — Miami

EXP MLB DEBUT: 2018 | H/W: 6-2 185 | FUT: Setup reliever | **7C**

Thrws R Age 25
2012 (11) Illinois

Velo	Pitch	Grade
91-94	FB	++++
82-85	CB	++++

Year	Lev	Team	W	L	Sv	IP	K	ERA	WHIP	BF/G	OBA	H%	S%	xERA	Ctl	Dom	Cmd	hr/9	BPV
2012	A-	Jamestown	2	3	0	35	30	4.11	1.54	17.0	239	29	75	4.12	5.9	7.7	1.3	0.8	-3
2013	A	Greensboro	0	2	0	57	59	5.52	1.68	15.1	281	36	67	5.04	5.2	9.3	1.8	0.8	45
2014	A	Greensboro	6	3	0	63	87	2.57	1.06	17.5	198	32	74	1.77	3.3	12.4	3.8	0.1	153
2014	A+	Jupiter	2	9	0	50	37	7.20	1.74	19.0	258	30	57	4.83	6.8	6.7	1.0	0.7	-47
2015	A+	Jupiter	6	2	2	61	80	3.25	1.57	7.4	236	36	79	3.66	6.3	11.8	1.9	0.3	59

Strong-armed reliever overpowers hitters with a nice one-two punch. FB tops out a 95 mph with good, late life and he backs it up with a plus mid-80s SL. K'd 80 in 61 IP, but also walked 43 and the lack of control kept him at High-A all year. Has the stuff to be an impact reliever, but it won't happen unless he learns to throw strikes.

Mitchell,Bryan — SP — New York (A)

EXP MLB DEBUT: 2014 | H/W: 6-2 200 | FUT: #4 starter | 7C

Thrws R Age 24	Year	Lev	Team	W	L	Sv	IP	K	ERA	WHIP	BF/G	OBA	H%	S%	xERA	Ctl	Dom	Cmd	hr/9	BPV
2009 (16) HS (NC)	2014	AA	Trenton	2	5	0	61	60	4.86	1.52	19.0	271	34	69	4.59	4.3	8.8	2.1	0.9	62
90-95 FB ++++	2014	AAA	Scranton/WB	4	2	0	41	34	3.71	1.48	19.7	279	33	79	4.81	3.5	7.4	2.1	1.1	57
80-84 CB +++	2014	MLB	NY Yankees	0	1	0	11	7	2.45	1.18	14.7	244	29	77	2.56	2.5	5.7	2.3	0.0	55
85-89 CT +++	2015	AAA	Scranton/WB	5	5	0	75	61	3.12	1.33	20.8	230	29	75	2.86	4.4	7.3	1.6	0.1	30
82-86 CU +	2015	MLB	NY Yankees	0	2	1	29	29	6.47	1.82	6.8	310	38	65	6.24	4.9	8.9	1.8	1.2	46

Big, strong pitcher who was SP in minors before moving to pen in NYY. Has deep repertoire to be SP, but fringy command and sub-par CU may keep him in pen. Delivery can get out of whack and has tendency to overthrow. Limits flyballs with power sinker and can get Ks with hard CB. Added CT to repertoire to give hitters different look.

Molina,Marcos — SP — New York (N)

EXP MLB DEBUT: 2018 | H/W: 6-3 188 | FUT: #3 Starter/Closer | 8D

Thrws R Age 21	Year	Lev	Team	W	L	Sv	IP	K	ERA	WHIP	BF/G	OBA	H%	S%	xERA	Ctl	Dom	Cmd	hr/9	BPV
2012 FA (DR)																				
93-95 FB ++++	2013	Rk	GCL Mets	4	3	0	53	43	4.41	1.32	20.0	272	33	66	3.76	2.4	7.3	3.1	0.5	85
85-87 SL +++	2014	A-	Brooklyn	7	3	0	76	91	1.77	0.84	23.2	177	26	79	1.07	2.1	10.8	5.1	0.2	154
84-86 CU +++	2015	Rk	GCL Mets	0	0	0	3	3	0.00	0.00	8.5	0	0			0.0	9.0		0.0	180
	2015	A+	St. Lucie	1	5	0	41	36	4.60	1.46	22.0	297	38	66	4.20	2.4	7.9	3.3	0.2	95

Hard-throwing RHP will miss 2016 season after TJS. Electric FB has touched 97 in past. Enhances sinking action by throwing at a downhill angle. SL developing into solid breaking pitch. Advanced deceptive CU keeps hitters away from sitting FB. Generates swings and misses with all 3-pitches.

Moll,Sam — RP — Colorado

EXP MLB DEBUT: 2016 | H/W: 5-10 185 | FUT: Setup reliever | 7C

Thrws L Age 24	Year	Lev	Team	W	L	Sv	IP	K	ERA	WHIP	BF/G	OBA	H%	S%	xERA	Ctl	Dom	Cmd	hr/9	BPV
2013 (3) Memphis	2013	NCAA	Memphis	9	3	0	94		2.30	1.04	24.2	199	29	76	1.62	3.1	10.1	3.3	0.0	118
94-96 FB ++++	2013	A-	Tri-City	3	1	0	30	29	1.80	1.00	11.5	191	26	80	1.43	3.0	8.7	2.9	0.0	94
CB +++	2014	A-	Tri-City	0	1	0	13	7	4.15	1.62	6.4	317	35	75	5.38	2.8	4.8	1.8	0.7	30
84-86 SL ++	2015	A+	Modesto	0	1	2	53	57	3.05	0.98	8.1	210	26	76	2.71	2.0	9.6	4.8	1.2	137
	2015	AA	New Britain	0	0	0	14	17	1.27	0.77	3.9	149	23	82	0.38	2.5	10.8	4.3	0.0	143

Lefty RP was fully recovered after an injury shortened '14. Shows good Cmd of his 94-96 mph heater. Mixes in a power CB and shelved his below average CU. Mechanics and release point need to be more consistent, but showed huge improvement and walked just 16 in 68.1 IP while striking out 74 and posting an oppBAA of .193

Montas,Frankie — SP — Los Angeles (N)

EXP MLB DEBUT: 2015 | H/W: 6-2 185 | FUT: #2 starter / Closer | 8C

Thrws R Age 23	Year	Lev	Team	W	L	Sv	IP	K	ERA	WHIP	BF/G	OBA	H%	S%	xERA	Ctl	Dom	Cmd	hr/9	BPV
2009 FA (DR)	2014	Rk	Azl White Sox	1	0	0	14	23	1.29	0.93	13.1	132	23	92	1.16	4.5	14.8	3.3	0.6	163
93-98 FB ++++	2014	A+	Winston-Salem	4	0	0	62	56	1.60	0.95	23.4	205	27	84	1.75	2.0	8.1	4.0	0.3	109
84-88 SL ++++	2014	AA	Birmingham	0	0	0	5	1	0.00	0.40	16.1	66	7	100		1.8	1.8	1.0	0.0	2
83-87 CU ++	2015	AA	Birmingham	5	5	0	112	108	2.97	1.22	19.7	220	29	75	2.56	3.9	8.7	2.3	0.2	70
	2015	MLB	Chi White Sox	0	2	0	15	20	4.80	1.53	9.3	249	37	68	4.02	5.4	12.0	2.2	0.6	88

Big-bodied pitcher who showed off plus arm strength in MLB trial. Achieves velocity easily and can hit triple digits with FB. Loses velocity late which may result in future RP role. Keeps ball down and can wipe out hitters with nasty SL. Improvement of CU, as well as refinement of release point and command, is key to his future.

Montgomery,Jordan — SP — New York (A)

EXP MLB DEBUT: 2017 | H/W: 6-4 225 | FUT: #4 starter | 7D

Thrws L Age 23	Year	Lev	Team	W	L	Sv	IP	K	ERA	WHIP	BF/G	OBA	H%	S%	xERA	Ctl	Dom	Cmd	hr/9	BPV
2014 (4) South Carolina	2014	NCAA	South Carolina	8	5	0	100	95	3.42	1.22	25.3	248	32	73	3.28	2.6	8.6	3.3	0.6	101
88-92 FB +++	2014	Rk	GCL Yankees 2	0	1	0	5	5	5.19	1.35	7.2	254	34	57	3.09	3.5	8.7	2.5	0.0	80
72-77 CB ++	2014	A-	Staten Island	1	0	0	13	15	3.44	1.15	7.4	229	33	67	2.24	2.7	10.3	3.8	0.0	129
77-81 CU +++	2015	A	Charleston (Sc)	4	3	0	43	55	2.71	1.11	18.9	228	34	74	2.32	2.5	11.5	4.6	0.2	157
	2015	A+	Tampa	6	5	0	90	77	3.09	1.18	22.5	244	31	74	2.90	2.4	7.7	3.2	0.4	92

Consistent, durable SP who succeeds with pitch location and ability to get groundballs. Has posted a high K rate in career despite fringe-average stuff. FB has below average velocity, but bottom drops out late. CU is best secondary offering and features depth and fade. Needs to stay on top of CB and throw for strikes.

Moore,Andrew — SP — Seattle

EXP MLB DEBUT: 2018 | H/W: 6-0 185 | FUT: #4 starter | 7D

Thrws R Age 21	Year	Lev	Team	W	L	Sv	IP	K	ERA	WHIP	BF/G	OBA	H%	S%	xERA	Ctl	Dom	Cmd	hr/9	BPV
2015 (2) Oregon St																				
87-92 FB +++																				
74-75 CB ++																				
79-82 CU +++	2015	NCAA	Oregon St	4	1	0	77	70	1.40	0.81	27.9	187	25	82	1.01	1.4	8.2	5.8	0.1	127
	2015	A-	Everett	1	1	0	39	43	2.08	1.00	10.6	252	34	81	2.60	0.5	9.9	21.5	0.5	184

Short, versatile pitcher who thrives with smarts and understanding of craft. Throws pinpoint strikes and can induce weak contact, but doesn't own out pitch. Nifty CU can be tough to elevate and FB appears quicker than radar gun indicates. CB is distant third pitch and will need if he intends to remain SP.

Moreno,Gerson — RP — Detroit

EXP MLB DEBUT: 2019 | H/W: 6-0 175 | FUT: Closer | 7E

Thrws R Age 20	Year	Lev	Team	W	L	Sv	IP	K	ERA	WHIP	BF/G	OBA	H%	S%	xERA	Ctl	Dom	Cmd	hr/9	BPV
2012 FA (DR)																				
93-98 FB ++++	2013	Rk	DSL Tigers	2	1	1	50	35	2.88	1.28	13.7	234	29	75	2.68	3.8	6.3	1.7	0.0	29
77-80 CB +++	2014	Rk	GCL Tigers	1	1	0	28	22	4.47	1.74	9.2	287	36	71	4.55	5.4	7.0	1.3	0.0	-2
CU +	2015	A-	Connecticut	2	5	2	28	29	3.86	1.43	7.9	262	36	70	3.39	3.9	9.3	2.4	0.0	82
	2015	A	West Michigan	0	0	1	9	9	0.00	0.66	6.3	105	15	100		3.0	8.9	3.0	0.0	98

Short, quick-armed RP who can succeed by FB alone. Showed improved walk rate and higher K rate by repeating arm slot better. CB developing into potential plus offering, but rarely changes speeds. Size will likely keep him in pen as will questionable stamina. Will need to continue to keep ball low in zone.

Morimando,Shawn — SP — Cleveland

EXP MLB DEBUT: 2016 | H/W: 5-11 195 | FUT: #5 starter | 6B

Thrws L Age 23	Year	Lev	Team	W	L	Sv	IP	K	ERA	WHIP	BF/G	OBA	H%	S%	xERA	Ctl	Dom	Cmd	hr/9	BPV
2011 (19) HS (VA)	2012	A	Lake County	7	6	0	110	69	3.60	1.34	20.8	236	26	76	3.72	4.3	5.6	1.3	0.9	5
90-94 FB +++	2013	A+	Carolina	8	13	0	135	102	3.73	1.41	21.2	232	28	74	3.49	5.1	6.8	1.3	0.5	4
77-79 CB +++	2014	A+	Carolina	8	3	0	96	70	3.00	1.11	21.0	210	24	75	2.58	3.3	6.6	2.0	0.7	48
81-84 SL ++	2014	AA	Akron	2	6	0	56	38	3.85	1.43	23.8	285	34	72	4.05	2.7	6.1	2.2	0.3	54
CU ++	2015	AA	Akron	10	12	0	158	128	3.19	1.29	23.2	238	29	76	3.22	3.7	7.3	2.0	0.5	49

Short, consistent SP who produces average velocity from easy arm action and mechanics. Posted solid numbers and could eventually become lefty specialist due to dominance of LHH. Tight CB is best pitch, though often leaves short SL and CU up in zone for flyballs and HR. Can nibble when behind in count.

Morris,Akeel — RP — New York (N)

EXP MLB DEBUT: 2015 | H/W: 6-1 195 | FUT: Set-up Reliever | 8E

Thrws R Age 23	Year	Lev	Team	W	L	Sv	IP	K	ERA	WHIP	BF/G	OBA	H%	S%	xERA	Ctl	Dom	Cmd	hr/9	BPV
2010 (10) HS (VG)	2013	A-	Brooklyn	4	1	1	45	60	1.00	1.16	12.8	186	30	92	1.92	4.6	12.0	2.6	0.2	110
91-94 FB ++++	2014	A	Savannah	4	1	16	57	89	0.63	0.72	4.9	106	20	93		3.5	14.1	4.0	0.2	177
78-80 SL ++	2015	A+	St. Lucie	0	1	13	32	46	1.69	0.78	4.8	109	18	79	0.25	3.9	12.9	3.3	0.3	145
75-77 CU ++++	2015	AA	Binghamton	0	1	0	29	35	2.47	1.10	5.0	172	25	77	1.73	4.6	10.8	2.3	0.3	88
	2015	MLB	NY Mets	0	0	0	0	0		30.00	6.6	842	78	20			0.0	0.0	45.0	-3627

Had disastrous MLB debut as an emergency call-up from High-A. Delivery is all arms and legs. Hides baseball well. FB sits in low-90s but looks like mid-90s to hitters. Plus CU takes off 15 mph from FB. Very deceptive. SL is serviceable and a distraction to hitters sitting on FB/CU combo.

Morris,Elliot — SP — San Diego

EXP MLB DEBUT: 2017 | H/W: 6-4 210 | FUT: #4 starter | 7D

Thrws R Age 23	Year	Lev	Team	W	L	Sv	IP	K	ERA	WHIP	BF/G	OBA	H%	S%	xERA	Ctl	Dom	Cmd	hr/9	BPV
2013 (4) Pierce JC	2014	A	Burlington	2	1	0	40	44	2.25	1.05	19.4	205	28	80	2.12	2.9	9.9	3.4	0.5	117
90-94 FB +++	2014	A+	Inland Empire	3	3	0	45	40	4.19	1.44	21.4	225	27	73	3.90	5.6	8.0	1.4	1.0	11
78-82 SL ++	2014	A+	Lake Elsinore	3	3	0	48	33	3.56	1.06	23.3	228	24	73	3.29	2.1	6.2	3.0	1.3	74
81-85 CU ++	2015	Rk	Azl Padres	0	0	0	1	0	0.00	0.00	2.8	0	0			0.0	0.0		0.0	18
	2015	AA	San Antonio	5	9	0	101	72	4.89	1.55	21.1	284	33	68	4.54	3.9	6.4	1.6	0.5	28

Big-bodied SP with potential for 3 above average pitches. Has difficulty throwing consistent strikes and has tendency to slow arm speed with secondary offerings. Spots solid-average FB to both sides of plate, but K rate low despite decent SL. LHH have been problematic and will need CU to succeed. Could move to pen and be righty specialist.

Morris,Jacob — RP — Chicago (A)

EXP MLB DEBUT: 2017 | H/W: 6-3 215 | FUT: Setup reliever | 7E

Thrws R Age 25	Year	Lev	Team	W	L	Sv	IP	K	ERA	WHIP	BF/G	OBA	H%	S%	xERA	Ctl	Dom	Cmd	hr/9	BPV
2013 (24) Arkansas																				
90-95 FB +++																				
80-84 SL ++																				
CU +																				
	2015	A	Kannapolis	5	3	0	56	60	4.49	1.35	6.7	181	24	67	2.81	6.6	9.6	1.5	0.6	14

Converted OF who enjoyed first year on mound. Exhibited raw command as expected, but impressed with arm strength and pitch movement. Has strong frame and arm to generate velocity and FB is tough to make hard contact against. Low oppBA (.178) a result of FB and max effort delivery. Development of SL key to future role.

Moscot,Jon — SP — Cincinnati

EXP MLB DEBUT: 2015 | H/W: 6-4 210 | FUT: #5 starter | 6B

Thrws R Age 24	Year	Lev	Team	W	L	Sv	IP	K	ERA	WHIP	BF/G	OBA	H%	S%	xERA	Ctl	Dom	Cmd	hr/9	BPV
2012 (4) Pepperdine	2013	AA	Pensacola	2	1	0	31	28	3.19	1.48	22.2	280	34	81	4.62	3.5	8.1	2.3	0.9	70
89-93 FB +++	2014	AA	Pensacola	7	10	0	149	111	3.14	1.26	24.3	256	30	77	3.55	2.6	6.7	2.6	0.7	69
75-77 CB ++	2014	AAA	Louisville	1	1	0	17	9	5.79	1.29	23.4	237	20	65	5.23	3.7	4.7	1.3	2.6	4
80-84 SL ++	2015	AAA	Louisville	7	1	0	54	34	3.16	1.28	24.6	247	28	78	3.62	3.2	5.7	1.8	0.8	34
80-83 CU ++	2015	MLB	Cincinnati	1	1	0	11	6	4.82	1.43	15.9	258	26	71	4.90	4.0	4.8	1.2	1.6	-4

Made 3 starts for CIN before dislocating left shoulder that required surgery. Throws four pitches & can command them all for strikes. Stuff tops out average at best. Works CU & SL off a low-nineties FB to keep hitters off-balance. CU has good deception and solid runs away from LH hitters. SL keeps RH hitters honest.

Musgrave,Harrison — SP — Colorado

EXP MLB DEBUT: 2018 | H/W: 6-1 205 | FUT: #5 starter | 7C

Thrws L Age 24	Year	Lev	Team	W	L	Sv	IP	K	ERA	WHIP	BF/G	OBA	H%	S%	xERA	Ctl	Dom	Cmd	hr/9	BPV
2014 (8) West Virginia	2013	NCAA	West Virginia	9	1	0	95	81	2.18	0.99	25.9	195	25	79	1.81	2.7	7.7	2.8	0.4	82
88-91 FB ++	2014	NCAA	West Virginia	5	3	0	106	87	2.63	1.06	27.4	231	29	76	2.47	1.9	7.4	4.0	0.4	100
85-86 SL ++	2014	Rk	Grand Junction	2	4	0	48	50	5.44	1.54	16.1	307	37	70	6.10	2.6	9.4	3.6	1.9	116
75-78 CB ++	2015	A+	Modesto	10	1	0	90	83	2.89	1.11	22.1	242	30	76	2.98	1.9	8.3	4.4	0.7	116
80-83 CU ++	2015	AA	New Britain	3	4	0	56	53	3.20	1.21	20.6	258	31	79	3.85	2.1	8.5	4.1	1.1	115

Has a chance to develop into a back-end starter with a decent 4-pitch mix. FB sits at 88-91 mph, with a SL, CB, and CU. None are plus offerings, but he keeps the ball around the plate, Not particularly athletic and delivery is a bit mechanical, but he knows how to pitch.

Musgrove,Joe — SP — Houston

EXP MLB DEBUT: 2016 | H/W: 6-5 255 | FUT: #3 starter | 8C

Thrws R Age 23	Year	Lev	Team	W	L	Sv	IP	K	ERA	WHIP	BF/G	OBA	H%	S%	xERA	Ctl	Dom	Cmd	hr/9	BPV
2011 (1) HS (CA)	2013	Rk	GCL Astros	1	3	0	32		4.47	1.46	12.5	321	41	67	4.63	1.1	8.4	7.5	0.3	139
91-95 FB ++++	2014	A-	Tri City	7	1	0	77	67	2.81	0.96	19.4	228	29	71	2.22	1.2	7.8	6.7	0.5	127
81-83 SL +++	2015	A	Quad Cities	4	1	0	25	23	0.71	0.91	18.8	236	31	91	1.77	0.4	8.2	23.0	0.0	156
82-84 CU ++	2015	A+	Lancaster	4	0	0	30	43	2.40	0.97	18.9	249	38	78	2.58	0.3	12.9	43.0	0.6	242
	2015	AA	Corpus Christi	4	0	1	45	33	2.20	0.91	21.0	216	23	88	2.84	1.2	6.6	5.5	1.4	104

Sleeper prospect who was consistently good in first full season. Dominated three levels of minors with quality pitches and ability to keep ball down in zone. Rarely walks hitters and can get hitters to flail at solid SL and FB that is rarely straight. CU shows promise and repeats arm speed and slot effectively.

Neidert,Nick — SP — Seattle

EXP MLB DEBUT: 2020 | H/W: 6-1 180 | FUT: #3 starter | 8D

Thrws R Age 19	Year	Lev	Team	W	L	Sv	IP	K	ERA	WHIP	BF/G	OBA	H%	S%	xERA	Ctl	Dom	Cmd	hr/9	BPV
2015 (2) HS (GA)																				
89-94 FB +++																				
79-83 SL ++																				
84-85 CU ++																				
	2015	Rk	Azl Mariners	0	2	0	35	23	1.54	0.97	12.1	202	24	85	1.74	2.3	5.9	2.6	0.3	62

Athletic SP who was impressive upon signing by showing mature sequencing and ability to repeat delivery. Doesn't wow with any one pitch, but all three work well in tandem. Throws strikes with nice command and hitters rarely make hard contact. SL could evolve into plus pitch, but needs more power. Pitch movement will assist him in lower minors.

Newcomb,Sean — SP — Atlanta

EXP MLB DEBUT: 2016 | H/W: 6-5 245 | FUT: #1 starter | 9D

Thrws L Age 22	Year	Lev	Team	W	L	Sv	IP	K	ERA	WHIP	BF/G	OBA	H%	S%	xERA	Ctl	Dom	Cmd	hr/9	BPV
2014 (1) Hartford	2014	Rk	Azl Angels	0	0	0	3	3	3.00	1.33	6.2	262	27	100	5.98	3.0	9.0	3.0	3.0	99
93-95 FB ++++	2014	A	Burlington	0	1	0	11	15	7.23	1.61	12.4	292	42	53	5.00	4.0	12.1	3.0	0.8	126
78-80 CB +++	2015	A	Burlington	1	0	0	34	45	1.85	1.29	20.0	206	32	86	2.56	5.0	11.9	2.4	0.3	96
81-83 CU ++++	2015	A+	Inland Empire	6	1	0	65	84	2.48	1.27	20.5	214	32	80	2.62	4.6	11.6	2.5	0.3	104
	2015	AA	Arkansas	2	2	0	36	39	2.75	1.28	21.1	178	24	80	2.45	6.0	9.8	1.6	0.5	32

Acquired by ATL this offseason in trade with LAA, had a breakout season in '15. FB command improved immensely, especially with corralling late movement down in the zone. His CU remains his best secondary pitch. FB and CU are lethal 1-2 punch. Ditching the SL, his 12-6 CB has emerged as a weapon against LH hitters.

Nielsen,Trey — SP — St. Louis

EXP MLB DEBUT: 2019 | H/W: 6-1 190 | FUT: #4 starter | 7D

Thrws R Age 24	Year	Lev	Team	W	L	Sv	IP	K	ERA	WHIP	BF/G	OBA	H%	S%	xERA	Ctl	Dom	Cmd	hr/9	BPV
2013 (30) Utah																				
90-94 FB +++																				
SL ++	2013	NCAA	Utah	0	0	0	6	7	6.00	2.83	8.5	394	53	76	9.13	9.0	10.5	1.2	0.0	-36
CU ++	2014	A-	State College	3	2	1	50	49	2.51	1.00	12.8	203	26	77	2.07	2.5	8.8	3.5	0.5	109
	2015	A+	Palm Beach	9	6	0	111	78	2.59	1.22	17.9	244	29	78	2.88	2.8	6.3	2.3	0.2	57

Surprisingly effective as a pro despite the lack of overpowering stuff. Had TJS in '13, but is fully recovered. Low-90s sinking FB is his best offering and he consistently gets hitters to beat the ball into the ground. Complements the sinker with a SL and CU, both of which are works in progress.

Nikorak,Mike — SP — Colorado

EXP MLB DEBUT: 2020 | H/W: 6-5 205 | FUT: #2 starter | 8D

Thrws R Age 19	Year	Lev	Team	W	L	Sv	IP	K	ERA	WHIP	BF/G	OBA	H%	S%	xERA	Ctl	Dom	Cmd	hr/9	BPV
2015 (1) HS (PA)																				
92-95 FB ++++																				
80-83 CB ++																				
78-81 CU ++																				
	2015	Rk	Grand Junction	0	4	0	17	14	12.03	3.37	13.3	349	42	61	10.16	16.7	7.3	0.4	0.5	-302

Has a plus 92-95 mph FB with good sink and run. Mixes in a potentially plus CB and a solid-avg CU. Has an ideal power pitching frame with good athleticism. Inconsistent release point from high 3/4 arm slot results in the ball being up in the zone and below-avg Cmd. Is stiff on the mound, but has good long-term potential.

Nix,Jacob — SP — San Diego

EXP MLB DEBUT: 2020 | H/W: 6-3 220 | FUT: #3 starter | 8D

Thrws R Age 20	Year	Lev	Team	W	L	Sv	IP	K	ERA	WHIP	BF/G	OBA	H%	S%	xERA	Ctl	Dom	Cmd	hr/9	BPV
2015 (3) HS (FL)																				
89-95 FB +++																				
77-81 CB +++																				
CU ++																				
	2015	Rk	Azl Padres	0	2	0	19	19	5.63	1.56	12.0	298	38	62	4.70	3.3	8.9	2.7	0.5	90

Projectable hurler whose production doesn't match his stuff. Has the mix and tenacity to be great, but needs to repeat delivery, maintain velocity, and command FB more efficiently. Could add ticks to FB to project to plus, but can be too straight. CU has tendency to be too firm, though CB projects very well. Has size and frame to front rotation.

Nolin,Sean — SP — Oakland

EXP MLB DEBUT: 2013 | H/W: 6-4 230 | FUT: #4 starter | 7B

Thrws L Age 26	Year	Lev	Team	W	L	Sv	IP	K	ERA	WHIP	BF/G	OBA	H%	S%	xERA	Ctl	Dom	Cmd	hr/9	BPV
2010 (6) San Jacinto JC	2014	A+	Dunedin	0	1	0	7	9	3.80	1.13	14.0	167	27	63	1.45	5.1	11.4	2.3	0.0	86
89-94 FB +++	2014	AAA	Buffalo	4	6	0	87	74	3.51	1.25	20.9	232	28	73	3.15	3.6	7.6	2.1	0.6	58
79-82 CB ++	2014	MLB	Toronto	0	0	0	1	0	9.00	1.00	3.8	262	0		10.87	0.0	0.0		9.0	18
81-84 SL ++	2015	AAA	Nashville	2	2	0	47	38	2.68	1.25	13.7	231	27	83	3.47	3.6	7.3	2.0	1.0	51
80-82 CU +++	2015	MLB	Oakland	1	2	0	29	15	5.28	1.62	21.5	300	32	70	5.64	3.7	4.7	1.3	1.2	1

Tall, strong SP who missed time with minor injuries. Has appeared in majors each of last 3 seasons and is ready to stick. Uses four pitches, all thrown with arm speed and high 3/4 slot. FB shows hard sink down in zone and above average CU is second top offering. Can hang CB and has flyball tendencies. Needs to clean up control to be in rotation.

Null,Jeremy — SP — Chicago (N)

EXP MLB DEBUT: 2019 | H/W: 6-7 200 | FUT: #3 starter | 7C

Thrws R Age 22	Year	Lev	Team	W	L	Sv	IP	K	ERA	WHIP	BF/G	OBA	H%	S%	xERA	Ctl	Dom	Cmd	hr/9	BPV
2014 (15) Western Carolina	2014	NCAA	Western Carolina	6	4	0	101	93	2.94	1.15	26.7	234	29	78	3.17	2.6	8.3	3.2	0.9	97
91-93 FB +++	2014	Rk	Azl Cubs	0	0	0	2	2	9.00	1.50	4.3	347	45	33	4.90	0.0	9.0		0.0	180
SL +++	2014	A-	Boise	2	0	0	14	11	1.29	1.00	10.7	233	30	86	1.96	1.3	7.1	5.5	0.0	111
CU ++	2015	A	South Bend	6	2	0	65	48	2.35	1.10	21.3	270	33	79	2.98	0.6	6.6	12.0	0.3	122
	2015	A+	Myrtle Beach	2	3	0	51	34	4.75	1.31	21.1	294	33	65	4.41	1.2	6.0	4.9	0.9	92

Big, strong hurler fell to the 15th round due to concerns about a back injury. Now healthy and FB velo sits 91-93 mph, topping out at 95 mph with good downward tilt. Mixes in a decent SL. Improved CU and plus Cmd resulted in breakout in the MWL. Definite sleeper.

Okert,Steven — RP — San Francisco

EXP MLB DEBUT: 2016 | H/W: 6-2 210 | FUT: Setup reliever | 7C

Thrws L Age 24	Year	Lev	Team	W	L	Sv	IP	K	ERA	WHIP	BF/G	OBA	H%	S%	xERA	Ctl	Dom	Cmd	hr/9	BPV
2012 (4) Oklahoma	2012	A-	Salem-Kaizer	2	0	0	26	22	2.40	1.41	7.4	260	33	81	3.35	3.8	7.6	2.0	0.0	52
92-95 FB ++++	2013	A	Augusta	2	2	2	60	59	2.99	1.31	5.7	245	32	78	3.30	3.6	8.8	2.5	0.4	80
82-85 SL ++++	2014	A+	San Jose	1	2	19	35	54	1.54	1.25	4.3	250	41	90	3.23	2.8	13.8	4.9	0.5	191
83-86 CU ++	2014	AA	Richmond	1	0	5	33	38	2.73	1.06	5.3	205	28	78	2.50	3.0	10.4	3.5	0.8	124
	2015	AAA	Sacramento	5	3	3	61	69	3.83	1.49	5.1	265	35	77	4.54	4.3	10.2	2.4	1.0	86

Lanky LH withstood some Ctl erosion in AAA debut, but still has late RP-type profile. Settles 92-95 mph (T97) with FB, which is good bat-misser up in zone. Has mid-80s SL with good late bite to keep both LH/RH at bay; will mix in fringy CU vs. RHH at times. Smooth, online delivery with repeatable low 3/4 slot should help cut down on those walks.

Ortiz,Luis — SP — Texas

EXP MLB DEBUT: 2018 | H/W: 6-3 230 | FUT: #3 starter | 8C

Thrws R Age 20
2014 (1) HS (CA)
91-95 FB ++++
81-84 SL +++
78-80 CB ++
80-84 CU +++

Year	Lev	Team	W	L	Sv	IP	K	ERA	WHIP	BF/G	OBA	H%	S%	xERA	Ctl	Dom	Cmd	hr/9	BPV
2014	Rk	Azl Rangers	1	1	0	13	15	2.06	1.15	8.7	245	35	80	2.44	2.1	10.3	5.0	0.0	148
2014	A	Hickory	0	0	1	7	4	1.29	1.00	8.9	168	16	100	2.42	3.9	5.1	1.3	1.3	6
2015	A	Hickory	4	1	0	50	46	1.80	1.08	15.0	242	32	83	2.43	1.6	8.3	5.1	0.2	123

Strong-framed SP who missed time late with fatigue. Has repeatable delivery with some deception. FB and SL serve as K pitches and CU vastly improved. Can dominate at times when sequencing well and challenging hitters. More of a flyball pitcher and will need to address stamina issues. Raw ingredients to be dynamite mid-rotation guy.

Osich,Josh — RP — San Francisco

EXP MLB DEBUT: 2015 | H/W: 6-2 230 | FUT: Setup reliever | 8C

Thrws L Age 27
2011 (6) Oregon St
94-97 FB ++++
90-92 CT +++
85-87 CU ++

Year	Lev	Team	W	L	Sv	IP	K	ERA	WHIP	BF/G	OBA	H%	S%	xERA	Ctl	Dom	Cmd	hr/9	BPV
2013	AA	Richmond	2	3	3	29	28	4.93	1.30	5.5	240	31	61	3.37	3.7	8.6	2.3	0.6	73
2014	AA	Richmond	1	0	0	33	27	3.81	1.45	5.0	231	27	77	4.08	5.4	7.3	1.4	1.1	3
2015	AA	Richmond	0	1	19	34	34	1.59	0.97	4.2	193	26	84	1.63	2.6	9.0	3.4	0.3	109
2015	AAA	Sacramento	0	0	2	7	11	0.00	0.71	4.1	132	26	100	0.03	2.6	14.1	5.5	0.0	203
2015	MLB	SF Giants	2	0	0	28	27	2.23	1.13	3.2	232	28	89	3.46	2.6	8.6	3.4	1.3	104

Strong, polished LH impressed (18% SwK, 112 BPV in 29 IP) in stint with SF bullpen. Shows good command of plus FB, which touches 99 mph and sits 94-97. Hard SL/CT is quality source of ground balls; CU flashes ability to miss bats. If he can stay healthy, and it's been a problem in the past, he could have solid-avg impact as late, setup-type RP.

Overton,Dillon — SP — Oakland

EXP MLB DEBUT: 2016 | H/W: 6-2 172 | FUT: #3 starter | 8C

Thrws L Age 24
2013 (2) Oklahoma
86-92 FB +++
76-79 CB +++
81-84 CU +++

Year	Lev	Team	W	L	Sv	IP	K	ERA	WHIP	BF/G	OBA	H%	S%	xERA	Ctl	Dom	Cmd	hr/9	BPV
2013	NCAA	Oklahoma	9	3	0	92		3.03	1.24	23.4	259	33	74	3.08	2.2	7.7	3.4	0.2	96
2014	Rk	Azl Athletics	0	2	0	22	31	1.64	1.00	12.0	234	38	82	1.92	1.2	12.7	10.3	0.0	213
2014	A-	Vermont	0	1	0	15	22	2.40	0.80	10.9	206	35	67	1.06	0.6	13.2	22.0	0.0	239
2015	A+	Stockton	2	4	0	61	59	3.83	1.21	17.6	265	33	72	3.86	1.8	8.7	4.9	1.0	127
2015	AA	Midland	5	2	0	64	47	3.08	1.25	20.1	264	31	76	3.52	2.1	6.6	3.1	0.6	80

Savvy SP who bypassed Low-A and reached AA in July despite velocity not all the way back after TJ surgery. Thrives with deceptive delivery and solid-average secondary offerings. Gets hitters to chase CB when on and has pinpoint location of pitches. Can pitch up too often and often gets hit hard by RHH. If velocity comes back, could come quickly.

Parsons,Wes — SP — Atlanta

EXP MLB DEBUT: 2017 | H/W: 6-5 190 | FUT: #4 starter | 7C

Thrws R Age 23
2012 NDFA Jackson St CC
90-93 FB +++
80-83 SL +++
80-82 CU ++

Year	Lev	Team	W	L	Sv	IP	K	ERA	WHIP	BF/G	OBA	H%	S%	xERA	Ctl	Dom	Cmd	hr/9	BPV
2013	A	Rome	7	7	0	109	101	2.64	1.03	22.1	228	29	75	2.33	1.7	8.3	4.8	0.4	121
2014	A+	Lynchburg	4	7	0	113	96	5.01	1.35	20.5	272	33	63	4.10	2.7	7.6	2.8	0.8	82
2015	Rk	GCL Braves	0	0	0	9	14	0.98	0.76	11.0	212	37	86	1.03	0.0	13.7		0.0	265
2015	A	Rome	1	0	0	5	2	1.80	0.40	16.1	124	8	100	0.96	0.0	3.6		1.8	83
2015	A+	Carolina	1	0	0	5	0	7.20	1.80	23.1	362	36	56	6.01	1.8	0.0	0.0	0.0	-31

Made only 5 starts in '15 due to injury. NDFA came out of nowhere in '13 to establish his prospect status. However, he's struggled mightily since due to command issues and injuries. FB is straight and needs pinpoint location to be effective. His best pitch is a CB with depth and bend. A below-average CU rounds out package.

Paulino,David — SP — Houston

EXP MLB DEBUT: 2018 | H/W: 6-7 215 | FUT: #3 starter | 8C

Thrws R Age 22
2010 FA (DR)
90-95 FB +++
77-79 CB ++++
83-84 CU ++

Year	Lev	Team	W	L	Sv	IP	K	ERA	WHIP	BF/G	OBA	H%	S%	xERA	Ctl	Dom	Cmd	hr/9	BPV
2015	A-	Tri City	1	0	0	9	10	0.00	0.66	15.8	135	20	100		2.0	9.9	5.0	0.0	143
2015	A	Quad Cities	3	2	0	28	32	1.60	0.99	21.5	209	31	82	1.61	2.2	10.2	4.6	0.0	142
2015	A+	Lancaster	1	1	1	29	30	4.95	1.17	19.3	226	31	55	2.56	3.1	9.3	3.0	0.3	102

Angular SP who has flown under radar due to rash of injuries. Began season in June after missing '14 due to TJ surgery. Has great size in lean frame and one of best pure CB in org. Drives ball down in zone and hitters rarely elevate pitches. Shows surprising control despite limited experience and only needs to hone CU to become top prospect.

Pazos,James — RP — New York (A)

EXP MLB DEBUT: 2015 | H/W: 6-3 230 | FUT: Setup reliever | 6B

Thrws L Age 24
2012 (13) San Diego
89-95 FB +++
82-84 SL +++
84-88 CU +

Year	Lev	Team	W	L	Sv	IP	K	ERA	WHIP	BF/G	OBA	H%	S%	xERA	Ctl	Dom	Cmd	hr/9	BPV
2014	A+	Tampa	0	2	4	25	33	3.96	1.16	5.5	246	38	62	2.48	2.2	11.9	5.5	0.0	174
2014	AA	Trenton	0	1	6	42	42	1.50	1.12	5.9	191	27	85	1.73	4.1	9.0	2.2	0.0	70
2015	AA	Trenton	0	0	1	9	12	1.96	0.43	5.0	134	18	67	0.28	0.0	11.7		1.0	229
2015	AAA	Scranton/WB	3	1	2	33	37	1.09	1.21	6.3	212	31	90	2.20	4.1	10.1	2.5	0.0	89
2015	MLB	NY Yankees	0	0	0	5	3	0.00	1.20	1.8	175	21	100	1.79	5.4	5.4	1.0	0.0	-31

Durable-framed RP with power arm and improving stuff. Can be guilty of throwing too many strikes. Uses tough angle to plate and is tough to make hard contact against. Can get on side of SL, but still shows velocity and break. Has retired LHH with ease and may end up as situational RP. Pitches aggressively inside, though FB can be too straight.

Pena,Felix — SP — Chicago (N)

EXP MLB DEBUT: 2017 | H/W: 6-2 190 | FUT: #4 starter | 7D

Thrws R Age 26
2009 FA (DR)
90-93 FB +++
CU ++
SL ++

Year	Lev	Team	W	L	Sv	IP	K	ERA	WHIP	BF/G	OBA	H%	S%	xERA	Ctl	Dom	Cmd	hr/9	BPV
2012	A	Peoria	0	0	0	10	10	4.50	1.40	7.0	242	31	69	3.90	4.5	9.0	2.0	0.9	59
2013	A	Kane County	4	7	1	103	77	3.93	1.30	20.2	260	31	69	3.48	2.8	6.7	2.4	0.4	64
2014	A+	Daytona	4	6	0	96	76	3.19	1.27	20.7	245	30	76	3.32	3.2	7.1	2.2	0.6	60
2014	AA	Tennessee	2	4	0	27	26	7.61	1.73	20.6	281	33	57	5.98	5.6	8.6	1.5	1.7	21
2015	AA	Tennessee	7	8	0	129	140	3.76	1.24	21.0	234	31	71	3.19	3.4	9.8	2.9	0.7	101

Late developing Dominican hurler continues to impress. Pitches off a good low-90s FB and mixes in an average SL and CU. Keeps hitters off balance and throws plenty of strikes. Nothing stands out as plus, but hard to argue with the results.

Perdomo,Angel — SP — Toronto

EXP MLB DEBUT: 2018 | H/W: 6-6 200 | FUT: #4 SP / Setup RP | 7D

Thrws L Age 21
2011 FA (DR)
89-94 FB +++
82-85 SL ++
80-82 CU ++

Year	Lev	Team	W	L	Sv	IP	K	ERA	WHIP	BF/G	OBA	H%	S%	xERA	Ctl	Dom	Cmd	hr/9	BPV
2013	Rk	DSL Blue Jays	0	1	2	26	43	3.09	1.30	9.0	178	33	76	2.30	6.2	14.8	2.4	0.3	117
2014	Rk	GCL Blue Jays	3	2	1	46	57	2.54	1.24	14.4	217	32	79	2.50	4.1	11.2	2.7	0.2	108
2015	Rk	Bluefield	4	1	0	48	36	2.63	1.17	21.3	237	28	79	2.95	2.6	6.8	2.6	0.6	69
2015	A-	Vancouver	2	0	0	21	31	2.56	1.23	17.1	144	24	80	1.86	6.8	13.2	1.9	0.4	72

Tall, improving SP who has never pitched in full season, but has dominant stuff when on. Can be tough to make hard contact against when all three pitches working in tandem. Lively FB has been tough to control, but rarely elevated. SL and CU show glimpses, but may eventually move to pen due to arm strength.

Perdomo,Luis — SP — San Diego

EXP MLB DEBUT: 2018 | H/W: 6-2 160 | FUT: #4 SP / Setup RP | 7D

Thrws R Age 22
2010 FA (DR)
93-95 FB ++++
83-85 SL ++
CU ++

Year	Lev	Team	W	L	Sv	IP	K	ERA	WHIP	BF/G	OBA	H%	S%	xERA	Ctl	Dom	Cmd	hr/9	BPV
2014	A-	State College	1	0	0	12	13	1.50	1.00	22.9	245	32	91	2.79	0.8	9.8	13.0	0.8	173
2014	A	Peoria	3	6	0	57	41	5.05	1.49	22.3	285	33	65	4.50	3.3	6.5	2.0	0.6	45
2014	A+	Palm Beach	0	0	0	3	3	0.00	0.67	10.5	191	27	100	0.59	0.0	9.0		0.0	180
2015	A	Peoria	5	9	0	100	100	3.69	1.34	24.5	267	34	73	3.84	2.8	9.0	3.2	0.6	105
2015	A+	Palm Beach	1	3	0	26	18	5.17	1.42	18.4	296	35	61	4.22	2.1	6.2	3.0	0.3	74

Projectable hurler who appeared in Futures Game. Improved from time in '14 in MWL. Has quick arm that generates easy velocity to plus FB. Tinkered with mechanics and arm slot that resulted in better velocity. Backs up FB with hard, inconsistent SL. CU and command are below average. May move to pen. Selected from STL in Rule 5.

Perez,David — RP — Texas

EXP MLB DEBUT: 2017 | H/W: 6-5 200 | FUT: Setup reliever | 8E

Thrws R Age 23
2009 FA (DR)
90-96 FB ++++
75-78 CB +++
84-88 CU +

Year	Lev	Team	W	L	Sv	IP	K	ERA	WHIP	BF/G	OBA	H%	S%	xERA	Ctl	Dom	Cmd	hr/9	BPV
2012	A-	Spokane	1	1	0	9	11	13.00	2.56	16.1	321	43	45	8.04	11.0	11.0	1.0	1.0	-81
2013	Rk	Azl Rangers	0	1	0	2	3	8.18	2.27	3.7	326	48	60	6.46	8.2	12.3	1.5	0.0	18
2014	A-	Spokane	1	0	0	27	24	3.97	1.47	8.3	199	24	74	3.33	6.9	7.9	1.1	0.7	-27
2015	A	Hickory	2	1	0	29	37	0.93	1.17	7.2	197	29	97	2.48	4.3	11.5	2.6	0.6	107
2015	A+	High Desert	4	3	1	55	60	4.42	1.18	13.8	247	32	64	3.49	2.3	9.8	4.3	1.0	133

Tall pitcher who spent first year in full-season ball after 5 years in short-season. Moved to SP late and showed surprising command. Live arm and long limbs offer projection, but needs to continue to polish control. Tends to overthrow and overuse nice CB and CU in nascent stage. Has cleaned up delivery and has upside.

Perry,Chris — RP — St. Louis

EXP MLB DEBUT: 2017 | H/W: 6-2 215 | FUT: Middle reliever | 6C

Thrws R Age 25
2012 (17) Methodist
90-93 FB +++
CB +++
CU ++

Year	Lev	Team	W	L	Sv	IP	K	ERA	WHIP	BF/G	OBA	H%	S%	xERA	Ctl	Dom	Cmd	hr/9	BPV
2013	A	Peoria	2	4	0	48	40	3.93	1.35	22.3	269	33	71	3.85	2.8	7.5	2.7	0.6	77
2014	A	Peoria	4	0	3	49	80	2.20	0.90	6.5	173	30	80	1.61	2.8	14.7	5.3	0.7	208
2014	A+	Palm Beach	1	1	5	14	18	1.93	0.86	4.0	132	19	82	1.02	3.9	11.6	3.0	0.6	122
2014	A+	Palm Beach	1	3	11	32	34	1.97	0.97	4.8	143	21	77	0.82	4.5	9.6	2.1	0.0	69
2015	AA	Springfield	1	3	1	28	24	6.11	1.61	6.9	255	32	59	4.07	5.8	7.7	1.3	0.3	1

Comes after hitters with a live 90-93 mph FB and an above-average, but inconsistent CB. Mechanics are not ideal and he has struggled with control, but continues to rack up plenty of Ks. Looked good at High-A, but struggled when he moved up to Double-A.

Petrick,Zach — SP — St. Louis

EXP MLB DEBUT: 2016 | H/W: 6-3 195 | FUT: #5 starter | 6C

Thrws R Age 26 — 2012 Northwestern Ohio

Velo	Pitch	Grade
87-90	FB	++
	CB	+++
	CU	+++

Year	Lev	Team	W	L	Sv	IP	K	ERA	WHIP	BF/G	OBA	H%	S%	xERA	Ctl	Dom	Cmd	hr/9	BPV
2013	A+	Palm Beach	3	0	1	33	32	0.27	0.76	13.1	184	26	96	0.73	1.1	8.7	8.0	0.0	145
2013	AA	Springfield	3	3	0	47	44	4.01	1.25	21.3	249	32	68	3.32	2.9	8.4	2.9	0.6	92
2014	AA	Springfield	2	0	0	18	15	0.49	0.77	21.8	149	20	93	0.41	2.5	7.4	3.0	0.0	85
2014	AAA	Memphis	7	6	1	115	82	4.62	1.35	20.0	268	30	69	4.49	2.8	6.4	2.3	1.3	57
2015	AAA	Memphis	7	7	0	157	113	4.53	1.34	23.3	290	34	67	4.35	1.7	6.5	3.9	0.8	90

Finesse RHP rarely breaks 90 mph with his FB, but does a good job of keeping hitters off-balance. Gets good deception from a funky delivery and mixes in a good CB and CU. Keeps the ball down in the zone and limits damage against. Walked just 27 in 157.1 IP but Triple-A hitters mashed when he came into the zone—.287 oppBAA.

Pike,Tyler — SP — Seattle

EXP MLB DEBUT: 2017 | H/W: 6-0 180 | FUT: #4 starter | 7D

Thrws L Age 22 — 2012 (3) HS (FL)

Velo	Pitch	Grade
88-91	FB	+++
73-78	CB	++
80-83	CU	+++

Year	Lev	Team	W	L	Sv	IP	K	ERA	WHIP	BF/G	OBA	H%	S%	xERA	Ctl	Dom	Cmd	hr/9	BPV
2013	A	Clinton	7	4	0	110	90	2.37	1.18	20.0	190	24	81	2.28	4.7	7.4	1.6	0.4	25
2014	A+	High Desert	2	4	0	61	57	5.74	1.67	19.6	245	29	68	5.17	6.8	8.4	1.2	1.5	-14
2014	AA	Jackson	3	4	0	49	33	7.35	1.86	17.6	292	33	59	5.80	6.2	6.1	1.0	0.9	-42
2015	A+	Bakersfield	6	6	0	122	114	4.27	1.49	21.1	257	30	76	4.73	4.6	8.4	1.8	1.3	44
2015	AA	Jackson	0	2	0	11	7	4.91	2.09	18.0	262	31	74	5.10	9.8	5.7	0.6	0.0	-144

Athletic, deceptive SP who struggled to control average pitch mix in sub-par season. Repeats easy delivery well, but tends to overthrow and can't throw CB for strikes. Was victimized by HR in '15 despite solid sinker with life. Can also nibble at corners at times. Has look of back-end SP, but needs work on CB.

Pineyro,Ivan — SP — Miami

EXP MLB DEBUT: 2016 | H/W: 6-1 200 | FUT: #5 starter | 6C

Thrws R Age 24 — 2010 FA (DR)

Velo	Pitch	Grade
91-93	FB	+++
73-77	CB	++
	CU	++

Year	Lev	Team	W	L	Sv	IP	K	ERA	WHIP	BF/G	OBA	H%	S%	xERA	Ctl	Dom	Cmd	hr/9	BPV
2014	Rk	Azl Cubs	0	2	0	11		5.68	1.53	12.1	324	39	63	5.37	1.6	7.3	4.5	0.8	106
2014	AA	Tennessee	0	4	0	48	41	5.60	1.68	19.7	299	35	69	5.81	4.3	7.7	1.8	1.3	40
2015	AA	Jacksonville	0	1	0	2	0	13.50	3.00	11.6	347	35	50	8.77	13.5	0.0	0.0	0.0	-347
2015	AA	Tennessee	7	5	0	107	92	3.70	1.25	22.9	256	32	70	3.36	2.5	7.7	3.1	0.5	89
2015	AAA	New Orleans	2	2	0	36	26	2.73	1.08	23.5	233	28	76	2.62	2.0	6.5	3.3	0.5	81

Short Dominican hurler rebounded nicely at Double-A and was then traded to the Marlins in the Dan Haren deal. Showed improved Ctl and was able to keep hitters off-balance. FB sits at 91-93 with a curve and change-up, none of which project as above-average. Profiles as back-end starter.

Pinto,Ricardo — SP — Philadelphia

EXP MLB DEBUT: 2018 | H/W: 6-0 165 | FUT: #3 starter | 8C

Thrws R Age 22 — 2011 FA (VZ)

Velo	Pitch	Grade
91-94	FB	+++
79-82	CU	+++
	SL	++

Year	Lev	Team	W	L	Sv	IP	K	ERA	WHIP	BF/G	OBA	H%	S%	xERA	Ctl	Dom	Cmd	hr/9	BPV
2014	A-	Williamsport	1	5	0	47	48	2.11	1.09	20.4	214	27	85	2.63	2.9	9.2	3.2	0.8	106
2015	A	Lakewood	6	2	0	67	60	3.09	1.24	24.7	256	32	76	3.35	2.4	8.1	3.3	0.5	98
2015	A+	Clearwater	9	2	0	78	45	2.88	1.06	23.3	225	25	75	2.68	2.2	5.2	2.4	0.7	52

Success at both levels of A-ball in 2015. Low-90s FB can be straight, but commands it and earns plus marks. Likewise on CU; sells it by repeating arm speed and slot. SL flashes average; with more consistency, he'll have a solid mid-rotation arsenal. Pitches confidently, attacking hitters. Not much physical projection left.

Pivetta,Nick — SP — Philadelphia

EXP MLB DEBUT: 2016 | H/W: 6-5 220 | FUT: #4 starter | 7C

Thrws R Age 23 — 2013 (4) New Mexico JC

Velo	Pitch	Grade
92-94	FB	+++
72-76	CB	++
85-86	SL	++
85-87	CU	++

Year	Lev	Team	W	L	Sv	IP	K	ERA	WHIP	BF/G	OBA	H%	S%	xERA	Ctl	Dom	Cmd	hr/9	BPV
2013	A-	Auburn	0	1	0	21	17	3.41	1.42	17.9	242	30	76	3.53	4.7	7.3	1.5	0.4	22
2014	A	Hagerstown	13	8	0	132	98	4.22	1.37	21.3	276	32	72	4.43	2.7	6.7	2.5	1.0	66
2015	A+	Potomac	7	4	0	86	72	2.30	1.15	22.8	224	28	81	2.60	3.0	7.5	2.5	0.4	72
2015	AA	Harrisburg	0	2	0	15	6	7.20	1.87	23.4	310	29	67	7.52	5.4	3.6	0.7	2.4	-63
2015	AA	Reading	2	2	0	28	25	7.37	1.81	18.6	288	34	60	5.95	6.1	8.0	1.3	1.3	-2

Tall pitcher who throws downhill with high three-quarters delivery. FB is low-90s with some sink. Also throws two breaking pitches; SL is harder, while CB has significant break, it can get loose and loopy; lack of consistency stands out. Also throws CU that lags behind. Can get hit when misses with FB up.

Plutko,Adam — SP — Cleveland

EXP MLB DEBUT: 2016 | H/W: 6-3 195 | FUT: #4 starter | 7B

Thrws R Age 24 — 2013 (11) UCLA

Velo	Pitch	Grade
89-93	FB	+++
74-75	CB	+++
82-84	SL	+++
81-82	CU	+++

Year	Lev	Team	W	L	Sv	IP	K	ERA	WHIP	BF/G	OBA	H%	S%	xERA	Ctl	Dom	Cmd	hr/9	BPV
2013	NCAA	UCLA	10	3	0	124	81	2.25	0.98	24.8	208	24	78	2.03	2.2	5.9	2.7	0.4	65
2014	A	Lake County	3	1	0	52	66	3.97	1.17	20.8	250	37	63	2.72	2.1	11.4	5.5	0.2	167
2014	A+	Carolina	4	9	0	97	78	4.08	1.21	21.7	266	31	69	3.87	1.7	7.2	4.3	1.0	103
2015	A+	Lynchburg	4	2	0	49	47	1.28	0.71	21.7	178	23	88	1.07	0.9	8.6	9.4	0.5	148
2015	AA	Akron	9	5	0	116	90	2.87	1.02	23.5	227	27	75	2.59	1.8	7.0	3.9	0.7	95

Breakout prospect who dominated High-A before promotion to AA in May. Tough to hit due to deep arsenal and ability to sequence. Locates FB to both sides of plate and mixes in two breakers with varying speeds. May not have out pitch, but keeps hitters off guard and doesn't beat himself. Flyball pitcher, but not yet susceptible to HR.

Polanco,Anderson — SP — Cleveland

EXP MLB DEBUT: 2018 | H/W: 6-3 190 | FUT: #4 SP / Setup RP | 7D

Thrws L Age 23 — 2011 FA (DR)

Velo	Pitch	Grade
87-93	FB	+++
78-80	CB	++
81-83	CU	+++

Year	Lev	Team	W	L	Sv	IP	K	ERA	WHIP	BF/G	OBA	H%	S%	xERA	Ctl	Dom	Cmd	hr/9	BPV
2012	Rk	AZL Indians	1	2	0	22	26	6.49	2.03	9.0	277	34	73	7.01	8.5	10.5	1.2	2.0	-22
2013	Rk	AZL Indians	2	0	0	25	37	1.79	1.12	8.2	175	31	82	1.50	4.7	13.3	2.8	0.0	131
2013	A	Lake County	1	2	0	14	23	5.11	1.56	7.7	185	26	74	4.51	8.3	14.7	1.8	1.9	58
2014	A	Lake County	3	0	0	50	62	1.97	0.98	10.0	184	28	79	1.44	3.0	11.1	3.6	0.2	136
2015	A	Lake County	8	8	0	126	119	4.14	1.44	20.6	257	33	71	3.83	4.1	8.5	2.1	0.5	59

Long, projectable hurler who moved to rotation full-time in 2nd year in Low-A. Has head jerk in delivery that impacts command, but throws with quick arm and has sink to solid-average FB. May return to pen, but development of CU has been key for success. Moves FB around well, but can't find consistency with mediocre CB.

Ponce,Cody — SP — Milwaukee

EXP MLB DEBUT: 2018 | H/W: 6-6 240 | FUT: #3 starter | 8E

Thrws R Age 21 — 2015 (2) Cal Poly Pomona

Velo	Pitch	Grade
91-94	FB	++++
86-89	CT	+++
78-82	CB	++
82-86	CU	++

Year	Lev	Team	W	L	Sv	IP	K	ERA	WHIP	BF/G	OBA	H%	S%	xERA	Ctl	Dom	Cmd	hr/9	BPV
2015	Rk	Helena	0	0	0	5	4	3.60	0.80	9.1	221	28	50	1.30	0.0	7.2		0.0	148
2015	A	Wisconsin	2	1	3	46	36	2.15	1.13	15.1	249	31	80	2.67	1.8	7.0	4.0	0.2	97

Big-bodied RH sits mid-90s with straight FB and good feel for cutter. Secondaries are less refined, as CB action is slurvy and CU doesn't get enough separation from FB at times. Strong, durable build with clean mechanics. Works low in the zone. Future horse with Dom upside if CB/CU can develop well enough.

Rainey,Tanner — SP — Cincinnati

EXP MLB DEBUT: 2018 | H/W: 6-2 235 | FUT: Closer | 8C

Thrws R Age 22 — 2015 (2) West Alabama

Velo	Pitch	Grade
93-96	FB	++++
83-86	SL	+++
	CU	+

Year	Lev	Team	W	L	Sv	IP	K	ERA	WHIP	BF/G	OBA	H%	S%	xERA	Ctl	Dom	Cmd	hr/9	BPV
2015	Rk	Billings	2	2	0	59	57	4.27	1.46	16.8	258	34	69	3.71	4.3	8.7	2.0	0.3	59

Strong with electric FB, he was one of the hottest prospects coming out of Division II in '15. FB is clearly best pitch, but when pro, couldn't tap into the plus-plus velocity often. SL true out pitch with 2-plane break. Has a feel for CU but didn't throw it until pro debut. Will need to improve greatly to be effective.

Ramirez,Emmanuel — SP — San Diego

EXP MLB DEBUT: 2019 | H/W: 6-2 190 | FUT: #3 starter | 8E

Thrws R Age 21 — 2012 FA (DR)

Velo	Pitch	Grade
89-94	FB	+++
75-79	CB	+++
82-84	CU	++

Year	Lev	Team	W	L	Sv	IP	K	ERA	WHIP	BF/G	OBA	H%	S%	xERA	Ctl	Dom	Cmd	hr/9	BPV
2015	Rk	Azl Padres	4	2	0	41	37	1.53	0.87	19.0	200	25	85	1.63	1.5	8.1	5.3	0.4	122
2015	A-	Tri-City	2	1	0	24	25	3.00	1.17	19.1	228	31	74	2.64	3.0	9.4	3.1	0.4	106

Tall, thin SP who had nice showing in first year in U.S. Hides ball in deceptive delivery and allows sneaky FB to play up. Secondary pitches are crude, but show promise. CB has decent velocity while CU has depth and fade. Has trouble repeating complicated mechanics and arm slot varies. Does nice job of keeping ball low.

Ramirez,Jose — RP — Atlanta

EXP MLB DEBUT: 2014 | H/W: 6-3 190 | FUT: Closer | 7C

Thrws R Age 26 — 2009 FA (DR)

Velo	Pitch	Grade
92-97	FB	++++
82-85	SL	++
83-85	CU	+++

Year	Lev	Team	W	L	Sv	IP	K	ERA	WHIP	BF/G	OBA	H%	S%	xERA	Ctl	Dom	Cmd	hr/9	BPV
2014	MLB	NY Yankees	0	2	0	10	10	5.40	1.80	5.8	281	33	75	6.29	6.3	9.0	1.4	1.8	10
2015	AAA	Scranton/WB	3	0	10	49	56	2.93	1.28	6.3	224	32	76	2.68	4.2	10.2	2.4	0.2	89
2015	AAA	Tacoma	1	1	0	13	10	9.00	1.77	6.6	304	29	56	8.14	4.8	6.9	1.4	3.5	12
2015	MLB	NY Yankees	0	0	0	3	2	15.00	3.33	6.2	415	48	50	10.88	12.0	6.0	0.5	0.0	-198
2015	MLB	Seattle	1	0	0	4	3	12.86	3.57	5.4	432	50	60	11.86	12.9	6.4	0.5	0.0	-213

Power pitcher who was moved to bullpen in '14 to take advantage of electric stuff, but can't stay healthy. Uses FB/CU combo to keep hitters off guard. Ability to move ball in and out of zone and change speeds. CU has lots of fade, though can be tough to control. Tends to overthrow FB and needs to enhance SL to give third weapon.

Ramirez,Noe — RP — Boston

EXP MLB DEBUT: 2015 | H/W: 6-3 205 | FUT: Middle reliever | **6A**

Thrws R Age 26 — 2011 (4) Cal St Fullerton

Velo	Pitch	Grade
89-94	FB	+++
80-81	SL	++
81-84	CU	+++

Year	Lev	Team	W	L	Sv	IP	K	ERA	WHIP	BF/G	OBA	H%	S%	xERA	Ctl	Dom	Cmd	hr/9	BPV
2013	A+	Salem	2	1	1	47	44	2.11	1.06	8.7	236	32	78	2.14	1.7	8.4	4.9	0.0	123
2013	AA	Portland	1	1	5	28	31	2.87	1.06	7.3	217	27	81	3.08	2.6	9.9	3.9	1.3	127
2014	AA	Portland	2	1	18	67	56	2.15	1.07	6.2	228	30	78	2.07	2.1	7.5	3.5	0.0	95
2015	AAA	Pawtucket	4	1	3	42	38	2.35	1.21	5.7	217	28	80	2.47	3.8	8.1	2.1	0.2	60
2015	MLB	Boston	0	1	0	13	13	4.15	1.54	3.3	262	30	82	5.62	4.8	9.0	1.9	2.1	49

Sinkerballer who reached BOS for first time despite increasing walk rate. FB shows vicious, late action and can be tough to command. Low 3/4 slot helps pitch movement and provides deception. Induces groundballs and can register Ks with FB and solid-average CU. SL can be too loose and slurvy. Lacks upside, but has ability to get double plays.

Ravenelle,Adam — RP — Detroit

EXP MLB DEBUT: 2017 | H/W: 6-3 185 | FUT: Setup reliever | **7D**

Thrws R Age 23 — 2014 (4) Vanderbilt

Velo	Pitch	Grade
92-95	FB	+++
80-85	SL	+++
	CU	+

Year	Lev	Team	W	L	Sv	IP	K	ERA	WHIP	BF/G	OBA	H%	S%	xERA	Ctl	Dom	Cmd	hr/9	BPV
2014	NCAA	Vanderbilt	3	2	3	40	37	1.35	0.83	6.1	144	19	84	0.70	3.2	8.3	2.6	0.2	83
2014	Rk	GCL Tigers	0	0	0	1	1	0.00	0.00	2.8	0	0			0.0	9.0		0.0	180
2014	A	West Michigan	0	0	1	3	5	0.00	0.00	4.2	0	0			0.0	15.0		0.0	288
2015	Rk	GCL Tigers	0	0	0	4	1	0.00	0.75	7.1	0	0	100		6.8	2.3	0.3	0.0	-124
2015	A	West Michigan	2	0	0	34	40	3.96	1.47	7.7	244	34	73	3.73	5.0	10.6	2.1	0.5	73

Projectable RP who began season in June. Developing SL turning into true swing and miss pitch while FB command needs work. Gets good, late sink on FB and is difficult to control. K rate could be higher if he got ahead in count more consistently. Has clean, quick arm action to generate velocity. Needs work on LHH and control.

Ravin,Josh — RP — Los Angeles (N)

EXP MLB DEBUT: 2015 | H/W: 6-4 230 | FUT: Setup reliever | **6B**

Thrws R Age 28 — 2006 (5) HS (CA)

Velo	Pitch	Grade
95-98	FB	++++
85-87	SL	++

Year	Lev	Team	W	L	Sv	IP	K	ERA	WHIP	BF/G	OBA	H%	S%	xERA	Ctl	Dom	Cmd	hr/9	BPV
2013	AAA	Louisville	0	0	0	10	9	7.06	2.25	5.2	294	36	68	6.79	9.7	7.9	0.8	0.9	-101
2014	AA	Chattanooga	1	1	4	14	17	3.17	1.34	4.9	231	32	78	3.33	4.4	10.8	2.4	0.6	92
2014	AAA	Albuquerque	1	0	2	10	8	4.41	1.86	4.3	294	35	78	5.81	6.2	7.1	1.1	0.9	-22
2015	AAA	Oklahoma City	3	1	3	28	38	3.86	1.39	5.4	226	34	73	3.40	5.1	12.2	2.4	0.6	99
2015	MLB	LA Dodgers	2	1	0	9	12	6.92	1.87	4.7	336	42	71	8.40	4.0	11.9	3.0	3.0	125

Older prospect finally made his MLB debut after nine seasons in the minors. RH reliever features a quality 95-98 mph FB, topping out at 100 mph. Ditched his CB and CU for a nice cutter/slider. FB can be straight, but he does a good job of keeping it down in the zone.

Rea,Colin — SP — San Diego

EXP MLB DEBUT: 2015 | H/W: 6-5 220 | FUT: #4 starter | **7B**

Thrws R Age 25 — 2011 (12) Indiana State

Velo	Pitch	Grade
90-93	FB	+++
75-78	CB	++
83-85	CT	+++
81-82	CU	+++

Year	Lev	Team	W	L	Sv	IP	K	ERA	WHIP	BF/G	OBA	H%	S%	xERA	Ctl	Dom	Cmd	hr/9	BPV
2013	A+	Lake Elsinore	0	5	0	43	45	6.07	1.91	13.6	262	34	67	5.19	8.2	9.4	1.2	0.6	-33
2014	A+	Lake Elsinore	11	9	0	139	118	3.88	1.35	20.7	278	34	72	4.12	2.4	7.6	3.2	0.7	91
2015	AA	San Antonio	3	2	0	75	60	1.08	0.81	22.7	191	24	87	1.09	1.3	7.2	5.5	0.1	112
2015	AAA	El Paso	2	2	0	26	20	4.47	1.56	19.1	282	33	72	4.69	4.1	6.9	1.7	0.7	30
2015	MLB	San Diego	2	2	0	31	26	4.33	1.28	21.3	248	30	66	3.40	3.2	7.5	2.4	0.6	67

Tall, angular SP who reached majors after breakout season. Lacks dominant offering, but thrives with pitch movement, deception, and angle to plate. Throws all offerings for strikes and keeps ball low in zone consistently. Slow CB is fringy pitch, but can register Ks with CU that features plus, late action.

Reed,Chris — RP — Miami

EXP MLB DEBUT: 2015 | H/W: 6-3 225 | FUT: Middle reliever | **6C**

Thrws L Age 25 — 2011 (1) Stanford

Velo	Pitch	Grade
91-93	FB	+++
73-77	CB	++
	CU	++

Year	Lev	Team	W	L	Sv	IP	K	ERA	WHIP	BF/G	OBA	H%	S%	xERA	Ctl	Dom	Cmd	hr/9	BPV
2014	AAA	Albuquerque	0	3	0	21	18	11.09	2.27	21.5	383	44	51	9.55	4.7	7.7	1.6	2.1	30
2015	AA	Tulsa	2	2	1	23	16	7.37	1.72	6.6	252	29	55	4.76	7.0	6.2	0.9	0.8	-59
2015	AAA	New Orleans	1	0	0	20	23	4.01	1.53	6.3	240	31	79	4.62	5.8	10.2	1.8	1.3	46
2015	AAA	Oklahoma City	0	0	0	11	5	3.27	1.36	5.8	262	30	73	3.28	3.3	4.1	1.3	0.0	3
2015	MLB	Miami	0	0	0	4	1	4.50	1.75	9.1	347	37	71	5.60	2.3	2.3	1.0	0.0	-2

Tall lefty struggled with control and was traded to the Marlins for G. Dayton. Has some funk in his delivery that creates deception, but also inconsistency in his release point, which results in below-avg control. FB sits in the low-90s with good sink. Complements it with a plus SL and a below avg CU. The move to relief seems likely to stick.

Reed,Cody — SP — Arizona

EXP MLB DEBUT: 2019 | H/W: 6-3 245 | FUT: #3 starter | **8E**

Thrws L Age 19 — 2014 (2) HS (AL)

Velo	Pitch	Grade
91-94	FB	++++
82-84	SL	+++
	CU	++

Year	Lev	Team	W	L	Sv	IP	K	ERA	WHIP	BF/G	OBA	H%	S%	xERA	Ctl	Dom	Cmd	hr/9	BPV
2014	Rk	Azl DBacks	0	1	0	20	26	2.23	1.09	7.9	230	35	77	2.09	2.2	11.6	5.2	0.0	166
2014	Rk	Missoula	0	1	0	12	14	2.25	0.83	11.0	81	9	78	0.59	5.3	10.5	2.0	0.8	65
2015	A-	Hillsboro	5	4	0	63	72	3.28	1.14	16.7	223	30	73	2.82	3.0	10.3	3.4	0.7	122

Big-boned LHP at physical projection. Sits in low 90s with FB; touches 96. FB tails away from RH hitters. SL has potential of being swing-and-miss offering. Depth improved throughout NWL stint. Has feel for CU. Generates solid arm-side bore. Consistency is improving.

Reed,Cody A. — SP — Cincinnati

EXP MLB DEBUT: 2017 | H/W: 6-5 220 | FUT: #2 starter | **9D**

Thrws L Age 22 — 2013 (2) NW Mississippi CC

Velo	Pitch	Grade
92-95	FB	++++
82-84	CU	+++
	SL	+++

Year	Lev	Team	W	L	Sv	IP	K	ERA	WHIP	BF/G	OBA	H%	S%	xERA	Ctl	Dom	Cmd	hr/9	BPV
2013	Rk	Idaho Falls	0	1	0	29	25	6.16	1.85	9.1	274	35	63	4.63	7.1	7.7	1.1	0.0	-35
2014	A	Lexington	3	9	0	84	58	5.46	1.68	19.9	307	36	66	5.22	3.9	6.2	1.6	0.5	26
2015	A+	Wilmington	5	5	1	67	65	2.15	1.19	20.7	247	32	83	2.98	2.4	8.7	3.6	0.4	110
2015	AA	NW Arkansas	2	2	0	28	19	3.51	1.21	22.7	246	28	74	3.56	2.6	6.1	2.4	1.0	58
2015	AA	Pensacola	6	2	0	49	60	2.20	1.12	24.2	219	33	80	2.21	2.9	11.0	3.8	0.2	137

Acquired by CIN mid-season in the Johnny Cueto trade. Commands plus FB for strikes; SL is quickly becoming an out pitch. Hard SL has always had strong break but the added depth in '15 has pushed pitch to plus potential. Has a good feel for CU. Has solid deception & movement but struggles with command.

Reed,Jake — RP — Minnesota

EXP MLB DEBUT: 2016 | H/W: 6-2 190 | FUT: Setup reliever | **7D**

Thrws R Age 23 — 2014 (5) Oregon

Velo	Pitch	Grade
91-95	FB	+++
81-83	SL	+++
	CU	++

Year	Lev	Team	W	L	Sv	IP	K	ERA	WHIP	BF/G	OBA	H%	S%	xERA	Ctl	Dom	Cmd	hr/9	BPV
2014	NCAA	Oregon	4	1	13	37	34	1.95	1.00	4.6	174	23	81	1.47	3.6	8.3	2.3	0.2	68
2014	Rk	Elizabethton	0	0	3	6	8	0.00	0.17	4.5	56	10	100		0.0	12.0		0.0	234
2014	A	Cedar Rapids	3	0	5	25	31	0.36	0.52	5.2	124	20	92		1.1	11.2	10.3	0.0	190
2015	A+	Fort Myers	1	0	1	12	7	0.00	0.74	4.8	190	23	100	0.81	0.7	5.2	7.0	0.0	92
2015	AA	Chattanooga	4	4	1	47	39	6.32	1.62	6.0	293	36	59	4.88	4.0	7.5	1.9	0.6	44

Lean, athletic hurler who was demoted in August after lackluster season. Has plus arm strength that produces lively FB with good velocity, but K rate dropped as SL regressed. Has difficulty commanding secondary pitches and rarely uses CU. Throws from low 3/4 slot that gives him some deception. Key will be return of slider and FB command.

Reid-Foley,Sean — SP — Toronto

EXP MLB DEBUT: 2018 | H/W: 6-3 220 | FUT: #2 starter | **8C**

Thrws R Age 20 — 2014 (2) HS (FL)

Velo	Pitch	Grade
91-97	FB	++++
82-86	SL	+++
84-87	CU	++

Year	Lev	Team	W	L	Sv	IP	K	ERA	WHIP	BF/G	OBA	H%	S%	xERA	Ctl	Dom	Cmd	hr/9	BPV
2014	Rk	GCL Blue Jays	1	2	0	22	25	4.86	1.40	10.4	251	36	61	3.16	4.1	10.1	2.5	0.0	91
2015	A	Lansing	3	5	0	63	90	3.71	1.58	16.3	243	38	76	3.90	6.1	12.8	2.1	0.4	83
2015	A+	Dunedin	1	5	0	32	35	5.31	1.52	17.5	216	30	63	3.29	6.7	9.8	1.5	0.3	13

Strong-framed SP who has dazzling stuff, but will need to work on mechanics and control. Has deceptive delivery with quick, strong arm and can fire plus FB on downhill plane. Holds velocity late and can eat innings. Posts very high K rate and also induces groundballs. Needs to add polish to rudimentary CU.

Reyes,Alex — SP — St. Louis

EXP MLB DEBUT: 2016 | H/W: 6-3 175 | FUT: #1 starter | **10D**

Thrws R Age 21 — 2012 FA (DR)

Velo	Pitch	Grade
96-97	FB	+++++
75-78	CB	++++
88-90	CU	++++

Year	Lev	Team	W	L	Sv	IP	K	ERA	WHIP	BF/G	OBA	H%	S%	xERA	Ctl	Dom	Cmd	hr/9	BPV
2013	Rk	Johnson City	6	4	0	58	68	3.41	1.41	20.5	248	36	74	3.29	4.3	10.5	2.4	0.2	90
2014	A	Peoria	7	7	0	109	137	3.63	1.31	21.5	210	31	72	2.88	5.0	11.3	2.2	0.5	86
2015	Rk	GCL Cardinals	0	0	0	3	3	0.00	0.00	8.5	0	0			0.0	9.0		0.0	180
2015	A+	Palm Beach	2	5	0	63	96	2.28	1.27	19.9	216	37	80	2.34	4.4	13.7	3.1	0.0	145
2015	AA	Springfield	3	2	0	34	52	3.16	1.14	16.9	179	31	71	1.84	4.7	13.7	2.9	0.3	136

Top prospect in the system will miss 50 games due to 2nd drug violation. Stuff is highlighted by a plus-plus 96-97 mph FB that tops at 102 mph with good arm-side run. Also has a hard 12-6 CB and an improved CU. Mechanics have been smoothed out and now draws on the plus velo with ease. One of the best pitching prospects in baseball.

Reynolds,Danny — RP — Houston

EXP MLB DEBUT: 2016 | H/W: 6-0 190 | FUT: Setup reliever | **6B**

Thrws R Age 24 — 2009 (6) HS (NV)

Velo	Pitch	Grade
92-95	FB	++++
85-88	SL	++
82-83	CU	+

Year	Lev	Team	W	L	Sv	IP	K	ERA	WHIP	BF/G	OBA	H%	S%	xERA	Ctl	Dom	Cmd	hr/9	BPV
2013	A+	Inland Empire	11	10	0	145	114	5.40	1.43	23.7	260	30	64	4.51	4.0	7.1	1.8	1.2	38
2014	A+	Inland Empire	0	0	0	20	19	1.80	0.90	6.8	163	23	78	0.87	3.2	8.6	2.7	0.0	87
2014	AA	Arkansas	3	2	2	40	41	3.60	1.43	5.7	271	36	73	3.73	3.4	9.2	2.7	0.2	93
2014	AAA	Salt Lake	1	0	0	2	3	0.00	1.00	7.6	151	27	100	0.94	4.5	13.5	3.0	0.0	140
2015	AA	Arkansas	2	3	10	43	50	4.59	1.44	4.3	219	32	66	3.04	5.8	10.4	1.8	0.2	48

Short, aggressive RP who has spent most of last 2 years in AA, but on verge of majors. Converted to RP in '14 and showed increased K rate and success against RHH (.180). Has athletic delivery and quick arm to add movement to plus FB. Walk rate increased as he tends to overthrow both FB and SL. Size and inconsistency will keep him in bullpen.

Rhame,Jacob — RP — Los Angeles (N)

EXP MLB DEBUT: 2016 | H/W: 6-0 190 | FUT: Setup reliever | 7C

Thrws R Age 23	Year	Lev	Team	W	L	Sv	IP	K	ERA	WHIP	BF/G	OBA	H%	S%	xERA	Ctl	Dom	Cmd	hr/9	BPV
2013 (6) Grayson County CC	2013	NCAA	Grayson County	2	0	0	75	58	2.16	1.00	23.9	232	29	78	2.17	1.3	7.0	5.3	0.2	108
94-98 FB ++++	2013	Rk	Ogden	1	2	8	19	21	4.69	1.46	4.1	260	34	69	4.32	4.2	9.8	2.3	0.9	81
85-88 SL ++	2014	A	Great Lakes	5	4	9	67	90	2.01	0.92	4.9	202	31	80	1.72	1.9	12.1	6.4	0.4	185
CU ++	2015	A+	RanchoCuca	0	0	1	7	13	0.00	0.43	4.5	92	23	100	-1.10	1.3	16.7	13.0	0.0	284
	2015	AA	Tulsa	3	3	2	50	57	3.06	1.06	5.0	194	26	75	2.45	3.4	10.3	3.0	0.9	110

Thrives with a plus sinking FB that now sits at 94-98 mph and is difficult to square up. Mixes in a decent CU and ditched the CB in favor of a hard SL. Hooks the ball behind his back before release, creating some deception, but also leads to below-avg control.

Rhoades,Jeremy — SP — Los Angeles (A)

EXP MLB DEBUT: 2017 | H/W: 6-4 225 | FUT: #4 starer | 7D

Thrws R Age 23	Year	Lev	Team	W	L	Sv	IP	K	ERA	WHIP	BF/G	OBA	H%	S%	xERA	Ctl	Dom	Cmd	hr/9	BPV
2014 (4) Illinois St																				
90-94 FB +++	2014	NCAA	Illinois St	6	4	4	76	92	2.36	1.17	16.0	229	34	78	2.29	3.0	10.9	3.7	0.0	134
81-83 SL +++	2014	Rk	Orem	2	1	0	38	40	4.48	1.52	11.8	285	37	71	4.61	3.5	9.4	2.7	0.7	92
CU +	2015	A	Burlington	5	5	0	87	78	2.69	1.08	21.2	234	30	76	2.55	2.0	8.1	4.1	0.4	110
	2015	A+	Inland Empire	4	5	0	50	57	8.43	1.65	22.5	315	38	52	7.09	3.2	10.2	3.2	2.5	115

Tall SP who was solid in Low-A before being hit hard in High-A in July. Has two solid offerings in quick FB and SL that features late break. Throws with effort and has limited deception in mechanics. Has difficulty repeating complicated delivery, but could enhance stuff with more smooth arm action. Sequencing and changing speeds need work.

Richy,John — SP — Philadelphia

EXP MLB DEBUT: 2018 | H/W: 6-4 215 | FUT: #4 starter | 7C

Thrws R Age 23	Year	Lev	Team	W	L	Sv	IP	K	ERA	WHIP	BF/G	OBA	H%	S%	xERA	Ctl	Dom	Cmd	hr/9	BPV
2014 (3) UNLV	2014	NCAA	UNLV	11	4	0	121		3.20	1.13	29.9	249	33	70	2.62	1.8	8.4	4.7	0.1	121
89-91 FB +++	2014	Rk	Ogden	0	0	0	17	17	5.79	1.40	9.0	293	38	57	4.28	2.1	8.9	4.3	0.5	122
81-84 CB ++	2014	A	Great Lakes	0	0	0	16	14	1.68	1.30	16.6	236	31	86	2.75	3.9	7.8	2.0	0.0	53
84-86 CU ++	2015	A+	Clearwater	0	0	0	12	10	2.95	0.90	22.7	225	27	70	2.30	0.7	7.4	10.0	0.7	131
	2015	A+	RanchoCuca	10	5	0	124	105	4.21	1.43	24.0	290	35	72	4.56	2.5	7.6	3.1	0.8	88

Sports a refined three-pitch mix. Commands everything well; FB struggles to get to 90 mph, but is lively with heavy sink and is at its best when he locates it down. CB, CU are good complements. Sturdy frame built to soak up innings, especially effective when drives out over his front knee. Could move quickly due to polished repetoire.

Robichaux,Austin — SP — Los Angeles (A)

EXP MLB DEBUT: 2017 | H/W: 6-5 170 | FUT: #4 starter | 7E

Thrws R Age 23	Year	Lev	Team	W	L	Sv	IP	K	ERA	WHIP	BF/G	OBA	H%	S%	xERA	Ctl	Dom	Cmd	hr/9	BPV
2014 (18) Louisiana-Laf	2012	NCAA	Louisiana-Laf	2	4	0	43	21	2.92	1.25	14.6	261	29	77	3.38	2.3	4.4	1.9	0.4	35
89-92 FB +++	2013	NCAA	Louisiana-Laf	9	2	0	109	88	3.05	1.08	26.6	238	29	72	2.68	1.8	7.3	4.0	0.5	100
75-77 CB ++	2014	NCAA	Louisiana-Laf	8	3	0	89	80	3.13	1.04	24.6	215	27	70	2.30	2.4	8.1	3.3	0.5	98
78-80 CU ++	2014	Rk	Orem	2	3	0	40	27	4.94	1.30	11.0	280	31	64	4.41	1.8	6.1	3.4	1.1	79
	2015	A	Burlington	9	8	0	142	92	3.74	1.31	20.9	254	29	73	3.73	3.2	5.8	1.8	0.8	37

Long and lanky SP who enjoyed moderate success in first full season. Disappointing K rate, but doesn't have velocity or plus pitch to increase. Uses height to pitch on tough, downhill plane and gets high amount of groundballs. Shows feel for control and using all pitches. CB and CU only show average potential at peak.

Robinson,Alex — RP — Minnesota

EXP MLB DEBUT: 2018 | H/W: 6-3 220 | FUT: Setup reliever | 7D

Thrws L Age 21	Year	Lev	Team	W	L	Sv	IP	K	ERA	WHIP	BF/G	OBA	H%	S%	xERA	Ctl	Dom	Cmd	hr/9	BPV
2015 (5) Maryland																				
91-96 FB ++++																				
80-82 SL ++																				
CU +	2015	NCAA	Maryland	1	1	3	27	32	1.65	1.18	4.3	135	20	87	1.57	6.6	10.6	1.6	0.3	30
	2015	Rk	Elizabethton	0	3	0	12	15	9.00	2.17	6.0	228	35	54	4.79	12.0	11.3	0.9	0.0	-104

Big-framed RP who is all about power with plus FB and fringy SL. Has difficulty controlling pitches due to movement and max effort delivery. Lively FB registers Ks, but needs to throw more strikes. SL shows flashes of becoming solid offering, but needs to repeat slot. Rarely changes speed and will need time to polish mechanics.

Robson,Tom — SP — Toronto

EXP MLB DEBUT: 2018 | H/W: 6-4 210 | FUT: #4 starter | 7D

Thrws R Age 22	Year	Lev	Team	W	L	Sv	IP	K	ERA	WHIP	BF/G	OBA	H%	S%	xERA	Ctl	Dom	Cmd	hr/9	BPV
2011 (4) HS (BC)	2013	A-	Vancouver	3	0	0	38	29	0.94	1.02	20.9	207	26	90	1.69	2.6	6.9	2.6	0.0	71
89-94 FB +++	2014	A	Lansing	2	4	0	31	22	6.35	1.76	17.9	296	35	61	5.03	5.2	6.3	1.2	0.3	-8
75-79 CB +++	2015	Rk	GCL Blue Jays	0	0	0	4	5	4.29	2.38	7.3	432	54	89	10.83	2.1	10.7	5.0	2.1	153
81-83 SL ++	2015	A-	Vancouver	0	1	0	5	9	5.29	1.18	10.2	122	27	50	1.08	7.1	15.9	2.3	0.0	113
84-87 CU ++	2015	A	Lansing	0	2	0	26	21	5.15	1.72	17.0	296	35	70	5.27	4.8	7.2	1.5	0.7	18

Slowly developing prospect who has been beset by injuries, including TJ surgery in '14. Average pitch mix enhanced by high 3/4 slot and sinker induces high amount of groundballs. Has trouble commanding plate, somewhat attributable to pitch movement. Mixes in very good CB that is tough on RHH. Has occasional SL and CU that is too firm.

Rodgers,Brady — SP — Houston

EXP MLB DEBUT: 2016 | H/W: 6-2 205 | FUT: #4 starter | 7E

Thrws R Age 25	Year	Lev	Team	W	L	Sv	IP	K	ERA	WHIP	BF/G	OBA	H%	S%	xERA	Ctl	Dom	Cmd	hr/9	BPV
2012 (3) Arizona St	2013	AA	Corpus Christi	1	0	0	5	6	0.00	1.00	19.1	262	38	100	2.30	0.0	10.8		0.0	212
89-93 FB +++	2013	AAA	Oklahoma City	0	0	0	5	4	1.80	1.00	19.1	262	33	80	2.33	0.0	7.2		0.0	148
80-83 SL +++	2014	AA	Corpus Christi	5	12	2	120	87	4.79	1.28	19.0	285	32	65	4.43	1.4	6.5	4.6	1.1	97
74-77 CB ++	2014	AAA	Oklahoma City	1	0	0	6	4	0.00	0.50	19.9	106	13	100		1.5	6.0	4.0	0.0	86
81-84 CU +++	2015	AAA	Fresno	9	7	0	115	89	4.53	1.40	23.1	295	34	70	4.77	2.0	7.0	3.6	1.0	90

Low-ceiling SP who has advanced one level per year. Relies more on guile and savvy than stuff, though he exhibits strong command of four-pitch arsenal. Impeccably spots FB despite late movement and sink and SL flashes plus at times. Mixes in slower CB and deceptive CU with fading action. Has starter arsenal, but can be hittable.

Rodriguez,Helmis — SP — Colorado

EXP MLB DEBUT: 2019 | H/W: 5-11 155 | FUT: #4 starter | 7D

Thrws L Age 21	Year	Lev	Team	W	L	Sv	IP	K	ERA	WHIP	BF/G	OBA	H%	S%	xERA	Ctl	Dom	Cmd	hr/9	BPV
2010 FA (VZ)																				
87-91 FB +++																				
80-83 CU +++	2013	Rk	Grand Junction	2	4	0	54	36	5.15	1.40	15.3	282	32	63	4.42	2.7	6.0	2.3	0.8	54
CB +	2014	A-	Tri-City	4	7	0	91	41	1.98	1.10	23.8	242	27	82	2.53	1.8	4.1	2.3	0.2	43
	2015	A	Asheville	9	8	0	147	101	3.37	1.36	22.8	248	29	76	3.58	3.9	6.2	1.6	0.6	25

Short lefty had mixed results posting a 3.36 ERA at Low-A, but Cmd took at step back. Best offering is a 87-90 mph sinking FB that he pounds down in the zone. CU is plus with above-avg potential and good late sink, but his CB remains inconsistent. Pitches to contact and needs to throw strikes to be successful. Little margin for error.

Rodriguez,Jefry — SP — Washington

EXP MLB DEBUT: 2018 | H/W: 6-5 185 | FUT: #4 starter / reliever | 7C

Thrws R Age 22	Year	Lev	Team	W	L	Sv	IP	K	ERA	WHIP	BF/G	OBA	H%	S%	xERA	Ctl	Dom	Cmd	hr/9	BPV
2012 FA (DR)	2013	Rk	GCL Nationals	3	0	0	47	43	2.48	1.27	16.1	231	30	80	2.78	3.8	8.2	2.2	0.2	63
91-93 FB +++	2014	A-	Auburn	1	0	0	16	9	2.80	1.24	21.8	261	31	75	2.95	2.2	5.0	2.3	0.0	48
78-80 CB +++	2014	A	Hagerstown	0	2	0	17	11	6.88	1.88	20.0	360	42	59	6.13	2.6	5.8	2.2	0.0	51
83 CU ++	2015	A-	Auburn	3	5	0	68	67	4.62	1.54	22.9	272	35	69	4.32	4.4	8.8	2.0	0.5	60
	2015	A	Hagerstown	1	5	0	42	27	6.82	1.66	18.9	274	31	57	4.79	5.3	5.8	1.1	0.6	-22

Tough year overall, which included demotion to NYPL. FB/CB combination has potential, as both could be bat-missing pitches. But rough present mechanics hinder control, and durability/long term health still a question. Excellent size, but much work to do. Could end up as RP.

Rogers,Taylor — SP — Minnesota

EXP MLB DEBUT: 2016 | H/W: 6-3 180 | FUT: #5 starter | 6B

Thrws L Age 25	Year	Lev	Team	W	L	Sv	IP	K	ERA	WHIP	BF/G	OBA	H%	S%	xERA	Ctl	Dom	Cmd	hr/9	BPV
2012 (11) Kentucky	2012	A	Beloit	2	2	0	33	35	2.72	1.36	15.4	261	32	88	4.49	3.3	9.5	2.9	1.4	101
89-93 FB +++	2013	A	Cedar Rapids	0	1	0	10	10	7.20	1.80	15.4	332	42	59	6.24	3.6	9.0	2.5	0.9	83
78-82 SL +++	2013	A+	Fort Myers	11	6	0	130	83	2.56	1.16	23.6	245	29	78	2.85	2.2	5.7	2.6	0.3	62
79-83 CU ++	2014	AA	New Britain	11	6	0	145	113	3.29	1.29	24.8	268	33	73	3.39	2.3	7.0	3.1	0.2	82
	2015	AAA	Rochester	11	12	0	174	126	3.98	1.34	25.9	279	33	70	3.89	2.3	6.5	2.9	0.5	74

Tall, thin SP who finished 2nd in IL in Ks despite limited, fringy stuff. Throws with smooth delivery and clean arm while showcasing ability to move pitches around strike zone. Struggled with RHH (.330 oppBA) as he pitches to contact with sinker/SL combo. Can spot SL for strikes and keeps ball on ground.

Rollins,David — RP — Seattle

EXP MLB DEBUT: 2015 | H/W: 6-1 210 | FUT: Setup reliever | 6B

Thrws L Age 26	Year	Lev	Team	W	L	Sv	IP	K	ERA	WHIP	BF/G	OBA	H%	S%	xERA	Ctl	Dom	Cmd	hr/9	BPV
2011 (24) San Jacinto	2013	AA	Corpus Christi	0	3	0	33	33	4.36	1.45	23.5	290	36	73	4.89	2.7	9.0	3.3	1.1	106
91-95 FB ++++	2013	AAA	Oklahoma City	1	0	0	6	8	0.00	0.67	20.9	151	25	100	0.12	1.5	12.0	8.0	0.0	194
83-85 SL +++	2014	AA	Corpus Christi	3	4	1	78	77	3.81	1.23	11.7	252	32	71	3.52	2.5	8.9	3.5	0.8	109
	2015	AAA	Tacoma	0	0	0	9	8	0.00	0.88	4.8	214	28	100	1.41	1.0	7.9	8.0	0.0	134
	2015	MLB	Seattle	0	2	0	25	21	7.56	1.80	5.8	344	41	57	6.64	2.9	7.6	2.6	1.1	76

Hard-throwing RP who began year late after PED suspension. Reached majors on basis of pure arm strength and ability to miss bats with FB and SL. Has a lot of effort in delivery and will likely stay in pen long-term. Can pitch multiple innings and has decent control to warrant high-leverage role. Doesn't change speeds and can get on side of SL.

Romano,Sal — SP — Cincinnati

EXP MLB DEBUT: 2017 | H/W: 6-4 250 | FUT: #3 starter | 8E

Thrws R Age 22
2011 (23) HS (CT)

Velo	Pitch	Grade
92-95	FB	+ + + +
82-83	CB	+ + +
	CU	+ +

Year	Lev	Team	W	L	Sv	IP	K	ERA	WHIP	BF/G	OBA	H%	S%	xERA	Ctl	Dom	Cmd	hr/9	BPV
2012	Rk	Billings	5	6	0	64	52	5.34	1.51	18.5	290	36	61	4.17	3.2	7.3	2.3	0.1	62
2013	A	Dayton	7	11	0	120	89	4.87	1.59	21.2	283	33	70	4.84	4.3	6.7	1.6	0.7	23
2014	A	Dayton	8	11	0	148	128	4.13	1.42	22.5	288	36	71	4.28	2.6	7.8	3.0	0.5	89
2015	A+	Daytona	6	5	0	104	79	3.46	1.31	22.6	260	32	72	3.25	2.9	6.8	2.4	0.2	64
2015	AA	Pensacola	0	4	0	23	9	10.96	2.04	16.0	350	36	44	7.86	4.7	3.5	0.8	1.6	-45

Scouts are still waiting for him to take off. Tailing FB is best when working up in zone. Hard CB became 2nd viable pitch, adding additional depth in '15. CU is still very inconsistent. Successful season in High-A but struggled in AA.

Romero,Enny — RP — Tampa Bay

EXP MLB DEBUT: 2013 | H/W: 6-3 215 | FUT: Setup reliever | 7C

Thrws L Age 25
2008 FA (DR)

Velo	Pitch	Grade
88-96	FB	+ + + +
82-86	SL	+ + +
80-83	CU	+

Year	Lev	Team	W	L	Sv	IP	K	ERA	WHIP	BF/G	OBA	H%	S%	xERA	Ctl	Dom	Cmd	hr/9	BPV
2013	MLB	Tampa Bay	0	0	0	4	0	0.00	1.19	16.8	78	8	100	0.86	8.6	0.0	0.0	0.0	-213
2014	AAA	Durham	5	11	0	126	117	4.50	1.43	21.4	265	33	70	4.32	3.7	8.4	2.3	0.9	68
2015	A+	Charlotte	0	1	0	6	5	7.26	1.94	14.7	314	39	58	5.46	5.8	7.3	1.3	0.0	-8
2015	AAA	Durham	1	1	1	46	45	4.88	1.41	11.5	270	34	67	4.38	3.3	8.8	2.6	1.0	87
2015	MLB	Tampa Bay	0	2	0	30	31	5.10	1.73	5.9	316	41	69	5.24	3.9	9.3	2.4	0.3	80

Strong-framed pitcher who converted to RP in '15. Has pure arm strength with live arm that whips FB into high 90s at times. FB exhibits hard movement, though pitches up in zone. Hard SL is legitimate out pitch, but uses FB as go to pitch. Inconsistent release point impacts SL while CU has been discarded in short stints.

Romero,Fernando — SP — Minnesota

EXP MLB DEBUT: 2018 | H/W: 6-0 215 | FUT: #3 starter | 8E

Thrws R Age 21
2011 FA (DR)

Velo	Pitch	Grade
91-94	FB	+ + + +
78-81	CB	+ +
84-87	CB	+ + +

Year	Lev	Team	W	L	Sv	IP	K	ERA	WHIP	BF/G	OBA	H%	S%	xERA	Ctl	Dom	Cmd	hr/9	BPV
2013	Rk	GCL Twins	2	0	0	45	47	1.60	1.00	14.3	201	29	82	1.54	2.6	9.4	3.6	0.0	117
2014	A	Cedar Rapids	0	0	0	12	9	3.00	1.50	17.3	278	33	82	4.52	3.8	6.8	1.8	0.8	38
2015			*Did not pitch; injured*																

Powerful SP who missed season after TJ surgery in June '14. Injury history is only flaw. Owns loose arm to generate easy velocity with plus FB and uses power CB to miss bats. Repeats delivery that has some effort, but generally throws strikes. Has potential to develop plus CU, but needs to shore up consistency of breaking ball to ascend quickly.

Rucinski,Drew — SP — Chicago (N)

EXP MLB DEBUT: 2014 | H/W: 6-2 190 | FUT: Middle reliever | 6C

Thrws R Age 27
2011 (NDFA) Ohio St

Velo	Pitch	Grade
90-94	FB	+ + +
84-87	SP	+ + +
81-82	SL	+ +
78-80	CU	+ +

Year	Lev	Team	W	L	Sv	IP	K	ERA	WHIP	BF/G	OBA	H%	S%	xERA	Ctl	Dom	Cmd	hr/9	BPV
2013	A+	Inland Empire	2	2	0	29	21	1.86	1.14	23.0	262	32	82	2.69	1.2	6.5	5.3	0.0	102
2014	AA	Arkansas	10	6	0	148	140	3.16	1.23	23.1	254	33	74	3.20	2.5	8.5	3.4	0.4	104
2014	MLB	LA Angels	0	0	0	7	8	5.07	1.55	10.3	310	43	64	4.40	2.5	10.1	4.0	0.0	132
2015	AAA	Salt Lake	5	7	0	112	87	5.70	1.65	22.8	308	34	70	6.24	3.5	7.0	2.0	1.7	48
2015	MLB	LA Angels	0	2	0	7	4	7.71	2.29	8.9	336	36	67	7.94	7.7	5.1	0.7	1.3	-98

Deceptive SP who has MLB experience after stint in indy leagues. Not overpowering with average FB, but riding life makes it tough to elevate. Uses hard SP as out pitch, though SL and CU remain below average. Control regressed, but generally is around plate. Has chance to carve out role due to stamina and deep repertoire. Repeats delivery well.

Rumbelow,Nick — RP — New York (A)

EXP MLB DEBUT: 2015 | H/W: 6-0 190 | FUT: Middle reliever | 6B

Thrws R Age 24
2013 (7) Louisiana St

Velo	Pitch	Grade
90-94	FB	+ + +
79-82	CB	+ + +
	CU	+

Year	Lev	Team	W	L	Sv	IP	K	ERA	WHIP	BF/G	OBA	H%	S%	xERA	Ctl	Dom	Cmd	hr/9	BPV
2014	A+	Tampa	5	1	1	26	29	2.41	1.07	5.3	214	31	75	1.87	2.8	10.0	3.6	0.0	124
2014	AA	Trenton	0	0	1	7	15	3.80	0.70	3.6	167	44	40	0.31	1.3	19.0	15.0	0.0	326
2014	AAA	Scranton/WB	0	1	1	15	19	4.14	1.45	6.5	284	39	75	4.85	3.0	11.3	3.8	1.2	141
2015	AAA	Scranton/WB	2	3	8	52	57	4.31	1.15	5.6	242	32	63	3.07	2.2	9.8	4.4	0.7	134
2015	MLB	NY Yankees	1	1	0	15	15	4.14	1.38	3.8	272	33	74	4.53	3.0	8.9	3.0	1.2	98

Short, quick-armed RP who has spent entire career in pen. Lacks ideal frame for late-innings dominance, but exhibits pitch movement and above average command. Doesn't change speeds much, but doesn't have to in short stints. Big-breaking CB flashes plus and he has the durability to pitch multiple innings.

Russell,Ashe — SP — Kansas City

EXP MLB DEBUT: 2019 | H/W: 6-4 201 | FUT: #2 starter | 8D

Thrws R Age 19
2015 (1) HS (IN)

Velo	Pitch	Grade
91-94	FB	+ + + +
80-84	SL	+ + +
	CU	+

Year	Lev	Team	W	L	Sv	IP	K	ERA	WHIP	BF/G	OBA	H%	S%	xERA	Ctl	Dom	Cmd	hr/9	BPV
2015	Rk	Burlington	0	3	0	36	24	4.24	1.25	13.3	239	24	76	4.54	3.2	6.0	1.8	2.0	38

Quick-armed pitcher with lean, wiry frame and high ceiling. Locates FB to both sides of plate and has potential plus SL in arsenal. Can leave SL up in zone too often and will need to develop CU to battle LHH. Delivery is clean and fast, but has inconsistent release point which negatively impacts SL.

Sanchez,Ricardo — SP — Atlanta

EXP MLB DEBUT: 2019 | H/W: 5-11 170 | FUT: #3 starter | 8E

Thrws L Age 18
2013 FA (VZ)

Velo	Pitch	Grade
90-92	FB	+ + +
78-80	CB	+ + +
84-85	CU	+

Year	Lev	Team	W	L	Sv	IP	K	ERA	WHIP	BF/G	OBA	H%	S%	xERA	Ctl	Dom	Cmd	hr/9	BPV
2014	Rk	Azl Angels	2	2	0	38	43	3.53	1.62	14.1	271	38	76	4.00	5.2	10.1	2.0	0.0	60
2015	A	Rome	1	6	0	39	31	5.51	1.48	16.9	251	30	62	4.04	4.8	7.1	1.5	0.7	16

Struggled in his first taste of full season ball after being acquired by ATL in trade with LAA. Battled arm tenderness for most of the season. When healthy, he flashed two potential plus pitches, a heavy 2-seam FB and a 12-6 CB. Throwing strikes consistently is a big issue. His CU was non-existent in '15.

Sandoval,Patrick — SP — Houston

EXP MLB DEBUT: 2020 | H/W: 6-3 190 | FUT: #4 starter | 7E

Thrws L Age 19
2015 (11) HS (CA)

Velo	Pitch	Grade
87-91	FB	+ +
74-76	CB	+ + +
78-80	CU	+ +

Year	Lev	Team	W	L	Sv	IP	K	ERA	WHIP	BF/G	OBA	H%	S%	xERA	Ctl	Dom	Cmd	hr/9	BPV
2015	Rk	GCL Astros	0	3	0	13	11	6.18	1.98	10.5	373	45	68	7.26	2.7	7.6	2.8	0.7	80

Lean SP who has significant development time ahead of him. Offers some projection which will be needed as his FB is below average. Excellent CB shows promise of becoming plus pitch, but needs to stay on top of it. Crude delivery needs work and inability to repeat hinders control. Doesn't own out pitch and will need strength to thin frame.

Sands,Carson — SP — Chicago (N)

EXP MLB DEBUT: 2019 | H/W: 6-3 205 | FUT: #3 starter | 8D

Thrws L Age 21
2014 (4) HS (FL)

Velo	Pitch	Grade
90-95	FB	+ + +
73-75	CB	+ + +
76-78	CU	+ + +

Year	Lev	Team	W	L	Sv	IP	K	ERA	WHIP	BF/G	OBA	H%	S%	xERA	Ctl	Dom	Cmd	hr/9	BPV
2014	Rk	Azl Cubs	3	1	0	19	20	1.89	1.16	8.4	219	31	82	2.15	3.3	9.5	2.9	0.0	99
2015	A-	Eugene	3	4	0	57	41	3.94	1.45	17.4	278	34	70	3.71	3.3	6.5	2.0	0.0	45

Has a plus 90-94 mph FB, with good late life. Mixes in an improved CU and CB, both of which project as above-average offerings. Front-side mechanics are inconsistent, leading to fringy Cmd. Cubs have been cautious and limited his IP. Lots of potential, but needs to show more in '16.

Santillan,Antonio — SP — Cincinnati

EXP MLB DEBUT: 2019 | H/W: 6-3 240 | FUT: #3 starter | 8E

Thrws R Age 18
2015 (2) HS (TX)

Velo	Pitch	Grade
93-95	FB	+ + + +
82-84	CB	+ + +
	CU	+

Year	Lev	Team	W	L	Sv	IP	K	ERA	WHIP	BF/G	OBA	H%	S%	xERA	Ctl	Dom	Cmd	hr/9	BPV
2015	Rk	AZL Reds	0	2	0	19	19	5.16	1.35	10.0	217	28	60	3.07	5.2	8.9	1.7	0.5	39

Features plus FB with late action that hitters struggle to square up. Lacks consistent FB command; arm gets too quick for body and base. Calming down mechanics will help harness arm speed. Throws a 12-6 CB that projects plus. Has a remedial feel for CU. As mechanics improve, so will CU.

Santos,Michael — SP — San Francisco

EXP MLB DEBUT: 2018 | H/W: 6-4 170 | FUT: #3 starter | 8E

Thrws R Age 20
2012 FA (DR)

Velo	Pitch	Grade
90-93	FB	+ + +
72-76	CB	+ + +
80-82	CU	+ + +

Year	Lev	Team	W	L	Sv	IP	K	ERA	WHIP	BF/G	OBA	H%	S%	xERA	Ctl	Dom	Cmd	hr/9	BPV
2013	Rk	DSL Giants	1	2	0	19	18	2.81	1.25	19.5	250	33	75	2.78	2.8	8.4	3.0	0.0	94
2014	Rk	Azl Giants	4	3	0	59	50	2.58	1.22	19.9	261	32	80	3.29	2.0	7.6	3.8	0.5	101
2015	Rk	Azl Giants	0	0	0	3	5	0.00	0.67	5.2	0	0	100		6.0	15.0	2.5	0.0	126
2015	A	Augusta	0	2	0	36	23	3.48	1.33	16.7	271	31	74	3.77	2.5	5.7	2.3	0.5	54

Tall, lean RH has a projectable build and good feel for three-pitch mix. Fills zone with low-90s FB that could add a tick more with maturity. CB has slow 11-5 break, but projects as solid-avg pitch. CU is raw, but athleticism should allow him to hone it. Stays online with fluid, effortless delivery; repeatable mechanics. Guy to watch for in 2016.

Sborz,Joshua — SP — Los Angeles (N)

EXP MLB DEBUT: 2018 | H/W: 6-3 225 | FUT: Closer | 7C

Thrws R Age 22
2015 (2) Virginia

Velo	Pitch	Grade
92-95	FB	++++
	SL	++
	CU	+

Year	Lev	Team	W	L	Sv	IP	K	ERA	WHIP	BF/G	OBA	H%	S%	xERA	Ctl	Dom	Cmd	hr/9	BPV
2015	NCAA	Virginia	7	2	15	73	62	1.60	0.90	8.2	166	19	90	1.73	3.1	7.6	2.5	0.9	72
2015	Rk	Ogden	0	1	0	4	4	2.25	1.25	8.1	81	12	80	0.95	9.0	9.0	1.0	0.0	-63
2015	A	Great Lakes	0	1	0	6	9	2.95	1.15	12.1	225	27	100	4.94	3.0	13.3	4.5	3.0	177
2015	A+	RanchoCuca	0	0	2	12	12	1.50	1.25	5.4	262	33	93	3.65	2.3	9.0	4.0	0.8	119

2nd rounder was the MVP of the 2015 CWS. Strong-armed hurler has a plus 92-95 mph FB that tops out at 98 mph and has good late life. Backs it up with an avg SL that has potential. Mixes in an occasional CU to keep hitters off-balance. Dodgers used him mostly in relief in his debut, but haven't settled on his long-term role yet.

Schultz,Jaime — SP — Tampa Bay

EXP MLB DEBUT: 2016 | H/W: 5-10 200 | FUT: #4 starter | 7D

Thrws R Age 24
2013 (14) High Point

Velo	Pitch	Grade
89-95	FB	+++
81-84	SL	++
77-81	CB	+++
	CU	+++

Year	Lev	Team	W	L	Sv	IP	K	ERA	WHIP	BF/G	OBA	H%	S%	xERA	Ctl	Dom	Cmd	hr/9	BPV
2013	NCAA	High Point	1	6	0	60	59	3.59	1.30	17.7	198	27	70	2.40	5.4	8.8	1.6	0.1	31
2013	A-	Hudson Valley	1	2	0	44	55	3.06	1.38	10.9	205	29	79	3.11	5.9	11.2	1.9	0.6	60
2014	A	Bowling Green	2	1	0	37	58	1.95	1.11	16.1	206	35	85	2.28	3.4	14.1	4.1	0.5	180
2014	A+	Charlotte	2	0	0	23	21	3.13	1.48	19.8	227	30	76	3.07	5.9	8.2	1.4	0.0	7
2015	AA	Montgomery	9	5	0	135	168	3.67	1.44	21.3	216	31	76	3.51	6.0	11.2	1.9	0.7	58

Short, strong SP who led SL in Ks. Doesn't look part of dynamic pitcher, but has live arm that generates easy velocity. Holds velocity deep into games and has posted low oppBA with high K rates. Repeats delivery well, but has trouble throwing strikes. Walks far too many hitters and may eventually shelve one of breaking balls.

Scott,Tanner — RP — Baltimore

EXP MLB DEBUT: 2017 | H/W: 6-2 220 | FUT: Setup reliever | 7D

Thrws L Age 21
2014 (6) Howard JC

Velo	Pitch	Grade
92-97	FB	++++
84-88	SL	++

Year	Lev	Team	W	L	Sv	IP	K	ERA	WHIP	BF/G	OBA	H%	S%	xERA	Ctl	Dom	Cmd	hr/9	BPV
2014	Rk	GCL Orioles	1	5	0	23	23	6.26	1.78	10.6	245	33	61	4.06	7.8	9.0	1.2	0.0	-31
2015	A-	Aberdeen	4	0	0	21	31	3.41	1.33	9.7	212	36	71	2.46	5.1	13.2	2.6	0.0	118
2015	A	Delmarva	0	3	2	21	29	4.29	1.38	9.8	243	39	66	2.99	4.3	12.4	2.9	0.0	126

Aggressive RP with strong frame and plus velocity. Generates velocity with pure strength and above average arm speed. Can reach triple digits, though FB can be straight and thrown with violent mechanics. Registers high K rate with FB and SL that could become at least average. Erratic command needs to get better.

Seddon,Joel — SP — Oakland

EXP MLB DEBUT: 2017 | H/W: 6-1 165 | FUT: #4 SP / Middle RP | 7E

Thrws R Age 23
2014 (11) South Carolina

Velo	Pitch	Grade
88-92	FB	+++
74-78	CB	+++
80-83	SL	++
81-83	CU	++

Year	Lev	Team	W	L	Sv	IP	K	ERA	WHIP	BF/G	OBA	H%	S%	xERA	Ctl	Dom	Cmd	hr/9	BPV
2013	NCAA	South Carolina	1	1	0	18	20	4.50	1.89	7.7	330	44	76	6.05	4.5	10.0	2.2	0.5	77
2014	NCAA	South Carolina	3	2	14	48	59	1.68	1.02	6.8	214	32	83	1.90	2.2	11.0	4.9	0.2	156
2014	Rk	Azl Athletics	0	0	0	2	4	4.50	1.50	8.6	151	38	67	2.16	9.0	18.0	2.0	0.0	99
2014	A	Beloit	2	2	1	25	20	2.87	1.12	5.2	220	26	77	2.76	2.9	7.2	2.5	0.7	70
2015	A+	Stockton	8	8	0	105	82	3.60	1.14	12.2	258	30	72	3.52	1.5	7.0	4.8	0.9	105

Lean, light pitcher who was converted to RP in mid-July despite deep repertoire. Throws four pitches for strikes and likes to use sinker early in count. Velocity is short to be top SP or late innings RP, but commands plate and keeps hitters off-guard with multiple pitches. Needs to polish CU where he can slow arm speed.

Selman,Sam — RP — Kansas City

EXP MLB DEBUT: 2016 | H/W: 6-3 195 | FUT: Setup reliever | 7D

Thrws L Age 25
2012 (2) Vanderbilt

Velo	Pitch	Grade
90-95	FB	+++
80-85	SL	+++
82-84	CU	+

Year	Lev	Team	W	L	Sv	IP	K	ERA	WHIP	BF/G	OBA	H%	S%	xERA	Ctl	Dom	Cmd	hr/9	BPV
2012	Rk	Idaho Falls	5	4	0	60	89	2.10	1.11	18.2	210	35	80	2.03	3.3	13.3	4.0	0.1	169
2013	A+	Wilmington	11	9	0	125	128	3.38	1.38	19.5	200	27	74	2.69	6.1	9.2	1.5	0.2	19
2014	AA	NW Arkansas	4	6	0	93	87	3.87	1.40	14.0	236	30	73	3.62	4.7	8.4	1.8	0.7	42
2014	AAA	Omaha	0	0	0	4	7	13.50	3.50	5.1	383	62	57	10.54	15.8	15.8	1.0	0.0	-124
2015	AA	NW Arkansas	3	5	3	56	69	5.29	1.75	6.2	261	37	68	4.62	6.7	11.1	1.6	0.5	35

Hard-throwing RP who converted to pen in mid '14 due to command issues. Spent 2nd year in AA and failed to produce strikes. Has dynamic stuff when on. Has been menace to LHH with high hard stuff and offers deceptive delivery that allows stuff to play up. SL has moments of brilliance, but struggles to repeat high effort delivery impacts command.

Senzatela,Antonio — SP — Colorado

EXP MLB DEBUT: 2019 | H/W: 6-1 180 | FUT: #3 starter | 7D

Thrws R Age 21
2011 FA (VZ)

Velo	Pitch	Grade
92-95	FB	++++
78-80	CB	+++
82-85	CU	++

Year	Lev	Team	W	L	Sv	IP	K	ERA	WHIP	BF/G	OBA	H%	S%	xERA	Ctl	Dom	Cmd	hr/9	BPV
2013	Rk	DSL Rockies	6	1	0	51	46	1.76	0.69	22.4	182	24	74	0.71	0.5	8.1	15.3	0.2	150
2013	A-	Tri-City	2	4	0	42	20	3.85	1.45	22.5	288	32	72	4.07	2.8	4.3	1.5	0.2	20
2014	A	Asheville	15	2	0	144	89	3.12	1.18	22.2	248	28	75	3.26	2.2	5.6	2.5	0.2	57
2015	A+	Modesto	9	9	0	154	143	2.51	1.06	23.0	232	29	79	2.64	1.9	8.4	4.3	0.6	116

RHP had a breakout season. Comes after hitters from a high 3/4 arm slot and gets late run on his plus 92-95 mph FB. Backs up the heater with a quality SL and serviceable CU. Attacks the strike zone. Jump in Dom gives him the potential to be an impact starter in the majors.

Sever,John — SP — Pittsburgh

EXP MLB DEBUT: 2019 | H/W: 6-4 190 | FUT: #5 starter/reliever | 7D

Thrws L Age 22
2014 (20) Bethune-Cookman

Velo	Pitch	Grade
90-93	FB	+++
	SL	+++
	CU	+

Year	Lev	Team	W	L	Sv	IP	K	ERA	WHIP	BF/G	OBA	H%	S%	xERA	Ctl	Dom	Cmd	hr/9	BPV
2014	NCAA	BethuneCookmn	3	5	4	59	49	4.27	1.49	12.1	238	30	69	3.40	5.5	7.5	1.4	0.2	4
2014	Rk	Bristol	1	3	1	40	63	1.34	1.17	10.0	209	37	89	2.23	3.8	14.1	3.7	0.2	169
2015	A	West Virginia	3	3	4	86	84	2.92	1.25	12.1	241	31	78	3.26	3.2	8.8	2.7	0.6	88

Tall, lanky LHP was a 20th round pick in '14. Split time between starting and relieving and put up solid numbers. FB sits in the low-90s and he tends to pitch up in the zone. Mixes in a good wipe-out SL that gets swings and misses. CU remains a work in progress and will need to develop for him to remain a starter.

Sheffield,Justus — SP — Cleveland

EXP MLB DEBUT: 2018 | H/W: 5-10 196 | FUT: #3 starter | 8C

Thrws L Age 19
2014 (1) HS (TN)

Velo	Pitch	Grade
91-95	FB	++++
75-78	CB	+++
82-85	SL	+++
81-82	CU	+

Year	Lev	Team	W	L	Sv	IP	K	ERA	WHIP	BF/G	OBA	H%	S%	xERA	Ctl	Dom	Cmd	hr/9	BPV
2014	Rk	AZL Indians	3	1	0	20	29	4.90	1.63	11.2	296	46	67	4.37	4.0	12.9	3.2	0.0	142
2015	A	Lake County	9	4	0	127	138	3.33	1.36	20.5	273	37	76	3.91	2.7	9.8	3.6	0.6	121

Short, yet powerful prospect who was 2nd in MWL in K and was outstanding late. Throws lively FB with conviction early in count and uses hard SL to wipe out hitters from both sides. Has surprising angle to plate and has velocity to pitch up in zone. Can be in strike zone too much and has been hittable. Needs to upgrade CU to realize vast potential.

Sherfy,Jimmie — RP — Arizona

EXP MLB DEBUT: 2016 | H/W: 6-0 175 | FUT: Setup reliever | 7D

Thrws R Age 24
2013 (10) Oregon

Velo	Pitch	Grade
94-97	FB	++++
83-85	SL	+++

Year	Lev	Team	W	L	Sv	IP	K	ERA	WHIP	BF/G	OBA	H%	S%	xERA	Ctl	Dom	Cmd	hr/9	BPV
2013	A-	Hillsboro	0	0	5	9	17	0.00	0.44	3.3	106	26	100		1.0	17.0	17.0	0.0	297
2013	A	South Bend	1	1	2	8	12	2.22	1.60	4.0	304	48	85	4.42	3.3	13.3	4.0	0.0	168
2014	A+	Visalia	2	0	6	11	23	3.27	1.00	3.8	162	33	78	2.55	4.1	18.8	4.6	1.6	246
2014	AA	Mobile	3	1	1	38	45	4.97	1.37	4.3	241	33	65	3.84	4.3	10.7	2.5	0.9	95
2015	AA	Mobile	1	6	2	49	50	6.59	1.59	4.9	265	35	56	4.35	5.1	9.1	1.8	0.5	44

Short statured, max-effort reliever who struggles commanding 2-pitch arsenal. Has trouble repeating low 3/4's delivery. FB sits in the mid-to-upper 90s. In a 20-pitch scouted sequence, hit target only 3 times. FB has late arm-side run. SL is inconsistent, swing-and-miss offering. Solid, 2-plane break. Like FB, has no idea where it is going.

Shipley,Braden — SP — Arizona

EXP MLB DEBUT: 2016 | H/W: 6-2 185 | FUT: #2 starter | 8C

Thrws R Age 24
2013 (1) Nevada

Velo	Pitch	Grade
92-94	FB	++++
78-80	CB	+++
83-86	CU	++++

Year	Lev	Team	W	L	Sv	IP	K	ERA	WHIP	BF/G	OBA	H%	S%	xERA	Ctl	Dom	Cmd	hr/9	BPV
2013	A	South Bend	0	1	0	20	16	2.67	1.09	19.7	197	23	80	2.58	3.6	7.1	2.0	0.9	50
2014	A	South Bend	4	2	0	45	41	3.78	1.26	23.1	265	34	68	3.22	2.2	8.2	3.7	0.2	106
2014	A+	Visalia	2	4	0	60	68	4.04	1.30	24.7	252	33	72	3.90	3.1	10.2	3.2	1.0	116
2014	AA	Mobile	1	2	0	20	18	3.60	1.20	20.1	199	22	76	3.30	4.5	8.1	1.8	1.4	42
2015	AA	Mobile	9	11	0	156	118	3.51	1.30	23.0	250	30	72	3.31	3.2	6.8	2.1	0.4	53

Plus FB sits 92-94 with slight arm-side run and drop. Will work to all four quadrants, but FB command is sometimes elusive. Throws hard 12-6 CB that's a swing-and-miss offering on its best days. Struggles with release point. CU is best pitch; deceptive with kitchen sink-like drop. Reaches ceiling by cleaning up command.

Simmons,Shae — RP — Atlanta

EXP MLB DEBUT: 2014 | H/W: 5-11 175 | FUT: Setup reliever | 8B

Thrws R Age 25
2012 (22) SE Missouri St

Velo	Pitch	Grade
95-97	FB	+++++
83-86	SL	+++

Year	Lev	Team	W	L	Sv	IP	K	ERA	WHIP	BF/G	OBA	H%	S%	xERA	Ctl	Dom	Cmd	hr/9	BPV
2013	AA	Mississippi	0	0	0	11	16	2.45	1.09	3.9	139	25	75	1.06	5.7	13.1	2.3	0.0	99
2014	AA	Mississippi	0	0	14	23	30	0.78	0.91	4.3	188	30	90	1.15	2.3	11.7	5.0	0.0	166
2014	AAA	Gwinnett	0	1	0	1	1	36.00	5.00	3.9	515	62	20	17.71	18.0	9.0	0.5	0.0	-306
2014	MLB	Atlanta	1	2	1	21	23	2.97	1.23	3.3	201	28	76	2.50	4.7	9.8	2.1	0.4	68
2015	MLB	Atlanta	*Did not pitch; injured*																

Missed all of the '15 season recovering from TJS. A max-effort thrower will likely struggle with arm fatigue as he progresses in his career. When healthy, he featured a plus-plus FB with late action that missed bats. His SL is an under-appreciated offering, which also generates swings and misses. Health could hold him back from realizing potential.

Sims,Lucas — SP — Atlanta

EXP MLB DEBUT: 2017 | H/W: 6-1 225 | FUT: #3 starter | 8C

Thrws R Age 21 — 2012 (1) HS (GA)

Velo	Pitch	Grade
91-95	FB	++++
76-78	CB	++++
83-85	CU	++

Year	Lev	Team	W	L	Sv	IP	K	ERA	WHIP	BF/G	OBA	H%	S%	xERA	Ctl	Dom	Cmd	hr/9	BPV
2013	A	Rome	12	4	0	116	134	2.63	1.11	16.3	202	29	75	2.04	3.6	10.4	2.9	0.2	109
2014	A+	Lynchburg	8	11	0	156	107	4.21	1.30	23.0	249	29	68	3.57	3.3	6.2	1.9	0.7	40
2015	Rk	GCL Braves	0	0	0	5	7	9.00	1.80	11.6	332	50	44	5.36	3.6	12.6	3.5	0.0	148
2015	A+	Carolina	3	4	0	40	37	5.18	1.55	19.4	257	33	65	4.06	5.2	8.3	1.6	0.5	28
2015	AA	Mississippi	4	2	0	47	56	3.24	1.23	21.2	179	27	72	2.03	5.5	10.7	1.9	0.2	61

Former 1st rd pick had a breakout '15, making it to AA for first time in career. His FB sits in the low to mid 90s with good action. He commanded the pitch in the strike zone, changing eye levels to enhance its production. His best pitch is a 12-6 CB which causes feeble swings. His CU lags behind the rest of his package but showed promise.

Skoglund,Eric — SP — Kansas City

EXP MLB DEBUT: 2017 | H/W: 6-7 200 | FUT: #4 starter | 7E

Thrws L Age 23 — 2014 (3) Central Florida

Velo	Pitch	Grade
88-92	FB	+++
80-83	SL	+++
77-81	CU	++

Year	Lev	Team	W	L	Sv	IP	K	ERA	WHIP	BF/G	OBA	H%	S%	xERA	Ctl	Dom	Cmd	hr/9	BPV
2012	NCAA	Central Florida	5	3	0	47	45	3.24	1.63	12.4	303	39	79	4.70	3.6	8.6	2.4	0.2	75
2013	NCAA	Central Florida	1	4	0	56	26	5.12	1.55	17.5	268	29	66	4.43	4.6	4.2	0.9	0.6	-32
2014	NCAA	Central Florida	9	3	0	110	94	2.54	1.03	28.2	217	28	73	1.89	2.2	7.7	3.5	0.1	97
2014	Rk	Idaho Falls	0	2	0	23	25	5.09	1.70	11.5	316	41	70	5.60	3.5	9.8	2.8	0.8	99
2015	A+	Wilmington	6	3	0	84	66	3.53	1.12	22.1	259	32	66	2.80	1.2	7.1	6.0	0.2	113

Lanky, lean SP who ended season in July. Locates pitches well despite moving parts in delivery. Not much projection in arm action and could be hit hard with pitch-to-contact philosophy. Keeps ball on ground and allows few HR due to lively sinker. SL is an average offering, but more for strikes than as chaser. Below average CU can be too firm.

Smith,Austin — SP — San Diego

EXP MLB DEBUT: 2020 | H/W: 6-4 220 | FUT: #2 starter | 8D

Thrws R Age 19 — 2015 (2) HS (FL)

Velo	Pitch	Grade
90-95	FB	+++
75-79	CB	+++
82-84	CU	++

Year	Lev	Team	W	L	Sv	IP	K	ERA	WHIP	BF/G	OBA	H%	S%	xERA	Ctl	Dom	Cmd	hr/9	BPV
2015	Rk	Azl Padres	0	3	0	17	11	7.94	2.12	9.3	360	42	58	6.73	4.8	5.8	1.2	0.0	-6

Tall, athletic SP who has advanced feel for power stuff. Needs to add more strength and stamina in order to realize potential. Uses easy delivery and fast arm to generate velocity and can counter FB with CB that could grow into plus pitches. Velocity declined late in season, but should be OK with more pro innings. Has some projection remaining.

Smith,Drew — RP — Detroit

EXP MLB DEBUT: 2018 | H/W: 6-1 190 | FUT: Closer | 8E

Thrws R Age 22 — 2015 (3) Dallas Baptist

Velo	Pitch	Grade
93-97	FB	++++
77-79	CB	++
	CU	+

Year	Lev	Team	W	L	Sv	IP	K	ERA	WHIP	BF/G	OBA	H%	S%	xERA	Ctl	Dom	Cmd	hr/9	BPV
2015	NCAA	Dallas Baptist	3	2	4	45	38	3.99	1.40	7.6	266	33	72	3.95	3.4	7.6	2.2	0.6	63
2015	Rk	GCL Tigers	0	0	0	1	3	0.00	0.83	4.4	228	72	100	1.32	0.0	22.5		0.0	423
2015	A-	Connecticut	2	0	2	27	33	0.33	0.70	8.7	164	26	95	0.35	1.3	10.9	8.3	0.0	179
2015	A	West Michigan	1	0	0	1	2	0.00	1.67	5.4	228	42	100	3.49	7.5	15.0	2.0	0.0	86

Athletic RP who dominated in pro debut. Throws with a lot of effort and will stick in pen, but can blow ball by hitters upstairs. Hides ball well which makes plus FB even better. Exhibited better command as pro, but inconsistent mechanics need clean up. FB often lacks life and will need to develop breaking ball to be dynamic RP at upper levels.

Smith,Kyle — SP — Houston

EXP MLB DEBUT: 2017 | H/W: 6-0 170 | FUT: #4 starter | 6B

Thrws R Age 23 — 2011 (4) HS (FL)

Velo	Pitch	Grade
87-91	FB	+++
77-80	CB	+++
79-82	CU	++

Year	Lev	Team	W	L	Sv	IP	K	ERA	WHIP	BF/G	OBA	H%	S%	xERA	Ctl	Dom	Cmd	hr/9	BPV
2012	A	Kane County	4	3	0	67	87	2.95	1.22	20.9	247	37	76	3.02	2.7	11.7	4.4	0.4	156
2013	A+	Lancaster	1	1	0	23	21	7.40	1.52	20.0	285	33	52	5.42	3.5	8.2	2.3	1.6	71
2013	A+	Wilmington	5	4	0	104	96	2.85	1.17	21.9	241	30	79	3.20	2.5	8.3	3.3	0.8	100
2014	A+	Lancaster	4	0	0	27	31	2.65	1.10	15.2	190	25	81	2.60	4.0	10.3	2.6	1.0	95
2014	AA	Corpus Christi	5	5	0	95	96	4.35	1.23	18.3	255	31	69	4.05	2.4	9.1	3.8	1.3	118

Short hurler who did not pitch in '15 due to TJ surgery in April. Never had plus velocity so feel and pitchability should return in short order. Sequences pitches well and aggressively spots FB within strike zone. Compact, clean delivery allow for command. CB is best pitch and can use as chase pitch. Not much projection in size or arm action.

Smith,Myles — RP — Arizona

EXP MLB DEBUT: 2018 | H/W: 6-1 175 | FUT: Middle reliever | 7E

Thrws R Age 24 — 2013 (4) Missouri

Velo	Pitch	Grade
93-96	FB	++++
86-88	SL	+++
	CU	+

Year	Lev	Team	W	L	Sv	IP	K	ERA	WHIP	BF/G	OBA	H%	S%	xERA	Ctl	Dom	Cmd	hr/9	BPV
2014	A	Greenville	5	10	1	103	73	5.84	1.77	18.2	294	34	67	5.49	5.4	6.4	1.2	0.8	-13
2015	A-	Hillsboro	0	1	3	7	12	2.57	0.86	4.3	132	11	100	2.79	3.9	15.4	4.0	2.6	192
2015	A	Kane County	2	0	0	21	29	1.28	0.90	7.1	144	25	84	0.63	3.8	12.4	3.2	0.0	137
2015	A+	Visalia	0	1	0	9	12	4.95	1.10	4.5	214	34	50	1.92	3.0	11.9	4.0	0.0	152
2015	AAA	Reno	0	0	0	1	1	0.00	1.00	3.8	0	0	100		9.0	9.0	1.0	0.0	-63

Made full-time conversion to reliever in '15. Prior to trade to ARI, worked on changing delivery to fix command/control issues. Control has vastly improved. Command needs work. Relies on late arm-side bore to blow mid-90s FB by hitters. SL has taken step forward as well. Has flashed plus 2-plane break. CU is flat and hittable.

Smith,Nate — SP — Los Angeles (A)

EXP MLB DEBUT: 2016 | H/W: 6-3 205 | FUT: #4 starter | 7D

Thrws L Age 24 — 2013 (8) Furman

Velo	Pitch	Grade
87-91	FB	++
80-82	SL	+++
75-78	CU	+++

Year	Lev	Team	W	L	Sv	IP	K	ERA	WHIP	BF/G	OBA	H%	S%	xERA	Ctl	Dom	Cmd	hr/9	BPV
2013	Rk	Orem	2	2	0	35	31	3.86	1.17	9.3	256	31	70	3.65	1.8	8.0	4.4	1.0	113
2014	A+	Inland Empire	6	3	0	55	51	3.10	1.00	21.1	208	27	69	2.09	2.3	8.3	3.6	0.5	106
2014	AA	Arkansas	5	3	0	62	67	2.90	1.26	23.0	215	29	77	2.76	4.3	9.7	2.2	0.4	75
2015	AA	Arkansas	8	4	0	101	81	2.49	1.09	23.3	223	26	82	2.88	2.5	7.2	2.9	0.9	80
2015	AAA	Salt Lake	2	4	0	36	23	7.75	1.75	23.5	321	34	57	6.77	3.8	5.8	1.5	1.8	20

Tall, deceptive SP who has been good as pro until hit hard in AAA. Very tough on LHH (under .200) and has poise and moxie to succeed despite limited heat on FB. Spots FB to both sides of plate and counters with average SL and CU that flashes plus. Has low ceiling, but has durability and stamina.

Smoker,Josh — RP — New York (N)

EXP MLB DEBUT: 2016 | H/W: 6-2 195 | FUT: Setup Reliever | 8C

Thrws L Age 27 — 2007 (1) HS (GA)

Velo	Pitch	Grade
95-97	FB	+++++
87-89	SL	+++

Year	Lev	Team	W	L	Sv	IP	K	ERA	WHIP	BF/G	OBA	H%	S%	xERA	Ctl	Dom	Cmd	hr/9	BPV
2015	A	Savannah	1	0	0	6	8	8.71	2.10	5.1	386	54	54	7.11	2.9	11.6	4.0	0.0	149
2015	A+	St. Lucie	1	0	6	21	26	1.71	0.85	5.5	168	25	82	1.18	2.6	11.1	4.3	0.4	149
2015	AA	Binghamton	1	0	0	21	26	3.00	1.29	4.1	213	33	74	2.38	4.7	11.1	2.4	0.0	91

2015 was first season in affiliated ball since '12. Pitched in Frontier LG in '14. Struggled with shoulder issues until last year, when he re-discovered velocity. Touched 100 in a few late season appearances. Slight mechanical adjustment with hands has lead to better command of FB. SL hasn't regained pre-injury form; flashed plus early in career.

Smoral,Matthew — RP — Toronto

EXP MLB DEBUT: 2017 | H/W: 6-8 220 | FUT: #3 SP / Closer | 8E

Thrws L Age 22 — 2012 (1) HS (OH)

Velo	Pitch	Grade
90-95	FB	++++
80-85	SL	+++
83-86	CU	+

Year	Lev	Team	W	L	Sv	IP	K	ERA	WHIP	BF/G	OBA	H%	S%	xERA	Ctl	Dom	Cmd	hr/9	BPV
2013	Rk	GCL Blue Jays	0	2	0	25	27	7.14	1.90	7.9	236	32	60	4.59	9.3	9.6	1.0	0.4	-59
2014	Rk	Bluefield	2	3	0	33	51	3.52	1.48	15.8	249	42	73	3.29	4.9	13.8	2.8	0.0	135
2014	A-	Vancouver	2	0	0	20	19	2.70	1.45	17.1	199	27	79	2.66	6.8	8.6	1.3	0.0	-10
2015	Rk	Bluefield	0	0	0	10	16	5.29	2.06	6.2	196	35	71	4.10	12.4	14.1	1.1	0.0	-61
2015	A+	Dunedin	1	0	0	3	5	16.88	4.06	4.4	437	63	54	13.13	16.9	14.1	0.8	0.0	-185

Very tall, angular pitcher who pitched out of pen in limited action in '15. Has extreme K potential due to arm strength, pitch movement, and angle to plate. Gets ton of groundballs as he pitches downhill and hitters can't elevate ball. Has big-breaking SL that can miss bats. Needs to clean up issues: control, erratic delivery, CU, and durability.

Snell,Blake — SP — Tampa Bay

EXP MLB DEBUT: 2016 | H/W: 6-4 180 | FUT: #2 starter | 9C

Thrws L Age 23 — 2011 (1) HS (WA)

Velo	Pitch	Grade
90-95	FB	+++
82-84	SL	++++
87-89	CT	+++
82-85	CU	++++

Year	Lev	Team	W	L	Sv	IP	K	ERA	WHIP	BF/G	OBA	H%	S%	xERA	Ctl	Dom	Cmd	hr/9	BPV
2014	A	Bowling Green	3	2	0	40	42	1.80	1.12	19.8	187	26	84	1.90	4.3	9.4	2.2	0.2	73
2014	A+	Charlotte	5	6	0	75	77	3.95	1.41	19.9	246	34	70	3.25	4.4	9.2	2.1	0.1	64
2015	A+	Charlotte	3	0	0	21	27	0.00	1.00	20.1	144	24	100	0.90	4.7	11.6	2.5	0.0	99
2015	AA	Montgomery	6	2	0	68	79	1.58	1.09	22.2	190	26	90	2.23	3.8	10.4	2.7	0.7	102
2015	AAA	Durham	6	2	0	44	57	1.84	0.95	18.5	189	29	83	1.64	2.7	11.6	4.4	0.4	156

Tall, lean SP who did not allow ER in first 8 starts and was dominant all season. Fulfilling projection with electric FB that features late sinking action. Has velocity and sequencing ability to pitch up while mixing in plus SL and CU. Can cut FB effectively and repeat arm speed and slot on all pitches. Could use better control.

Soroka,Mike — SP — Atlanta

EXP MLB DEBUT: 2019 | H/W: 6-4 195 | FUT: #3 starter | 8D

Thrws R Age 18 — 2015 (1) HS (AB)

Velo	Pitch	Grade
91-92	FB	+++
82-84	CU	+++
	CB	++

Year	Lev	Team	W	L	Sv	IP	K	ERA	WHIP	BF/G	OBA	H%	S%	xERA	Ctl	Dom	Cmd	hr/9	BPV
2015	Rk	Danville	0	2	0	24	26	3.75	1.33	16.6	293	40	69	3.59	1.5	9.8	6.5	0.0	153
2015	Rk	GCL Braves	0	0	0	10	11	1.80	0.60	8.6	151	23	67		0.9	9.9	11.0	0.0	172

Canadian RH selected with the 28th pick in the '15 draft had a solid professional debut. Long bodied, there is room to grow into frame. 2-seam FB has tremendous boring action in on RHH. CU is best secondary pitch, featuring solid drop. A 12-6 CB lags behind other two offerings at present but shows potential to become a barrel missing pitch.

Stanek,Ryne — SP — Tampa Bay
EXP MLB DEBUT: 2016 | H/W: 6-4 180 | FUT: #3 starter | 8E

Thrws R Age 24	Year	Lev	Team	W	L	Sv	IP	K	ERA	WHIP	BF/G	OBA	H%	S%	xERA	Ctl	Dom	Cmd	hr/9	BPV
2013 (1) Arkansas	2014	Rk	GCL Rays	0	0	0	1	0	0.00	0.00	2.8	0	0			0.0	0.0		0.0	18
90-95 FB ++++	2014	A	Bowling Green	3	4	0	44	46	3.67	1.36	20.5	274	36	72	3.76	2.6	9.4	3.5	0.4	115
82-86 SL +++	2014	A+	Charlotte	1	1	0	13	4	5.54	1.38	18.2	262	28	56	3.35	3.5	2.8	0.8	0.0	-26
75-78 CB ++	2015	A+	Charlotte	4	2	0	50	38	1.79	0.96	21.1	189	23	83	1.65	2.7	6.8	2.5	0.4	68
CU ++	2015	AA	Montgomery	4	3	1	61	41	4.12	1.36	16.0	232	25	72	3.81	4.6	6.0	1.3	1.0	3

Tall, power-armed SP who sequences pitches well and thrives despite surprisingly low K rate. Has injury history that hinders durability, but throws hard with loose arm action. Delivery adds deception and allows plus FB to play up. LHH have hit him hard and may not have CU to stick as SP.

Stankiewicz,Teddy — SP — Boston
EXP MLB DEBUT: 2017 | H/W: 6-4 200 | FUT: #4 starter | 7D

Thrws R Age 22	Year	Lev	Team	W	L	Sv	IP	K	ERA	WHIP	BF/G	OBA	H%	S%	xERA	Ctl	Dom	Cmd	hr/9	BPV
2013 (2) Seminole St JC																				
90-94 FB +++	2013	NCAA	Seminole St	4	5	0	60	70	2.54	1.00	20.9	228	31	78	2.54	1.5	10.5	7.0	0.7	166
78-83 SL +++	2013	A-	Lowell	0	0	0	19	15	2.34	0.99	8.1	239	29	78	2.44	0.9	7.0	7.5	0.5	119
75-78 CB +++	2014	A	Greenville	11	8	0	140	102	3.73	1.21	22.6	263	31	70	3.44	1.9	6.6	3.5	0.6	86
81-83 CU ++	2015	A+	Salem	5	11	0	141	77	4.02	1.28	23.2	272	30	69	3.88	2.0	4.9	2.4	0.7	51

Athletic SP who was consistent all season. Provides durability and stamina to rotation with repeatable delivery and strong arm. Has command of four pitches, though doesn't own out pitch in arsenal. Pitches to contact and has very low K rate. Sequences well and pitches with tough angle to plate. Holds velocity deep into games.

Staumont,Josh — RP — Kansas City
EXP MLB DEBUT: 2018 | H/W: 6-3 200 | FUT: #2 starter / Closer | 9E

Thrws R Age 22	Year	Lev	Team	W	L	Sv	IP	K	ERA	WHIP	BF/G	OBA	H%	S%	xERA	Ctl	Dom	Cmd	hr/9	BPV
2015 (2) Azusa Pacific																				
94-98 FB ++++																				
82-84 CB +++																				
	2015	Rk	Idaho Falls	3	1	1	31	51	3.18	1.35	9.3	170	33	74	2.02	6.9	14.8	2.1	0.0	96

Fireballer who was mostly RP upon signing. Easily registers triple-digits on FB due to clean arm action and pure arm strength. Didn't allow HR in pro debut and keeps ball down. Big-breaking CB is handy 2nd pitch, but neither thrown for consistent strikes. Has no change-of-pace offering, but wouldn't be needed in short stints. May be tried as SP.

Steele,Justin — SP — Chicago (N)
EXP MLB DEBUT: 2019 | H/W: 6-2 195 | FUT: #3 starter | 7C

Thrws L Age 20	Year	Lev	Team	W	L	Sv	IP	K	ERA	WHIP	BF/G	OBA	H%	S%	xERA	Ctl	Dom	Cmd	hr/9	BPV
2014 (5) HS (MS)																				
90-93 FB ++++																				
75-78 SL +++																				
CU ++	2014	Rk	Azl Cubs	0	0	0	18	25	2.97	1.26	8.3	226	36	74	2.48	4.0	12.4	3.1	0.0	134
	2015	A-	Eugene	3	1	0	40	38	2.69	1.32	16.6	251	34	77	2.98	3.4	8.5	2.5	0.0	80

Athletic lefty was solid in the NWL, attacking hitters with a plus 90-93 sinkng FB that hits 95 mph with some deception. Flashes potentially plus CB that needs to be more consistent, and an avg CU. Has yet to give up a HR since turning pro. Logged just 40.2 IP as the Cubs attempt to limit his innings.

Stephens,Jackson — SP — Cincinnati
EXP MLB DEBUT: 2017 | H/W: 6-3 205 | FUT: #4 starter | 7C

Thrws R Age 21	Year	Lev	Team	W	L	Sv	IP	K	ERA	WHIP	BF/G	OBA	H%	S%	xERA	Ctl	Dom	Cmd	hr/9	BPV
2012 (18) HS (AL)																				
92-94 FB +++	2012	Rk	AZL Reds	1	1	2	21	22	4.69	1.23	4.3	279	36	63	3.94	1.3	9.4	7.3	0.9	152
CB +++	2013	A	Dayton	3	7	1	64	55	4.63	1.51	19.9	304	37	70	5.02	2.5	7.7	3.1	0.8	89
83-85 SL ++	2014	A	Dayton	2	7	0	67	54	4.83	1.37	20.1	270	31	67	4.39	3.0	7.2	2.5	1.1	69
82-85 CU +++	2015	A+	Daytona	12	7	0	145	97	2.98	1.29	22.9	277	32	79	3.93	1.9	6.0	3.2	0.7	76

Bounced back from injury-plagued '14 to put up solid numbers in the FSL. Best pitch is a 2-seam FB with solid arm-side run. CB & SL are borderline average offerings. CU made a biggest jump in '14. Previously poor, it is now a solid pitch, mimicking the movement of his FB with additional sink.

Stephens,Jordan — SP — Chicago (A)
EXP MLB DEBUT: 2018 | H/W: 6-1 190 | FUT: #4 starter | 7D

Thrws R Age 23	Year	Lev	Team	W	L	Sv	IP	K	ERA	WHIP	BF/G	OBA	H%	S%	xERA	Ctl	Dom	Cmd	hr/9	BPV
2015 (5) Rice																				
88-92 FB +++																				
80-82 SL ++	2015	NCAA	Rice	6	5	1	59	75	3.19	1.15	13.8	234	35	70	2.44	2.6	11.4	4.4	0.2	153
75-79 CB +++	2015	Rk	Great Falls	0	0	0	3	3	0.00	1.00	5.7	191	27	100	1.43	3.0	9.0	3.0	0.0	99
CU ++	2015	Rk	Azl White Sox	0	0	0	14	18	0.63	0.63	5.4	149	24	89	0.02	1.3	11.4	9.0	0.0	189

Small-framed SP with deep repertoire on knowledge of pitching. Gets ample movement to pitches thanks to quick arm action. Induces groundballs with sinker and can rear back and add ticks to FB as needed. CB can be neutralizer against RHH and has power to both breaking balls. CU is far from polished.

Stephenson,Robert — SP — Cincinnati
EXP MLB DEBUT: 2016 | H/W: 6-2 200 | FUT: #2 starter | 9C

Thrws R Age 23	Year	Lev	Team	W	L	Sv	IP	K	ERA	WHIP	BF/G	OBA	H%	S%	xERA	Ctl	Dom	Cmd	hr/9	BPV
2011 (1) HS (CA)	2013	A+	Bakersfield	2	2	0	20	22	3.12	1.04	19.5	250	31	78	3.51	0.9	9.8	11.0	1.3	170
93-96 FB ++++	2013	AA	Pensacola	0	2	0	16	18	5.00	1.85	18.9	271	35	75	5.63	7.2	10.0	1.4	1.1	3
79-82 CB ++++	2014	AA	Pensacola	7	10	0	136	140	4.76	1.38	21.2	229	28	68	3.96	4.9	9.3	1.9	1.2	52
86-88 CU ++	2015	AA	Pensacola	4	7	0	78	89	3.69	1.23	22.6	194	26	73	2.89	5.0	10.3	2.1	0.9	69
	2015	AAA	Louisville	4	4	0	55	51	4.08	1.41	21.2	247	32	70	3.47	4.4	8.3	1.9	0.3	49

Power pitcher with 2 potential plus-plus offerings. 2-Seam FB has heavy sink & moderate arm-side run. Struggles keeping FB down. Gets hit up in the zone when pitch flattens out. CB has taken a step forward in '15. Previously slurvy, it's a true 12-6 breaking CB now. CU is improving. More of a CT than CU. 40-grade command & control.

Stewart,Kohl — SP — Minnesota
EXP MLB DEBUT: 2017 | H/W: 6-3 195 | FUT: #3 starter | 8D

Thrws R Age 21	Year	Lev	Team	W	L	Sv	IP	K	ERA	WHIP	BF/G	OBA	H%	S%	xERA	Ctl	Dom	Cmd	hr/9	BPV
2013 (1) HS (TX)																				
91-95 FB +++	2013	Rk	GCL Twins	0	0	0	16	16	1.69	0.94	10.0	210	29	80	1.49	1.7	9.0	5.3	0.0	134
82-85 SL +++	2013	Rk	Elizabethton	0	0	0	4	8	0.00	0.50	13.3	81	23	100		2.3	18.0	8.0	0.0	281
75-79 CB +++	2014	A	Cedar Rapids	3	5	0	87	62	2.59	1.14	18.1	234	28	78	2.71	2.5	6.4	2.6	0.4	66
CU +++	2015	A+	Fort Myers	7	8	0	129	71	3.21	1.39	24.7	269	31	75	3.56	3.1	4.9	1.6	0.1	22

Strong starter who repeats clean delivery, but doesn't miss the bats that his stuff would suggest. Induces groundballs with lively FB and has hard SL that could become plus. Changes speeds well with sinking CU and also mixes in CB. Could stand to mix better as well as using all quadrants of strike zone.

Stinnett,Jake — SP — Chicago (N)
EXP MLB DEBUT: 2018 | H/W: 6-4 200 | FUT: #3 starter | 8D

Thrws R Age 23	Year	Lev	Team	W	L	Sv	IP	K	ERA	WHIP	BF/G	OBA	H%	S%	xERA	Ctl	Dom	Cmd	hr/9	BPV
2014 (2) Maryland	2013	NCAA	Maryland	6	5	2	63	48	2.85	1.11	15.5	205	26	71	1.89	3.4	6.8	2.0	0.0	49
92-95 FB +++	2014	NCAA	Maryland	8	6	1	118	132	2.67	0.97	26.3	203	28	75	2.07	2.3	10.1	4.4	0.6	137
83-85 SL +++	2014	Rk	Azl Cubs	0	1	0	4	3	8.57	2.14	6.9	432	50	56	8.26	0.0	6.4		0.0	134
CU ++	2014	A-	Boise	0	0	0	6	7	2.95	0.82	11.1	149	16	75	1.88	3.0	10.3	3.5	1.5	124
	2015	A	South Bend	7	6	0	117	91	4.46	1.43	22.6	262	32	68	3.85	3.8	7.0	1.8	0.5	40

Strong bodied RHP generates good velocity. Best offering is a good 92-95 mph sinking FB, which he sometimes leaves up in the zone. Also has a plus 78-80 mph SL that has good late break. Needs to develop a more consistent release point and refine his approach and walks killed him in '15. Raw stuff remains plus, so look for better results in '16.

Strahan,Wyatt — SP — Cincinnati
EXP MLB DEBUT: 2017 | H/W: 6-3 190 | FUT: #4 SP / Setup RP | 8C

Thrws R Age 22	Year	Lev	Team	W	L	Sv	IP	K	ERA	WHIP	BF/G	OBA	H%	S%	xERA	Ctl	Dom	Cmd	hr/9	BPV
2014 (3) USC	2012	NCAA	USC	3	3	2	26	18	1.38	1.38	5.0	197	24	89	2.47	6.2	6.2	1.0	0.0	-38
92-95 FB ++++	2013	NCAA	USC	4	3	0	80	45	2.47	1.41	26.1	241	27	83	3.54	4.6	5.0	1.1	0.4	-15
77-83 CB +++	2014	NCAA	USC	6	5	1	104	89	3.29	1.34	27.1	237	31	73	2.86	4.2	7.7	1.8	0.0	42
CU ++	2014	Rk	Billings	0	3	0	42	40	2.78	1.43	12.8	288	38	78	3.76	2.6	8.6	3.3	0.0	103
	2015	A	Dayton	9	10	0	164	132	2.80	1.29	24.1	255	31	80	3.47	2.9	7.2	2.5	0.5	70

Strong RHP with an arsenal of pitches to start but an arm, suited for the pen. Doesn't use body in delivery. Arm strength propels velocity. Advanced command of sinking FB makes him GB machine. Able to change speeds with his CB without tipping to opposition. Can get slurvy at times. CU is deceptive but extremely inconsistent.

Strahm,Matthew — SP — Kansas City
EXP MLB DEBUT: 2017 | H/W: 6-4 180 | FUT: #4 SP / Setup RP | 7D

Thrws L Age 24	Year	Lev	Team	W	L	Sv	IP	K	ERA	WHIP	BF/G	OBA	H%	S%	xERA	Ctl	Dom	Cmd	hr/9	BPV
2012 (21) Neosho Co CC	2012	NCAA	Neosho Co CC	9	3	0	99	129	1.91	0.97	26.8	210	32	81	1.80	2.0	11.7	5.9	0.3	175
90-94 FB +++	2012	Rk	Idaho Falls	1	3	0	30	42	5.68	1.69	7.2	286	43	64	4.65	5.1	12.6	2.5	0.3	107
76-79 CB +++	2014	Rk	Idaho Falls	1	0	1	19	27	2.34	1.04	7.4	156	25	79	1.55	4.7	12.7	2.7	0.5	119
CU ++	2015	A	Lexington	2	1	4	26	38	2.08	0.92	7.0	141	24	78	0.98	4.2	13.2	3.2	0.3	143
	2015	A+	Wilmington	1	6	1	68	83	2.78	0.99	17.3	200	27	77	2.35	2.5	11.0	4.4	0.9	148

Projectable pitcher who has flown under radar despite dominance. Used as RP in Low-A before promotion to High-A rotation. Has three pitches to be potent SP and throws with loose arm and deceptive delivery. Keeps ball down in zone with sinking FB and can wipe out hitters with CB. Posts low oppBA and will need to maintain ability to hit spots.

Stratton,Chris — SP — San Francisco

EXP MLB DEBUT: 2016 | H/W: 6-2 190 | FUT: #4 starter | 8E

Thrws R Age 25
2012 (1) Mississippi St

Velo	Pitch	Grade
89-93	FB	++++
82-84	SL	+++
77-79	CB	+++
80-82	CU	++

Year	Lev	Team	W	L	Sv	IP	K	ERA	WHIP	BF/G	OBA	H%	S%	xERA	Ctl	Dom	Cmd	hr/9	BPV
2013	A	Augusta	9	3	0	132	123	3.27	1.33	24.9	256	33	75	3.38	3.2	8.4	2.6	0.3	82
2014	A+	San Jose	7	8	0	99	102	5.09	1.40	22.0	269	34	66	4.54	3.3	9.3	2.8	1.2	96
2014	AA	Richmond	1	1	0	23	18	3.52	1.78	21.2	309	37	82	5.74	4.7	7.0	1.5	0.8	18
2015	AA	Richmond	1	5	0	50	39	4.14	1.24	22.6	221	27	66	2.92	4.0	7.0	1.8	0.5	37
2015	AAA	Sacramento	4	5	0	98	72	3.86	1.31	23.8	242	29	70	3.36	3.7	6.6	1.8	0.6	38

Former 1st rounder has good size, clean 3/4 arm action and track record for durability. Can run FB up to 95 mph, sitting an easy 89-93. Promising SL with good, late bite; CB projects as average; CU not quite there. Works low in zone for avg ground ball contact. Throws strikes, but command still needs refinement.

Stripling,Ross — SP — Los Angeles (N)

EXP MLB DEBUT: 2016 | H/W: 6-3 190 | FUT: #4 starter | 7C

Thrws R Age 26
2012 (5) Texas A&M

Velo	Pitch	Grade
90-94	FB	+++
73-75	CB	+++
83-85	SL	+++
	CU	++

Year	Lev	Team	W	L	Sv	IP	K	ERA	WHIP	BF/G	OBA	H%	S%	xERA	Ctl	Dom	Cmd	hr/9	BPV
2015	A	Great Lakes	0	0	0	4	4	0.00	0.75	14.3	81	12	100		4.5	9.0	2.0	0.0	59
2015	AA	Tulsa	3	6	0	67	55	3.89	1.19	20.7	244	29	70	3.46	2.5	7.4	2.9	0.9	82

Good mix of stuff and pitchability. Missed all of '14 with TJS. Pounds the zone with a nice four-pitch mix highlighted by a 90-94 mph FB that he controls well to both sides. 12-6 CB and tight SL are above-average and have swing-and-miss potential. CU remains below average. Not overpowering, but plus command gives him potential as a back-end starter.

Suarez,Andrew — SP — San Francisco

EXP MLB DEBUT: 2017 | H/W: 6-2 210 | FUT: #4 starter | 8D

Thrws L Age 23
2015 (2) Miami

Velo	Pitch	Grade
89-93	FB	+++
82-84	SL	++++
79-82	CB	+++
82-83	CU	++

Year	Lev	Team	W	L	Sv	IP	K	ERA	WHIP	BF/G	OBA	H%	S%	xERA	Ctl	Dom	Cmd	hr/9	BPV
2015	NCAA	Miami	9	2	0	85	78	3.49	1.28	21.8	266	34	72	3.49	2.3	8.2	3.5	0.4	104
2015	Rk	Azl Giants	0	0	0	5	6	1.80	0.60	5.7	124	20	67		1.8	10.8	6.0	0.0	164
2015	A-	Salem-Kaizer	1	0	0	19	15	1.41	0.99	14.6	240	28	94	2.92	0.9	7.1	7.5	0.9	120
2015	A+	San Jose	1	0	0	15	16	1.80	1.00	19.1	235	29	92	3.08	1.2	9.6	8.0	1.2	158

Athletic, quick-armed LH moved quickly after signing as 2nd-round pick. Best pitch is SL, which has plus late bite and is filthy vs. LHH. Offers low-90s FB with arm-side tail and a CB/CU tandem that project as avg. Fills the zone with repeatable mechanics. If he can maintain his velo deep into starts, could have impact as #4 SP with quality Cmd.

Suarez,Jose — SP — Los Angeles (A)

EXP MLB DEBUT: 2020 | H/W: 5-10 170 | FUT: #4 starter | 7E

Thrws L Age 18
2014 FA (VZ)

Velo	Pitch	Grade
85-89	FB	++
74-77	CB	+++
77-79	CU	+++

Year	Lev	Team	W	L	Sv	IP	K	ERA	WHIP	BF/G	OBA	H%	S%	xERA	Ctl	Dom	Cmd	hr/9	BPV
2015	Rk	DSL Angels	2	2	0	55	34	2.13	0.93	18.7	217	26	75	1.59	1.3	5.6	4.3	0.0	83
2015	Rk	AZL Angels	1	1	0	17	12	5.76	1.86	20.1	366	43	66	6.18	2.1	6.3	3.0	0.0	75

Short SP who has limited experience in US, but has advanced feel. Gets by with below average FB, but plays up due to late movement and command. Should have more velocity when body matures. Big-breaking CB is best pitch and nice CU is neutralizer against RHH. Rarely allows hit balls in air.

Suggs,Colby — RP — Miami

EXP MLB DEBUT: 2016 | H/W: 5-11 235 | FUT: Setup reliever | 7B

Thrws R Age 24
2013 (2) Arkansas

Velo	Pitch	Grade
93-98	FB	++++
78-83	CB	+++
	CU	++

Year	Lev	Team	W	L	Sv	IP	K	ERA	WHIP	BF/G	OBA	H%	S%	xERA	Ctl	Dom	Cmd	hr/9	BPV
2013	Rk	GCL Marlins	0	0	0	1	1	9.00	3.00	5.8	262	35	67	7.36	18.0	9.0	0.5	0.0	-306
2013	A-	Batavia	1	0	3	8	11	1.13	0.88	4.2	181	30	86	0.97	2.3	12.4	5.5	0.0	180
2013	A+	Jupiter	1	3	0	18	26	3.98	1.27	5.3	150	26	65	1.62	7.0	12.9	1.9	0.0	63
2014	A+	Jupiter	1	6	3	58	47	5.11	1.45	5.4	265	32	63	3.93	3.9	7.3	1.9	0.5	44
2015	A	Greensboro	0	0	1	5	6	0.00	0.78	3.7	173	26	100	0.66	1.8	10.6	6.0	0.0	161

Short, big-bodied reliever missed all but 5 games due a forearm strain. Uses lower half to generate mid-90s FB up to 98. Pairs it with a power CB with tight spin and downward action. The combo generates plus Dom, though his max effort delivery has led to control issues. His arsenal has closer potential, but needs to prove he's healthy.

Supak,Trey — SP — Milwaukee

EXP MLB DEBUT: 2019 | H/W: 6-5 210 | FUT: #3 starter | 8D

Thrws R Age 19
2014 (2) HS (TX)

Velo	Pitch	Grade
90-93	FB	+++
73-75	CB	+++
	CU	++

Year	Lev	Team	W	L	Sv	IP	K	ERA	WHIP	BF/G	OBA	H%	S%	xERA	Ctl	Dom	Cmd	hr/9	BPV
2014	Rk	GCL Pirates	1	3	0	24	21	4.88	1.58	13.2	285	33	74	5.54	4.1	7.9	1.9	1.5	48
2015	Rk	Bristol	1	2	0	28	23	6.73	1.42	14.9	306	37	50	4.65	1.6	7.4	4.6	0.6	107

Tall righty struggled in pro debut. Started the season late and then missed a month with a sore shoulder. FB sits at 90-93 mph, topping out at 94 mph. Gets good downhill tilt from a high 3/4 arm slot, but throws with effort and FB command is an issue. Shows some ability to spin a breaking ball and has a good mid-70s CB and CU that needs refinement.

Szapucki,Thomas — SP — New York (N)

EXP MLB DEBUT: 2019 | H/W: 6-2 190 | FUT: #3 SP / Setup RP | 7E

Thrws L Age 19
2015 (5) HS (FL)

Velo	Pitch	Grade
91-93	FB	++++
82-84	SL	+++
	CU	+

Year	Lev	Team	W	L	Sv	IP	K	ERA	WHIP	BF/G	OBA	H%	S%	xERA	Ctl	Dom	Cmd	hr/9	BPV
2015	Rk	GCL Mets	0	0	0	2	3	17.14	2.38	3.6	458	63	20	9.42	0.0	12.9		0.0	249

Strong-armed LHP with max-effort delivery, worrying scouts. FB sits in low 90s. Flattens out at higher velocities. Late biting SL flashes plus. Has reported feel for CU but arm action may limit future growth.

Taillon,Jameson — SP — Pittsburgh

EXP MLB DEBUT: 2016 | H/W: 6-5 240 | FUT: #1 starter | 9D

Thrws R Age 24
2010 (1) HS (TX)

Velo	Pitch	Grade
93-97	FB	++++
83-85	CB	++++
83-86	CU	+++

Year	Lev	Team	W	L	Sv	IP	K	ERA	WHIP	BF/G	OBA	H%	S%	xERA	Ctl	Dom	Cmd	hr/9	BPV
2012	AA	Altoona	3	0	0	17	18	1.59	0.71	20.0	187	27	75	0.63	0.5	9.5	18.0	0.0	175
2013	AA	Altoona	4	7	0	110	106	3.68	1.34	22.9	265	34	74	3.85	2.9	8.7	2.9	0.7	95
2013	AAA	Indianapolis	1	3	0	37	37	3.89	1.27	25.2	229	31	67	2.79	3.9	9.0	2.3	0.2	75
2014		*Did not pitch; injured*																	
2015		*Did not pitch; injured*																	

Missed his 2nd straight season, this time with a sports hernia. When healthy, has a plus 93-97 mph sinking FB that tops out at 99 mph. Also hads a good mid-80s power CB. Flashes a plus CU, but the pitch remains inconsistent. Has the size and power frame to dominate and gets good downhill tilt that makes FB difficult to elevate.

Tarpley,Stephen — SP — Pittsburgh

EXP MLB DEBUT: 2019 | H/W: 6-1 180 | FUT: #3 starter | 8D

Thrws L Age 23
2013 (3) Scottsdale CC

Velo	Pitch	Grade
92-94	FB	+++
	CB	+++
	SL	++
	CU	+++

Year	Lev	Team	W	L	Sv	IP	K	ERA	WHIP	BF/G	OBA	H%	S%	xERA	Ctl	Dom	Cmd	hr/9	BPV
2012	NCAA	USC	5	4	0	78	67	3.23	1.28	22.9	244	32	72	2.79	3.3	7.7	2.3	0.0	67
2013	NCAA	Scottsdale CC	3	2	0	92	108	2.35	1.11	22.6	193	28	80	2.08	3.9	10.6	2.7	0.4	103
2013	Rk	GCL Orioles	0	1	0	21	25	2.14	1.10	11.7	252	37	78	2.41	1.3	10.7	8.3	0.0	176
2014	A-	Aberdeen	3	5	0	66	60	3.68	1.41	21.5	270	34	74	3.98	3.3	8.2	2.5	0.5	77
2015	A	West Virginia	11	4	0	116	105	2.48	1.15	23.0	248	32	77	2.66	1.9	8.1	4.2	0.2	112

Hard throwing lefty came over from the Orioles in the T. Snider deal. Comes after hitters with a good 92-94 mph sinking FB and a decent four-pitch mix. CB and CU both show above-avg potential with a SL that lags behind. Mechanics and release point can be inconsistent, but he showed improvement in '15, which led to better results on the field.

Tate,Dillon — SP — Texas

EXP MLB DEBUT: 2017 | H/W: 6-2 165 | FUT: #1 starter | 9C

Thrws R Age 21
2015 (1) UC-Santa Barbara

Velo	Pitch	Grade
93-96	FB	++++
85-88	SL	++++
81-84	CU	++

Year	Lev	Team	W	L	Sv	IP	K	ERA	WHIP	BF/G	OBA	H%	S%	xERA	Ctl	Dom	Cmd	hr/9	BPV
2015	NCAA	UC Santa Barbara	8	5	0	103	111	2.27	0.91	27.5	185	26	75	1.38	2.4	9.7	4.0	0.3	126
2015	A-	Spokane	0	0	0	2	3	0.00	1.50	4.3	0	0	100	0.88	13.5	13.5	1.0	0.0	-104
2015	A	Hickory	0	0	0	7	5	1.29	0.43	5.7	132	12	100	0.59	0.0	6.4		1.3	134

Fast arm action generates plus pitch movement and no pitch is straight. Can be very tough to make hard contact against. Owns two plus pitches in sinking FB and vicious SL; both serve as true out pitches. Can also cut FB for different look. Some effort in delivery, but maintains arm speed on CU. Has the repertoire to become an ace.

Taylor,Blake — SP — New York (N)

EXP MLB DEBUT: 2020 | H/W: 6-3 220 | FUT: #4 starter | 7E

Thrws L Age 20
2013 (2) HS (CA)

Velo	Pitch	Grade
88-90	FB	+++
75-77	CB	+++
86-87	SL	+
81-82	CU	++

Year	Lev	Team	W	L	Sv	IP	K	ERA	WHIP	BF/G	OBA	H%	S%	xERA	Ctl	Dom	Cmd	hr/9	BPV
2013	Rk	GCL Pirates	0	2	0	21	13	2.57	0.76	9.4	106	13	63		3.9	5.6	1.4	0.0	14
2014	Rk	GCL Mets	2	0	0	10	10	0.00	0.78	12.3	34	5	100		6.2	8.8	1.4	0.0	10
2014	Rk	Kingsport	2	1	0	30	20	5.38	2.13	18.6	326	38	73	6.43	6.9	6.0	0.9	0.3	-60
2015	Rk	GCL Mets	0	0	0	3	3	6.00	1.33	6.2	321	42	50	4.04	0.0	9.0		0.0	180
2015	A-	Brooklyn	0	0	0	9	5	1.00	1.00	11.5	191	23	89	1.47	3.0	5.0	1.7	0.0	27

Had TJS surgery during '15 season. Tall LHP at physical projection. Has struggled with command of FB since pro debut. Thrown at downward angle. Has significant arm-side run. 1-7 CB has best potential of secondary offerings. PIT played around with grips. Returned to amateur grip with NYM. Has feel for CU. SL mimics bad cutter.

Taylor,Jacob | SP | Pittsburgh | EXP MLB DEBUT: 2020 | H/W: 6-3 205 | FUT: #3 starter/reliever | 9E

Thrws R Age 20
2015 (4) Pearl River CC

93-95	FB	++++
	SL	+++
	CU	++

Year	Lev	Team	W	L	Sv	IP	K	ERA	WHIP	BF/G	OBA	H%	S%	xERA	Ctl	Dom	Cmd	hr/9	BPV
2015	Rk	GCL Pirates	0	0	0	2	2	0.00	1.50	8.6	0	0	100	0.92	13.5	9.0	0.7	0.0	-185

4th round JuCo pick was limited to just 2 IP before an elbow injury that resulted in TJ surgery. Prior to the injury he showed a good 93-95 mph FB that topped out at 97 mph. He backs up the FB with a slurvy SL and a below-avg CU. Taylor is still relatively new to pitching and was drafted more for his athleticism and potential than his polish.

Thompson,Dylan | SP | Seattle | EXP MLB DEBUT: 2019 | H/W: 6-2 180 | FUT: #4 starter | 7C

Thrws R Age 19
2015 (4) HS (SC)

88-92	FB	+++
77-79	SL	++
80-83	CU	++

Year	Lev	Team	W	L	Sv	IP	K	ERA	WHIP	BF/G	OBA	H%	S%	xERA	Ctl	Dom	Cmd	hr/9	BPV
2015	Rk	Azl Mariners	2	1	0	26	25	2.40	0.99	11.1	196	27	73	1.47	2.7	8.6	3.1	0.0	98

Advanced arm who has athleticism and relative polish for age. Doesn't amaze with plus velocity, but knows how to set up hitters by changing speeds and mixing. Shows feel for secondary pitches and throws strikes with all. Will need to add strength to improve stamina. Repeats delivery and could be big-time sleeper.

Thompson,Jake | SP | Philadelphia | EXP MLB DEBUT: 2016 | H/W: 6-4 235 | FUT: #3 starter | 8C

Thrws R Age 22
2012 (2) HS (TX)

90-94	FB	+++
84-87	SL	++++
77-80	CB	+++
80-83	CU	+++

Year	Lev	Team	W	L	Sv	IP	K	ERA	WHIP	BF/G	OBA	H%	S%	xERA	Ctl	Dom	Cmd	hr/9	BPV
2014	A+	Lakeland	6	4	0	83		3.14	1.20	20.9	243	32	73	2.89	2.7	8.6	3.2	0.3	99
2014	AA	Erie	1	0	0	11	7	2.45	1.27	22.5	244	29	79	2.79	3.3	5.7	1.8	0.0	33
2014	AA	Frisco	3	1	0	35	44	3.32	1.31	20.8	220	31	77	3.24	4.6	11.3	2.4	0.8	96
2015	AA	Frisco	6	6	0	87	78	4.75	1.42	21.8	277	34	67	4.27	3.1	8.1	2.6	0.7	79
2015	AA	Reading	5	1	0	45	34	1.80	1.00	24.6	206	24	86	2.19	2.4	6.8	2.8	0.6	76

He seemed to stall at Double-A early in the season, but flourished after trade to Philadelphia. Arsenal highlighted by heavy low-90s fastball and a plus slider, but also used change-up, curveball for a four-pitch mix. Walks too many and continues to have trouble with LHH, but has a durable frame for future innings.

Thorpe,Lewis | SP | Minnesota | EXP MLB DEBUT: 2018 | H/W: 6-1 160 | FUT: #3 starter | 8D

Thrws L Age 20
2012 FA (AU)

89-94	FB	+++
78-80	CB	+++
81-83	SL	++
80-83	CU	+++

Year	Lev	Team	W	L	Sv	IP	K	ERA	WHIP	BF/G	OBA	H%	S%	xERA	Ctl	Dom	Cmd	hr/9	BPV
2013	Rk	GCL Twins	4	1	0	44	64	2.05	0.86	13.5	205	33	78	1.59	1.2	13.1	10.7	0.4	221
2014	A	Cedar Rapids	3	2	0	71	80	3.54	1.38	18.7	236	31	77	3.74	4.6	10.1	2.2	0.9	77
2015	A	Cedar Rapids	*Did not pitch; injured*																

Sneaky quick hurler who underwent TJ surgery in April and missed entire season. Has advanced skills for age and should regain average velocity and command. CU could develop into plus offering while CB shows solid break. Needs to add more strength to pitch deeper into games, but has the ingredients to be mid-rotation guy.

Thurman,Andrew | SP | Atlanta | EXP MLB DEBUT: 2017 | H/W: 6-3 225 | FUT: #4 starter | 7C

Thrws R Age 24
2013 (2) UC-Irvine

91-94	FB	+++
72-75	CB	++
80-81	SL	+++
81-83	CU	+++

Year	Lev	Team	W	L	Sv	IP	K	ERA	WHIP	BF/G	OBA	H%	S%	xERA	Ctl	Dom	Cmd	hr/9	BPV
2013	A-	Tri City	4	2	1	39	43	3.90	1.38	13.7	280	36	76	4.59	2.5	9.9	3.9	1.1	128
2014	A	Quad Cities	7	9	1	115	107	5.40	1.41	18.7	273	34	61	4.17	3.1	8.4	2.7	0.7	84
2015	Rk	GCL Braves	1	0	0	8	9	3.38	0.88	9.9	210	27	67	2.38	1.1	10.1	9.0	1.1	170
2015	A+	Carolina	5	4	0	57	43	3.78	1.19	20.8	261	32	67	3.11	1.7	6.8	3.9	0.3	93
2015	AA	Mississippi	1	4	0	24	14	5.23	1.87	22.6	299	35	69	5.08	6.0	5.2	0.9	0.0	-49

Incredibly solid prospect with potentially 4 MLB quality pitches acquired in trade with HOU last offseason. Does not have a plus offering but his low 90s FB with pinpoint command comes close. CU and SL are solid secondaries but CB lags behind. Season ended in May with injuries sustained in team bus accident.

Tinoco,Jesus | SP | Colorado | EXP MLB DEBUT: 2019 | H/W: 6-4 190 | FUT: #3 starter | 8D

Thrws R Age 20
2011 FA (VZ)

92-95	FB	++++
83-85	SL	+++
88-90	CU	++

Year	Lev	Team	W	L	Sv	IP	K	ERA	WHIP	BF/G	OBA	H%	S%	xERA	Ctl	Dom	Cmd	hr/9	BPV
2012	Rk	GCL Blue Jays	1	1	0	6	8	6.00	1.33	12.5	293	44	50	3.57	1.5	12.0	8.0	0.0	194
2013	Rk	GCL Blue Jays	0	5	1	46	45	5.09	1.52	16.6	274	37	63	3.80	4.1	8.8	2.1	0.0	66
2014	Rk	Bluefield	1	9	1	56	47	4.97	1.46	18.5	282	34	65	4.38	3.2	7.5	2.4	0.6	67
2015	A	Asheville	5	0	0	40	37	1.80	1.10	22.4	242	31	86	2.73	1.8	8.3	4.6	0.5	119
2015	A	Lansing	2	6	0	81	68	3.55	1.36	22.6	278	35	72	3.56	2.4	7.5	3.1	0.1	88

Tall, projectable hurler came over as part of the Tulowitzki deal. FB already sits at 92-95 mph, topping out at 97 mph. Gets good late sink and has room for more as he fills out. Mixes in a SL that shows potential and an avg CU. Throws all three for strikes and keeps the ball down in the zone. Some work to do, but lots to like here.

Tirado,Alberto | RP | Philadelphia | EXP MLB DEBUT: 2017 | H/W: 6-1 180 | FUT: Setup reliever | 7C

Thrws R Age 21
2011 FA (DR)

92-96	FB	++++
82-84	SL	+++
81-82	CU	+++

Year	Lev	Team	W	L	Sv	IP	K	ERA	WHIP	BF/G	OBA	H%	S%	xERA	Ctl	Dom	Cmd	hr/9	BPV
2013	Rk	Bluefield	3	0	0	48	44	1.68	1.27	16.4	232	30	87	2.78	3.7	8.2	2.2	0.2	65
2014	A-	Vancouver	1	0	0	35	36	3.58	1.51	9.0	201	28	75	3.06	7.2	9.2	1.3	0.3	-10
2014	A	Lansing	1	2	1	40	40	6.30	2.10	15.1	285	37	69	6.05	8.8	9.0	1.0	0.7	-57
2015	A+	Clearwater	1	0	0	15	16	0.60	1.60	7.4	124	19	96	2.23	10.8	9.6	0.9	0.0	-101
2015	A+	Dunedin	4	3	3	61	61	3.24	1.31	8.1	207	27	76	2.95	5.2	9.0	1.7	0.6	41

Converted starter can now focus on two potentially plus pitches—a mid-90s FB and developing hard swing-and-miss slider that has flashed plus in the past. Control of the arsenal is a weak link at the moment, though. Great arm speed and still some physical projection; added strength would be a plus.

Torres,Jose | RP | San Diego | EXP MLB DEBUT: 2018 | H/W: 6-2 175 | FUT: Setup reliever | 7D

Thrws L Age 22
2010 FA (VZ)

92-96	FB	+++
83-86	SL	++
	CU	+

Year	Lev	Team	W	L	Sv	IP	K	ERA	WHIP	BF/G	OBA	H%	S%	xERA	Ctl	Dom	Cmd	hr/9	BPV
2012	Rk	Azl Athletics	3	1	0	52	41	4.33	1.56	19.0	262	32	71	4.06	5.0	7.1	1.4	0.3	10
2013	A-	Vermont	3	2	0	30	21	2.68	1.32	13.9	247	29	82	3.53	3.6	6.3	1.8	0.6	34
2014	A-	Vermont	0	6	2	61	47	4.41	1.37	18.3	264	32	68	3.86	3.2	6.9	2.1	0.6	55
2015	A	Beloit	4	5	8	73	80	2.70	1.07	6.5	210	29	76	2.27	2.8	9.8	3.5	0.5	119
2015	A+	Stockton	0	0	0	3	4	0.00	0.31	3.3	0	0	100		2.8	11.3	4.0	0.0	145

Improving RP who was moved to pen in 1st full season. Showed excellent feel for strike zone and has two potential average to plus offerings. Quick and lively FB is best current pitch, but quality SL isn't far behind. SL has inconsistent break and can be left up. Rarely uses CU, but may not need. Will need time to polish craft.

Torrez,Daury | SP | Chicago (N) | EXP MLB DEBUT: 2018 | H/W: 6-3 210 | FUT: #4 starter | 6C

Thrws R Age 22
2010 FA (DR)

90-92	FB	+++
83-85	SL	+++
	CB	+

Year	Lev	Team	W	L	Sv	IP	K	ERA	WHIP	BF/G	OBA	H%	S%	xERA	Ctl	Dom	Cmd	hr/9	BPV
2013	Rk	Azl Cubs	4	2	1	49	49	3.31	1.10	16.0	262	35	69	2.92	0.9	9.0	9.8	0.4	155
2013	A	Kane County	0	1	0	5	2	5.40	1.20	20.1	262	25	60	4.57	1.8	3.6	2.0	1.8	34
2014	A	Kane County	11	7	0	131	81	2.75	1.00	21.8	229	26	74	2.44	1.4	5.6	3.9	0.5	79
2015	A+	Myrtle Beach	10	6	0	134	86	3.76	1.18	22.3	266	30	69	3.55	1.4	5.8	4.1	0.7	84

Dominican hurler thrives despite the lack of overpowering stuff. FB sits in the 89-92 mph range with good sink. Mixes in a decent SL and a below-avg CU. Pounds the strike zone, inducing weak contact and tons of GB outs. Career Ctl of 1.18 and a WHIP of 1.05 are worth noting.

Toussaint,Touki | SP | Atlanta | EXP MLB DEBUT: 2018 | H/W: 6-3 185 | FUT: #1 starter | 9E

Thrws R Age 19
2014 (1) HS (FL)

91-94	FB	+++
74-75	CB	++++
84-85	CU	+++
82-86	SL	++

Year	Lev	Team	W	L	Sv	IP	K	ERA	WHIP	BF/G	OBA	H%	S%	xERA	Ctl	Dom	Cmd	hr/9	BPV
2014	Rk	Azl DBacks	1	1	0	15	17	4.80	1.73	9.8	249	36	69	3.97	7.2	10.2	1.4	0.0	7
2014	Rk	Missoula	1	3	0	13	15	12.95	2.27	13.4	392	46	44	10.89	4.1	10.2	2.5	3.4	92
2015	A	Rome	3	5	0	48	38	5.79	1.51	20.9	227	26	63	4.23	6.2	7.1	1.2	1.1	-21
2015	A	Kane County	2	2	0	39	29	3.69	1.18	22.3	220	25	71	3.11	3.5	6.7	1.9	0.9	45

Acquired by ATL in a mid-season deal with ARI. Former 1st rd pick fell out of favor in previous organization. A slight mechanical adjustments improved his FB velocity and command. The break and depth of a potentially plus-plus CB is special. SL is slurvy and doesn't complement package. CU has deception but lacks consistency. Could be plus offering.

Travieso,Nicholas | SP | Cincinnati | EXP MLB DEBUT: 2017 | H/W: 6-2 225 | FUT: #3 starter | 8C

Thrws R Age 22
2012 (1) HS (FL)

93-95	FB	++++
86-88	SL	+++
84-85	CU	++

Year	Lev	Team	W	L	Sv	IP	K	ERA	WHIP	BF/G	OBA	H%	S%	xERA	Ctl	Dom	Cmd	hr/9	BPV
2012	Rk	AZL Reds	0	2	0	21	14	4.71	1.19	10.5	252	27	64	3.91	2.1	6.0	2.8	1.3	68
2013	A	Dayton	7	4	0	81	61	4.66	1.35	19.9	266	31	66	4.02	3.0	6.8	2.3	0.8	59
2014	A	Dayton	14	5	0	142	114	3.04	1.17	21.8	235	28	76	3.01	2.8	7.2	2.6	0.6	73
2015	A+	Daytona	6	6	0	93	76	2.71	1.20	19.7	238	29	78	2.89	2.9	7.3	2.5	0.4	72

Strong-armed tough SP is not intimidated by hitters. Not afraid to challenge with plus sinking FB. SL took a step forward in '15. Previously, threw SL in 82-85 range. Harder SL has contributed to sharper depth. Has a feel for a sparingly-used CU. Must work on CU to have real shot sticking as a SP.

Trexler,David — RP — Chicago (A)

EXP MLB DEBUT: 2017 | H/W: 6-3 185 | FUT: Setup reliever | 7E

Thrws R Age 25 — 2014 (17) North Florida

Velo	Pitch	Grade
91-95	FB	++++
78-80	CB	++
83-86	CU	+

Year	Lev	Team	W	L	Sv	IP	K	ERA	WHIP	BF/G	OBA	H%	S%	xERA	Ctl	Dom	Cmd	hr/9	BPV
2013	NCAA	North Florida	5	4	2	56	38	3.52	1.44	15.0	275	32	75	3.94	3.4	6.1	1.8	0.3	37
2014	NCAA	North Florida	6	4	0	87	59	3.62	1.51	26.9	273	32	76	4.16	4.0	6.1	1.5	0.4	19
2014	Rk	Azl White Sox	0	0	0	7	6	0.00	0.71	6.2	202	27	100	0.85	0.0	7.7		0.0	157
2014	Rk	Great Falls	1	2	0	23	27	3.49	1.42	7.0	268	33	86	5.28	3.5	10.5	3.0	1.9	112
2015	A	Kannapolis	0	3	7	69	76	4.95	1.52	8.3	259	35	67	4.19	4.8	9.9	2.1	0.7	66

Aggressive power arm that has spent entire career in bullpen. Old for level, but has arm strength and FB to ascend quickly if he can harness his power arsenal. Has trouble retiring LHH with below average CU, though hard CB is true out pitch. Likes to challenge hitters inside and shows capacity to keep ball on ground.

Tseng,Jen-Ho — SP — Chicago (N)

EXP MLB DEBUT: 2017 | H/W: 6-1 195 | FUT: #3 starter | 8D

Thrws R Age 21 — 2013 FA (TW)

Velo	Pitch	Grade
90-93	FB	+++
75-78	CB	+++
80-82	CU	+++

Year	Lev	Team	W	L	Sv	IP	K	ERA	WHIP	BF/G	OBA	H%	S%	xERA	Ctl	Dom	Cmd	hr/9	BPV
2014	A	Kane County	6	1	0	105	85	2.40	0.87	20.4	204	25	75	1.83	1.3	7.3	5.7	0.6	114
2015	A+	Myrtle Beach	7	7	0	119	87	3.55	1.22	21.8	255	31	70	3.16	2.3	6.6	2.9	0.4	75

Taiwanese hurler has a good 90-93 mph FB and backs it up with a mid-70s CB, and a plus change-up. Tseng hides the ball well and locates all three offerings. He comes inside effectively vs. RHH, but has a fairly slow tempo and throws with some effort. Held his own at A+, but AA will give him a true test.

Tuivailala,Sam — RP — St. Louis

EXP MLB DEBUT: 2014 | H/W: 6-3 195 | FUT: Closer | 7C

Thrws R Age 23 — 2010 (3) HS (CA)

Velo	Pitch	Grade
94-97	FB	++++
79-81	CB	+++
	CU	++

Year	Lev	Team	W	L	Sv	IP	K	ERA	WHIP	BF/G	OBA	H%	S%	xERA	Ctl	Dom	Cmd	hr/9	BPV
2014	AA	Springfield	2	1	1	21		2.57	1.29	5.1	233	38	78	2.62	3.9	12.9	3.3	0.0	145
2014	AAA	Memphis	0	0	1	1	3	0.00	0.91	2.1	244	91	100	1.69	0.0	24.5		0.0	460
2014	MLB	St. Louis	0	0	0	1	1	36.00	7.00	4.9	639	62	60	44.98	18.0	9.0	0.5	18.0	-306
2015	AAA	Memphis	3	1	17	45	43	1.60	1.20	4.2	181	24	88	2.20	5.2	8.6	1.7	0.4	32
2015	MLB	St. Louis	0	1	0	14	20	3.17	1.48	4.4	245	35	84	4.45	5.1	12.7	2.5	1.3	109

Dominant reliever comes after hitters with a blazing upper-90s FB that has good late life. Improved power CB gives him a 2nd plus offering. CU remains inconsistent, but has potential. FB command is the only red flag, but if he can master it he has the tools to dominate in the majors.

Turley,Josh — SP — Detroit

EXP MLB DEBUT: 2016 | H/W: 5-11 190 | FUT: #5 starter | 6B

Thrws L Age 25 — 2012 (16) Baylor

Velo	Pitch	Grade
85-90	FB	++
77-80	CB	++
80-85	SL	++
	CU	++++

Year	Lev	Team	W	L	Sv	IP	K	ERA	WHIP	BF/G	OBA	H%	S%	xERA	Ctl	Dom	Cmd	hr/9	BPV
2012	A-	Connecticut	4	0	0	34	25	1.06	0.82	10.3	193	24	86	1.04	1.3	6.6	5.0	0.0	101
2013	A	West Michigan	8	4	2	77	79	2.10	1.05	5.9	227	30	83	2.53	2.0	9.2	4.6	0.6	130
2014	A+	Lakeland	7	1	0	97	81	1.85	0.96	20.4	204	26	80	1.66	2.1	7.5	3.5	0.2	96
2014	AA	Erie	3	4	0	50	28	3.78	1.38	23.3	273	28	79	4.83	2.9	5.0	1.8	1.4	31
2015	AA	Erie	13	8	0	153	103	3.29	1.22	24.7	259	29	76	3.68	2.1	6.1	2.9	0.9	71

Light-throwing SP with deep repertoire who can handle LHH. Converted to SP in '14 and can pitch deep into games while maintaining stuff. CU is plus offering, but not out pitch. Mixes in two breaking balls with varying shapes. Can cut FB and locate within strike zone. Won't fan many batters and has tendency to allow HR.

Turnbull,Spencer — SP — Detroit

EXP MLB DEBUT: 2017 | H/W: 6-3 215 | FUT: #3 SP / Setup RP | 8D

Thrws R Age 23 — 2014 (2) Alabama

Velo	Pitch	Grade
92-95	FB	++++
83-87	SL	+++
	CU	++

Year	Lev	Team	W	L	Sv	IP	K	ERA	WHIP	BF/G	OBA	H%	S%	xERA	Ctl	Dom	Cmd	hr/9	BPV
2013	NCAA	Alabama	4	3	0	90	51	3.70	1.44	25.6	266	31	73	3.72	3.8	5.1	1.3	0.2	7
2014	NCAA	Alabama	5	7	0	93	61	2.22	1.16	24.7	189	22	81	2.11	4.5	5.9	1.3	0.3	1
2014	Rk	GCL Tigers	0	0	0	3	4	3.00	1.00	11.5	191	18	100	4.22	3.0	12.0	4.0	3.0	153
2014	A-	Connecticut	0	2	0	28	19	4.48	1.60	11.3	281	33	70	4.43	4.5	6.1	1.4	0.3	6
2015	A	West Michigan	11	3	0	116	106	3.02	1.36	22.1	244	32	75	3.00	4.0	8.2	2.0	0.0	57

Big, physical SP who didn't allow HR in 2015. Lives in lower half of zone by using 2-seam FB with heavy sink. Power SL has incrementally improved, but CU lags behind. Has significant effort in delivery, which some scouts see as a future move to the bullpen. Next step is to increase number and quality of strikes.

Underwood,Duane — SP — Chicago (N)

EXP MLB DEBUT: 2017 | H/W: 6-2 215 | FUT: #3 starter | 8C

Thrws R Age 21 — 2012 (2) HS (GA)

Velo	Pitch	Grade
91-95	FB	++++
86-88	CT	++
82-84	CU	++
80-83	CB	+++

Year	Lev	Team	W	L	Sv	IP	K	ERA	WHIP	BF/G	OBA	H%	S%	xERA	Ctl	Dom	Cmd	hr/9	BPV
2012	Rk	Azl Cubs	0	1	0	8	7	5.49	1.59	7.2	232	27	67	4.45	6.6	7.7	1.2	1.1	-22
2013	A-	Boise	3	4	0	54	36	4.99	1.65	17.3	289	33	69	4.98	4.5	6.0	1.3	0.7	5
2014	A	Kane County	6	4	0	100	84	2.51	1.21	18.3	231	27	84	3.29	3.2	7.5	2.3	0.9	67
2015	Rk	Azl Cubs	0	0	0	5	6	0.00	0.60	8.6	175	27	100	0.23	0.0	10.8		0.0	212
2015	A+	Myrtle Beach	6	3	0	73	48	2.59	1.04	20.2	201	23	79	2.37	3.0	5.9	2.0	0.7	45

Hard thrower has some of the best velocity in the system. Attacks hitters with a good 91-95 mph FB that tops at 99 mph. Also has a hard CB and an inconsistent CU. Showed improved mechanics, but still struggles with control. Missed action with a balky right shoulder, but avoided surgery. When healthy, he generates weak contact.

Urias,Julio — SP — Los Angeles (N)

EXP MLB DEBUT: 2016 | H/W: 6-2 205 | FUT: #1 starter | 9C

Thrws L Age 19 — 2012 FA (MX)

Velo	Pitch	Grade
92-95	FB	++++
75-81	CB	++++
	CU	+++

Year	Lev	Team	W	L	Sv	IP	K	ERA	WHIP	BF/G	OBA	H%	S%	xERA	Ctl	Dom	Cmd	hr/9	BPV
2014	A+	RanchoCuca	2	2	0	87	109	2.37	1.11	13.7	196	29	80	2.14	3.8	11.3	2.9	0.4	117
2015	Rk	Azl Dodgers	0	0	0	3	5	0.00	1.00	5.7	191	37	100	1.37	3.0	15.0	5.0	0.0	207
2015	A+	RanchoCuca	0	0	0	4	4	8.57	1.67	18.8	371	43	50	7.78	0.0	8.6		2.1	172
2015	AA	Tulsa	3	4	0	68	74	2.78	1.00	20.0	216	29	73	2.21	2.0	9.8	4.9	0.5	141
2015	AAA	Oklahoma City	0	1	0	4	5	19.76	4.15	14.3	488	63	47	14.69	13.2	11.0	0.8	0.0	-140

Smallish lefty was limited to 80.1 IP after opting to have surgery to remove a mass under his left eye. When healthy attacks hitters with a plus 92-95 mph FB that tops out at 97 mph. Mixes in a plus CU and a hard CB that has the potential to be plus. Understands how to change speeds and keep hitters off-balance.

Valdez,Jose — RP — Detroit

EXP MLB DEBUT: 2015 | H/W: 6-1 200 | FUT: Setup reliever | 7D

Thrws R Age 26 — 2009 FA (DR)

Velo	Pitch	Grade
93-98	FB	+++
84-87	SL	+++
	CU	+

Year	Lev	Team	W	L	Sv	IP	K	ERA	WHIP	BF/G	OBA	H%	S%	xERA	Ctl	Dom	Cmd	hr/9	BPV
2013	A	West Michigan	1	1	16	26	35	2.76	1.38	4.1	179	29	78	2.21	6.9	12.1	1.8	0.0	49
2013	A+	Lakeland	1	1	17	23	32	2.74	1.30	4.1	198	31	79	2.61	5.5	12.5	2.3	0.4	95
2014	AA	Erie	2	3	18	57	66	4.11	1.44	5.2	258	35	74	4.25	4.1	10.4	2.5	0.9	95
2015	AAA	Toledo	4	5	5	57	43	3.32	1.53	5.9	234	28	79	3.74	6.0	6.8	1.1	0.5	-22
2015	MLB	Detroit	0	1	0	9	4	4.00	1.56	5.6	283	27	83	5.94	4.0	4.0	1.0	2.0	-18

Stocky RP who has spent entire career in pen, but can't master art of control. Throws vicious FB with good angle, but exhibits little command. K rate fell dramatically despite hard stuff. Has long arm action and max-effort delivery, but little deception as he tends to overthrow. Hard SL can be wipeout offering, though lacks pitch vs. LHH.

Varga,Cameron — SP — Tampa Bay

EXP MLB DEBUT: 2018 | H/W: 6-3 190 | FUT: #4 starter | 7D

Thrws R Age 21 — 2014 (2) HS (OH)

Velo	Pitch	Grade
89-94	FB	+++
75-79	CB	+++
80-83	CU	++

Year	Lev	Team	W	L	Sv	IP	K	ERA	WHIP	BF/G	OBA	H%	S%	xERA	Ctl	Dom	Cmd	hr/9	BPV
2014	Rk	Princeton	1	1	0	19	11	4.74	1.74	17.3	327	37	72	5.63	3.3	5.2	1.6	0.5	22
2014	Rk	GCL Devil Rays	2	0	0	14	14	2.55	0.92	10.6	232	32	69	1.72	0.6	8.9	14.0	0.0	162
2015	A-	Hudson Valley	3	6	0	57	39	2.99	1.35	19.9	290	34	77	3.92	1.7	6.1	3.5	0.3	82

Athletic SP who repeated short-season ball and has yet to pitch in full season. Has ingredients to be potent back-end starter with lively pitch mix. Generates easy velocity with clean mechanics and repeats delivery. CU needs attention, though shows signs of improvement. More of a pitch-to-contact guy than K guy.

VerHagen,Drew — RP — Detroit

EXP MLB DEBUT: 2014 | H/W: 6-6 230 | FUT: Middle reliever | 6B

Thrws R Age 25 — 2012 (4) Vanderbilt

Velo	Pitch	Grade
90-94	FB	+++
76-78	CB	+++
80-83	CU	++

Year	Lev	Team	W	L	Sv	IP	K	ERA	WHIP	BF/G	OBA	H%	S%	xERA	Ctl	Dom	Cmd	hr/9	BPV
2014	AAA	Toledo	6	7	0	110	63	3.68	1.29	23.8	274	31	71	3.63	2.0	5.1	2.5	0.4	56
2014	MLB	Detroit	0	1	0	5	4	5.40	1.60	22.1	262	33	63	3.85	5.4	7.2	1.3	0.0	2
2015	AA	Erie	2	0	2	6	5	2.90	1.29	5.1	255	29	86	4.34	2.9	7.3	2.5	1.5	70
2015	AAA	Toledo	1	3	1	27	21	3.64	1.36	7.6	253	32	70	3.13	3.6	6.9	1.9	0.0	45
2015	MLB	Detroit	2	0	0	26	13	2.07	1.23	5.3	197	22	84	2.43	4.8	4.5	0.9	0.3	-32

Tall, strong pitcher who converted to RP in '15. Has huge frame and added a few ticks to FB in bullpen. Keeps ball down with sinker and has deception with crossfire delivery. CB has glimpses of plus break, but CU lags behind. K rate improved in pen, but still not strikeout guy, even in short stints. Pitches to contact and gets groundballs.

Voelker,Paul — RP — Detroit

EXP MLB DEBUT: 2016 | H/W: 5-10 185 | FUT: Setup reliever | 6B

Thrws R Age 23 — 2014 (10) Dallas Baptist

Velo	Pitch	Grade
91-95	FB	+++
83-87	SL	++
	CU	+

Year	Lev	Team	W	L	Sv	IP	K	ERA	WHIP	BF/G	OBA	H%	S%	xERA	Ctl	Dom	Cmd	hr/9	BPV
2014	Rk	GCL Tigers	0	0	1	2	4	0.00	0.00	2.8	0	0			0.0	18.0		0.0	342
2014	A-	Connecticut	0	1	1	25	31	2.52	1.08	6.1	203	30	77	2.09	3.2	11.2	3.4	0.4	131
2015	A	West Michigan	2	0	2	16	20	2.25	0.81	5.8	166	26	69	0.66	2.3	11.3	5.0	0.0	160
2015	A+	Lakeland	3	0	7	22	26	1.64	1.05	6.1	215	31	86	2.19	2.5	10.6	4.3	0.4	143
2015	AA	Erie	1	1	9	17	17	2.63	1.40	4.5	225	29	83	3.35	5.3	8.9	1.7	0.5	37

Short RP who served as closer in breakout season. Put himself on map with command of two pitches, FB and SL. Hard SL has chance to become plus, but leaves up in zone often. Doesn't throw with good angle to plate because of height, but commands quick FB to both sides. Rarely uses change-up.

Voth,Austin | SP | Washington | EXP MLB DEBUT: 2016 | H/W: 6-1 189 | FUT: #3 starter | 8C

Thrws R Age 23	Year	Lev	Team	W	L	Sv	IP	K	ERA	WHIP	BF/G	OBA	H%	S%	xERA	Ctl	Dom	Cmd	hr/9	BPV
2013 (5) Washington	2013	A	Hagerstown	1	0	0	10	9	3.53	0.98	19.4	218	29	60	1.70	1.8	7.9	4.5	0.0	113
90-92 FB +++	2014	A	Hagerstown	4	3	0	69	74	2.47	1.05	20.6	207	29	75	1.87	2.9	9.6	3.4	0.1	114
83-85 SL +++	2014	A+	Potomac	2	1	0	37	40	1.45	0.62	21.3	132	18	81	0.29	1.7	9.7	5.7	0.5	146
CU +++	2014	AA	Harrisburg	1	3	0	19	19	6.60	1.62	17.0	290	34	63	6.06	4.2	9.0	2.1	1.9	65
	2015	AA	Harrisburg	6	7	0	157	148	2.92	1.11	22.0	232	30	75	2.74	2.3	8.5	3.7	0.6	109

Polished starter who improved all facets of his game at AA, and lead the Eastern League in strikeouts. Relies more on location and command of all three pitches, rather than pure stuff. CU is best secondary pitch, and has the frame to withstand rigors of a full MLB season.

Waddell,Brandon | SP | Pittsburgh | EXP MLB DEBUT: 2018 | H/W: 6-3 180 | FUT: #5 starter | 6C

Thrws L Age 21	Year	Lev	Team	W	L	Sv	IP	K	ERA	WHIP	BF/G	OBA	H%	S%	xERA	Ctl	Dom	Cmd	hr/9	BPV
2015 (5) Virginia																				
88-91 FB ++																				
CB ++																				
CU ++	2015	NCAA	Virginia	5	5	0	110	89	3.93	1.48	24.9	269	33	72	3.95	4.0	7.3	1.8	0.3	41
	2015	A-	West Virginia	1	1	0	20	18	5.82	1.54	14.6	297	38	58	4.21	3.1	8.1	2.6	0.0	78

Was inconsistent in his junior year, showing an ability to keep hitters off-balance but then struggling with control in other starts. Raw stuff is not overpowering. Cut FB sits 88-91 mph. CB shows some potential with good 11-5 tilt and an average CU. Could develop into a decent back-end starter or lefty reliever.

Wagner,Tyler | SP | Milwaukee | EXP MLB DEBUT: 2015 | H/W: 6-3 195 | FUT: #5 starter | 7B

Thrws R Age 25	Year	Lev	Team	W	L	Sv	IP	K	ERA	WHIP	BF/G	OBA	H%	S%	xERA	Ctl	Dom	Cmd	hr/9	BPV
2012 (4) Utah																				
89-92 FB +++	2013	A	Wisconsin	10	8	0	148		3.22	1.25	22.3	236	28	75	3.19	3.4	7.0	2.1	0.6	53
88-91 CT +++	2014	A+	Brevard County	13	6	0	150	118	1.86	1.11	23.6	218	26	87	2.60	2.9	7.1	2.5	0.6	68
83-87 CU ++	2015	AA	Biloxi	11	5	0	152	120	2.25	1.15	24.2	233	28	82	2.72	2.7	7.1	2.7	0.4	74
75-79 CB +++	2015	MLB	Milwaukee	0	2	0	13	5	7.50	2.20	22.1	371	39	64	7.80	4.8	3.4	0.7	0.7	-50

Converted college reliever who led SL in ERA. Primary weapon is low-90s FB with heavy sink and now complements it with good CT to induce heaps of GBs. Command of CB and CU have improved, but project as average MLB pitches. Fluid delivery with minimal torque should allow for more Ctl gains. Gets ahead of hitters and attacks lower third of the zone.

Wahl,Bobby | RP | Oakland | EXP MLB DEBUT: 2016 | H/W: 6-3 210 | FUT: Setup reliever | 8E

Thrws R Age 24	Year	Lev	Team	W	L	Sv	IP	K	ERA	WHIP	BF/G	OBA	H%	S%	xERA	Ctl	Dom	Cmd	hr/9	BPV
2013 (5) Mississippi	2013	Rk	Azl Athletics	0	0	0	1	1	9.00	2.00	4.8	0	0	50	2.18	18.0	9.0	0.5	0.0	-306
92-97 FB +++	2013	A-	Vermont	0	0	2	20	27	4.01	1.29	9.2	260	36	74	4.24	2.7	12.0	4.5	1.3	162
82-84 SL +++	2014	A	Beloit	0	4	4	42	43	5.12	1.54	9.2	279	35	68	4.92	4.1	9.2	2.3	1.1	74
80-82 CU +++	2014	A+	Stockton	0	0	0	10	19	4.41	1.37	4.8	218	38	75	4.26	5.3	16.8	3.2	1.8	177
	2015	AA	Midland	2	0	4	32	36	4.21	1.56	5.9	285	38	73	4.56	3.9	10.1	2.6	0.6	94

Aggressive pitcher who was moved to pen in '15. Missed significant time with minor injuries, but showcased electric FB in short stints. Can be dominant at times, but FB is flat at higher velocity. Hard SL is go-to pitch when ahead in count, though struggles with changing speeds and LHH. Effort in delivery will keep him as RP.

Watson,Nolan | SP | Kansas City | EXP MLB DEBUT: 2019 | H/W: 6-2 195 | FUT: #3 starter | 8D

Thrws R Age 19	Year	Lev	Team	W	L	Sv	IP	K	ERA	WHIP	BF/G	OBA	H%	S%	xERA	Ctl	Dom	Cmd	hr/9	BPV
2015 (1) HS (IN)																				
89-95 FB ++++																				
81-84 SL ++																				
CU ++																				
	2015	Rk	Burlington	0	3	0	29	16	4.95	1.72	12.0	322	36	71	5.65	3.4	4.9	1.5	0.6	15

Promising SP who was hit hard in pro debut, but has repertoire and easy velocity to have significant upside. Has frame to add strength and velocity while quick arm adds hint of pitch movement. Tendency to pitch up in zone could hurt him and lack of consistent secondaries need attention. Upgrade to CU is in order.

Weaver,Luke | SP | St. Louis | EXP MLB DEBUT: 2018 | H/W: 6-1 170 | FUT: #3 starter | 8C

Thrws R Age 22	Year	Lev	Team	W	L	Sv	IP	K	ERA	WHIP	BF/G	OBA	H%	S%	xERA	Ctl	Dom	Cmd	hr/9	BPV
2014 (1) Florida St	2013	NCAA	Florida St	7	2	0	98	119	2.29	0.99	22.0	220	32	78	2.15	1.7	10.9	6.3	0.5	167
91-93 FB ++++	2014	NCAA	Florida St	8	4	0	106	85	2.63	1.05	25.6	227	27	78	2.63	2.0	7.2	3.7	0.7	95
79-81 SL ++	2014	Rk	GCL Cardinals	0	0	0	6	9	0.00	0.67	5.2	191	34	100	0.54	0.0	13.5		0.0	261
78-81 CU ++++	2014	A+	Palm Beach	0	1	0	3	3	23.23	4.84	11.9	557	64	50	21.49	11.6	8.7	0.8	2.9	-139
	2015	A+	Palm Beach	8	5	0	105	88	1.63	1.11	21.8	248	32	85	2.60	1.6	7.5	4.6	0.2	110

Velocity is down from his college days, but still has a good 90-93 mph FB. Keeps the ball down in the zone and gets late action from a high ¾ arm slot. Improved mechanics results in plus command and he walked just 19 batters. Mixes in a decent SL and a plus CU that has good late fade and sink.

Wells,Nick | SP | Seattle | EXP MLB DEBUT: 2019 | H/W: 6-5 185 | FUT: #3 starter | 8E

Thrws L Age 20	Year	Lev	Team	W	L	Sv	IP	K	ERA	WHIP	BF/G	OBA	H%	S%	xERA	Ctl	Dom	Cmd	hr/9	BPV
2014 (3) HS (VA)																				
87-94 FB +++																				
75-79 CB +++	2014	Rk	GCL Blue Jays	1	3	0	34	18	5.79	1.61	13.8	313	35	61	4.90	2.9	4.7	1.6	0.3	25
CU ++	2015	Rk	Bluefield	1	2	0	32	31	4.78	1.28	18.7	250	31	65	3.92	3.1	8.7	2.8	1.1	91
	2015	A-	Everett	1	0	0	18	16	1.00	0.56	15.2	106	15	80		2.0	8.0	4.0	0.0	108

Long, projectable hurler has arm speed and loose delivery to become solid contributor. Needs lot of development time as he fails to repeat mechanics and arm slot. Has good control, but needs better FB command within strike zone. CB has big bending action, but CU can be too firm. When on, he's tough to hit and could register Ks with FB and CB.

Whalen,Rob | SP | Atlanta | EXP MLB DEBUT: 2017 | H/W: 6-2 200 | FUT: #4 starter | 7C

Thrws R Age 22	Year	Lev	Team	W	L	Sv	IP	K	ERA	WHIP	BF/G	OBA	H%	S%	xERA	Ctl	Dom	Cmd	hr/9	BPV
2012 (12) HS (FL)	2013	Rk	Kingsport	3	2	0	72	76	1.87	0.93	22.5	197	28	79	1.44	2.1	9.5	4.5	0.1	131
88-91 FB ++	2014	Rk	GCL Mets	0	1	0	7	10	1.29	0.86	8.6	168	29	83	0.78	2.6	12.9	5.0	0.0	180
77-79 CB ++++	2014	A	Savannah	9	1	0	62	53	2.03	1.01	21.7	201	26	80	1.86	2.7	7.7	2.8	0.3	82
80-81 CU ++	2015	A+	Carolina	1	2	0	13	7	3.41	1.14	17.4	228	23	77	3.54	2.7	4.8	1.8	1.4	30
	2015	A+	St. Lucie	4	5	0	83	61	3.36	1.28	22.7	235	28	74	3.09	3.7	6.6	1.8	0.4	38

Acquired by ATL in a trade sending playoff pieces to NYM. Has struggled the past two seasons battling the injury bug. Had surgery in '14 & '15 to clear out infections in his hand. When healthy, he is a command/control RH with average stuff. With good deception, break and velocity differential off his FB, the CU is his only exceptional offering.

Wheeler,Andre | RP | Chicago (A) | EXP MLB DEBUT: 2017 | H/W: 6-1 170 | FUT: Setup reliever | 7D

Thrws L Age 24	Year	Lev	Team	W	L	Sv	IP	K	ERA	WHIP	BF/G	OBA	H%	S%	xERA	Ctl	Dom	Cmd	hr/9	BPV
2013 (15) Texas Tech	2013	NCAA	Texas Tech	4	1	0	32	21	6.19	1.63	6.2	274	33	58	4.09	5.1	5.9	1.2	0.0	-12
88-94 FB +++	2013	Rk	Bristol	0	1	2	13	20	2.06	0.69	5.1	119	19	75	0.48	2.7	13.7	5.0	0.7	191
78-82 SL ++	2013	A	Kannapolis	1	0	3	17	18	4.19	1.10	7.5	224	27	69	3.56	2.6	9.4	3.6	1.6	117
80-84 CU ++	2014	A	Kannapolis	3	3	0	98	111	2.84	1.19	14.1	235	33	77	2.87	2.9	10.2	3.5	0.5	122
	2015	A+	Winston-Salem	4	2	1	63	61	3.86	1.44	8.4	262	34	73	3.84	4.0	8.7	2.2	0.4	67

Versatile and athletic RP who is menace to LHH thanks to quick arm action and sneaky quick FB. SL may lack power, but is good complement to heater. Could be full-time SP with better CU and it shows promise. Delivery remains crude, but adds deception. Needs to throw more consistent and better strikes to advance.

Wieland,Joe | SP | Los Angeles (N) | EXP MLB DEBUT: 2012 | H/W: 6-3 205 | FUT: #4 starter | 7B

Thrws R Age 26	Year	Lev	Team	W	L	Sv	IP	K	ERA	WHIP	BF/G	OBA	H%	S%	xERA	Ctl	Dom	Cmd	hr/9	BPV
2008 (4) HS (NV)	2014	AA	San Antonio	0	1	0	9	6	2.00	1.00	17.2	240	27	88	2.99	1.0	6.0	6.0	1.0	99
88-92 FB +++	2014	AAA	El Paso	2	1	0	23	20	3.49	1.12	22.9	252	32	68	2.86	1.6	7.8	5.0	0.4	116
80-83 CB +++	2014	MLB	San Diego	1	0	0	11	8	7.30	1.89	13.1	338	36	67	8.05	4.1	6.5	1.6	2.4	25
79-82 CU +++	2015	AAA	Oklahoma City	10	5	0	113	92	4.61	1.41	21.8	297	36	67	4.41	2.0	7.3	3.7	0.6	96
	2015	MLB	LA Dodgers	0	1	0	8	4	8.78	1.83	19.1	302	29	54	7.10	5.5	4.4	0.8	2.2	-51

Injuries have taken their toll and once promising hurler now looks like a back-end-type. TJS cost him two years. In 2014 he had surgery to remove scar tissue and didn't return until August. When healthy, has plus control of a nice three-pitch mix. Has walked only 111 in 590.1 IP. Should fare better in '16 and still has a chance.

Williams,Austen | SP | Washington | EXP MLB DEBUT: 2018 | H/W: 6-3 220 | FUT: #5 starter/RP | 7C

Thrws R Age 23	Year	Lev	Team	W	L	Sv	IP	K	ERA	WHIP	BF/G	OBA	H%	S%	xERA	Ctl	Dom	Cmd	hr/9	BPV
2014 (6) Texas St	2014	Rk	GCL Nationals	0	0	0	4	1	2.14	1.67	9.4	297	32	86	4.57	4.3	2.1	0.5	0.0	-59
89-91 FB +++	2014	A-	Auburn	4	3	0	38	26	4.71	1.31	17.5	281	33	63	3.83	1.9	6.1	3.3	0.5	77
79-81 CB ++	2015	A	Hagerstown	8	1	0	73	63	2.10	1.10	22.0	243	31	81	2.55	1.7	7.8	4.5	0.2	111
81-82 CU ++	2015	A+	Potomac	4	6	0	62	41	2.60	1.09	22.1	225	27	76	2.37	2.5	5.9	2.4	0.3	58
	2015	AAA	Syracuse	0	1	0	4	2	11.25	1.50	17.3	262	24	20	5.74	4.5	4.5	1.0	2.3	-23

Breakout season in two A-ball stops, though average arsenal will be tested at higher levels. Lacks true out pitch or physical projection, and control ahead of command at this point. Delivery still has enough rough edges that many suggest bullpen will be his final destination.

Williams,Devin — SP — Milwaukee
EXP MLB DEBUT: 2018 | H/W: 6-3 165 | FUT: #3 starter | 8D

Thrws R Age 23 — 2013 (2) HS (MO)

90-95 FB ++++ | 81-83 SL +++ | CU +++

Year	Lev	Team	W	L	Sv	IP	K	ERA	WHIP	BF/G	OBA	H%	S%	xERA	Ctl	Dom	Cmd	hr/9	BPV
2013	Rk	Azl Brewers	1	3	1	34	39	3.42	1.46	11.3	225	33	74	2.99	5.8	10.3	1.8	0.0	46
2014	Rk	Helena	4	7	0	66	66	4.49	1.42	18.7	284	36	69	4.34	2.7	9.0	3.3	0.7	106
2015	A	Wisconsin	3	9	0	89	89	3.44	1.25	16.5	230	31	71	2.81	3.6	9.0	2.5	0.3	82

Long right hander with projectable build. Shows plus fastball, quality feel for a changeup and a slider that continues to progress with tweaks to his delivery. Athleticism should allow for more control improvements. Keeps the ball down effectively. Stuff consistently plays up in the bullpen. Versatile arm with intriguing upside.

Williams,Ronnie — SP — St. Louis
EXP MLB DEBUT: 2019 | H/W: 6-0 170 | FUT: #3 starter | 8E

Thrws R Age 20 — 2014 (2) HS (FL)

95-97 FB ++++ | CB ++ | CU ++

Year	Lev	Team	W	L	Sv	IP	K	ERA	WHIP	BF/G	OBA	H%	S%	xERA	Ctl	Dom	Cmd	hr/9	BPV
2014	Rk	GCL Cardinals	0	5	1	36	30	4.74	1.33	15.0	277	35	62	3.61	2.2	7.5	3.3	0.2	92
2015	Rk	Johnson City	3	3	0	56	43	3.70	1.25	19.0	222	26	72	3.20	4.0	6.9	1.7	0.8	34

Pounds the strike zone with a plus 95-97 mph FB. Backs up the heater with a SL and CB that show potential, but remain below average. Shows some feel for a CU, which will be key to his development. There is some effort to his high ¾ delivery, but he has good front-side mechanics and a compact motion.

Williams,Ryan — SP — Chicago (N)
EXP MLB DEBUT: 2017 | H/W: 6-4 220 | FUT: #4 starter | 7B

Thrws R Age 24 — 2014 (10) East Carolina

90-92 FB +++ | 82-84 SL +++ | 78-80 CB +++

Year	Lev	Team	W	L	Sv	IP	K	ERA	WHIP	BF/G	OBA	H%	S%	xERA	Ctl	Dom	Cmd	hr/9	BPV
2014	NCAA	East Carolina	11	3	7	99		1.81	1.00	11.8	239	30	81	2.12	1.0	6.9	6.9	0.1	115
2014	Rk	Azl Cubs	1	0	0	2	3	0.00	0.50	3.3	151	27	100		0.0	13.5		0.0	261
2014	A-	Boise	1	1	1	24	26	1.49	0.95	10.1	227	30	90	2.42	1.1	9.7	8.7	0.7	162
2015	A	South Bend	4	1	0	53	37	1.18	0.71	20.9	194	24	82	0.76	0.3	6.3	18.5	0.0	122
2015	AA	Tennessee	10	2	0	88	61	2.76	1.01	19.8	227	28	71	2.11	1.6	6.2	3.8	0.2	86

Thrives despite not being overpowering. FB sits at 88-91 mph, but he keeps the ball down in the zone and induces tons of GB out (2.3 GB/FB). Walked just 18 in 141.2 IP and now has a WHIP of 0.90 and an ERA of 2.03 after two pro seasons.

Williams,Taylor — SP — Milwaukee
EXP MLB DEBUT: 2018 | H/W: 5-11 195 | FUT: #4 SP / Setup RP | 8D

Thrws R Age 25 — 2013 (4) Kent State

89-93 FB ++++ | 81-84 SL +++ | CU ++

Year	Lev	Team	W	L	Sv	IP	K	ERA	WHIP	BF/G	OBA	H%	S%	xERA	Ctl	Dom	Cmd	hr/9	BPV
2013	NCAA	Kent State	10	1	0	105	110	2.48	0.96	26.5	219	31	72	1.73	1.5	9.4	6.1	0.1	146
2013	Rk	Helena	3	1	0	42	42	4.28	1.40	14.8	261	33	72	4.33	3.6	9.0	2.5	1.1	81
2014	A	Wisconsin	8	1	4	107	112	2.36	0.94	18.3	205	28	75	1.77	1.9	9.4	4.9	0.3	135
2014	A+	Brevard Cnty	1	2	0	25	25	4.30	1.35	21.0	291	35	73	4.97	1.8	9.0	5.0	1.4	131
2015			*Did not pitch; injured*																

Underwent TJS in August after sitting out 2015 with ligament injury in throwing elbow. Smallish 5'11" frame, but sits low to mid-90s with good FB command. SL flashes plus late break and regularly induces whiffs vs. RHH; CU not quite there. Fills the zone and goes after hitters. Some effort in delivery. FB/SL combo could play well in the bullpen.

Williams,Trevor — SP — Pittsburgh
EXP MLB DEBUT: 2016 | H/W: 6-3 230 | FUT: #4 starter | 6C

Thrws R Age 23 — 2013 (2) Arizona St

90-93 FB +++ | CB ++ | 83-85 SL ++ | 77-80 CU +++

Year	Lev	Team	W	L	Sv	IP	K	ERA	WHIP	BF/G	OBA	H%	S%	xERA	Ctl	Dom	Cmd	hr/9	BPV
2013	A	Greensboro	0	0	0	3	3	0.00	0.67	10.5	191	27	100	0.59	0.0	9.0		0.0	180
2014	A+	Jupiter	8	6	0	129	90	2.79	1.29	23.1	275	33	78	3.60	2.0	6.3	3.1	0.3	76
2014	AA	Jacksonville	0	1	0	15	14	6.00	1.87	23.4	342	44	64	5.74	3.6	8.4	2.3	0.0	72
2015	AA	Jacksonville	7	8	0	117	88	4.00	1.38	22.4	276	33	72	4.16	2.8	6.8	2.4	0.7	65
2015	AAA	New Orleans	0	2	0	14	13	2.57	1.57	20.5	275	36	82	3.95	4.5	8.4	1.9	0.0	47

Was acquired by the Pirates in October 2015. FB sits in the low-90s and he complements with an above-avg CU that has good fade. Also mixes in a SL and a get-me-over CB. None of his offerings are plus. Has a good idea of how to set up hitters and throws tons of strikes.

Wilson,Tyler — SP — Baltimore
EXP MLB DEBUT: 2015 | H/W: 6-1 185 | FUT: #5 starter | 6B

Thrws R Age 26 — 2011 (10) Virginia

88-92 FB +++ | 80-82 SL +++ | 81-83 CU ++

Year	Lev	Team	W	L	Sv	IP	K	ERA	WHIP	BF/G	OBA	H%	S%	xERA	Ctl	Dom	Cmd	hr/9	BPV
2013	AA	Bowie	7	5	0	89	70	3.84	1.20	22.4	253	28	73	3.95	2.2	7.1	3.2	1.3	85
2014	AA	Bowie	10	5	0	96	91	3.74	1.28	24.6	271	34	73	4.03	2.1	8.5	4.1	0.9	116
2014	AAA	Norfolk	4	3	0	70	66	3.60	1.17	23.3	236	29	73	3.38	2.7	8.5	3.1	1.0	98
2015	AAA	Norfolk	5	5	0	94	63	3.25	1.19	22.2	262	30	75	3.54	1.7	6.0	3.5	0.8	80
2015	MLB	Baltimore	2	2	0	36	13	3.50	1.39	16.8	278	30	73	3.81	2.8	3.3	1.2	0.3	2

Command/control pitcher who is as consistent as they come. Doesn't have much upside or ceiling, but thrives with solid-average FB and nifty SL that has great depth. Can be too precise at times, but velocity held late in games. Won't be strikeout pitcher and will need to command all pitches to pitch at back-end of rotation.

Winkler,Daniel — RP — Atlanta
EXP MLB DEBUT: 2015 | H/W: 6-3 200 | FUT: Setup reliever | 7B

Thrws R Age 26 — 2011 (20) Central Florida

88-90 FB +++ | 83-86 SL ++++ | 85-87 CU +

Year	Lev	Team	W	L	Sv	IP	K	ERA	WHIP	BF/G	OBA	H%	S%	xERA	Ctl	Dom	Cmd	hr/9	BPV
2012	A	Asheville	11	10	0	145	136	4.47	1.37	24.3	271	33	69	4.32	2.9	8.4	2.9	1.0	91
2013	A+	Modesto	12	5	0	130	152	2.97	0.93	22.2	186	24	74	2.16	2.6	10.5	4.1	1.0	138
2013	AA	Tulsa	1	2	0	26	23	3.09	1.26	21.4	237	28	80	3.62	3.4	7.9	2.3	1.0	67
2014	AA	Tulsa	5	2	0	70	71	1.41	0.71	20.6	143	18	87	0.79	2.2	9.1	4.2	0.6	123
2015	MLB	Atlanta	0	0	0	1	2	15.00	2.50	3.2	371	0	100	21.91	7.5	15.0	2.0	15.0	86

A Rule 5 selection in 2014 from COL, he spent much of '15 on the DL. He was unable to accumulate enough service time and must stay on the 25-man roster in 2016 to remain ATL property. Profiles as a situational RHP. His best pitch is a sweeping SL, which is difficult for LHH to pick up. His FB generates ground balls.

Wittgren,Nick — RP — Miami
EXP MLB DEBUT: 2016 | H/W: 6-3 210 | FUT: Setup reliever | 7B

Thrws R Age 24 — 2012 (9) Purdue

90-93 FB +++ | CB +++ | CU ++

Year	Lev	Team	W	L	Sv	IP	K	ERA	WHIP	BF/G	OBA	H%	S%	xERA	Ctl	Dom	Cmd	hr/9	BPV
2013	A+	Jupiter	2	1	25	54	59	0.83	0.96	4.3	216	30	92	1.77	1.7	9.8	5.9	0.2	150
2013	AA	Jacksonville	0	0	1	4	4	0.00	0.00	2.8	0	0			0.0	9.0		0.0	180
2014	AA	Jacksonville	5	5	20	66	56	3.55	1.32	5.3	282	34	75	4.18	1.9	7.6	4.0	0.8	104
2015	AA	Jacksonville	0	0	1	1	3	0.00	0.00	1.7	0	0			0.0	22.5		0.0	423
2015	AAA	New Orleans	1	6	19	62	64	3.04	1.06	4.7	249	32	75	3.11	1.2	9.3	8.0	0.9	154

Big, athletic reliever continues to display plus Cmd and Ctl in closer role. Lacks plus velocity, but attacks hitters with a deceptive, low-90s sinking FB and a good power CB. Commands both pitches well and can throw the CB for strikes or get hitters to chase. Plus command gives him a chance and he's walked just 37 in 4 pro seasons.

Wojciechowski,Asher — SP — Houston
EXP MLB DEBUT: 2015 | H/W: 6-4 235 | FUT: #4 starter | 7C

Thrws R Age 27 — 2010 (1) The Citadel

89-94 FB +++ | 80-85 SL +++ | 81-84 CU +++

Year	Lev	Team	W	L	Sv	IP	K	ERA	WHIP	BF/G	OBA	H%	S%	xERA	Ctl	Dom	Cmd	hr/9	BPV
2013	AA	Corpus Christi	2	1	1	26	27	2.08	0.92	16.2	188	26	78	1.52	2.4	9.3	3.9	0.3	121
2013	AAA	Oklahoma City	9	7	0	134	104	3.56	1.19	24.4	235	28	71	3.10	3.0	7.0	2.4	0.7	64
2014	AAA	Oklahoma City	4	4	0	76	59	4.74	1.45	21.6	293	34	70	5.03	2.5	7.0	2.8	1.2	77
2015	AAA	Fresno	8	4	0	115	87	4.93	1.48	24.7	284	33	68	4.82	3.2	6.8	2.1	1.0	54
2015	MLB	Houston	0	1	0	16	16	7.27	1.86	15.1	336	42	61	6.68	3.9	8.9	2.3	1.1	73

Strong, durable SP who spent 3rd season in AAA. Hasn't made progress with ideal pitch mix and may move to pen. Lacks out pitch, but can sequence three average offerings. Keeps walks to minimum and can spot FB to both sides of plate. SL won't miss bats, but can drop in zone for strikes. Prone to flyballs and hasn't been effective against LHH.

Woodford,Jake — SP — St. Louis
EXP MLB DEBUT: 2019 | H/W: 6-4 210 | FUT: #3 starter | 8D

Thrws R Age 19 — 2015 (1) HS (FL)

90-93 FB +++ | SL ++ | CU ++

Year	Lev	Team	W	L	Sv	IP	K	ERA	WHIP	BF/G	OBA	H%	S%	xERA	Ctl	Dom	Cmd	hr/9	BPV
2015	Rk	GCL Cardinals	1	0	1	26	21	2.41	1.26	13.3	261	32	81	3.31	2.4	7.2	3.0	0.3	83

Advanced prep hurler features a good 90-93 mph sinking FB that hits 95 mph. Also has an improved SL and CU, both of which have upside. Tall and strong, he has the potential to add a bit more velocity once he fills out.

Woodruff,Brandon — SP — Milwaukee
EXP MLB DEBUT: 2018 | H/W: 6-4 215 | FUT: #4 SP / Setup RP | 8D

Thrws R Age 23 — 2014 (11) Mississippi St

93-96 FB ++++ | CB +++ | CU +++

Year	Lev	Team	W	L	Sv	IP	K	ERA	WHIP	BF/G	OBA	H%	S%	xERA	Ctl	Dom	Cmd	hr/9	BPV
2012	NCAA	Mississippi St	1	2	0	34	37	2.38	1.24	11.5	207	30	79	2.20	4.5	9.8	2.2	0.0	73
2013	NCAA	Mississippi St	1	1	0	18	15	4.45	1.43	11.0	249	32	65	3.24	4.5	7.4	1.7	0.0	31
2014	NCAA	Mississippi St	1	3	0	37	29	6.79	1.94	11.8	310	38	61	5.41	6.1	7.0	1.2	0.0	-19
2014	Rk	Helena	1	2	0	46	37	3.31	1.39	13.9	269	33	76	3.77	3.1	7.2	2.3	0.4	64
2015	A+	Brevard County	4	7	0	109	71	3.46	1.33	21.6	267	32	72	3.40	2.7	5.9	2.2	0.2	50

Lean, quick-armed LH who jumped to the FSL straight from rookie ball. Best pitch is his mid-90s fastball, which has good life and misses bats up in the zone. CU can be effective with good arm speed; CB a touch behind but flashes decent 11-5 bite. Control has improved from college. Good size and intriguing three-pitch mix with upside as SP and RP.

Wotell,Max

SP | New York (N) | EXP MLB DEBUT: 2020 | H/W: 6-3 180 | FUT: #4 starter | 7E

Thrws L Age 19
2015 (3) HS (NC)

Velo	Pitch	Grade
88-91	FB	+ + + +
	CB	+ + +
	CU	+

Year	Lev	Team	W	L	Sv	IP	K	ERA	WHIP	BF/G	OBA	H%	S%	xERA	Ctl	Dom	Cmd	hr/9	BPV
2015	Rk	GCL Mets	0	1	0	10	16	2.65	1.08	4.4	65	14	73	0.33	7.9	14.1	1.8	0.0	58

Signed away from commitment to Arizona, LHP with some projection. Throws from funky, low 3/4 angle that puts a lot of stress on shoulder. FB is best pitch. Sits in low 90s now but should increase velocity as strength is added. CB is close to an average offering. Without a serious change in delivery, pitch doesn't have anywhere else to go.

Wright,Mike

SP | Baltimore | EXP MLB DEBUT: 2015 | H/W: 6-5 215 | FUT: #4 SP / Setup RP | 7C

Thrws R Age 26
2011 (3) East Carolina

Velo	Pitch	Grade
88-94	FB	+ + +
80-83	SP	+ + +
77-80	CB	+ +
81-82	CB	+ + +

Year	Lev	Team	W	L	Sv	IP	K	ERA	WHIP	BF/G	OBA	H%	S%	xERA	Ctl	Dom	Cmd	hr/9	BPV
2013	AA	Bowie	11	3	0	143	136	3.27	1.33	22.9	273	35	76	3.86	2.5	8.5	3.5	0.6	106
2013	AAA	Norfolk	0	0	0	6	2	0.00	0.97	23.5	255	28	100	2.21	0.0	2.9		0.0	70
2014	AAA	Norfolk	5	11	0	142	103	4.62	1.41	23.1	284	33	67	4.27	2.6	6.5	2.5	0.6	65
2015	AAA	Norfolk	9	1	0	81	63	2.22	1.04	20.8	205	25	80	2.13	2.8	7.0	2.5	0.4	69
2015	MLB	Baltimore	3	5	0	44	26	6.11	1.58	16.2	294	30	66	6.01	3.7	5.3	1.4	1.8	14

Tall, strong SP who put things together to reach BAL in '15. Has durable frame to maintain velocity deep into games. Delivery can be stiff, but showed dramatic improvement in control and command. Arm angle tough to pick up which makes sinking FB play up. Can be subject to HR with flyball tendencies. Uses two breaking balls with SL trumping CB.

Yarbrough,Ryan

SP | Seattle | EXP MLB DEBUT: 2017 | H/W: 6-6 205 | FUT: #4 starter | 7C

Thrws L Age 24
2014 (4) Old Dominion

Velo	Pitch	Grade
88-92	FB	+ + +
81-83	CB	+ +
80-82	CU	+ + +

Year	Lev	Team	W	L	Sv	IP	K	ERA	WHIP	BF/G	OBA	H%	S%	xERA	Ctl	Dom	Cmd	hr/9	BPV
2014	Rk	Pulaski	0	0	1	4		0.00	0.50	6.6	81	14	100		2.3	11.3	5.0	0.0	160
2014	A-	Everett	0	1	0	38	53	1.41	0.76	11.4	188	30	82	0.98	0.9	12.5	13.3	0.2	217
2015	Rk	Azl Mariners	0	0	0	10	13	1.80	1.20	10.1	281	42	83	3.06	0.9	11.7	13.0	0.0	204
2015	A	Clinton	0	1	0	5	1	14.12	3.14	15.2	455	47	50	11.37	7.1	1.8	0.3	0.0	-141
2015	A+	Bakersfield	4	7	0	81	74	3.77	1.28	20.8	273	34	72	3.93	2.0	8.2	4.1	0.8	112

Long, lanky SP who missed time with groin strain, but continues to pepper strike zone with quality strikes. Has deceptive, crossfire delivery and is menace to LHH. Uses tough angle to plate which allows sinking FB to play up. Arm speed enhances CU, but CB lags behind as third pitch. K rate should decline as he doesn't own true out pitch.

Ynoa,Gabriel

SP | New York (N) | EXP MLB DEBUT: 2016 | H/W: 6-2 160 | FUT: #4 starter | 7C

Thrws R Age 22
2009 FA (DR)

Velo	Pitch	Grade
91-94	FB	+ + +
82-84	SL	+ +
82-84	CU	+ + +
77-79	CB	+ +

Year	Lev	Team	W	L	Sv	IP	K	ERA	WHIP	BF/G	OBA	H%	S%	xERA	Ctl	Dom	Cmd	hr/9	BPV
2012	A-	Brooklyn	5	2	0	76	64	2.24	0.93	22.0	221	28	74	1.74	1.2	7.6	6.4	0.1	122
2013	A	Savannah	15	4	0	135	106	2.73	1.03	23.6	244	29	75	2.73	1.1	7.1	6.6	0.6	116
2014	A+	St. Lucie	8	2	0	82	64	3.95	1.32	24.2	291	34	71	4.28	1.4	7.0	4.9	0.8	106
2014	AA	Binghamton	3	2	0	66	42	4.22	1.30	24.8	284	31	71	4.58	1.6	5.7	3.5	1.2	77
2015	AA	Binghamton	9	9	0	152	82	3.91	1.24	24.7	268	29	70	3.82	1.8	4.9	2.6	0.8	56

4 pitch command/control RHP most effective when FB/CU are complementing each other. FB velocity improved as the season wore on. Learning to throw quality strikes. CU flashes plus with good deception and solid arm-side bore. Should concentrate on one breaking ball. Both below average offerings at this time. SL has more potential.

Ynoa,Michael

RP | Chicago (A) | EXP MLB DEBUT: 2016 | H/W: 6-7 210 | FUT: Setup reliever | 7D

Thrws R Age 24
2008 FA (DR)

Velo	Pitch	Grade
92-97	FB	+ + + +
82-84	SL	+ + +
82-85	CU	+ +

Year	Lev	Team	W	L	Sv	IP	K	ERA	WHIP	BF/G	OBA	H%	S%	xERA	Ctl	Dom	Cmd	hr/9	BPV
2012	A-	Vermont	1	3	0	20	19	7.13	1.78	11.6	260	32	59	5.10	7.1	8.5	1.2	0.9	-22
2013	A	Beloit	2	1	0	54	48	2.16	1.16	14.4	227	29	83	2.75	3.0	8.0	2.7	0.5	81
2013	A+	Stockton	1	2	1	21	20	7.71	1.90	14.2	280	35	58	5.66	7.3	8.6	1.2	0.9	-24
2014	A+	Stockton	4	2	0	45	64	5.58	1.39	6.1	248	37	60	4.02	4.2	12.7	3.0	1.0	134
2015	A+	Winston-Salem	0	2	6	38	40	2.61	1.39	5.7	257	34	82	3.68	3.8	9.5	2.5	0.5	86

Tall pitcher who was converted to RP in '14. Has been prospect for years, but can't get past High-A. Throws with great angle to plate which enhances FB and SL. Generates easy velocity to plus FB in short stints and counters with power SL. Can change speeds with CU, but doesn't mix well. FB can be straight at times.

Young,Alex

SP | Arizona | EXP MLB DEBUT: 2018 | H/W: 6-2 205 | FUT: #3 starter | 8D

Thrws L Age 22
2015 (2) Texas Christian

Velo	Pitch	Grade
89-91	FB	+ + +
82-84	SL	+ + + +
80-83	CU	+ + +

Year	Lev	Team	W	L	Sv	IP	K	ERA	WHIP	BF/G	OBA	H%	S%	xERA	Ctl	Dom	Cmd	hr/9	BPV
2015	NCAA	Texas Christian	9	3	0	97	103	2.22	1.00	21.8	215	28	84	2.57	2.0	9.5	4.7	0.9	135
2015	Rk	Azl DBacks	0	0	0	1	1	0.00	0.00	2.8	0	0			0.0	9.0		0.0	180
2015	A-	Hillsboro	0	0	1	6	5	1.50	1.00	3.8	228	30	83	1.89	1.5	7.5	5.0	0.0	113

Former college RP who converted to rotation as senior. FB is fringe-average offering. Has solid movement but will rely on location to keep hitters off pitch. SL is best pitch, effective due to excellent depth and break. Can be slurvy at times. Feel for CU is advanced for level. Can use CU to keep RH hitters off balance.

Ysla,Luis

SP | Boston | EXP MLB DEBUT: 2017 | H/W: 6-1 185 | FUT: #3 SP / Setup RP | 8E

Thrws L Age 23
2012 FA (VZ)

Velo	Pitch	Grade
89-94	FB	+ + +
78-82	SL	+ +
82-84	CU	+ + +

Year	Lev	Team	W	L	Sv	IP	K	ERA	WHIP	BF/G	OBA	H%	S%	xERA	Ctl	Dom	Cmd	hr/9	BPV
2013	Rk	Azl Giants	4	0	0	51	52	2.65	1.00	16.2	209	29	72	1.80	2.3	9.2	4.0	0.2	121
2014	A	Augusta	6	7	0	121	115	2.45	1.23	20.4	233	30	82	3.08	3.3	8.5	2.6	0.6	82
2015	A+	Salem	0	0	0	5	6	0.00	0.40	8.1	0	0	100		3.6	10.8	3.0	0.0	115
2015	A+	San Jose	3	6	0	79	95	6.25	1.89	11.3	328	44	67	6.51	4.7	10.8	2.3	1.0	87

Versatile, power-armed pitcher who has stuff to be dynamic, but lacks consistency with max effort delivery. Has been used as both SP and RP, though may be headed to bullpen to let pitches fly. Slings ball to plate from low slot, but can't seem to master SL. Dominates LHH and has CU that flashes plus.

Zastryzny,Rob

SP | Chicago (N) | EXP MLB DEBUT: 2016 | H/W: 6-3 205 | FUT: #4 starter | 7C

Thrws L Age 24
2013 (2) Missouri

Velo	Pitch	Grade
90-93	FB	+ + +
80-83	SL	+ + +
	CB	+ +

Year	Lev	Team	W	L	Sv	IP	K	ERA	WHIP	BF/G	OBA	H%	S%	xERA	Ctl	Dom	Cmd	hr/9	BPV
2013	A-	Boise	0	0	0	14	16	3.19	1.35	7.3	274	39	74	3.35	2.6	10.2	4.0	0.0	133
2013	A	Kane County	1	0	0	9	6	0.98	1.41	13.0	258	31	92	3.33	3.9	5.9	1.5	0.0	18
2014	A+	Daytona	4	6	0	110	110	4.66	1.40	20.2	281	36	67	4.36	2.7	9.0	3.3	0.8	107
2015	Rk	Azl Cubs	0	0	0	4	4	2.25	1.25	16.3	210	29	80	2.28	4.5	9.0	2.0	0.0	59
2015	AA	Tennessee	2	5	0	60	48	6.28	1.74	19.6	312	36	66	6.21	4.2	7.2	1.7	1.3	34

Projectable lefty was hit hard in his first exposure to AA. FB sits at 90-92 maxing out at 94 mph, but he found too much of the plate and SL batters hit him at a .310 clip. Also has an above-average CU and a usable breaking ball. Will need to prove that '15 was a fluke.

Zimmer,Kyle

SP | Kansas City | EXP MLB DEBUT: 2016 | H/W: 6-3 215 | FUT: #1 starter | 9D

Thrws R Age 24
2012 (1) San Francisco

Velo	Pitch	Grade
93-96	FB	+ + + +
80-81	CB	+ + + +
82-84	SL	+ +
83-85	CU	+ + +

Year	Lev	Team	W	L	Sv	IP	K	ERA	WHIP	BF/G	OBA	H%	S%	xERA	Ctl	Dom	Cmd	hr/9	BPV
2013	A+	Wilmington	4	8	0	89	113	4.84	1.24	20.1	241	34	62	3.49	3.1	11.4	3.6	0.9	139
2013	AA	NW Arkansas	2	1	0	18	27	1.98	0.88	16.8	176	27	86	1.85	2.5	13.4	5.4	1.0	192
2014	Rk	Idaho Falls	0	0	0	4	5	2.14	2.14	3.5	297	42	89	5.68	8.6	10.7	1.3	0.0	-21
2015	A	Lexington	1	0	0	16	21	1.13	1.06	6.9	196	29	94	2.14	3.4	11.8	3.5	0.6	140
2015	AA	NW Arkansas	2	5	3	48	51	2.81	1.17	12.8	237	31	79	3.10	2.6	9.6	3.6	0.8	119

Dominant pitcher who began in late June afer limited action in '14. Stuff not all the way back after shoulder issues, but has frontline arsenal led by double-plus FB and sharp CB. Mixes in hard SL and average CU to post impressive K rate. Uses height to pitch downhill and throws constructive strikes. Only needs health and sky is limit.

Ziomek,Kevin

SP | Detroit | EXP MLB DEBUT: 2016 | H/W: 6-3 200 | FUT: #4 starter | 7B

Thrws L Age 24
2013 (2) Vanderbilt

Velo	Pitch	Grade
87-94	FB	+ + +
80-82	SL	+ + +
75-78	CB	+ +
	CU	+ + +

Year	Lev	Team	W	L	Sv	IP	K	ERA	WHIP	BF/G	OBA	H%	S%	xERA	Ctl	Dom	Cmd	hr/9	BPV
2012	NCAA	Vanderbilt	5	6	0	79	79	5.23	1.49	18.0	262	33	65	4.30	4.4	9.0	2.0	0.8	60
2013	NCAA	Vanderbilt	11	3	0	119	115	2.12	1.00	26.7	191	26	78	1.64	3.0	8.7	2.9	0.2	93
2013	A-	Connecticut	0	1	0	8	3	4.50	1.25	8.1	181	20	60	2.01	5.6	3.4	0.6	0.0	-73
2014	A	West Michigan	10	6	0	123	152	2.27	1.15	21.3	204	30	81	2.29	3.9	11.1	2.9	0.4	113
2015	A+	Lakeland	9	11	0	154	143	3.44	1.14	22.6	246	32	68	2.63	2.0	8.3	4.2	0.2	115

Angular and mature SP who led FSL in Ks while keeping ball on ground consistently. Showed much improved control with more consistent delivery. Hits spots with four pitches and has ability to change speeds. K rate fell in '15 and may eventually scrap CB. Profiles as back-end SP who can eat innings and retire LHH.

Zych,Tony

RP | Seattle | EXP MLB DEBUT: 2015 | H/W: 6-3 190 | FUT: Setup reliever | 6B

Thrws R Age 25
2011 (4) Louisville

Velo	Pitch	Grade
93-97	FB	+ + + +
83-86	SL	+ + +

Year	Lev	Team	W	L	Sv	IP	K	ERA	WHIP	BF/G	OBA	H%	S%	xERA	Ctl	Dom	Cmd	hr/9	BPV
2013	AA	Tennessee	5	5	3	56	40	3.05	1.29	4.9	244	29	76	3.13	3.4	6.4	1.9	0.3	43
2014	AA	Tennessee	4	5	2	58	35	5.11	1.60	5.7	314	36	67	5.07	2.8	5.4	1.9	0.5	40
2015	AA	Jackson	0	0	5	16	18	2.22	0.68	3.8	194	28	64	0.64	0.0	10.0		0.0	198
2015	AAA	Tacoma	1	2	4	31	37	3.46	1.38	5.2	279	39	76	4.03	2.6	10.7	4.1	0.6	140
2015	MLB	Seattle	0	0	0	18	24	2.49	1.10	5.5	250	37	79	2.86	1.5	11.9	8.0	0.5	193

Strong-armed RP who has spent entire career in pen. Has arm strength to generate plus velocity on FB that features great, late life. Arm action isn't clean and has effort, but provides deception to make FB and SL better. Hard SL can be flat, but FB rarely straight. Misses bats and gets groundball outs. Spent 3 years in AA before breakout in '15.

MAJOR LEAGUE EQUIVALENTS

In his 1985 *Baseball Abstract,* Bill James introduced the concept of major league equivalencies. His assertion was that, with the proper adjustments, a minor leaguer's statistics could be converted to an equivalent major league level performance with a great deal of accuracy.

Because of wide variations in the level of play among different minor leagues, it is difficult to get a true reading on a player's potential. For instance, a .300 batting average achieved in the high-offense Pacific Coast League is not nearly as much of an accomplishment as a similar level in the Eastern League. MLEs normalize these types of variances, for all statistical categories.

The actual MLEs are not projections. They represent how a player's previous performance might look at the major league level. However, the MLE stat line can be used in forecasting future performance in just the same way as a major league stat line would.

The model we use contains a few variations to James' version and updates all of the minor league and ballpark factors. In addition, we designed a module to convert pitching statistics, which is something James did not originally do.

Do MLEs really work?

Used correctly, MLEs are excellent indicators of potential. But just like we cannot take traditional major league statistics at face value, the same goes for MLEs. The underlying measures of base skill—batting eye ratios, pitching command ratios, etc.—are far more accurate in evaluating future talent than raw home runs, batting averages or ERAs.

The charts we present here also provide the unique perspective of looking at up to five years' worth of data. Ironically, the longer the history, the less likely the player is a legitimate prospect—he should have made it to the majors before compiling a long history in AA and/or AAA ball. Of course, the shorter trends are more difficult to read despite them often belonging to players with higher ceilings. But even here we can find small indications of players improving their skills, or struggling, as they rise through more difficult levels of competition. Since players—especially those with any talent—are promoted rapidly through major league systems, a two or three-year scan is often all we get to spot any trends.

Here are some things to look for as you scan these charts:

Target players who...

- spent a full year in AA and then a full year in AAA
- had consistent playing time from one year to the next
- improved their base skills as they were promoted

Raise the warning flag for players who...

- were stuck at a level for multiple seasons, or regressed
- displayed marked changes in playing time from one year to the next
- showed large drops in BPIs from one year to the next

Players are listed on the charts if they spent at least part of 2011-2015 in Triple-A or Double-A and had at least 100 AB or 30 IP within those two levels. Each is listed with the organization with which they finished the season.

Only statistics accumulated in Triple-A and Double-A ball are included (players who split a season are indicated as a/a); Single-A stats are excluded.

Each player's actual AB and IP totals are used as the base for the conversion. However, it is more useful to compare performances using common levels, so rely on the ratios and sabermetric gauges. Complete explanations of these formulas appear in the Glossary.

BATTER	B	Yr	Age	Pos	Lvl	Tm	AB	R	H	D	T	HR	RBI	BB	K	SB	CS	BA	OB	Slg	OPS	bb%	ct%	Eye	PX	SX	RC/G	BPV
Adames,Cristhian	B	13	22	SS	aa	COL	389	36	100	19	2	3	29	27	77	10	7	257	305	337	642	7%	80%	0.35	62	86	2.81	11
		14	23	SS	a/a	COL	475	42	123	19	4	2	36	29	86	8	11	258	301	329	630	6%	82%	0.34	54	77	2.63	8
		15	24	SS	aaa	COL	463	41	126	17	3	8	34	24	61	7	8	271	306	374	681	5%	87%	0.38	62	70	3.31	29
Adams,Lane	R	13	24	RF	aa	KC	156	23	33	6	1	4	20	14	49	12	0	213	277	333	611	8%	69%	0.28	94	150	2.89	14
		14	25	CF	aa	KC	405	50	94	22	3	8	27	34	95	29	10	232	292	358	650	8%	76%	0.36	97	131	2.84	40
		15	26	CF	a/a	KC	488	55	116	22	3	12	47	37	135	23	8	237	290	365	656	7%	72%	0.27	93	115	3.01	14
Aguilar,Jesus	R	13	23	1B	aa	CLE	499	49	116	25	0	11	78	41	123	0	1	233	291	352	643	8%	75%	0.33	90	24	2.89	-2
		14	24	1B	aaa	CLE	427	53	111	28	0	14	59	48	113	0	0	260	335	423	758	10%	74%	0.43	131	24	4.14	29
		15	25	1B	aaa	CLE	510	49	120	27	1	16	79	39	136	0	0	235	289	385	674	7%	73%	0.29	107	25	3.19	3
Alberto,Hanser	R	13	21	SS	aa	TEX	356	32	73	6	4	4	34	14	42	11	5	205	236	274	510	4%	88%	0.33	39	115	1.77	28
		14	22	SS	aa	TEX	178	19	45	6	1	2	12	5	18	6	4	255	275	326	601	3%	90%	0.27	47	92	2.52	32
		15	23	SS	aaa	TEX	310	34	86	17	3	3	26	7	36	4	6	279	295	386	681	2%	88%	0.20	68	91	3.04	41
Alfaro,Jorge	R	15	22	C	aa	TEX	190	17	43	13	2	4	16	7	66	2	1	225	253	374	628	4%	65%	0.11	126	89	2.36	-2
Almora,Albert	R	14	20	CF	aa	CHC	142	15	30	6	2	2	8	2	23	0	1	212	221	313	534	1%	84%	0.07	72	94	1.68	24
		15	21	CF	aa	CHC	405	56	101	25	3	5	37	22	52	7	4	249	295	361	657	6%	87%	0.51	74	108	2.81	55
Alvarez,Dariel	R	13	25	RF	aa	BAL	31	1	5.1	0	0	1	1	1	10	0	0	163	182	240	422	2%	67%	0.07	51	6	1.33	-83
		14	26	CF	a/a	BAL	532	52	134	30	2	12	60	15	74	6	6	251	271	380	651	3%	86%	0.20	89	70	2.81	44
		15	27	RF	aaa	BAL	512	54	125	21	1	16	64	14	73	6	4	245	266	384	649	3%	86%	0.20	82	76	2.98	39
Anderson,Tim	R	15	22	SS	aa	CHW	513	70	150	20	10	5	41	23	126	43	14	292	322	396	718	4%	75%	0.18	70	169	3.76	19
Aplin,Andrew	L	14	23	CF	aa	HOU	452	46	102	12	2	5	48	59	82	19	12	226	316	290	606	12%	82%	0.72	46	87	2.61	15
		15	24	CF	a/a	HOU	338	46	84	8	5	2	29	50	64	23	12	248	345	314	660	13%	81%	0.78	41	135	3.06	25
Arcia,Orlando	R	15	21	SS	aa	MIL	512	67	152	35	6	9	63	28	79	23	8	297	334	440	774	5%	85%	0.36	94	132	4.18	66
Asuaje,Carlos	L	15	24	2B	aa	BOS	495	47	112	24	5	6	48	44	97	7	7	226	290	331	620	8%	80%	0.46	71	92	2.42	24
Bandy,Jett	R	13	23	C	aa	LAA	245	22	52	15	1	3	24	12	44	0	1	213	248	325	573	4%	82%	0.26	83	56	1.98	23
		14	24	C	aa	LAA	312	32	68	10	0	11	34	27	72	2	5	219	282	354	636	8%	77%	0.38	95	36	2.79	13
		15	25	C	aaa	LAA	309	31	70	17	0	7	39	10	77	0	0	227	252	346	597	3%	75%	0.13	88	33	2.42	-11
Barnes,Austin	R	13	24	C	aa	MIA	62	8	19	2	2	1	6	10	11	0	0	307	404	431	835	14%	82%	0.90	73	75	5.05	39
		14	25	2B	aa	MIA	284	41	70	17	2	7	32	37	42	6	0	245	333	397	730	12%	85%	0.90	104	99	3.77	79
		15	26	C	aaa	LA	292	29	75	14	1	7	31	24	44	9	2	257	314	385	699	8%	85%	0.55	80	87	3.60	47
Barnes,Barrett	R	15	24	LF	aa	PIT	126	13	26	5	0	2	13	12	27	3	5	210	279	301	579	9%	78%	0.44	65	66	2.07	5
Bauers,Jake	L	15	20	1B	aa	TAM	257	30	64	16	0	4	30	18	45	5	3	249	297	357	654	6%	83%	0.39	78	70	2.90	29
Bell,Josh	B	10	24	5	aa	BAL	316	34	79	22	0	12	40	18	63	2	5	251	291	431	722	5%	80%	0.28	118	40	4.13	39
		11	25	3B	aaa	BAL	395	47	87	10	1	16	43	29	133	3	0	220	274	374	648	7%	66%	0.22	89	76	3.56	-25
		12	26	3B	aaa	ARI	360	36	81	22	2	8	45	22	94	2	6	226	271	360	631	6%	74%	0.24	100	58	2.41	7
		15	23	1B	a/a	PIT	489	57	140	22	7	5	66	52	70	8	4	285	354	389	744	10%	86%	0.75	65	101	3.97	47
Bernard,Wynton	R	15	25	CF	aa	DET	534	60	139	24	8	3	28	30	80	33	18	261	300	356	656	5%	85%	0.37	61	141	2.76	44
Blandino,Alex	R	15	23	SS	aa	CIN	115	13	25	6	0	3	15	16	24	2	2	214	307	349	656	12%	79%	0.64	92	50	2.78	30
Bohn,Justin	R	15	23	2B	aa	MIA	87	4	12	0	1	1	5	5	32	0	0	143	188	190	378	5%	63%	0.15	29	57	0.94	-95
Bonifacio,Jorge	R	13	20	RF	aa	KC	93	13	26	7	0	2	16	9	23	2	1	283	348	405	753	9%	75%	0.39	102	59	4.05	19
		14	21	RF	aa	KC	505	40	108	19	4	3	42	41	130	7	3	213	272	285	557	7%	74%	0.31	59	87	2.04	-13
		15	22	RF	aa	KC	483	49	105	28	2	13	52	34	131	2	2	218	269	365	634	7%	73%	0.26	108	62	2.59	11
Boyd,Jayce	R	14	24	1B	aa	NYM	413	43	97	17	1	6	40	37	82	1	1	235	297	325	623	8%	80%	0.45	68	51	2.74	9
		15	25	LF	a/a	NYM	299	22	68	22	0	1	21	18	47	1	4	226	271	307	579	6%	84%	0.39	67	37	2.00	15
Brett,Ryan	R	13	22	2B	aa	TAM	105	16	22	5	1	2	13	7	16	3	0	211	257	347	603	6%	85%	0.42	87	132	2.45	64
		14	23	2B	aa	TAM	422	51	112	22	5	6	30	19	85	22	8	265	297	385	682	4%	80%	0.22	88	140	3.17	43
		15	24	2B	aaa	TAM	328	39	70	15	1	4	25	12	74	3	3	212	241	300	541	4%	77%	0.17	65	86	1.87	-3
Brinson,Lewis	R	15	21	CF	a/a	TEX	140	19	41	8	1	6	22	11	37	4	1	295	345	489	834	7%	74%	0.29	133	95	5.25	46
Brito,Socrates	L	15	23	RF	aa	ARI	490	58	138	15	15	8	47	24	92	17	7	283	315	425	741	5%	81%	0.26	81	138	3.70	42
Brugman,Jaycob	L	15	23	LF	aa	OAK	500	45	111	24	7	4	46	47	98	8	8	222	289	320	609	9%	80%	0.48	67	98	2.25	24
Burns,Andy	R	13	23	3B	aa	TOR	265	30	59	18	2	6	24	17	62	9	6	223	270	365	635	6%	76%	0.27	108	106	2.44	38
		14	24	3B	aa	TOR	495	56	113	30	4	13	50	32	113	14	9	228	275	383	658	6%	77%	0.28	117	111	2.67	50
Buxton,Byron	R	15	22	CF	a/a	MIN	292	45	84	9	13	5	37	24	66	18	3	289	343	465	809	8%	77%	0.37	101	161	4.46	56
Calixte,Orlando	R	13	21	SS	aa	KC	484	48	112	23	4	6	29	34	135	11	12	231	282	334	615	7%	72%	0.25	82	96	2.34	-2
		14	22	SS	aa	KC	374	35	81	14	1	8	30	22	96	7	5	216	260	325	584	6%	74%	0.23	83	74	2.30	-1
		15	23	SS	aaa	KC	354	31	73	10	2	6	22	22	89	18	3	206	252	298	550	6%	75%	0.25	62	118	2.21	-2
Candelario,Jeimer	B	15	22	3B	aa	CHC	158	17	42	9	1	4	20	18	23	0	0	264	340	410	750	10%	85%	0.77	92	40	4.01	49
Cave,Jake	L	15	23	CF	a/a	NYY	529	64	135	23	4	2	35	42	119	15	3	256	310	325	635	7%	78%	0.35	53	117	2.92	4
Cecchini,Garin	L	13	22	3B	aa	BOS	240	28	66	14	2	2	22	39	56	6	2	276	378	376	754	14%	77%	0.70	80	98	3.99	31
		14	23	3B	aa	NYM	407	31	80	15	1	4	34	26	120	7	1	196	245	268	513	6%	71%	0.22	64	72	1.82	-31
		15	24	LF	aaa	BOS	422	29	85	15	0	6	24	35	109	8	0	201	262	277	539	8%	74%	0.32	58	69	2.10	-19
Cecchini,Gavin	R	15	22	SS	aa	NYM	439	55	125	23	3	6	44	36	62	3	4	286	340	395	735	8%	86%	0.58	72	65	3.87	38
Coats,Jason	R	15	25	LF	a/a	CHW	536	50	129	33	1	15	67	26	116	9	5	241	276	390	667	5%	78%	0.22	103	70	2.99	28
Cole,Hunter	R	15	23	RF	aa	SF	192	22	53	15	4	2	20	13	51	1	1	276	323	437	760	7%	74%	0.27	120	97	3.50	35
Contreras,Willson	R	15	23	C	aa	CHC	454	56	135	32	3	6	59	46	71	3	4	298	363	423	786	9%	84%	0.65	86	69	4.35	48
Cooper,Garrett	R	15	25	1B	aa	MIL	29	3	15	2	1	0	4	6	2	0	0	504	592	624	001	18%	92%	2.65	71	58	15.32	79
Cordell,Ryan	R	15	23	CF	aa	TEX	221	20	42	4	2	4	14	9	80	8	1	191	223	285	508	4%	64%	0.12	69	134	1.79	-39
Cowart,Kaleb	B	13	21	3B	aa	LAA	498	42	100	18	1	5	37	32	134	12	5	201	249	270	520	6%	73%	0.24	57	80	1.84	-24
		14	22	3B	aa	LAA	435	43	89	16	3	5	48	37	108	23	8	204	266	290	556	8%	75%	0.34	68	121	2.10	9
		15	23	3B	aaa	LAA	220	24	59	11	2	4	31	19	75	1	1	266	324	385	709	8%	66%	0.25	97	80	3.54	-18
Coyle,Sean	R	14	22	2B	aa	BOS	336	50	94	24	1	13	50	31	101	11	1	279	340	470	809	8%	70%	0.30	158	99	4.86	54
		15	23	2B	aaa	BOS	126	19	19	3	0	4	14	18	47	4	1	150	256	276	532	12%	63%	0.38	97	90	1.95	-18
Cozens,Dylan	L	15	21	RF	aa	PHI	40	5	13	2	0	3	7	2	8	2	1	318	358	564	922	6%	80%	0.31	146	54	6.45	67
Crawford,J.P.	L	15	20	SS	aa	PHI	351	43	84	19	5	4	27	40	50	6	2	241	319	364	683	10%	86%	0.81	78	110	3.00	61

BATTER	B	Yr	Age	Pos	Lvl	Tm	AB	R	H	D	T	HR	RBI	BB	K	SB	CS	BA	OB	Slg	OPS	bb%	ct%	Eye	PX	SX	RC/G	BPV
Cuthbert,Cheslor	R	13	21	3B	aa	KC	237	20	46	15	0	4	23	16	52	4	2	196	247	315	563	6%	78%	0.31	93	63	1.96	20
		14	22	3B	a/a	KC	446	36	109	22	1	8	49	34	83	8	4	244	298	354	652	7%	81%	0.42	82	63	2.98	26
		15	23	3B	aaa	KC	397	45	99	20	1	9	42	30	64	4	2	250	303	371	674	7%	84%	0.47	79	69	3.22	36
Dahl,David	L	15	21	CF	aa	COL	288	38	79	16	3	6	20	9	73	18	7	274	296	410	706	3%	75%	0.12	96	152	3.38	29
Davidson,Matt	R	12	21	3B	aa	ARI	486	65	119	28	2	19	62	54	133	2	4	245	320	428	748	10%	73%	0.40	129	59	3.81	33
		13	22	3B	aaa	ARI	443	35	104	28	2	11	47	29	148	1	0	235	282	385	667	6%	67%	0.19	128	51	2.93	-2
		14	23	3B	aaa	CHW	478	39	78	15	0	15	37	36	189	0	0	164	222	290	512	7%	61%	0.19	112	21	1.76	-46
Diaz,Elias	R	14	24	C	a/a	PIT	359	33	94	18	0	4	39	23	63	2	3	261	307	345	651	6%	83%	0.37	66	38	3.02	8
		15	25	C	aaa	PIT	325	28	77	14	3	3	40	23	52	1	5	237	288	326	614	7%	84%	0.45	59	61	2.39	17
Diaz,Yandy	R	15	24	3B	a/a	CLE	495	55	138	14	3	6	50	67	80	8	8	279	365	359	724	12%	84%	0.83	49	75	3.95	23
Dickerson,Alex	L	13	23	RF	aa	PIT	451	48	113	32	2	12	54	21	95	8	8	251	284	413	697	4%	79%	0.22	118	84	3.03	46
		14	24	RF	aa	SD	137	16	37	9	2	2	19	7	34	0	1	273	309	416	726	5%	75%	0.21	113	79	3.41	27
		15	25	LF	aaa	SD	459	54	109	27	6	8	46	30	119	3	0	237	284	372	656	6%	74%	0.25	98	105	2.76	20
Difo,Wilmer	R	15	23	SS	aa	WAS	359	40	92	20	4	2	32	10	84	22	1	256	276	346	621	3%	77%	0.12	69	157	2.80	16
Dixon,Brandon	R	15	23	2B	aa	LA	336	29	75	15	1	8	34	10	110	14	7	223	245	341	587	3%	67%	0.09	93	109	2.27	-16
Dosch,Drew	L	15	23	3B	aa	BAL	231	14	50	6	2	1	18	13	49	2	1	217	258	275	533	5%	79%	0.26	40	71	1.92	-19
Dozier,Hunter	R	14	23	3B	aa	KC	234	26	43	11	0	3	17	25	74	2	2	186	263	270	533	9%	68%	0.33	79	60	1.80	-24
		15	24	3B	aa	KC	475	50	87	24	1	9	41	34	163	5	2	182	238	293	531	7%	66%	0.21	94	81	1.77	-22
Drury,Brandon	R	14	22	3B	aa	ARI	105	10	29	7	0	3	11	6	20	0	0	274	310	434	744	5%	81%	0.27	118	16	4.02	33
		15	23	2B	a/a	ARI	524	48	139	36	1	4	45	23	86	3	9	265	296	360	656	4%	84%	0.27	73	42	2.75	16
Evans,Zane	R	15	24	C	aa	KC	238	16	52	13	0	4	32	6	69	1	0	219	239	329	568	3%	71%	0.09	87	34	2.17	-30
Farmer,Kyle	R	15	25	C	aa	LA	283	21	67	23	1	2	33	11	64	0	1	238	267	343	610	4%	77%	0.18	89	38	2.25	1
Field,Johnny	R	15	23	RF	aa	TAM	432	54	94	28	3	10	52	29	125	14	3	218	267	370	637	6%	71%	0.23	116	133	2.58	32
Fields,Roemon	L	15	25	CF	a/a	TOR	225	24	51	3	1	1	10	18	45	21	6	227	283	260	543	7%	80%	0.39	22	128	2.41	-7
Flores,Ramon	L	13	21	LF	aa	NYY	534	67	129	23	4	6	47	67	105	6	6	241	326	332	658	11%	80%	0.64	65	80	2.92	22
		14	22	RF	aaa	NYY	235	23	51	15	2	6	18	26	49	2	2	217	294	377	671	10%	79%	0.52	117	80	2.75	55
		15	23	LF	aaa	SEA	328	38	83	14	1	6	29	34	58	2	2	254	324	361	684	9%	82%	0.58	70	60	3.37	24
Fontana,Nolan	L	14	23	2B	aa	HOU	229	25	52	18	1	1	20	47	88	4	9	225	356	321	678	17%	62%	0.53	113	57	2.48	-10
		15	24	SS	aaa	HOU	361	38	71	17	4	2	27	51	117	4	13	196	296	286	582	12%	68%	0.44	75	87	1.78	-17
Fuenmayor,Balbino	R	15	26	1B	a/a	KC	360	47	110	24	2	12	50	9	68	1	0	305	322	486	808	2%	81%	0.13	118	66	4.84	46
Fuentes,Reymond	L	12	21	OF	aa	SD	473	42	87	17	3	3	27	44	152	28	10	184	253	252	505	8%	68%	0.29	56	123	1.68	-28
		13	22	RF	a/a	SD	400	57	113	20	2	5	33	40	96	27	12	282	347	377	724	9%	76%	0.41	75	113	3.86	18
		14	23	CF	a/a	SD	327	38	78	11	4	4	23	23	77	18	3	239	289	330	619	7%	76%	0.30	68	137	2.78	16
		15	24	CF	aaa	KC	396	56	109	9	4	7	37	24	78	23	7	275	316	368	684	6%	80%	0.30	56	139	3.70	21
Gallo,Joey	L	14	21	3B	aa	TEX	250	36	55	9	0	18	45	30	120	2	0	218	301	478	779	11%	52%	0.25	252	46	4.36	47
		15	22	3B	a/a	TEX	321	33	69	17	1	19	50	41	150	2	0	215	304	446	749	11%	53%	0.27	210	47	3.86	20
Garcia,Greg	L	12	23	SS	aa	STL	412	62	99	17	2	7	39	64	93	8	6	241	343	342	685	13%	77%	0.68	70	84	3.29	20
		13	24	SS	aaa	STL	354	37	81	20	3	2	26	37	80	10	2	228	301	315	616	9%	78%	0.47	71	107	2.52	20
		14	25	2B	a/a	STL	397	45	88	12	2	5	30	31	115	6	6	221	277	300	577	7%	71%	0.26	63	83	2.28	-25
		15	26	SS	aaa	STL	330	33	79	16	1	0	26	33	65	11	4	240	310	297	607	9%	80%	0.52	48	96	2.57	9
Garcia,Willy	R	14	22	RF	aa	PIT	439	44	102	24	3	12	47	17	153	6	4	232	262	385	647	4%	65%	0.11	133	93	2.66	5
		15	23	RF	a/a	PIT	480	52	117	17	4	11	56	18	131	3	7	245	273	365	638	4%	73%	0.14	83	86	2.72	-8
Goeddel,Tyler	R	15	23	LF	aa	TAM	473	54	115	15	9	9	57	38	112	22	10	243	300	366	665	7%	76%	0.34	77	142	2.98	26
Gonzalez,Erik	R	14	23	SS	aa	CLE	129	17	41	6	2	1	13	6	27	5	1	315	343	406	749	4%	79%	0.21	68	127	4.35	20
		15	24	SS	a/a	CLE	549	62	127	23	5	8	61	22	118	16	8	231	261	332	593	4%	79%	0.19	69	123	2.33	16
Goodwin,Brian	L	12	22	OF	aa	WAS	166	14	34	7	1	4	12	14	52	2	3	203	265	332	597	8%	68%	0.27	98	65	2.21	-11
		13	23	CF	aa	WAS	457	66	104	17	8	8	32	51	129	15	12	227	305	354	659	10%	72%	0.40	91	136	2.67	22
		14	24	CF	aaa	WAS	275	23	51	9	3	3	24	35	104	4	5	186	279	269	547	11%	62%	0.34	76	90	1.83	-39
		15	25	CF	aa	WAS	429	46	85	15	3	6	36	30	103	12	8	197	250	286	535	6%	76%	0.29	62	111	1.83	2
Gregor,Conrad	L	14	22	1B	aa	HOU	109	11	23	3	1	2	10	10	24	0	1	210	277	323	600	8%	78%	0.43	78	59	2.36	12
		15	23	1B	aa	HOU	435	44	90	25	2	8	56	50	117	4	1	206	288	326	614	10%	73%	0.43	92	71	2.43	10
Guerrero,Gabriel	R	15	22	RF	aa	ARI	460	43	95	24	4	6	39	19	115	9	2	207	239	320	559	4%	75%	0.16	83	117	1.95	11
Hager,Jake	R	14	21	SS	aa	TAM	447	34	108	24	4	3	39	24	101	3	4	242	281	333	614	5%	77%	0.24	76	71	2.41	4
Haniger,Mitch	R	14	24	RF	aa	ARI	267	36	62	9	1	8	30	17	50	3	0	233	278	365	642	6%	81%	0.33	88	88	3.03	35
		15	25	CF	aa	ARI	153	18	38	9	1	1	15	13	37	3	5	249	306	339	645	8%	76%	0.34	72	93	2.52	7
Hanson,Alen	B	13	21	SS	aa	PIT	137	11	32	4	4	1	8	6	27	5	2	231	264	327	592	4%	81%	0.24	59	123	2.15	17
		14	22	SS	aa	PIT	482	48	117	19	8	7	43	22	93	19	12	242	276	360	636	4%	81%	0.24	80	128	2.53	36
		15	23	2B	aaa	PIT	475	58	114	16	9	4	38	31	96	31	13	240	286	341	627	6%	80%	0.32	63	160	2.56	32
Harrison,Travis	R	15	23	RF	aa	MIN	396	48	83	21	4	4	40	48	110	2	10	210	295	307	602	11%	72%	0.44	77	75	2.05	-3
Hawkins,Courtney	R	15	22	LF	aa	CHW	300	34	68	18	2	9	36	19	110	1	4	227	273	383	656	6%	63%	0.17	130	68	2.65	-8
Healy,Ryon	R	15	23	3B	aa	OAK	507	47	130	27	1	7	46	23	91	0	1	257	289	355	644	4%	82%	0.25	70	31	2.92	4
Hernandez,Marco	L	15	23	SS	a/a	BOS	463	48	134	32	5	7	45	14	95	4	2	290	311	426	738	3%	80%	0.15	97	93	3.73	32
Hernandez,Teoscar	R	15	23	CF	aa	HOU	470	70	89	10	2	14	37	25	144	25	8	189	230	305	535	5%	69%	0.18	79	151	2.02	-2
Hicks,John	R	13	24	C	aa	SEA	296	35	64	14	1	3	26	19	71	11	4	215	262	300	562	6%	76%	0.26	67	108	2.13	4
		14	25	C	a/a	SEA	290	29	68	10	2	3	33	18	80	5	4	235	280	316	597	6%	72%	0.23	67	87	2.45	-17
		15	26	C	aaa	SEA	298	25	56	12	1	4	23	11	88	6	2	187	215	268	483	3%	70%	0.12	65	90	1.52	-31
Hinshaw,Chad	R	15	25	CF	aa	LAA	263	41	66	15	0	1	22	30	88	23	6	252	328	318	647	10%	66%	0.34	68	119	3.16	-22
Jagielo,Eric	L	15	23	3B	aa	NYY	222	32	59	15	1	9	31	16	65	0	0	265	315	465	781	7%	71%	0.25	145	61	4.24	33
Jankowski,Travis	L	14	23	CF	aa	SD	100	11	21	3	1	0	8	6	16	8	2	206	254	255	509	6%	84%	0.39	39	138	1.82	21
		15	24	CF	a/a	SD	379	51	105	14	5	1	18	37	60	23	13	277	341	347	687	9%	84%	0.61	45	136	3.31	33
Johnson,Micah	L	13	23	2B	aa	CHW	21	2	4.5	0	0	0	1	0	5	1	0	212	212	212	425	0%	78%	0.00	0	74	1.61	-62
		14	24	2B	a/a	CHW	419	33	102	16	4	4	31	28	82	15	15	242	290	326	616	6%	80%	0.34	61	94	2.40	13
		15	25	2B	aaa	CHW	311	43	85	15	2	7	29	27	74	22	8	274	333	404	737	8%	76%	0.37	89	129	4.01	32
Jones,JaCoby	R	15	23	SS	aa	DET	146	22	35	6	2	5	18	15	55	9	3	242	311	414	726	9%	63%	0.27	133	153	3.57	23

BATTER	B	Yr	Age	Pos	Lvl	Tm	AB	R	H	D	T	HR	RBI	BB	K	SB	CS	BA	OB	Slg	OPS	bb%	ct%	Eye	PX	SX	RC/G	BPV
Judge,Aaron	R	15	23	RF	a/a	NYY	478	56	113	23	2	20	63	48	161	6	2	237	306	419	726	9%	66%	0.30	137	81	3.71	20
Kemp,Tony	L	14	23	2B	aa	HOU	233	32	59	10	3	3	16	21	37	10	7	254	317	363	680	8%	84%	0.58	73	125	3.05	51
Kepler,Max	L	15	22	1B	aa	MIN	407	58	120	29	12	7	54	51	67	14	4	294	372	474	846	11%	84%	0.76	112	135	4.66	88
Kivlehan,Patrick	R	14	25	3B	aa	SEA	377	44	94	21	4	8	50	31	94	7	5	250	307	386	693	8%	75%	0.33	105	99	3.16	31
		15	26	LF	aaa	SEA	472	38	93	19	1	14	47	23	141	9	4	196	233	329	562	5%	70%	0.16	97	73	2.10	-9
Knapp,Andrew	B	15	24	C	aa	PHI	214	30	66	18	1	9	43	17	52	1	0	311	362	540	902	7%	76%	0.33	160	66	5.93	68
Kubitza,Kyle	L	14	24	3B	aa	ATL	440	60	113	27	9	6	43	61	156	16	7	258	348	400	748	12%	65%	0.39	128	132	3.61	27
		15	25	3B	aaa	LAA	457	41	97	34	3	4	33	37	152	5	1	212	271	327	599	8%	67%	0.25	105	88	2.12	-5
Lambo,Andrew	L	10	22	8	aa	PIT	272	31	67	11	1	5	29	19	55	1	1	246	296	349	645	7%	80%	0.35	68	59	3.63	6
		11	23	OF	aa	PIT	437	43	90	25	0	8	46	33	113	4	3	207	263	321	584	7%	74%	0.30	80	54	2.81	-7
		13	23	LF	a/a	PIT	444	51	104	21	3	22	76	32	141	5	1	234	285	446	731	7%	68%	0.23	157	92	3.66	41
		14	26	1B	aaa	PIT	238	31	63	16	1	7	30	15	54	2	2	264	308	431	739	6%	77%	0.28	126	76	3.66	47
Lara,Jordy	R	14	23	RF	aa	SEA	126	11	31	13	0	3	18	6	22	0	0	250	283	420	704	4%	83%	0.27	135	19	3.06	55
		15	24	3B	aa	SEA	443	39	92	24	4	6	45	29	99	0	0	207	256	315	571	6%	78%	0.29	78	58	2.02	4
Lee,Hak-Ju	L	11	21	SS	aa	TAM	100	12	17	1	3	1	5	8	24	4	2	172	235	272	507	8%	76%	0.35	50	240	2.02	13
		12	22	SS	aa	TAM	475	55	111	13	9	3	30	41	114	30	10	233	294	318	612	8%	76%	0.36	55	147	2.57	10
		13	23	SS	aaa	TAM	45	11	17	3	1	1	6	9	10	5	2	380	485	535	001	17%	77%	0.87	110	147	8.34	75
		14	24	SS	aaa	TAM	315	30	55	8	1	3	19	30	99	10	6	176	248	237	485	9%	69%	0.31	52	94	1.57	-36
		15	25	SS	aaa	TAM	313	26	58	13	1	2	22	28	124	11	3	185	253	252	505	8%	61%	0.23	66	111	1.76	-53
Leonard,Patrick	R	15	23	3B	aa	TAM	446	57	98	27	3	7	34	43	147	9	3	219	288	341	629	7%	67%	0.29	103	108	2.53	2
Lindsey,Taylor	L	13	22	2B	aa	LAA	508	59	126	20	5	14	49	40	100	3	4	248	303	388	691	7%	80%	0.40	90	77	3.32	33
		14	23	2B	aaa	SD	441	41	79	13	3	6	29	24	71	4	5	180	222	267	490	5%	84%	0.34	59	87	1.48	21
		15	24	2B	a/a	SD	291	21	44	11	1	3	16	28	66	3	1	150	226	228	454	9%	77%	0.43	56	63	1.27	-7
Liriano,Rymer	R	12	21	OF	aa	SD	183	19	39	8	2	2	16	17	58	8	1	214	281	314	595	8%	69%	0.29	80	119	2.42	-7
		14	23	LF	a/a	SD	433	49	102	24	2	10	46	30	140	14	9	235	285	369	654	7%	68%	0.22	117	99	2.76	9
		15	24	RF	aa	SD	472	57	108	24	2	9	43	44	160	12	9	229	294	345	639	8%	66%	0.27	96	96	2.67	-12
Lopez,Jesus	R	10	23	6	aa	SD	114	11	19	2	0	0	9	10	15	0	0	163	230	181	410	8%	87%	0.64	15	38	1.42	-12
Machado,Dixon	R	14	22	SS	aa	DET	292	33	78	20	1	4	24	29	38	6	6	267	333	380	713	9%	87%	0.76	85	68	3.37	56
		15	23	SS	aaa	DET	509	47	117	19	1	3	37	28	90	12	3	230	271	290	560	5%	82%	0.32	44	91	2.26	4
Mahtook,Mikie	R	12	23	OF	aa	TAM	153	14	33	9	1	3	20	9	35	3	3	215	257	343	600	5%	77%	0.25	92	79	2.14	18
		13	24	RF	aa	TAM	511	56	111	26	7	5	54	34	118	20	9	218	266	327	593	6%	77%	0.28	80	135	2.15	26
		14	25	CF	aaa	TAM	489	46	123	28	6	9	56	37	162	15	6	251	304	390	694	7%	67%	0.23	121	113	3.20	14
		15	26	RF	aaa	TAM	385	27	79	22	3	3	35	17	118	8	1	206	241	300	541	4%	69%	0.15	81	102	1.83	-17
Mancini,Trey	R	15	23	1B	BAL	326	52	108	27	2	12	49	19	64	2	1	332	369	540	909	6%	80%	0.30	138	79	6.23	69
Margot,Manuel	R	15	21	CF	aa	BOS	258	31	68	23	3	2	27	17	38	16	8	263	310	402	713	6%	85%	0.46	98	137	3.00	76
Marlette,Tyler	R	15	22	C	aa	SEA	178	13	41	12	1	2	10	8	35	0	0	232	266	348	614	4%	80%	0.23	85	33	2.42	10
Marrero,Deven	R	13	23	SS	aa	BOS	72	5	15	0	0	0	4	8	17	5	0	211	285	211	496	9%	76%	0.43	0	76	2.27	-53
		14	24	SS	a/a	BOS	454	51	107	30	2	5	46	35	104	13	9	235	291	339	629	7%	77%	0.34	89	92	2.48	24
		15	25	SS	aaa	BOS	375	42	89	14	1	5	25	28	97	10	6	236	290	315	605	7%	74%	0.29	59	88	2.61	-14
Marzilli,Evan	L	14	23	CF	aa	ARI	285	26	64	12	5	2	27	23	73	6	5	225	283	329	612	7%	74%	0.32	79	112	2.25	12
		15	24	CF	a/a	ARI	152	15	34	5	3	1	7	14	40	5	7	221	286	305	592	8%	74%	0.35	59	121	1.93	-2
May,Jacob	B	15	23	CF	aa	CHW	389	41	98	14	1	2	28	27	82	32	19	251	299	305	604	6%	79%	0.33	42	110	2.52	-3
Mazara,Nomar	L	15	20	RF	a/a	TEX	490	56	135	24	2	12	57	43	107	2	0	276	335	403	738	8%	78%	0.40	87	59	4.12	18
McKinney,Billy	L	15	21	RF	aa	CHC	274	23	72	25	1	2	31	22	52	0	0	262	318	384	702	8%	81%	0.43	97	30	3.16	28
Meadows,Austin	L	15	20	CF	aa	PIT	25	4	8.5	2	2	0	1	2	5	1	0	340	380	596	976	6%	79%	0.32	151	131	5.27	92
Miller,Ian	L	15	23	CF	aa	SEA	347	33	77	12	3	0	19	23	61	24	14	223	271	275	546	6%	83%	0.38	37	130	1.89	13
Mondesi,Raul	B	15	20	SS	aa	KC	304	30	70	11	5	5	27	14	89	16	6	230	264	343	606	4%	71%	0.16	79	149	2.41	2
Moran,Colin	L	14	22	3B	aa	HOU	112	9	30	5	0	2	17	7	26	0	1	268	312	359	671	6%	77%	0.27	75	25	3.25	-12
		15	23	3B	aaa	HOU	366	36	97	22	2	7	52	34	92	1	0	266	328	395	723	8%	75%	0.37	95	53	3.73	10
Moroff,Max	B	15	22	2B	aa	PIT	523	65	138	26	4	5	42	55	117	14	14	264	334	358	692	10%	78%	0.47	69	99	3.16	17
Moya,Steven	L	14	23	RF	aa	DET	515	58	121	28	3	25	75	16	174	11	5	235	259	446	704	3%	66%	0.09	172	104	3.24	42
		15	24	RF	aaa	DET	500	40	103	25	0	16	56	21	175	4	5	205	237	349	586	4%	65%	0.12	116	44	2.19	-24
Murphy,Tom	R	15	24	C	a/a	COL	394	39	91	23	3	16	45	20	132	4	3	231	268	429	697	5%	66%	0.15	150	80	3.07	21
Naquin,Tyler	L	13	22	CF	aa	CLE	80	7	15	3	0	1	5	4	25	1	3	193	229	254	483	4%	69%	0.15	54	60	1.29	-51
		14	23	CF	aa	CLE	304	43	83	11	3	3	24	23	82	11	3	274	325	362	686	7%	73%	0.28	69	127	3.53	2
		15	24	CF	a/a	CLE	327	44	89	24	1	6	24	34	84	11	3	272	341	405	745	9%	74%	0.41	104	96	3.98	31
Ngoepe,Gift	B	13	23	SS	aa	PIT	220	23	34	9	1	2	12	21	86	8	3	152	227	234	461	9%	61%	0.25	78	124	1.26	-37
		14	24	2B	aa	PIT	437	41	86	14	6	6	37	35	147	9	9	196	256	295	550	7%	66%	0.24	82	111	1.80	-19
		15	25	SS	a/a	PIT	307	29	68	14	1	2	21	23	90	3	9	221	275	296	571	7%	71%	0.26	63	69	1.92	-30
Nimmo,Brandon	L	14	21	CF	aa	NYM	240	28	47	10	2	5	19	27	62	4	1	198	278	317	595	10%	74%	0.43	90	103	2.29	22
		15	22	CF	a/a	NYM	360	35	85	13	3	4	19	34	86	4	7	237	303	321	624	9%	76%	0.40	59	71	2.58	-7
Nunez,Renato	R	15	21	3B	aa	OAK	381	47	92	21	0	13	47	22	71	1	0	242	283	397	680	5%	81%	0.31	100	47	3.27	32
Olivera,Hector	R	15	30	3B	a/a	ATL	92	10	22	3	1	1	8	4	16	0	0	243	273	342	615	4%	83%	0.24	62	60	2.67	8
Olson,Matt	L	15	21	1B	aa	OAK	466	62	101	33	0	12	57	82	149	4	1	216	333	364	697	15%	68%	0.55	123	57	3.19	20
Patterson,Jordan	L	15	23	RF	aa	COL	185	21	50	18	0	6	26	9	44	7	4	271	304	473	777	4%	76%	0.20	149	81	3.79	60
Peraza,Jose	R	14	20	2B	aa	ATL	185	30	58	7	3	1	14	6	16	21	9	315	336	391	728	3%	91%	0.36	49	159	3.98	60
		15	21	2B	aaa	LA	481	51	125	12	5	3	34	13	50	26	8	260	279	325	605	3%	90%	0.26	37	136	2.78	36
Perez,Fernando	R	10	27	8	aaa	TAM	385	33	68	9	2	3	23	21	87	17	7	178	220	231	451	5%	77%	0.24	36	116	1.64	-15
		11	28	OF	aaa	NYM	364	43	63	11	2	3	17	32	125	15	6	172	239	237	477	8%	66%	0.26	43	135	1.91	-44
Peterson,D.J.	R	14	22	3B	aa	SEA	222	25	51	8	0	9	30	17	58	1	1	229	282	390	672	7%	74%	0.29	115	37	3.26	15
		15	23	1B	aaa	SEA	372	29	70	17	1	5	33	22	107	4	1	187	234	281	515	6%	71%	0.21	74	75	1.69	-20
Phillips,Brett	L	15	21	CF	aa	MIL	214	33	61	14	6	1	22	21	61	8	3	285	348	425	773	9%	72%	0.34	105	143	3.75	33
Pinder,Chad	R	15	23	SS	aa	OAK	477	53	129	28	2	10	64	21	115	5	6	270	302	402	704	4%	76%	0.19	96	71	3.41	12

BATTER	B	Yr	Age	Pos	Lvl	Tm	AB	R	H	D	T	HR	RBI	BB	K	SB	CS	BA	OB	Slg	OPS	bb%	ct%	Eye	PX	SX	RC/G	BPV
Polanco,Jorge	B	14	21	SS	aa	MIN	146	11	38	6	0	1	13	7	30	6	3	258	293	312	605	5%	80%	0.25	47	65	2.68	-12
		15	22	SS	a/a	MIN	482	51	128	22	3	5	44	32	77	16	11	266	311	353	665	6%	84%	0.41	59	96	3.07	27
Powell,Boog	L	15	22	CF	a/a	TAM	444	55	118	14	8	2	33	51	88	15	15	266	342	351	693	10%	80%	0.58	53	121	3.11	22
Quinn,Roman	B	15	22	CF	a/a	PHI	232	35	63	5	4	4	12	14	48	23	11	272	314	379	693	6%	79%	0.30	63	171	3.28	32
Ramirez,Nick	L	14	25	1B	aa	MIL	490	52	96	18	4	16	61	42	181	1	5	197	260	345	605	8%	63%	0.23	126	62	2.32	-11
		15	26	1B	aaa	MIL	432	52	93	19	0	14	52	55	136	2	0	215	303	353	657	11%	69%	0.40	104	47	3.07	-4
Ramos,Henry	B	14	22	RF	aa	BOS	181	21	56	10	2	2	19	9	41	2	4	310	342	408	750	5%	78%	0.22	78	77	3.90	7
		15	23	RF	aa	BOS	131	6	30	12	1	0	6	11	28	0	0	231	292	342	634	8%	79%	0.40	91	46	2.24	19
Ramsey,James	L	13	24	CF	a/a	STL	350	45	72	9	1	10	32	39	124	6	5	205	286	327	612	10%	65%	0.32	95	87	2.61	-17
		14	25	CF	aa	CLE	352	49	87	20	1	12	40	33	119	4	2	247	311	411	722	9%	66%	0.27	141	77	3.62	19
		15	26	LF	aaa	CLE	440	38	92	19	1	10	35	43	153	3	5	209	279	326	605	9%	65%	0.28	94	50	2.40	-29
Ravelo,Rangel	R	14	22	1B	aa	CHW	476	55	129	32	3	10	50	47	88	8	7	272	337	411	748	9%	82%	0.53	105	75	3.80	53
		15	23	1B	a/a	OAK	189	18	49	10	2	2	27	13	43	0	1	260	307	365	673	6%	77%	0.30	76	60	3.03	3
Reed,A.J.	L	15	22	1B	aa	HOU	205	30	61	13	1	9	36	22	56	0	0	296	363	499	863	10%	73%	0.39	142	48	5.66	40
Reed,Michael	R	15	23	RF	a/a	MIL	439	49	105	29	5	5	55	60	126	20	8	239	330	361	691	12%	71%	0.47	97	126	3.05	27
Refsnyder,Rob	R	14	23	2B	NYY		515	64	144	33	4	12	49	44	118	7	10	279	335	429	764	8%	77%	0.37	115	76	3.90	41
		15	24	2B	aaa	NYY	450	57	110	25	1	9	48	49	84	10	2	244	318	363	681	10%	81%	0.59	81	91	3.31	39
Reinheimer,Jack	R	15	23	SS	aa	ARI	485	53	121	23	3	4	35	42	102	17	7	249	309	337	646	8%	79%	0.41	64	111	2.93	18
Renda,Tony	R	15	24	2B	aa	NYY	480	64	117	27	1	3	39	38	45	21	7	243	299	323	623	7%	91%	0.86	55	114	2.71	58
Renfroe,Hunter	R	14	22	LF	aa	SD	224	14	45	10	0	4	19	21	61	2	1	201	269	302	570	8%	73%	0.34	83	32	2.19	-14
		15	23	RF	aa	SD	511	48	115	22	4	14	58	28	154	4	1	226	266	367	633	5%	70%	0.18	102	85	2.72	-1
Reynolds,Matt	R	14	24	SS	a/a	NYM	478	57	128	16	4	4	40	33	127	13	8	267	314	343	657	7%	74%	0.26	60	105	3.12	-12
		15	25	SS	aaa	NYM	445	47	92	25	3	4	44	21	113	9	5	208	244	304	548	5%	75%	0.19	76	111	1.83	4
Riddle,J.T.	L	15	24	SS	a/a	MIA	176	23	46	6	1	3	16	8	27	0	0	260	293	363	656	4%	85%	0.31	61	61	3.24	17
Rivera,T.J.	R	14	26	SS	aa	NYM	201	19	56	10	0	1	19	8	35	1	0	278	305	338	643	4%	83%	0.22	53	41	3.13	-5
		15	27	3B	a/a	NYM	403	45	102	21	1	5	34	13	60	1	1	254	278	348	626	3%	85%	0.22	65	51	2.75	16
Rivera,Yadiel	R	14	22	SS	aa	MIL	183	24	44	8	5	2	10	8	40	4	2	239	271	366	638	4%	78%	0.20	89	137	2.40	35
		15	23	SS	a/a	MIL	473	43	106	15	5	5	34	22	94	9	11	223	258	289	547	4%	80%	0.23	45	103	1.85	-2
Roache,Victor	R	15	24	LF	aa	MIL	223	20	51	10	3	8	30	21	72	2	1	229	294	405	699	8%	68%	0.28	127	78	3.26	14
Robertson,Daniel	R	11	26	OF	aa	SD	438	67	94	17	3	3	30	40	66	14	7	214	280	289	570	8%	85%	0.61	52	128	2.77	39
		12	27	OF	aaa	SD	490	45	108	20	3	1	24	33	77	12	10	220	268	279	548	6%	84%	0.42	44	86	1.90	13
		15	30	CF	aa	LAA	245	16	46	11	0	1	12	13	43	4	8	187	229	240	470	5%	82%	0.31	44	52	1.21	-7
		15	21	SS	aa	TAM	299	40	73	18	4	3	33	27	64	2	3	245	308	364	672	8%	78%	0.42	84	100	2.76	30
Robinson,Drew	L	14	22	RF	a/a	TEX	354	32	63	15	4	10	33	32	140	7	5	177	246	324	570	8%	61%	0.23	132	107	1.90	-1
		15	23	2B	a/a	TEX	455	64	94	21	4	17	51	68	157	12	10	208	311	383	694	13%	66%	0.44	132	110	3.03	29
Rodriguez,Nelson	R	15	21	1B	aa	CLE	93	6	10	2	0	4	13	8	40	0	0	112	183	254	437	8%	57%	0.20	115	14	1.23	-56
Rodriguez,Ronny	R	13	21	SS	aa	CLE	468	48	108	23	4	4	40	12	85	9	3	231	251	319	570	3%	82%	0.14	65	110	2.13	20
		14	22	2B	aa	CLE	413	42	83	23	0	4	27	20	102	3	5	202	238	286	524	5%	75%	0.19	75	60	1.66	-10
		15	23	1B	aa	CLE	269	31	71	14	3	10	26	9	67	4	5	265	288	448	736	3%	75%	0.13	121	94	3.49	33
Rodriguez,Yorman	R	13	21	RF	aa	CIN	262	27	67	14	2	4	28	23	83	4	0	256	315	372	687	8%	68%	0.27	98	86	3.37	-5
		14	22	CF	aa	CIN	450	54	105	18	4	8	31	37	132	9	5	234	292	344	636	8%	71%	0.28	88	103	2.75	1
		15	23	RF	aa	CIN	308	36	77	12	3	10	35	15	92	9	3	249	284	405	689	5%	70%	0.16	108	94	3.38	6
Rondon,Jose	R	15	21	SS	aa	SD	100	5	17	2	1	0	7	3	17	1	3	168	196	203	398	3%	83%	0.20	22	74	0.84	-18
Ruiz,Rio	L	15	21	3B	aa	ATL	420	42	92	20	1	4	41	56	105	2	2	218	310	301	611	12%	75%	0.53	65	49	2.49	-8
Sanchez,Gary	R	13	21	C	aa	NYY	92	10	21	5	0	2	9	11	17	0	0	232	316	354	670	11%	81%	0.66	89	24	3.09	28
		14	22	C	aa	NYY	429	39	105	17	0	12	53	35	99	1	1	246	303	368	671	8%	77%	0.36	89	26	3.34	4
		15	23	C	a/a	NYY	365	44	93	21	0	18	55	26	87	6	2	256	305	459	764	7%	76%	0.30	135	65	4.19	47
Schebler,Scott	L	14	24	LF	aaa	LA	489	57	111	19	7	20	51	31	129	7	5	227	273	417	690	6%	74%	0.24	132	110	3.07	47
		15	25	RF	aaa	LA	432	42	85	13	5	10	37	28	111	11	2	198	247	322	569	6%	74%	0.25	81	122	2.16	13
Seager,Corey	L	14	20	SS	aa	LA	148	21	45	14	2	2	21	7	43	1	1	304	337	455	792	5%	71%	0.17	140	96	4.04	35
		15	21	SS	a/a	LA	501	69	135	34	2	16	65	30	84	3	1	269	311	444	754	6%	83%	0.36	112	79	3.99	60
Severino,Pedro	R	15	22	C	aa	WAS	329	28	76	12	0	4	29	16	53	1	2	230	265	303	568	5%	84%	0.30	50	36	2.27	-3
Shaffer,Richie	R	14	23	3B	aa	TAM	427	46	82	24	4	14	51	44	135	3	0	191	266	365	632	9%	68%	0.32	142	88	2.49	34
		15	24	3B	a/a	TAM	393	51	89	23	1	19	58	44	144	3	1	226	303	435	738	10%	63%	0.30	166	65	3.71	28
Sisco,Chance	L	15	20	C	aa	BAL	74	8	18	4	0	2	7	8	14	0	1	248	322	379	702	10%	80%	0.56	88	33	3.38	24
Skole,Matt	L	14	25	1B	aa	WAS	461	39	90	24	1	9	46	50	144	2	1	194	274	309	583	10%	69%	0.35	101	43	2.20	-10
		15	26	3B	a/a	WAS	465	44	93	20	1	15	65	56	144	2	2	200	287	341	628	11%	69%	0.39	104	41	2.66	-5
Slater,Austin	R	15	23	2B	aa	SF	199	20	55	10	1	0	12	14	53	1	1	278	324	342	666	6%	73%	0.26	57	62	3.14	-28
Smith,Dwight	L	15	23	LF	aa	TOR	460	62	113	26	2	6	37	39	73	3	3	246	305	352	657	8%	84%	0.53	73	76	2.92	35
Smith,Mallex	L	15	22	CF	a/a	ATL	484	75	139	16	7	2	31	45	96	51	14	288	349	360	709	9%	80%	0.47	49	163	3.94	28
Starling,Bubba	R	15	23	CF	aa	KC	331	40	75	17	4	8	25	24	97	3	6	227	279	370	649	7%	71%	0.24	105	100	2.56	13
Stassi,Max	R	13	22	C	aa	HOU	289	32	72	18	1	14	48	15	77	1	1	248	286	463	748	5%	73%	0.20	154	50	3.78	44
		14	23	C	aaa	HOU	392	35	81	17	1	7	32	16	119	1	0	208	239	309	548	4%	70%	0.13	86	57	2.00	-26
		15	24	C	aaa	HOU	294	25	50	6	1	9	29	18	109	1	1	171	218	298	516	6%	63%	0.16	94	63	1.76	-41
Story,Trevor	R	14	22	SS	aa	COL	205	23	39	8	1	8	16	22	81	2	1	191	268	355	623	10%	60%	0.27	144	79	2.59	2
		15	23	SS	a/a	COL	512	60	133	36	10	17	58	37	148	16	3	260	309	467	776	7%	71%	0.25	149	140	3.88	61
Sweeney,Darnell	B	14	23	2B	aa	LA	490	63	117	28	3	10	41	53	135	11	18	239	314	370	684	10%	73%	0.40	108	81	2.81	22
		15	24	2B	aaa	LA	472	52	108	26	2	7	37	30	136	24	15	229	275	339	614	6%	71%	0.22	87	117	2.37	4
Taylor,Tyrone	R	15	21	CF	aa	MIL	454	44	113	19	3	3	39	29	59	9	6	250	295	325	620	6%	87%	0.49	50	86	2.66	28
Telis,Tomas	B	13	22	C	aa	TEX	348	27	87	18	0	4	37	9	48	7	2	251	269	336	605	2%	86%	0.18	62	67	2.61	21
		14	23	C	a/a	TEX	406	36	114	21	3	4	37	17	45	6	2	281	310	377	687	4%	89%	0.38	67	83	3.42	44
		15	24	C	aaa	MIA	330	39	87	14	1	4	24	16	41	3	2	265	299	346	645	5%	88%	0.39	53	67	3.03	24

BATTER	B	Yr	Age	Pos	Lvl	Tm	AB	R	H	D	T	HR	RBI	BB	K	SB	CS	BA	OB	Slg	OPS	bb%	ct%	Eye	PX	SX	RC/G	BPV
Thompson,Trayce	R	13	22	CF	aa	CHW	507	65	107	22	4	14	61	55	154	21	9	210	288	352	640	10%	70%	0.36	108	123	2.74	23
		14	23	CF	aa	CHW	518	63	105	29	4	13	43	53	174	15	6	203	277	352	628	9%	66%	0.30	128	116	2.50	24
		15	24	CF	aaa	CHW	388	43	90	20	3	12	32	20	91	9	6	231	269	388	656	5%	77%	0.22	105	103	2.76	33
Travis,Sam	R	15	22	1B	aa	BOS	243	29	70	18	2	3	31	27	36	7	6	287	359	413	772	10%	85%	0.76	88	85	3.94	59
Turner,Stuart	R	15	24	C	aa	MIN	327	29	62	11	1	3	27	32	76	4	2	190	263	255	518	9%	77%	0.43	49	66	1.77	-14
Turner,Trea	R	15	22	SS	a/a	WAS	454	59	138	23	5	6	47	32	102	25	6	304	350	419	769	7%	78%	0.32	80	134	4.55	30
Vasquez,Danry	L	15	21	LF	aa	HOU	277	24	60	12	1	0	15	13	47	2	8	217	252	265	517	4%	83%	0.27	39	61	1.57	-7
Villalona,Angel	R	13	23	1B	aa	SF	196	17	38	10	0	5	21	6	67	0	0	195	219	323	541	3%	66%	0.09	109	29	1.90	-34
		14	24	1B	aa	SF	365	28	71	16	3	7	43	18	106	1	1	195	233	313	546	5%	71%	0.17	95	25	1.83	-8
		15	25	1B	aa	SF	56	3	7.1	2	0	0	5	3	19	0	0	127	168	159	327	5%	65%	0.14	36	25	0.62	-91
Villanueva,Christian	R	13	22	3B	aa	CHC	490	47	116	38	2	15	57	28	127	4	8	236	277	413	689	5%	74%	0.22	137	58	2.86	36
		14	23	3B	a/a	CHC	457	39	91	34	0	8	43	31	118	1	2	199	249	322	570	6%	74%	0.26	108	40	1.93	10
		15	24	3B	a/a	CHC	479	46	106	21	1	15	72	30	98	2	3	221	267	364	632	6%	79%	0.31	92	50	2.68	20
Wade,Tyler	L	15	21	SS	aa	NYY	113	6	22	4	0	1	3	2	26	2	1	194	207	254	461	2%	77%	0.07	46	50	1.42	-35
Waldrop,Kyle	L	14	23	RF	aa	CIN	232	21	65	15	2	7	27	13	51	2	4	278	317	453	769	5%	78%	0.26	127	66	3.85	46
		15	24	RF	a/a	CIN	447	24	94	17	3	7	37	16	135	2	3	210	237	306	543	3%	70%	0.12	73	51	1.91	-38
Walker,Christian	R	13	22	1B	aa	BAL	62	5	13	4	0	0	1	5	11	0	0	214	269	285	554	7%	83%	0.43	65	28	1.87	7
		14	23	1B	a/a	BAL	532	54	134	21	1	21	71	41	146	1	1	252	306	417	723	7%	72%	0.28	123	41	3.85	17
		15	24	1B	aaa	BAL	534	64	130	31	1	19	70	47	148	1	3	243	304	410	714	8%	72%	0.32	120	38	3.49	14
White,Tyler	R	15	25	3B	a/a	HOU	403	50	108	21	1	10	70	60	89	1	1	267	362	400	762	13%	78%	0.67	91	40	4.31	24
Williams,Mason	L	13	22	CF	aa	NYY	72	6	10	3	1	1	3	1	19	0	0	139	149	234	382	1%	73%	0.04	72	88	0.78	-19
		14	23	CF	aa	NYY	507	53	99	16	3	4	32	38	75	17	9	196	252	263	515	7%	85%	0.50	47	108	1.76	27
		15	24	CF	a/a	NYY	201	23	58	12	1	0	19	24	26	11	8	288	364	356	720	11%	87%	0.91	54	87	3.55	40
Williams,Nick	L	15	22	CF	aa	PHI	475	61	128	23	4	15	43	28	111	10	9	270	310	432	742	6%	77%	0.25	107	101	3.75	35
Wilson,Jacob	R	14	24	2B	aa	STL	131	12	34	11	0	4	16	9	26	2	1	259	304	426	730	6%	80%	0.33	131	50	3.52	54
		15	25	3B	a/a	STL	427	42	80	17	1	12	55	28	106	1	3	188	237	317	555	6%	75%	0.26	88	48	1.97	0
Winker,Jesse	L	15	22	LF	aa	CIN	443	60	117	22	2	14	48	65	95	7	4	264	359	414	773	13%	79%	0.69	99	73	4.37	43
Wisdom,Patrick	R	14	23	3B	aa	STL	452	38	83	17	3	10	41	31	164	4	1	183	235	298	533	6%	64%	0.19	100	82	1.84	-26
		15	24	3B	aa	STL	414	37	82	17	3	10	44	25	120	8	3	198	243	323	566	6%	71%	0.21	91	97	2.05	0
Wren,Kyle	L	14	23	CF	aa	ATL	205	22	52	10	3	0	13	13	46	10	6	252	296	330	626	6%	78%	0.28	64	135	2.49	16
		15	24	CF	a/a	MIL	518	45	122	15	2	1	30	34	86	28	15	235	282	277	559	6%	83%	0.40	31	103	2.22	4
Yarbrough,Alex	B	14	23	2B	aa	LAA	544	58	140	34	3	4	67	28	139	5	7	256	293	353	646	5%	74%	0.20	86	75	2.70	1
		15	24	2B	aaa	LAA	500	37	93	23	2	2	32	16	160	1	1	187	213	252	465	3%	68%	0.10	60	57	1.31	-55
Yastrzemski,Mike	L	14	24	CF	aa	BAL	184	17	39	11	3	2	9	10	38	1	2	213	254	340	594	5%	79%	0.27	96	85	1.97	32
		15	25	LF	aa	BAL	476	52	102	26	4	5	48	36	113	7	8	215	269	321	590	7%	76%	0.31	79	95	2.07	12
Yrizarri,Yeyson	R	15	18	SS	aaa	TEX	33	2	9.2	1	1	0	4	1	5	0	1	278	297	366	663	3%	85%	0.18	50	85	2.53	14
Zimmer,Bradley	L	15	23	CF	aa	CLE	187	22	38	9	1	5	22	16	60	11	2	202	265	344	608	8%	68%	0.26	107	119	2.58	10

PITCHER	Th	Yr	Age	LvL	Org	W	L	G	Sv	IP	H	ER	HR	BB	K	ERA	WHIP	BF/G	OBA	bb/9	k/9	Cmd	hr/9	H%	S%	BPV
Adam,Jason	R	13	22	aa	KC	8	11	26	0	144	171	97	12	52	106	6.04	1.55	24.2	297	3.3	6.6	2.0	0.7	35%	60%	55
		14	23	a/a	MIN	5	9	29	0	121	154	75.9	9	35.9	85.4	5.66	1.58	18.3	312	2.7	6.4	2.4	0.7	36%	63%	60
Almonte,Miguel	R	15	22	a/a	KC	6	6	28	0	104	112	62.4	7	41.4	79.6	5.42	1.48	15.9	276	3.6	6.9	1.9	0.6	33%	62%	62
Alvarez,Dario	L	15	26	a/a	NYM	3	2	48	0	42	31	15.8	2	21.1	50.7	3.38	1.24	3.6	208	4.5	10.9	2.4	0.5	30%	73%	115
Alvarez,R.J.	R	14	23	aa	SD	0	1	38	7	43.3	31.9	6.61	0	12.5	54.2	1.37	1.03	4.4	207	2.6	11.3	4.3	0.0	32%	85%	172
		15	24	aaa	OAK	3	3	31	5	35	42.2	19.6	2	18	33.3	5.04	1.72	5.1	300	4.6	8.6	1.9	0.5	38%	70%	70
Anderson,Chris	R	15	23	a/a	LA	9	10	26	0	133	154	80.6	16	63.7	86.3	5.46	1.64	22.8	291	4.3	5.8	1.4	1.1	32%	68%	28
Appel,Mark	R	14	23	aa	HOU	1	2	7	0	39	38.6	17.6	2	12.7	33.1	4.07	1.31	23.0	260	2.9	7.6	2.6	0.5	32%	68%	89
Armstrong,Shawn	R	13	23	aa	CLE	2	3	30	0	33	35	16	2	19	37	4.33	1.64	4.9	271	5.3	10.0	1.9	0.5	37%	73%	85
		14	24	a/a	CLE	6	2	49	15	56	48.7	17.1	4	21.4	60.9	2.75	1.25	4.7	236	3.4	9.8	2.8	0.6	32%	80%	107
		15	25	aaa	CLE	1	2	46	16	49.7	46.1	17.6	0	27.5	66.2	3.18	1.48	4.6	247	5.0	12.0	2.4	0.0	38%	76%	128
Aro,Jonathan	R	15	25	a/a	BOS	3	3	34	2	74	73.1	34.6	2	20	57.9	4.21	1.26	8.9	259	2.4	7.0	2.9	0.3	32%	65%	97
Asher,Alec	R	14	23	aa	TEX	11	11	28	0	154	165	82.8	23	33.8	101	4.84	1.29	22.6	275	2.0	5.9	3.0	1.3	30%	66%	58
		15	24	a/a	PHI	6	10	24	0	134	158	70.1	26	41.3	94	4.72	1.49	24.0	296	2.8	6.3	2.3	1.8	32%	75%	28
Banuelos,Manny	L	14	23	a/a	NYY	2	3	21	0	64	61.7	36.7	12	29.6	48.2	5.16	1.43	12.9	255	4.2	6.8	1.6	1.7	27%	69%	28
Barrett,Jake	R	14	23	a/a	ARI	2	2	55	28	55.3	51.6	20.8	3	25.4	39.4	3.38	1.39	4.2	248	4.1	6.4	1.5	0.5	29%	76%	61
		15	24	a/a	ARI	3	3	47	15	53	69.3	31.1	3	22.4	42.3	5.27	1.73	5.1	317	3.8	7.2	1.9	0.6	38%	69%	57
Barrios,Yhonathan	R	15	24	a/a	MIL	4	5	49	17	60.3	68.7	23.7	3	23.7	31.3	3.54	1.53	5.4	288	3.5	4.7	1.3	0.4	32%	77%	41
Beck,Chris	R	14	24	a/a	CHW	6	11	27	0	150	169	65.3	9	47.2	72.6	3.92	1.44	23.7	286	2.8	4.4	1.5	0.6	31%	73%	40
		15	25	aaa	CHW	3	2	10	0	54.3	62.5	25.9	4	16.4	33.1	4.28	1.45	23.2	290	2.7	5.5	2.0	0.7	33%	71%	52
Beede,Tyler	R	15	22	aa	SF	3	8	13	0	72.3	72.7	53.6	4	37	42.7	6.67	1.52	24.1	263	4.6	5.3	1.2	0.5	30%	53%	44
Berrios,Jose	R	14	20	a/a	MIN	3	5	9	0	43.7	43.8	25.2	2	14.2	27	5.20	1.33	20.1	263	2.9	5.6	1.9	0.4	30%	58%	64
		15	21	a/a	MIN	14	5	27	0	166	154	63.6	13	37.3	148	3.44	1.15	24.5	247	2.0	8.0	4.0	0.7	31%	71%	117
Berry,Tim	L	14	23	aa	BAL	7	23	0	133	137	59.6	14	44.3	90.5	4.02	1.36	24.2	267	3.0	6.1	2.0	0.9	30%	73%	53
Biddle,Jesse	L	13	22	aa	PHI	5	14	27	0	138	111	59	10	77	134	3.86	1.36	21.4	222	5.0	8.7	1.7	0.7	28%	72%	80
		14	23	aa	PHI	3	10	16	0	82.3	87.1	53.2	12	43.4	69.1	5.82	1.58	22.7	273	4.7	7.5	1.6	1.3	32%	65%	40
		15	24	a/a	PHI	9	6	24	0	125	170	81.9	13	62.9	76.7	5.88	1.86	24.4	325	4.5	5.5	1.2	1.0	36%	69%	20
Binford,Christian	R	14	22	a/a	KC	3	3	12	0	58	66.7	25.5	7	10.5	39	3.95	1.33	20.1	290	1.6	6.0	3.7	1.2	32%	74%	77
		15	23	a/a	KC	5	11	22	0	119	173	84.5	11	38.2	56.1	6.39	1.78	24.9	340	2.9	4.2	1.5	0.8	37%	63%	19
Blach,Ty	L	14	24	aa	SF	8	8	25	0	141	161	55.8	7	38.6	75.4	3.56	1.41	23.9	288	2.5	4.8	2.0	0.5	32%	75%	53
		15	25	aaa	SF	11	12	27	0	165	208	86.7	13	30.8	76.3	4.72	1.45	26.1	309	1.7	4.2	2.5	0.7	33%	67%	49
Black,Corey	R	14	23	aa	CHC	6	7	26	0	124	112	55	14	72	101	3.99	1.48	20.6	243	5.2	7.3	1.4	1.0	28%	76%	50
		15	24	aa	CHC	3	5	37	0	86	86.2	56.8	8	49.4	85.4	5.94	1.58	10.2	262	5.2	8.9	1.7	0.8	33%	62%	68
Blackburn,Clayton	R	14	21	aa	SF	5	6	18	0	93	101	36.8	1	18.8	74.1	3.56	1.29	21.2	278	1.8	7.2	3.9	0.1	35%	70%	123
		15	22	aaa	SF	10	4	23	0	123	130	36.8	5	29.9	85.5	2.69	1.30	22.1	273	2.2	6.3	2.9	0.3	33%	79%	88
Blair,Aaron	R	14	22	aa	ARI	4	1	8	0	46.3	34.3	12.1	5	15.7	39.3	2.36	1.08	22.6	208	3.0	7.6	2.5	0.9	25%	83%	85
		15	23	a/a	ARI	13	5	26	0	160	153	58.6	14	47.8	102	3.29	1.25	25.1	252	2.7	5.7	2.1	0.8	28%	69%	59
Bonilla,Lisalverto	R	14	24	aaa	TEX	4	2	39	1	74.7	81	37.3	10	24.8	74.8	4.49	1.42	8.1	278	3.0	9.0	3.0	1.2	34%	71%	82
Bradley,Archie	R	13	21	aa	ARI	12	5	21	0	123	111	36	6	60	104	2.62	1.38	24.7	242	4.4	7.6	1.7	0.5	30%	82%	75
		14	22	a/a	ARI	3	7	17	0	79	76.3	41.8	2	44.3	59	4.76	1.53	20.2	255	5.0	6.7	1.3	0.2	31%	66%	65
		15	23	aaa	ARI	1	0	4	0	21.3	27.1	6.9	3	4.47	16.9	2.91	1.48	22.9	310	1.9	7.1	3.8	1.2	36%	86%	79
Bradley,Jed	L	14	24	aa	MIL	5	8	17	0	87	123	52.7	10	37.6	60.6	5.45	1.85	23.9	334	3.9	6.3	1.6	1.0	38%	72%	29
		15	25	a/a	MIL	3	5	43	0	58.7	89.5	48.5	3	22	38.1	7.44	1.90	6.4	351	3.4	5.8	1.7	0.4	41%	58%	43
Brault,Steven	L	15	23	aa	PIT	9	3	15	0	90	80	22.5	1	17.6	65	2.25	1.08	23.4	240	1.8	6.5	3.7	0.1	30%	78%	121
Brice,Austin	R	15	23	aa	MIA	6	9	25	0	125	132	79.7	10	70.2	105	5.72	1.62	22.2	273	5.0	7.6	1.5	0.7	33%	64%	55
Bridwell,Parker	R	15	24	aa	BAL	4	5	18	0	97	118	57.9	9	41.3	76.3	5.38	1.64	24.1	302	3.8	7.1	1.8	0.9	36%	68%	55
Bundy,Dylan	R	15	23	aa	BAL	0	3	8	0	22	25.3	11.9	0	5.33	20.9	4.86	1.39	11.6	290	2.2	8.6	3.9	0.0	38%	61%	131
Burdi,Nick	R	15	22	aa	MIN	3	4	30	2	43.7	43.9	24.5	3	30.4	45.2	5.06	1.70	6.6	263	6.3	9.3	1.5	0.6	34%	70%	72
Butler,Ryan	R	15	23	aa	SD	0	3	3	0	17	17.7	10.1	0	8.91	6.1	5.33	1.57	24.9	270	4.7	3.2	0.7	0.0	30%	62%	35
Cabrera,Mauricio	R	15	22	aa	ATL	0	1	13	0	17.3	13.9	13.8	1	18.3	22.7	7.14	1.86	6.2	222	9.5	11.8	1.2	0.6	33%	59%	90
Cash,Ralston	R	15	24	a/a	LA	2	6	50	3	58	50.6	25.9	8	26.8	49	4.01	1.33	4.8	236	4.2	7.6	1.8	1.2	27%	74%	55
Cessa,Luis	R	15	23	a/a	DET	8	10	25	0	139	189	85.2	8	37.2	95.7	5.51	1.62	24.8	324	2.4	6.2	2.6	0.5	38%	65%	66
Chargois,J.T.	R	15	25	aa	MIN	1	1	32	11	33	30.3	11.9	1	20.2	26.8	3.24	1.53	4.5	246	5.5	7.3	1.3	0.3	31%	78%	69
Clevinger,Michael	R	15	25	aa	CLE	9	8	27	0	158	160	66.6	10	42.8	120	3.79	1.29	24.0	264	2.4	6.8	2.8	0.6	32%	71%	85
Cochran-Gill,Trey	R	15	23	a/a	SEA	4	4	35	4	55.7	66.8	33.8	0	31.1	28.8	5.46	1.76	7.3	299	5.0	4.7	0.9	0.0	34%	66%	43
Cole,A.J.	R	13	21	aa	WAS	4	2	7	0	45	35	13	3	9	41	2.54	0.96	24.5	213	1.8	8.2	4.5	0.6	27%	76%	138
		14	22	a/a	WAS	13	3	25	0	134	158	49.5	9	28.7	93	3.32	1.39	22.6	294	1.9	6.2	3.2	0.6	34%	77%	83
		15	23	aaa	WAS	5	6	21	0	106	110	48.8	10	35.5	62.4	4.16	1.37	21.1	269	3.0	5.3	1.8	0.8	30%	71%	45
Cole,Taylor	R	15	26	aa	TOR	7	10	28	0	164	222	102	25	60.7	106	5.62	1.72	26.6	324	3.3	5.8	1.7	1.4	36%	70%	21
Cooney,Tim	L	13	23	aa	STL	7	10	20	0	118	142	53	7	17	105	4.02	1.35	24.7	299	1.3	8.0	6.0	0.5	37%	70%	153
		14	24	aaa	STL	14	6	26	0	158	170	62.7	18	44.6	97.7	3.57	1.36	25.4	276	2.5	5.6	2.2	1.0	30%	77%	48
		15	25	aaa	STL	6	4	14	0	88.7	69.5	30.6	9	15.6	50.1	3.10	0.96	23.9	218	1.6	5.1	3.2	0.9	23%	72%	82
Coshow,Cale	R	15	23	aa	NYY	2	3	6	0	33.3	35.3	17.5	1	14.1	18.1	4.73	1.48	23.9	273	3.8	4.9	1.3	0.4	31%	66%	46
Cotton,Jharel	R	15	23	aa	LA	5	2	16	0	70	65.3	23	4	21.5	69.1	2.96	1.24	17.8	249	2.8	8.9	3.2	0.6	32%	77%	109
Cravy,Tyler	R	15	26	aaa	MIL	7	7	17	0	95.3	107	48.7	7	32.9	60.8	4.59	1.47	24.1	285	3.1	5.7	1.8	0.7	32%	69%	50
Crick,Kyle	R	14	22	aa	SF	6	7	23	0	90.3	84.7	41.6	6	58	95.9	4.14	1.58	17.3	250	5.8	9.6	1.7	0.6	33%	74%	79
		15	23	aa	SF	3	4	36	0	63	56.3	30	2	71.2	62.4	4.28	2.02	8.5	241	10.2	8.9	0.9	0.3	32%	78%	70
Danish,Tyler	R	15	21	aa	CHW	8	12	26	0	142	207	93.3	17	66.6	80.1	5.91	1.93	25.9	341	4.2	5.1	1.2	1.1	37%	70%	10
Davies,Zach	R	14	21	aa	BAL	10	7	21	0	110	116	45.6	9	30.5	94.1	3.73	1.33	21.7	271	2.5	7.7	3.1	0.7	33%	73%	90

PITCHER	Th	Yr	Age	LvL	Org	W	L	G	Sv	IP	H	ER	HR	BB	K	ERA	WHIP	BF/G	OBA	bb/9	k/9	Cmd	hr/9	H%	S%	BPV
Davis,Rookie	R	15	22	aa	NYY	2	1	6	0	33.3	45.4	21.1	1	8.53	21.1	5.71	1.62	24.6	325	2.3	5.7	2.5	0.4	38%	62%	65
De Leon,Jose	R	15	23	aa	LA	2	6	16	0	76.7	71.5	38.7	13	28.2	90.6	4.54	1.30	19.7	248	3.3	10.6	3.2	1.6	32%	71%	90
de los Santos,Abel	R	15	23	aa	WAS	4	4	39	8	57.7	62.6	27.9	6	12.3	45.2	4.35	1.30	6.1	278	1.9	7.0	3.7	1.0	32%	69%	89
Diaz,Edwin	R	15	21	aa	SEA	5	10	20	0	104	112	60.3	5	34.6	92.5	5.20	1.41	22.1	276	3.0	8.0	2.7	0.4	35%	61%	91
Diaz,Jairo	R	14	23	aa	LAA	2	1	27	11	32.7	35	9.89	2	9.91	41	2.73	1.37	5.1	275	2.7	11.3	4.1	0.6	39%	82%	137
		15	24	aaa	COL	3	5	47	8	55	60.5	35	8	38	39.8	5.73	1.79	5.4	280	6.2	6.5	1.0	1.3	31%	70%	22
Dull,Ryan	R	15	26	a/a	OAK	3	2	47	12	61	46.1	5.95	2	17	56.8	0.88	1.03	5.0	211	2.5	8.4	3.3	0.3	28%	94%	124
Edwards,C.J.	R	14	23	aa	CHC	1	2	10	0	48	33.7	14.9	1	21.3	38.9	2.80	1.15	19.0	200	4.0	7.3	1.8	0.2	25%	74%	91
Eflin,Zach	R	15	21	aa	PHI	8	6	23	0	132	147	59.2	13	22.2	61.7	4.04	1.29	23.5	284	1.5	4.2	2.8	0.9	30%	71%	55
Ellington,Brian	R	15	25	a/a	MIA	4	1	26	0	44.3	34.3	15.7	0	14	38.2	3.19	1.09	6.7	215	2.8	7.8	2.7	0.0	28%	67%	116
Escobar,Edwin	L	13	21	aa	SF	5	4	10	0	54	44	15	1	11	47	2.52	1.03	20.8	225	1.9	7.8	4.1	0.2	29%	75%	136
		14	22	aaa	BOS	3	10	25	0	138	186	94.3	21	44.7	99.2	6.14	1.67	24.8	323	2.9	6.5	2.2	1.3	36%	65%	36
		15	23	aaa	BOS	3	3	19	0	49.7	64.7	39.3	10	27.5	20.1	7.13	1.86	12.2	316	5.0	3.6	0.7	1.7	31%	64%	-23
Faulkner,Andrew	L	15	23	a/a	TEX	7	4	34	1	100	99	51.8	10	48.9	86.3	4.65	1.47	12.7	259	4.4	7.7	1.8	0.9	31%	70%	60
Feliz,Michael	R	15	22	aa	HOU	6	3	15	1	78.7	57.1	21.2	5	19.4	62.3	2.43	0.97	19.9	205	2.2	7.1	3.2	0.6	24%	78%	106
Ferrell,Jeff	R	15	25	aa	DET	0	1	48	16	38.3	35	14	8	9.7	34.7	3.28	1.17	5.5	245	2.3	8.1	3.6	1.9	27%	84%	72
Flores,Kendry	R	15	24	a/a	MIA	6	5	19	0	115	98.5	38.5	6	30.5	68.3	3.00	1.12	23.9	232	2.4	5.3	2.2	0.5	26%	74%	74
Flynn,Brian	L	12	22	aa	MIA	3	1	9	0	50	63	28	4	15	30	5.01	1.56	24.3	308	2.8	5.4	2.0	0.7	35%	68%	47
		13	23	a/a	MIA	7	12	27	0	161	172	60	10	48	134	3.38	1.37	25.0	275	2.7	7.5	2.8	0.6	34%	76%	86
		14	24	aaa	MIA	8	10	25	0	140	181	64.3	10	47.8	85.4	4.14	1.64	24.9	315	3.1	5.5	1.8	0.7	36%	75%	43
Gant,John	R	15	23	aa	ATL	8	5	18	0	100	113	48.5	3	41.5	76.4	4.36	1.54	24.2	285	3.7	6.9	1.8	0.3	35%	70%	69
Garcia,Jarlin	L	15	22	aa	MIA	1	3	7	0	36.7	43.3	24	4	16.9	29.6	5.90	1.64	23.4	295	4.2	7.3	1.7	0.9	35%	64%	49
Garcia,Onelki	L	13	24	a/a	LA	2	4	35	1	62	51	22	3	35	56	3.23	1.39	7.5	227	5.0	8.1	1.6	0.4	29%	77%	79
		15	26	a/a	CHW	1	1	38	3	56	82.5	42.5	4	35	58.4	6.83	2.10	7.2	343	5.6	9.4	1.7	0.7	44%	66%	57
Gibson,Daniel	L	15	24	aa	ARI	1	0	26	2	24	22.1	5.37	2	14.7	16.6	2.01	1.53	4.0	246	5.5	6.2	1.1	0.0	30%	85%	67
Giolito,Lucas	R	15	21	aa	WAS	4	2	8	0	47.3	55	24.6	2	16.9	38.1	4.68	1.52	25.7	292	3.2	7.2	2.3	0.4	36%	68%	76
Givens,Mychal	R	15	25	aa	BAL	4	2	35	15	57.3	47.7	15.1	1	17.8	63.5	2.38	1.14	6.5	228	2.8	10.0	3.6	0.2	32%	79%	138
Glasnow,Tyler	R	15	22	a/a	PIT	7	4	20	0	104	82.5	31.1	3	38	108	2.69	1.16	20.7	220	3.3	9.3	2.8	0.2	30%	76%	120
Goforth,David	R	13	25	aa	MIL	4	3	20	5	47	39	22	1	20	30	4.33	1.27	9.5	230	3.9	5.8	1.5	0.3	27%	64%	67
		14	26	aa	MIL	5	4	54	27	64.7	72.6	33.7	3	31.6	37.6	4.69	1.61	5.3	285	4.4	5.2	1.2	0.4	33%	69%	44
		15	27	aaa	MIL	0	4	38	4	47	42.9	16.6	3	29.3	27	3.18	1.54	5.4	244	5.6	5.2	0.9	0.5	28%	80%	42
Gonzalez,Marco	R	09	25	aa	STL	0	5	49	0	67	89	43	5	32	20	5.79	1.80	6.5	313	4.2	2.7	0.6	0.7	33%	67%	0
Green,Chad	R	15	24	aa	DET	5	14	27	0	149	203	82.4	11	45.8	108	4.99	1.67	24.7	326	2.8	6.5	2.4	0.6	38%	70%	59
Greene,Conner	R	15	20	aa	TOR	3	1	5	0	25	28.4	16.1	1	11.8	13.9	5.78	1.61	22.2	287	4.3	5.0	1.2	0.4	32%	62%	39
Gregorio,Joan	R	15	23	aa	SF	3	2	37	1	78.7	76.6	35.2	6	34.5	61.5	4.02	1.41	9.0	257	4.0	7.0	1.8	0.7	31%	72%	63
Gsellman,Robert	R	15	22	aa	NYM	7	7	16	0	92.3	99.3	41.6	4	25.4	43.6	4.05	1.35	24.1	276	2.5	4.2	1.7	0.4	30%	69%	48
Guaipe,Mayckol	R	15	25	aaa	SEA	0	4	38	5	47	52.5	15	3	9.1	30.1	2.88	1.31	5.1	284	1.7	5.8	3.3	0.5	33%	79%	87
Guduan,Reymin	L	15	23	aa	HOU	1	3	16	0	16.3	22.4	24	3	18.8	16.6	13.20	2.52	5.5	327	10.4	9.1	0.9	1.8	39%	45%	9
Guerrero,Tayron	R	15	24	a/a	SD	1	5	48	14	56	43.9	19.4	3	29.6	52.1	3.11	1.31	4.8	217	4.8	8.4	1.8	0.4	28%	76%	86
Guerrieri,Taylor	R	15	23	aa	TAM	1	8	0	36	31.2	6.77	2	7.88	24.2	1.69	1.09	17.6	235	2.0	6.0	3.1	0.5	27%	87%	94
Gunkel,Joe	R	15	24	aa	BAL	10	5	21	0	123	137	51.2	11	25	74.7	3.76	1.32	24.2	283	1.8	5.5	3.0	0.8	32%	73%	70
Gustave,Jandel	R	15	23	aa	HOU	5	2	46	20	58.7	57.2	16	2	24.8	42.7	2.45	1.40	5.4	257	3.8	6.6	1.7	0.3	31%	83%	69
Hall,Cody	R	15	27	aaa	SF	1	3	43	3	67.7	77.1	28.7	3	27	43.2	3.82	1.54	6.9	288	3.6	5.7	1.6	0.3	34%	74%	56
Hancock,Justin	R	15	25	a/a	SD	8	6	24	0	131	155	53.1	8	51.7	81.1	3.66	1.58	24.0	296	3.6	5.6	1.6	0.6	34%	77%	45
Hoffman,Jeff	R	15	22	aa	COL	2	2	9	0	48	45.2	22	5	13.1	30.7	4.12	1.21	21.5	250	2.5	5.8	2.3	0.9	28%	68%	63
Holdzkom,John	R	15	28	aaa	PIT	2	0	21	2	22.3	20.8	11	0	18.4	19.7	4.43	1.75	4.9	248	7.4	7.9	1.1	0.0	32%	72%	76
Houser,Adrian	R	15	22	aa	MIL	3	14	30	0	70.3	87.5	48	15	23.2	48.5	6.14	1.57	22.1	306	3.0	6.2	2.1	1.9	33%	65%	18
Hoyt,James	R	13	27	aa	ATL	0	1	22	1	33	22	13	1	15	26	3.48	1.13	5.9	193	4.1	7.3	1.8	0.3	24%	68%	87
		14	28	a/a	ATL	3	3	52	7	59.7	70.4	26.2	6	26.2	60.3	3.95	1.62	5.1	295	4.0	9.1	2.3	0.8	38%	77%	74
		15	29	aaa	HOU	0	1	47	9	49	58.3	22.3	1	11.8	50.5	4.10	1.43	4.4	297	2.2	9.3	4.3	0.2	39%	69%	135
Hursh,Jason	R	14	23	aa	ATL	11	7	27	0	148	172	69.2	5	43.2	72.4	4.20	1.45	23.4	291	2.6	4.4	1.7	0.3	32%	69%	49
		15	24	a/a	ATL	4	6	34	2	97.3	154	73.8	6	39.4	56.6	6.82	1.99	13.8	360	3.6	5.2	1.4	0.5	41%	64%	28
Jackson,Luke	R	14	23	a/a	TEX	9	5	26	1	123	129	86.2	16	52.6	105	6.29	1.47	20.4	271	3.8	7.6	2.0	1.2	32%	58%	53
		15	24	aaa	TEX	2	3	39	0	66.3	73.7	40.3	3	36.8	64.8	5.47	1.67	7.6	283	5.0	8.8	1.8	0.5	37%	66%	74
Jaime,Juan	R	14	27	aaa	ATL	1	0	43	18	41	31.9	18.6	1	37.6	50.4	4.09	1.69	4.3	216	8.2	11.1	1.3	0.2	32%	74%	100
Jaye,Myles	R	15	23	CHW	12	9	26	0	148	168	74.7	11	54.9	88	4.55	1.51	24.6	288	3.3	5.4	1.6	0.7	32%	70%	43
Jenkins,Tyrell	R	15	23	a/a	ATL	8	9	25	0	138	151	63.2	8	63.6	78.2	4.11	1.55	24.2	280	4.1	5.1	1.2	0.5	31%	73%	40
Jerez,Williams	L	15	23	aa	BOS	1	2	22	1	37	40	18.9	2	17.7	26	4.59	1.56	7.4	277	4.3	6.3	1.5	0.5	33%	70%	53
Johnson,Brian	L	14	24	aa	BOS	10	2	20	0	118	94.4	30	7	33.2	81.3	2.29	1.08	23.0	221	2.5	6.2	2.4	0.5	26%	81%	84
		15	25	aaa	BOS	9	6	18	0	96	95.9	39.5	8	36.7	72.3	3.71	1.38	22.4	262	3.4	6.8	2.0	0.7	31%	74%	64
Johnson,Hobbs	L	15	24	aa	MIL	7	8	25	0	117	114	71.4	8	88.8	79.5	5.47	1.73	21.3	256	6.8	6.1	0.9	0.6	30%	67%	41
Johnson,Pierce	R	14	23	aa	CHC	5	4	18	0	91.7	67.5	29.9	8	54.8	77	2.93	1.33	21.2	207	5.4	7.6	1.4	0.8	25%	81%	64
		15	24	aa	CHC	6	2	16	0	95	88.6	26.6	4	33.6	60.9	2.52	1.29	24.4	248	3.2	5.8	1.8	0.4	29%	81%	66
Jones,Zach	R	15	25	aa	MIN	2	2	27	10	27	28	21.4	3	18.2	23.6	7.12	1.71	4.5	269	6.1	7.9	1.3	1.0	32%	58%	45
Kelly,Casey	R	10	21	aa	BOS	3	5	21	0	95	124	60	10	31	72	5.68	1.63	20.6	309	3.0	6.9	2.3	0.9	37%	65%	56
		11	22	aa	SD	11	6	27	0	142	153	58	6	43	95	3.70	1.38	22.6	269	2.7	6.0	2.2	0.4	32%	72%	73
		15	26	a/a	SD	2	10	30	1	95.7	125	59.6	7	38.9	58.9	5.61	1.71	14.5	317	3.7	5.5	1.5	0.6	36%	66%	38
Kingham,Nick	R	14	23	a/a	PIT	6	11	26	0	159	152	62	8	47.5	95.7	3.51	1.25	24.9	253	2.7	5.4	2.0	0.4	29%	72%	66
		15	24	aaa	PIT	1	2	6	0	31.3	40.5	18.9	3	6.93	25.5	5.43	1.51	22.6	314	2.0	7.3	3.7	0.8	37%	64%	88

PITCHER	Th	Yr	Age	LvL	Org	W	L	G	Sv	IP	H	ER	HR	BB	K	ERA	WHIP	BF/G	OBA	bb/9	k/9	Cmd	hr/9	H%	S%	BPV
Kline,Branden	R	15	24	aa	BAL	3	3	8	0	39.3	43.1	21.6	5	20.7	22.2	4.93	1.62	21.8	280	4.7	5.1	1.1	1.2	30%	72%	15
Kubitza,Austin	R	15	24	aa	DET	9	13	27	0	134	228	109	7	51.1	75.6	7.34	2.09	24.3	377	3.4	5.1	1.5	0.5	42%	63%	27
Kuhl,Chad	R	15	23	aa	PIT	11	5	26	0	153	149	47.2	9	37.9	82.1	2.78	1.22	23.7	257	2.2	4.8	2.2	0.5	29%	78%	63
Kurcz,Aaron	R	12	22	aa	BOS	3	4	29	4	50	50	22	5	27	62	3.95	1.53	7.6	260	4.9	11.0	2.2	0.8	36%	76%	92
		15	25	aaa	OAK	6	4	49	7	59	69.5	30	4	38.9	54.9	4.58	1.84	5.6	295	5.9	8.4	1.4	0.6	37%	75%	57
Lail,Brady	R	15	22	a/a	NYY	9	6	27	0	143	162	62.6	8	45.5	66.9	3.93	1.45	22.7	287	2.9	4.2	1.5	0.5	31%	73%	39
Lamb,John	L	10	20	aa	KC	2	1	7	0	33	38	21	2	11	24	5.71	1.50	20.8	283	3.1	6.6	2.1	0.5	34%	60%	67
		11	21	aa	KC	1	2	8	0	35	35	12	3	12	18	3.20	1.33	18.6	254	3.0	4.7	1.6	0.7	29%	77%	46
		14	24	aaa	KC	8	10	27	0	138	151	66.1	17	65.7	104	4.30	1.57	22.5	279	4.3	6.8	1.6	1.1	32%	76%	40
		15	25	aaa	CIN	10	2	20	0	111	117	44.7	10	40.1	99.7	3.61	1.41	23.6	272	3.2	8.1	2.5	0.8	33%	77%	76
Leclerc,Jose	R	15	22	aa	TEX	6	8	26	0	103	108	76.2	9	72	83.8	6.65	1.75	18.1	271	6.3	7.3	1.2	0.7	33%	61%	47
Lee,Nick	L	15	24	aa	WAS	2	0	20	1	24	24.1	12.9	0	19.9	23.3	4.85	1.83	5.6	263	7.4	8.7	1.2	0.0	35%	71%	80
Lee,Zach	R	12	21	aa	LA	4	3	13	0	66	75	35	6	20	44	4.74	1.46	21.6	289	2.8	6.1	2.2	0.8	33%	68%	55
		13	22	aa	LA	10	10	28	0	143	152	62	15	36	114	3.94	1.31	21.1	274	2.2	7.2	3.2	0.9	32%	72%	83
		14	23	aaa	LA	7	13	28	0	151	169	74.6	14	43.8	82.9	4.45	1.41	22.8	285	2.6	5.0	1.9	0.8	31%	69%	43
		15	24	aaa	LA	11	6	19	0	113	119	37.2	5	17.5	68.5	2.95	1.20	24.0	271	1.4	5.4	3.9	0.4	31%	76%	103
Leyer,Robinson	R	15	22	aa	CHW	3	1	12	0	38.3	50.3	27.9	4	19.1	26.4	6.55	1.81	14.8	317	4.5	6.2	1.4	0.9	36%	63%	30
Light,Pat	R	15	24	a/a	BOS	3	5	47	5	62.7	60.4	36.6	6	40.4	55	5.25	1.61	5.9	255	5.8	7.9	1.4	0.9	31%	68%	55
Lindgren,Jacob	L	15	22	aaa	NYY	1	1	15	3	22	18.9	3.86	0	10.5	25.5	1.58	1.33	6.1	233	4.3	10.5	2.4	0.0	34%	87%	122
Lively,Ben	R	14	22	aa	CIN	3	6	13	0	72	66.2	34.9	8	34.7	67.6	4.37	1.40	23.4	246	4.3	8.5	1.9	1.0	30%	71%	66
		15	23	aa	PHI	8	7	25	0	144	178	74.5	16	44.8	97.7	4.67	1.55	25.1	306	2.8	6.1	2.2	1.0	35%	72%	46
Lopez,Frank	L	15	21	aa	TEX	3	7	16	0	75	96.1	46.8	9	33.2	50.1	5.62	1.72	21.3	312	4.0	6.0	1.5	1.1	35%	69%	26
Lopez,Jorge	R	15	22	aa	MIL	12	5	24	0	143	128	49.3	13	57.5	121	3.10	1.29	24.6	240	3.6	7.6	2.1	0.8	29%	79%	71
Lopez,Yoan	R	15	22	aa	ARI	1	6	10	0	48	54.2	32.2	5	24.3	27.6	6.04	1.63	21.4	286	4.5	5.2	1.1	0.9	31%	63%	25
Lugo,Seth	R	15	26	a/a	NYM	8	7	24	0	136	155	65.3	12	35.2	104	4.32	1.40	23.9	288	2.3	6.9	3.0	0.8	34%	70%	77
Mahle,Greg	L	15	22	aa	LAA	3	3	31	16	35.3	39	14.7	1	10.5	31.7	3.74	1.40	4.8	282	2.7	8.1	3.0	0.3	36%	72%	103
Manaea,Sean	L	15	23	aa	OAK	6	1	9	0	49.7	46.1	13.6	4	20.3	51.4	2.46	1.34	22.9	248	3.7	9.3	2.5	0.6	32%	84%	95
Mantiply,Joe	L	15	24	a/a	DET	4	2	39	3	63.3	65	19.9	5	13.7	40.2	2.83	1.24	6.6	267	1.9	5.7	2.9	0.7	30%	79%	78
Martinez,Juancito	R	15	26	aa	MIA	2	2	32	7	38.7	42.1	30	3	32.5	14	6.99	1.93	5.7	278	7.6	3.3	0.4	0.7	29%	62%	7
Matz,Steven	L	14	23	aa	NYM	6	5	12	0	71.3	68.5	17.6	3	12.7	60.7	2.23	1.14	23.5	254	1.6	7.7	4.8	0.4	32%	81%	140
		15	24	a/a	NYM	8	4	17	0	102	78.2	23.7	6	31.8	88.8	2.10	1.08	23.3	214	2.8	7.9	2.8	0.5	27%	83%	102
Mazzoni,Cory	R	12	23	aa	NYM	5	5	14	0	81	96	42	9	18	46	4.66	1.42	24.4	298	2.0	5.1	2.5	1.0	33%	69%	51
		13	24	aa	NYM	5	3	13	0	66	77	34	4	18	63	4.66	1.43	21.6	292	2.5	8.6	3.5	0.6	37%	67%	105
		14	25	a/a	NYM	7	1	11	0	64	65.6	30.2	5	14.4	49.8	4.25	1.25	23.7	267	2.0	7.0	3.5	0.7	32%	67%	94
		15	26	aaa	SD	1	3	26	5	34	26.5	14.4	0	11.4	37.6	3.82	1.12	5.1	217	3.0	10.0	3.3	0.0	31%	62%	141
McCurry,Brendan	R	15	23	aa	OAK	0	1	14	6	16.7	9.66	3.14	1	5.8	21.6	1.69	0.93	4.5	170	3.1	11.6	3.7	0.5	26%	85%	155
McGowin,Kyle	R	15	24	aa	LAA	9	9	27	0	154	176	95.5	17	49.7	106	5.58	1.46	24.4	288	2.9	6.2	2.1	1.0	33%	62%	49
Mejia,Adalberto	L	14	21	aa	SF	7	9	22	0	108	124	60.6	8	29.2	71.5	5.05	1.46	21.0	296	2.4	6.0	2.5	0.6	34%	65%	64
		15	22	aa	SF	5	2	12	0	51.3	44.6	17.9	2	19	33.1	3.13	1.24	17.4	235	3.3	5.8	1.7	0.3	28%	74%	69
Merritt,Ryan	L	15	23	a/a	CLE	12	7	27	0	171	220	90.6	11	22.5	90.6	4.77	1.42	26.8	313	1.2	4.8	4.0	0.6	35%	66%	89
Meyer,Alex	R	13	23	aa	MIN	4	3	13	0	70	66	28	3	29	70	3.58	1.36	22.5	252	3.7	9.0	2.5	0.4	33%	73%	100
		14	24	aaa	MIN	7	7	27	0	130	138	64	10	65.8	124	4.42	1.56	21.2	273	4.5	8.6	1.9	0.7	34%	72%	70
		15	25	aaa	MIN	4	5	38	0	92	128	69.1	5	52.9	78.7	6.76	1.97	11.6	331	5.2	7.7	1.5	0.5	41%	64%	52
Mitchell,Bryan	R	14	23	a/a	NYY	6	7	23	0	103	124	59.2	13	45.9	79.6	5.17	1.65	20.0	300	4.0	7.0	1.7	1.2	35%	71%	38
		15	24	aaa	NYY	5	5	15	0	75	77.3	34.9	1	40.5	51.6	4.18	1.57	22.0	268	4.9	6.2	1.3	0.2	32%	71%	60
Montas,Frankie	R	15	22	aa	CHW	5	5	23	0	112	106	49.1	5	43.8	95.1	3.95	1.43	20.7	252	4.3	7.6	1.8	0.3	32%	71%	78
Morimando,Shawn	L	14	22	aa	CLE	2	6	10	0	56.3	68.8	26.6	2	15.9	33.5	4.24	1.50	24.4	302	2.5	5.3	2.1	0.3	35%	70%	61
		15	23	aa	CLE	10	12	28	0	159	168	74.5	11	66.8	111	4.23	1.48	24.4	273	3.8	6.3	1.7	0.6	32%	72%	54
Morris,Akeel	R	15	23	aa	NYM	0	1	23	0	29.3	19.4	9.43	1	15	30.5	2.89	1.17	5.1	190	4.6	9.4	2.0	0.3	26%	75%	106
Morris,Elliot	R	15	23	aa	SD	5	9	21	0	102	125	61.5	6	43.6	62.8	5.44	1.66	21.7	304	3.9	5.6	1.4	0.5	35%	66%	42
Moscot,Jon	R	13	22	aa	CIN	2	1	6	0	31	41	15	4	13	25	4.29	1.72	23.5	319	3.6	7.2	2.0	1.2	37%	79%	38
		14	23	a/a	CIN	8	11	28	0	167	176	69.2	18	48.1	105	3.74	1.34	24.8	272	2.6	5.6	2.2	1.0	30%	75%	50
		15	24	aaa	CIN	7	1	9	0	54.3	61	25.2	7	20.7	29.6	4.17	1.50	26.1	285	3.4	4.9	1.4	1.2	30%	76%	21
Musgrave,Harrison	L	15	23	aa	COL	3	4	11	0	56.7	70.5	29.9	11	14.4	43.1	4.75	1.50	22.3	306	2.3	6.8	3.0	1.7	34%	74%	46
Musgrove,Joe	R	15	23	aa	HOU	4	0	8	1	45	39.2	12.6	8	5.94	28.8	2.51	1.00	21.5	236	1.2	5.8	4.8	1.5	24%	87%	98
Newcomb,Sean	L	15	22	aa	LAA	2	2	7	0	36	25.3	13.5	2	22.9	34.4	3.36	1.34	21.4	199	5.7	8.6	1.5	0.5	26%	75%	83
Nolin,Sean	L	13	24	a/a	TOR	9	4	20	0	110	119	41	8	35	96	3.37	1.39	23.2	277	2.8	7.8	2.8	0.7	34%	77%	85
		14	25	aaa	TOR	4	6	17	0	87.3	91.7	45.5	8	37.6	61.3	4.69	1.48	22.1	271	3.9	6.3	1.6	0.8	31%	69%	49
		15	26	aaa	OAK	2	2	14	0	47.3	49	17.9	5	21	29.6	3.40	1.48	14.5	268	4.0	5.6	1.4	1.0	30%	81%	34
Okert,Steven	L	14	23	aa	SF	1	0	24	5	33	26.6	11.2	3	10.7	32.2	3.04	1.13	5.4	222	2.9	8.8	3.0	0.7	28%	75%	105
		15	24	aaa	SF	4	3	52	3	61.3	66.9	26.9	6	28.2	57.8	3.95	1.55	5.2	279	4.1	8.5	2.0	0.8	35%	76%	69
Osich,Josh	L	15	27	a/a	SF	1	1	37	20	41	31.7	7.45	1	13.2	35.3	1.64	1.10	4.3	215	2.9	7.8	2.7	0.2	28%	85%	108
Overton,Dillon	L	15	24	aa	OAK	5	2	13	0	64.7	71.2	23.5	4	14.8	38.2	3.27	1.33	20.6	281	2.1	5.3	2.6	0.5	32%	76%	70
Pazos,James	L	15	24	a/a	NYY	3	1	27	3	42.7	35.8	8.15	1	16.5	41.4	1.72	1.23	6.4	229	3.5	8.7	2.5	0.3	30%	87%	105
Pena,Felix	R	15	25	aa	CHC	7	8	25	0	130	132	66.6	11	52.6	116	4.63	1.42	22.0	265	3.6	8.0	2.2	0.8	33%	68%	73
Perdomo,Luis	R	10	26	aaa	SD	4	6	58	1	82	79	31	5	33	43	3.39	1.37	6.1	249	3.6	4.7	1.3	0.6	28%	76%	44
		11	27	aaa	SD	0	8	65	10	72	85	35	4	42	42	4.45	1.78	5.2	290	5.3	5.2	1.0	0.5	34%	75%	34
		12	28	a/a	MIN	8	5	45	9	73	69	28	4	25	51	3.49	1.30	6.6	253	3.1	6.3	2.1	0.5	30%	73%	70
		13	29	aaa	MIN	5	4	45	6	65	84	54	10	48	43	7.53	2.04	7.0	315	6.7	6.0	0.9	1.3	35%	64%	7

PITCHER	Th	Yr	Age	LvL	Org	W	L	G	Sv	IP	H	ER	HR	BB	K	ERA	WHIP	BF/G	OBA	bb/9	k/9	Cmd	hr/9	H%	S%	BPV
Petrick,Zach	R	14	25	a/a	STL	9	6	27	1	134	144	65.9	15	40.7	78	4.44	1.38	20.8	276	2.7	5.2	1.9	1.0	30%	70%	42
Pike,Tyler	L	14	20	aa	SEA	3	4	13	0	49	60.2	42.6	5	30.5	30.2	7.83	1.85	17.6	304	5.6	5.6	1.0	0.8	34%	56%	23
Pineyro,Ivan	R	14	23	aa	CHC	0	4	11	0	48.7	65.2	34.5	7	23.3	34.7	6.38	1.82	20.5	322	4.3	6.4	1.5	1.4	36%	67%	19
		15	24	a/a	MIA	9	8	26	0	146	166	74.4	8	43.1	95.9	4.59	1.43	23.9	287	2.7	5.9	2.2	0.5	33%	67%	65
Plutko,Adam	R	15	24	aa	CLE	9	5	19	0	116	119	50.2	11	24.1	76.1	3.89	1.23	24.8	265	1.9	5.9	3.2	0.9	30%	70%	78
Ramirez,Jose	R	13	23	a/a	NYY	2	6	17	1	74	69	40	14	38	65	4.87	1.45	18.5	249	4.7	8.0	1.7	1.7	28%	72%	39
		15	25	aaa	SEA	4	1	41	10	62.7	60	29.1	5	27.3	55.2	4.17	1.39	6.4	254	3.9	7.9	2.0	0.8	31%	71%	71
Ramirez,Noe	R	14	25	aa	BOS	2	1	42	18	67.3	69.2	21.3	0	17	45	2.85	1.28	6.6	267	2.3	6.0	2.7	0.0	32%	75%	93
		15	26	aaa	BOS	4	1	30	3	42.7	43.7	16.5	1	21.1	29.9	3.47	1.52	6.2	266	4.4	6.3	1.4	0.3	32%	76%	61
Rea,Colin	R	15	25	a/a	SD	5	4	18	0	102	86.4	21.9	3	22.4	66.9	1.94	1.07	22.0	231	2.0	5.9	3.0	0.2	28%	82%	99
Reed,Chris	L	12	22	aa	LA	0	4	12	0	35	34	21	2	19	25	5.46	1.50	12.7	255	4.8	6.4	1.3	0.5	30%	62%	55
		13	23	aa	LA	4	11	29	0	138	150	74	10	65	91	4.82	1.57	20.8	279	4.3	5.9	1.4	0.7	32%	69%	43
		14	24	a/a	LA	4	11	28	0	158	153	68.9	13	56.9	112	3.91	1.33	23.5	256	3.2	6.4	2.0	0.7	30%	72%	62
		15	25	a/a	MIA	3	2	38	1	55.3	62.5	41.9	5	37.6	35	6.82	1.81	6.7	286	6.1	5.7	0.9	0.8	32%	61%	27
Reed,Cody (CIN)	L	15	22	aa	CIN	8	4	13	0	78.3	75.7	28.9	6	24.9	71.6	3.32	1.28	24.7	255	2.9	8.2	2.9	0.6	32%	75%	95
Reed,Jake	R	15	23	aa	MIN	4	4	35	1	47	61.5	37.5	3	20.4	32	7.19	1.74	6.1	317	3.9	6.1	1.6	0.6	37%	56%	44
Rhame,Jacob	R	15	22	aa	LA	3	3	39	2	50	39	20.8	6	18.1	50.2	3.74	1.14	5.1	217	3.3	9.0	2.8	1.1	27%	71%	92
Rodgers,Brady	R	15	25	aaa	HOU	9	7	21	0	116	151	62.3	13	24.5	74.4	4.85	1.52	23.9	316	1.9	5.8	3.0	1.0	35%	70%	59
Rogers,Taylor	R	13	26	aa	SF	5	9	26	1	104	119	65	4	54	56	5.63	1.65	18.0	288	4.6	4.8	1.0	0.3	33%	64%	38
		14	24	aa	MIN	11	6	24	0	145	175	64	4	37.4	91.8	3.97	1.46	25.9	299	2.3	5.7	2.5	0.3	35%	71%	73
		15	25	aaa	MIN	11	12	28	0	174	242	109	11	48.5	99.2	5.62	1.67	27.9	330	2.5	5.1	2.0	0.6	37%	65%	46
Rollins,David	L	13	24	a/a	HOU	1	3	7	0	39	46	18	4	11	34	4.22	1.48	23.9	297	2.6	7.9	3.1	1.0	36%	74%	78
Romero,Enny	L	14	23	aaa	TAM	5	11	25	0	126	147	75.1	14	51.6	101	5.36	1.57	22.1	292	3.7	7.2	2.0	1.0	34%	67%	52
Rucinski,Drew	R	14	26	aa	LAA	10	6	26	0	149	176	68.5	8	43.3	112	4.15	1.48	24.6	296	2.6	6.8	2.6	0.5	35%	71%	77
		15	26	aaa	LAA	5	7	22	0	112	152	70.7	17	39.5	70.5	5.67	1.71	23.1	325	3.2	5.6	1.8	1.4	35%	69%	20
Rumbelow,Nick	R	15	24	aaa	NYY	2	3	37	8	52.7	57.7	33.5	5	14.2	48.2	5.73	1.37	6.0	280	2.4	8.2	3.4	0.9	34%	58%	91
Schultz,Jaime	R	15	24	aa	TAM	9	5	27	0	135	119	63.3	11	90.5	142	4.22	1.56	21.9	239	6.0	9.5	1.6	0.7	31%	74%	76
Selman,Sam	L	14	24	a/a	KC	4	6	33	0	97	100	53.1	7	55.8	74.8	4.93	1.61	13.0	268	5.2	6.9	1.3	0.6	32%	69%	52
		15	25	aa	KC	3	5	41	3	56.3	67.3	41.5	3	43.7	53.8	6.63	1.97	6.6	298	7.0	8.6	1.2	0.5	38%	65%	57
Sherfy,Jimmie	R	14	23	aa	ARI	3	1	37	1	38	39.7	26	5	18	37.7	6.16	1.52	4.5	270	4.3	8.9	2.1	1.1	34%	60%	65
		15	24	aa	ARI	1	6	44	2	49.7	61.4	48.3	4	29.5	41.5	8.75	1.83	5.2	305	5.3	7.5	1.4	0.7	37%	49%	47
Shipley,Braden	R	15	23	aa	ARI	9	11	28	0	157	176	80.1	9	57.8	99.9	4.60	1.49	24.1	284	3.3	5.7	1.7	0.5	33%	68%	53
Sims,Lucas	R	15	21	aa	ATL	4	2	9	0	47.7	33.3	21.1	1	29.2	51.3	3.97	1.31	21.9	199	5.5	9.7	1.8	0.2	28%	68%	104
Smith,Kyle	R	14	22	aa	HOU	5	5	21	0	95.3	99.3	49.7	14	23.9	85.4	4.69	1.29	18.7	270	2.3	8.1	3.6	1.4	32%	68%	84
Smith,Nate	L	14	23	aa	LAA	5	3	11	0	62.3	56	24.7	3	29.7	57.3	3.57	1.38	23.8	242	4.3	8.3	1.9	0.5	31%	74%	83
		15	24	a/a	LAA	10	8	24	0	138	144	64.4	15	39.6	88	4.21	1.33	23.8	270	2.6	5.7	2.2	1.0	30%	71%	52
Smoker,Josh	L	15	27	aa	NYM	1	0	21	0	21	19.8	8.98	0	11.9	20.8	3.85	1.51	4.3	251	5.1	8.9	1.7	0.0	34%	72%	95
Snell,Blake	L	15	23	a/a	TAM	12	4	21	0	113	83.8	24.5	7	42.1	117	1.95	1.11	21.2	208	3.4	9.4	2.8	0.5	28%	85%	112
Stanek,Ryne	R	15	24	aa	TAM	4	3	16	1	61.7	59.1	32.2	7	31.2	34.7	4.71	1.46	16.5	254	4.5	5.1	1.1	1.0	27%	70%	28
Stephenson,Robert	R	14	21	aa	CIN	7	10	27	0	137	124	80.3	21	70.7	126	5.29	1.43	21.5	244	4.7	8.3	1.8	1.4	28%	66%	52
		15	22	a/a	CIN	8	11	25	0	134	121	72.1	14	73	127	4.84	1.45	22.9	243	4.9	8.5	1.7	0.9	30%	68%	66
Stratton,Chris	R	15	25	a/a	SF	5	10	26	0	148	149	77.3	8	65.3	91	4.70	1.45	24.3	264	4.0	5.5	1.4	0.5	30%	67%	50
Stripling,Ross	R	13	24	aa	LA	6	4	21	1	94	109	37	5	20	70	3.54	1.37	18.8	291	1.9	6.7	3.5	0.5	35%	74%	96
		15	26	aa	LA	3	6	13	0	67.3	76.1	38.5	9	19.7	44.6	5.15	1.42	22.0	286	2.6	6.0	2.3	1.2	32%	66%	45
Taillon,Jameson	R	13	22	a/a	PIT	5	10	26	0	147	156	67	8	48	117	4.12	1.38	23.8	273	2.9	7.2	2.5	0.5	33%	70%	80
Thompson,Jake	R	14	20	aa	TEX	4	1	9	0	46.7	42.8	19.4	4	22.1	44.5	3.74	1.39	21.8	245	4.3	8.6	2.0	0.7	31%	74%	79
		15	21	aa	PHI	11	7	24	0	133	137	60.3	11	40.6	102	4.09	1.34	23.0	269	2.8	6.9	2.5	0.8	32%	71%	73
Thurman,Andrew	R	15	24	aa	ATL	1	4	5	0	24.3	35.1	18.2	0	16.9	12.2	6.75	2.14	24.1	338	6.3	4.5	0.7	0.0	38%	65%	29
Tuivailala,Sam	R	15	23	aaa	STL	3	1	43	17	45	30.6	8.69	2	24.4	35.7	1.74	1.22	4.2	194	4.9	7.1	1.5	0.4	24%	87%	78
Turley,Josh	L	14	24	aa	DET	3	4	9	0	50	59	23.2	8	15.4	22.3	4.17	1.49	23.9	295	2.8	4.0	1.4	1.4	30%	77%	7
		15	25	aa	DET	13	8	25	0	153	184	72.5	18	38.1	79.4	4.26	1.45	26.1	299	2.2	4.7	2.1	1.1	32%	73%	35
Urias,Julio	L	15	19	a/a	LA	3	5	15	0	72.7	68.3	32.3	4	18.4	73.1	3.99	1.19	19.4	250	2.3	9.1	4.0	0.5	33%	66%	127
Valdez,Jose	R	13	25	aa	SF	3	2	38	0	56	69	34	2	45	43	5.54	2.03	7.2	304	7.2	7.0	1.0	0.2	37%	71%	49
		14	24	aa	DET	2	1	47	18	57	62.3	28.7	6	25.1	52.5	4.53	1.53	5.3	279	4.0	8.3	2.1	0.9	34%	72%	65
		14	31	a/a	BOS	0	2	24	4	35.7	51.8	11.7	3	12.9	20.3	2.96	1.81	6.9	340	3.2	5.1	1.6	0.6	38%	85%	32
		15	25	aaa	DET	4	5	43	5	57	58.6	26.2	3	40.6	33.2	4.13	1.74	6.0	267	6.4	5.2	0.8	0.5	30%	76%	34
VerHagen,Drew	R	13	23	aa	DET	2	5	12	0	60	61	24	3	16	32	3.60	1.29	20.5	265	2.5	4.8	2.0	0.5	30%	72%	58
		14	24	aaa	DET	6	7	19	0	110	138	56	6	25.6	50.1	4.56	1.49	25.0	308	2.1	4.1	2.0	0.5	34%	68%	45
		15	25	a/a	DET	3	3	20	3	34.3	38.6	16.5	1	14	20.1	4.33	1.53	7.5	285	3.7	5.3	1.4	0.3	33%	70%	50
Voelker,Paul	R	15	23	aa	DET	1	1	16	9	17.3	16.4	6.21	1	10.4	13.7	3.22	1.55	4.7	251	5.4	7.1	1.3	0.6	30%	80%	57
Voth,Austin	R	15	23	aa	WAS	6	7	28	0	157	158	64.6	11	40.9	122	3.70	1.27	23.0	263	2.3	7.0	3.0	0.6	31%	71%	88
Wagner,Tyler	R	15	24	aa	MIL	11	5	25	0	152	165	54.2	11	51.9	101	3.20	1.42	25.8	277	3.1	6.0	2.0	0.6	32%	79%	58
Wahl,Bobby	R	15	23	aa	OAK	2	0	24	4	32.3	38.6	15.7	2	13.5	29.9	4.37	1.61	6.0	298	3.8	8.3	2.2	0.5	38%	72%	77
Wieland,Joe	R	14	24	a/a	SD	2	2	6	0	32.7	30.9	10.4	2	4.51	22.6	2.87	1.08	21.3	251	1.2	6.2	5.0	0.5	30%	74%	133
		15	25	aaa	LA	10	5	22	0	114	153	64.7	8	23.5	76.2	5.13	1.55	22.6	323	1.9	6.0	3.2	0.6	37%	66%	77
Williams,Ryan	R	15	24	aa	CHC	10	2	17	0	88	85.1	32.6	2	16.8	51.6	3.34	1.16	20.6	255	1.7	5.3	3.1	0.2	30%	69%	93
Williams,Trevor	R	15	23	a/a	MIA	7	10	25	0	131	166	70.4	9	44.3	83.8	4.84	1.60	23.2	310	3.0	5.8	1.9	0.6	35%	69%	49

PITCHER	Th	Yr	Age	LvL	Org	W	L	G	Sv	IP	H	ER	HR	BB	K	ERA	WHIP	BF/G	OBA	bb/9	k/9	Cmd	hr/9	H%	S%	BPV
Wilson,Tyler	R	13	24	aa	BAL	7	5	16	0	89	99	46	16	23	57	4.59	1.36	23.3	281	2.3	5.8	2.5	1.6	30%	72%	39
		14	25	a/a	BAL	14	8	28	0	167	188	79.9	21	43.7	126	4.32	1.39	25.1	286	2.4	6.8	2.9	1.2	33%	72%	65
		15	26	aaa	BAL	5	5	17	0	94.3	129	55	13	21.9	49.6	5.25	1.60	24.6	327	2.1	4.7	2.3	1.2	35%	70%	28
Winkler,Daniel	R	14	24	aa	COL	5	2	12	0	70	41.4	15.4	7	18.5	54.7	1.98	0.85	21.4	173	2.4	7.0	3.0	0.9	19%	84%	97
Wittgren,Nick	R	14	23	aa	MIA	5	5	52	20	66	81.5	29.5	5	14	46.9	4.02	1.45	5.4	305	1.9	6.4	3.4	0.7	35%	73%	82
		15	24	a/a	MIA	1	6	53	20	64	69.6	27	6	8.41	54.4	3.79	1.22	4.9	278	1.2	7.7	6.5	0.8	34%	71%	156
Wojciechowski,Asher	R	12	24	aa	HOU	2	2	8	0	44	33	12	0	13	29	2.38	1.05	21.1	209	2.7	5.9	2.2	0.0	26%	75%	94
		13	25	a/a	HOU	11	8	28	1	160	154	69	12	53	110	3.87	1.29	23.5	254	3.0	6.2	2.1	0.7	29%	71%	65
		14	26	aaa	HOU	4	4	15	0	76	101	44.1	10	21.1	48.3	5.22	1.61	22.4	321	2.5	5.7	2.3	1.2	35%	70%	36
		15	27	aaa	HOU	8	4	20	0	115	150	70.7	14	42	69.7	5.52	1.66	25.8	315	3.3	5.4	1.7	1.1	35%	68%	27
Wright,Mike	R	12	22	aa	BAL	5	3	12	0	62	79	39	8	16	38	5.68	1.53	22.6	311	2.4	5.5	2.3	1.2	34%	64%	40
		13	23	a/a	BAL	11	3	27	0	150	183	63	11	40	116	3.79	1.48	24.0	301	2.4	6.9	2.9	0.7	36%	75%	77
		14	24	aaa	BAL	5	11	26	0	143	179	82.7	11	40.5	84.5	5.22	1.54	23.9	308	2.6	5.3	2.1	0.7	35%	66%	47
		15	25	aaa	BAL	9	1	15	0	81	79.5	31.7	6	29.8	50.6	3.52	1.35	22.5	258	3.3	5.6	1.7	0.7	29%	75%	52
Ynoa,Gabriel	R	14	21	aa	NYM	3	2	11	0	66.3	74.6	29.5	8	10.6	38.1	4.00	1.28	24.7	285	1.4	5.2	3.6	1.1	31%	72%	71
		15	22	aa	NYM	9	9	25	0	152	175	76.2	15	30.3	72.9	4.50	1.35	25.4	290	1.8	4.3	2.4	0.9	31%	68%	46
Zastryzny,Rob	L	15	23	aa	CHC	2	5	14	0	60.7	87.9	49.7	10	28.8	41.4	7.38	1.92	20.6	339	4.3	6.1	1.4	1.4	38%	63%	11
Zimmer,Kyle	R	15	24	aa	KC	2	5	15	3	48	49.4	18.5	4	14.3	40.6	3.46	1.33	13.3	267	2.7	7.6	2.8	0.8	32%	76%	83
Zych,Tony	R	13	23	aa	CHC	5	5	47	3	56	58	22	2	22	34	3.58	1.42	5.1	268	3.5	5.5	1.6	0.3	31%	74%	57
		14	24	aa	CHC	4	5	45	2	58.3	86.1	38.7	3	18.6	29	5.97	1.80	6.0	344	2.9	4.5	1.6	0.5	38%	65%	31
		15	25	a/a	SEA	1	2	40	9	48.3	50.6	17.6	2	8.59	46	3.28	1.22	4.9	271	1.6	8.6	5.4	0.4	35%	73%	154

This section of the book may be the smallest as far as word count is concerned, but may be the most important, as this is where players' skills and potential are tied together and ranked against their peers. The rankings that follow are divided into long-term potential in the major leagues and shorter-term fantasy value.

HQ100: Lists the top 100 minor league prospects in terms of long-range potential in the major leagues. The overall list is the work of five minor-league analysts at BaseballHQ.com (Rob Gordon, Jeremy Deloney, Brent Hershey, Chris Blessing and Alec Dopp). Gordon and Deloney also provide their own personal lists.

ORGANIZATIONAL: Lists the top 15 minor league prospects within each organization in terms of long-range potential in the major leagues.

POSITIONAL: Lists the top 15 prospects, by position, in terms of long-range potential in the major leagues.

TOP POWER: Lists the top 25 prospects that have the potential to hit for power in the major leagues, combining raw power, plate discipline, and at the ability to make their power game-usable.

TOP BA: Lists the top 25 prospects that have the potential to hit for high batting average in the major leagues, combining contact ability, plate discipline, hitting mechanics and strength.

TOP SPEED: Lists the top 25 prospects that have the potential to steal bases in the major leagues, combining raw speed and base-running instincts.

TOP FASTBALL: Lists the top 25 pitchers that have the best fastball, combining velocity and pitch movement.

TOP BREAKING BALL: Lists the top 25 pitchers that have the best breaking ball, combining pitch movement, strikeout potential, and consistency.

2016 TOP FANTASY PROSPECTS: Lists the top 75 minor league prospects that will have the most value to their respective fantasy teams in 2016. This list is ranked in terms of short-term value only.

TOP 100 ARCHIVE: Takes a look back at the top 100 lists from the past eight years.

The rankings in this book are the creation of the minor league department at BaseballHQ.com. While several baseball personnel contributed player information to the book, no opinions were solicited or received in comparing players.

THE HQ100: TOP PROSPECTS OF 2016

1	Byron Buxton	OF	MIN		51	A.J. Reed	1B	HOU
2	Corey Seager	SS	LA		52	Jeff Hoffman	RHP	COL
3	Lucas Giolito	RHP	WAS		53	Jesse Winker	OF	CIN
4	J.P. Crawford	SS	PHI		54	Brent Honeywell	RHP	TAM
5	Alex Reyes	RHP	STL		55	Josh Bell	1B	PIT
6	Julio Urias	LHP	LA		56	Anthony Alford	OF	TOR
7	Yoan Moncada	2B	BOS		57	Tyler Kolek	RHP	MIA
8	Tyler Glasnow	RHP	PIT		58	Max Kepler	OF	MIN
9	Joey Gallo	3B	TEX		59	Hunter Renfroe	OF	SD
10	Steven Matz	LHP	NYM		60	Mark Appel	RHP	PHI
11	Rafael Devers	3B	BOS		61	Kyle Zimmer	RHP	KC
12	Jose Berrios	RHP	MIN		62	Jose Peraza	2B	CIN
13	Orlando Arcia	SS	MIL		63	Kyle Tucker	OF	HOU
14	Blake Snell	LHP	TAM		64	Cody Reed	LHP	CIN
15	Trea Turner	SS	WAS		65	Billy McKinney	OF	CHC
16	Bradley Zimmer	OF	CLE		66	Nick Gordon	SS	MIN
17	Jose De Leon	RHP	LA		67	Braden Shipley	RHP	ARI
18	Brendan Rodgers	SS	COL		68	Jorge Lopez	RHP	MIL
19	Dansby Swanson	SS	ATL		69	Touki Toussaint	RHP	ATL
20	Robert Stephenson	RHP	CIN		70	Hector Olivera	3B	ATL
21	Nomar Mazara	OF	TEX		71	Derek Fisher	OF	HOU
22	Victor Robles	OF	WAS		72	Jorge Alfaro	C	PHI
23	Aaron Judge	OF	NYY		73	Raimel Tapia	OF	COL
24	Manuel Margot	OF	SD		74	Grant Holmes	RHP	LA
25	Clint Frazier	OF	CLE		75	Dominic Smith	1B	NYM
26	Lewis Brinson	OF	TEX		76	Daz Cameron	OF	HOU
27	Alex Bregman	SS	HOU		77	Alex Jackson	OF	SEA
28	Jon Gray	RHP	COL		78	Sean Manaea	LHP	OAK
29	Ryan McMahon	3B	COL		79	Amed Rosario	SS	NYM
30	Austin Meadows	OF	PIT		80	Reynaldo Lopez	RHP	WAS
31	Nick Williams	OF	PHI		81	Javier Guerra	SS	SD
32	Franklin Barreto	SS	OAK		82	Hunter Harvey	RHP	BAL
33	David Dahl	OF	COL		83	Luis Ortiz	RHP	TEX
34	Brett Phillips	OF	MIL		84	Brady Aiken	LHP	CLE
35	Gleyber Torres	SS	CHC		85	Matt Olson	1B	OAK
36	Sean Newcomb	LHP	ATL		86	Jorge Mateo	SS	NYY
37	Carson Fulmer	RHP	CHW		87	Daniel Robertson	SS	TAM
38	Ozhaino Albies	SS	ATL		88	Taylor Guerrieri	RHP	TAM
39	Dillon Tate	RHP	TEX		89	Amir Garrett	LHP	CIN
40	Andrew Benintendi	OF	BOS		90	Willson Contreras	C	CHC
41	Jameson Taillon	RHP	PIT		91	Renato Nunez	3B	OAK
42	Raul Mondesi	SS	KC		92	Tyler Jay	LHP	MIN
43	Archie Bradley	RHP	ARI		93	Tyler Stephenson	C	CIN
44	Tim Anderson	SS	CHW		94	Christian Arroyo	SS	SF
45	Kolby Allard	LHP	ATL		95	Josh Naylor	1B	MIA
46	Jake Thompson	RHP	PHI		96	Brian Johnson	LHP	BOS
47	Dylan Bundy	RHP	BAL		97	Tyler Beede	RHP	SF
48	Willy Adames	SS	TAM		98	Garrett Whitley	OF	TAM
49	Anderson Espinoza	RHP	BOS		99	Cody Bellinger	1B	LA
50	Aaron Blair	RHP	ATL		100	Michael Fulmer	RHP	DET

ROB GORDON'S TOP 100

1	Corey Seager	SS	LA		51	Raul Mondesi	SS	KC
2	Byron Buxton	OF	MIN		52	Alex Jackson	OF	SEA
3	Lucas Giolito	RHP	WAS		53	Brian Johnson	LHP	BOS
4	J.P. Crawford	SS	PHI		54	Brent Honeywell	RHP	TAM
5	Yoan Moncada	2B	BOS		55	Josh Naylor	1B	MIA
6	Alex Reyes	RHP	STL		56	Andrew Benintendi	OF	BOS
7	Joey Gallo	3B	TEX		57	Jake Thompson	RHP	PHI
8	Julio Urias	LHP	LA		58	Dillon Tate	RHP	TEX
9	Nomar Mazara	OF	TEX		59	Frankie Montas	RHP	LA
10	Brendan Rodgers	SS	COL		60	A.J. Reed	1B	HOU
11	Steven Matz	LHP	NYM		61	Grant Holmes	RHP	LA
12	Tyler Glasnow	RHP	PIT		62	Hunter Harvey	RHP	BAL
13	Trea Turner	SS	WAS		63	Dylan Bundy	RHP	BAL
14	Orlando Arcia	SS	MIL		64	Tyler Kolek	RHP	MIA
15	Austin Meadows	OF	PIT		65	Mark Appel	RHP	PHI
16	Rafael Devers	3B	BOS		66	Kyle Tucker	OF	HOU
17	Jose Berrios	RHP	MIN		67	Nick Gordon	SS	MIN
18	Sean Newcomb	LHP	ATL		68	Tyler Jay	LHP	MIN
19	Bradley Zimmer	OF	CLE		69	Daz Cameron	OF	HOU
20	Aaron Judge	OF	NYY		70	Trent Clark	OF	MIL
21	Dansby Swanson	SS	ATL		71	Albert Almora	OF	CHC
22	Clint Frazier	OF	CLE		72	Touki Toussaint	RHP	ATL
23	Franklin Barreto	SS	OAK		73	Garrett Whitley	OF	TAM
24	Manuel Margot	OF	SD		74	Aaron Blair	RHP	ATL
25	Alex Bregman	SS	HOU		75	Duane Underwood	RHP	CHC
26	Josh Bell	1B	PIT		76	Cody Bellinger	1B	LA
27	Brett Phillips	OF	MIL		77	Hunter Renfroe	OF	SD
28	Robert Stephenson	RHP	CIN		78	Jorge Polanco	SS	MIN
29	David Dahl	OF	COL		79	Dominic Smith	1B	NYM
30	Jose De Leon	RHP	LA		80	Kolby Allard	LHP	ATL
31	Jesse Winker	OF	CIN		81	Amed Rosario	SS	NYM
32	Jose Peraza	2B	CIN		82	Amir Garrett	LHP	CIN
33	Gleyber Torres	SS	CHC		83	Ian Happ	OF	CHC
34	Ryan McMahon	3B	COL		84	Gavin Cecchini	SS	NYM
35	Ozhaino Albies	SS	ATL		85	Jorge Mateo	SS	NYY
36	Jon Gray	RHP	COL		86	Brandon Nimmo	OF	NYM
37	Nick Williams	OF	PHI		87	Tyler Stephenson	C	CIN
38	Archie Bradley	RHP	ARI		88	Braden Shipley	RHP	ARI
39	Tim Anderson	SS	CHW		89	Javier Guerra	SS	SD
40	Hector Olivera	3B	ATL		90	Daniel Robertson	SS	TAM
41	Billy McKinney	OF	CHC		91	Cornelius Randolph	OF	PHI
42	Blake Snell	LHP	TAM		92	Luis Ortiz	RHP	TEX
43	Jeff Hoffman	RHP	COL		93	Michael Fulmer	RHP	DET
44	Jorge Alfaro	C	PHI		94	Max Kepler	OF	MIN
45	Jameson Taillon	RHP	PIT		95	Kyle Zimmer	RHP	KC
46	Carson Fulmer	RHP	CHW		96	Anthony Alford	OF	TOR
47	Willy Adames	SS	TAM		97	Keury Mella	RHP	CIN
48	Lewis Brinson	OF	TEX		98	Jon Harris	RHP	TOR
49	Raimel Tapia	OF	COL		99	Trevor Story	SS	COL
50	Victor Robles	OF	WAS		100	Ashe Russell	RHP	KC

JEREMY DELONEY'S TOP 100

1	Byron Buxton	OF	MIN		51	Matt Olson	1B	OAK
2	Corey Seager	SS	LA		52	Victor Robles	OF	WAS
3	Alex Reyes	RHP	STL		53	Tyler Kolek	RHP	MIA
4	J.P. Crawford	SS	PHI		54	Jameson Taillon	RHP	PIT
5	Lucas Giolito	RHP	WAS		55	Kyle Tucker	OF	HOU
6	Julio Urias	LHP	LA		56	Taylor Guerrieri	RHP	TAM
7	Tyler Glasnow	RHP	PIT		57	Renato Nunez	3B	OAK
8	Yoan Moncada	2B	BOS		58	Manuel Margot	OF	SD
9	Joey Gallo	3B	TEX		59	Reynaldo Lopez	RHP	WAS
10	Raul Mondesi	SS	KC		60	Daniel Robertson	SS	TAM
11	Blake Snell	LHP	TAM		61	Jeff Hoffman	RHP	COL
12	Jon Gray	RHP	COL		62	Aaron Blair	RHP	ATL
13	Dansby Swanson	SS	ATL		63	Brett Phillips	OF	MIL
14	Rafael Devers	3B	BOS		64	Derek Fisher	OF	HOU
15	Dylan Bundy	RHP	BAL		65	Erick Fedde	RHP	WAS
16	Bradley Zimmer	OF	CLE		66	Ozhaino Albies	SS	ATL
17	Orlando Arcia	SS	MIL		67	Jorge Mateo	SS	NYY
18	Brendan Rodgers	SS	COL		68	Jake Thompson	RHP	PHI
19	Steven Matz	LHP	NYM		69	Jon Harris	RHP	TOR
20	Dillon Tate	RHP	TEX		70	Archie Bradley	RHP	ARI
21	Jose Berrios	RHP	MIN		71	Anderson Espinoza	RHP	BOS
22	Robert Stephenson	RHP	CIN		72	A.J. Reed	1B	HOU
23	Ryan McMahon	3B	COL		73	Nick Gordon	SS	MIN
24	Tim Anderson	SS	CHW		74	Duane Underwood	RHP	CHC
25	Alex Bregman	SS	HOU		75	Miguel Almonte	RHP	KC
26	Gleyber Torres	SS	CHC		76	Garrett Whitley	OF	TAM
27	Franklin Barreto	SS	OAK		77	Anthony Alford	OF	TOR
28	Clint Frazier	OF	CLE		78	Jack Flaherty	RHP	STL
29	Sean Newcomb	LHP	ATL		79	Nomar Mazara	OF	TEX
30	Brent Honeywell	RHP	TAM		80	Max Kepler	OF	MIN
31	David Dahl	OF	COL		81	Michael Feliz	RHP	HOU
32	Carson Fulmer	RHP	CHW		82	Tyler Beede	RHP	SF
33	Jose De Leon	RHP	LA		83	Grant Holmes	RHP	LA
34	Trea Turner	SS	WAS		84	Tyler Jay	LHP	MIN
35	Nick Williams	OF	PHI		85	Josh Naylor	1B	MIA
36	Willy Adames	SS	TAM		86	Christian Arroyo	SS	SF
37	Aaron Judge	OF	NYY		87	Brian Johnson	LHP	BOS
38	Hector Olivera	3B	ATL		88	Michael Fulmer	RHP	DET
39	Andrew Benintendi	OF	BOS		89	Luke Weaver	RHP	STL
40	Kyle Zimmer	RHP	KC		90	Amir Garrett	LHP	CIN
41	Mark Appel	RHP	PHI		91	Luis Ortiz	RHP	TEX
42	Hunter Renfroe	OF	SD		92	Joe Musgrove	RHP	HOU
43	Jorge Lopez	RHP	MIL		93	Trent Clark	OF	MIL
44	Braden Shipley	RHP	ARI		94	Gary Sanchez	C	NYY
45	Lewis Brinson	OF	TEX		95	Kyle Freeland	LHP	COL
46	Kolby Allard	LHP	ATL		96	Josh Bell	1B	PIT
47	Sean Manaea	LHP	OAK		97	Wilmer Difo	SS	WAS
48	Brady Aiken	LHP	CLE		98	Cody Bellinger	1B	LA
49	Austin Meadows	OF	PIT		99	Phil Bickford	RHP	SF
50	Alex Jackson	OF	SEA		100	Hunter Harvey	RHP	BAL

TOP PROSPECTS BY ORGANIZATION

AL EAST

BALTIMORE ORIOLES
1. Dylan Bundy, RHP
2. Hunter Harvey, RHP
3. Jomar Reyes, 3B
4. Chance Sisco, C
5. Mychal Givens, RHP
6. D.J. Stewart, OF
7. Ryan Mountcastle, SS
8. Dariel Alvarez, OF
9. Trey Mancini, 1B
10. Mike Wright, RHP
11. David Hess, RHP
12. Christian Walker, 1B
13. Parker Bridwell, RHP
14. Jason Garcia, RHP
15. Tyler Wilson, RHP

BOSTON RED SOX
1. Yoan Moncada, 2B
2. Rafael Devers, 3B
3. Andrew Benintendi, OF
4. Anderson Espinoza, RHP
5. Brian Johnson, LHP
6. Michael Kopech, RHP
7. Sam Travis, 1B
8. Trey Ball, LHP
9. Edwin Escobar, LHP
10. Michael Chavis, 3B
11. Mauricio Dubon, 2B/SS
12. Deven Marrero, INF
13. Luis Basabe, OF
14. Luis Ysla, LHP
15. Ty Buttrey, RHP

NEW YORK YANKEES
1. Aaron Judge, OF
2. Jorge Mateo, SS
3. Gary Sanchez, C
4. James Kaprielian, RHP
5. Rob Refsnyder, 2B
6. Jacob Lindgren, LHP
7. Domingo Acevedo, RHP
8. Tyler Wade, 2B/SS
9. Ian Clarkin, LHP
10. Kyle Holder, SS
11. Brady Lail, RHP
12. Domingo German, RHP
13. Bryan Mitchell, RHP
14. Luis Torrens, C
15. Abiatal Avelino, 2B/SS

TAMPA BAY RAYS
1. Blake Snell, LHP
2. Brent Honeywell, RHP
3. Willy Adames, SS
4. Taylor Guerrieri, RHP
5. Daniel Robertson, SS
6. Garrett Whitley, OF
7. Casey Gillaspie, 1B
8. Adrian Rondon, SS
9. Richie Shaffer, 3B
10. Jake Bauers, 1B
11. Mikie Mahtook, OF
12. Justin O'Conner, C
13. Ryan Brett, 2B
14. Chris Betts, C
15. Justin Williams, OF

TORONTO BLUE JAYS
1. Jonathan Harris, RHP
2. Anthony Alford, OF
3. Richard Urena, SS
4. Sean Reid-Foley, RHP
5. Max Pentecost, C
6. Vladimir Guerrero, OF
7. Dwight Smith, OF
8. Rowdy Tellez, 1B
9. Conner Greene, RHP
10. Justin Maese, RHP
11. Matt Dean, 1B/3B
12. Ryan Borucki, LHP
13. Andy Burns, INF
14. D.J. Davis, OF
15. Matthew Smoral, LHP

AL CENTRAL

CHICAGO WHITE SOX
1. Tim Anderson, SS
2. Carson Fulmer, RHP
3. Spencer Adams, RHP
4. Trey Michalczewski, 3B
5. Tyler Danish, RHP
6. Courtney Hawkins, OF
7. Micker Adolfo, OF
8. Chris Beck, RHP
9. Jordan Guerrero, LHP
10. Brandon Brennan, RHP
11. Jake Peter, 2B
12. Corey Zangari, 1B
13. Adam Engel, OF
14. Andre Wheeler, LHP
15. Jacob May, OF

CLEVELAND INDIANS
1. Bradley Zimmer, OF
2. Clint Frazier, OF
3. Brady Aiken, LHP
4. Justus Sheffield, LHP
5. Michael Clevinger, RHP
6. Rob Kaminsky, LHP
7. Francisco Mejia, C
8. Bobby Bradley, 1B
9. Adam Plutko, RHP
10. Tyler Naquin, OF
11. James Ramsey, OF
12. Triston McKenzie, RHP
13. Dylan Baker, RHP
14. Mike Papi, 1B/OF
15. Mark Mathias, 2B

DETROIT TIGERS
1. Michael Fulmer, RHP
2. Beau Burrows, RHP
3. Spencer Turnbull, RHP
4. Steven Moya, OF
5. Kevin Ziomek, LHP
6. Jairo Labourt, LHP
7. Derek Hill, OF
8. Michael Gerber, OF
9. Christin Stewart, OF
10. Tyler Alexander, LHP
11. Joe Jimenez, RHP
12. JaCoby Jones, SS
13. Zach Shepherd, 3B
14. Dixon Machado, SS
15. Artie Lewicki, RHP

KANSAS CITY ROYALS
1. Raul Mondesi, SS
2. Kyle Zimmer, RHP
3. Miguel Almonte, RHP
4. Ashe Russell, RHP
5. Nolan Watson, RHP
6. Bubba Starling, OF
7. Jorge Bonifacio, OF
8. Scott Blewett, RHP
9. Foster Griffin, LHP
10. Josh Staumont, RHP
11. Cheslor Cuthbert, 3B
12. Ryan O'Hearn, 1B
13. Pedro Fernandez, RHP
14. Hunter Dozier, 3B
15. Elier Hernandez, OF

MINNESOTA TWINS
1. Byron Buxton, OF
2. Jose Berrios, RHP
3. Nick Gordon, SS
4. Max Kepler, OF
5. Tyler Jay, LHP
6. Jorge Polanco, 2B/SS
7. Kohl Stewart, RHP
8. Stephen Gonsalves, LHP
9. Alex Meyer, RHP
10. Nick Burdi, RHP
11. J.T. Chargois, RHP
12. Adam Brett Walker, OF
13. Lewin Diaz, 1B
14. Felix Jorge, RHP
15. Lewis Thorpe, LHP

AL WEST

HOUSTON ASTROS
1. Alex Bregman, SS
2. Kyle Tucker, OF
3. Derek Fisher, OF
4. A.J. Reed, 1B
5. Michael Feliz, RHP
6. Joe Musgrove, RHP
7. Daz Cameron, OF
8. Francis Martes, RHP
9. David Paulino, RHP
10. Colin Moran, 3B
11. J.D. Davis, 3B
12. Reymin Guduan, LHP
13. Tony Kemp, 2B
14. Akeem Bostick, RHP
15. Riley Ferrell, RHP

LOS ANGELES ANGELS
1. Taylor Ward, C
2. Victor Alcantara, RHP
3. Kaleb Cowart, 3B
4. Kyle Kubitza, 3B/OF
5. Joe Gatto, RHP
6. Hunter Green, LHP
7. Roberto Baldoquin, SS
8. Jake Jewell, RHP
9. Jahmai Jones, OF
10. Julio Garcia, SS
11. Natanael Delgado, OF
12. Nate Smith, LHP
13. Grayson Long, RHP
14. Greg Mahle, LHP
15. Chad Hinshaw, OF

OAKLAND ATHLETICS
1. Franklin Barreto, SS
2. Sean Manaea, LHP
3. Matt Olson, 1B
4. Renato Nunez, 3B
5. Richie Martin, SS
6. Matt Chapman, 3B
7. Jacob Nottingham, C/1B
8. Chad Pinder, SS
9. Yairo Munoz, SS
10. Dakota Chalmers, RHP
11. Dillon Overton, LHP
12. Sean Nolin, LHP
13. Raul Alcantara, RHP
14. Joey Wendle, 2B
15. R.J. Alvarez, RHP

SEATTLE MARINERS
1. Alex Jackson, OF
2. Edwin Diaz, RHP
3. D.J. Peterson, 1B
4. Luiz Gohara, LHP
5. Tyler O'Neill, OF
6. Nick Neidert, RHP
7. Ryan Yarbrough, LHP
8. Luis Liberato, OF
9. Austin Wilson, OF
10. Brayan Hernandez, OF
11. Dylan Thompson, RHP
12. Boog Powell, OF
13. Tyler Marlette, C
14. Gareth Morgan, OF
15. Nick Wells, LHP

TEXAS RANGERS
1. Joey Gallo, 3B
2. Dillon Tate, RHP
3. Lewis Brinson, OF
4. Nomar Mazara, OF
5. Luis Ortiz, RHP
6. Michael Matuella, RHP
7. Ryan Cordell, 3B/OF
8. Ariel Jurado, RHP
9. Yohander Mendez, LHP
10. Luke Jackson, RHP
11. Jose Leclerc, RHP
12. Patrick Kivlehan, UT
13. Josh Morgan, INF
14. Jairo Beras, OF
15. Ti'quan Forbes, 3B

TOP PROSPECTS BY ORGANIZATION

NL EAST

ATLANTA BRAVES
1. Dansby Swanson, SS
2. Kolby Allard, LHP
3. Sean Newcomb, LHP
4. Ozhaino Albies, SS
5. Aaron Blair, RHP
6. Touki Toussaint, RHP
7. Hector Olivera, 3B/OF
8. Lucas Sims, RHP
9. Austin Riley, 3B
10. Max Fried, LHP
11. Tyrell Jenkins, RHP
12. Mallex Smith, OF
13. Mike Soroka, RHP
14. Braxton Davidson, OF
15. Manny Banuelos, LHP

MIAMI MARLINS
1. Josh Naylor, 1B
2. Tyler Kolek, RHP
3. Stone Garrett, OF
4. Jarlin Garcia, LHP
5. Kendry Flores, RHP
6. Anfernee Seymour, SS
7. Brian Anderson, UT
8. Brett Lilek, LHP
9. Isael Soto, OF
10. Isaiah White, OF
11. Nick Wittgren, RHP
12. Austin Dean, OF
13. Juancito Martinez, RHP
14. J.T. Riddle, SS
15. Justin Twine, SS

NEW YORK METS
1. Steven Matz, LHP
2. Amed Rosario, SS
3. Dominic Smith, 1B
4. Gavin Cecchini, SS
5. Luis Carpio, SS
6. Marcos Molina, RHP
7. Brandon Nimmo, OF
8. Ali Sanchez, C,
9. Desmond Lindsay, OF
10. Matt Reynolds, INF
11. Wuilmer Becerra, OF
12. Robert Gsellman, RHP
13. Josh Smoker, LHP
14. Akeel Morris, RHP
15. Jhoan Urena, 3B

PHILADELPHIA PHILLIES
1. J.P. Crawford, SS
2. Nick Williams, OF
3. Mark Appel, RHP
4. Jake Thompson, RHP
5. Roman Quinn, OF
6. Jorge Alfaro, C
7. Corneilus Randolph, OF
8. Franklyn Kilome, RHP
9. Adonis Medina, RHP
10. Andrew Knapp, C
11. Ricardo Pinto, RHP
12. Scott Kingery, 2B
13. Zach Eflin, RHP
14. Jhailyn Ortiz, OF
15. Jose Pujols, OF

WASHINGTON NATIONALS
1. Lucas Giolito, RHP
2. Victor Robles, OF
3. Trea Turner, SS
4. Erick Fedde, RHP
5. Reynaldo Lopez, RHP
6. Wilmer Difo, SS
7. A.J. Cole, RHP
8. Austin Voth, RHP
9. Anderson Franco, 3B
10. Andrew Stevenson, OF
11. Jakson Reetz, C
12. Drew Ward, 3B
13. Rafael Bautista, OF
14. Max Schrock, 2B
15. Juan Soto, OF

NL CENTRAL

CHICAGO CUBS
1. Gleyber Torres, SS
2. Billy McKinney, OF
3. Albert Almora, OF
4. Duane Underwood, RHP
5. Ian Happ, 2B
6. Willson Contreras, C
7. Pierce Johnson, RHP
8. Dylan Cease, RHP
9. Mark Zagunis, OF
10. Donnie Dewees, OF
11. Eloy Jimenez, OF
12. C.J. Edwards, RHP
13. Oscar De La Cruz, RHP
14. Dan Vogelbach, 1B
15. Jeimer Candelario, 3B

CINCINNATI REDS
1. Robert Stephenson, RHP
2. Jesse Winker, OF
3. Cody Reed, LHP
4. Tyler Stephenson, C
5. Amir Garrett, LHP
6. Jose Peraza, 2B,
7. Alex Blandino, INF
8. Rookie Davis, RHP
9. Keury Mella, RHP
10. Nicholas Travieso, RHP
11. Tyler Mahle, RHP
12. Blake Trahan, 2B/SS
13. Sal Romano, RHP
14. Eric Jagielo, 3B
15. Antonio Santillan, RHP

MILWAUKEE BREWERS
1. Orlando Arcia, SS
2. Brett Phillips, OF
3. Trent Clark, OF
4. Jorge Lopez, RHP
5. Tyrone Taylor, OF
6. Kodi Medeiros, LHP
7. Gilbert Lara, SS
8. Devin Williams, RHP
9. Clint Coulter, OF
10. Josh Hader, LHP
11. Cody Ponce, RHP
12. Monte Harrison, OF
13. Zach Davies, RHP
14. Jake Gatewood, SS
15. Nathan Kirby, LHP

PITTSBURGH PIRATES
1. Tyler Glasnow, RHP
2. Austin Meadows, OF
3. Josh Bell, 1B
4. Jameson Taillon, RHP
5. Harold Ramirez, OF
6. Cole Tucker, SS
7. Alen Hanson, 2B
8. Ke'Bryan Hayes, 3B
9. Willy Garcia, OF
10. Elias Diaz, C
11. Reese McGuire, C
12. Nick Kingham, RHP
13. Kevin Newman, SS
14. Mitch Keller, RHP
15. Jordan Luplow, 3B

ST. LOUIS CARDINALS
1. Alex Reyes, RHP
2. Magneuris Sierra, OF
3. Jack Flaherty, RHP
4. Luke Weaver, RHP
5. Marco Gonzales, LHP
6. Tim Cooney, LHP
7. Edmundo Sosa, SS
8. Harrison Bader, OF
9. Charlie Tilson, OF
10. Junior Fernandez, RHP
11. Nick Plummer, OF
12. Ronnie Williams, RHP
13. Sandy Alcantara, RHP
14. Jake Woodford, RHP
15. Sam Tuivailala, RHP

NL WEST

ARIZONA DIAMONDBACKS
1. Archie Bradley, RHP
2. Braden Shipley, RHP
3. Alex Young, LHP
4. Brandon Drury, 2B/3B
5. Isan Diaz, SS
6. Socrates Brito, OF
7. Jamie Westbrook, 2B
8. Cody Reed, LHP
9. Peter O'Brien, 1B/OF
10. Domingo Leyba, SS
11. Marcus Wilson, OF
12. Wei-Chieh Huang, RHP
13. Yoan Lopez, RHP
14. Gabriel Guerrero, OF
15. Ryan Burr, RHP

COLORADO ROCKIES
1. David Dahl, OF
2. Ryan McMahon, 3B
3. Brendan Rodgers, SS
4. Jon Gray, RHP
5. Jeff Hoffman, RHP
6. Raimel Tapia, OF
7. Trevor Story, SS
8. Forrest Wall, 2B
9. Kyle Freeland, LHP
10. Dom Nunez, C
11. Tom Murphy, C
12. Tyler Nevin, 3B
13. Jordan Patterson, OF
14. Miguel Castro, RHP
15. Antonio Senzatela, RHP

LOS ANGELES DODGERS
1. Corey Seager, SS
2. Julio Urias, LHP
3. Jose De Leon, RHP
4. Frankie Montas, RHP
5. Grant Holmes, RHP
6. Cody Bellinger, 1B
7. Yadier Alvarez, RHP
8. Alex Verdugo, OF
9. Jharel Cotton, RHP
10. Austin Barnes, C
11. Starling Heredia, OF
12. Walker Buehler, RHP
13. Chris Anderson, RHP
14. Zach Lee, RHP
15. Micah Johnson, 2B

SAN DIEGO PADRES
1. Hunter Renfroe, OF
2. Manuel Margot, OF
3. Javier Guerra, SS
4. Michael Gettys, OF
5. Colin Rea, RHP
6. Ruddy Giron, SS
7. Travis Jankowski, OF
8. Austin Smith, RHP
9. Enyel de los Santos, RHP
10. Rymer Liriano, OF
11. Cory Mazzoni, RHP
12. Jacob Nix, RHP
13. Dinelson Lamet, RHP
14. Jose Rondon, SS
15. Jose Castillo, LHP

SAN FRANCISCO GIANTS
1. Christian Arroyo, SS
2. Tyler Beede, RHP
3. Phil Bickford, RHP
4. Lucius Fox, SS
5. Samuel Coonrod, RHP
6. Christopher Shaw, 1B
7. Kyle Crick, RHP
8. Clayton Blackburn, RHP
9. Aramis Garcia, C,
10. Adalberto Mejia, LHP
11. Mac Williamson, OF
12. Jalen Miller, SS
13. Steven Okert, LHP
14. Chris Stratton, RHP
15. Ray Black, RHP

TOP PROSPECTS BY POSITION

CATCHER
1. Jorge Alfaro, PHI
2. Willson Contreras, CHC
3. Tyler Stephenson, CIN
4. Gary Sanchez, NYY
5. Chance Sisco, BAL
6. Max Pentecost, TOR
7. Jacob Nottingham, OAK
8. Reese McGuire, PIT
9. Taylor Ward, LAA
10. Aramis Garcia, SF
11. Andrew Knapp, PHI
12. Justin O'Conner, TAM
13. Francisco Mejia, CLE
14. Dom Nunez, COL
15. Tom Murphy, COL

FIRST BASEMEN
1. A.J. Reed, HOU
2. Josh Bell, PIT
3. Dominic Smith, NYM
4. Matt Olson, OAK
5. Josh Naylor, MIA
6. Cody Bellinger, LA
7. D.J. Peterson, SEA
8. Casey Gillaspie, TAM
9. Bobby Bradley, CLE
10. Chris Shaw, SF
11. Sam Travis, BOS
12. Jake Bauers, TAM
13. Trey Mancini, BAL
14. Dan Vogelbach, CHC
15. Rowdy Tellez, TOR

SECOND BASEMEN
1. Yoan Moncada, BOS
2. Jose Peraza, CIN
3. Forrest Wall, COL
4. Alen Hanson, PIT
5. Scott Kingery, PHI
6. Rob Refsnyder, NYY
7. Micah Johnson, LA
8. Tony Kemp, HOU
9. Ryan Brett, TAM
10. Jamie Westbrook, ARI
11. Kean Wong, TAM
12. Joey Wendle, OAK
13. Travis Demeritte, TEX
14. Mauricio Dubon, BOS
15. Sean Coyle, BOS

SHORTSTOP
1. Corey Seager, LA
2. J.P. Crawford, PHI
3. Orlando Arcia, MIL
4. Trea Turner, WAS
5. Brendan Rodgers, COL
6. Dansby Swanson, ATL
7. Alex Bregman, HOU
8. Franklin Barreto, OAK
9. Gleyber Torres, CHC
10. Ozhaino Albies, ATL
11. Raul Mondesi, KC
12. Tim Anderson, CHW
13. Willy Adames, TAM
14. Nick Gordon, MIN
15. Amed Rosario, NYM

THIRD BASEMEN
1. Joey Gallo, TEX
2. Rafael Devers, BOS
3. Ryan McMahon, COL
4. Hector Olivera, ATL
5. Renato Nunez, OAK
6. Jomar Reyes, BAL
7. Matt Chapman, OAK
8. Colin Moran, HOU
9. Richie Shaffer, TAM
10. Brandon Drury, ARI
11. Trey Michalczewski, CHW
12. Ke'Bryan Hayes, PIT
13. Eric Jagielo, CIN
14. Kaleb Cowart, LAA
15. Austin Riley, ATL

OUTFIELDERS
1. Byron Buxton, MIN
2. Bradley Zimmer, CLE
3. Nomar Mazara, TEX
4. Victor Robles, WAS
5. Aaron Judge, NYY
6. Manuel Margot, SD
7. Clint Frazier, CLE
8. Lewis Brinson, TEX
9. Austin Meadows, PIT
10. Nick Williams, PHI
11. David Dahl, COL
12. Brett Phillips, MIL
13. Andrew Benintendi, BOS
14. Jesse Winker, CIN
15. Anthony Alford, TOR
16. Max Kepler, MIN
17. Hunter Renfroe, SD
18. Kyle Tucker, HOU
19. Billy McKinney, CHC
20. Derek Fisher, HOU
21. Raimel Tapia, COL
22. Daz Cameron, HOU
23. Alex Jackson, SEA
24. Garrett Whitley, TAM
25. Trent Clark, MIL
26. Albert Almora, CHC
27. Ian Happ, CHC
28. Roman Quinn, PHI
29. Bubba Starling, KC
30. Brandon Nimmo, NYM
31. Harold Ramirez, PIT
32. Cornelius Randolph, PHI
33. Magneuris Sierra, STL
34. Alex Verdugo, LA
35. Mallex Smith, ATL
36. Mikie Mahtook, TAM
37. Ryan Cordell, TEX
38. Mark Zagunis, CHC
39. Michael Gettys, SD
40. Jairo Beras, TEX
41. Travis Jankowski, SD
42. Tyler Naquin, CLE
43. Adam Brett Walker, MIN
44. Vladimir Guerrero, Jr, TOR
45. Steven Moya, DET

STARTING PITCHERS
1. Lucas Giolito, WAS
2. Alex Reyes, STL
3. Julio Urias, LA
4. Tyler Glasnow, PIT
5. Steven Matz, NYM
6. Jose Berrios, MIN
7. Blake Snell, TAM
8. Jose De Leon, LA
9. Robert Stephenson, CIN
10. Jon Gray, COL
11. Sean Newcomb, ATL
12. Carson Fulmer, CHW
13. Dillon Tate, TEX
14. Jameson Taillon, PIT
15. Archie Bradley, ARI
16. Kolby Allard, ATL
17. Jake Thompson, PHI
18. Dylan Bundy, BAL
19. Anderson Espinoza, BOS
20. Aaron Blair, ATL
21. Jeff Hoffman, COL
22. Brent Honeywell, TAM
23. Tyler Kolek, MIA
24. Mark Appel, PHI
25. Kyle Zimmer, KC
26. Cody Reed, CIN
27. Braden Shipley, ARI
28. Jorge Lopez, MIL
29. Touki Toussaint, ATL
30. Grant Holmes, LA
31. Sean Manaea, OAK
32. Reynaldo Lopez, WAS
33. Hunter Harvey, BAL
34. Luis Ortiz, TEX
35. Brady Aiken, CLE
36. Taylor Guerrieri, TAM
37. Amir Garrett, CIN
38. Tyler Jay, MIN
39. Brian Johnson, BOS
40. Tyler Beede, SF
41. Michael Fulmer, DET
42. Erick Fedde, WAS
43. Rob Kaminsky, CLE
44. Frankie Montas, LA
45. Duane Underwood, CHC
46. Miguel Almonte, KC
47. Jon Harris, TOR
48. Ashe Russell, KC
49. Jack Flaherty, STL
50. Michael Feliz, HOU
51. Nick Travieso, CIN
52. Yadier Alvarez, LA
53. Phil Bickford, SF
54. Luke Weaver, STL
55. Joe Musgrove, HOU
56. Kyle Freeland, COL
57. Keury Mella, CIN
58. Marco Gonzales, STL
59. Sean Reid-Foley, TOR
60. Justus Sheffield, CLE
61. Pierce Johnson, CHC
62. Sam Coonrod, SF
63. Colin Rea, SD
64. Lucas Sims, ATL
65. Michael Kopech, BOS
66. Beau Burrows, DET
67. James Kaprielian, NYY
68. Edwin Diaz, SEA
69. Tim Cooney, STL
70. Clayton Blackburn, SF
71. Michael Clevinger, CLE
72. Jarlin Garcia, MIA
73. Kohl Stewart, MIN
74. Nick Kingham, PIT
75. Domingo Acevedo, NYY

RELIEF PITCHERS
1. Alex Meyer, MIN
2. Miguel Castro, COL
3. Mychal Givens, BAL
4. Luke Jackson, TEX
5. Cory Mazzoni, SD
6. Jacob Lindgren, NYY
7. Corey Black, CHC
8. Joe Jimenez, DET
9. Nick Burdi, MIN
10. Brian Ellington, MIA
11. Shae Simmons, ATL
12. Sam Tuivailala, STL
13. R.J.Alvarez, OAK
14. Chance Adams, NYY
15. Jake Barrett, ARI

TOP PROSPECTS BY SKILLS

2016 TOP FANTASY IMPACT

TOP POWER

Joey Gallo, 3B, TEX
Aaron Judge, OF, NYY
Adam Brett Walker, OF, MIN
Josh Naylor, 1B, MIA
A.J. Reed, 1B, HOU
Ryan McMahon, 3B, COL
Corey Seager, SS, LA
Steven Moya, OF, DET
Brendan Rodgers, SS, COL
Rafael Devers, 3B, BOS
Gary Sanchez, C, NYY
Bobby Bradley, 1B, CLE
Austin Meadows, OF, PIT
Hunter Renfroe, OF, SD
Chris Shaw, 1B, SF
Dan Vogelbach, 1B, CHC
Matt Olson, 1B, OAK
Alex Jackson, OF, SEA
Clint Frazier, OF, CLE
Jesse Winker, OF, CIN
Casey Gillaspie, 1B, TAM
Renato Nunez, 3B, OAK
Josh Bell, 1B, PIT
Andrew Benintendi, OF, BOS
Austin Riley, 3B, ATL

TOP SPEED

Byron Buxton, OF, MIN
Tim Anderson, SS, CHW
Mallex Smith, OF, ATL
Ozhaino Albies, SS, ATL
Jorge Mateo, SS, NYY
Roman Quinn, OF, PHI
Rafael Bautista, OF, WAS
Alen Hanson, 2B, PIT
Tony Kemp, 2B, HOU
Jose Peraza, 2B, CIN
Manuel Margot, OF, SD
Monte Harrison, OF, MIL
Adam Engel, OF, CHW
Derek Hill, OF, DET
Travis Jankowski, OF, SD
Wilmer Difo, SS, WAS
Trea Turner, SS, WAS
Raimel Tapia, OF, COL
Victor Robles, OF, WAS
Yoan Moncada, 2B, BOS
D.J. Davis, OF, TOR
Raul Mondesi, SS, KC
Jacob May, OF, CHW
Anthony Alford, OF, TOR
Orlando Arcia, SS, MIL

TOP BREAKING BALL

Blake Snell, LHP, TAM
Julio Urias, LHP, LA
Lucas Giolito, RHP, WAS
Alex Reyes, RHP, STL
Kyle Zimmer, RHP, KC
Dylan Bundy, RHP, BAL
Steven Matz, LHP, NYM
Dillon Tate, RHP, TEX
Aaron Blair, RHP, ATL
Carson Fulmer, RHP, CHW
Robert Stephenson, RHP, CIN
Jameson Taillon, RHP, PIT
Touki Toussaint, RHP, ATL

TOP BA

Corey Seager, SS, LA
Byron Buxton, OF, MIN
Christian Arroyo, SS, SF
Tim Anderson, SS, CHW
J.P. Crawford, SS, PHI
Dansby Swanson, SS, ATL
Dominic Smith, 1B, NYM
Alex Bregman, SS, HOU
Ozhaino Albies, SS, ATL
Jesse Winker, OF, CIN
Franklin Barreto, SS, OAK
David Dahl, OF, COL
Orlando Arcia, SS, MIL
Max Kepler, OF, MIN
Colin Moran, 3B, HOU
Forrest Wall, 2B, COL
Austin Meadows, OF, PIT
Trent Clark, OF, MIL
Nick Gordon, SS, MIN
Josh Bell, 1B, PIT
Victor Robles, OF, WAS
Trey Mancini, 1B, BAL
Cornelius Randolph, OF, PHI
Kevin Newman, SS, PIT
Billy McKinney, OF, CHC

TOP FASTBALL

Lucas Giolito, RHP, WAS
Tyler Glasnow, RHP, PIT
Alex Reyes, RHP, STL
Kyle Zimmer, RHP, KC
Steven Matz, LHP, NYM
Carson Fulmer, RHP, CHW
Michael Kopech, RHP, BOS
Julio Urias, LHP, LA
Jose De Leon, RHP, LA
Jon Gray, RHP, COL
Robert Stephenson, RHP, CIN
Jameson Taillon, RHP, PIT
Sean Newcomb, LHP, ATL
Jeff Hoffman, RHP, COL
Grant Holmes, RHP, LA
Dillon Tate, RHP, TEX
Jose Berrios, RHP, MIN
Anderson Espinoza, RHP, BOS
Braden Shipley, RHP, ARI
Domingo Acevedo, RHP, NYY
Archie Bradley, RHP, ARI
Frankie Montas, RHP, LA
Tyler Jay, LHP, MIN
Reynaldo Lopez, RHP, WAS
Tyler Kolek, RHP, MIA

Grant Holmes, RHP, LA
Taylor Guerrieri, RHP, TAM
Jon Gray, RHP, COL
Jake Thompson, RHP, PHI
Archie Bradley, RHP, ARI
James Kaprielian, RHP, NYY
Erick Fedde, RHP, WAS
Pierce Johnson, RHP, CHC
Frankie Montas, RHP, LA
Alex Meyer, RHP, MIN
Kolby Allard, LHP, ATL
Rob Kaminsky, LHP, CLE
C.J. Edwards, RHP, CHC

1   Corey Seager (SS, LA)
2   Byron Buxton (OF, MIN)
3   Steven Matz (LHP, NYM)
4   Trea Turner (SS, WAS)
5   Joey Gallo (3B, TEX)
6   Hector Olivera (3B/OF, ATL)
7   J.P. Crawford (SS, PHI)
8   Jose Berrios (RHP, MIN)
9   Blake Snell (LHP, TAM)
10 Tyler Glasnow (RHP, PIT)
11 Orlando Arcia (SS, MIL)
12 Lucas Giolito (RHP, WAS)
13 Jose Peraza (2B, CIN)
14 Alex Reyes (RHP, STL)
15 Robert Stephenson (RHP, CIN)

16 Nomar Mazara (OF, TEX)
17 Archie Bradley (RHP, ARI)
18 Tim Anderson (SS, CHW)
19 Trevor Story (SS, COL)
20 A.J. Reed (1B, HOU)
21 Nick Williams (OF, PHI)
22 Josh Bell (1B, PIT)
23 Julio Urias (LHP, LA)
24 Jake Thompson (RHP, PHI)
25 Lewis Brinson (OF, TEX)
26 Pete O'Brien (OF, ARI)
27 Aaron Judge (OF, NYY)
28 Brett Phillips (OF, MIL)
29 Brian Johnson (LHP, BOS)
30 Sean Newcomb (LHP, ATL)

31 Richie Shaffer (3B, TAM)
32 Mikie Mahtook (OF, TAM)
33 Dylan Bundy (RHP, BAL)
34 Jesse Winker (OF, CIN)
35 Mark Appel (RHP, PHI)
36 Hunter Renfroe (OF, SD)
37 Brandon Drury (2B/3B, ARI)
38 Manuel Margot (OF, SD)

39 Jameson Taillon (RHP, PIT)
40 Frankie Montas (RHP, LA)
41 Jorge Polanco (SS, MIN)
42 Jon Gray (RHP, COL)
43 Marco Gonzales (LHP, STL)
44 David Dahl (OF, COL)
45 Alen Hanson (2B, PIT)

46 Bradley Zimmer (OF, CLE)
47 Tommy Murphy (C, COL)
48 Aaron Blair (RHP, ATL)
49 Miguel Almonte (RHP, KC)
50 Roman Quinn (OF, PHI)
51 Max Kepler (OF, MIN)
52 A.J. Cole (RHP, WAS)
53 Billy McKinney (OF, CHC)
54 Michael Fulmer (RHP, DET)
55 Micah Johnson (2B, LA)
56 Braden Shipley (RHP, ARI)
57 Jose De Leon (RHP, LA)
58 Alex Meyer (RHP, MIN)
59 Colin Rea (RHP, SD)
60 Albert Almora (OF, CHC)

61 Manny Banuelos (LHP, ATL)
62 Daniel Robertson (SS, TAM)
63 Steven Moya (OF, DET)
64 Gary Sanchez (C, NYY)
65 Zach Davies (RHP, MIL)
66 Sean Manaea (LHP, OAK)
67 Matt Olson (1B, OAK)
68 Gavin Cecchini (SS, NYM)
69 John Lamb (LHP, CIN)
70 Jorge Lopez (RHP, MIL)
71 Trayce Thompson (OF, CHW)
72 Willson Contreras (C, CHC)
73 Mallex Smith (OF, ATL)
74 Jeff Hoffman (RHP, COL)
75 Robert Refsnyder (2B, NYY)

TOP 100 PROSPECTS ARCHIVE

2015

1. Kris Bryant (3B, CHC)
2. Byron Buxton (OF, MIN)
3. Carlos Correa (SS, HOU)
4. Addison Russell (SS, CHC)
5. Corey Seager (SS, LAD)
6. Francisco Lindor (SS, CLE)
7. Joc Pederson (OF, LAD)
8. Miguel Sano (3B, MIN)
9. Lucas Giolito (P, WAS)
10. Joey Gallo (3B, TEX)

11. Dylan Bundy (P, BAL)
12. Jorge Soler (OF, CHC)
13. Archie Bradley (P, ARI)
14. Julio Urias (P, LAD)
15. Jon Gray (P, COL)
16. Daniel Norris (P, TOR)
17. Carlos Rodon (P, CHW)
18. Tyler Glasnow (P, PIT)
19. Noah Syndergaard (P, NYM)
20. Blake Swihart (C, BOS)

21. Aaron Sanchez (P, TOR)
22. Henry Owens (P, BOS)
23. Jameson Taillon (P, PIT)
24. Robert Stephenson (P, CIN)
25. Andrew Heaney (P, LAA)
26. David Dahl (OF, COL)
27. Jose Berrios (P, MIN)
28. Jorge Alfaro (C, TEX)
29. Hunter Harvey (P, BAL)
30. Alex Meyer (P, MIN)

31. Kohl Stewart (P, MIN)
32. J.P. Crawford (SS, PHI)
33. Alex Jackson (OF, SEA)
34. Jesse Winker (OF, CIN)
35. Raul Mondesi (SS, KC)
36. D.J. Peterson (3B, SEA)
37. Austin Meadows (OF, PIT)
38. Josh Bell (OF, PIT)
39. Kyle Crick (P, SF)
40. Luis Severino (P, NYY)

41. Nick Gordon (SS, MIN)
42. Kyle Schwarber (OF, CHC)
43. Aaron Nola (P, PHI)
44. Kyle Zimmer (P, KC)
45. Alex Reyes (P, STL)
46. Braden Shipley (P, ARI)
47. Albert Almora (OF, CHC)
48. Clint Frazier (OF, CLE)
49. Tyler Kolek (P, MIA)
50. Mark Appel (P, HOU)

51. Rusney Castillo (OF, BOS)
52. Sean Manaea (P, KC)
53. A.J. Cole (P, WAS)
54. Matt Wisler (P, SD)
55. Raimel Tapia (OF, COL)
56. C.J. Edwards (P, CHC)
57. Dalton Pompey (OF, TOR)
58. Hunter Renfroe (OF, SD)
59. Hunter Dozier (3B, KC)
60. Brandon Nimmo (OF, NYM)

61. Tim Anderson (SS, CHW)
62. Maikel Franco (3B, PHI)
63. Mike Foltynewicz (P, HOU)
64. Nick Kingham (P, PIT)
65. Eddie Butler (P, COL)
66. Steven Matz (P, NYM)
67. Domingo Santana (OF, HOU)
68. Aaron Judge (OF, NYY)
69. Daniel Robertson (SS, OAK)
70. Stephen Piscotty (OF, STL)

71. Kyle Freeland (P, COL)
72. Kevin Plawecki (C, NYM)
73. Lucas Sims (P, ATL)
74. Yasmany Tomas (OF, ARI)
75. Jose Peraza (2B, ATL)
76. Eduardo Rodriguez (P, BOS)
77. Max Fried (P, ATL)
78. Manuel Margot (OF, BOS)
79. Matt Olson (1B, OAK)
80. Ryan McMahon (3B, COL)

81. Alex Gonzalez (P, TEX)
82. Tyler Beede (P, SF)
83. Alen Hanson (SS, PIT)
84. Grant Holmes (P, LAD)
85. Aaron Blair (P, ARI)
86. Michael Taylor (OF, WAS)
87. Trea Turner (SS, SD/WAS)
88. Christian Bethancourt (C, ATL)
89. Marco Gonzales (P, STL)
90. Michael Conforto (OF, NYM)

91. Sean Newcomb (P, LAA)
92. Alex Colome (P, TAM)
93. Jeff Hoffman (P, TOR)
94. Luke Jackson (P, TEX)
95. Lewis Brinson (OF, TEX)
96. Willy Adames (SS, TAM)
97. Jake Thompson (P, TEX)
98. Nick Williams (OF, TEX)
99. Colin Moran (3B, HOU)
100. Bradley Zimmer (OF, CLE)

2014

1. Byron Buxton (OF, MIN)
2. Oscar Taveras (OF, STL)
3. Xander Bogaerts (SS, BOS)
4. Taijuan Walker (RHP, SEA)
5. Miguel Sano (3B, MIN)
6. Francisco Lindor (SS, CLE)
7. Javier Baez (SS, CHC)
8. Archie Bradley (RHP, ARI)
9. Carlos Correa (SS, HOU)
10. Gregory Polanco (OF, PIT)

11. Addison Russell (SS, OAK)
12. Jameson Taillon (RHP, PIT)
13. Kris Bryant (3B, CHC)
14. Dylan Bundy (RHP, BAL)
15. George Springer (OF, HOU)
16. Nick Castellanos (3B, DET)
17. Noah Syndergaard (RHP, NYM)
18. Kevin Gausman (RHP, BAL)
19. Carlos Martinez (RHP, STL)
20. Robert Stephenson (RHP, CIN)

21. Yordano Ventura (RHP, KC)
22. Jonathan Gray (RHP, COL)
23. Kyle Zimmer (RHP, KC)
24. Albert Almora (OF, CHC)
25. Mark Appel (RHP, HOU)
26. Aaron Sanchez (RHP, TOR)
27. Travis d'Arnaud (C, NYM)
28. Kyle Crick (RHP, SF)
29. Joc Pederson (OF, LA)
30. Alex Meyer (RHP, MIN)

31. Garin Cecchini (3B, BOS)
32. Jorge Soler (OF, CHC)
33. Jonathan Singleton (1B, HOU)
34. Maikel Franco (3B, PHI)
35. Lucas Giolito (RHP, WAS)
36. Eddie Butler (RHP, COL)
37. Andrew Heaney (LHP, MIA)
38. Jackie Bradley (OF, BOS)
39. Taylor Guerrieri (RHP, TAM)
40. Corey Seager (SS, LA)

41. Adalberto Mondesi (SS, KC)
42. Billy Hamilton (OF, CIN)
43. Clint Frazier (OF, CLE)
44. Tyler Glasnow (RHP, PIT)
45. Kolten Wong (2B, STL)
46. Henry Owens (LHP, BOS)
47. Gary Sanchez (C, NYY)
48. Jorge Alfaro (C, TEX)
49. Austin Meadows (OF, PIT)
50. Austin Hedges (C, SD)

51. Alen Hanson (SS, PIT)
52. Marcus Stroman (RHP, TOR)
53. Kohl Stewart (RHP, MIN)
54. Max Fried (LHP, SD)
55. Jake Odorizzi (RHP, TAM)
56. Michael Choice (OF, TEX)
57. C.J. Edwards (RHP, CHC)
58. Trevor Bauer (RHP, CLE)
59. Julio Urias (LHP, LA)
60. Jake Marisnick (OF, MIA)

61. Jesse Biddle (LHP, PHI)
62. Eddie Rosario (2B, MIN)
63. Lucas Sims (RHP, ATL)
64. Lance McCullers (RHP, HOU)
65. A.J. Cole (RHP, WAS)
66. Rougned Odor (2B, TEX)
67. Colin Moran (3B, MIA)
68. Mike Foltynewicz (RHP, HOU)
69. Allen Webster (RHP, BOS)
70. Chris Owings (SS, ARI)

71. Eduardo Rodriguez (LHP, BAL)
72. Miguel Almonte (RHP, KC)
73. Blake Swihart (C, BOS)
74. Jose Abreu (1B, CHW)
75. Zach Lee (RHP, LA)
76. Danny Hultzen (LHP, SEA)
77. Matt Wisler (RHP, SD)
78. Matt Barnes (RHP, BOS)
79. James Paxton (LHP, SEA)
80. Rosell Herrera (SS, COL)

81. Erik Johnson (RHP, CHW)
82. David Dahl (OF, COL)
83. Hak-Ju Lee (SS, TAM)
84. D.J. Peterson (3B, SEA)
85. Luke Jackson (RHP, TEX)
86. Delino DeShields (OF, HOU)
87. Brian Goodwin (OF, WAS)
88. Hunter Dozier (SS, KC)
89. Matt Davidson (3B, CHW)
90. Anthony Ranaudo (RHP, BOS)

91. Jimmy Nelson (RHP, MIL)
92. Bubba Starling (OF, KC)
93. Christian Bethancourt (C, ATL)
94. Courtney Hawkins (OF, CHW)
95. Domingo Santana (OF, HOU)
96. Kaleb Cowart (3B, LAA)
97. Jose Berrios (RHP, MIN)
98. Braden Shipley (RHP, ARI)
99. Justin Nicolino (LHP, MIA)
100. Alex Colome (RHP, TAM)

TOP 100 PROSPECTS ARCHIVE

2013

1. Jurickson Profar (SS, TEX)
2. Dylan Bundy (RHP, BAL)
3. Wil Myers (OF, TAM)
4. Gerrit Cole (RHP, PIT)
5. Oscar Taveras (OF, STL)
6. Taijuan Walker (RHP, SEA)
7. Trevor Bauer (RHP, CLE)
8. Jose Fernandez (RHP, MIA)
9. Travis d'Arnaud (C, NYM)
10. Miguel Sano (3B, MIN)

11. Zack Wheeler (RHP, NYM)
12. Christian Yelich (OF, MIA)
13. Tyler Skaggs (LHP, ARI)
14. Francisco Lindor (SS, CLE)
15. Javier Baez (SS, CHC)
16. Shelby Miller (RHP, STL)
17. Nick Castellanos (OF, DET)
18. Xander Bogaerts (SS, BOS)
19. Jameson Taillon (RHP, PIT)
20. Danny Hultzen (LHP, SEA)

21. Jonathan Singleton (1B, HOU)
22. Mike Zunino (C, SEA)
23. Billy Hamilton (OF, CIN)
24. Anthony Rendon (3B, WAS)
25. Mike Olt (3B, TEX)
26. Byron Buxton (OF, MIN)
27. Nolan Arenado (3B, COL)
28. Carlos Correa (SS, HOU)
29. Archie Bradley (RHP, ARI)
30. Julio Teheran (RHP, ATL)

31. Matt Barnes (RHP, BOS)
32. Gary Sanchez (C, NYY)
33. Jackie Bradley (OF, BOS)
34. Carlos Martinez (RHP, STL)
35. Bubba Starling (OF, KC)
36. Jake Odorizzi (RHP, TAM)
37. Jedd Gyorko (3B, SD)
38. Alen Hanson (SS, PIT)
39. George Springer (OF, HOU)
40. Nick Franklin (2B, SEA)

41. Aaron Sanchez (RHP, TOR)
42. Albert Almora (OF, CHC)
43. Kaleb Cowart (3B, LAA)
44. Taylor Guerrieri (RHP, TAM)
45. Kyle Zimmer (RHP, KC)
46. Noah Syndergaard (RHP, NYM)
47. Kolten Wong (2B, STL)
48. Tyler Austin (OF, NYY)
49. James Paxton (LHP, SEA)
50. Rymer Liriano (OF, SD)

51. Jake Marisnick (OF, MIA)
52. Trevor Story (SS, COL)
53. Kevin Gausman (RHP, BAL)
54. Trevor Rosenthal (RHP, STL)
55. Alex Meyer (RHP, MIN)
56. Jorge Soler (OF, CHC)
57. Matt Davidson (3B, ARI)
58. Brett Jackson (OF, CHC)
59. Michael Choice (OF, OAK)
60. David Dahl (OF, COL)

61. Mason Williams (OF, NYY)
62. Robert Stephenson (RHP, CIN)
63. Chris Archer (RHP, TAM)
64. Oswaldo Arcia (OF, MIN)
65. Zach Lee (RHP, LA)
66. Tony Cingrani (LHP, CIN)
67. Jesse Biddle (LHP, PHI)
68. Gregory Polanco (OF, PIT)
69. Addison Russell (SS, OAK)
70. Robbie Erlin (RHP, SD)

71. Courtney Hawkins (OF, CHW)
72. Brian Goodwin (OF, WAS)
73. Martin Perez (LHP, TEX)
74. Luis Heredia (RHP, PIT)
75. Yasiel Puig (OF, LA)
76. Wilmer Flores (3B, NYM)
77. Justin Nicolino (LHP, MIA)
78. Max Fried (LHP, SD)
79. Adam Eaton (OF, ARI)
80. Gary Brown (OF, SF)

81. Casey Kelly (RHP, SD)
82. Lucas Giolito (RHP, WAS)
83. Wily Peralta (RHP, MIL)
84. Michael Wacha (RHP, STL)
85. Austin Hedges (C, SD)
86. Kyle Gibson (RHP, MIN)
87. Hak-Ju Lee (SS, TAM)
88. Dan Straily (RHP, OAK)
89. Kyle Crick (RHP, SF)
90. Avisail Garcia (OF, DET)

91. Cody Buckel (RHP, TEX)
92. Tyler Thornburg (RHP, MIL)
93. Allen Webster (RHP, BOS)
94. Jarred Cosart (RHP, HOU)
95. Bruce Rondon (RHP, DET)
96. Delino DeShields (2B, HOU)
97. A.J. Cole (RHP, OAK)
98. Manny Banuelos (LHP, NYY)
99. Yordano Ventura (RHP, KC)
100. Trevor May (RHP, MIN)

2012

1. Bryce Harper (OF, WAS)
2. Matt Moore (LHP, TAM)
3. Mike Trout (OF, LAA)
4. Julio Teheran (RHP, ATL)
5. Jesus Montero (C, NYY)
6. Jurickson Profar (SS, TEX)
7. Manny Machado (SS, BAL)
8. Gerrit Cole (RHP, PIT)
9. Devin Mesoraco (C, CIN)
10. Wil Myers (OF, KC)

11. Miguel Sano (3B, MIN)
12. Jacob Turner (RHP, DET)
13. Anthony Rendon (3B, WAS)
14. Trevor Bauer (RHP, ARI)
15. Nolan Arenado (3B , COL)
16. Jameson Taillon (RHP, PIT)
17. Shelby Miller (RHP, STL)
18. Dylan Bundy (RHP, BAL)
19. Brett Jackson (OF, CHC)
20. Drew Pomeranz (LHP, COL)

21. Martin Perez (LHP, TEX)
22. Yonder Alonso (1B, SD)
23. Taijuan Walker (RHP, SEA)
24. Danny Hultzen (LHP, SEA)
25. Gary Brown (OF, SF)
26. Anthony Rizzo (1B, CHC)
27. Bubba Starling (OF, KC)
28. Travis d'Arnaud (C, TOR)
29. Mike Montgomery (LHP, KC)
30. Jake Odorizzi (RHP, KC)

31. Hak-Ju Lee (SS, TAM)
32. Jonathan Singleton (1B, HOU)
33. Garrett Richards (RHP, LAA)
34. Manny Banuelos (LHP, NYY)
35. James Paxton (LHP, SEA)
36. Jarrod Parker (RHP, OAK)
37. Carlos Martinez (RHP, STL)
38. Jake Marisnick (OF, TOR)
39. Yasmani Grandal (C, SD)
40. Trevor May (RHP, PHI)

41. Gary Sanchez (C, NYY)
42. Mike Olt (3B, TEX)
43. Wilin Rosario (C, COL)
44. John Lamb (LHP, KC)
45. Francisco Lindor (SS, CLE)
46. Dellin Betances (RHP, NYY)
47. Michael Choice (OF, OAK)
48. Arodys Vizcaino (RHP, ATL)
49. Trayvon Robinson (OF, SEA)
50. Matt Harvey (RHP, NYM)

51. Will Middlebrooks (3B, BOS)
52. Jedd Gyorko (3B, SD)
53. Randall Delgado (RHP, ATL)
54. Zack Wheeler (RHP, NYM)
55. Zach Lee (RHP, LA)
56. Tyler Skaggs (LHP, ARI)
57. Nick Castellanos (3B, DET)
58. Robbie Erlin (LHP, SD)
59. Christian Yelich (OF, MIA)
60. Anthony Gose (OF, TOR)

61. Addison Reed (RHP, CHW)
62. Javier Baez (SS, CHC)
63. Starling Marte (OF, PIT)
64. Kaleb Cowart (3B, LAA)
65. George Springer (OF, HOU)
66. Jarred Cosart (RHP, HOU)
67. Jean Segura (2B, LAA)
68. Kolten Wong (2B, STL)
69. Nick Franklin (SS, SEA)
70. Alex Torres (RHP, TAM)

71. Rymer Liriano (OF, SD)
72. Josh Bell (OF, PIT)
73. Leonys Martin (OF, TEX)
74. Joe Wieland (RHP, SD)
75. Joe Benson (OF, MIN)
76. Wily Peralta (RHP, MIL)
77. Tim Wheeler (OF, COL)
78. Oscar Taveras (OF, STL)
79. Xander Bogaerts (SS, BOS)
80. Archie Bradley (RHP, ARI)

81. Kyle Gibson (RHP, MIN)
82. Allen Webster (RHP, LA)
83. C.J. Cron (1B, LAA)
84. Grant Green (OF, OAK)
85. Brad Peacock (RHP, OAK)
86. Chris Dwyer (LHP, KC)
87. Billy Hamilton (SS, CIN)
88. A.J. Cole (RHP, OAK)
89. Aaron Hicks (OF, MIN)
90. Noah Syndergaard (RHP, TOR)

91. Tyrell Jenkins (RHP, STL)
92. Anthony Ranaudo (RHP, BOS)
93. Jed Bradley (LHP, MIL)
94. Nathan Eovaldi (RHP, LA)
95. Andrelton Simmons (SS, ATL)
96. Taylor Guerrieri (RHP, TAM)
97. Cheslor Cuthbert (3B, KC)
98. Edward Salcedo (3B, ATL)
99. Domingo Santana, OF, HOU)
100. Jesse Biddle (LHP, PHI)

TOP 100 PROSPECTS ARCHIVE

2011

1. Bryce Harper (OF, WAS)
2. Domonic Brown (OF, PHI)
3. Jesus Montero (C, NYY)
4. Mike Trout (OF, LAA)
5. Jeremy Hellickson (RHP, TAM)
6. Aroldis Chapman (LHP, CIN)
7. Eric Hosmer (1B, KC)
8. Dustin Ackley (2B, SEA)
9. Desmond Jennings (OF, TAM)
10. Julio Teheran (RHP, ATL)

11. Mike Moustakas (3B, KC)
12. Brandon Belt (1B, SF)
13. Freddie Freeman (1B, ATL)
14. Michael Pineda (RHP, SEA)
15. Matt Moore (LHP, TAM)
16. Mike Montgomery (LHP, KC)
17. Brett Jackson (OF, CHC)
18. Nick Franklin (SS, SEA)
19. Jameson Taillon (RHP, PIT)
20. Jacob Turner (RHP, DET)

21. Shelby Miller (RHP, STL)
22. Martin Perez (LHP, TEX)
23. Wil Myers (C, KC)
24. Kyle Gibson (RHP, MIN)
25. Lonnie Chisenhall (3B, CLE)
26. Tyler Matzek (LHP, COL)
27. Brett Lawrie (2B, TOR)
28. Yonder Alonso (1B, CIN)
29. Jarrod Parker (RHP, ARI)
30. Jonathan Singleton (1B, PHI)

31. Tanner Scheppers (RHP,TEX)
32. Kyle Drabek (RHP, TOR)
33. Jason Knapp (RHP, CLE)
34. Manny Banuelos (LHP, NYY)
35. Alex White (RHP, CLE)
36. Jason Kipnis (2B, CLE)
37. Wilin Rosario (C, COL)
38. Manny Machado (SS, BAL)
39. Chris Sale (LHP, CHW)
40. Devin Mesoraco (C, CIN)

41. Tyler Chatwood (RHP, LAA)
42. John Lamb (LHP, KC)
43. Danny Duffy (LHP, KC)
44. Trevor May (RHP, PHI)
45. Mike Minor (LHP, ATL)
46. Jarred Cosart (RHP, PHI)
47. Tony Sanchez (C, PIT)
48. Brody Colvin (RHP, PHI)
49. Zach Britton (LHP, BAL)
50. Dee Gordon (SS, LA)

51. Miguel Sano (3B, MIN)
52. Grant Green (SS, OAK)
53. Danny Espinosa (SS, WAS)
54. Simon Castro (RHP, SD)
55. Derek Norris (C, WAS)
56. Chris Archer (RHP, CHC)
57. Jurickson Profar (SS, TEX)
58. Zack Cox (3B, STL)
59. Billy Hamilton (2B, CIN)
60. Gary Sanchez (C, NYY)

61. Zach Lee (RHP, LA)
62. Drew Pomeranz (LHP, CLE)
63. Randall Delgado (RHP, ATL)
64. Michael Choice (OF, OAK)
65. Nick Weglarz (OF, CLE)
66. Nolan Arenado (3B, COL)
67. Chris Carter (1B/OF, OAK)
68. Arodys Vizcaino (RHP, ATL)
69. Trey McNutt (RHP, CHC)
70. Dellin Betances (RHP, NYY)

71. Aaron Hicks (OF, MIN)
72. Aaron Crow (RHP, KC)
73. Jake McGee (LHP, TAM)
74. Lars Anderson (1B, BOS)
75. Fabio Martinez (RHP, LAA)
76. Ben Revere (OF, MIN)
77. Jordan Lyles (RHP, HOU)
78. Casey Kelly (RHP, SD)
79. Trayvon Robinson (OF, LA)
80. Craig Kimbrel (RHP, ATL)

81. Jose Iglesias (SS, BOS)
82. Garrett Richards (RHP, LAA)
83. Allen Webster (RHP, LA)
84. Chris Dwyer (LHP, KC)
85. Alex Colome (RHP, TAM)
86. Zack Wheeler (RHP, SF)
87. Andy Oliver (LHP, DET)
88. Andrew Brackman (RHP,NYY)
89. Wilmer Flores (SS, NYM)
90. Christian Friedrich (LHP, COL)

91. Anthony Ranaudo (RHP, BOS)
92. Aaron Miller (LHP, LA)
93. Matt Harvey (RHP, NYM)
94. Mark Rogers (RHP, MIL)
95. Jean Segura (2B, LAA)
96. Hank Conger (C, LAA)
97. J.P. Arencibia (C, TOR)
98. Matt Dominguez (3B, FLA)
99. Jerry Sands (1B, LA)
100. Nick Castellanos (3B, DET)

2010

1. Stephen Strasburg (RHP, WAS)
2. Jason Heyward (OF, ATL)
3. Jesus Montero (C, NYY)
4. Buster Posey (C, SF)
5. Justin Smoak (1B, TEX)
6. Pedro Alvarez (3B, PIT)
7. Carlos Santana (C, CLE)
8. Desmond Jennings (OF, TAM)
9. Brian Matusz (LHP, BAL)
10. Neftali Feliz (RHP, TEX)

11. Brett Wallace (3B, TOR)
12. Mike Stanton (OF. FLA)
13. M. Bumgarner (LHP, SF)
14. J. Hellickson (RHP, TAM)
15. Dustin Ackley (1B/OF, SEA)
16. Aroldis Chapman (LHP, CIN)
17. Yonder Alonso (1B, CIN)
18. Alcides Escobar (SS, MIL)
19. Brett Lawrie (2B, MIL)
20. Starlin Castro (SS, CHC)

21. Logan Morrison (1B, FLA)
22. Mike Montgomery (LHP, KC)
23. Domonic Brown (OF, PHI)
24. Josh Vitters (3B, CHC)
25. R. Westmoreland (OF, BOS)
26. Todd Frazier (3B/OF, CIN)
27. Eric Hosmer (1B, KC)
28. Freddie Freeman (1B, ATL)
29. Derek Norris (C, WAS)
30. Martin Perez (LHP, TEX)

31. Wade Davis (RHP, TAM)
32. Trevor Reckling (LHP, LAA)
33. Jordan Walden (RHP, LAA)
34. Mat Gamel (3B, MIL)
35. Tyler Flowers (C, CHW)
36. T. Scheppers (RHP, TEX)
37. Casey Crosby (LHP, DET)
38. Austin Jackson (OF, DET)
39. Devaris Gordon (SS, LA)
40. Kyle Drabek (RHP, TOR)

41. Ben Revere (OF, MIN)
42. Michael Taylor (OF, OAK)
43. Jacob Turner (RHP, DET)
44. Tim Beckham (SS, TAM)
45. Carlos Triunfel (SS, SEA)
46. Aaron Crow (RHP, KC)
47. Matt Moore (LHP, TAM)
48. Jarrod Parker (RHP, ARI)
49. F. Martinez (OF, NYM)
50. C. Friedrich (LHP, COL)

51. Jenrry Mejia (RHP, NYM)
52. Tyler Matzek (LHP, COL)
53. Brett Jackson (OF, CHC)
54. Aaron Hicks (OF, MIN)
55. Jhoulys Chacin (RHP, COL)
56. Josh Bell (3B, BAL)
57. Brandon Allen (1B, ARI)
58. Chris Carter (1B, OAK)
59. Jason Knapp (RHP, CLE)
60. Danny Duffy (LHP, KC)

61. Tim Alderson (RHP, PIT)
62. Matt Dominguez (3B, FLA)
63. Mike Moustakas (3B, KC)
64. Jake Arrieta (RHP, BAL)
65. Carlos Carrasco (RHP, CLE)
66. Wilmer Flores (SS, NYM)
67. Drew Storen (RHP, WAS)
68. Lonnie Chisenhall (3B, CLE)
69. Aaron Poreda (LHP, SD)
70. A. Cashner (RHP, CHC)

71. Tony Sanchez (C, PIT)
72. Julio Teheran (RHP, ATL)
73. Jose Tabata (OF, PIT)
74. Jason Castro (C, HOU)
75. Casey Kelly (RHP, BOS)
76. Alex White (RHP, CLE)
77. Jay Jackson (RHP, CHC)
78. Dan Hudson (RHP, CHW)
79. Brandon Erbe (RHP, BAL)
80. Zack Wheeler (RHP, SF)

81. Shelby Miller (RHP, STL)
82. Jordan Lyles (RHP, HOU)
83. Simon Castro (RHP, SD)
84. Aaron Miller (LHP, LA)
85. Michael Ynoa (RHP, OAK)
86. Ethan Martin (RHP, LA)
87. Scott Elbert (LHP, LA)
88. Nick Weglarz (OF, CLE)
89. Donavan Tate (OF, SD)
90. Jordan Danks (OF, CHW)

91. Hector Rondon (RHP, CLE)
92. Chris Heisey (OF, CIN)
93. Kyle Gibson (RHP, MIN)
94. Mike Leake (RHP, CIN)
95. Mike Trout (OF, LAA)
96. Jake McGee (LHP, TAM)
97. Chad James (LHP, FLA)
98. C. Bethancourt (C, NYY)
99. Miguel Sano (SS, MIN)
100. Noel Arguelles (LHP, KC)

TOP 100 PROSPECTS ARCHIVE

2009

1. Matt Wieters (C, BAL)
2. David Price (LHP, TAM)
3. Rick Porcello (RHP, DET)
4. Colby Rasmus (OF, STL)
5. Madison Bumgarner (LHP, SF)
6. Neftali Feliz (RHP, TEX)
7. Jason Heyward (OF, ATL)
8. Andrew McCutchen (OF, PIT)
9. Pedro Alvarez (3B, PIT)
10. Cameron Maybin (OF, FLA)
11. Trevor Cahill (RHP, OAK)
12. Mike Moustakas (3B/SS, KC)
13. Jordan Zimmermann (RHP, WAS)
14. Travis Snider (OF, TOR)
15. Tim Beckham (SS, TAM)
16. Eric Hosmer (1B, KC)
17. Tommy Hanson (RHP, ATL)
18. Dexter Fowler (OF, COL)
19. Brett Anderson (LHP, OAK)
20. Carlos Triunfel (SS/2B, SEA)
21. Buster Posey (C, SF)
22. Chris Tillman (RHP, BAL)
23. Brian Matusz (LHP, BAL)
24. Justin Smoak (1B, TEX)
25. Jarrod Parker (RHP, ARI)
26. Derek Holland (LHP, TEX)
27. Lars Anderson (1B, BOS)
28. Michael Inoa (RHP, OAK)
29. Mike Stanton (OF, FLA)
30. Taylor Teagarden (C, TEX)
31. Gordon Beckham (SS, CHW)
32. Brett Wallace (3B, STL)
33. Matt LaPorta (OF, CLE)
34. Jordan Schafer (OF, ATL)
35. Carlos Santana (C, CLE)
36. Aaron Hicks (OF, MIN)
37. Adam Miller (RHP, CLE)
38. Elvis Andrus (SS, TEX)
39. Alcides Escobar (SS, MIL)
40. Wade Davis (RHP, TAM)
41. Austin Jackson (OF, NYY)
42. Jesus Montero (C, NYY)
43. Tim Alderson (RHP, SF)
44. Jhoulys Chacin (RHP, COL)
45. Phillippe Aumont (RHP, SEA)
46. James McDonald (RHP, LA)
47. Reid Brignac (SS, TAM)
48. Desmond Jennings (OF, TAM)
49. Fernando Martinez (OF, NYM)
50. JP Arencibia (C, TOR)

51. Wilmer Flores (SS, NYM)
52. Brett Cecil (LHP, TOR)
53. Aaron Poreda (LHP, CHW)
54. Jeremy Jeffress (RHP, MIL)
55. Michael Main (RHP, TEX)
56. Josh Vitters (3B, CHC)
57. Mat Gamel (3B, MIL)
58. Yonder Alonso (1B, CIN)
59. Gio Gonzalez (LHP, OAK)
60. Michael Bowden (RHP, BOS)
61. Angel Villalona (1B, SF)
62. Carlos Carrasco (RHP, PHI)
63. Jake Arrieta (RHP, BAL)
64. Jordan Walden (RHP, LAA)
65. Freddie Freeman (1B, ATL)
66. Logan Morrison (1B, FLA)
67. Shooter Hunt (RHP, MIN)
68. Junichi Tazawa (RHP, BOS)
69. Nick Adenhart (RHP, LAA)
70. Jose Tabata (OF, PIT)
71. Adrian Cardenas (SS/2B, OAK)
72. Chris Carter (3B/OF, OAK)
73. Ben Revere (OF, MIN)
74. Josh Reddick (OF, BOS)
75. Jeremy Hellickson (RHP, TAM)
76. Justin Jackson (SS, TOR)
77. Wilson Ramos (C, MIN)
78. Jason Castro (C, HOU)
79. Julio Borbon (OF, TEX)
80. Tyler Flowers (C, CHW)
81. Gorkys Hernandez (OF, ATL)
82. Neftali Soto (3B, CIN)
83. Henry Rodriguez (RHP, OAK)
84. Dan Duffy (LHP, KC)
85. Daniel Cortes (RHP, KC)
86. Dayan Viciedo (3B, CHW)
87. Matt Dominguez (3B, FLA)
88. Jordan Danks (OF, CHW)
89. Chris Coghlan (2B, FLA)
90. Brian Bogusevic (OF, HOU)
91. Ryan Tucker (RHP, FLA)
92. Jonathon Niese (LHP, NYM)
93. Martin Perez (LHP, TEX)
94. James Simmons (RHP, OAK)
95. Nick Weglarz (OF/1B, CLE)
96. Daniel Bard (RHP, BOS)
97. Yamaico Navarro (SS, BOS)
98. Jose Ceda (RHP, FLA)
99. Jeff Samardzija (RHP, CHC)
100. Jason Donald (SS, PHI)

2008

1. Jay Bruce (OF, CIN)
2. Evan Longoria (3B, TAM)
3. Clay Buchholz (RHP, BOS)
4. Clayton Kershaw (LHP, LAD)
5. Joba Chamberlain (RHP, NYY)
6. Colby Rasmus (OF, STL)
7. Cameron Maybin (OF, FLA)
8. Homer Bailey (RHP, CIN)
9. David Price (LHP, TAM)
10. Andrew McCutchen (OF, PIT)
11. Brandon Wood (3B/SS, LAA)
12. Matt Wieters (C, BAL)
13. Jacoby Ellsbury (OF, BOS)
14. Travis Snider (OF, TOR)
15. Reid Brignac (SS, TAM)
16. Jacob McGee (LHP, TAM)
17. Wade Davis (RHP, TAM)
18. Adam Miller (RHP, CLE)
19. Rick Porcello (RHP, DET)
20. Franklin Morales (LHP, COL)
21. Carlos Triunfel (SS, SEA)
22. Andy LaRoche (3B/OF, LAD)
23. Jordan Schafer (OF, ATL)
24. Kosuke Fukodome (OF, CHC)
25. Jose Tabata (OF, NYY)
26. Carlos Gonzalez (OF, OAK)
27. Joey Votto (1B/OF, CIN)
28. Daric Barton (1B, OAK)
29. Angel Villalona (3B, SF)
30. Eric Hurley (RHP, TEX)
31. Nick Adenhart (RHP, LAA)
32. Fernando Martinez (OF, NYM)
33. Ross Detwiler (LHP, WAS)
34. Johnny Cueto (RHP, CIN)
35. Chris Marrero (OF, WAS)
36. Jason Heyward (OF, ATL)
37. Mike Moustakas (SS, KC)
38. Elvis Andrus (SS, TEX)
39. Taylor Teagarden (C, TEX)
40. Ian Kennedy (RHP, NYY)
41. Kasey Kiker (LHP, TEX)
42. Scott Elbert (LHP, LAD)
43. Justin Masterson (RHP, BOS)
44. Max Scherzer (RHP, ARI)
45. Brandon Jones (OF, ATL)
46. Josh Vitters (3B, CHC)
47. Jarrod Parker (RHP, ARI)
48. Matt Antonelli (2B, SD)
49. Gio Gonzalez (LHP, CHW)
50. Ian Stewart (3B, COL)

51. Chase Headley (3B, SD)
52. Anthony Swarzak (RHP, MIN)
53. Jair Jurrjens (RHP, DET)
54. Billy Rowell (3B, BAL)
55. Jeff Clement (C, SEA)
56. Tyler Colvin (OF, CHC)
57. Neil Walker (3B, PIT)
58. Geovany Soto (C/1B, CHC)
59. Steven Pearce (1B/OF, PIT)
60. Fautino de los Santos (RHP, CHW)
61. Manny Parra (LHP, MIL)
62. Matt LaPorta (OF, MIL)
63. Austin Jackson (OF, NYY)
64. Carlos Carrasco (RHP, PHI)
65. Jed Lowrie (SS/2B, BOS)
66. Deolis Guerra (RHP, NYM)
67. Jonathon Meloan (RHP, LAD)
68. Chin-Lung Hu (SS, LAD)
69. Blake Beaven (RHP, TEX)
70. Michael Main (RHP, TEX)
71. Gorkys Hernandez (OF, ATL)
72. Jeff Niemann (RHP, TAM)
73. Desmond Jennings (OF, TAM)
74. Radhames Liz (RHP, BAL)
75. Chuck Lofgren (LHP, CLE)
76. Luke Hochevar (RHP, KC)
77. Brent Lillibridge (SS, ATL)
78. Jaime Garcia (LHP, STL)
79. Bryan Anderson (C, STL)
80. Troy Patton (LHP, BAL)
81. Nolan Reimold (OF, BAL)
82. Matt Latos (RHP, SD)
83. Tommy Hanson (RHP, ATL)
84. Aaron Poreda (LHP, CHW)
85. Cole Rohrbough (LHP, ATL)
86. Lars Anderson (1B, BOS)
87. Chris Volstad (RHP, FLA)
88. Henry Sosa (RHP, SF)
89. Madison Bumgarner (LHP, SF)
90. Michael Bowden (RHP, BOS)
91. Hank Conger (C, LAA)
92. JR Towles (C, HOU)
93. Greg Reynolds (RHP, COL)
94. Adrian Cardenas (2B/SS, PHI)
95. Chris Nelson (SS, COL)
96. Ryan Kalish (OF, BOS)
97. Dexter Fowler (OF, COL)
98. James McDonald (RHP, LAD)
99. Beau Mills (3B/1B, CLE)
100. Michael Burgess (OF, WAS)

AVG: Batting Average (see also BA)

BA: Batting Average (see also AVG)

Base Performance Indicator (BPI): A statistical formula that measures an isolated aspect of a player's situation-independent raw skill or a gauge that helps capture the effects of random chance has on a skill. Although there are many such formulas, there are only a few that we are referring to when the term is used in this book. For pitchers, our BPI's are control (bb%), dominance (k/9), command (k/bb), opposition on base average (OOB), ground/line/fly ratios (G/L/F), and expected ERA (xERA). Random chance is measured witih the hit rate (H%) and strand rate (S%).

*Base Performance Value (BPV): A single value that describes a pitcher's overall raw skill level. This is more useful than any traditional statistical gauge to track performance trends and project future statistical output. The BPV formula combines and weights several BPIs:

(Dominance Rate x 6) + (Command ratio x 21) – Opposition HR Rate x 30) – ((Opp. Batting Average - .275) x 200)

The formula combines the individual raw skills of power, command, the ability to keep batters from reaching base, and the ability to prevent long hits, all characteristics that are unaffected by most external team factors. In tandem with a pitcher's strand rate, it provides a complete picture of the elements that contribute to a pitcher's ERA, and therefore serves as an accurate tool to project likely changes in ERA. **BENCHMARKS:** We generally consider a BPV of 50 to be the minimum level required for long-term success. The elite of bullpen aces will have BPV's in the excess of 100 and it is rare for these stoppers to enjoy long-term success with consistent levels under 75.

Batters Faced per Game *(Craig Wright)*

((IP x 2.82) + H + BB) / G

A measure of pitcher usage and one of the leading indicators for potential pitcher burnout.

Batting Average (BA, or AVG)

(H/AB)

Ratio of hits to at-bats, though it is a poor evaluative measure of hitting performance. It neglects the offensive value of the base on balls and assumes that all hits are created equal.

Batting Eye (Eye)

(Walks / Strikeouts)

A measure of a player's strike zone judgment, the raw ability to distinguish between balls and strikes. **BENCHMARKS:** The best hitters have eye ratios over 1.00 (indicating more walks than strikeouts) and are the most likely to be among a league's .300 hitters. At the other end of the scale are ratios

less than 0.50, which represent batters who likely also have lower BAs.

bb%: Walk rate (hitters)

bb/9: Opposition Walks per 9 IP

BF/Gm: Batters Faced Per Game

BPI: Base Performance Indicator

*BPV: Base Performance Value

Cmd: Command ratio

Command Ratio (Cmd)

(Strikeouts / Walks)

This is a measure of a pitcher's raw ability to get the ball over the plate. There is no more fundamental a skill than this, and so it is accurately used as a leading indicator to project future rises and falls in other gauges, such as ERA. Command is one of the best gauges to use to evaluate minor league performance. It is a prime component of a pitcher's base performance value. **BENCHMARKS:** Baseball's upper echelon of command pitchers will have ratios in excess of 3.0. Pitchers with ratios under 1.0 — indicating that they walk more batters than they strike out — have virtually no potential for long term success. If you make no other changes in your approach to drafting a pitching staff, limiting your focus to only pitchers with a command ratio of 2.0 or better will substantially improve your odds of success.

Contact Rate (ct%)

((AB - K) / AB)

Measures a batter's ability to get wood on the ball and hit it into the field of play. BENCHMARK: Those batters with the best contact skill will have levels of 90% or better. The hackers of society will have levels of 75% or less.

Control Rate (bb/9), or Opposition Walks per Game

BB Allowed x 9 / IP

Measures how many walks a pitcher allows per game equivalent. **BENCHMARK:** The best pitchers will have bb/9 levels of 3.0 or less.

ct%: Contact rate

Ctl: Control Rate

Dom: Dominance Rate

Dominance Rate (k/9), or Opposition Strikeouts per Game

(K Allowed x 9 / IP)

Measures how many strikeouts a pitcher allows per game equivalent. **BENCHMARK:** The best pitchers will have k/9 levels of 6.0 or higher.

*Expected Earned Run Average *(Gill and Reeve)*

(.575 x H [per 9 IP]) + (.94 x HR [per 9 IP]) + (.28 x BB [per 9 IP]) - (.01 x K [per 9 IP]) - Normalizing Factor

"xERA represents the expected ERA of the pitcher based on a normal distribution of his statistics. It is not influenced by situation-dependent factors." xERA erases the inequity between starters' and relievers' ERA's, eliminating the effect that a pitcher's success or failure has on another pitcher's ERA.

Similar to other gauges, the accuracy of this formula changes with the level of competition from one season to the next. The normalizing factor allows us to better approximate a pitcher's actual ERA. This value is usually somewhere around 2.77 and varies by league and year. **BENCHMARKS:** In general, xERA's should approximate a pitcher's ERA fairly closely. However, those pitchers who have large variances between the two gauges are candidates for further analysis.

Extra-Base Hit Rate (X/H)

(2B + 3B + HR) / Hits

X/H is a measure of power and can be used along with a player's slugging percentage and isolated power to gauge a player's ability to drive the ball. **BENCHMARKS:** Players with above average power will post X/H of greater than 38% and players with moderate power will post X/H of 30% or greater. Weak hitters with below average power will have a X/H level of less than 20%.

Eye: Batting Eye

h%: Hit rate (batters)

H%: Hits Allowed per Balls in Play (pitchers)

Hit Rate (h% or H%)

(H—HR) / (AB – HR - K)

The percent of balls hit into the field of play that fall for hits.

hr/9: Opposition Home Runs per 9 IP

ISO: Isolated Power

Isolated Power (ISO)

(Slugging Percentage - Batting Average)

Isolated Power is a measurement of power skill. Subtracting a player's BA from his SLG, we are essentially pulling out all the singles and single bases from the formula. What remains are the extra-base hits. ISO is not an absolute measurement as it assumes that two doubles is worth one home run, which certainly is not the case, but is another statistic that is a good measurement of raw power. **BENCHMARKS:** The game's top sluggers will tend to have ISO levels over .200. Weak hitters will be under .100.

k/9: Dominance rate (opposition strikeouts per 9 IP)

Major League Equivalency *(Bill James)*

A formula that converts a player's minor or foreign league statistics into a comparable performance in the major leagues. These are not projections, but conversions of current performance.

Contains adjustments for the level of play in individual leagues and teams. Works best with Triple-A stats, not quite as well with Double-A stats, and hardly at all with the lower levels. Foreign conversions are still a work in process. James' original formula only addressed batting. Our research has devised conversion formulas for pitchers, however, their best use comes when looking at BPI's, not traditional stats.

MLE: Major League Equivalency

OBP: On Base Percentage (batters)

OBA: Opposition Batting Average (pitchers)

On Base Percentage (OBP)

(H + BB) / (AB + BB)

Addressing one of the two deficiencies in BA, OBP gives value to those events that get batters on base, but are not hits. By adding walks (and often, hit batsmen) into the basic batting average formula, we have a better gauge of a batter's ability to reach base safely. An OBP of .350 can be read as "this batter gets on base 35% of the time."

Why this is a more important gauge than batting average? When a run is scored, there is no distinction made as to how that runner reached base. So, two thirds of the time—about how often a batter comes to the plate with the bases empty—a walk really is as good as a hit. **BENCHMARKS:** We all know what a .300 hitter is, but what represents "good" for OBP? That comparable level would likely be .400, with .275 representing the level of futility.

On Base Plus Slugging Percentage (OPS): A simple sum of the two gauges, it is considered as one of the better evaluators of overall performance. OPS combines the two basic elements of offensive production — the ability to get on base (OBP) and the ability to advance baserunners (SLG). **BENCHMARKS:** The game's top batters will have OPS levels over .900. The worst batters will have levels under .600.

Opposition Batting Average (OBA)

(Hits Allowed / ((IP x 2.82) + Hits Allowed))

A close approximation of the batting average achieved by opposing batters against a particular pitcher. **BENCHMARKS:** The converse of the benchmark for batters, the best pitchers will have levels under .250; the worst pitchers levels over .300.

Opposition Home Runs per Game (hr/9)

(HR Allowed x 9 / IP)

Measures how many home runs a pitcher allows per game equivalent. **BENCHMARK:** The best pitchers will have hr/9 levels of under 1.0.

Opposition On Base Average (OOB)

(Hits Allowed + BB) / ((IP x 2.82) + H + BB)

A close approximation of the on base average achieved by opposing batters against a particular pitcher. **BENCHMARK:** The best pitchers will have levels under .300; the worst pitchers levels over .375.

Opposition Strikeouts per Game: See Dominance Rate.

Opposition Walks per Game: See Control Rate.

OPS: On Base Plus Slugging Percentage

RC: Runs Created

RC/G: Runs Created Per Game

Runs Created *(Bill James)*

(H + BB - CS) x (Total bases + (.55 x SB)) / (AB + BB)

A formula that converts all offensive events into a total of runs scored. As calculated for individual teams, the result approximates a club's actual run total with great accuracy.

Runs Created Per Game *(Bill James)*

Runs Created / ((AB - H + CS) / 25.5)

RC expressed on a per-game basis might be considered the hypothetical ERA compiled against a particular batter. **BENCHMARKS:** Few players surpass the level of a 10.00 RC/G in any given season, but any level over 7.50 can still be considered very good. At the bottom are levels below 3.00.

S%: Strand Rate

Save: There are six events that need to occur in order for a pitcher to post a single save...

1. The starting pitcher and middle relievers must pitch well.
2. The offense must score enough runs.
3. It must be a reasonably close game.
4. The manager must choose to put the pitcher in for a save opportunity.
5. The pitcher must pitch well and hold the lead.
6. The manager must let him finish the game.

Of these six events, only one is within the control of the relief pitcher. As such, projecting saves for a reliever has little to do with skill and a lot to do with opportunity. However, pitchers with excellent skills sets may create opportunity for themselves.

Situation Independent: Describing a statistical gauge that measures performance apart from the context of team, ballpark, or other outside variables. Strikeouts and Walks, inasmuch as they are unaffected by the performance of a batter's surrounding team, are considered situation independent stats.

Conversely, RBIs are situation dependent because individual performance varies greatly by the performance of other batters on the team (you can't drive in runs if there is nobody on base). Similarly, pitching wins are as much a measure of the success of a pitcher as they are a measure of the success of the offense and defense performing behind that pitcher, and are therefore a poor measure of pitching performance alone.

Situation independent gauges are important for us to be able to separate a player's contribution to his team and isolate his performance so that we may judge it on its own merits.

Slg: Slugging Percentage

Slugging Percentage (Slg)

(Singles + (2 x Doubles) + (3 x Triples) + (4 x HR)) / AB

A measure of the total number of bases accumulated per at bat. It is a misnomer; it is not a true measure of a batter's slugging ability because it includes singles. SLG also assumes that each type of hit has proportionately increasing value (i.e. a double is twice as valuable as a single, etc.) which is not true. **BENCHMARKS:** The top batters will have levels over .500. The bottom batters will have levels under .300.

Strand Rate (S%)

(H + BB - ER) / (H + BB - HR)

Measures the percentage of allowed runners a pitcher strands, which incorporates both individual pitcher skill and bullpen effectiveness. **BENCHMARKS:** The most adept at stranding runners will have S% levels over 75%. Once a pitcher's S% starts dropping down below 65%, he's going to have problems with his ERA. Those pitchers with strand rates over 80% will have artificially low ERAs, which will be prone to relapse.

Strikeouts per Game: See Opposition Strikeouts per game.

Walks + Hits per Innings Pitched (WHIP): The number of baserunners a pitcher allows per inning. **BENCHMARKS:** Usually, a WHIP of under 1.20 is considered top level and over 1.50 is indicative of poor performance. Levels under 1.00 — allowing fewer runners than IP — represent extraordinary performance and are rarely maintained over time.

Walk rate (bb%)

(BB / (AB + BB))

A measure of a batter's eye and plate patience. BENCHMARKS: The best batters will have levels of over 10%. Those with the least plate patience will have levels of 5% or less.

Walks per Game: See Opposition Walks per Game.

WHIP: Walks + Hits per Innings Pitched

Wins: There are five events that need to occur in order for a pitcher to post a single win...

1. He must pitch well, allowing few runs.
2. The offense must score enough runs.
3. The defense must successfully field all batted balls.
4. The bullpen must hold the lead.
5. The manager must leave the pitcher in for 5 innings, and not remove him if the team is still behind.

X/H: Extra-base Hit Rate

*xERA: Expected ERA

* Asterisked formulas have updated versions in the Baseball Forecaster. However, those updates include statistics like Ground Ball Rate, Fly Ball Rate or Line Drive Rate, for which we do not have reliable data for minor leaguers. So we use the previous version of those formulas, as listed here, for the players in this book.

TEAM AFFILIATIONS

TEAM	ORG	LEAGUE	LEV	TEAM	ORG	LEAGUE	LEV
Aberdeen	BAL	New York-Penn League	SS	Colorado Springs	MIL	Pacific Coast League	AAA
Akron	CLE	Eastern League	AA	Columbia	NYM	South Atlantic League	A-
Albuquerque	COL	Pacific Coast League	AAA	Columbus	CLE	International League	AAA
Altoona	PIT	Eastern League	AA	Connecticut	DET	New York-Penn League	SS
Arkansas	LAA	Texas League	AA	Corpus Christi	HOU	Texas League	AA
Asheville	COL	South Atlantic League	A-	Danville	ATL	Appalachian League	Rk
Auburn	WAS	New York-Penn League	SS	Dayton	CIN	Midwest League	A-
Augusta	SF	South Atlantic League	A-	Daytona	CIN	Florida State League	A+
AZL Angels	LAA	Arizona League	Rk	Delmarva	BAL	South Atlantic League	A-
AZL Athletics	OAK	Arizona League	Rk	Dunedin	TOR	Florida State League	A+
AZL Brewers	MIL	Arizona League	Rk	Durham	TAM	International League	AAA
AZL Cubs	CHC	Arizona League	Rk	El Paso	SD	Pacific Coast League	AAA
AZL Diamondbacks	ARI	Arizona League	Rk	Elizabethton	MIN	Appalachian League	Rk
AZL Dodgers	LAD	Arizona League	Rk	Erie	DET	Eastern League	AA
AZL Giants	SF	Arizona League	Rk	Eugene	CHC	Northwest League	SS
AZL Indians	CLE	Arizona League	Rk	Everett	SEA	Northwest League	SS
AZL Mariners	SEA	Arizona League	Rk	Fort Myers	MIN	Florida State League	A+
AZL Padres	SD	Arizona League	Rk	Fort Wayne	SD	Midwest League	A-
AZL Rangers	TEX	Arizona League	Rk	Frederick	BAL	Carolina League	A+
AZL Reds	CIN	Arizona League	Rk	Fresno	HOU	Pacific Coast League	AAA
AZL Royals	KC	Arizona League	Rk	Frisco	TEX	Texas League	AA
AZL White Sox	CHW	Arizona League	Rk	GCL Astros	HOU	Gulf Coast League	Rk
Bakersfield	SEA	California League	A+	GCL Blue Jays	TOR	Gulf Coast League	Rk
Batavia	MIA	New York-Penn League	SS	GCL Braves	ATL	Gulf Coast League	Rk
Beloit	OAK	Midwest League	A-	GCL Cardinals	STL	Gulf Coast League	Rk
Billings	CIN	Pioneer League	Rk	GCL Marlins	MIA	Gulf Coast League	Rk
Biloxi	MIL	Southern League	AA	GCL Mets	NYM	Gulf Coast League	Rk
Binghamton	NYM	Eastern League	AA	GCL Nationals	WAS	Gulf Coast League	Rk
Birmingham	CHW	Southern League	AA	GCL Orioles	BAL	Gulf Coast League	Rk
Bluefield	TOR	Appalachian League	Rk	GCL Phillies	PHI	Gulf Coast League	Rk
Boise	COL	Northwest League	SS	GCL Pirates	PIT	Gulf Coast League	Rk
Bowie	BAL	Eastern League	AA	GCL Rays	TAM	Gulf Coast League	Rk
Bowling Green	TAM	Midwest League	A-	GCL Red Sox	BOS	Gulf Coast League	Rk
Bradenton	PIT	Florida State League	A+	GCL Tigers	DET	Gulf Coast League	Rk
Brevard County	MIL	Florida State League	A+	GCL Twins	MIN	Gulf Coast League	Rk
Bristol	PIT	Appalachian League	Rk	GCL Yankees 1	NYY	Gulf Coast League	Rk
Brooklyn	NYM	New York-Penn League	SS	GCL Yankees 2	NYY	Gulf Coast League	Rk
Buffalo	TOR	International League	AAA	Grand Junction	COL	Pioneer League	Rk
Burlington	KC	Appalachian League	Rk	Great Falls	CHW	Pioneer League	Rk
Burlington	LAA	Midwest League	A-	Great Lakes	LAD	Midwest League	A-
Carolina	ATL	Carolina League	A+	Greeneville	HOU	Appalachian League	Rk
Cedar Rapids	MIN	Midwest League	A-	Greensboro	MIA	South Atlantic League	A-
Charleston	NYY	South Atlantic League	A-	Greenville	BOS	South Atlantic League	A-
Charlotte	CHW	International League	AAA	Gwinnett	ATL	International League	AAA
Charlotte	TAM	Florida State League	A+	Hagerstown	WAS	South Atlantic League	A-
Chattanooga	MIN	Southern League	AA	Harrisburg	WAS	Eastern League	AA
Clearwater	PHI	Florida State League	A+	Hartford	COL	Eastern League	AA
Clinton	SEA	Midwest League	A-	Helena	MIL	Pioneer League	Rk

TEAM	ORG	LEAGUE	LEV	TEAM	ORG	LEAGUE	LEV
Hickory	TEX	South Atlantic League	A-	Peoria	STL	Midwest League	A-
High Desert	TEX	California League	A+	Portland	BOS	Eastern League	AA
Hillsboro	ARI	Northwest League	SS	Potomac	WAS	Carolina League	A+
Hudson Valley	TAM	New York-Penn League	SS	Princeton	TAM	Appalachian League	Rk
Idaho Falls	KC	Pioneer League	Rk	Pulaski	NYY	Appalachian League	Rk
Indianapolis	PIT	International League	AAA	Quad Cities	HOU	Midwest League	A-
Inland Empire	LAA	California League	A+	Rancho Cucamonga	LAD	California League	A+
Iowa	CHC	Pacific Coast League	AAA	Reading	PHI	Eastern League	AA
Jackson	SEA	Southern League	AA	Reno	ARI	Pacific Coast League	AAA
Jacksonville	MIA	Southern League	AA	Richmond	SF	Eastern League	AA
Johnson City	STL	Appalachian League	Rk	Rochester	MIN	International League	AAA
Jupiter	MIA	Florida State League	A+	Rome	ATL	South Atlantic League	A-
Kane County	ARI	Midwest League	A-	Round Rock	TEX	Pacific Coast League	AAA
Kannapolis	CHW	South Atlantic League	A-	Sacramento	SF	Pacific Coast League	AAA
Kingsport	NYM	Appalachian League	Rk	Salem	BOS	Carolina League	A+
Lake County	CLE	Midwest League	A-	Salem-Keizer	SF	Northwest League	SS
Lake Elsinore	SD	California League	A+	Salt Lake	LAA	Pacific Coast League	AAA
Lakeland	DET	Florida State League	A+	San Antonio	SD	Texas League	AA
Lakewood	PHi	South Atlantic League	A-	San Jose	SF	California League	A+
Lancaster	HOU	California League	A+	Scranton/Wilkes-Barre	NYY	International League	AAA
Lansing	TOR	Midwest League	A-	South Bend	CHC	Midwest League	A-
Las Vegas	NYM	Pacific Coast League	AAA	Spokane	TEX	Northwest League	SS
Lehigh Valley	PHI	International League	AAA	Springfield	STL	Texas League	AA
Lexington	KC	South Atlantic League	A-	St. Lucie	NYM	Florida State League	A+
Louisville	CIN	International League	AAA	State College	STL	New York-Penn League	SS
Lowell	BOS	New York-Penn League	SS	Staten Island	NYY	New York-Penn League	SS
Lynchburg	CLE	Carolina League	A+	Stockton	OAK	California League	A+
Mahoning Valley	CLE	New York-Penn League	SS	Syracuse	WAS	International League	AAA
Memphis	STL	Pacific Coast League	AAA	Tacoma	SEA	Pacific Coast League	AAA
Midland	OAK	Texas League	AA	Tampa	NYY	Florida State League	A+
Mississippi	ATL	Southern League	AA	Tennessee	CHC	Southern League	AA
Missoula	ARI	Pioneer League	Rk	Toledo	DET	International League	AAA
Mobile	ARI	Southern League	AA	Trenton	NYY	Eastern League	AA
Modesto	COL	California League	A+	Tri-City	HOU	New York-Penn League	SS
Montgomery	TAM	Southern League	AA	Tri-City	SD	Northwest League	SS
Myrtle Beach	CHC	Carolina League	A+	Tulsa	LAD	Texas League	AA
Nashville	OAK	Pacific Coast League	AAA	Vancouver	TOR	Northwest League	SS
New Hampshire	TOR	Eastern League	AA	Vermont	OAK	New York-Penn League	SS
New Orleans	MIA	Pacific Coast League	AAA	Visalia	ARI	California League	A+
Norfolk	BAL	International League	AAA	West Michigan	DET	Midwest League	A-
Northwest Arkansas	KC	Texas League	AA	West Virginia	PIT	New York-Penn League	SS
Ogden	LAD	Pioneer League	Rk	West Virginia	PIT	South Atlantic League	A-
Oklahoma City	LAD	Pacific Coast League	AAA	Williamsport	PHI	New York-Penn League	SS
Omaha	KC	Pacific Coast League	AAA	Wilmington	KC	Carolina League	A+
Orem	LAA	Pioneer League	Rk	Winston-Salem	CHW	Carolina League	A+
Palm Beach	STL	Florida State League	A+	Wisconsin	MIL	Midwest League	A-
Pawtucket	BOS	International League	AAA				
Pensacola	CIN	Southern League	AA				

FIRST PITCH 2016
Fantasy Baseball Forums

PRESENTED BY:  BASEBALL **HQ**.COM

Read everything you want.
The best advice is live advice.

Get ready for an unforgettable experience—*in some new cities in 2016!*—BaseballHQ.com's **First Pitch Forums**. These 3+ hour events are packed full of fantasy baseball talk, interactive activities and fun! Top national baseball analysts disclose competitive secrets unique to 2016: Players to watch, trends to monitor, new strategies to employ and more! Plus, they answer YOUR questions as you look for the edge that will lead to a 2016 championship.

BaseballHQ.com founder Ron Shandler, along with current co-GMs Brent Hershey and Ray Murphy chair the sessions and bring a dynamic energy to every event. They are joined by experts from BaseballHQ.com as well as other sports media sources, such as ESPN.com, MLB.com, RotoWire, FanGraphs, Baseball Prospectus, Mastersball, Sirius/XM Radio and more.

Don't forget **First Pitch Arizona:** Nov. 4-6, 2016 in Phoenix, at the AFL!

FIRST PITCH **ARIZONA**
FANTASY BASEBALL SYMPOSIUM

2016 FIRST PITCH FORUM DATES, SITES AND REGISTRATION

Sat, February 27	CHICAGO
Sun, February 28	ST. LOUIS
Sat, March 5	HOUSTON
Sun, March 6	ATLANTA
Fri, March 11	WASHINGTON DC
Sat, March 12	NEW YORK
Sat, March 12	LOS ANGELES
Sun, March 13	BOSTON

Find complete description and details at:

www.firstpitchforums.com

Registration:
$39 per person in advance
$49 per person at the door

Get Baseball Insights
Every Single Day.

The *Minor League Baseball Analyst* provides a head-start in evaluating and selecting up-and-coming prospects for your fantasy team. You can maintain that edge all season long.

From spring training to the season's last pitch, **BaseballHQ.com** covers all aspects of what's happening on and off the field—all with the most powerful fantasy slant on the Internet:

- Nationally-renowned baseball analysts.
- MLB news analysis; including anticipating the *next* move.
- Dedicated columns on starting pitching, relievers, batters, and our popular Fact or Fluke? player profiles.
- Minor-league coverage beyond just scouting and lists.
- FAAB targets, starting pitcher reports, strategy articles, daily game resources, call-up profiles and more!

Plus, **BaseballHQ.com** gets personal, with customizable tools and valuable resources:

- Team Stat Tracker and Power Search tools
- Custom Draft Guide for YOUR league's parameters
- Sortable and downloadable stats and projection files
- Subscriber forums, the friendliest on the baseball Internet

Visit **www.baseballhq.com/subscribe**
to lock down your path to a 2016 championship!

Full Season subscription **$89**
(prorated at the time of order; auto-renews each October)

Draft Prep subscription **$39**
(complete access from January through April 30, 2016)

Please read our Terms of service at www.baseballhq.com/terms.html

Minor League Baseball Analyst & BaseballHQ.com:
Your season-long championship lineup.

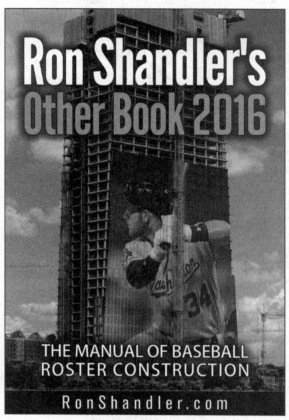

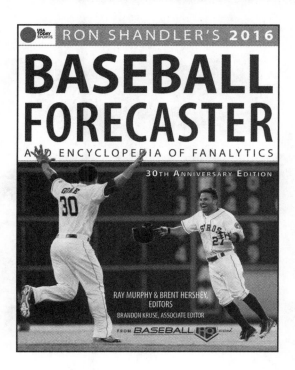